AUTOMOTIVE HEATING AND AIR CONDITIONING

Fourth Edition

Tom Birch

Upper Saddle River, New Jersey
Columbus, Ohio

Library of Congress Cataloging-in-Publication Data
Birch, Thomas W. (Thomas Wesley)
    Automotive heating and air conditioning / Tom Birch.—4th ed.
      p. cm.
    Includes index.
    ISBN 0-13-118491-1 (pbk.)
    1. Automobiles—Heating and ventilation. 2. Automobiles—Air conditioning. I. Title.
TL271.B57 2006
629.2′772—dc22

                                                                2004058643

Director of Development: Vernon R. Anthony
Production Editor: Christine M. Buckendahl
Production Coordination: Carlisle Publishers Services
Design Coordinator: Diane Ernsberger
Cover Designer: Ali Mohrman
Production Manager: Deidra Schwartz
Marketing Manager: Ben Leonard

This book was set in Century by Carlisle Communications, Ltd., and was printed and bound by Banta Book Group. The cover was printed by The Lehigh Press, Inc.

Pearson Prentice Hall™ is a trademark of Pearson Education, Inc.
Pearson® is a registered trademark of Pearson plc
Prentice Hall® is a registered trademark of Pearson Education, Inc.

Pearson Education Ltd.
Pearson Education Singapore Pte. Ltd.
Pearson Education Canada, Ltd.
Pearson Education—Japan

Pearson Education Australia Pty. Limited
Pearson Education North Asia Ltd.
Pearson Educación de Mexico, S.A. de C.V.
Pearson Education Malaysia Pte. Ltd

10 9 8 7 6 5 4 3 2
ISBN: 0-13-118491-1

PREFACE

This fourth edition of *Automotive Heating and Air Conditioning* is organized around the ASE, National Institute for Automotive Service Excellence, service area of Heating and Air Conditioning. The ASE task list is included in Appendix A. The text information and task list should prepare you to take the A7, Heating and Air Conditioning, test.

This comprehensive textbook provides a diagnostic and repair approach to this area of automotive service and repair. The theory chapters are organized to provide an understanding of the operating theory of automotive air conditioning, heating, and engine cooling systems. The service chapters describe the most modern system maintenance, diagnostic, and repair procedures. Service Cautions, Service Tips, and Real World Fixes are included in these chapters to aid your understanding.

ASE AND NATEF CORRELATED

This textbook and worktext are designed to aid students in achieving the skills listed in the ASE Task List for A7, Heating and Air Conditioning (see Appendix A). The worktext includes normal lab exercises needed to complete all of the NATEF tasks. A correlation chart for NATEF tasks is provided in Appendix I.

MULTIMEDIA SYSTEM

The multimedia CD-ROM that accompanies and supplements this textbook should make learning more fun. This CD includes:

1. PowerPoint presentations that illustrate both theory and service topics

2. Flash animations that illustrate complex actions
3. Live-action videos of A/C service operations
4. Sample ASE-style test questions in an interactive form for immediate correct-answer feedback
5. Student worksheets
6. A crossword puzzle for each chapter
7. A glossary of automotive terms
8. A Spanish-language translation of the textbook

WORKTEXT

A separate worktext accompanies this textbook. Each exercise is a real-world task performed by HVAC (heating, ventilation, and air conditioning) technicians. The exercises help students and instructors apply the textbook information to everyday-type service and testing procedures. The exercises include typical results and where the problem might be if test results were not within the acceptable range. These exercises should help build diagnosis, testing, and repair skills.

CHAPTER COMPONENTS

- Each chapter opens with a list of *Learning Objectives* for information contained in that chapter. They identify the goals to be achieved.
- Next is the *Terms to Learn* list, which includes the new words you might encounter that are commonly used in this field of automotive repair.
- Each chapter is divided numerically into topical sections that should help you understand their relationship and move through the textbook more easily.

- The service chapters contain *Service Cautions*, *Service Tips*, *Problem Solving*, and *Real World Fixes* to relate the printed information to real-world tasks encountered in HVAC service and repair.
- Each chapter ends with a *Chapter Quiz* and *Review Questions* that are written in the style of ASE-type questions.

Bold type is used for new terms as they appear for the first time. *Italic type* is used to emphasize important words and terms. These terms are often defined as they are introduced, and most of them are listed in the glossary at the end of the book.

NEW FEATURES OF THE FOURTH EDITION

1. An index of "How To" Service Operations on p. xi
2. Expanded content describing possible future refrigerants
3. Expanded A/C and HVAC testing, diagnosis, and service procedures to reflect new tools, equipment, and service procedures
4. Expanded electrical/electronic content for testing, diagnosis, and repair
5. Expanded engine cooling system testing, diagnosis, and service procedures to reflect new tools, equipment, and service procedures
6. A Spanish-language glossary
7. A key to the *Problem Solving* challenges is included as Appendix J

INSTRUCTOR PACKAGE

A comprehensive *Instructor Package* is available free when this text is adopted for classroom use. Instructors should contact Prentice Hall (call 1-800-526-0485 or visit Prentice Hall online at **www.prenhall.com**). The instructor package includes the following:

- *Instructor Manual* with answers to all of the textbook questions
- Computerized testing program

ACKNOWLEDGMENTS

This book has the support of much of the HVAC and cooling system repair industry. I am grateful and wish to express sincere thanks to the following individuals and organizations for their special contributions:

ACDelco
Acme Radiator & Air Conditioning
Airsept, Inc.
American Lokring Corporation
Appollo America Corporation, Lorie Homolish
BLR Enterprises
Bright Solutions
John Brunner
Castrol North America
Cliplight Manufacturing Company
DaimlerChrysler Corporation
Dayco Products, Inc.
Delphi Corporation
Environmental Test Systems, Inc.
The Ergonomics Society
Everco Industries
Fedco Automotive Components, Patrick L. O'Conner
Four Seasons
The Gates Rubber Company
General Motors Corporation
Goodyear Tire & Rubber Company
INFICON
International Mobile Air Conditioning Association (IMACA), Executive Director, Frank Allison
James Halderman
James Johnson, Four Seasons
John Fluke Mfg. Co.
Kent-Moore
Mastercool
Mobile Air Conditioning Society (MACS), Paul De Guiseppi
Mobile Air Conditioning Society (MACS), Simon Oulouhojian, Past President
Modine Manufacturing
Nartron Corp./Smart Power Products
Neutronics Inc.
Nissan Motor Corporation
Purdue University, Frederick Peacock
Raytek Corp.
Red Dot Corp.
Robinaire Division/SPX Corp.
Sanden International (USA)
Santech Industries
Saturn Corporation
Selective Technology, Seltec
Sercon Spectronics Corporation
Society of Automotive Engineers (SAE)
Stant Manufacturing
System Guard
TDR Stabilizer Clamp Company

Technical Chemical Company (TCC)
TIF Instruments
Toyota Motor Corporation
Tracer Products
UView Ultraviolet Systems
Visteon Corporation
Waekon Industries
Warner Electric
White Industries
Wynn Oil Company
Yokogawa Corporation of America
Yuba College, Bill Steen
Zexel Illinois

Portions of materials contained herein have been reprinted with permission of General Motors Corporation, Service Operations.

Finally, I would like to thank the following reviewers for their helpful suggestions: Mark Durivage, Owens Community College; John Eichelberger, St. Philip's College; and Mitchell Walker, St. Louis Community College.

Tom Birch

CONTENTS

Chapter 1 SERVICE INFORMATION, FASTENERS, TOOLS, AND SAFETY 1

Learning Objectives 1
Terms to Learn 1
1.1 Vehicle Identification 1
1.2 Service Information 3
1.3 Steel Classification 4
1.4 Threaded Fasteners 5
1.5 Basic Tool List 8
1.6 Measuring Tools 13
1.7 Safety Tips for Technicians 15
1.8 Electrical Cord Safety 20
1.9 Fire Extinguishers 20

Review Questions 24

Chapter Quiz 24

Chapter 2 ENVIRONMENTAL AND HAZARDOUS MATERIALS 25

Learning Objectives 26
Terms to Learn 26
2.1 Introduction 26
2.2 Occupational Safety and Health Act 26
2.3 Hazardous Waste 27
2.4 Resource Conservation and Recovery Act (RCRA) 27
2.5 Clean Air Act 28
2.6 Material Safety Data Sheets (MSDS) 28
2.7 Asbestos Exposure Hazard 28
2.8 Proper Disposal 30

Review Questions 37
Chapter Quiz 37

Chapter 3 BASICS OF HEATING AND AIR CONDITIONING 39

Learning Objectives 39
Terms to Learn 39
3.1 Introduction 39
3.2 Heat 40
3.3 Heat Measurement 42
3.4 Comfort 44

Review Questions 45

Chapter Quiz 46

Chapter 4 HEAT MOVEMENT THEORY 47

Learning Objectives 47
Terms to Learn 47
4.1 Introduction 47
4.2 Heat Movement 48
4.3 States of Matter 50
4.4 Latent and Sensible Heat 51
4.5 Boiling Points 52
4.6 Saturated Vapors and the Pressure–Temperature Relationship 53
4.7 Pressure: Gauge and Absolute 54
4.8 Refrigerants 55

Review Questions 60

Chapter Quiz 60

Chapter 5 **REFRIGERANTS AND THE ENVIRONMENT 62**

Learning Objectives 62
Terms to Learn 62
5.1 Introduction 62
5.2 Legislation 64
5.3 Additional Concerns 64
5.4 Recovery and Recycling 65
5.5 Refrigerants 67
Review Questions 74
Chapter Quiz 74

Chapter 6 **MOVING HEAT: HEATING AND AIR CONDITIONING PRINCIPLES 76**

Learning Objectives 76
Terms to Learn 76
6.1 Introduction 76
6.2 Heating Load 76
6.3 Cooling Load 77
6.4 Compression Heating 79
6.5 Expansion Cooling 80
Review Questions 81
Chapter Quiz 81

Chapter 7 **AIR CONDITIONING SYSTEMS 83**

Learning Objectives 83
Terms to Learn 83
7.1 Introduction 83
7.2 Low Side Operation 85
7.3 High Side Operation 94
7.4 Lines and Hoses 102
Review Questions 104
Chapter Quiz 105

Chapter 8 **AIR CONDITIONING SYSTEM COMPONENTS 106**

Learning Objectives 106
Terms to Learn 106
8.1 Introduction 106
8.2 Compressors 106
8.3 Condensers 127
8.4 Expansion Devices 128
8.5 Evaporators 132
8.6 Receiver–Driers and Accumulators 132
8.7 Hoses and Lines 136

8.8 Electrical Switches and Evaporator Temperature Controls 138
8.9 Rear A/C Systems 144
8.10 Aftermarket A/C Units 144
Review Questions 147
Chapter Quiz 147

Chapter 9 **HEATING SYSTEMS 149**

Learning Objectives 149
Terms to Learn 149
9.1 Introduction 149
9.2 Operation 149
9.3 Heater Core 152
9.4 Hoses 152
9.5 Control Valves 153
9.6 Dual Heating Systems 154
9.7 Aftermarket Heating Systems 154
Review Questions 155
Chapter Quiz 155

Chapter 10 **AIR MANAGEMENT SYSTEM 157**

Learning Objectives 157
Terms to Learn 157
10.1 Introduction 157
10.2 Cases and Ducts 160
10.3 Control Head 163
10.4 Rear Air Distribution Systems 169
10.5 Automatic Temperature Control and Semiautomatic Temperature Control 170
10.6 Rear Window Defroster 178
Review Questions 178
Chapter Quiz 179

Chapter 11 **HVAC SYSTEM INSPECTION AND TROUBLE DIAGNOSIS PROCEDURES 180**

Learning Objectives 180
Terms to Learn 180
11.1 Introduction 180
11.2 HVAC System Inspection 181
11.3 Problem Diagnosis 188
11.4 HVAC System Problems 193
Review Questions 196
Chapter Quiz 197

Chapter 12 A/C SYSTEM INSPECTION AND DIAGNOSIS 198

Learning Objectives 198
Terms to Learn 198
12.1 Introduction 198
12.2 A/C Pressure Checks 201
12.3 Performance Test 214
12.4 A/C System Refrigerant Leak Tests 234
Review Questions 246
Chapter Quiz 246

Chapter 13 HEATING AND AIR MANAGEMENT SYSTEMS INSPECTION AND DIAGNOSIS 248

Learning Objectives 248
Terms to Learn 248
13.1 Introduction 248
13.2 HVAC Air Filter Replacement 254
13.3 Air Management System Checks 255
Review Questions 261
Chapter Quiz 262

Chapter 14 HVAC SYSTEM ELECTRICAL OR ELECTRONIC CONTROLS: THEORY, INSPECTION, DIAGNOSIS, AND REPAIR 263

Learning Objectives 263
Terms to Learn 263
14.1 Introduction 263
14.2 Basic Electricity 264
14.3 Basic Electronics 268
14.4 A/C Clutch Circuits 274
14.5 Blower Motor Circuits 277
14.6 Cooling Fan Circuits 278
14.7 Electrical Circuit Problems 280
14.8 Measuring Electrical Values 282
14.9 Electrical System Repair 298
Review Questions 301
Chapter Quiz 301

Chapter 15 REFRIGERANT SERVICE OPERATIONS 303

Learning Objectives 303
Terms to Learn 303
15.1 Introduction 303
15.2 Preventive Maintenance and Adjustment Operations 304
15.3 A/C Service Operations 304
15.4 Retrofitting R-134a into an R-12 System 335
15.5 Using and Installing Sealants and Stop Leaks 341
Review Questions 342
Chapter Quiz 343

Chapter 16 A/C SYSTEM REPAIR 345

Learning Objectives 345
Terms to Learn 345
16.1 Introduction 345
16.2 Compressor Repair 346
16.3 Hose and Fitting Repair 368
16.4 A/C System Component Replacement 380
Review Questions 383
Chapter Quiz 384

Chapter 17 COOLING SYSTEM THEORY 385

Learning Objectives 385
Terms to Learn 385
17.1 Introduction 385
17.2 Water Jackets 387
17.3 Thermostat 387
17.4 Water Pump 390
17.5 Radiator 393
17.6 Fan 397
17.7 Hoses 401
17.8 Gauges 402
17.9 Coolant 404
17.10 Engine Block Heater 406
Review Questions 407
Chapter Quiz 408

Chapter 18 COOLING SYSTEM INSPECTION, TROUBLE DIAGNOSIS, AND SERVICE 409

Learning Objectives 409
Terms to Learn 409
18.1 Introduction 409
18.2 Preventive Maintenance Operations 410
18.3 Trouble Diagnosis 426
18.4 Cooling System Service and Repair 439

Review Questions 447

Chapter Quiz 448

Appendix A ASE CERTIFICATION AND TASK LIST 449

Appendix B TEMPERATURE–PRESSURE CHARTS 452

Appendix C A/C SERVICE PROCEDURE DOCUMENTS 453

Appendix D EPA SNAP-APPROVED REFRIGERANTS AS SUBSTITUTES FOR CFC-12 455

Appendix E POTENTIAL COMPRESSOR PROBLEMS WITH R-134A 458

Appendix F ENGLISH–METRIC CONVERSION TABLE 459

Appendix G BOLT TORQUE TIGHTENING CHART 460

Appendix H REFRIGERANT NUMBERING SYSTEM 461

Appendix I NATEF TASKS: AREA VII, HEATING AND AIR CONDITIONING 462

Appendix J KEY TO PROBLEM SOLVING 464

ENGLISH-LANGUAGE GLOSSARY 466

SPANISH-LANGUAGE GLOSSARY 472

INDEX 483

"HOW TO" SERVICE OPERATIONS

Chapter 11 HVAC SYSTEM INSPECTION AND TROUBLE DIAGNOSIS PROCEDURES

Inspect HVAC System   181

Chapter 12 A/C SYSTEM INSPECTION AND DIAGNOSIS

Connect a Gauge Set to a System   213
Disconnect a Gauge Set from a
     System   214
Test System Performance   217
Measure Relative Humidity   220
Perform a Stress Test   224
Verify Refrigerant Charge Level, Hands-
     on Check   231
Verify Refrigerant Charge Level,
     Delta T   231
Verify Refrigerant Charge Level, Sub-
     Cooling   231
Check TXV Operation   232
Locate Refrigerant Leak, Electronic
     Detector or Soap Solution   240
Locate Refrigerant Leak, Fluorescent
     Tracer   242
Vacuum Test a Single A/C Component for
     Leaks   245

Chapter 13 HEATING AND AIR MANAGEMENT SYSTEMS INSPECTION AND DIAGNOSIS

Check Heater Core Coolant
     Circulation   251
Check Heater Core for Leaks   252

Troubleshoot Vacuum Control
     System   260

Chapter 14 HVAC SYSTEM ELECTRICAL OR ELECTRONIC CONTROLS: THEORY, INSPECTION, DIAGNOSIS, AND REPAIR

Measure Voltage   285
Measure Voltage Drop   287
Measure Resistance   288
Measure Amperage Using an Inductive
     Pickup   289
Measure Amperage Using Meter
     Leads   289
Splice a Wire   299

Chapter 15 REFRIGERANT SERVICE OPERATIONS

Identify Refrigerant in a System   307
Identify Sealant in a System   309
Recover Refrigerant   313
Recover Contaminated Refrigerant
     Without Using a Recovery
     Machine   315
Recycle Refrigerant   316
Check PT Relationship   316
Install an In-Line Filter   322
Install an In-Line Filter in a Metal
     Line   322
Determine Oil Charge   323
Evacuate a System   327
Charge a System Using a Charging
     Station   332

Charge a System Using Small Cans   334
Retrofit a System   340
Install a Sealant   342

Chapter 16   A/C SYSTEM REPAIR

Remove a Compressor   349
Replace a Compressor   349
Remove a Clutch Assembly   352
Replace a Clutch Assembly   354
Remove a Lip-Type Seal   358
Replace a Lip-Type Seal   358
Remove a Two-Part Seal   359
Replace a Two-Part Seal   362
Remove a Reed Valve Assembly   363
Replace a Reed Valve Assembly   363
Make a Rotating Compressor Check   364
Make Compressor Leak Checks   365
Check Oil Level in a Compressor with a
    Dipstick   366
Check Oil Level in a Compressor
    Without a Dipstick   367
Repair a Leaky Line Fitting, Threaded
    Connector   369
Repair a Leaky Line Fitting, Spring Lock
    Connector   370
Remove and Replace Refrigerant Hose
    or Metal Line   373
Attach a Barb Fitting Using a Finger-
    Style Crimp   378
Attach a Beadlock Fitting Using a
    Bubble-Style Crimp   379
Repair a Refrigerant Hose   379
Remove and Replace a Major A/C
    Component   381

**Chapter 18   COOLING SYSTEM INSPECTION,
             TROUBLE DIAGNOSIS, AND
             SERVICE**

Measure Coolant Concentration and
    Condition Using Test Strips   414

Measure Coolant Concentration Using a
    Refractometer   415
Measure Coolant Concentration Using a
    Hydrometer   415
Measure Cooling System Voltage   415
Change Coolant   417
Change Coolant Using a Coolant
    Exchange Unit   419
Fill a Cooling System Using an Airlift
    Tool   420
Quick-Check Cause of Drive Belt
    Noise   421
Remove and Replace a Drive Belt, Set
    Tensioner   421
Remove and Replace a Drive Belt,
    Automatic Tensioner   424
Check Belt Tensioner Operation   424
Remove and Replace a Hose   425
Check a Cooling System   427
Pressure Test a Radiator Cap, Hand
    Pump Tester   432
Pressure Test a Cooling System, Hand
    Pump Tester   432
Pressure Test a Cooling System,
    Pressure Regulator and Shop
    Air   433
Test for Combustion Leak, Pressure
    Tester   435
Test for Combustion Leak, Gas
    Bubbles   436
Test for Combustion Leak, CO_2
    Presence   436
Test for Thermostat   437
Quick-Check a Fan Clutch   438
Test a Fan Clutch   438
Test a Fan for Cavitation   439
Test a Water Pump   439
Flush a Cooling System, Handheld
    Flushing Gun   440
Remove and Replace a Core Plug   442
Check for Fan Runout   443
Remove and Replace a Radiator   444
Remove and Replace a Thermostat   445
Remove and Replace a Water Pump   446

Chapter I

SERVICE INFORMATION, FASTENERS, TOOLS, AND SAFETY

LEARNING OBJECTIVES

After completing this chapter, you should:

1. Be able to retrieve vehicle service information.
2. Know the strength ratings of threaded fasteners.
3. Know how to safely use hand tools.
4. Know how to safely hoist a vehicle.
5. Know the personal safety equipment that all service technicians should wear.
6. Know the ASE requirements for vehicle identification and the proper use of tools and shop equipment.

TERMS TO LEARN

aftermarket	OEM
bolt	pitch
bump cap	spontaneous combustion
cap screw	stud
dial indicator	telescopic gauge
grade	TSB
iATN	UNC
lock washer	UNF
Loctite	VECI
micrometer	vernier dial caliper washer
nut	VIN

1.1 VEHICLE IDENTIFICATION

All service work requires that the vehicle, including the engine and accessories, be properly identified. The most common identification method is knowing the make, model, and year of the vehicle.

> **Make:** e.g., Chevrolet, **Model:** e.g., Trailblazer, **Year:** e.g., 2003

The year of the vehicle is often difficult to determine exactly. Typically, a new model year starts in September or October of the year prior to the actual new year, but not always. A model may be introduced as the next year's model as soon as January of the previous year. This is why the **vehicle identification number,** usually abbreviated **VIN,** is so important (Figure 1-1). Since 1981 all vehicle manufacturers have used a VIN that is 17 characters long. Although every vehicle manufacturer assigns various letters or numbers within these 17 characters, there are some constants, including:

- The first number or letter designates the country of origin.

1 = United States	K = Korea
2 = Canada	L = Taiwan
3 = Mexico	S = England
4 = United States	V = France
6 = Australia	W = Germany
9 = Brazil	Y = Sweden
J = Japan	Z = Italy

- The model of the vehicle is commonly the fourth or fifth character.
- The eighth character is often the engine code. (Some engines cannot be determined by the VIN number.)

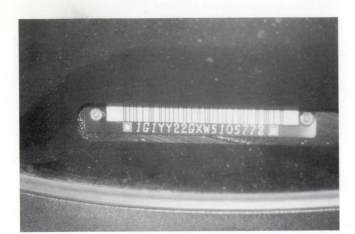

FIGURE 1-1 The VIN, vehicle identification number, is at the top front of the instrument panel and is visible through the windshield. (*Courtesy of James Halderman*)

- The tenth character represents the year on all vehicles.

A = 1980	L = 1990	Y = 2000
B = 1981	M = 1991	1 = 2001
C = 1982	N = 1992	2 = 2002
D = 1983	P = 1993	3 = 2003
E = 1984	R = 1994	4 = 2004
F = 1985	S = 1995	5 = 2005
G = 1986	T = 1996	6 = 2006
H = 1987	V = 1997	7 = 2007
J = 1988	W = 1998	8 = 2008
K = 1989	X = 1999	9 = 2009

1.1.1 VECI Label

The *vehicle emissions control information* (**VECI**) label located under the hood of the vehicle shows informative settings and emission hose routing information (Figure 1-2). The VECI label (sticker) can be located on the underside of the hood, the radiator fan shroud, radiator core support, or on the strut towers. The VECI label usually includes the following information:

Engine identification	Base ignition timing
Emissions standard	(if adjustable)
for vehicle	Spark plug type and gap
Vacuum hose routing	Valve lash
diagram	Emission calibration code

1.1.2 Calibration Codes

Calibration codes are usually located on power train control modules (PCMs) or other controllers. When-

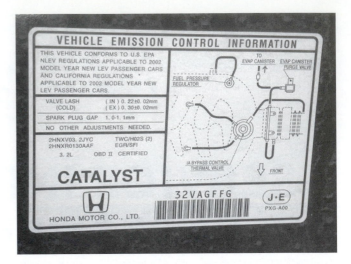

FIGURE 1-2 The VECI, vehicle emission control information, label is attached to an underhood portion of the vehicle. (*Courtesy of James Halderman*)

ever diagnosing an engine operating fault, it may be necessary to know the calibration code to determine if the vehicle is the subject of a technical service bulletin or other service procedure (Figure 1-3).

FIGURE 1-3 The sticker attached to this control module indicates the calibration code. (*Courtesy of James Halderman*)

1.1.3 Casting Numbers

Whenever an engine part such as a block is cast, a number is put into the mold to identify the casting (Figure 1-4). These casting numbers can be used to check dimensions such as the cubic inch displacement as well as other information such as year of manufacture. Sometimes changes are made to the mold, yet the casting number is not changed. The casting number is often the best piece of identifying information that the service technician can use.

1.2 SERVICE INFORMATION

Service information is needed by the service technician to determine specifications and service procedures and to learn about any necessary special tools needed.

1.2.1 Service Manuals

The original equipment manufacturer, **OEM,** and **aftermarket** service manuals contain specifications and service procedures. While OEM service manuals cover just one year and one or more model of the same vehicle, most aftermarket service manufacturers cover multiple years and/or models in one manual (Figure 1-5). Included in most service manuals are the following:

- Capacities and recommended specifications for all fluids
- Specifications including engine and routine maintenance items
- Testing procedures
- Service procedures including the use of special tools if needed

1.2.2 Electronic Service Information

Electronic service information is available mostly by subscription and provides access to an Internet site where service manual information is available (Figure 1-6). Most vehicle manufacturers also offer electronic service information to their dealers and to schools that offer corporate training programs.

FIGURE 1-5   The factory service manual is considered to be the most complete source of service and repair information for a vehicle. (*Courtesy of James Halderman*)

Casting Number   ID Tag

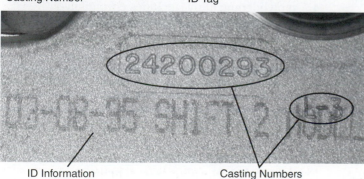

ID Information   Casting Numbers

FIGURE 1-4   The two transmission cases show casting numbers that are cast as part of the case. They also have an ID tag or painted-on ID information. (*Courtesy of James Halderman*)

FIGURE 1-6 Electronic service information, available from several independent sources, is read using a computer and monitor. (*Courtesy of James Halderman*)

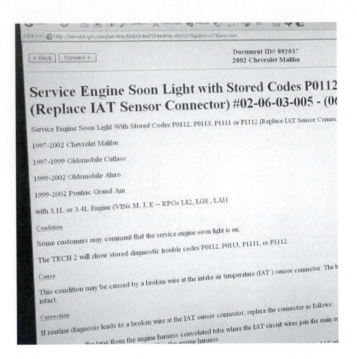

FIGURE 1-7 This TSB, technical service bulletin, describes a condition that causes the "Service Engine Soon Light" to come on for certain vehicles, and it describes the correction procedure for this concern. Note that it is in an electronic form. (*Courtesy of James Halderman*)

1.2.3 Technical Service Bulletins

Technical service bulletins, often called **TSBs**, are issued by the vehicle manufacturer to notify service technicians of a problem, and include the necessary corrective action. Technical service bulletins are designed for OEM dealership technicians but are republished by aftermarket companies and made available along with other service information to shops and vehicle repair facilities (Figure 1-7).

1.2.4 Internet

The Internet has opened the field for information exchange and access to technical advice. A very useful site is the international Automotive Technicians' Network (**iATN**) at www.iatn.net. This is a free site, but service technicians need to register to join. If a small monthly sponsor fee is paid, the shop or service technician can gain access to the archives, which include thousands of successful repairs in the searchable data base.

1.3 STEEL CLASSIFICATION

Steel is the base material for automotive parts that require high strength. Steel is iron that has been refined to

the point where little carbon remains. Even a very small percentage of carbon in steel has a great deal of significance in the physical characteristics of any steel. The classifications of steel were established by the Society of Automotive Engineers (SAE) and are referred to as the SAE numbers.

The classification number usually contains four numbers, such as SAE 1040 steel. The first number (on the left) identifies the basic type (alloy) of the steel.

1 carbon steel (no other alloy)
2 nickel alloy
3 nickel-chromium (includes stainless steels)
4 molybdenum alloy (includes chromium-molybdenum alloys)
5 chromium
6 chromium-vanadium
9 silicon-manganese

(Other numbers are used to represent triple alloy steels.)

The second number represents the percent of alloy in the steel or is used to identify percentage ranges of alloy if more than one alloy is used in the steel.

The last two numbers represent the points of carbon. A small change in carbon content means a big difference in the characteristics of the steel (1% contains 100 points; therefore, 35 points of carbon means the steel contains 0.35% carbon). Generally, the higher the carbon content of the steel, the harder the steel.

Low carbon steels	0.08% to 0.20% (8 to 20 points) carbon
Medium carbon steels	0.20% to 0.45% (20 to 45 points) carbon
High carbon steels	0.45% to 0.65% (45 to 65 points) carbon
Tool steel	above 0.65% (65 points) carbon

1.3.1   Steel Classification Examples

SAE 4130 is commonly used for high-strength tubing for race car roll cages:

4	chromium molybdenum
1	1% alloy
30	0.30% carbon

SAE 5140 is commonly used as the billet (block) of steel for some stabilizer bars:

5	chromium
1	1% alloy
40	0.40% carbon

Besides carbon content, the hardness of the steel is determined by heat treatment procedures, cooling times, temperatures, and even by what material is used to cool the steel. For example, *water-hardened* steel is quenched (cooled) by submerging the hot steel in water.

1.3.1.1 Rockwell Hardness Test   The harder the steel, the more it resists the penetration of another object. A Rockwell hardness tester uses this principle by using a hard 1/16″ diameter ball on a diamond cone and measuring the distance this ball dents into the metal sample under a given load. Different scales are used to test various types of materials. The *C* scale is the most commonly used Rockwell hardness tester scale used for hardened and alloy steels. A typical camshaft lobe in an automotive engine should have a hardness of 45 on the Rockwell *C* scale. This is often abbreviated as 45 HRC.

1.4   THREADED FASTENERS

Most of the threaded fasteners used on vehicles are **cap screws,** which are fasteners that are threaded into a casting or part. Automotive service technicians usually refer to these fasteners as **bolts,** regardless of how they are used. In this book, they are called bolts although bolts are normally used with nuts. Sometimes **studs,** a short rod with threads on both ends, are used for threaded fasteners. Often, a stud will have coarse threads on one end and fine threads on the other end. The end of the stud with coarse threads is screwed into the casting, and a nut is used on the opposite end to hold the parts together (Figure 1-8).

The fastener threads *must* match the threads in the casting or nut. The threads, which may be measured either in fractions of an inch (called *fractional*) or in metric units, are either coarse or fine. The coarse threads are called Unified National Coarse **(UNC),** and the fine threads are called Unified National Fine **(UNF).** Standard combinations of sizes and number of threads per inch (called **pitch**) are used. Pitch can be measured with a thread pitch gauge, as shown in Figure 1-9.

Bolts are identified by their diameter and length as measured from below the head, as shown in Figure 1-10. Fractional thread sizes are specified by the diameter in

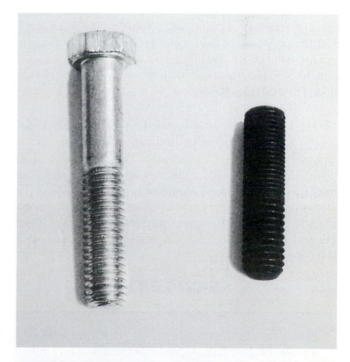

FIGURE 1-8   Typical bolt on the left and stud on the right. Note the different thread pitch on the top and bottom portions of the stud. (*Courtesy of James Halderman*)

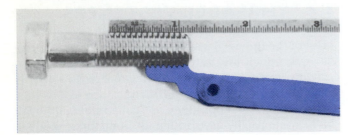

FIGURE 1-9 Thread pitch gauge used to measure the pitch of the thread. This is a 1/2-in. diameter bolt with 13 threads to the inch (1/2–13). (*Courtesy of James Halderman*)

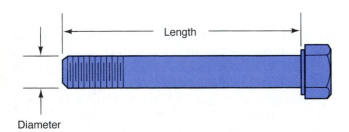

FIGURE 1-10 Bolt size identification. (*Courtesy of James Halderman*)

fractions of an inch and the number of threads per inch. For example, a 5/16–18 bolt has threads that are 5/16 of an inch in diameter and 18 threads per inch of length. Typical UNC thread sizes would be 5/16–18 and 1/2–13. Similar UNF thread sizes would be 5/16–24 and 1/2–20.

1.4.1 Metric Bolts

The size of a metric bolt is specified by the letter *M* followed by the diameter in millimeters (mm) across the outside (crest) of the threads. Typical metric sizes would be M8 and M12. Fine metric threads (pitch) are specified by the thread diameter followed by X and the distance between the threads measured in millimeters (M8 X 1.5). Typical metric sizes would be M8 X 1.5 (coarse thread), M8 X 1.25 (medium thread), and M8 X 1.0 (fine thread).

◀ SERVICE TIP ▶

Synthetic wintergreen oil, available at drugstores, makes an excellent penetrating oil. The next time you can't get that rusted bolt loose, head for the drugstore (Figure 1-11).

FIGURE 1-11 Synthetic wintergreen oil can be used as a penetrating oil to loosen rusted bolts or nuts. (*Courtesy of James Halderman*)

1.4.2 Bolt Grade

Bolts are made from many different types of steel, and for this reason some are stronger than others. The strength or classification of a bolt is called the **grade** and is marked on the bolt head. Fractional bolts have lines on the head to indicate the grade, as shown in Figure 1-12, the actual grade being two more than the number of lines on the bolt head. More lines or a higher grade number indicate a stronger bolt. Grade 5 and better bolts usually have threads that are rolled rather than cut, which also makes them stronger. In some cases, nuts and machine screws have similar grade markings. Metric bolts are marked with a decimal number to indicate the grade.

◀ CAUTION ▶

Never use hardware store (nongraded) bolts, studs, or nuts on any vehicle steering, suspension, brake, or clutch component (Figure 1-13). Always use the exact size and grade of hardware that is specified and used by the vehicle manufacturer.

1.4.3 Nuts

Most **nuts** used on bolts have the same hex size as the bolt head. Some inexpensive nuts use a hex size larger than the cap screw head. Metric nuts are often marked with dimples to show their strength—more dimples indicate stronger nuts. Some nuts, commonly called *self-locking nuts*, use interference fit threads to keep them from accidentally loosening. They are made so that the shape of the nut is slightly

FIGURE 1-12 Typical bolt (cap screw) grade markings and approximate strength. (*Courtesy of James Halderman*)

1	5	7	8	Inch Grade
4.6	8.8	9.8	10.9	Metric Class
60,000	120,000	130,000	150,000	Approximate Maximum Pound Force Per Square Inch

◄ SERVICE TIP ►

A common mistake made by new technicians is to think that the size of a bolt or nut is the size of the head. The size of the bolt or nut (outside diameter of the threads) is usually smaller than the size of the wrench or socket that fits the head of the bolt or nut. Examples are given in the following table:

Wrench Size	Thread Size
7/16 in.	1/4 in.
1/2 in.	5/16 in.
9/16 in.	3/8 in.
5/8 in.	7/16 in.
3/4 in.	1/2 in.
10 mm	6 mm
12 mm or 13 mm*	8 mm
14 mm or 17 mm*	10 mm

* European (Système International d'Unités-SI) metric.

distorted or a section of the threads is deformed. Nuts can also be kept from loosening with a nylon washer fastened in the nut or with a nylon patch or strip on the threads (Figure 1-14).

FIGURE 1-13 Every shop should have an assortment of high-quality bolts and nuts to replace those damaged during vehicle service procedures. (*Courtesy of James Halderman*)

FIGURE 1-14 Types of lock nuts. On the left, a nylon ring; in the center, a distorted shape; and on the right, a castle used with a cotter key. (*Courtesy of James Halderman*)

◀ **SERVICE TIP** ▶

An open-end wrench can be used to gauge bolt sizes by placing the wrench opening across the threads. For example, a 3/8-in. wrench will closely fit the threads of a 3/8-in. bolt.

Most of these "locking nuts" are grouped together and are commonly referred to as *prevailing torque* nuts. This means that the nut will hold its tightness or torque and not loosen with movement or vibration. Most prevailing torque nuts should be replaced whenever removed to ensure that the nut will not loosen during service. Always follow manufacturer's recommendations. Anaerobic sealers, such as **Loctite,** are used on the threads where the nut or cap screw must be both locked and sealed.

1.4.4 Washers

Washers are often used under cap screw heads and under nuts. Plain, flat washers are used to provide an even clamping load around the fastener and to protect that part. **Lock washers** are added to prevent accidental loosening. Some manufacturers lock the washer onto a cap screw by placing it into position before rolling the threads.

1.5 BASIC TOOL LIST

Every automotive technician should possess the hand tools to turn fasteners (bolts, nuts, and screws). The following list does not include specialty tools, and items marked with an asterisk (*) are only needed if working on older vehicles.

Tool chest

1/4-in. drive socket set (Figure 1-15):
 1/4- to 9/16-in. standard and deep sockets (Figure 1-16)*
 6- to 15-mm standard and deep sockets
 1/4-in. drive ratchet
 1/4-in. drive 2-in. and 6-in. extension
 1/4-in. drive handle
3/8-in. drive socket set:
 *3/8- to 7/8-in. standard and deep sockets (Figure 1-17)
 10- to 19-mm standard and deep sockets
 3/8-in. drive Torx set, T40, T45, T50, and T55
 3/8-in. drive 5/8-in. and 13/16-in. spark plug socket

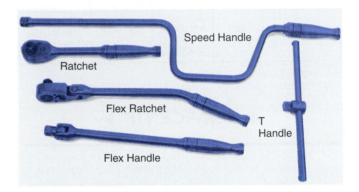

FIGURE 1-15 Typical drive handles for sockets. (*Courtesy of James Halderman*)

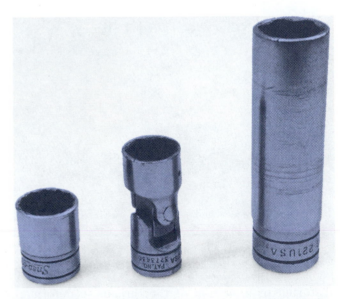

FIGURE 1-16 Standard 12-point short socket (left), universal joint socket (center), and deep-well socket (right). Both the universal and deep-well are 6-point sockets. (*Courtesy of James Halderman*)

3/8-in. drive ratchet
3/8-in. drive 1 1/2-in., 3-in., 6-in., and 12-in. extension (Figure 1-18)
3/8-in. drive universal
Crowfoot set (fractional inch* and metric)
Hex/Allen socket
1/2-in. drive socket set:
   1/2- to 1-in. standard and deep sockets*
   1/2-in. drive ratchet
   1/2-in. drive breaker bar
   1/2-in. drive 5-in. and 10-in. extension
   3/8- to 1/4-in. adapter (Figure 1-19)
   1/2- to 3/8-in. adapter
   3/8- to 1/2-in. adapter
3/8- through 1-in. combination wrench set (Figure 1-20)
10- to 19-mm combination wrench set

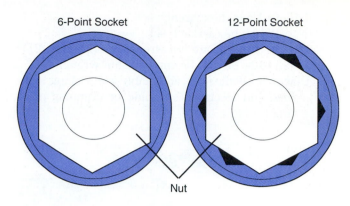

FIGURE 1-17 A 6-point socket fits the head of the bolt or nut on all sides. A 12-point socket can round off the head of a bolt or nut if a lot of force is applied. (*Courtesy of James Halderman*)

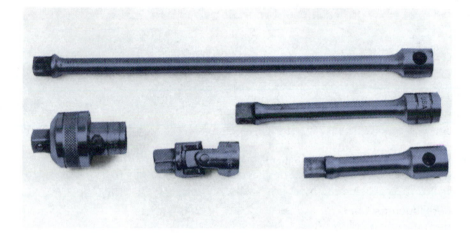

FIGURE 1-18 Various socket extensions. The universal joint (U-joint) in the center (bottom) is useful for gaining access in tight areas. (*Courtesy of James Halderman*)

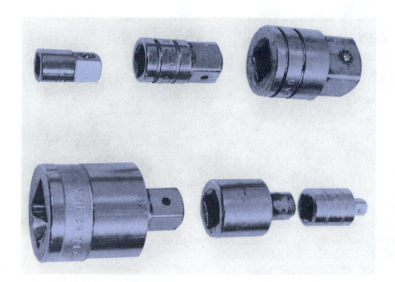

FIGURE 1-19 Socket drive adapters. These adapters permit the use of a 3/8-in. drive ratchet with 1/2-in. drive sockets, or other combinations as the various adapters permit. Adapters should *not* be used where a larger tool used with excessive force could break or damage a smaller-sized socket. (*Courtesy of James Halderman*)

1/16- to 1/4-in. hex wrench set
2- to 12-mm hex wrench set
5/16- to 9/16-in. flare-nut wrench set (Figure 1-21)*
10- and 12-, 14- and 17-mm flare-nut wrench set
Diagonal, needle nose, adjustable-jaw, locking, snap-ring, and electrical stripping or crimping pliers (Figure 1-22)

Ball-peen, rubber, and dead-blow hammers (Figure 1-23)
Five-piece standard screwdriver set (Figure 1-24)
Four-piece Phillips screwdriver set
#15 and #20 Torx screwdriver
Awl
Mill file

FIGURE 1-20   Combination wrench. The openings are the same size at both ends. Notice the angle of the open end to permit use in close spaces. (*Courtesy of James Halderman*)

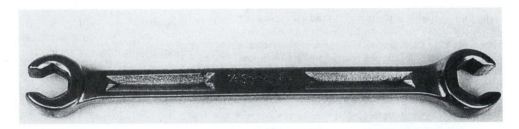

FIGURE 1-21   Flare-nut wrench. Also known as a *line wrench, fitting wrench,* or *tube-nut wrench.* This style of wrench is designed to grasp most of the flats of a six-sided (hex) tubing fitting to provide the most grip without damage to the fitting. (*Courtesy of James Halderman*)

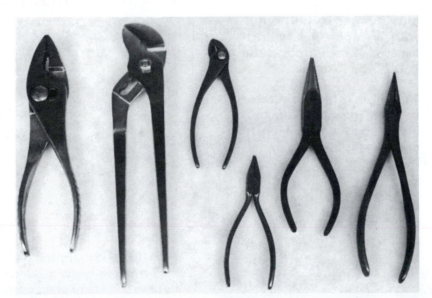

FIGURE 1-22   Assortment of pliers. Slip-joint pliers (far left) are often confused with water pump pliers (second from left). (*Courtesy of James Halderman*)

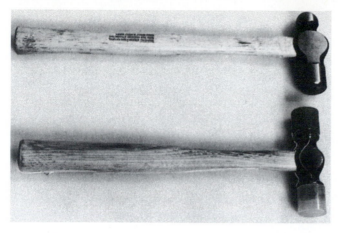

FIGURE 1-23 A ball-peen hammer (top) is purchased according to the weight (usually in ounces) of the head of the hammer. At bottom is a soft-faced (plastic) hammer. Always use a hammer that is softer than the material being driven. Use a block of wood or similar material between a steel hammer and steel or iron engine parts to prevent damage to the engine parts. (*Courtesy of James Halderman*)

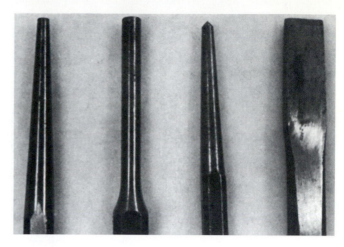

FIGURE 1-25 From the left, a starting punch, pin punch, center punch, and chisel. (*Courtesy of James Halderman*)

Center and pin punches (Figure 1-25)
Chisel
Utility knife
Valve core tool
Filter wrench (large and small filters)
Safety glasses
Circuit tester
Feeler gauge set
Gasket scraper
Pinch bar
Magnet

1.5.1 Tool Sets and Accessories

A beginning service technician may wish to start with a small set of tools before spending a lot of money on an expensive, extensive tool set (Figure 1-26).

◀ **SERVICE TIP** ▶

An apprentice technician started working for a dealership and put his top tool box on a workbench. Another technician observed that along with a complete set of good-quality tools, the box contained several adjustable wrenches. The more experienced technician said, "Hide those from the boss." If any adjustable wrench is used on a bolt or nut, the movable jaw often moves or loosens and starts to round the head of the fastener. If the head of the bolt or nut becomes rounded, it becomes that much more difficult to remove.

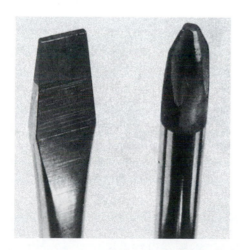

FIGURE 1-24 A flat-blade (or straight-blade) screwdriver (on the left) is specified by the length of the screwdriver and width of the blade. The width of the blade should match the width of the screw slot of the fastener. A Phillips-head screwdriver (on the right) is specified by the length of the handle and the size of the point at the tip. A #1 is a sharp point; #2 is most common (as shown), and a #3 Phillips is blunt and is only used for larger sizes of Phillips-head fasteners. (*Courtesy of James Halderman*)

(a)

(b)

FIGURE 1-26 (*a*) A beginning technician can start with some simple basic hand tools. (*b*) An experienced, serious technician often spends several thousand dollars a year for tools such as found in this large (and expensive) tool box. (*Courtesy of James Halderman*)

◀ **SERVICE TIP** ▶

Most service technicians agree that it is okay for a beginning technician to borrow a tool occasionally. However, if a tool has to be borrowed more than twice, then be sure to purchase it as soon as possible. Also, whenever a tool is borrowed, be sure that you return the tool clean and show the technician you borrowed the tool from that you are returning the tool. These actions will help in any future dealings with other technicians.

◀ **SERVICE TIP** ▶

Apply a small amount of valve grinding compound to a Phillips or Torx screw or bolt head. The gritty valve grinding compound "grips" the screwdriver or tool bit and prevents the tool from slipping up and out of the screw head. Valve grinding compound is available in a tube from most automotive parts stores.

1.5.2   Brand Name versus Proper Term

Technicians often use slang or brand names of tools rather than the proper term. This results in some confusion for new technicians. Some examples are given in the following table.

Brand Name	Proper Term	Slang Name
Crescent wrench	Adjustable wrench	Monkey wrench
Vise Grips	Locking pliers	
Channel Locks	Water pump pliers or multigroove adjustable pliers	Pump pliers
	Diagonal cutting pliers	Dikes or side cuts

◀ **SERVICE TIP** ▶

Whenever removing any automotive component, it is wise to quickly note the length, diameter, and thread pitch of each bolt so you will have a good idea of which bolt goes where.

◀ **SERVICE TIP** ▶

Normally, a bolt should be long enough to thread into the part a distance that is equal to or about half-again the bolt diameter.

1.5.3   Safety Tips for Using Hand Tools

The following safety tips should be kept in mind whenever you are working with hand tools:

- Always *pull* a wrench toward you for best control and safety. Avoid pushing a wrench.
- Keep wrenches and all hand tools clean to help prevent rust and for a better, firmer grip.
- Always use a 6-point socket or a box-end wrench to break loose a tight bolt or nut.
- Use a box-end wrench for torque and the open-end wrench for speed.
- Never use a pipe extension or other type of "cheater bar" on a wrench or ratchet handle. If more force is required, use a larger tool or use penetrating oil and/or heat on the frozen fastener. (If heat is used on a bolt or nut to remove it, always replace it with a new part.)
- Always use the proper tool for the job. If a specialized tool is required, use the proper tool and do not try to use another tool improperly.
- Never expose any tool to excessive heat. High temperatures can reduce the strength ("draw the temper") of metal tools.
- Never use a hammer on any wrench or socket handle unless you are using a special wrench designed to be used with a hammer.
- Replace any tools that are damaged or worn.

◀ **SERVICE TIP** ▶

If you must strike or pound on something, be sure to use a tool that is softer than what you are about to strike to avoid damage. Examples are given in the following table.

The Material Being Pounded	What to Pound With
Steel or cast iron	Brass or aluminum hammer or punch
Aluminum	Plastic or rawhide mallet or plastic-covered dead-blow hammer
Plastic	Rawhide mallet or plastic dead-blow hammer

◀ **SERVICE TIP** ▶

Punches, made from soft materials like brass or aluminum, are available for striking a shaft, gear, or other object.

1.6   MEASURING TOOLS

The purpose of any repair is to restore the vehicle to factory-specified tolerance. Every repair procedure involves measuring. The service technician must measure twice:

- The original components must be measured to see if correction is necessary to restore the component or part to factory specifications.
- The replacement parts and finished machined areas must be measured to ensure proper dimension before the component is assembled or replaced on the vehicle.

1.6.1   Micrometer

A **micrometer** is a commonly used measuring instrument (Figure 1-27). The *thimble* rotates over the *barrel*

FIGURE 1-27 Typical micrometers used for dimensional measurements. *(Courtesy of James Halderman)*

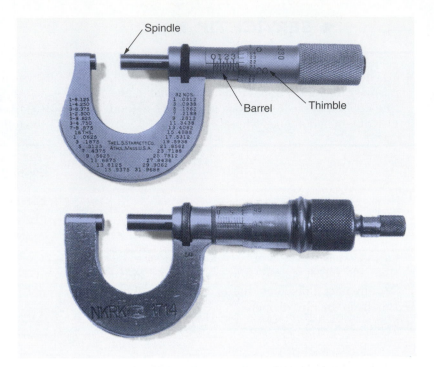

on a screw that has 40 threads per inch. Every revolution of the thimble moves the *spindle* 0.025 in. The thimble is graduated into 25 equally spaced lines; therefore, each line represents 0.001 in. Every micrometer should be checked for calibration on a regular basis (Figure 1-28).

1.6.2 Telescopic Gauge

A **telescopic gauge** is used with a micrometer to measure the inside diameter of a hole or bore.

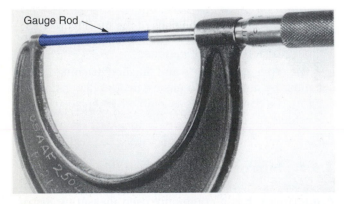

FIGURE 1-28 All micrometers should be checked and calibrated as needed using a gauge rod. *(Courtesy of James Halderman)*

◀ **FREQUENTLY ASKED** ▶
QUESTION

The word *gauge* means "measurement or dimension to a standard of reference." The word *gauge* can also be spelled *gage*. Therefore, in most cases, the words mean the same.

INTERESTING NOTE: One vehicle manufacturing representative mentioned that *gage* was used rather than *gauge* because even though it is the second acceptable spelling of the word, it is correct and it saved the company a lot of money in printing costs because the word *gage* has one less letter! One letter multiplied by millions of vehicles with gauges and the word *gage* used in service manuals adds up to a big savings to the manufacturer.

1.6.3 Vernier Dial Caliper

A **vernier dial caliper** can be used to measure gear diameter, bearing race inside diameter, as well as the depth of a bolt hole. Although not as accurate as a micrometer, a vernier caliper is faster and covers a wider measuring range (Figure 1-29).

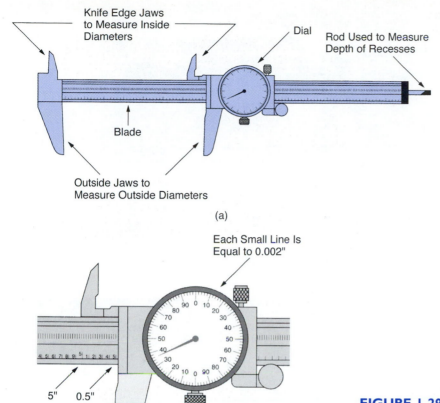

Knife Edge Jaws
to Measure Inside
Diameters

Dial

Rod Used to Measure
Depth of Recesses

Blade

Outside Jaws to
Measure Outside Diameters

(a)

Each Small Line Is
Equal to 0.002"

5"   0.5"

Add Reading on Blade (5.5")
to Reading on Dial (0.036") to
Get Final Total Measurement (5.536")

(b)

FIGURE 1-29 *(a)* A typical vernier dial caliper. This is a very useful measuring tool for automotive engine work because it is capable of measuring inside and outside measurements. *(b)* To read a vernier dial caliper, simply add the reading on the blade to the reading on the dial. *(Courtesy of James Halderman)*

1.6.4 Dial Indicator

A **dial indicator** is used to measure movement like shaft runout or gear lash/clearance (see Figure 16-15).

1.7 SAFETY TIPS FOR TECHNICIANS

Safety is not just a buzzword on a poster in the work area. Safe work habits can reduce accidents and injuries, ease the workload, and keep employees pain-free. Suggested safety tips include the following:

- *Wear safety glasses at all times while servicing any vehicle* (Figure 1-30).
- Watch your toes—always keep your toes protected with steel-toed safety shoes (Figure 1-31). If safety shoes are not available, then leather-topped shoes offer more protection than canvas or cloth.

- Wear gloves to protect your hands from rough or sharp surfaces. Thin rubber gloves are recommended when working around automotive liquids such as engine oil, antifreeze, transmission fluid, or any other liquids that may be hazardous.
- Service technicians working under a vehicle should wear a **bump cap** to protect the head against under-vehicle objects and the pads of the lift (Figure 1-32).
- Remove all jewelry that may get caught on something or act as a conductor to an exposed electrical circuit (Figure 1-33).
- Take care of your hands. Keep your hands clean by washing frequently with soap and hot water of at least 110°F (43°C).
- Avoid loose or dangling clothing.
- Ear protection should be worn if the sound around you requires that you raise your voice (sound level higher than 90 dB). (A typical lawn mower produces noise at a level of about 110 dB. This means that everyone who uses a lawn mower or other lawn or garden equipment should wear ear protection.)

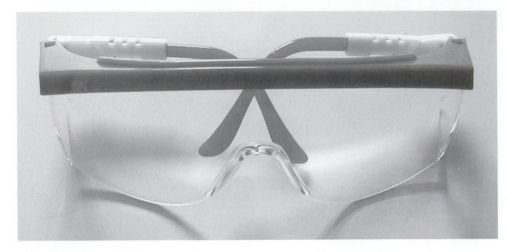

FIGURE 1-30   Safety glasses should be worn at all times when working on or around any vehicle or servicing any component. (*Courtesy of James Halderman*)

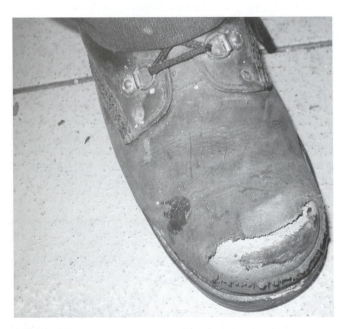

FIGURE 1-31   Steel-toed shoes are a worthwhile investment to help prevent foot injury due to falling objects. Even these well-worn shoes can protect the feet of this service technician. (*Courtesy of James Halderman*)

FIGURE 1-32   A bump cap provides a shield and padding to protect the head while working under a vehicle. (*Courtesy of James Halderman*)

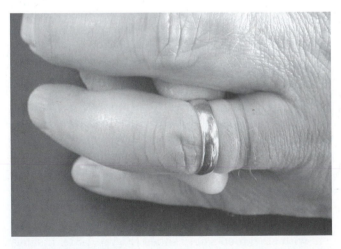

FIGURE 1-33   All jewelery like rings and watches should be removed when working on vehicles. (*Courtesy of James Halderman*)

- When lifting any object, get a secure grip with solid footing. Keep the load close to your body to minimize the strain. Lift with your legs and arms, not your back.
- Do not twist your body when carrying a load. Instead, pivot your feet to help prevent strain on the spine.
- Ask for help when moving or lifting heavy objects.
- Push a heavy object rather than pull it. (This is opposite to the way you should work with tools. Remember, never push a wrench! If you do and a bolt

or nut loosens, your entire weight is used to propel your hand(s) forward. This usually results in cuts, bruises, or other painful injury.)

- Always connect an exhaust hose to the tailpipe of any running vehicle to help prevent the buildup of carbon monoxide inside a closed garage space (Figure 1-34).

- When standing, keep objects, parts, and tools with which you are working between chest height and waist height. If seated, work at tasks that are at elbow height.

- Always be sure the hood is securely held open (Figure 1-35).

◀ SAFETY TIP ▶

Always dispose of oily shop cloths in an enclosed container to prevent a fire (Figure 1-36). Whenever oily cloths are thrown together on the floor or workbench, a chemical reaction can occur which can ignite the cloth even without an open flame. This process of ignition without an open flame is called **spontaneous combustion.**

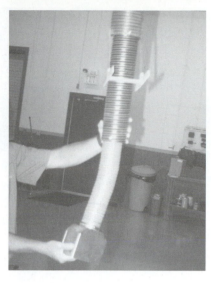

FIGURE 1-34 Always connect an exhaust hose to the tailpipe of the engine of a vehicle to be run inside a building. (*Courtesy of James Halderman*)

(a)

Hood Strut Clamp

(b)

FIGURE 1-35   (a) A crude but effective method is to use locking pliers on the chrome-plated shaft of a hood strut. Locking pliers should only be used on defective struts because the jaws of the pliers can damage the strut shaft. (b) A commercially available hood clamp. This tool uses a bright orange tag to help remind the technician to remove the clamp before attempting to close the hood. The hood could be bent if force is used to close the hood with the clamp in place. (*Courtesy of James Halderman*)

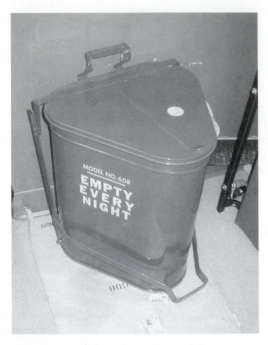

FIGURE 1-36   All oily shop cloths should be stored in a metal container equipped with a lid to help prevent spontaneous combustion. (*Courtesy of James Halderman*)

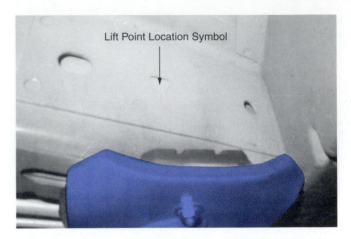

Lift Point Location Symbol

FIGURE 1-37   Most newer vehicles have a triangle symbol indicating the recommended hoisting lift points. (*Courtesy of James Halderman*)

Standard JRP–2184. These recommendations typically include the following points:

1. The vehicle, with the doors, hood, and trunk closed, should be centered on the lift or hoist so as not to overload one side or put too much force either forward or rearward.
2. The pads of the lift should be spread as far apart as possible to provide a stable platform.
3. Each pad should be placed under a part of the vehicle that is strong and capable of supporting the weight of the vehicle.
   a. Pinch welds at the bottom edge of the body are generally considered to be strong.

◄ **TECH TIP** ►

SHOCK CONTROL

To avoid impact damage from your impact wrench on your hand, take the rubber covering from an old electric fuel pump and fit it on the handle of the gun to soften the blow.

1.7.1   Vehicle Lifting (Hoisting) Safety

Many chassis and underbody service procedures require that the vehicle be hoisted or lifted off the ground. The simplest methods involve the use of drive-on ramps or a floor jack and safety (jack) stands, whereas in-ground or surface-mounted lifts provide greater access. **Setting the pads is a critical part of the lifting procedure.**

All automobile and light-truck service manuals include recommended locations to be used when hoisting (lifting) a vehicle. Newer vehicles have a triangle decal on the driver's door indicating the recommended lift points (Figure 1-37). The recommended standards for the lift points and lifting procedures are found in SAE

◄ **CAUTION** ►

Even though pinch weld seams are the recommended location for hoisting many vehicles with unitized bodies (unit-body), care should be taken not to place the pad(s) too far forward or rearward. Incorrect placement of the vehicle on the lift could cause the vehicle to be imbalanced, and the vehicle could fall. This is exactly what happened to the vehicle in Figure 1-38. Be aware that a tall vehicle might hit the ceiling or suspended lights.

   b. Boxed areas of the body are the best places to position the pads on a vehicle without a frame. Be careful to note whether the arms of the lift might come into contact with other parts of the vehicle before the pad touches the intended

FIGURE 1-38   This vehicle fell from the hoist because the pads were not set correctly. No one was hurt, but the vehicle was a total loss. *(Courtesy of James Halderman)*

location. Commonly damaged areas include the following:

1. rocker panel moldings,
2. exhaust system (including catalytic converter), and
3. tires or body panels (Figure 1-39).
4. The vehicle should be raised about a foot [30 centimeters (cm)] off the floor, then stopped and shaken to check for stability. If the vehicle seems to be stable when checked at a short distance from the floor, continue raising the vehicle and watch until it has reached the desired height.

◄ CAUTION ►

Do not look away from the vehicle while it is being raised (or lowered) on a hoist. One side or one end of the hoist can stop or fail, resulting in the vehicle being slanted enough to slip or fall, creating physical damage not only to the vehicle and/or hoist but also to the technician or others who may be nearby.

◄ HINT ►

Most hoists can be safely placed at any desired height. For ease while working, the area in which you are working should be at chest level. When removing and replacing components like an axle, it is not necessary to work on them down near the floor or over your head. Raise the hoist so that the components are at chest level.

5. Before lowering the hoist, the safety latch(es) must be released and the direction of the controls reversed. The speed downward is often adjusted to be as slow as possible for additional safety.

(a)

(b)

FIGURE 1-39   (a) In this photo the pad arm is just contacting the rocker panel of the vehicle. (b) This photo shows what can occur if the technician places the pad too far inward underneath the vehicle. The arm of the hoist has dented the rocker panel. *(Courtesy of James Halderman)*

1.8 ELECTRICAL CORD SAFETY

Use correctly grounded three-prong sockets and extension cords to operate power tools. Use only double insulated power tools. Some modern tools use polarized two-prong plugs that have one wide and one narrow prong. When not in use, keep electrical cords off the floor to prevent tripping over them. Tape the cords to the floor if they are placed in high foot traffic areas.

◀ SAFETY TIP ▶

Improper use of an air nozzle can cause blindness or deafness. If an air nozzle is used to dry and clean parts, make sure the airstream is directed away from anyone else in the immediate area. Clean, coil, and store air hoses when they are not in use.

1.9 FIRE EXTINGUISHERS

There are four classes of fire extinguishers. Each class should be used on specific fires only:

- **Class A** is designed for use on general combustibles, such as cloth, paper, and wood.
- **Class B** is designed for use on flammable liquids and greases, including gasoline, oil, thinners, and solvents.
- **Class C** is used only on electrical fires.
- **Class D** is effective only on combustible metals such as powdered aluminum, sodium, or magnesium.

The class rating is clearly marked on the side of every fire extinguisher. Many extinguishers are good for multiple types of fires (Figure 1-40).

When using a fire extinguisher, remember the word "PASS":

P = Pull the safety pin.
A = Aim the nozzle of the extinguisher at the base of the fire.
S = Squeeze the lever to actuate the extinguisher.
S = Sweep the nozzle from side-to-side at the base of the flame.

See Figure 1-41.

1.9.1 Types of Fire Extinguishers

The variety of fire extinguishers include:

- **Water**—A water fire extinguisher is usually in a pressurized container and is good to use on Class A

fires because it reduces the temperature to the point where a fire cannot be sustained.

- **Carbon Dioxide (CO₂)**—A carbon dioxide fire extinguisher is good for almost any type of fire, especially Class B or Class C materials. A CO_2 fire extinguisher works by removing the oxygen from the fire; the cold CO_2 also helps reduce the temperature of the fire.
- **Dry Chemical (yellow)**—A dry chemical fire extinguisher is good for Class A, B, or C fires by coating the flammable materials to eliminate the oxygen from the fire. A dry chemical fire extinguisher tends to be very corrosive and will cause damage to electronic devices.

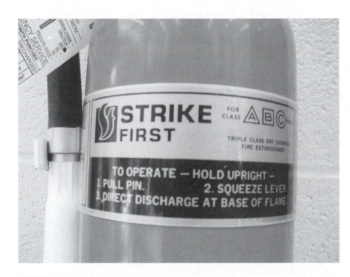

FIGURE 1-40 A typical fire extinguisher designed to be used on type A, B, or C fires. (*Courtesy of James Halderman*)

FIGURE 1-41 A CO₂ fire extinguisher being used on a fire set in an open steel drum during a demonstration at a fire department training center. (*Courtesy of James Halderman*)

(Photos courtesy of James Halderman)

PS-1 The first step in hoisting a vehicle is to properly align the vehicle in the center of the stall.

PS-2 Most vehicles will be correctly positioned when the left front tire is centered on the tire pad.

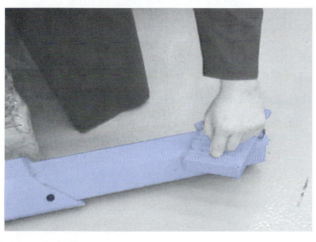

PS-3 Most pads at the end of the hoist arms can be rotated to allow for many different types of vehicle construction.

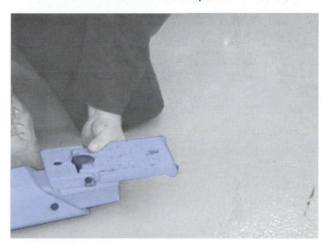

PS-4 The arms of the lifts can be retracted or extended to accommodate vehicles of many different lengths.

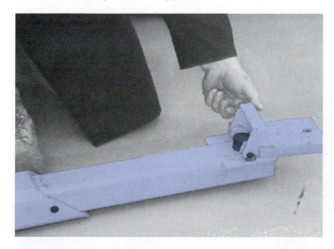

PS-5 Most lifts are equipped with short pad extensions that are often necessary to use to allow the pad to contact the frame of a vehicle without causing the arm of the lift to hit and damage parts of the body.

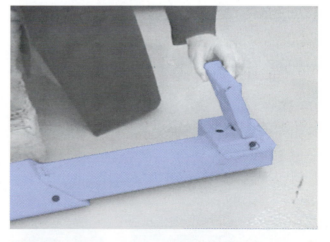

PS-6 Tall pad extensions can also be used to gain access to the frame of a vehicle. This position is needed to safely hoist many pickup trucks, vans, and sport utility vehicles (SUVs).

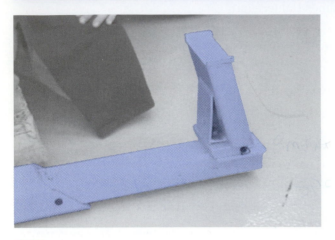

PS-7 An additional extension may be necessary to hoist a truck or van equipped with running boards to give the necessary clearance.

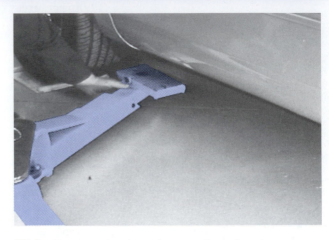

PS-8 Position the front hoist pads under the recommended locations as specified in the owner's manual and/or service information for the vehicle being serviced.

PS-9 Position the rear pads under the vehicle in the recommended locations.

PS-10 This photo shows an asymmetrical lift where the front arms are shorter than the rear arms. This design is best used for passenger cars and allows the driver to exit the vehicle more easily because the door can be opened wide without it hitting the vertical support column.

PS-11 After being sure all pads are correctly positioned, use the electromechanical controls to raise the vehicle.

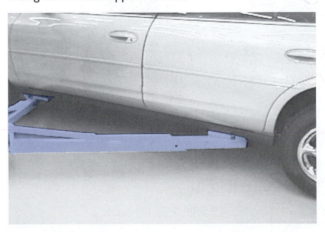

PS-12 Raise the vehicle about 1 foot (30 cm) and stop to double check that all pads contact the body or frame in the correct positions.

PS-13 With the vehicle raised about 1 foot off the ground, push down on the vehicle to check to see if it is stable on the pads. If the vehicle rocks, lower the vehicle and reset the pads. If the vehicle is stable, the vehicle can be raised to any desired working level. Be sure the safety is engaged before working on or under the vehicle.

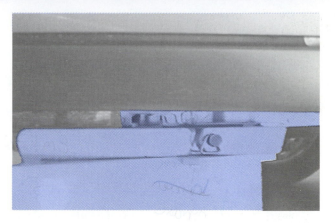

PS-14 This photo shows the pads set flat and contacting the pinch welds of the body. This method spreads the load over the entire length of the pad and is less likely to dent or damage the pinch weld area.

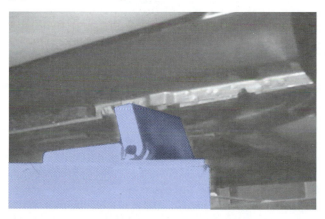

PS-15 Where additional clearance is necessary for the arms to clear the rest of the body, the pads can be raised and placed under the pinch weld area as shown.

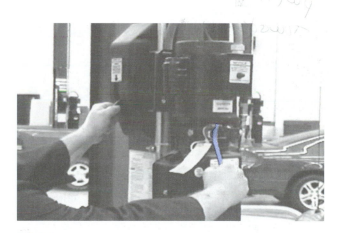

PS-16 When the service work is completed, the hoist should be raised slightly and the safety released before using the hydraulic lever to lower the vehicle.

PS-17 After lowering the vehicle, be sure all arms of the lift are moved out of the way before driving the vehicle out of the work stall.

PS-18 Carefully back the vehicle out of the stall. Notice that all of the lift arms have been neatly moved out of the way to provide clearance so that the tires will not contact the arms when the vehicle is driven out of the stall.

REVIEW QUESTIONS

The following questions are provided to help you study as you read the chapter.

1. The two common types of bolt sizes are _____ and _____.

2. A 5/16–18 bolt has _____ threads and a _____ diameter of 5/16″.

3. A M8 X 1.5 bolt has a thread diameter of _8 millimeter_ _____ and a _pitch_ of 1.5 mm.

4. A grade 8 bolt is _harder_ than a grade 5 bolt. _Strouzer_

5. Loctite is an _thread_ compound used to _____ the nut on the bolt.

6. A Crescent wrench should properly be called an _adj_ _wrench_

7. When you loosen a tight nut or bolt, you should _pull_ _____ on the wrench.
Towards you

8. The best tool to loosen a really tight nut is either a _six_ _point_ socket or a _box_ _end_ wrench.

9. A _____ is a good tool to measure a shaft to see if it is worn. _micrometer or_

10. A _dial_ _ind_ _____ can be used to measure shaft end play or flywheel runout.

11. An oily shop cloth can ignite and burn without an open flame because of _spon_ _comb_ .

12. A critical step in lifting a car on a hoist is to _____ the _____.

13. The third prong of a three-prong electrical plug is for _____.

14. Class B fire extinguishers are designed to extinguish _____ _____ fires.

15. A _____ _____ fire extinguisher is good for most types of fire.

CHAPTER QUIZ

The following questions will help you check the facts you have learned. Select the answer that completes each statement correctly.

1. Technician A says that if a micrometer thimble is rotated two complete revolutions, the spindle will move 0.050″. Technician B says the micrometer barrel has 40 threads per inch. Who is correct?
   a. Technician A   c. Both A and B
   b. Technician B   d. Neither A nor B

2. Two technicians are discussing bolts. Technician A says that the wrench used with a bolt is the same size as the bolt. Technician B says the thread diameter is the bolt size. Who is correct?
   a. Technician A   c. Both A and B
   b. Technician B   d. Neither A nor B

3. Two technicians are discussing measuring tools. Technician A says that a micrometer can be used to measure parts to 0.001″. Technician B says vernier calipers can be used to measure depth as well as the inside and outside diameter of a part. Who is correct?
   a. Technician A   c. Both A and B
   b. Technician B   d. Neither A nor B

4. Technician A says that it is a good idea to get help when you need to lift a heavy object. Technician B says that you should lift heavy objects using your legs, not your back. Who is correct?
   a. Technician A   c. Both A and B
   b. Technician B   d. Neither A nor B

5. Two technicians are discussing the hoisting of a vehicle. Technician A says to put the pads of a lift under a notch at the pinch weld of a unit-body vehicle. Technician B says to place the pads on the four corners of the frame of a full-frame vehicle. Who is correct?
   a. Technician A   c. Both A and B
   b. Technician B   d. Neither A nor B

6. The correct location for the pads when hoisting or jacking the vehicle can often be found in the _____.
   a. service manual   c. owner's manual
   b. shop manual   d. all of the above

7. For the best working position, the work should be _____.
   a. at neck or head level   c. overhead by about 1 foot
   b. at knee or ankle level   d. at chest or elbow level

8. When working with hand tools, always _____.
   a. push the wrench—don't pull toward you
   b. pull a wrench—don't push a wrench

9. Technician A says that the fire extinguisher should be aimed at the base of a fire. Technician B says that fire extinguishers remove either heat or oxygen from the burning material. Who is correct?

    a. Technician A   **c.** Both A and B

    b. Technician B   **d.** Neither A nor B

    PG 20

10. A high-strength bolt is identified by _____.

    a. a UNC symbol   **c.** strength letter codes

    b. lines on the head   **d.** the coarse threads

    PG 6

11. A fastener that uses threads on both ends is called a _____.

    a. cap screw   **c.** machine screw

    b. stud   **d.** crest fastener

    PG 7

12. The proper term for Channel Locks is _____.

    a. Vise Grips

    b. Crescent wrench

    c. locking pliers

    d. multigroove adjustable pliers

    PG 12

13. The proper term for Vise Grips is _____.

    a. locking pliers

    b. slip-joint pliers

    c. side cuts

    d. multigroove adjustable pliers

    PG 12

14. What is *not* considered to be personal safety equipment?

    a. air impact wrench   **c.** rubber gloves

    b. safety glasses   **d.** hearing protection

Chapter 2

ENVIRONMENTAL AND HAZARDOUS MATERIALS

LEARNING OBJECTIVES

After completing this chapter, you should:

1. Be able to define the Occupational Safety and Health Act (OSHA).
2. Be able to explain the term material safety data sheet (MSDS).
3. Identify hazardous waste materials in accordance with state and federal regulations.
4. Describe the steps required to safely handle and store automotive chemicals and waste.
5. Follow proper safety precautions while handling hazardous waste materials.
6. Know the ASE requirements for all service technicians in order to adhere to environmentally appropriate actions and behavior.

TERMS TO LEARN

asbestosis	OSHA
DOT	right-to-know laws
EPA	solvent
hazardous waste materials	used brake fluid
HEPA	used coolant
lung cancer	used oil
mesothelioma	WHIMS
MSDS	

2.1 INTRODUCTION

The safe handling of hazardous waste materials is extremely important in the automotive shop. The improper handling of hazardous material affects us all, not just those in the shop. Shop personnel must be familiar with their rights and responsibilities regarding hazardous waste disposal required by right-to-know laws. Shop personnel must also be familiar with hazardous materials in the automotive shop and the proper disposal methods for these materials according to state and federal regulations.

2.2 OCCUPATIONAL SAFETY AND HEALTH ACT

The United States Congress passed the **Occupational Safety and Health Act (OSHA)** in 1970. The purpose of this legislation is to assist and encourage the citizens of the United States in their efforts to assure safe and healthful working conditions by providing research, information, education, and training in the field of occupational safety and health, and to assure safe and healthful working conditions for working men and women by authorizing enforcement of the standards developed under the act. Since approximately 25% of workers are exposed to health and safety hazards on the job, the OSHA standards are necessary to monitor, control, and educate workers regarding health and safety in the workplace.

2.2.1   Health Care Rights

The OSHA regulations concerning on-the-job safety place certain responsibilities on the employer and give employees specific rights. Any person who feels there might be unsafe conditions in the workplace, whether asbestos exposure, chemical poisoning, or any other problem, should discuss the issue with fellow workers, the union representative (where applicable), and the supervisor or employer. If no action is taken and there is reason to believe the employer is not complying with OSHA standards, a complaint can be filed with OSHA, which will be investigated. The law forbids employers from taking action against employees who file a complaint concerning a health or safety hazard. However, if workers fear reprisal as the result of a complaint, they may request that OSHA withhold their names from the employer.

2.3   HAZARDOUS WASTE

Hazardous waste materials are chemicals, or components, that the shop no longer needs and that pose a danger to the environment and people if they are disposed of in ordinary garbage cans or sewers. However, one should note that no material is considered hazardous waste until the shop has finished using it and is ready to dispose of it. The **Environmental Protection Agency (EPA)** publishes a list of hazardous materials that is included in the Code of Federal Regulations. The EPA considers waste hazardous if it is included on the EPA list of hazardous materials or if it can be described in one or more of the following ways:

Reactive. Any material that reacts violently with water or other chemical is considered hazardous.

Corrosive. If a material burns the skin or dissolves metals and other materials, a technician should consider it hazardous. A pH scale is used, with the number 7 indicating neutral. Pure water has a pH of 7. Lower numbers indicate an acidic solution and higher numbers indicate a caustic solution. If when exposed to low pH acid solutions, a material releases cyanide gas, hydrogen sulfide gas, or similar gases, it is considered hazardous.

Toxic. Materials are hazardous if they leak one or more of eight different heavy metals in concen-

trations greater than 100 times the primary drinking water standard.

Ignitable. A liquid is hazardous if it has a flash point below 140°F (60°C), and a solid is hazardous if it ignites spontaneously.

Radioactive. Any substance that emits measurable levels of radiation is hazardous. When individuals bring containers of highly radioactive substances into the shop environment, qualified personnel with the appropriate equipment must test them.

◄ CAUTION ►

When handling hazardous waste material, one must always wear proper protective clothing and use equipment detailed in the right-to-know laws, including respirator equipment when needed. All recommended procedures must be followed accurately. Personal injury may result from improper clothing, equipment, and procedures when handling hazardous materials.

◄ WARNING ►

Hazardous waste disposal laws include serious penalties for anyone responsible for breaking these laws.

2.4   RESOURCE CONSERVATION AND RECOVERY ACT (RCRA)

Federal and state laws control the disposal of hazardous waste materials. Every shop employee must be familiar with these laws. Hazardous waste disposal laws include the Resource Conservation and Recovery Act (RCRA), which states that hazardous material users are responsible for hazardous materials from the time they become a waste until the proper waste disposal is completed. Many shops hire an independent hazardous waste hauler to dispose of hazardous waste material. The shop owner, or manager, should have a written contract with the waste hauler. In this case, the user must store hazardous waste material properly and safely and be responsible for its transportation until it arrives at an approved hazardous waste disposal site and is processed according to the law. A shop may also choose to recycle the hazardous waste material in the shop rather than have it hauled to an approved hazardous waste disposal site. The RCRA controls these types of automotive waste:

- paint and body repair products waste,
- solvents for parts and equipment cleaning,
- batteries and battery acid,
- mild acids used for metal cleaning and preparation,
- waste oil and engine coolants or antifreeze,
- air conditioning refrigerants and oils, and
- engine oil filters.

The **right-to-know laws** state that employees have a right to know when the materials they use at work are hazardous. The right-to-know laws started with the *Hazard Communication Standard* published by the Occupational Safety and Health Administration (OSHA) in 1983. Originally, this document was intended for chemical companies and manufacturers that required employees to handle hazardous materials in their work situation. Meanwhile, the federal courts have decided to apply these laws to all companies, including automotive service shops. Under the right-to-know laws, the employer has responsibilities regarding the handling of hazardous materials by employees. All employees must be trained about the types of hazardous materials they will encounter in the workplace, and the employees must be informed about their rights under legislation regarding the handling of hazardous materials.

2.5 CLEAN AIR ACT

Air-conditioning (A/C) systems and refrigerant are regulated by the Clean Air Act, Title VI, Section 609. Technician certification and service equipment is also regulated. Any technician working on automotive A/C systems must be certified. A/C refrigerants must not be released or vented into the atmosphere, and used refrigerants must be recovered.

2.6 MATERIAL SAFETY DATA SHEETS (MSDS)

All hazardous materials must be properly labeled, and information about each hazardous material must be posted on **material safety data sheets (MSDS),**

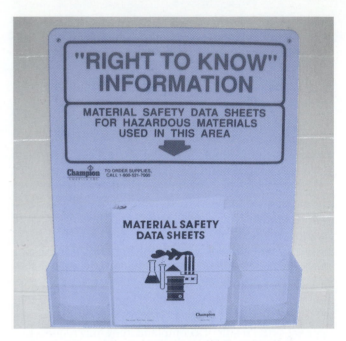

FIGURE 2-1 Material safety data sheets (MSDS) should be readily available for use by anyone in the area who may come into contact with hazardous materials. (*Courtesy of James Halderman*)

available from the manufacturer (Figure 2-1). In Canada, MSDS sheets are called **workplace hazardous materials information systems (WHMIS).**

The employer has a responsibility to place MSDS sheets where they are easily accessible by all employees. The MSDS sheets provide the following information about the hazardous material: chemical name, physical characteristics, protective handling equipment, explosion/fire hazards, incompatible materials, health hazards, medical conditions aggravated by exposure, emergency and first-aid procedures, safe handling, and spill/leak procedures.

The employer also has a responsibility to make sure that all hazardous materials are properly labeled. The label information must include health, fire, and reactivity hazards posed by the material and the protective equipment necessary to handle the material. The manufacturer must supply all warning and precautionary information about hazardous materials, and this information must be read and understood by the employee before handling the material.

2.7 ASBESTOS EXPOSURE HAZARD

Friction materials such as brake and clutch linings may contain asbestos. Although asbestos has been eliminated from most original equipment friction materials, the automotive service technician cannot know whether the vehicle being serviced is or is not equipped with friction materials containing asbestos. It is important that all friction materials be handled as if they do contain asbestos.

Asbestos exposure can cause scar tissue to form in the lungs. This condition, called **asbestosis,** causes gradually increasing shortness of breath and permanent scarring of the lungs. Even low exposures to asbestos can cause **mesothelioma,** a type of fatal cancer of the lining of the chest or abdominal cavity. Asbestos exposure can also increase the risk of **lung cancer** as well as cancer of the voice box, stomach, and large intestine. It usually takes 15 to 30 years or more for cancer or asbestos lung scarring to show up after exposure. (Scientists call this the *latency period.*)

Government agencies recommend that asbestos exposure should be eliminated or controlled to the lowest level possible and have developed recommendations and standards that the automotive service technician and equipment manufacturers should follow. These agencies include the National Institute for Occupational Safety and Health (NIOSH), the Occupational Safety and Health Administration (OSHA), and the Environmental Protection Agency (EPA).

2.7.1   OSHA Asbestos Standards

The Occupational Safety and Health Administration (OSHA) has established three levels of asbestos exposure. Any vehicle service establishment that does either brake or clutch work must limit employee exposure to asbestos to less than 0.2 fibers per cubic centimeter (cc) as determined by an air sample. If the level of employee exposure is greater than specified, corrective measures must be taken and a large fine may be imposed.

Research has found that worn asbestos fibers, such as from automotive brakes or clutches, may not be as hazardous as first believed. Worn asbestos fibers do not have sharp flared ends that can latch onto tissue, but rather are worn down to a dust form that resembles talc. Grinding or sawing operations on unworn brake shoes or clutch discs *will* contain *harmful* asbestos fibers. To limit health damage, always use proper handling procedures while working around any component that may contain asbestos.

2.7.2   EPA Asbestos Regulations

The federal Environmental Protection Agency (EPA) has established procedures for the removal and disposal of asbestos. The EPA procedures require that products containing asbestos be "wetted" to prevent the asbestos fibers from becoming airborne. According to the EPA, asbestos-containing materials can be disposed of as regular waste—asbestos is only considered hazardous when it is airborne.

2.7.3   Asbestos Handling Guidelines

The air in the shop area can be tested by a testing laboratory, but this can be expensive. Tests have determined that asbestos levels can easily be kept below the recommended levels by using a solvent or a special vacuum.

◄ **NOTE** ►

Even though manufacturers are removing asbestos from brake and clutch lining materials, the service technician cannot tell whether the old brake pads or shoes or clutch discs contain asbestos. Therefore, to be safe, the technician should assume that all brake pads or shoes or clutch discs contain asbestos.

2.7.3.1 HEPA Vacuum   A special **high-efficiency particulate air (HEPA)** vacuum system has been proven to be effective in keeping asbestos exposure levels below 0.1 fibers per cubic centimeter.

2.7.3.2 Liquid/Solvent Brake Cleaners   Many technicians use an aerosol can of brake cleaning solvent to wet the brake dust and prevent it from becoming airborne. Some of the brake cleaning solvents may be hazardous; be sure to read the label on the product. Commercial brake cleaners are available that use a concentrated cleaner that is mixed with water (Figure 2-2). The waste liquid is filtered, and when dry, the filter can be disposed of as solid waste.

Never use compressed air to blow brake dust. The fine talclike brake dust can create a health hazard even if asbestos is not present or is present in dust rather than fiber form.

FIGURE 2-2   All brakes should be washed with liquid to help keep brake dust from becoming airborne. (*Courtesy of James Halderman*)

2.7.3.3 Disposal of Brake Dust and Brake Shoes   As mentioned, the hazard of asbestos occurs when asbestos fibers are airborne. Once the asbestos has been wetted down, it is (currently) considered to be solid waste, not hazardous waste. Old brake shoes and pads should be enclosed, preferably in a plastic bag, to help prevent any of the brake material from becoming airborne.

2.8   PROPER DISPOSAL

Always follow current federal and local laws considering disposal of all waste.

2.8.1   Used Brake Fluid

Most brake fluid is made from polyglycol; it is water soluble and can be considered hazardous if it has absorbed metals from the brake system.

- Collect **used brake fluid** in containers clearly marked to indicate that they are dedicated for that purpose.
- If your waste brake fluid is hazardous, manage it appropriately and use only an authorized waste receiver for its disposal.
- If your waste brake fluid is nonhazardous, determine from your local solid waste collection provider how to dispose of it properly.

- Do not mix brake fluid with used engine oil.
- Do not pour brake fluid down drains or onto the ground.
- Recycle brake fluid through a registered recycler.

2.8.2   Used Oil

Used oil is any petroleum-based or synthetic oil that has been used. During normal use, impurities such as dirt, metal scrapings, water, or chemicals can get mixed in with the oil. Eventually, this used oil must be replaced with virgin or re-refined oil. The EPA's used oil management standards include a three-pronged approach to determine if a substance meets the definition of used oil. To meet this definition, a substance must satisfy each of the following three criteria:

1. **Origin.**   The first criterion for identifying used oil is based on the origin of the oil. Used oil must have been refined from crude oil or made from synthetic materials. Animal and vegetable oils are excluded from the EPA's definition of used oil.

2. **Use.**   The second criterion is based on whether and how the oil is used. Oils used as lubricants, hydraulic fluids, heat transfer fluids, and for other similar purposes are considered used oil. Unused oil, such as bottom clean-out waste from virgin fuel oil storage tanks or virgin fuel oil recovered from a spill, do not meet the EPA's definition of used oil because these oils have never been "used." The EPA's definition also excludes products used as cleaning agents or solely for their solvent properties, as well as certain petroleum-derived products like antifreeze and kerosene.

3. **Contaminants.**   The third criterion is based on whether the oil is contaminated with either physical or chemical impurities. In other words, to meet the EPA's definition, used oil must become contaminated as a result of being used. This aspect of the EPA's definition includes residues and contaminants generated from handling, storing, and processing used oil.

◄ **NOTE** ►

The release of only 1 gallon of used oil (a typical oil change) can make a million gallons of fresh water undrinkable.

If used oil is dumped down the drain and enters a sewage treatment plant, concentrations as small as 50–100 PPM (parts per million) in the wastewater can foul sewage treatment processes. Never mix a listed hazardous waste, gasoline, wastewater, hologenated solvent, antifreeze, or an unknown waste material with used oil. Adding any of these substances will cause the used oil to become contaminated, which classifies it as hazardous waste.

2.8.2.1 Disposal of Used Oil

Once oil has been used, it can be collected, recycled, and used over and over again. An estimated 380 million gallons of used oil are recycled each year. Recycled used oil can sometimes be used again for the same job or for a completely different task. For example, used motor oil can be re-refined and sold at the store as motor oil or processed for heating fuel. After collecting used oil in an appropriate container (for example, a 55-gallon steel drum), the material must be disposed of in one of two ways:

- Shipped off-site for recycling
- Burned in an on-site or off-site EPA-approved heater for energy recovery

2.8.2.2 Used Oil Storage

Used oil must be stored in compliance with existing *underground storage tank (UST)* or an *aboveground storage tank (AGST)* standard or kept in separate containers. Containers are portable receptacles, such as a 55-gallon steel drum.

Keep used-oil storage drums in good condition. This means that they should be covered, secured from vandals, properly labeled, and maintained in compliance with local fire codes. Frequent inspections for leaks, corrosion, spillage, and so on are an essential part of container maintenance.

Never store used oil in anything other than the proper tanks and storage containers. Used oil may also be stored in containers that are permitted to store regulated hazardous waste.

Follow used oil filters disposal regulations. Used oil filters contain used engine oil that may be hazardous. Before an oil filter is placed in the trash or sent for recycling, it must be drained using one of the following hot-draining methods approved by the EPA:

- Puncture the filter antidrain back valve or filter dome end and hot-drain for at least 12 hours.
- Hot-drain and crush.
- Dismantle and hot-drain.
- Use any other hot-draining method that will remove all the used oil from the filter.

After the oil has been drained from the oil filter, the filter housing can be disposed of in any of the following ways:

- Recycling
- Pickup by a service contract company
- Disposed of in regular trash

2.8.3 Solvents

The major sources of chemical danger are liquid and aerosol brake cleaning fluids that contain chlorinated hydrocarbon solvents. The most common of these solvents are 1,1,1-trichloroethane, trichloroethylene, and tetrachloroethylene, which is also known as perchloroethylene, or "perk" for short. These solvents are all members of the same chemical family and share the same basic characteristics. They are colorless liquids with an odor of chloroform or ether. In large enough quantities these solvents can dull the senses, induce sleep, or cause a stupor. Very high levels of exposure over even a short period of time can be fatal. Repeated exposure to these solvents, in high concentrations and over long periods of time, can result in liver, kidney, and lung damage and may potentially cause cancer. Additionally, if these solvents are exposed to high heat or an open flame, they decompose into deadly gases such as hydrogen chloride, phosgene, and carbon monoxide.

Because 1,1,1-trichloroethane and trichloroethylene are known to be ozone depleters, the EPA prohibited their manufacture after January 1, 1996. Perks do not deplete the ozone and their use continues. Several other chemicals that do not deplete the ozone, such as heptane, hexane, and xylene, are now being used in nonchlorinated brake cleaning solvents. Some manufacturers are also producing solvents they describe as environmentally responsible that are biodegradable and noncarcinogenic.

Another solvent that can affect health is *n*-Hexane, a major component in several brands of automotive and industrial cleaners.

Some local areas like the South Coast Air Quality Management District in Southern California have regulations and standards for air quality and various chemicals that can affect air quality, including chemicals like solvents that evaporate into the air.

2.8.3.1 Sources of Chemical Poisoning

The health hazards presented by automotive cleaning solvents occur from three different forms of exposure: ingestion, inhalation, or physical contact. It should be obvious that swallowing automotive cleaning solvent is harmful, and such occurrences are not common. Automotive cleaning solvents should always be handled and stored properly and kept out of reach of children. The dangers of inhalation are perhaps the most serious problem—even very low levels of solvent vapors are hazardous. For example, the current OSHA standard (1910.1000) for airborne trichloroethylene is 100 parts per million (ppm) in the ambient air averaged over an 8-hour period. The ceiling level for exposure is 200 ppm, and there is a maximum acceptable peak level of 300 ppm for 5 minutes in any 2-hour period. The limits for other chlorinated hydrocarbon solvents, and for other chemicals replacing the chlorinated ones, are similar. These alternative chemicals are being used because they do not deplete the ozone layer, not because they are necessarily any safer to breathe, ingest, or touch.

Ingestion and inhalation are common forms of poisoning from many hazardous substances, but allowing automotive cleaning solvents to come in contact with the skin presents a danger unknown to many people. Not only do these solvents strip natural oils from the skin and cause irritation of the tissues, but they also have the ability to be absorbed through the skin directly into the bloodstream. The transfer begins immediately upon contact and continues until the liquid is wiped or washed away.

There is no specific standard for physical contact with chlorinated hydrocarbon solvents or the chemicals replacing them. All contact should be avoided whenever possible. The law requires an employer to provide appropriate protective equipment and ensure proper work practices by an employee handling these chemicals.

2.8.3.2 Effects of Chemical Poisoning   The effects of exposure to chlorinated hydrocarbon and other types of solvents can take many forms. Short-term exposure at low levels can cause headache, nausea, drowsiness, dizziness, lack of coordination, or unconsciousness. It may also cause irritation of the eyes, nose, and throat and flushing of the face and neck. Short-term exposure to higher concentrations can cause liver damage with symptoms such as yellow jaundice or dark urine. Liver damage may not become evident until several weeks after the exposure. Long-term or repeated exposure to perk may cause irritation or burning of the skin. It also increases the risk of damage to the liver or kidneys. If you experience any of these symptoms, seek medical treatment immediately, and tell the doctor about your exposure to brake cleaning solvents.

2.8.3.3 Chemical Precautions   Unlike many industrial applications of chlorinated hydrocarbon solvents, automotive parts/brake cleaning sprays and liquids present relatively limited opportunity for exposure to dangerous levels of contamination. The possibility still exists, however, and just as with asbestos, there are safety precautions that should be followed to minimize the risk.

Always use any automotive cleaning solvent in an open, well-ventilated area and avoid breathing the vapors. Take precautions to prevent physical contact with the liquid solvent and clean any spills from the skin promptly using soap and water. Wear protective clothing and immediately remove any piece of clothing that becomes dampened with solvent. Do not wear the item again until it has been cleaned. Wear safety goggles or other eye protection when spraying brake cleaning solvents. The safest procedure is to avoid using these chemicals completely.

◀ SAFETY TIP ▶

HAND SAFETY

Service technicians should wear protective rubber or rubberlike gloves or wash their hands with soap and water after handling engine oil, differential or transmission fluids, or other shop chemicals (Figure 2-3).

The service technician should not wear watches or rings or other jewelry that could come in contact with electrical or moving parts of a vehicle.

FIGURE 2-3   Protective gloves should be worn whenever working around grease or oil to help prevent possible skin problems. They help keep your hands clean, too! (*Courtesy of James Halderman*)

2.8.3.4 Status of Solvents as Hazardous and Regulatory Status Most used solvents are classified as hazardous wastes. Other characteristics include:

- Solvents with flash points below 140°F are considered flammable and, like gasoline, are federally regulated by the **Department of Transportation (DOT).**
- Solvents and oils with flash points above 140°F are considered combustible and, like engine oil, are also regulated by DOT.

It is the responsibility of the repair shop to determine if their spent solvent is hazardous waste. Waste solvents that are considered hazardous waste have a flash point below 140°F (60°C). Hot water or aqueous parts cleaners may be used to avoid disposing of spent solvent as hazardous waste. Solvent-type parts cleaners with filters are available to greatly extend solvent life and reduce spent solvent disposal costs. Solvent reclaimers are available that clean and restore the solvent so that it lasts indefinitely.

2.8.3.5 Used Solvents Used or spent solvents are liquid materials that have been generated as waste and may contain xylene, methanol, ethyl ether, and methyl isobutyl ketone (MIBK). These materials must be stored in OSHA-approved safety containers with tightly closed lids or caps (Figure 2-4). These storage receptacles must show no signs of leaks or significant damage due to dents or rust. In addition, the containers must be stored in a protected area equipped with secondary containment or spill protectors, such as a spill pallet. Additional requirements include:

- Containers should be clearly labeled "Hazardous Waste" and include the date the material was first placed into the storage receptacle.
- Labeling is not required for solvents being used in a parts washer.
- Used solvents will not be counted toward a facility's monthly output of hazardous waste if the vendor under contract removes the material.
- Used solvents may be disposed of by recycling with a local vendor, such as SafetyKleen, who removes the used solvent according to specific terms in the vendor agreement. See Figure 2-5.

2.8.4 Coolant Disposal

Coolant is a mixture of antifreeze and water. Proper **used coolant** disposal applies to all types of antifreeze coolant, including the following:

- **Ethylene glycol**—This is the type that has been used almost exclusively since the 1950s. It is

FIGURE 2-4 Typical fireproof flammable storage cabinet. (*Courtesy of James Halderman*)

FIGURE 2-5 All solvents and other hazardous waste should be disposed of properly. (*Courtesy of James Halderman*)

sweet-tasting and can harm or kill humans, wild animals, or pets if swallowed (usually yellow–green).

◄ NOTE ►

There is no universal color standard for antifreeze.

- **Propylene glycol**—Similar to ethylene glycol, this type of coolant is less harmful to pets and animals because it is not sweet-tasting, although it is still harmful if swallowed.
- **Organic acid technology (OAT)** antifreeze coolant (orange).
- **Hybrid organic acid technology (HOAT)** (orange or green).
- **VW/Audi pink**—Most of these coolants are HOAT (ethylene glycol-based with some silicate and containing an organic acid) and are phosphate-free.
- **Asian red**—This coolant is ethylene glycol-based and is silicate-free, yet contains phosphate.
- **Mercedes yellow**—This conventional ethylene glycol coolant has low amounts of silicate and no phosphates.
- **Korean or European blue**—This conventional ethylene glycol coolant has low amounts of silicate and no phosphates.

New antifreeze is not considered to be hazardous even though it can cause death if ingested. Used antifreeze may be hazardous due to dissolved metals from engine and other components of the cooling system. These metals can include iron, steel, aluminum, copper, brass, and lead (from older radiators and heater cores).

1. Coolant should be recycled either on-site or off-site.
2. Used coolant should be stored in a sealed and labeled container (Figure 2-6).
3. With a permit, used coolant can be disposed of by pouring into municipal sewers. Check with local authorities and obtain a permit before discharging used coolant into sanitary sewers.

2.8.5 Lead–Acid Battery Waste

About 70 million spent lead–acid batteries are disposed of each year in the United States alone. Lead is classified as a toxic metal and the acid used in lead–acid bat-

FIGURE 2-6 Used antifreeze coolants should be kept separate and stored in a leak-proof container until it can be recycled or disposed of according to federal, state, and local laws. Note that the storage barrel is placed inside another container to catch any coolant that may spill out of the inside barrel. (*Courtesy of James Halderman*)

teries is highly corrosive. The vast majority (95–98%) of these batteries are recycled through lead reclamation operations and secondary lead smelters for use in the manufacture of new batteries.

2.8.5.1 Status of Batteries as Hazardous and Regulatory Status
Used lead–acid batteries must be reclaimed or recycled. Leaking batteries must be stored and transported as hazardous waste. Some states have stricter regulations that require special handling procedures and transportation. According to the Battery Council International (BCI), battery laws usually include rules that:

- prohibit lead-acid battery disposal in landfills or incinerators,
- require batteries to be delivered to a battery retailer, wholesaler, recycling center, or lead smelter, and
- require all retailers of automotive batteries to post a sign that displays the universal recycling symbol and indicates the retailer's specific requirements for accepting used batteries.

◀ **CAUTION** ▶

Battery electrolyte contains sulfuric acid, which is a very corrosive substance capable of causing serious personal injury, such as skin burns and eye damage. In addition, the battery plates contain lead, which is highly poisonous. For this reason, disposing of batteries improperly can cause environmental contamination and lead to severe health problems.

2.8.5.2 Battery Handling and Storage Batteries, whether new or used, should be kept indoors if possible. The storage location should be an area specifically designated for battery storage and must be well ventilated (to the outside). If outdoor storage is the only alternative, a sheltered and secured area with acid-resistant secondary containment is strongly recommended. It is also advisable that acid-resistant secondary containment be used for indoor storage. In addition, batteries should be placed on acid-resistant pallets and never stacked!

2.8.6 Fuel Safety and Storage

Gasoline is very explosive. The expanding vapors are extremely dangerous and are present even in cold temperatures. The vapors that form in many vehicle gasoline tanks are controlled, but vapors from stored gasoline may escape from the can, resulting in a hazardous situation. Therefore, place gasoline storage containers in a well-ventilated space. Although diesel fuel is not as volatile as gasoline, the same basic rules apply.

- Approved gasoline storage cans have a flash-arresting screen at the outlet. These screens prevent external ignition sources from igniting the gasoline within the can when someone pours the gasoline or diesel fuel.
- Technicians must always use approved *red* gasoline containers to allow for proper hazardous substance identification (Figure 2-7).
- Do not fill gasoline containers completely full. Always leave the level of gasoline at least 1 inch from the top of the container. This will allow room for the gasoline to expand at higher temperatures. If the containers are completely full, the expanding gasoline will be forced from the can and create a dangerous spill.

FIGURE 2-7   This portable gasoline supply is a sealed steel container that is painted red. (*Courtesy of James Halderman*)

- If gasoline or diesel fuel containers must be stored, place them in a designated storage locker or facility.
- Never leave gasoline containers open except while filling or pouring gasoline from the container.
- Never use gasoline as a cleaning agent.
- Always connect a ground strap to containers when filling or transferring fuel or other flammable products from one container to another, in order to prevent static electricity that could result in explosion and fire. These ground wires prevent the buildup of a static electric charge, which could result in a spark and a disastrous explosion.

2.8.7 Air Bag Handling

Air bag modules are pyrometer devices that can be ignited if exposed to an electrical charge or if the front or sides of the vehicle are subjected to a sudden shock. Air bag safety should include the following precautions:

1. Disarm the air bag(s) if you will be working in the area where a discharged bag could make contact

with any part of your body. Consult service information for the exact procedure to follow for the vehicle being serviced.

2. Do not expose an air bag to extreme heat or fire.
3. Always carry an air bag pointing away from your body.
4. Place an air bag module facing upward.
5. Always follow the manufacturer's recommended procedure for air bag disposal or recycling, including the proper packaging to use during shipment.
6. Always wash your hands or body well if exposed to a deployed air bag. The chemicals involved can cause skin irritation and a possible rash to develop.
7. Wear protective gloves if handling a deployed air bag.

2.8.8 Used Tire Disposal

Used tires are an environmental concern for several reasons, including:

1. In a landfill, they tend to "float" up through the other trash and rise to the surface.
2. Tires trap and hold rainwater, which is a breeding ground for mosquitoes. Mosquito-borne diseases include encephalitis and dengue fever.
3. Used tires present a fire hazard and when they burn they create a large amount of black smoke that contaminates the air.

Used tires can be reused until the end of their useful life and then should be disposed of in one of the following ways:

1. Tires can be retreaded.
2. Tires can be recycled by shredding for use in asphalt.
3. Tires, removed from the wheel, can be sent to a landfill (most landfill operators will shred the tires because it is illegal in many states to landfill whole tires).
4. Tires can be burned in cement kilns or other power plants where the smoke can be controlled.

Use only a registered scrap tire handler to transport tires for disposal or recycling.

2.8.9 Air Conditioning Refrigerant Oil Disposal

Air conditioning refrigerant oil contains dissolved refrigerant and is therefore considered hazardous waste. This oil must be kept separate from other waste oil or the entire amount of oil must be treated as hazardous. Used refrigerant oil must be sent to a licensed hazardous waste disposal company for recycling or disposal (Figure 2-8).

◄ **SAFETY TIP** ►

INFECTION CONTROL PRECAUTIONS

Working on a vehicle can result in personal injury, including the possibility of being cut severely enough to cause serious bleeding. Some infections such as hepatitis B, HIV (which can cause acquired immunodeficiency syndrome, (AIDS)), hepatitis C virus, plus others are transmitted in the blood. These infections are commonly called *blood-borne pathogens*. Report any injury that involves blood to your supervisor and take the necessary precautions to avoid coming in contact with blood from another person.

FIGURE 2-8 Used refrigerant oil should be stored in a clearly labeled, secure container. (*Courtesy of James Halderman*)

REVIEW QUESTIONS

The following questions are provided to help you study as you read the chapter.

1. OSHA is short for _____ _____ and _____ _____.

2. Hazardous waste materials are _____ or _____that the shop no longer needs and that pose a danger.

3. EPA is short for _____ _____ _____.

4. A _____ material can burn skin or dissolve metal.

5. MSDS is short for _____ _____ _____ _____.

6. A MSDS contains information about a _____ _____.

7. _____ _____ or _____ _____ might contain asbestos.

8. Asbestos exposure can cause _____.

9. Used engine oil should be _____ so it can be used over and over.

10. Automotive solvents that contain _____ _____ solvents can cause health and environmental problems.

11. Cleaning solvents can strip _____ _____ from skin.

12. Some cleaning solvents have the ability to enter your _____ _____.

13. Technicians should wear _____ _____ and _____ _____.

14. Antifreeze can cause death if _____.

15. _____ is a very explosive liquid.

CHAPTER QUIZ

The following questions will help you check the facts you have learned. Select the answer that completes each statement correctly.

1. Technician A says that the Occupational Safety and Health Act was passed in 1970 to protect workers. Technician B says that the Environmental Protection Agency publishes a list of hazardous materials. Who is correct?
   a. Technician A
   b. Technician B
   c. Both A and B
   d. Neither A nor B

2. Hazardous materials include all of the following except _____.
   a. engine oil
   b. asbestos
   c. water
   d. brake cleaner

3. Technician A says that employees have a right to know if materials that they are working with are hazardous. Technician B says that all employees must be trained about hazardous materials. Who is correct?
   a. Technician A
   b. Technician B
   c. Both A and B
   d. Neither A nor B

4. Technician A says that any technician working on an automotive A/C system must be certified. Technician B says that all hazardous materials must be labeled. Who is correct?
   a. Technician A
   b. Technician B
   c. Both A and B
   d. Neither A nor B

5. To determine if a product or substance being used is hazardous, consult _____.
   a. a dictionary
   b. an MSDS
   c. EPA guidelines
   d. SAE standards

6. Technician A says that right-to-know laws state that employees have the right to know when they are working with hazardous materials. Technician B says that the right-to-know laws state that the employer has the responsibility to train employees about the hazardous wastes they will encounter in their workplace. Who is correct?
   a. Technician A
   b. Technician B
   c. Both A and B
   d. Neither A nor B

7. Technician A says that hazardous waste is material that the shop no longer needs that can pose a danger to people and the environment. Technician B says that material safety data sheets (MSDS) must be provided to all employees. Who is correct?
   a. Technician A
   b. Technician B
   c. Both A and B
   d. Neither A nor B

8. Technician A says that exposure to asbestos can cause serious health problems. Technician B says that all brake and clutch lining materials should be treated as if they contain asbestos. Who is correct?
   a. Technician A
   b. Technician B
   c. Both A and B
   d. Neither A nor B

9. Two technicians are discussing the disposal of used motor oil. Technician A says that used motor oil should be recycled. Technician B says that 1 gallon of used motor oil will make 1 million gallons of fresh water undrinkable. Who is correct?
   - **a.** Technician A
   - **b.** Technician B
   - **c.** Both A and B
   - **d.** Neither A nor B

10. Two technicians are discussing the solvents often used in automotive repair. Technician A says that physical contact with solvents should be avoided. Technician B says that all solvents should be used in open, well-ventilated areas. Who is correct?
    - **a.** Technician A
    - **b.** Technician B
    - **c.** Both A and B
    - **d.** Neither A nor B

11. Technician A says that used coolant can be recycled or, with a permit, disposed of by pouring it down a drain. Technician B says that new or used antifreeze can cause death if it is swallowed. Who is correct?
    - **a.** Technician A
    - **b.** Technician B
    - **c.** Both A and B
    - **d.** Neither A nor B

12. Technician A says that the lead in batteries is toxic and battery acid is corrosive. Technician B says that used batteries must be recycled. Who is correct?
    - **a.** Technician A
    - **b.** Technician B
    - **c.** Both A and B
    - **d.** Neither A nor B

13. Technician A says that gasoline vapors are very dangerous. Technician B says that gasoline should never be used to clean parts. Who is correct?
    - **a.** Technician A
    - **b.** Technician B
    - **c.** Both A and B
    - **d.** Neither A nor B

14. Two technicians are discussing how air bags should be handled. Technician A says that air bag systems should always be disarmed when working near them. Technician B says that air bags should never be exposed to extreme heat or fire. Who is correct?
    - **a.** Technician A
    - **b.** Technician B
    - **c.** Both A and B
    - **d.** Neither A nor B

15. Two technicians are discussing used tire disposal. Technician A says that recycled tires can be added to asphalt for roads. Technician B says that used tires are a fire hazard. Who is correct?
    - **a.** Technician A
    - **b.** Technician B
    - **c.** Both A and B
    - **d.** Neither A nor B

◀ Chapter 3 ▶

BASICS OF HEATING AND AIR CONDITIONING

LEARNING OBJECTIVES

After completing this chapter, you should:

1. Have a basic understanding of the purpose of the heating, ventilation, and air conditioning (HVAC) system in automobiles and other vehicles.
2. Have a basic understanding of temperature and humidity comfort zones.
3. Know how heat is measured in both temperature and quantity, using either metric or U.S./British units.

TERMS TO LEARN

air distribution	heat
air management	humidity
British thermal unit (Btu)	intensity
cabin filter	quantity
calorie	relative humidity (RH)
Celsius	thermal
comfort zone	watt
Fahrenheit	

3.1 INTRODUCTION

For the most part, the HVAC system of an automobile is designed to provide comfort for the driver and passengers. It is intended to maintain in-car temperature and humidity within a range that is comfortable for the people inside and provide fresh, clean air for ventilation. This temperature range also helps keep the driver alert and attentive.

Heating and air conditioning (A/C) systems control several aspects of an in-vehicle environment. This is often called *climate control*. Most people consider a comfortable temperature to be the most important climate control aspect. Two other major aspects are humidity and air cleanliness. We are all familiar with the temperature aspect—if it is too hot or too cold. Many of us realize the effects of humidity and how unpleasant a hot day can be if the humidity is too high. We all know that dusty, foul, or smelly conditions are unpleasant (Figure 3-1).

The HVAC system in a vehicle (Figure 3-2) can be divided into three closely related subsystems:

- **Air distribution,** also called **air management,** with the control system
- Heating
- Refrigeration, A/C

In this text, we will study these factors, concentrating for the most part on the ways that we can control air temperature. Because much of this study has to do with heat and how we move it, we need to cover the basic principles of heat. Air conditioning becomes relatively easy to understand when we are familiar with concepts such as latent heat and the pressure–temperature relationships of saturated vapors; it is almost impossible to understand A/C operation otherwise.

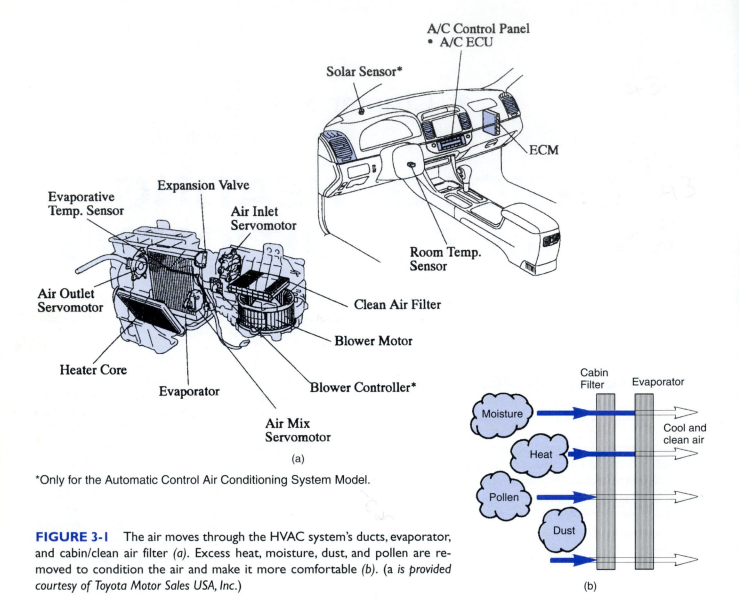

(a)

*Only for the Automatic Control Air Conditioning System Model.

FIGURE 3-1 The air moves through the HVAC system's ducts, evaporator, and cabin/clean air filter (a). Excess heat, moisture, dust, and pollen are removed to condition the air and make it more comfortable (b). (a is provided courtesy of Toyota Motor Sales USA, Inc.)

FIGURE 3-2 A typical HVAC system has a choice of two inlets (right), a blower to move the air, an A/C evaporator core and heater core, and several air discharge outlets.

3.2 HEAT

Heat is a form of basic energy, and, like other forms of energy, heat cannot be created or destroyed. It can, however, be converted to or from other forms of energy (Figure 3-3). Most automotive students realize that the engine converts the potential energy found in a fuel such as gasoline into heat. This **thermal** (heat) energy increases the air pressure in the cylinders, which in turn forces the crankshaft to revolve. Crankshaft rotation is mechanical energy, and this mechanical energy drives the car. The engine does not make the energy, but it transfers the energy from the gasoline to the rotating crankshaft (Figure 3-4).

FIGURE 3-3 Heat, like light and electricity, is one of the basic forms of energy. (*Courtesy of DaimlerChrysler Corporation*)

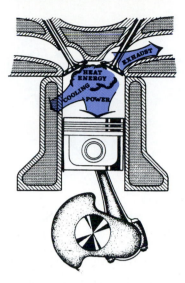

FIGURE 3-5 About one-third of the heat in an engine is converted into useful power. The other two-thirds is lost to the cooling and exhaust systems.

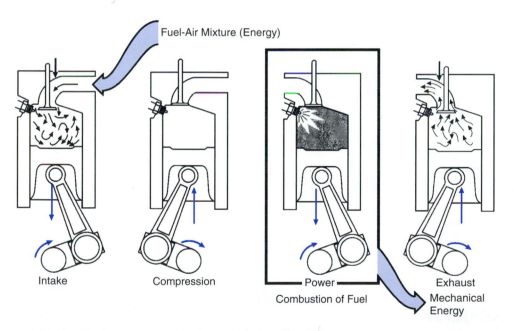

Fuel-Air Mixture (Energy)

Intake   Compression   Power   Exhaust
                          Combustion of Fuel   Mechanical Energy

FIGURE 3-4 An engine converts potential energy from fuel into mechanical energy.

An engine is not capable of converting all of the heat from the gasoline into mechanical energy in the short period of a combustion cycle. Because energy cannot be destroyed, this leftover heat energy is sent out the exhaust pipe or to the cooling system. We can feel the waste heat at both of these places (Figure 3-5).

Along with the concept of heat comes the concept of cold. Cold is merely the absence of heat. It is what is left if we remove all heat energy. Heat and cold are much like light and dark. Light is a form of energy, and dark is the absence of light. Light travels toward dark much like heat travels toward cold (Figure 3-6). The action of light is easy to see when we turn on a light in a dark room; the action of heat traveling toward cold can be felt as we come close to a hot stove. Heat is not affected by gravity, and its direction of travel can be upward as easily as downward, depending on where something is colder (Figure 3-7).

As we study heat further, we will find that it is relatively easy to measure and its methods of movement are very predictable and controllable.

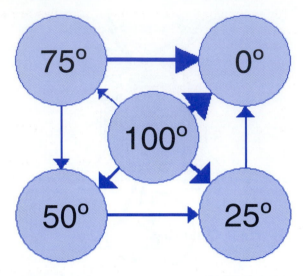

FIGURE 3-6 One of the basic principles of heat is that it always travels toward a colder area.

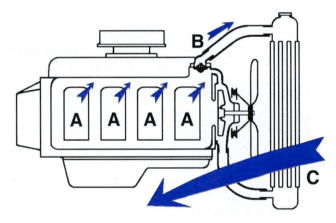

FIGURE 3-7 (A) In a cooling system, heat flows from the hot engine parts to the colder coolant (B), then to the colder radiator, and then to the colder ambient air (C).

3.3 HEAT MEASUREMENT

A heating and air conditioning technician is concerned with measuring two different aspects of heat: **intensity** and **quantity.** Intensity is what we feel; it is measured in degrees, on either a **Celsius** or **Fahrenheit** scale. Quantity is the actual amount of heat; it is measured in either **calories** or **British thermal units (Btu).**

3.3.1 Heat Intensity

Intensity of heat is important to us because it is what we feel. If it is too cold, we are uncomfortable. Ex-

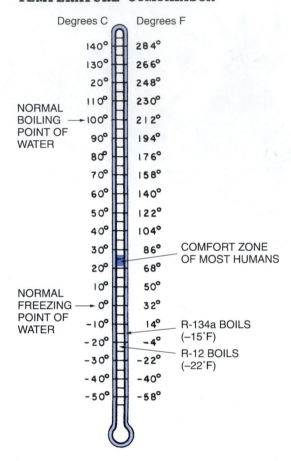

FIGURE 3-8 Heat intensity is measured using a thermometer. The two common measuring scales, Celsius and Fahrenheit, are shown here. This thermometer is also marked with important temperatures.

tremely cold temperatures can cause frostbite and hypothermia. The other end of the scale can also be uncomfortable and may cause heat stress and dehydration. Humans have a temperature **comfort zone** somewhere between 65 and 80°F (21 and 27°C). This comfort zone varies among individuals. Women tend to prefer slightly warmer temperatures than men, and older people tend to have a narrower comfort zone and prefer warmer temperatures than younger people (Figure 3-8).

Critical temperatures are also very important to us. A good example of this is the boiling point of many automotive cooling systems, about 260°F (126°C). If this temperature is exceeded, coolant will boil away, leaving the moving parts of the engine without protection. The next critical temperature is the breakdown point of the oil, a loss of lubrication, and probably bearing burnout or piston seizure to the cylinders.

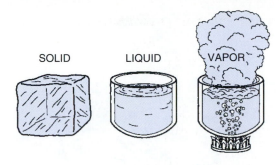

SOLID   LIQUID   VAPOR

FIGURE 3-9 Water is a solid, ice, below 32°F, and adding heat will change it to a liquid. Adding more heat will cause water to boil (above 212°F) and turn to vapor called steam.

Temperature or heat intensity scales allow us to discuss the amount of heat in an area or object and let us define the range of operation for people and objects.

3.3.1.1 Measuring Intensity Heat intensity is easily measured using a thermometer; as just mentioned, two different scales are in common usage. The Celsius scale, sometimes called the centigrade scale, is a metric measurement. The base for this scale, 0°C, is the freezing point of water; 100°C is the boiling point of water. The Fahrenheit scale has commonly been used in the United States and England. The freezing point of water on this scale is 32°F, and the boiling point is 212°F. We often use water when we discuss heat because we are familiar with it, and we can easily get an idea of its temperature by observing what state it is in: The temperature of ice must be 32°F (0°C) or lower and water as a liquid is usually between 32 and 212°F (0 and 100°C) (Figure 3-9). If we take away all heat, we are left with absolute cold or absolute zero. This temperature, which we will never encounter in the normal world, is −459.67°F (−273.15°C).

There are several ways to convert temperature between the Celsius and Fahrenheit scales. This conversion becomes easier if we remember these major points:

- 0°C = 32°F
- 100°C = 212°F
- The Celsius scale is 100° long from freezing to boiling
- The Fahrenheit scale is 180° long from freezing to boiling

The commonly used conversion formulas are as follows:

$$\text{Temperature in °C} \times 1.8 + 32 = \text{Temperature in °F } or$$
$$\frac{\text{Temperature in °C} \times 9 + 32}{5} = \text{Temperature in °F } or$$
$$\text{Temperature in °F} - 32 \times 0.556 = \text{Temperature in °C } or$$
$$\text{Temperature in °F} - 32 \times 5 \div 9 = \text{Temperature in °C}$$

The simplest way to convert between the Fahrenheit and Celsius scales is to use a conversion chart (Figure 3-10).

3.3.2 Heat Quantity

We use the concept of heat quantity to illustrate heat movement and transfer and to discuss efficiency. To heat or cool a person or object, we must move a certain amount of heat either to it or away from it. For example, when you buy a gallon of gasoline, you are really purchasing about 115,000 Btu of thermal energy, and your plan is to move that amount of heat into the engine to produce power (Figure 3-11).

Engineers rate heating and air conditioning units in calories—actually kilocalories (1,000 calorie units) (1 kilocalorie per second = 4.1868 kW)—or **watts** or Btu so that heating or air conditioning units can be sized to fit the load. Once they determine the expected heating or cooling load, they can select a unit with the correct size specification.

3.3.2.1 Measuring Quantity When we need to cool the interior of a vehicle that is at 122°F (50°C) down to 75°F (24°C), we become involved with removing a certain amount of heat energy from the car. This quantity depends on several factors: The size of the vehicle and the sun load are the most important. As mentioned earlier, we measure these quantities of heat in Btu, calories, or kilowatts.

A Btu is the amount of heat it takes to raise the temperature of 1 lb of water 1°F. Very similarly, a calorie is defined as the amount of heat it takes to increase the temperature of 1 g of water 1°C. A Btu is much larger: 1 Btu equals 252 calories. The burning of a kitchen-size wooden match gives off about 1 Btu when it burns completely (Figure 3-12).

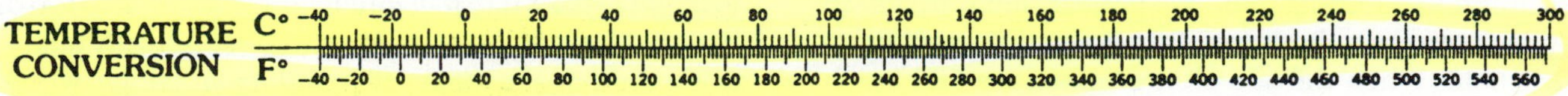

TEMPERATURE CONVERSION

C° −40 −20 0 20 40 60 80 100 120 140 160 180 200 220 240 260 280 300

F° −40 −20 0 20 40 60 80 100 120 140 160 180 200 220 240 260 280 300 320 340 360 380 400 420 440 460 480 500 520 540 560

FIGURE 3-10 A combined scale can be used to convert temperatures between the Celsius and Fahrenheit scales.

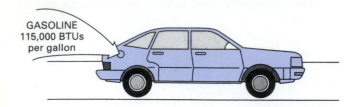

FIGURE 3-11 We put about 115,000 Btu of heat energy in the car with each gallon of gas we buy.

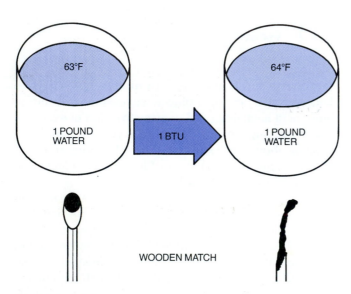

FIGURE 3-12 A wooden match produces about 1 Btu of heat when it burns. This amount of heat will increase the temperature of 1 lb of water 1°F. (*Courtesy of Fluke; reproduced with permission*)

3.4 COMFORT

Our goal in heating and air conditioning is to maintain a comfortable in-vehicle temperature and humidity. This is affected by the size of the vehicle, the number of passengers, and the amount of glass area, to name only a few variables. The internal body temperature of humans is about 98.6°F (37°C), which seems odd when our most comfortable temperature is 65 to 80°F (21 to 27°C). This means that in the summer we must continuously give off heat to be comfortable, but in the winter suitable clothing can keep heat next to us to maintain warmth. Body comfort is also affected by radiant heat: When the sun shines on us, we feel much warmer. Depending on the season of the year, this can be good or bad. Solar engineers are working on ways

FIGURE 3-13 Human comfort is greatly affected by temperature and humidity. (*Courtesy of www.ergonomics4schools.com*)

to control this heat flow as the amount of glass area of a vehicle increases.

The velocity of air past our bodies is another factor in human comfort. In the summer, this helps us feel cooler; in the winter, a chill factor can be created if the warm air that surrounds our bodies is blown away. Air movement is an important part of heating and A/C systems. (The blower motor and air registers are discussed more completely in Chapter 10.)

3.4.1 Humidity

A factor that greatly affects the heat flow to or from our bodies is **humidity**, the amount of water in the air around us. The amount of water vapor suspended in air can vary from a perfectly dry 0% to a foggy 100%, where drizzle or rain forms. The amount of water vapor air can hold varies with temperature and is referred to as **relative humidity (RH).** Air at 50°F (10°C) can hold a maximum of 0.33 oz (9.41 g) in a cubic meter (100% RH), but it can hold 0.61 oz (17.3 g) at 68°F (20°C). Warm air can hold much more water vapor than cold air. This is why dew forms as air cools and fog burns off as a day becomes warmer.

Humid cold air feels much colder than dry air at the same temperature. Humid hot air slows down our natural body cooling system (evaporation of perspiration), so it can make a day feel much hotter. Air that is too dry also tends to make us uncomfortable. As with temperature, we have a range of humidity in which we feel most comfortable, about 45 to 50% for most people (Figure 3-13).

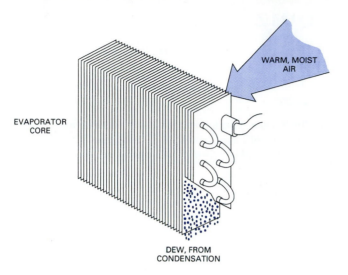

FIGURE 3-14 When air comes into contact with the cold evaporator, excess moisture forms dew. This condensed moisture leaves the car through the evaporator drain.

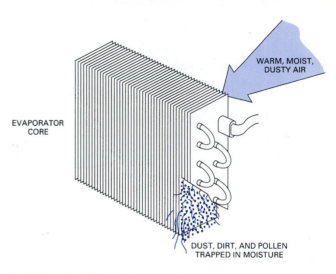

FIGURE 3-15 The dew on the evaporator traps dust and pollen that comes in contact with it; the dust and pollen drain out with the water.

As it operates, a vehicle's air conditioner dehumidifies, or removes moisture from, air. Water vapor condenses on the cold evaporator fins just as on the glass holding a cold drink. This condensed water then drops off the evaporator and runs out the drain at the bottom of the evaporator case. In-vehicle humidity becomes about 40 to 45% on even the most humid days if the A/C is operated long enough. This level, of course, will be higher if any wet, outside air enters. A good example of this dehumidification process occurs when a vehicle's A/C is operated on cold days when the windows are fogged up; it usually takes only a short time to dry the air and remove the fog from the windows (Figure 3-14).

3.4.2 Cleanliness

A side effect of air conditioning is the cleaning of the air coming into the car as it passes through the cooling ductwork. The act of cooling and dehumidifying air at the A/C evaporator causes water droplets to form on the evaporator fins. Dust and other contaminants in the air that come into contact with these droplets become trapped and are flushed out of the system as the water drops drain from the evaporator (Figure 3-15). Some new vehicles incorporate **cabin filters** into their A/C and heating systems to clean the air even more thoroughly by trapping dust and pollen particles before they enter the passenger compartment.

REVIEW QUESTIONS

The following questions are provided to help you study as you read the chapter.

1. HVAC is short for _____, _____, and _____ _____.

2. A typical HVAC system uses a(n) _____ to cool the air, a(n) _____ to warm the air, and _____ or _____ to control the air flow.

3. _____ is a form of energy that makes us feel warmer, and _____ is the absence of heat.

4. Heat intensity is commonly measured using either the _____ or _____ scale.

5. A temperature of 100° C is equal to _____ °F.

6. Heat quantity is commonly measured using units of _____ or _____.

7. Heat always moves from _____ to _____.

8. The A/C system can make air _____, _____, and _____.

9. RH is generally _____ as air warms up.

10. Moisture that collects on the evaporator reduces the _____ in the vehicle.

CHAPTER QUIZ

The following questions will help you check the facts you have learned. Select the answer that completes each statement correctly.

1. A vehicle's HVAC system contains a(n) _____ system.
   - **a.** A/C
   - **b.** heater
   - **c.** air distribution
   - **d.** All of these

2. Air conditioning systems control which of the following in a vehicle?
   - **a.** Temperature
   - **b.** Humidity
   - **c.** Air cleanliness
   - **d.** All of these

3. Two technicians are discussing heat movement. Technician A says that heat is a form of energy. Technician B says heat travels from hot to cold. Who is correct?
   - **a.** Technician A
   - **b.** Technician B
   - **c.** Both A and B
   - **d.** Neither A nor B

4. Heat intensity refers to which of the following?
   - **a.** The amount of heat in an area
   - **b.** The number of Btu in an area
   - **c.** The heat individuals feel
   - **d.** None of these

5. The freezing point of water is _____ on the Celsius scale.
   - **a.** 100°
   - **b.** 0°
   - **c.** 32°
   - **d.** 212°

6. The boiling point of water is _____ on the Fahrenheit scale.
   - **a.** 0°
   - **b.** 32°
   - **c.** 100°
   - **d.** 212°

7. Technician A says that 1 c of heat can increase the temperature of 1 g of water by 1°F. Technician B says the temperature will increase 1°C if 1 c is added. Who is correct?
   - **a.** Technician A
   - **b.** Technician B
   - **c.** Both A and B
   - **d.** Neither A nor B

8. The normal temperature for the average human is _____.
   - **a.** 80°F
   - **b.** 100°F
   - **c.** 60°F
   - **d.** 98.6°F

9. The amount of moisture contained by air is called _____.
   - **a.** temperature
   - **b.** ambient
   - **c.** humidity
   - **d.** None of these

10. In addition to cooling the passenger compartment, an air conditioning system _____.
    - **a.** heats the passengers
    - **b.** dehumidifies the air
    - **c.** puts moisture in the air
    - **d.** All of these

Chapter 4

HEAT MOVEMENT THEORY

LEARNING OBJECTIVES

After completing this chapter, you should:

1. Understand how heat can be transferred from one location to another.
2. Be familiar with the three states of matter and the effect that heat has on them.
3. Understand what latent heat is and why it is important to A/C.
4. Understand how pressure is measured.
5. Understand the effect that pressure has on boiling points.

TERMS TO LEARN

bar
boiling point
chlorofluorocarbon (CFC)
conduction
convection
critical pressure
critical temperature
gas
gauge pressures
heat exchanger
hydrochlorofluorocarbon (HCFC)
hydrofluorocarbon (HFC)
insulator
latent heat

latent heat of condensation
latent heat of evaporation
latent heat of fusion
liquid
kilopascal (kPa)
pounds per square inch absolute (psia)
pounds per square inch gauge (psig)
pressure
pressure–temperature (PT)
radiant heat
refrigerant

retrofit
saturated vapor
sensible heat
solid

subcool
superheat
vacuum

4.1 INTRODUCTION

In practical terms, an HVAC system moves heat. The A/C system simply transfers the heat out of a place where it is not wanted, and the heating system moves the heat into a place where it is wanted. Several physical principles are involved. If we understand these basic principles, the operation of the A/C system becomes easily understandable. This understanding, in turn, makes diagnosing and servicing an A/C system relatively easy and quite interesting.

Heat always moves from hot to cold. Remember that heat is energy, and cold is lack of energy. The rate or speed that heat moves, then, is simply a factor of the difference in the temperature between the hot and cold areas. A large temperature difference moves heat much faster than if the two areas are almost the same temperature. The heat flow tends to make the hot item cooler and the cool item warmer. If left alone, the two areas become the same temperature, and the heat flow stops (Figure 4-1).

Understanding heat flow shows us that if we want to cool a hot car, we have to create a place inside the car for the heat to go to; this place must be colder than our

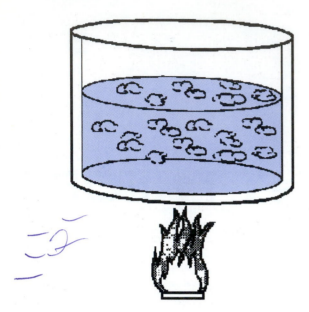

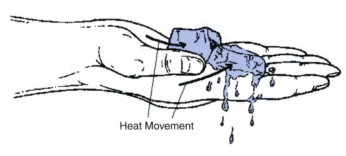

Heat Movement

FIGURE 4-1 Heat always moves from hot to cold. In this example, it will travel from the fire to the cooler water and from the hand to the cooler ice.

desired in-car temperature. Because cooling the car makes the hot place cooler, we have to move the heat elsewhere. The only other place to move it is outside the car, and the ambient air temperature around the car is often hotter than inside. This means we have to take the heat from inside the car and make it hotter than the air outside the car. As we shall see, this takes a little energy from the engine, but it is actually fairly easy to do once we learn a little about heat (Figure 4-2).

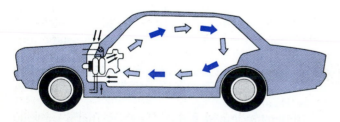

FIGURE 4-2 Heat can enter a vehicle's passenger compartment from several sources. The A/C system allows us to move excess heat out of the vehicle.

FIGURE 4-3 The transfer of heat directly through a material is called conduction. *(Courtesy of DaimlerChrysler Corporation)*

4.2   HEAT MOVEMENT

Heat can travel on one or more of three paths as it moves from hot to cold: *conduction, convection,* and *radiation.* Heat travel can be beneficial and intentional, or it can be detrimental. Understanding it allows us to either control its flow or avoid unwanted heat movement as we promote the desired movement; for example, to make living with radiant heat easier, many of us park our cars in the warm sunshine in the winter and the cooler shade in the summer.

4.2.1   Conduction

The simplest heat movement is **conduction,** by which heat travels through a medium such as a solid or liquid, moving from one molecule of the material to the next. If we heat one end of a wire, heat will go in one end and be conducted through the material, and the wire will become hot at the other end (Figure 4-3).

Some materials (most of the metals) are good heat conductors. Copper and aluminum are among the best of the commonly used metals, so we make most **heat exchangers** (radiators, evaporators, and condensers) from them. Some materials (wood, for example) are poor heat conductors, and some (styrofoam, for example) conduct heat so poorly that they are called **insulators.** Most good insulators incorporate a lot of air or gaseous material in their structure because air is a poor heat conductor.

4.2.2   Convection

Convection is a process of transferring heat by moving the heated medium. The medium is fluid, in either a liquid or gaseous state, so we can heat it in one location and move it to another location where the heat is re-

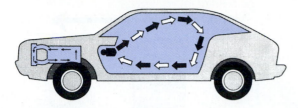

FIGURE 4-4 We move heat from the heater to the passengers or from the passengers to the A/C system by convection. Heat movement from the engine to the radiator using circulating coolant is also an example of convection.

leased. A convection current is a continuous flow of the medium and heat.

An example of convection is a vehicle's cooling system. Coolant (the medium) is heated in the water jackets next to the cylinders and combustion chambers. Then it is pumped to the radiator, where the heat is transferred to the air traveling through the radiator. Convection also occurs in the interior of the car, where we circulate air past the driver and passengers to pick up heat and move the air to the evaporator, where the heat is transferred to the cooler evaporator fins (Figure 4-4).

Convection can be forced by a fan or pump, or it can occur naturally. Most materials expand as they are heated, which decreases their weight per volume. Hotter liquids and gases tend to rise, and cooler ones tend to drop. When heating occurs in a liquid or gas, the warmer, lighter parts naturally rise and the cooler, heavier parts fall. Natural convection currents occur in every volume of liquid or gas that is not heated evenly. Sometimes we can feel this movement: If we were to stand next to a hot stove in a cold room, we would feel the warmed air rising above the stove and the cooler air moving horizontally, down low, toward the stove (Figure 4-5).

4.2.3 Radiation

Heat can travel through heat rays and pass from one location to another without warming the air through which it passes. The best example of this is the heat from the sun, which passes through cold space and warms our planet and everything it shines on. **Radiant heat** can pass from any warmer object through air to any cooler object. It is affected by the color and texture of both the heat emitter, where the heat leaves, and the collector, where the heat is absorbed. Dark, rough surfaces make better heat emitters and collectors than light-colored, smooth surfaces (Figure 4-6).

Radiant heat can be beneficial (for example, passing through the windows and warming the interior of a car or building in winter), but this same heat can be

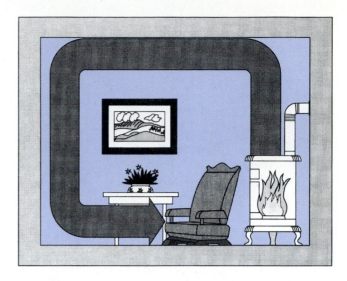

FIGURE 4-5 Heated air next to the stove will rise and cooler air will move in to replace it. This creates a convection current to move the air and heat. *(Courtesy of Daimler-Chrysler Corporation)*

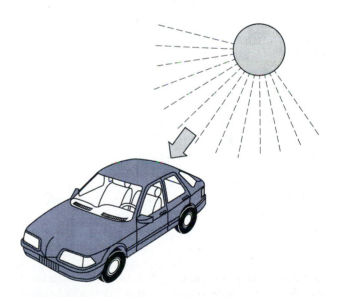

FIGURE 4-6 Heat is transferred from the sun to things on Earth through radiation. *(Courtesy of Toyota Motor Sales USA, Inc.)*

very detrimental in the summer. It is not unusual for sunlight to pass through a window, where it is absorbed by dark dash pads or upholstery, and produce in-car temperatures of 150°F (66°C) or higher (Figure 4-7). (At one time, California Highway Patrol cars were painted all black. Painting the tops white benefited the patrol officers by lowering the in-car temperature significantly.) The engine, radiator, and exhaust system all radiate heat, which can find its way into the passenger compartment.

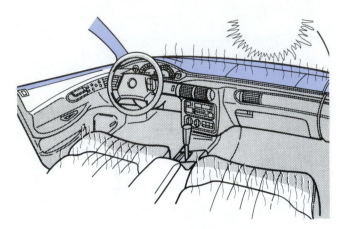

FIGURE 4-7   Radiant heat entering a vehicle through the windows can add a lot of heat to a car's interior. *(Courtesy of DaimlerChrysler Corporation)*

4.3   STATES OF MATTER

The air conditioning process works through a fluid, called a **refrigerant,** that continuously changes state from liquid to gas and back to liquid. These changes of state are where the movement of heat needed for cooling occurs. All basic materials exist in one of the states of matter—**solid, liquid,** or **gas**—and most of them can be changed from one state to another by adding or removing heat (Figure 4-8).

Molecules are the building blocks for all things we can see or feel. Molecules are combinations of atoms, which are in turn made up of electrons and protons. The protons are in the center, or nucleus, of the atom; the electrons travel in an orbit around them. There are about 100 basic elements or atoms, each having a different atomic number, that combine with other elements to make the many, varied molecules. The atomic number of an element is based on the number of electrons and protons in that element. The periodic table of elements seen in most chemistry laboratories shows the relationship of these elements.

In A/C we are primarily concerned with four different molecules: water, refrigerant 12 (R-12), refrigerant 22 (R-22), and refrigerant 134a (R-134a). Water molecules are H_2O; this is a combination of a single oxygen atom and two hydrogen atoms. Hydrogen has

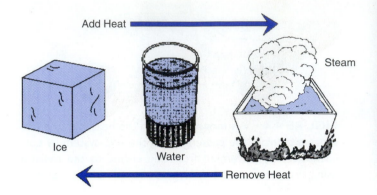

FIGURE 4-8   We can cause matter to change state by adding or removing heat.

an atomic number of 1 (1 proton and 1 electron), and oxygen has an atomic number of 8 (8 electrons and 8 protons). Again, we are describing water because we are familiar with it in all three states: solid ice, liquid water, and gaseous steam. R-12, R-22, and R-134a are described more completely at a later point in this chapter (Figure 4-9).

4.3.1   Solid

Solid matter is familiar; it has a definite shape and substance. Solids exert pressure in only one direction, and that is downward because of gravity.

Most of us know that ice is the solid form of water, will hold its shape, and is cold. Water is normally a solid at temperatures below 32°F (0°C), which is the normal freezing point. The electrons in the molecule's atoms are still orbiting around the protons, but the movement has been slowed because much of the heat energy has been removed (Figure 4-10).

4.3.2   Liquid

Adding heat to most solids produces a liquid as the solid material melts. It is the same material, but heat energy has broken the molecular bond and has made the matter fluid. A fluid has no shape and needs a container to hold it; a fluid takes the shape of its container. Liquid is affected by gravity but also exerts pressure sideways.

FIGURE 4-9   A water molecule contains two oxygen atoms and one hydrogen atom; R-12 is a combination of one carbon, two chlorine, and two fluorine atoms; and R-134a is a combination of two carbon, four fluorine, and two hydrogen atoms.

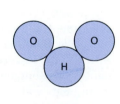

WATER–H_2O

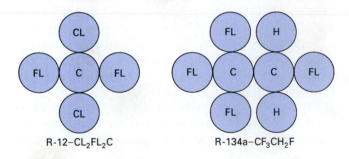

R-12–CL_2FL_2C R-134a–CF_3CH_2F

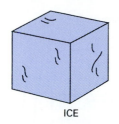

Solid:
H_2O at temperatures below 32°F, 0°C:
Solid, has definite shape
Exerts pressure downward

ICE

FIGURE 4-10   Ice is a solid form of water with a low temperature and slow molecular action.

Liquid:
H_2O at temperatures between 32° and 212°F (0° and 100°C):
Liquid/fluid, takes shape of container
Exerts pressure downward and to sides

WATER

FIGURE 4-11   Water is warmer than ice and has a much freer molecular action.

STEAM

Gas:
H_2O at temperatures above 212°F, 100°C:
Gas has no shape
Can exert pressure in all directions

FIGURE 4-12   Adding heat to water produces steam, the gas state, with a much freer molecular action.

Another point important to A/C is that liquids flow through a pipe or hose and can be pumped.

Water is normally a liquid between 32 and 212°F (0 and 100°C). It is the same molecule as ice, but heat energy has increased the movement of the electrons (Figure 4-11).

4.3.3   Gas

Adding heat to most liquids produces gas as the liquids boil. It is the same material, but the heat energy has freed the molecular bonds still further so that the molecule has no shape at all and has expanded so much that it has very little weight. A gas molecule exerts pressure in every direction. Gases can also be pumped through hoses and pipes, making them easy to move through an A/C system.

At temperatures above 212°F (100°C) water normally boils to become a gas, called steam. Again, this is

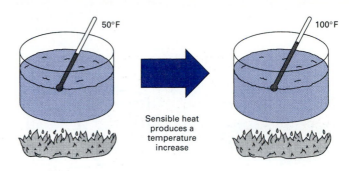

50°F   100°F

Sensible heat produces a temperature increase

FIGURE 4-13   Heat that causes a temperature increase is called *sensible heat.*

the same molecule as water or ice, but heat energy has greatly increased molecular movement (Figure 4-12).

4.4   LATENT AND SENSIBLE HEAT

Sensible heat makes sense; it can be felt and measured on a thermometer. If we have 1 lb of water at 40°F and add 1 Btu of heat to it, the temperature will increase to 41°F; adding another Btu of heat will increase the temperature to 42°F; and adding another 170 Btu (212 − 42) will increase the temperature to 212°F, the boiling point.

Sensible heat is fairly easy to understand, but if we add more heat, an odd thing occurs (Figure 4-13). If we add another Btu of heat to water at 212°F, some of the water will boil, but the temperature of both the water and the steam produced will remain at 212°F. The added heat has caused some of the water to change state, but it has not changed temperature. This is an example of **latent,** or *hidden,* **heat.** We can watch this happen each time we boil water. The water boils a little bit at a time. It takes a large amount of heat to get the water to change into steam, and we end up with steam that is the same temperature as the water. Latent heat causes a change in state but no change in temperature (Figure 4-14). Once water reaches 212°F, it cannot get any hotter; it simply boils.

To change 1 lb of water at 212°F into 1 lb of steam at 212°F, we must add 970 Btu of heat. Using metric terms, to change 1 g of water at 100°C into 1 g of steam at 100°C, we must add 540 calories of heat. This is called the **latent heat of evaporation.** To reverse this and change 1 lb of steam back into 1 lb of water, we have to remove this same 970 Btu of heat; this is called the **latent heat of condensation.** It should be noted that the latent heat of evaporation requires much more heat than the amount of heat required to raise the temperature from the freezing point to the boiling point (Figure 4-15).

This is the major principle through which A/C works. Heat added in the car's evaporator causes the liquid refrigerant to change state, and it absorbs the latent heat of evaporation. This heat is released from the

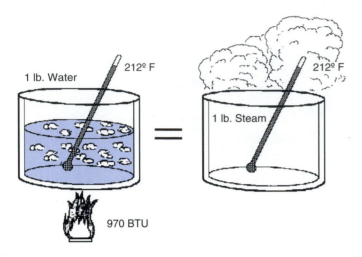

FIGURE 4-14   If we add 970 Btu of heat to 1 lb of water at 212°F, we will have 1 lb of steam at the same temperature.

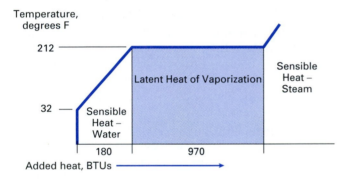

FIGURE 4-15   If we start with 1 lb of water at 32°F, adding 180 Btu will increase the temperature to 212°F. It will take another 970 Btu (the latent heat of evaporation) to boil that pound of water.

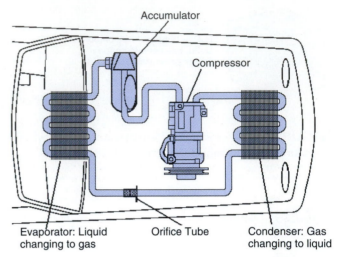

FIGURE 4-16   In an A/C system, the refrigerant changes state and absorbs heat in the evaporator and releases heat as it changes state again in the condenser.

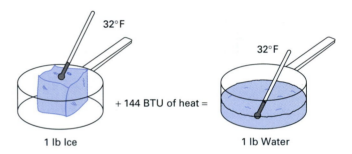

FIGURE 4-17   If we start with a 1-lb block of ice at 32°F, it will take 144 Btu (the latent heat of fusion) to melt all of the ice.

system in the condenser as the gas changes back into a liquid and latent heat of condensation is removed (Figure 4-16).

The change of state between a solid and liquid also requires a large amount of latent heat. This is called the **latent heat of fusion.** For water, it takes the removal of 144 Btu of heat to change 1 lb of water at 32°F into ice at 32°F (Figure 4-17). Using metric terms, it takes the removal of 79.7 calories of heat to change 1 g of water at 0°C into ice at 0°C. We need to add the same amount of heat to change the ice back into water. The latent heat of fusion is what makes ice chests effective in cooling things; ice can absorb a fairly large amount of heat as it melts (Figure 4-18).

All commercial forms of refrigeration or air conditioning utilize the principle of latent heat and the change of state that it causes. The liquid-to-gas-to-liquid change

is used because both media are fluid and can be easily moved by pumping. In addition, the greatest amount of heat energy is absorbed and released between these two states (Figure 4-19). With the solid-to-liquid change of state, the liquid can be pumped but solids must be moved using more cumbersome methods.

4.5   BOILING POINTS

Boiling points can be increased or decreased by raising or lowering the **pressure** on the liquid. With water, the boiling point will rise about 2 1/2°F for each pound per square inch (psi) of pressure, or about 1°C for each 5 kPa.

Note that raising the pressure increases the boiling point and lowering the pressure reduces it. A standard A/C service step is to evacuate the system before charg-

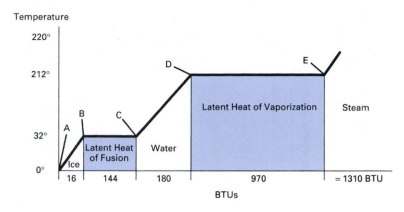

Adding 16 BTU of heat to ice @ 0°F (A) will increase the temperature to 32°F (B).
Adding 144 BTU of heat will cause a change of state to water @ 32°F (C).
Adding 180 BTU of heat will increase the temperature to 212°F (D).
Adding 970 BTU of heat will cause a change of state to steam @ 212°F (E).

FIGURE 4-18   The amount of heat movement required to change 0°F ice to steam, or vice versa.

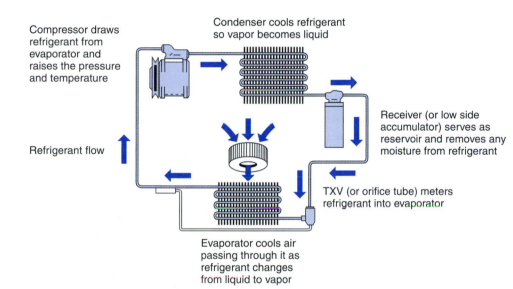

Compressor draws refrigerant from evaporator and raises the pressure and temperature

Condenser cools refrigerant so vapor becomes liquid

Refrigerant flow

Receiver (or low side accumulator) serves as reservoir and removes any moisture from refrigerant

TXV (or orifice tube) meters refrigerant into evaporator

Evaporator cools air passing through it as refrigerant changes from liquid to vapor

FIGURE 4-19 A refrigeration cycle absorbs heat as the refrigerant boils in the evaporator and removes heat as it changes state back to a liquid in the condenser.

ing it with new or reclaimed refrigerant. This is done to remove any water, which can cause rust or corrosion or mix with the refrigerant to form acids. At a vacuum of 30 inches of mercury (″Hg) (−103 kPa), the boiling point of water is lowered to 0°F (−18°C).

The condensing point of a gas is the same as the boiling point; the only difference is that we add heat to a liquid to make it boil, and we remove heat from a gas to make it condense. Raising the pressure of a gas allows the gas to condense at temperatures above the normal boiling point (Figure 4-20).

4.5.1   Critical Temperature

The **critical temperature** is the maximum point at which a gas can be liquefied or condensed by raising the pressure. The **critical pressure** is the pressure that is necessary to liquefy a gas at that temperature. Looking at Figure 4-27 shows us that R-134a has a critical tem-

perature of 101.15°C (214°F) and a critical pressure of 4.065 MPa (589 psi). This tells us what the upper limits are for the high side of an A/C system.

4.6   SATURATED VAPORS AND THE PRESSURE–TEMPERATURE RELATIONSHIP

Saturated vapor is the term used to describe a liquid and gas inside a closed chamber, which is the condition in an A/C system. When discussing saturated vapors, we need to learn two additional terms: **subcool** and **superheat**. Subcool refers to a liquid whose temperature is well below its boiling point. Superheat refers to the temperature increases of a vapor above its boiling point.

FIGURE 4-20 The boiling point of a liquid changes as the pressure changes. Water will boil at 183°F with a pressure of 13 psi on a mountain. It will boil at 212°F at an atmospheric pressure of 14.7 psi. In a radiator at a pressure of 30 psi (absolute), it will boil at 250°F.

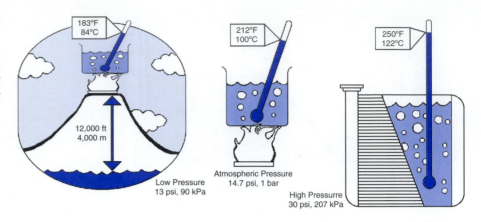

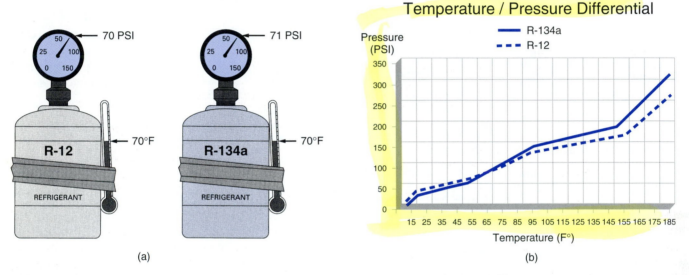

(a)

(b)

FIGURE 4-21 R-12 in a container is a saturated vapor with gas in contact with a liquid. The pressure in the container is in direct relation to the temperature *(a)*; a chart can be used to determine the temperature if we know the pressure or vice versa *(b)*. (a *courtesy of DaimlerChrysler Corporation*; b *courtesy of Four Seasons*)

If heat is added to the saturated vapor inside a closed container, some liquid will boil, which will increase the pressure within the container. This added pressure will, in turn, increase the boiling point. If heat is removed, the pressure will drop as some of the gas condenses back into a liquid because the boiling point will be lowered. The pressure increase is directly proportional to the temperature increase and is caused by the great increase in volume (about 1,000 times) as the liquid boils (Figure 4-21).

A **pressure–temperature (PT)** relationship chart (such as that shown in Figure 4-30) shows us the relative temperature–pressure relationship of a refrigerant when it is in a system. Once a technician has measured the pressure in a system, that part of the system should be the same temperature as indicated on the chart. The

temperature of a saturated vapor for a particular liquid will always be at a constant point relative to the pressure, and the pressure will always be relative to the temperature. If they do not match, something is wrong. Lower-than-normal pressure for a particular temperature can indicate starvation because there is no saturated vapor. Higher-than-normal pressure for a particular temperature usually indicates contamination from another chemical, air, or the wrong refrigerant.

4.7 PRESSURE: GAUGE AND ABSOLUTE

Pressure is defined as a certain amount of force exerted on a unit area. Traditionally in the United States,

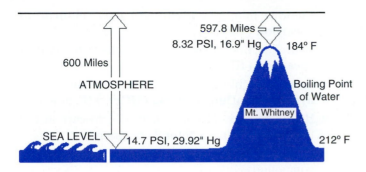

FIGURE 4-22 The weight of the air in our atmosphere generates a pressure of about 15 psi at sea level. Atmospheric pressure and the boiling point of water are lower at higher altitudes *(Courtesy of DaimlerChrysler Corporation)*

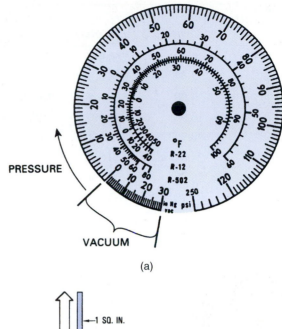

(a)

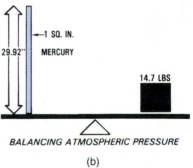

(b)

FIGURE 4-23 As shown on this compound gauge, pressures below atmospheric are commonly called a *vacuum (a)*. A perfect vacuum is **29.92** inches of mercury *(b)*. *(a courtesy of TIF Instruments; b courtesy of Robinair, SPX Corporation)*

pressure is given in pounds and the unit area in square inches, so pressure has been given in pounds per square inch (psi). Most pressure gauges disregard atmospheric pressure and are calibrated to read 0 at their starting point, which is the normal atmospheric pressure surrounding us. The pressure created by the weight of the air in our atmosphere generates a pressure of 14.7 psi at sea level, which is often rounded off to 15 psi (Figure 4-22).

Pressures below atmospheric are usually called a **vacuum** and are measured using a gauge calibrated in inches of mercury (″Hg) or millimeters of mercury (mmHg). Most of these gauges start from 0 at atmospheric pressure and read downward to 29.92 ″Hg (usually rounded off to 30 ″Hg); 29.92 ″Hg is a perfect vacuum where there is no pressure at all. A perfect vacuum is really zero pressure (Figure 4-23).

Deep or high vacuum is close to perfect vacuum and is measured in microns of mercury. A micron is one-millionth of a meter; atmospheric pressure is equal to 759,968 microns. Figure 4-24 illustrates the relative pressure in inches and microns, and how the boiling point of water relates to these pressures.

The pressures just discussed are often called **gauge pressures** because their zero points are atmospheric pressure, and zero on these gauges can be called 0 **psig, pounds per square inch gauge.** Some gauges are calibrated so their zero reading is at an absolute vacuum, and they read upward from this point. These gauges read *absolute pressures;* atmospheric pressure shows up on them as 15 **psia, pounds per square inch absolute.**

At one time, the metric system used kilograms per square centimeter (kg/cm^2) and **bar** as the pressure standard. Bar is still commonly used, and they have similar values. One bar is equal to 14.5 psi, atmospheric pressure. Today, the international unit for pressure is

pascal (Pa): 1 psi is equal to 0.006895 Pa. A pascal is very small, so **kilopascal (kPa)** (1,000 Pa) (1 thousand) or sometimes megapascal (MPa) (1,000,000 Pa) (1 million) are used. To convert from one standard to another, you can multiply a number in psi by 6.895 to get kilopascals or a number in kPa by 0.145 to get the reading in psi. An A/C system high-side pressure of 200 psi is equal to 1,379 kPa and 1.38 MPa. A conversion table is given in Appendix F (Figure 4-25).

4.8 REFRIGERANTS

The working fluid of an A/C system is refrigerant. Refrigerants were first developed by the Du Pont Corporation using the name *Freon.* This term is used improperly by

Temperature (°F)	Vacuum (inches)	Pressure* (microns)	Pressure (psi)
212°	0.00	759.968	14.696
205°	4.92	535,000	12.279
194°	9.23	525,526	10.162
176°	15.94	355,092	6.866
158°	20.72	233,680	4.519
140°	24.04	149,352	2.888
122°	26.28	92,456	1.788
104°	27.75	55,118	1.066
86°	28.67	31,750	0.614
80°	28.92	25,400	0.491
76°	29.02	22,860	0.442
72°	29.12	20,320	0.393
69°	29.22	17,780	0.344
64°	29.32	15,240	0.295
59°	29.42	12,700	0.246
53°	29.52	10,160	0.196
45°	29.62	7,620	0.147
32°	29.74	4,572	0.088
21°	29.82	2,540	0.049
6°	29.87	1,270	0.0245
−24°	29.91	254	0.0049
−35°	29.915	127	0.00245
−60°	29.919	25.4	0.00049
−70°	29.9195	12.7	0.00024
−90°	29.9199	2.54	0.000049

*Remaining pressure in system in microns:
1.000 inch = 25,400 microns = 2.540 cm = 25.40 mm
0.100 inch = 2,540 microns = 0.254 cm = 2.54 mm
0.039 inch = 1,000 microns = 0.100 cm = 1.00 mm

FIGURE 4-24 The boiling point of water drops as pressure is reduced. At a near-perfect vacuum of 29.9199 ″Hg or 2.54 microns, the boiling point is −90°F. *(Courtesy of Robinair, SPX Corporation)*

many people to mean refrigerant. A new term, *SUVA*, refers to Du Pont's newer refrigerants: Suva MP52 (a blend) and Suva Trans A/C (134a). There are many refrigerants, but the two main ones used in automotive and other mobile systems are R-12 and R-134a. R-22 is commonly used in refrigerators and stationary A/C units for buildings. A refrigerant compound can be a combination of the following:

- Chlorine, fluorine, and carbon, called a **chlorofluorocarbon (CFC)**
- Hydrogen, fluorine, and carbon, called a **hydrofluorocarbon (HFC)**
- Hydrogen, chlorine, fluorine, and carbon, called a **hydrochlorofluorocarbon (HCFC)** (Figure 4-26)
- Hydrogen and carbon, called a hydrocarbon (butane and propane, a natural compound)
- Hydrogen and oxygen, called CO_2 (a natural compound)

Technically, a refrigerant should be referred to as CFC-12, HFC-134a, or HCFC-22 to show the chemical prefix.

Refrigerants must have a low boiling point—below 32°F (0°C)—to boil and absorb latent heat at low temperatures. The lowest temperature we can use to cool a car's passenger compartment is 32°F. Temperatures below 32°F cause ice to form and block airflow through the fins of the evaporator. When a refrigerant is in a gaseous state, its vapor pressure must be high enough so that a sufficient quantity can be pumped efficiently, but the pressure should not be so high that containing it becomes a problem (Figure 4-27).

Even though the refrigerant's boiling point is well below ambient temperature, it can be contained in a liquid form in metal cans, canisters, and drums if the container is strong enough to hold the required pressure (Figure 4-28). Remember that this is a saturated vapor, so some of the liquid will boil and generate pressure in the container; the container must be able to contain the pressure generated by that particular chemical at normally encountered temperatures. Some additional potential hazards in handling refrigerants are discussed in Chapter 5.

A refrigerant should mix and become chemically stable with oil, so that the oil is moved through the system to keep the compressor and the expansion valve in some systems lubricated. The oil and refrigerant mixture must be compatible with the various metal, rubber, and plastic materials that make up the system. A refrigerant should also be safe to work with; flammability and toxicity are important concerns (Figure 4-29).

4.8.1 R-12

R-12, or more properly CFC-12, is a CFC, a compound of chlorine, fluorine, and carbon. The actual compound is Cl_2Fl_2C, two chlorine atoms combined with two fluorine atoms and one carbon atom. Its chemical name is dichlorodifluoromethane.

R-12 has a boiling point of −21.7°F (−29.8°C). This low temperature allows R-12 to boil easily in the evaporator and absorb the needed latent heat. Its vapor pressure

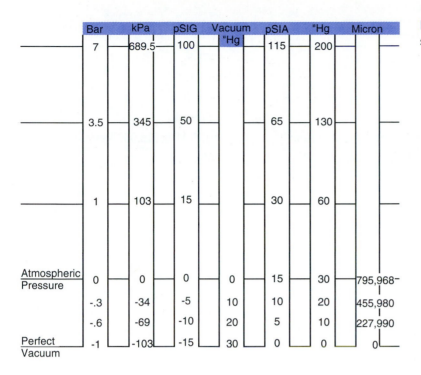

Bar	kPa	pSIG	Vacuum "Hg	pSIA	"Hg	Micron
7	689.5	100		115	200	
3.5	345	50		65	130	
1	103	15		30	60	
0 *(Atmospheric Pressure)*	0	0	0	15	30	795,968
-.3	-34	-5	10	10	20	455,980
-.6	-69	-10	20	5	10	227,990
-1 *(Perfect Vacuum)*	-103	-15	30	0	0	0

FIGURE 4-25 The relative pressures between seven different measuring systems.

HFC:	R-125, R-134a, other halogenated compounds
CFC:	R-12, R-11, R-13, R-113, R-114, R-500, R-503
HCFC:	R-22, R-123, R-124, R-502

FIGURE 4-26 Depending on the combination of carbon, chlorine, fluorine, or hydrogen, a refrigerant is classed as an HFC, CFC, or HCFC. *(Courtesy of TIF Instruments)*

in the evaporator will be about 30 psi and in the condenser about 150 to 300 psi (Figure 4-30). As we will learn, these pressures vary somewhat depending on the temperature. R-12 has a latent heat of vaporization of 70 Btu per lb.

R-12 is soluble in mineral oil and does not react to the metals, hoses, and gaskets used in the system. At one time, R-12 was very inexpensive. R-12 was considered an ideal refrigerant until it was discovered that its molecules can travel into the upper atmosphere before breaking down. Here, the chlorine atoms can react with ozone, O_3, in the ozone layer. This is discussed further in Chapter 5.

4.8.2   R-22

R-22, or more properly HCFC-22, is an HCFC; its chemical compound is monochlorodifluoromethane, $CHClF_2$. R-22 is closely related to R-12, and like R-12, R-22 was once fairly inexpensive.

R-22 has a boiling point of $-40°F$ ($-40°C$) and a vapor pressure that is about double that of R-12, which is why R-22 is normally used in freezers, which require colder temperatures—about $0°F$ ($-19°C$)—and in stationary installations, which use hermetically sealed compressors and metal tubing. A hermetically sealed compressor has both the motor and the compressor mounted in a well-sealed container, eliminating most possibilities for leakage.

R-22 should never be used in an R-12 system or mixed with R-12 or R-134a: It would have a greater tendency to leak from the compressor shaft seal and flexible hoses used in an automotive A/C system. R-22 is not compatible with the rubber hose and seal materials used in most R-12 systems. A mixture of R-12 and R-22 would cause higher pressure and damage to the desiccant, hoses, and O-rings. If a blend that contains R-22 is used to retrofit an R-12 system, the rubber hoses must be replaced with barrier hoses. If mixed, R-12 and R-22 cannot be separated by normal methods.

4.8.3   R-134a

R-134a, or more properly HFC-134a, is an HFC. Its full name is tetrafluoroethane, and its chemical compound is CF_3CH_2F. There is no chlorine in this compound, so it has no effect on Earth's ozone layer. This is one of the major reasons why the automotive industry converted to R-134a. Its cost was once about three times that of R-12, but this has changed. R-12 is much more

Item	R-134a	R-12
Molecular formula	CH_2FCF_3	CCl_2F_2
Molecular weight	102.03	120.91
Boiling point	$-26.8°C$	$-29.79°C$
Critical temperature	101.15°C	111.80°C
Critical pressure	4.065 MPa {41.452 kgf/cm^2}	4.125 MPa {42.063 kgf/cm^2}
Critical density	511 kg/cm^3	558 kg/cm^3
Saturated liquid density	1206.0 kg/cm^3	1310.9 kg/cm^3
Specific volume (saturated vapor)	0.031009 m^3/kg	0.027085 m^3/kg
Specific heat (saturated liquid at constant pressure)	1.4287 kJ/kg·K {0.3413 kcal/kgf·K}	0.9682 kJ/kg·K {0.2313 kcal/kgf·K}
Specific heat (saturated vapor at constant pressure)	0.8519 kJ/kg·K {0.2035 kcal/kgf·K}	0.6116 kJ/kg·K {0.1461 kcal/kgf·K}
Latent heat of vaporization	216.50 kJ/kg {51.72 kcal/kgf}	166.56 kJ/kg {39.79 kcal/kgf}
Thermal conductivity (saturated liquid)	0.0815 W/m·K {0.0701 kcal/m·h·K}	0.0702 W/m·K {0.0604 kcal/m·h·K}
Combustibility	Incombustible	Incombustible
Ozone depletion index (CFC-12 = 1.0)	0	1.0
Global warming index	0.24–0.29	2.8–3.4

FIGURE 4-27 Comparison of the physical characteristics of R-12 and R-134a. *(Courtesy of Zexel USA Corporation)*

FIGURE 4-28 R-134a refrigerant is commonly available in small (about 12-oz) or larger (30- or 50-lb) containers. R-12 is no longer available in small containers. KLEA is a registered trademark for R-134a. *(Courtesy of Sercon)*

expensive, and R-134a is much cheaper. The characteristics of R-134a are very similar to those of R-12, and, with some changes, an R-12 system can be converted or **retrofitted** to use R-134a.

R-134a has a boiling point of $-15.2°F$ ($-26.8°C$) and a latent heat of vaporization of 77.74 Btu per lb. The pressure–temperature relationship is also similar to that of R-12.

R-134a is lighter in weight than R-12. A cubic foot of R-12 weighs 82.7 lb (37.5 kg) at 70°F (21°C) while a cu-

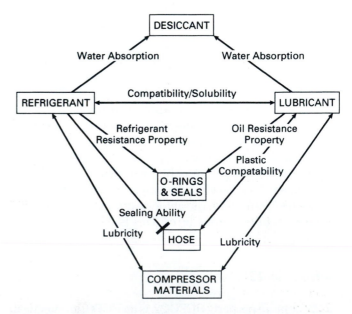

FIGURE 4-29 A refrigerant and its oil must be completely compatible with all of the materials and chemicals in the system.

Temperature		Pressure		
°F	°C	R-12	R-134a	R-22
0	−22	9	6	24
5	−15	12	9	28
10	−12	15	12	33
15	−9	18	15	38
20	−7	21	18	43
25	−4	25	22	49
30	−1	28.5	26	55
35	2	33	30.5	61
40	4	37	35	68
45	7	42	40	76
50	10	47	45	84
55	13	52	51	93
60	16	58	57	102
65	18	64	64	111
70	21	70	71	121
75	24	77	79	132
80	27	84	87	144
85	29	92	95	156
90	32	100	104	168
95	35	108	114	182
100	38	117	124	196
105	41	127	135	211
110	43	136	147	226
115	47	147	159	243
120	49	158	171	260
125	52	169	185	278
130	54	181	199	297
135	57	193	214	317
140	60	207	229	337
145	63	220	246	359
150	65	235	263	382

FIGURE 4-30 The boiling points for R-12, R-22, and R-134a vary depending on the pressure.

bic foot of R-134a weighs 76.2 lb (34.5 kg) at the same temperature. R-134a weighs about 90% as much as R-12. A comparison of the sizes of equal-weight bottles of R-12 and R-134a illustrates the weight differences. When we retrofit an R-12 system to R-134a, we usually decrease the amount of refrigerant charged into the system to compensate for this weight difference.

R-134a is not compatible with the mineral oil used to lubricate an R-12 system. Synthetic *polyalkaline glycol (PAG)* or *polyolester (POE)*, commonly called *ester*, lubricants are used with R-134a; these two lubricants do not mix well with R-12. R-134a is also not compatible with the desiccant used in R-12 systems. The process of retrofitting an R-12 system to use R-134a is described in Chapter 15. This process requires changing both the refrigerant and the oil. Other parts of the system need to be replaced if they are not compatible with R-134a or its oil.

During early tests, it was thought that mineral oil and PAG oils would not mix properly in a retrofitted R-12 system. Now it is believed that these early tests were adversely affected by residue left over from flushing the system with R-11; several vehicle manufacturers believe that PAG and mineral oil will mix with no chemical incompatibility.

4.8.4 Blends

Several refrigerant blends (a mixture of several different chemical compounds) are currently being marketed to replace R-12. The chemicals most commonly used are mixtures of HCFC-22, HCFC-124, HFC-134a, HCFC-142B, HCFC-152a, butane (R-600), isobutane (R-600a), and propane (R-290).

Three of these blend chemicals (butane, isobutane, and propane) are very flammable. At least one technician has been seriously burned when the escaping refrigerant has contacted flame. In 1995, the EPA found that all flammable refrigerants are unacceptable for R-12 replacement. Many states ban the use of flammable refrigerants.

Class II substances, which include HCFC-22, will be phased out of production on Jan. 1, 2015 because they add to environmental global warming problems. It is recommended that no new type of refrigerant be used unless it has been approved by the Environmental Protection Agency (EPA) and the Society of Automotive Engineers (SAE). The SNAP rule and the acceptable blends are described in Chapter 5. A list of SNAP approved blends is provided in Appendix D.

Blends offer the advantage of being supposedly "drop-in" replacements for R-12 in that they can be used in an R-12 system with little or no change. *However, there is no legal drop-in refrigerant for an R-12 system.* Blends also offer rather serious drawbacks: fractionation, glide, and contamination. Normally, a blend cannot be recycled in a shop; it has to be sent off for disposal or recovery. If a system is undercharged, instead of adding more refrigerant, the system has to be emptied and completely recharged. Blend refrigerants are discussed more thoroughly in Chapters 5 and 15.

Contamination is becoming the focus of every A/C technician who works on automotive systems. Abnormally high pressures in a system may be caused by several factors, one of which is the addition of a blend refrigerant. As we will learn, the recovery equipment used to remove the refrigerant from a system pulls the refrigerant out of the system and puts it into a container with other recovered refrigerant. Recycling equipment cannot separate out the blend compounds or even one type of refrigerant from another. Contaminated refrigerants must be disposed of through a rather expensive process. The recovery and recycling equipment may also become contaminated; this, in turn, can contaminate the systems in other vehicles.

4.8.5   Refrigerant Oils

Refrigerant oil is highly refined, with all wax particles and water removed. An R-12 system uses a mineral-based oil with a viscosity of 500–525 Saybolt universal seconds (SUS). (SAE 30 automotive oil has a viscosity of between 410 and 630 SUS.) An original equipment manufacturer (OEM) R-134a system probably uses 1 of

about 29 different PAG oils; the particular oil variety is selected by the vehicle or compressor manufacturer after many hours of very expensive testing to ensure that it works perfectly in that system and will last a long time. An oil that is not recommended by a particular manufacturer either has not been tested or has failed these tests. Almost every compressor and vehicle manufacturer recommends using a particular PAG oil. Some compressor manufacturers will void their warranty if the wrong oil is used.

Because they mix better with mineral oil and have a higher tolerance for any chlorine remaining in the system from R-12, ester oils are commonly used when an R-12 system is retrofitted to become an R-134a system. One expert recommends against using ester oils because he believes that if they are introduced into a system that is contaminated with moisture or R-12, they will break down into acid and alcohol, which will cause long-term system damage.

Aftermarket sources market two or three types of PAG oils and one or two types of ester oils. Both PAG and ester oils include high and low viscosities to suit the requirements of certain compressors.

REVIEW QUESTIONS

The following questions are provided to help you study as you read the chapter.

1. We must move _____ to the outside of the vehicle in order to cool it.

2. Heat transfer from one molecule to the one next to it is called _____, and moving heat by circulating hot air or water is called _____.

3. The three states of matter are _____, _____, and _____.

4. If we add enough heat to solid matter, it will change to a(n) _____.

5. Heat that is added to change water to gas is called _____ _____ of _____.

6. Adding pressure to a hot liquid will increase the _____ _____.

7. A liquid gas mixture in a closed container is called a(n) _____ _____, and heating this container will _____ the internal pressure.

8. Ten psi is equal to _____ kPa.

9. A pressure lower than atmospheric is called a(n) _____, and this pressure is measured in _____ or _____.

10. Most vehicle and compressor manufacturers recommend using _____ oil in R-134a systems.

CHAPTER QUIZ

The following questions will help you check the facts you have learned. Select the answer that completes each statement correctly.

1. Which of the following is true about heat?
   a. Heat always travels from something warm to something cold.
   b. Heat is a form of energy.
   c. Cold is the lack of heat.
   d. All of these are true.

2. _____ occurs when heat travels through a material, from one molecule to the one next to it.
   a. Radiation
   b. Convection
   c. Conduction
   d. None of these

3. The process of transferring heat by circulating the heated media is called _____.
   - **a.** radiation
   - **b.** convection
   - **c.** Conduction
   - **d.** None of these

   48

4. The movement of heat through heat rays is called _____.
   - **a.** radiation
   - **b.** convection
   - **c.** conduction
   - **d.** None of these

   49

5. Molecules are composed of _____.
   - **a.** atoms
   - **b.** protons
   - **c.** electrons
   - **d.** compounds

   50

6. Which of the following is a form of matter?
   - **a.** Solid
   - **b.** Liquid
   - **c.** Gas
   - **d.** All of these

   50-51

7. Which of the following describes sensible heat?
   - **a.** It causes a change of state.
   - **b.** It causes a temperature change.
   - **c.** It causes a liquid to boil.
   - **d.** All of these

   51

8. _____ causes a change of state in matter.
   - **A.** Sensible heat
   - **B.** Latent heat

   Which is correct?
   - **a.** A only
   - **b.** B only
   - **c.** Both A and B
   - **d.** Neither A nor B

   51

9. It takes _____ Btu of heat to cause a change of state from 1 lb of water to 1 lb of steam.
   - **a.** 100
   - **b.** 212
   - **c.** 970
   - **d.** 32

   51

10. The boiling point of a liquid can be increased by raising the _____.
    - **a.** temperature
    - **b.** latent heat
    - **c.** pressure
    - **d.** All of these

11. Superheat refers to temperature increases in a vapor after all of the liquid has boiled.
    - **a.** True
    - **b.** False

    53

12. Zero psig is _____.
    - **a.** the zero point on all gauges
    - **b.** the lowest point on a vacuum gauge
    - **c.** equal to about 15 psi on the absolute pressure scale
    - **d.** All of these

    55

13. Which of the following is not a CFC or HCFC?
    - **a.** R-12
    - **b.** R-22
    - **c.** R-134a
    - **d.** None of these

    56

14. Two technicians are discussing heat. Technician A says that heat always travels from hot to cold. Technician B says that heat is a form of energy. Who is correct?
    - **a.** Technician A
    - **b.** Technician B
    - **c.** Both A and B
    - **d.** Neither A nor B

15. R-12 is normally used with _____ oil.
    - **a.** mineral
    - **b.** PAG
    - **c.** POE
    - **d.** Any of these

    60

◀ **Chapter 5** ▶

REFRIGERANTS AND THE ENVIRONMENT

LEARNING OBJECTIVES

After completing this chapter, you should:

1. Be familiar with the ozone layer and the adverse effects of a CFC on it.
2. Be familiar with the effects of the Montreal Protocol on automotive A/C servicing.
3. Understand what refrigerants are and the important safety concerns related to them.
4. Be aware of the possible effects of the Kyoto Protocol.
5. Be aware of what the next generation of HVAC systems might be.

TERMS TO LEARN

azeotrope	recovery
blend	recycling
bubble point	SAE (Society of
Clean Air Act	Automotive Engineers)
dew point	Section 609
drop in	small can
EPA (Environmental	SNAP (Significant New
Protection Agency)	Alternatives Policy)
fractionizing	stratosphere
glide	topping off
global warming	vent
greenhouse effect	zeotrope
ozone	

5.1 INTRODUCTION

Planet Earth is unique in many ways. It has an atmosphere that contains a percentage of oxygen high enough to allow mammals, including humans, to live in it. This atmosphere extends outward from Earth for about 31 miles (50 km). The upper layer of the atmosphere is called the **stratosphere,** and it begins about 7 to 10 miles (11 to 16 km) up and extends to the outer limits. A layer of **ozone** (O_3) extends around the Earth in the stratosphere (Figure 5-1).

The ozone layer is important to us because it blocks out ultraviolet wavelengths of light generated by the sun. Ultraviolet rays can be very harmful to our way of life. In humans, an excess of these rays can cause an increase in skin cancer and cataracts of the eyes, as well as damage to our immune systems. These same problems can affect many animals. Ultraviolet rays can also damage plants and vegetables. This damage probably also extends to plankton and larvae in the sea, the base of the food chain for sea animals.

In the late 1900s, it was determined that the ozone layer is getting much thinner, and large holes are being created in it (mostly near the South Pole). The ozone layer is not providing the same protection from ultraviolet (UV) rays as it once did. It has been determined that (1) the breakup or depletion of the ozone layer is caused by human-made chemical pollution, (2) one of the major ozone-depleting chemicals is chlorine, and (3) one of the major sources of chlorine in the atmosphere is R-12.

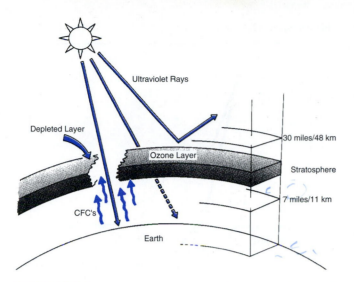

FIGURE 5-1 The ozone layer is in the stratosphere, and it blocks ultraviolet rays from the sun. CFCs from R-12 can cause a depletion of and holes in the ozone layer.

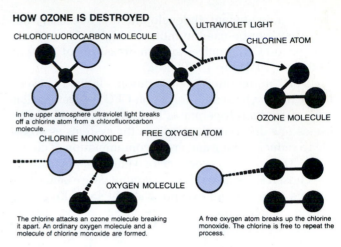

FIGURE 5-3 When CFC molecules break down in the stratosphere, a chlorine atom breaks free to attack ozone molecules. *(Courtesy of DaimlerChrysler Corporation)*

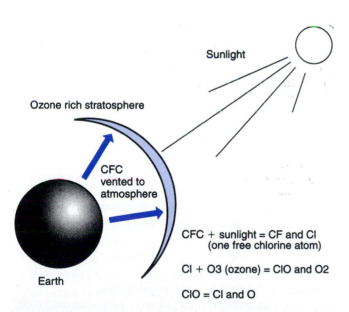

FIGURE 5-2 The ozone-rich stratosphere protects us from harmful rays coming from the sun. CFC that is vented can break down this layer.

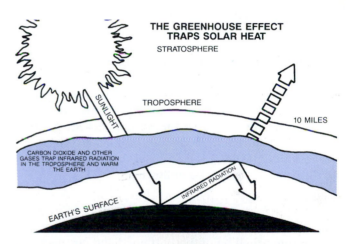

FIGURE 5-4 Greenhouse gases in the lower atmosphere reflect heat back onto Earth and increase temperatures. *(Courtesy of DaimlerChrysler Corporation)*

A chlorine atom from a chlorinated fluorocarbon (CFC) such as R-12 can travel into the stratosphere if it escapes or is released. There, under the effects of ice clouds and sunlight, it can combine with one of the oxygen atoms of an ozone molecule to form chlorine monoxide and an ordinary oxygen molecule, O_2. This destroys that ozone molecule (Figure 5-2). The effect does not end there; the chlorine can break away and attack other ozone molecules. It is believed that 1 chlorine atom can destroy 10,000 to 100,000 ozone molecules (Figure 5-3).

Another area of concern is a layer of gases that are causing a **greenhouse effect.** This gas layer traps heat at the Earth's surface and lower atmosphere, and it is increasing the temperature of our living area. This is called **global warming.** CFC and HC gases are considered greenhouse gases (Figure 5-4). Although only partially, R-134a does contribute to global warming. To become more environmentally friendly, vehicle manufacturers are currently testing two "natural" refrigerants: hydrocarbon (HC) and carbon dioxide (CO_2). Both of these are very difficult to use, and substantial development is necessary before they can be used in motor vehicles. HC is flammable, and CO_2 requires system pressures of 1,500 to 2,000 psi (10,342 to 13,790 kPa).

The automotive refrigeration industry went through a major search for a non-CFC refrigerant that was as good a refrigerant as R-12. Another goal was to use as few different chemicals in the systems as possible to reduce mixing and cross-contamination of chemicals. At this time, every major vehicle manufacturer has chosen R-134a; few other compounds are being considered or tested. An exception is that some European vehicle manufacturers are preparing to use carbon dioxide, CO_2, refrigerant.

5.2 LEGISLATION

At a conference in Montreal, Canada, in 1987, the United States, along with 22 other countries, agreed to limit the production of ozone-depleting chemicals. This agreement is referred to as the Montreal Protocol. In 1990, President Bush (senior) signed the **Clean Air Act,** which phased out the production of CFCs in the United States by the year 2000. In 1993, the phaseout of CFC-12 was moved forward; R-12 production in the United States ceased at the end of 1995 (Figure 5-5).

Section 609 is a portion of the Clean Air Act that places certain requirements on the mobile vehicle air conditioning (MVAC) service field. Important portions of this section require the following:

Effective January 1, 1992

- Technicians who repair or service automotive A/C systems shall be properly trained and certified and use approved refrigerant recovery and recycling equipment.
- Recovery and recycling equipment must be properly approved.
- Each shop that performs A/C service on motor vehicles shall certify to the **Environmental Protection Agency (EPA)** that it is using approved recycling equipment and that only properly trained and certified technicians are using this equipment.

Effective November 15, 1992

- Sales of small containers of R-12 (less than 20 lb) are restricted to certified technicians.

Effective November 14, 1994

- MVAC technicians must be certified to purchase EPA-acceptable blend refrigerants.

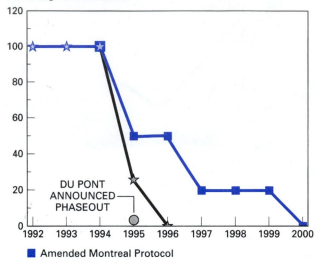

FIGURE 5-5 The time scale adopted as the Montreal Protocol was amended to speed up the phaseout of CFCs. *(Courtesy of Castrol North America)*

Effective January 29, 1998

- Equipment used to recover or recycle R-134a must meet SAE standards.
- MVAC service technicians must be certified to handle non-ozone-depleting refrigerants (including R-134a).

Some areas have local environmental control regulations that include even more restrictions. The European Community set 1995 as the date for a complete phaseout of R-12. At least two Canadian provinces have banned R-12, and a complete elimination of R-12 in Canada should occur within the next 10 years. R-12 is no longer produced in the United States.

Under the Montreal Protocol, phaseout of HCFC began in 2004 (a 35% reduction). This reduction began in 2003 in the United States. Manufacture of HCFC-22 will stop in 2010 in the United States and other developed countries.

5.3 ADDITIONAL CONCERNS

There is still a major concern about the global-warming effect from escaping refrigerants. Representatives from many nations met in Kyoto, Japan, in 1997 and established the Kyoto Protocol to address these concerns. The Total Environmental Warming Impact

(TEWI) index was developed; it rates the impact of various refrigerants along with the energy required to perform the cooling operation. In the future, it is hoped that each nation will reduce its negative impact on the environment to zero in order to reduce global change to zero. All factors concerning energy use and emissions will be considered. The United States has not signed the Kyoto Protocol.

5.4 RECOVERY AND RECYCLING

A major thrust of the Clean Air Act is to recycle R-12 instead of releasing it to enter the atmosphere. This makes economic sense. At one time, new (also called virgin) R-12 was inexpensive, well under $1.00 per pound. Now added taxes and increased demand due to limited production have raised the price significantly. When R-12 was inexpensive, it was standard practice to simply **vent** the contents of a system to the atmosphere when service was needed. Also, many people kept adding R-12 to a system rather than going through the trouble and expense of repairing a leak. This was called **topping off** a system. With the increased cost of R-12, it pays to repair small leaks and possibly retrofit the vehicle to use a less expensive refrigerant. It is also socially irresponsible not to repair any fixable leaks. Small containers of R-12 are no longer available to do-it-yourselfers. And service shops must now have equipment to recover R-12 from a system and recycle or clean it so it can be reused.

The **Society of Automotive Engineers (SAE)** has established important standards for the recovery and recycling of R-12, and these are listed in Appendix C. Other important and related standards are also listed in Appendix C.

Recovery means to remove all of the refrigerant from a system so it can be stored in a container in liquid form. **Recycling** is the process of removing moisture (water), oil, and noncondensable gases (air) from the recovered R-12 or R-134a so it meets the standards of new refrigerant. Recycled refrigerant should be at least 98% pure. Limits for these standards are as follows:

- Moisture: 15 parts per million (ppm) by weight
- Refrigerant oil: 4,000 ppm by weight
- Noncondensable gases: 330 ppm by weight

R-134a can also be recovered and recycled, but separate equipment, dedicated to R-134a, is required. Recycled R-12 or R-134a can be used in the same way as new refrigerant.

Blend refrigerants can also be recovered and recycled using a dedicated machine for that blend. However, this refrigerant can only be used in the vehicle from which the recovered mix came. In cases of fleet vehicles, recycled blend refrigerants can be used in other vehicles within that fleet.

Recovery equipment is available as a single unit or in combination with a recycling unit. Recovery-only units are simpler and less expensive than equipment that handles both recovery and recycling. The procedure used to recover and recycle R-12 and R-134a is described in Chapter 15 (Figure 5-6).

5.4.1 Recovering Contaminated Refrigerant

A service problem facing the modern MVAC technician concerns what to do with a system that contains the wrong or a contaminated refrigerant. If it is recovered using R-12 or R-134a recovery equipment, the equipment and the recovery container become contaminated. Recycling equipment is designed to remove only water, oil, and air; other refrigerant compounds cannot be removed. The equipment must be decontaminated, and any refrigerant in the recovery container must be sent off-site for reclaiming or disposal. Another fear is that if the recovery unit is electric powered, as most are, and if a flammable refrigerant is recovered, an explosion or other damage to the equipment is possible. Air-powered recovery machines or a special procedure can be used to recover flammable refrigerants.

An important step in any future recovery process is to identify what refrigerant is in the system: R-12, R-134a, a **blend,** or a contaminated mixture. Contaminated mixtures are called *unknown, junk,* or *Brand X.* Most larger shops have a separate recovery or recovery–recycling machine for R-12, another one for R-134a, and still another one for blends and unknowns. The technician has two ways of identifying the refrigerant: the label and service fittings on the vehicle and a refrigerant identifier. These labels and fittings are described in Appendix D. The label is the easiest method but is not always accurate. The identifier is the most reliable, but it must be capable of identifying whether the refrigerant contains hydrocarbon (flammable refrigerant) and the type of refrigerant (Figure 5-7). If a contaminated or unknown refrigerant is recovered, it should be recovered into a container that is gray with a yellow top that is labeled as a *mixed, junk, dirty R-12, dirty R-134a,* or *unknown refrigerant.* The mixture should be sent off to one of the several firms that specialize in disposal or recovery of the mixtures.

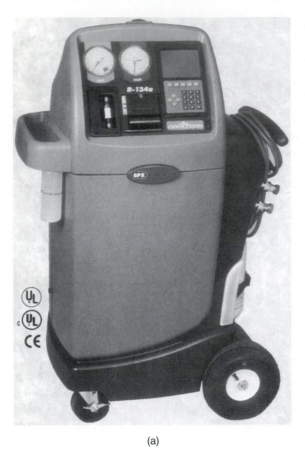

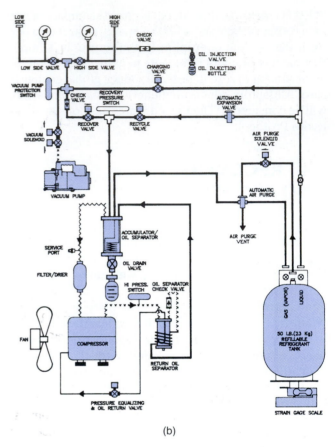

(a)

(b)

FIGURE 5-6 Recovery systems remove the refrigerant from a system so it can be recycled. Most are on a cart for easy movement to the vehicle *(a)*. A schematic of the internal portion is shown in *(b)*. *(Courtesy of Robinair Division, SPX Corporation)*

5.4.2 Recovery Container Certification

The tank used to recover refrigerant on a recovery-recycling machine must be safety checked every 5 years. This legal requirement is part of the refrigerant equipment certification requirement in the Clean Air Act. Tank testing is based on the Title 49 U.S. Department of Transportation (DOT) requirements, essentially an external and internal visual inspection and a hydrostatic pressure test. Failure to test the cylinders can put the owners at risk of a $25,000 fine. SAE standard J2296, Retest of Refrigerant Container, identifies the DOT standards that are required by law and also discusses other concerns for storage containers. The 5-year time period begins at the date of tank manufacture, which is stamped on the tank's collar (Figure 5-8).

FIGURE 5-7 A refrigerant identifier can be used to determine whether the refrigerant in a system is pure or contaminated. *(Courtesy of Neutronics Inc.)*

FIGURE 5-8 The circled portion of this recovery tank reads "Retest by 02."

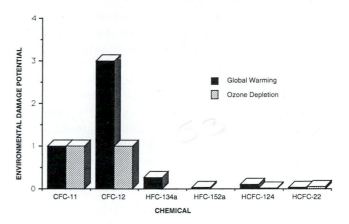

FIGURE 5-10 A comparison of potential atmospheric damage of refrigerants and flushing agents. *(Reprinted with permission from SAE Document M-106, © 1992, Society of Automotive Engineers, Inc.)*

5.5   REFRIGERANTS

As discussed in Chapter 2, before the early 1990s, R-12 was the refrigerant used in mobile A/C systems. R-134a is now being used (beginning in model year 1994) (Figure 5-9). R-22, commonly used in stationary units, is not for automotive use. R-22 has a lower ozone-depletion potential (ODP) of 0.05 than R-12, which is 0.9; R-134a has an ODP of 0 (Figure 5-10).

Refrigerants are colorless and odorless compounds. Usually the only way we know that they are present is how the container feels when we pick it up or shake it. We can also feel the temperature drop of the container as we release the refrigerant into a system. On gauge sets equipped with a sight glass, we can see bubbles in the clear liquid as it passes by the glass.

Two other refrigerants have been used in the automotive field as flushing agents. These refrigerants are R-11 and R-113, and they both have fairly high boiling points, 75°F (24°C) for R-11 and 118°F (48°C) for R-113. Their usage, basically to flush debris out of a system, has stopped because of their possible toxicity and their effect on the environment. Because they are CFCs, they should not be released into the atmosphere.

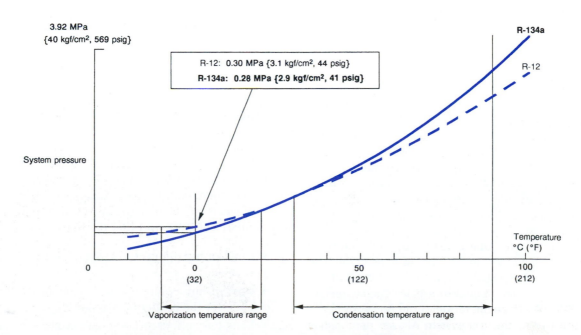

FIGURE 5-9 R-12 and R-134a have similar operating pressures. *(Courtesy of Zexel USA Corporation)*

Refrigerants are commonly available in several sizes of containers with a **small can** of 12 to 14 oz (400 g—at one time, this was 15 oz of R-12 and 1 oz of can, for a total of 1 lb) and larger drums or canisters of 15 or 30 lb (6.8 or 13.6 kg). As mentioned earlier, small containers of R-12 can only be purchased by certified technicians. Refrigerant containers are color coded: R-12 containers are white, R-22 containers are green, and R-134a containers are light blue (Figure 5-11).

The containers that refrigerants are purchased in are usually disposable (Figure 5-12). These containers should be evacuated into a recovery unit, marked empty, and properly disposed of when they are emptied. The storage containers for recycled refrigerant must be approved by the DOT and carry the proper marking to show this (Figure 5-13).

5.5.1 Alternate Refrigerants for R-12

Both R-12 and R-134a are good single-compound refrigerants. But R-12 adversely affects our environment, and some systems and compressors are not compatible with R-134a.

These problems can be solved by replacing the compressor, but this increases the cost of the retrofit. Retrofit procedure and potential problems are discussed more completely in Chapter 15. Approved alternate refrigerants are blend refrigerants that are combinations of molecules. They are an **azeotrope** or a **zeotrope;** both are mixtures or blends that cannot be easily separated. Azeotrope chemicals act like a single chemical with a single boiling point. Zeotrope chemicals are also blends, but they behave differently. They have a range of boiling points (called **bubble point**) that **glides** upward until the heavier compounds boil off. The amount of glide indicates the boiling point range. When a blend condenses, the lowest boiling point ingredient will condense first (called the **dew point**), and condensation will continue to the point where all of the ingredients are liquid. If a refrigerant leak should occur, the lighter elements will vaporize and escape first. This is called **fractionizing,** and it changes the characteristics of the refrigerant. Most of the problems with R-134a are caused by compressors that are not capable of handling the slightly higher pressures or by reactions with viton sealing materials.

It should be noted that R-134a is the only alternate product for an R-12 system that has addressed the SAE retrofit documents (SAE J1657, SAE J1658, SAE J1659, and SAE J1662). These standards are designed to ensure long-term, trouble-free operation of the A/C system.

Section 612 of the 1990 Clean Air Act established the **Significant New Alternatives Policy (SNAP)** program to determine acceptable replacements for Class I and Class II chemicals. Class I chemicals include CFCs, and Class II chemicals are HCFCs. SNAP is administered by the EPA and identifies refrigerants that are acceptable from their ozone-depleting potential, global warming potential, flammability, and toxicity characteristics. Alternate refrigerants are not tested on their refrigeration quality, only on their human health and environmental risks. Several alternate refrigerants have been declared acceptable by SNAP, and these are listed in Appendix D. All of these are blends of two or more compounds, and they have characteristics of zeotropic compounds: fractionation and glide. Some contain R-134a, which means they could cause some of the same problems to the system that R-134a does, and others contain R-22. R-22 causes serious seal swell (as great as 40%) with some of the sealing compounds used with R-12, and barrier hoses are required (Figure 5-14). Most of these compounds contain an HCFC, one of the interim refrigerants that will be banned in the near future because of their effect on global warming.

An alternate refrigerant can only be used under the following conditions:

- Each refrigerant must have its own unique set of fittings, and all ports not converted must be permanently disabled. (These fittings are described in Appendix D.)
- Each refrigerant must have a label with a unique color that specifies pertinent information.
- All original refrigerant must be removed before charging with the new refrigerant.
- With blends that contain HCFC-22, hoses must be replaced with less permeable barrier hoses.
- With systems that include a high-pressure release device, a high-pressure shutoff switch must be installed.
- Blends containing HCFC-22 will be phased out in the near future.

These requirements apply to every vehicle in the United States. It is fairly easy to see that there can be no **drop-in** refrigerant that will simply replace R-12 or that can be added to an R-12 system.

If you are considering retrofitting a vehicle to an alternate refrigerant, consider the following:

- Cost of refrigerant, fittings, and equipment to service it
- Cost of any components that might need replacement for the particular system
- Long-term effect on components, seals, and hoses in the system

R-12   # R-134a

REFRIGERANT

R-12	R-134a
CONTAINER COLOR White	**CONTAINER COLOR** Light blue
CONTAINER MARKING R-12, Freon®	**CONTAINER MARKING** R-134a, Suva® Trans A/C
PART NUMBER 999MP-A4001	**PART NUMBER** 999MP-R134A
CONTAINER FITTING SIZE 7/16" - 20, also known as "1/4 - flare"	**CONTAINER FITTING SIZE** 1/2" - 16 ACME
CHEMICAL NAME Dichlorodifluoromethane	**CHEMICAL NAME** Tetrafluoroethane
ODP (OZONE DEPLETION POTENTIAL) (R-11 = 1) 1	**ODP (OZONE DEPLETION POTENTIAL) (R-11 = 1)** 0
HGWP (HALOCARBON GLOBAL WARMING POTENTIAL) 3.0	**HGWP (HALOCARBON GLOBAL WARMING POTENTIAL)** Less than 0.3
BOILING POINT -21.62°F (-29.79°C)	**BOILING POINT** -15.07°F (-26.15°C)
LATENT HEAT OF VAPORIZATION (The amount of energy required to change state from vapor to liquid) 36.43 (Kcal/Kg @ 0°C)	**LATENT HEAT OF VAPORIZATION** (The amount of energy required to change state from vapor to liquid) 47.19 (Kcal/Kg @ 0°C)
CHEMICAL STRUCTURE	**CHEMICAL STRUCTURE**
MOLECULAR DIAMETER 4.4 angstroms	**MOLECULAR DIAMETER** 4.2 angstroms

Chemical structure R-12:

$$F - C - Cl$$ with F above and Cl below the central C

Chemical structure R-134a:

$$H - C - C - F$$ with H, F above and F, F below

FIGURE 5-11   A comparison of R-12 and R-134a; note differences in container and fittings. *(Courtesy of Nissan Motor Corporation in USA)*

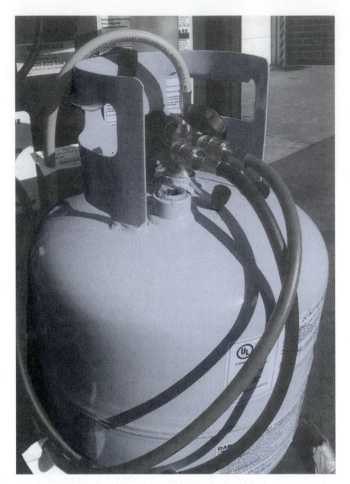

(a)   (b)

FIGURE 5-12 A disposable container of R-12 *(a)*. As mentioned on the printed portion *(b)*, this container should not be reused.

- If a refrigerant that contains R-22 is considered, barrier hoses must be installed (if not already used on the system).
- Cost of future disposal of refrigerant used (R-134a can be recovered and recycled; a blend can be recycled but only for reuse in the same vehicle or for reuse in the same fleet)
- Warranty for most vehicle and replacement parts; manufacturers only warranty parts and equipment used with R-12 or R-134a.
- Operating characteristics relative to R-12; whether the system controls need to be recalibrated (Figure 5-15)
- Availability of refrigerant in the future or in other parts of the country where the vehicle might end up.

R-134a is a good refrigerant, but it has a global warming potential, GWP, of 1300 (R-12 has a 8500 GWP). HFC-152a is a refrigerant with operating characteristics that are very similar to R-134a, and HFC-152a has a GWP of 120. HFC-152a is currently used in several refrigerant blends. HFC-152a is called difluoroethane, with a molecular formula of $C_2H_4F_2$. Being an ethane, HFC-152a is considered flammable so special precautions must be used in a HFC-152a system design.

5.5.2 Alternate Refrigerants, R-134a

At least one manufacturer has developed an alternate refrigerant for R-134a; this refrigerant is a zeotropic blend containing R-152a, R-134a, and R-125 and is claimed to

(a)

(b)

FIGURE 5-13 A DOT-approved refrigerant container has two valves, one for gas and one for liquid *(a)*. A portion of the upper band reads "DOT-4BA400 *(b)*.

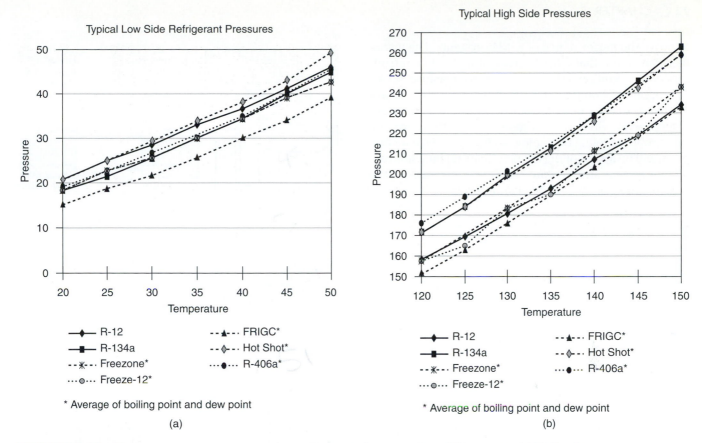

FIGURE 5-14 The pressure–temperature relationship varies between these EPA-approved SNAP refrigerants.

Refrigerant	ST4470 Nitrile O-ring	ST7470 HNBR O-ring	ST9670 Neoprene O-ring	HNBR Lathe Cut	Nitrile Lathe Cut
R-12 Mineral Oil	Good	Good	Good	Good	Good
R-134a Polyalkylene Glycol Oil	Good	Good	Good	Good	Good
Freez-12 Mineral Oil	Good	Marginal	Good	Marginal	Good
Freez-12 Polyol Ester Oil	Poor	Poor	Marginal	Poor	Marginal
RB-276 (Freezone) Mineral Oil	Marginal	Marginal	Good	Marginal	Good
FR-12 (Frig-c) Mineral Oil	Marginal	Poor	Good	Poor	Marginal
FR-12 (Frig-c) Polyol Ester Oil	Good	Marginal	Good	Poor	Good
GHG-X4 (Chill-it) Mineral Oil	Poor	Poor	Marginal	Poor	Poor
Hot Shot/Kar Kool Mineral Oil	Marginal Note 1	Marginal Note 1	Good Note 1	Poor Note 1	Good Note 1
R-406a (McCool) Mineral Oil	Good	Poor	Marginal	Poor	Good

Good = Volume Change ±15%   Marginal = Volume Change +16 to +40   Poor = Volume Change >40%
Note 1: The Hot Shot container received through retail channels contained only R-22 & R-142b.

FIGURE 5-15 This table shows how various refrigerants affect the elastomer seal materials commonly used in an A/C system. *(Courtesy of Santech Industries, Fort Worth, Texas)*

improve the performance of R-134a systems. The manufacturer states that SNAP approval and other retrofit procedure requirements do not apply because SNAP only applies to alternate refrigerants for R-12. (R-134a is neither a Class I or II chemical.) It is very important whenever an alternate refrigerant is used in a system that proper labeling be applied so future service technicians will be aware of the change. Many technicians prefer not to use an alternate for R-134a because of the possible fractionation and contamination problems.

5.5.3 Counterfeit and Bootleg Refrigerants

With the high cost and limited availability of R-12, a refrigerant buyer has to be more careful of where R-12 is purchased. Refrigerant is being illegally imported, and some of it is badly contaminated. There are stories of counterfeit refrigerant being sold in containers marked the same as those of a reputable, domestic manufacturer. Other stories tell of containers that contain nothing but water with air pressure. Refrigerant should be purchased only from a known source that handles reputable products; buyers must be certified.

5.5.4 Future Refrigerants and Systems

In order to meet the requirements of Total Environment Warming Impact (TEWI), several possible changes are being considered: improved R-134a efficiency and one of the new natural refrigerants, CO_2 and HC. There are potential problems with both of the natural refrigerants.

The European Community is very concerned about global warming. A ban on R-134a is proposed to begin in 2009. At this same time, extremely tight standards for refrigerant containment are expected; vehicles will be certified that the A/C system will leak less than 40 grams (1.4 oz per year).

One alternative refrigerant is R-152a, which has operating characteristics very similar to R-134a and a much lower GWP. R-152a is more efficient than R-134a and is able to produce the same cooling with about 7 to 22% less energy. R-152a has a Level 2 flammability rating and is commonly used in aerosol dust-off cans used to clean electronic gear. Because of the flammability and asphyxiation potential, an R-152a system will probably have two vent valves that will be able to vent all of the refrigerant from a system if an evaporator leak should occur.

A carbon dioxide (CO_2) system is similar to the present-day systems, but it requires extremely high pressures, 7 to 10 times that of an R-134a system.

A butane/propane (HC) system uses a very flammable gas that will function in present-day A/C systems, but the potential danger is too great to use it. A leak or

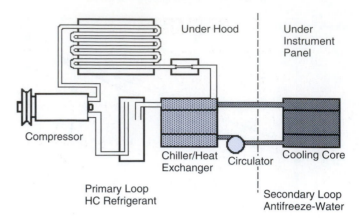

FIGURE 5-16 A secondary loop A/C system keeps the potentially dangerous HC refrigerant out of the passenger compartment by using a chiller/heat exchanger to cool an antifreeze and water mixture. This fluid then transfers heat from the cooling core in the air distribution section to the chiller.

rupture in the evaporator could easily result in a vehicle explosion. An HC system will probably use a secondary loop. The HC portion of the system will be entirely under the hood; a heat exchanger will provide a very cold fluid to connect with a liquid-to-air heat exchanger that will replace the evaporator (Figure 5-16).

On the whole, R-134a systems are not too bad, and they can get better if the efficiency of the present system can be improved and leakage can be reduced. At this time, a CO_2 system is up to 40% less efficient than an R-134a system and can cost about 30% more to produce. The efficiency of an HC, secondary loop system is about 20% lower than an R-134a system and will be about 20% more expensive to build. System efficiency is important in that less efficient systems require more power to do the same job, and this power comes from the engine. A less efficient system will cause the engine to work harder and burn more fuel, increasing its emissions.

5.5.5 Refrigerant Safety Precautions

Refrigerants should be handled only by trained and certified technicians because of potential safety hazards:

- Physiological reaction
- Asphyxiation
- Frostbite and blindness
- Poisoning
- Combustion
- Explosion of storage containers

◄ **CAUTION** ►

Refrigerants are asphyxiants; they do not contain oxygen so they cannot sustain life. Humans can live without food or water for days, but they can live without oxygen for only a few minutes.

◄ **CAUTION** ►

The wise technician is always prudent when working with modern chemicals and avoids breathing fumes and vapors, as well as skin contact, with refrigerants, oils and lubricants, cleaning agents, and other chemicals.

Human bodies react to chemicals in different ways, so exposure to chemicals is not completely predictable. In laboratory tests, a human subject lost consciousness and both his blood pressure and pulse dropped to zero after 4½ minutes of exposure to a concentration of 4,000 ppm of R-134a; other subjects experienced a rise in blood pressure and pulse rate as well as noticeable discomfort. The condition of these subjects returned to normal after the tests were stopped. With modern A/C service methods and recovery equipment, it should be easy to avoid breathing in refrigerants.

Refrigerants do not contain oxygen and are heavier than air. If they are released into a confined area, they fill the lower space, forcing air and its oxygen upward. Any humans or animals that breathe refrigerants can be asphyxiated, and lack of oxygen can cause loss of consciousness or death. Current regulations for recycling refrigerants should eliminate any intentional dumping of refrigerants, but in case of accidental release into a confined area, you should immediately move to an area with adequate ventilation.

If liquid refrigerant is splashed onto the skin or into the eye of a human or animal, it immediately boils and absorbs heat from the body part it is in direct contact with. The temperature of the area is reduced to the low boiling point of the refrigerant, which is cold enough to freeze that body part.

◄ **SAFETY NOTE** ►

A wise technician wears safety goggles or a clear face shield and protective clothing (gloves) when working with refrigerants. If refrigerant splashes into your eyes, blindness can occur. If refrigerant splashes into your eye or onto your skin, **do not** rub that body part; **flush it with cool, clean water** to restore the temperature. Place sterile gauze over the eye to keep it clean and get professional medical attention immediately.

If a CFC such as R-12 or R-22 comes into contact with flame or heated metal, *a poisonous gas similar to phosgene is formed*. This can occur while using a flame-type leak detector, if refrigerant is drawn into a running engine, or even if it is drawn through burning tobacco. An indication that a poisonous gas is forming is a bitter taste in your throat. Flame-type leak detectors should be used only in well-ventilated areas; if used, they should be held away from your face at arm's length.

Several flammable refrigerants have been marketed, and even though they have been banned and are illegal, they still show up. A mixture of more than 2% hydrocarbon (butane, isobutane, or propane) is considered flammable, and about 4 oz in a car interior can become an explosive mixture. R-134a can become combustible at higher pressures if mixed with air. Air should not be used to flush an R-134a system because of the remote chance of a fire or explosion.

When refrigerant containers are filled, reserve room is left for expansion and the container is marked with its critical temperature, the maximum that it should be subjected to. Refrigerant containers are designed to contain the refrigerant under pressures encountered under normal working and storage conditions. Container pressure is about the same as the vapor pressure for that refrigerant up to a certain temperature point, which is where the liquid has expanded to fill the entire container. Beyond this point, any further expansion of the liquid generates very high hydraulic pressures that will rupture the container. The chance of container rupture is generally low unless the container is overfilled or overheated. You should never apply direct heat to a storage container or place the container where it will be exposed to high temperatures. Containers of R-12 have exploded from the radiant heat of direct sunlight (Figure 5-17).

When working with PAG and ester oils, you should take care not to breathe the vapor that can escape from an open container or the mist discharging with refrigerant from a system. Avoid contact between these oils and your skin: Nonpermeable gloves should be worn to prevent skin contact with PAG oil. Another problem encountered with R-134a and PAG oil is damage to paint (possibly removing any paint that it is spilled onto), plastic parts, drive belts, and hoses.

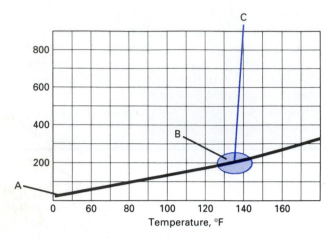

A Normal pressure-temperature for R-12
B Can fills with liquid and begins to generate
   hydrostatic pressure
C Explosive forces are developed

(a)

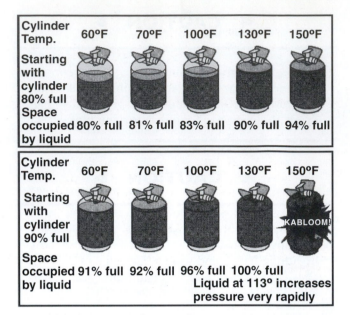

(b)

FIGURE 5-17   Pressure in a refrigerant container follows the pressure–temperature relationship until the contents expand to fill the container (a). When recovering refrigerant, the container should be filled to a maximum of about 80% (b).

REVIEW QUESTIONS

The following questions are provided to help you study as you read the chapter.

1. A chlorine atom in the stratosphere will combine with a(n) _____ molecule and _____ it.

2. A layer of gases that can trap heat in the Earth's lower atmosphere is called the _____ effect, and this can produce _____ _____.

3. One of the provisions of Section 609 of the Clean Air Act requires the technicians who _____ or _____ automotive A/C systems to be properly _____ and _____.

4. Removing refrigerant from a system is called _____; _____ removes water, oil, and air from that refrigerant so it can be reused.

5. A mixture of R-12 and R-22 is considered _____ and _____ be recycled.

6. The tank into which the refrigerant is recovered must be _____ every _____ years.

7. Both R-12 and R-134a are _____ _____ refrigerants; a mixture of two or more refrigerants is commonly called a(n) _____.

8. SNAP stands for _____ _____ _____ _____, and SNAP _____ refrigerants have acceptable global warming potential, flammability, and toxicity characteristics.

9. Care should be exercised while working with refrigerants because they present potential _____ _____.

10. If a liquid expands to the point where a container is filled with liquid, adding heat will _____ the _____ very rapidly.

CHAPTER QUIZ

The following questions will help you check the facts you have learned. Select the answer that completes each statement correctly.

1. _____ is thought to be the chemical chiefly responsible for depletion of the ozone layer.
   a. Hydrogen   c. Nitrogen
   b. Chlorine   d. Carbon

2. In 1987, 23 major countries agreed to phase out _____ at a conference in Montreal.
   a. R-22   c. R-11
   b. R-12   d. All of these

3. Two technicians are discussing Section 609 of the Clean Air Act. Technician A says that it requires that A/C technicians be properly trained and certified. Technician B says Section 609 requires that recovery and recycling equipment be of an approved type. Who is correct?

   a. Technician A   **c.** Both A and B

   b. Technician B   **d.** Neither A nor B

   64

4. Technician A says that the EPA ensures that all SNAP refrigerants are as good or better than R-12. Technician B says that the EPA checks possible new refrigerants to make sure they are safe to work with. Who is correct?

   a. Technician A   **c.** Both A and B

   b. Technician B   **d.** Neither A nor B

   68

5. Standards for A/C service procedures and equipment have been developed by the _____.

   a. EPA   **c.** SAE

   b. Clean Air Act   **d.** DOT

6. Two technicians are discussing the retrofit procedure. Technician A says that the service ports must be changed to match the new refrigerant. Technician B says a new label must be installed over the old one to identify the new refrigerant and oil. Who is correct?

   a. Technician A   **c.** Both A and B

   b. Technician B   **d.** Neither A nor B

7. Mixing two different refrigerants _____.

   a. is illegal

   b. makes a contaminated mixture that is expensive to dispose of

   c. creates a zeotrope

   d. All of these

8. Two technicians are discussing the practice of topping off an R-12 system. Technician A says that this practice is no longer profitable. Technician B says that it is not recommended because of ozone depletion. Who is correct?

   a. Technician A   **c.** Both A and B

   b. Technician B   **d.** Neither A nor B

9. A container of R-134a is color-coded _____.

   a. yellow   **c.** green

   b. white   **d.** light blue

10. A potential safety hazard when working with refrigerants is _____.

    a. frostbite and blindness

    b. asphyxiation

    c. container explosion

    d. All of these

11. When R-12 comes in contact with flame, a toxic gas called _____ is (are) formed.

    a. chlorine   **c.** fluorine

    b. phosgene   **d.** All of these

    73

12. When working with refrigerants and refrigerant oils, you should _____.

    A. avoid breathing the vapors

    B. avoid contact with your skin

    Which is correct?

    73

    a. A only   **c.** Both A and B

    b. B only   **d.** Neither A nor B

13. Technician A says that butane and propane will work as refrigerants. Technician B says that these gases present a fire hazard during service procedures. Who is correct?

    a. Technician A   **c.** Both A and B

    b. Technician B   **d.** Neither A nor B

    73

14. Technician A says that the recovery tank used in a recovery system must be checked and certified every 3 years. Technician B says that a disposable refrigerant tank should be properly evacuated before disposal. Who is correct?

    a. Technician A   **c.** Both A and B

    b. Technician B   **d.** Neither A nor B

Chapter 6

MOVING HEAT: HEATING AND AIR CONDITIONING PRINCIPLES

LEARNING OBJECTIVES

After completing this chapter, you should:

1. Have a basic understanding of heating and cooling loads.
2. Be familiar with the ways to handle a heating load.
3. Be familiar with the ways to handle a cooling load.
4. Understand the effect that compression and expansion have on the temperature of a gas.

TERMS TO LEARN

cooling load	heat exchanger
evaporative cooling	heating load
fossil fuel	mechanical refrigeration
heater core	RH (relative humidity)

6.1 INTRODUCTION

Heating and air conditioning must follow the basic rules of heat transfer. An understanding of these rules helps greatly in understanding the systems:

- Heat always flows toward cold.
- To warm a person or item, heat must be added.
- To cool a person or item, heat must be removed.
- Fuels can be burned to generate heat.

- A large amount of heat is absorbed when a liquid changes state to a vapor.
- A large amount of heat is released when a vapor changes state to a liquid.
- Compressing a gas concentrates the heat and increases the temperature.

6.2 HEATING LOAD

Heating load is the term used when we need to add heat. The actual load is the number of Btu or calories of heat energy that must be added. In a home or office, burning fuel is the usual way to generate heat; the fuel is usually a fossil fuel such as coal, gas, or oil. In most vehicles, the heat is provided by the heated coolant from the engine's cooling system. This coolant is at a temperature of 180 to 205°F (82 to 98°C) when the engine reaches its normal operating temperature (Figure 6-1).

In most vehicles, it is a fairly simple process to circulate heated coolant through a heat exchanger, called a heater core. Air is circulated through the heater core, where it absorbs heat. Then it is blown into the lower part of the passenger compartment, where the heat travels on to warm the car interior and occupants. Convection is used with the air as the medium to move heat from the heater core to the passengers (Figure 6-2). This system is described in more detail in Chapter 9.

Some very efficient hybrid vehicles do not run the engine enough to heat the coolant. These vehicles can add heat to the heater using PTC, positive temperature

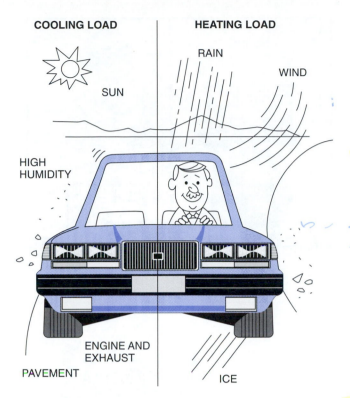

SUN

RAIN

WIND

HIGH
HUMIDITY

ENGINE AND
EXHAUST

PAVEMENT

ICE

FIGURE 6-1 Winter presents a heat load: Heat must be added for comfort (right). Summer presents a cooling load.

coefficient, heaters (Figure 6-3). A PTC is a ceramic and electronic element that produces heat when current is sent through it.

Another method of generating heat is through a thermoelectric (TE) device using the Peltier effect. This is a simple device, essentially two alloys of bismuth or tellurium with dissimilar free electron densities that are fused together. If an electric current is sent in one connector and out the other, the junction will heat up. If the current flow is reversed, the junction will become cold. This is the operating principle of picnic food chests that plug into a cigarette lighter socket and either cool or heat the inside. Some vehicles use this device plus a fan to circulate air inside of the driver and passenger seats. It can heat or cool the seat, circulating the air out through the seat cover.

6.3   COOLING LOAD

Cooling load describes the removal of heat, which is the purpose of air conditioners and evaporative coolers. We need to move heat to a cooler location in order to handle a cooling load.

One way to move heat is with a block of ice. A substantial amount of latent heat is required to change the

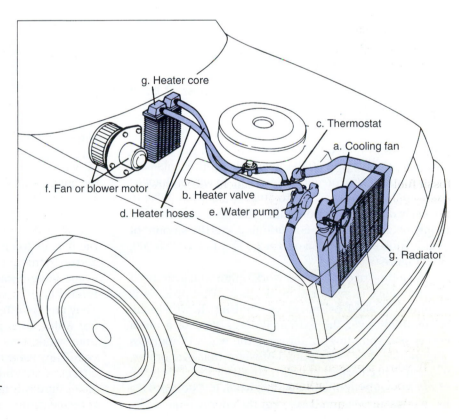

g. Heater core

c. Thermostat

a. Cooling fan

f. Fan or blower motor

b. Heater valve

d. Heater hoses   e. Water pump

g. Radiator

FIGURE 6-2 The components of an automotive heater system. *(Courtesy of Everco Industries)*

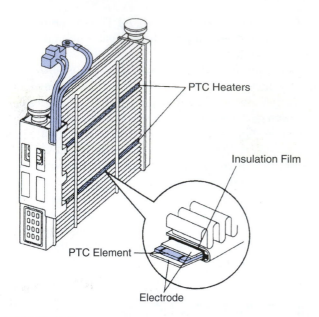

FIGURE 6-3   This hybrid vehicle component uses a pair of electric PTC (positive temperature coefficient) heaters to add heat to the heater core. *(Courtesy of Toyota Motor Sales USA, Inc.)*

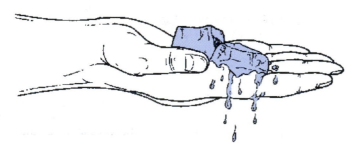

FIGURE 6-4   Ice has a cooling effect because of latent heat of fusion: It absorbs heat as it melts.

state of the solid ice into a liquid: 144 Btu per lb (79.7 calories per gram). A 50-lb block of ice represents 50×144, or 7,200 Btu of cooling power, when it changes from 50 lb of solid at 32°F to 50 lb of liquid at 32°F. In the early days of air conditioning, the term *ton* was commonly used. A ton of air conditioning was the amount of heat it took to melt a ton of ice: $2,000 \times 144$, or 288,000, Btu (Figure 6-4).

A method of cooling that works quite well in areas of low humidity is evaporation of water. This process is commonly called **evaporative cooling.** If we spread water thinly over the extremely large area of a mesh cooler pad and blow air across it, the water evaporates (Figure 6-5). For every pound of water that evaporates, 970 Btu (540 calories per gram) are absorbed. This is the *latent heat of evaporation*, just as when it is boiled. This is a natural process and uses only the energy required by

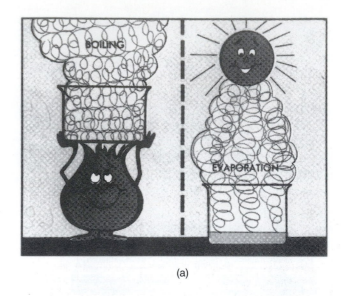

(a)

(b)

FIGURE 6-5   (a) Both boiling and evaporating liquids absorb the latent heat of vaporization as they change state. (b) This principle is used to cool water in a cloth Lister bag. *(Courtesy of DaimlerChrysler Corporation)*

the blower to circulate the air through the cooler pads and on to the space to be cooled. A possible drawback to evaporative coolers is that they increase the **relative humidity, RH;** they are often called "swamp" coolers. They are not effective in areas of very high RH because the water does not evaporate rapidly enough. At one time, window-mounted evaporative coolers were used in cars. They were not very popular because they were unattractive and only worked well in dry areas (Figure 6-6).

A third way to handle a cooling load is by **mechanical refrigeration:** air conditioning. This system also uses

FIGURE 6-6 At one time evaporative coolers were used to cool car interiors. Air forced through a water-wetted mesh produces evaporation and a cooling effect. *(Courtesy of International Mobile Air Conditioning Association, IMACA)*

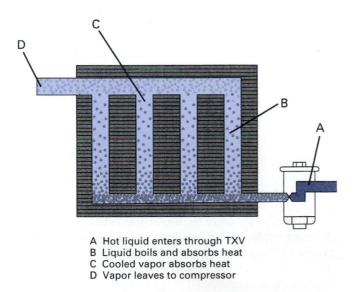

A Hot liquid enters through TXV
B Liquid boils and absorbs heat
C Cooled vapor absorbs heat
D Vapor leaves to compressor

FIGURE 6-7 Liquid refrigerant boils and absorbs heat as it enters the lower pressure of the evaporator. The absorbed heat comes from the air passing through the evaporator fins.

evaporation of a liquid and the large amount of heat required for the latent heat of evaporation. We boil the refrigerant so that it changes from a liquid to a gas, but we recycle the gas (Figure 6-7). An evaporative cooler must be continuously supplied with water, and new ice must be added to replace the ice in an ice chest. Mechanical refrigeration uses the gas to absorb and move heat from the

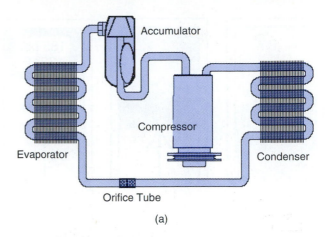

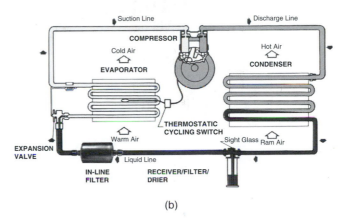

FIGURE 6-8 An automotive A/C system in a schematic *(a)* and somewhat realistic view *(b)*. These views show the relationship of the components and the circulation of the refrigerant.

evaporator to the condenser and sends the liquid back to the evaporator to boil again and absorb more heat. It requires energy to drive the compressor for this process to occur. As with a heating system, air convection is used to move the heat from the area to be cooled to the evaporator (Figure 6-8). Mechanical refrigeration is used in home and mobile A/C and is described fully in Chapter 7.

6.4 COMPRESSION HEATING

When we compress a gas into a higher pressure, we also increase the temperature of the gas. A given volume of gas has a certain temperature that, as we know, represents a certain amount of energy. Because this heat energy becomes more concentrated as the gas is compressed, heat intensity is increased. A good example of this process is the diesel engine. The operating principle of this engine is to compress air a relatively

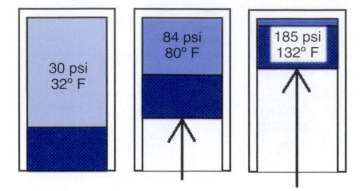

FIGURE 6-9 When a gas is compressed the heat energy is more concentrated, and this causes a temperature increase.

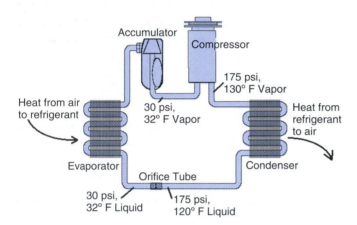

FIGURE 6-10 In a mechanical refrigeration system, the compressor increases the pressure and causes the refrigerant to circulate through the cycle as shown here.

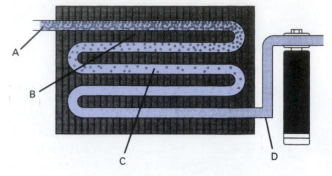

A Hot vapor enters from compressor
B Heat is transferred to air passing through
C Vapor condenses to liquid
D Liquid leaves through liquid line

FIGURE 6-11 Refrigerant enters the condenser as a hot, high-pressure gas and leaves as a liquid. Removing heat to ambient air causes the refrigerant to condense.

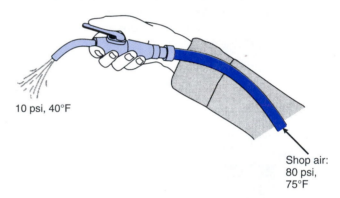

10 psi, 40°F

Shop air: 80 psi, 75°F

FIGURE 6-12 Releasing a compressed gas allows the air to expand; the air will be cooled because the heat energy is spread out.

large amount, about 20:1, so that the air becomes hot enough to ignite the fuel as it is injected into the cylinder (Figure 6-9). Another example is the discharge line of an operating air compressor, which is substantially warmer than the inlet line because of the heat of the compressed air. Some of these lines can be very hot.

Mechanical refrigeration uses a compressor to raise the pressure of the refrigerant that has boiled in the evaporator. R-12 is at a temperature of about 32°F in the evaporator, with a pressure of about 30 psi; R-134a has a slightly lower pressure of 27 psi at 32°F. Raising the pressure increases the gas temperature to a point above the ambient temperature. With R-12 and an ambient temperature of 100°F, we have to raise the pressure to about 205 psi. This pressure is slightly higher with R-134a, about 230 psi, and depends to a great extent on the design of the condenser and the airflow through it (Figure 6-10).

Raising the temperature of the refrigerant allows the required heat flow from the now warmer refrigerant to ambient air; this removal of heat causes the change of state back to liquid. We accomplish two things at the condenser: We remove all of the heat that was absorbed in the evaporator, and we recycle the gas back into a liquid (Figure 6-11).

6.5 EXPANSION COOLING

If we can raise the temperature of a gas by compressing it, we can lower the temperature if we allow it to expand. Expanding a volume of gas spreads out the heat energy over a larger area and lowers its temperature. An example can be felt with the coolness of an air nozzle as we use it to blow parts clean and dry (Figure 6-12).

In the past, a closed system using air compression and expansion was under development for use in cooling car interiors. Air was compressed and then cooled in a heat exchanger mounted in front of the car. Then this high-pressure, fairly cool air was allowed to expand in a heat exchanger mounted in the passenger compartment. The cooler air absorbed heat from the inside of the car as it expanded. This heat was then concentrated so that it could be released at the outer heat exchanger. This system worked, but it required much larger lines and a bigger heat exchanger to handle the volume of air. Furthermore, it was not as efficient as the mechanical refrigeration system currently in use (Figure 6-13).

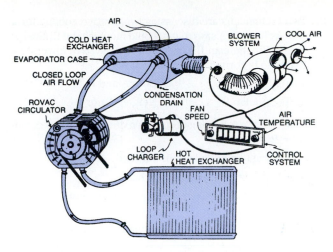

FIGURE 6-13 The Rovac system used a circulator to compress air and to allow the air to expand again. Heat from the compressed air was transferred to ambient air in the hot heat exchanger. Heat from the passenger compartment was absorbed by the expanded air in the cold heat exchanger.

REVIEW QUESTIONS

The following questions are provided to help you study as you read the chapter.

1. *Heating load* is the term used to describe the amount of _____ that must be _____ to make people comfortable.

2. The object where heat is transferred from one medium to another is called a(n) _____ _____.

3. It takes _____ Btu of heat to melt 1 lb of ice.

4. Evaporative coolers use the principle of _____ _____ of _____, the amount of heat that is required to evaporate water.

5. Mechanical refrigeration cools because of the amount of _____ _____ that is required to boil the _____ _____ in the evaporator.

6. An A/C system changes the refrigerant from a(n) _____ to a(n) _____ in the evaporator.

7. An A/C system changes the refrigerant from a(n) _____ to a(n) _____ in the condenser.

8. An A/C compressor increases the gas pressure in order to increase the _____.

9. As a gas is compressed, the temperature will _____.

10. There will be a(n) _____ effect when we allow compressed air to expand.

CHAPTER QUIZ

The following questions will help you check the facts you have learned. Select the answer that completes each statement correctly.

1. In the automobile, a heat load comes from _____. 76
   a. the engine cooling system
   b. the sun load on the car
   c. a cold winter day
   d. None of these

2. Which of the following is a method of handling a cooling load?
   a. A block of ice
   b. Evaporating water   78
   c. Mechanical refrigeration
   d. All of these

3. Two technicians are discussing evaporative cooling for a car. Technician A says that it would increase the RH inside the car. Technician B says that an A/C system lowers the RH. Who is correct?

   a. Technician A   **c.** Both A and B

   b. Technician B   **d.** Neither A nor B

4. Which of the following describes a drawback of mechanical refrigeration?

   a. Oil must be added continuously.

   b. R-12 must be added continuously.

   c. The passenger compartment does not get cool enough.

   d. It takes energy to drive the compressor.

5. Two technicians are discussing HVAC systems. Technician A says the evaporator moves heat from the passenger compartment to the refrigerant. Technician B says the refrigerant boils inside the evaporator. Who is correct?

   a. Technician A   **c.** Both A and B

   b. Technician B   **d.** Neither A nor B

6. In an A/C system, the refrigerant changes state from a _____ in the evaporator.

   A. liquid to a gas   **B.** gas to a liquid

   Which is correct?

   a. A only   **c.** Both A and B

   b. B only   **d.** Neither A nor B

7. When an A/C system is operating, the compressor _____ runs hot.

   A. inlet   **B.** outlet

   Which is correct?

   a. A only   **c.** Both A and B

   b. B only   **d.** Neither A nor B

8. Technician A says that some devices generate heat by compressing a gas to a higher pressure. Technician B says some devices generate cool air by allowing a compressed gas to expand. Who is correct?

   a. Technician A   **c.** Both A and B

   b. Technician B   **d.** Neither A nor B

◀ Chapter 7 ▶

AIR CONDITIONING SYSTEMS

LEARNING OBJECTIVES

After completing this chapter, you should:

1. Understand the relationship between the A/C cycle and the components on the low side and high side of a system.
2. Understand the functions for the low side and high side of a system.
3. Be familiar with the role of each A/C component.

TERMS TO LEARN

accumulator
axial
barrier hose
condenser
cut-in pressure
cutout pressure
cycling clutch orifice tube (CCOT)
cycling clutch system
discharge line
evaporator
evaporator pressure regulator (EPR)
fin and tube
fixed orifice tube (FOT)
flattened tube
flooded

high pressure cutoff (HPCO) switch
high side
liquid line
low side
orifice tube (OT)
overcharge
parallel flow
pilot operated absolute (POA)
pressure sensor
pressure switch
radial pistons
receiver–drier
reciprocating piston
rotary vane
Scotch yoke

scroll
serpentine flow
slugging
starved
sub-cooling
suction line
suction throttling valve (STV)
swash plate
temperature sensing thermistor

thermal expansion valve (TXV)
undercharge
variable displacement compressor
variable orifice valve (VOV)
wobble plate

7.1 INTRODUCTION

The automotive A/C system uses the physical principles described in earlier chapters to move heat from the passenger compartment to the condenser and then to the ambient air moving through the condenser. The heating system uses some of the same principles to move heat from the engine's cooling system to the passenger compartment (Figure 7-1).

Automotive A/C systems are either **orifice tube (OT) systems** or **thermal expansion valve (TXV) systems,** depending on which type of *flow control* or *expansion device* is used—either an OT or TXV (Figure 7-2). Orifice tube systems are also called **cycling clutch orifice tube (CCOT)** and **fixed orifice tube (FOT)** systems. A/C systems can be easily divided into two parts: the **low side,** with its low pressure and temperature, and the **high side,** with its higher pressures and temperatures (Figure 7-3). The low side begins at the expansion device—the OT or

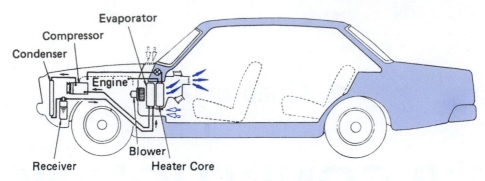

FIGURE 7-1 Air is circulated through the A/C and heating system and the car to either add or remove heat. *(Courtesy of Toyota Motor Sales USA, Inc.)*

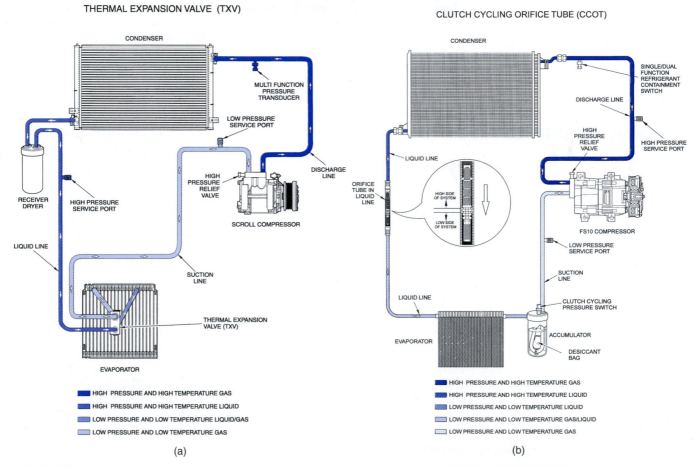

FIGURE 7-2 Automative A/C systems are either a TXV system with a receiver–drier *(a)* or an OT system with an accumulator *(b)*. A variety of compressors are used with both systems. *(Courtesy of Visteon)*

the TXV—and ends at the compressor; the high side begins at the compressor and ends at the OT or TXV.

Refrigerant boils or evaporates in the low side and it condenses in the high side (Figure 7-4). In an operating system, you can identify the low and high sides by:

- **Pressure:** A gauge set shows low pressure in the low side and high pressure in the high side.

- **Sight:** On high-humidity days, the cold low side tubing often collects water droplets and may even frost.

- **Temperature:** The low side is cool to cold, and the high side is hot.

- **Tubing size:** Low side tubes and hoses are larger (vapor), and high side tubes and hoses are smaller (liquid).

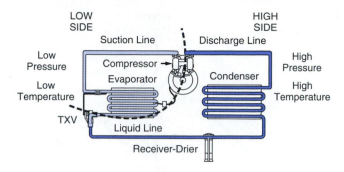

FIGURE 7-3 The high and low sides of an A/C system are divided by the compressor (where the pressure is increased) and either a TXV or OT (where the pressure drops).

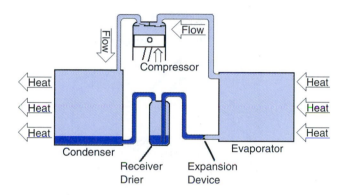

FIGURE 7-4 Refrigerant changes state to a vapor as it absorbs heat in the low side and into a liquid as it loses heat in the high side.

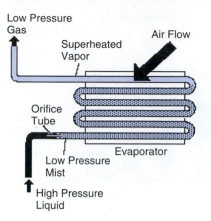

FIGURE 7-5 As liquid refrigerant enters the evaporator, the boiling point will try to drop as low as 32°F because of the drop in pressure. The cold temperature causes the refrigerant to absorb heat from the air circulated through the evaporator.

7.2 LOW SIDE OPERATION

When the A/C system is in full operation, the goal of most systems is to maintain an evaporator temperature just above the freezing point of water, 32°F (0°C). This temperature produces the greatest heat exchange without ice formation on the evaporator fins (evaporator icing significantly reduces the heat transfer).

The cold temperature in the evaporator is produced by boiling the refrigerant. Remember that R-12 and R-134a have very low boiling points, well below 0°F, and that when a liquid boils, it absorbs a large amount of heat, the latent heat of vaporization. To produce cooling, liquid refrigerant must enter the **evaporator,** and it must boil inside the evaporator. The amount of heat an evaporator absorbs is directly related to the amount of liquid refrigerant that boils inside it (Figure 7-5).

A properly operating evaporator has a temperature just above 32°F (0°C), and refrigerant pressure is directly related to temperature because the refrigerant is a saturated vapor. An A/C technician becomes familiar with normal low side temperatures and pressures. Abnormal temperatures and pressures indicate that something is wrong (e.g., a **starved** or **flooded** evaporator). An evaporator that has a low pressure but a temperature that is too warm is called starved; not enough refrigerant is entering to produce the desired cooling effect. A starved evaporator is usually caused by a restriction at or before the expansion device or an undercharge of refrigerant. If more refrigerant enters the evaporator than can boil, the evaporator floods. In this case the pressure is then higher than normal (Figure 7-6).

Major components in the low side are the evaporator and the expansion device. The evaporator is the heat exchanger and absorbs heat from the passenger compartment. The low side begins at the refrigerant expansion or flow metering device, either a TXV or an OT, which produces a pressure drop. The low side ends at the compressor, which causes the pressure to increase (Figure 7-7).

7.2.1 Expansion Devices

The expansion device separates the high-pressure liquid from the low-pressure evaporator. The liquid refrigerant becomes a mist as it passes through, and this allows it to absorb heat easily. The restriction of the expansion device limits the refrigerant flow so the compressor must generate the high side pressure.

7.2.1.1 Thermal Expansion Valves A TXV is a variable valve that changes the size of the valve opening

NORMAL OPERATION

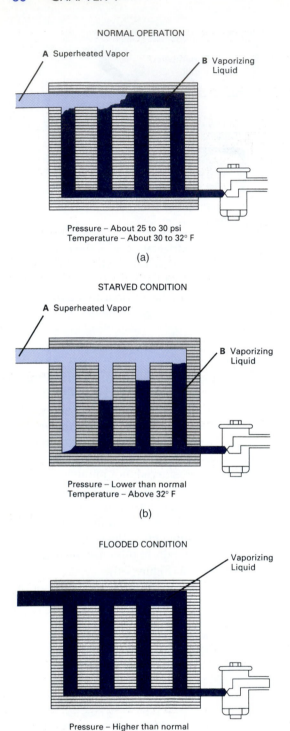

FIGURE 7-6   If the proper amount of refrigerant enters the evaporator, it has a slight superheat as it leaves (a). A starved condition, in which not enough refrigerant enters the evaporator, does not produce as much cooling (b). If too much refrigerant enters, the evaporator floods because the refrigerant will not all boil (c).

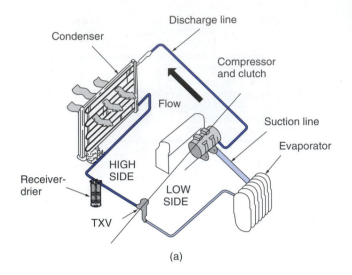

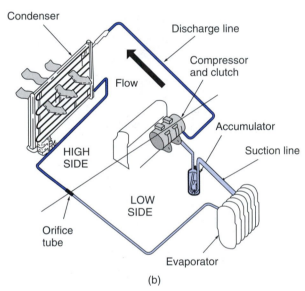

FIGURE 7-7   The low side begins at the TXV or OT and includes the evaporator and suction line to the compressor (a). The OT system includes an accumulator (b).

in response to the cooling load of the evaporator. A TXV is controlled by evaporator temperature and pressure so that it opens to flow as much refrigerant as possible when a lot of cooling is needed. But all of the refrigerant must boil in the evaporator, and the vapor must be slightly superheated when it reaches the evaporator outlet. Most TXVs are calibrated so that the outlet temperature is a few degrees above the inlet pressure and temperature: The refrigerant leaving the evaporator has boiled completely and has a few degrees of superheat. When there is a lower cooling load, the TXV must reduce the flow. The various types of TXVs and other system components are described more completely in Chapter 8 (Figure 7-8).

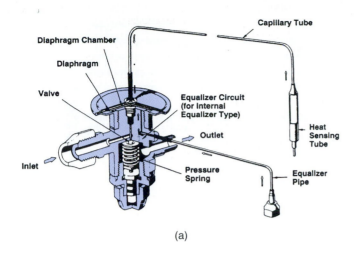

(a)

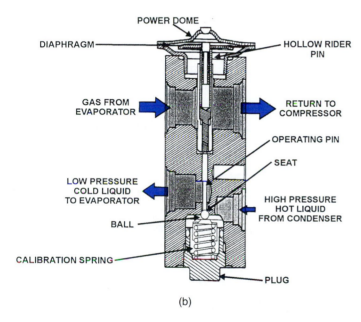

(b)

FIGURE 7-8   A TXV is controlled by the pressure on the diaphragm from the heat sensing tube, the pressure spring, and evaporator pressure through the equalizer pipe (*a*). An H-type valve is essentially the same except evaporator pressure goes through an internal passage to the bottom of the diaphragm (*b*). (a *Courtesy of Toyota Motor Sales USA, Inc.*, b *courtesy of DaimlerChrysler*)

In most systems that use a TXV, the evaporator outlet is connected to the compressor inlet by a line with an internal diameter (ID) of about 5/8 or 3/4 inch (16 or 19 mm). Some TXV systems use a suction throttling valve to prevent evaporator pressure from dropping below a certain pressure, about 30 psi (207 kPa). Lower

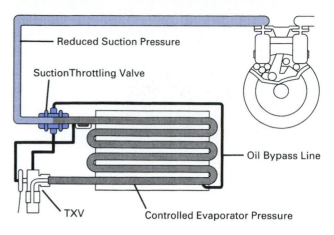

FIGURE 7-9   Some systems use a suction throttling valve to keep evaporator pressure from dropping to the point at which icing can occur.

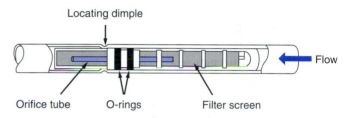

FIGURE 7-10   An OT is a simple restriction that limits the flow of refrigerant into the evaporator. The locating dimple keeps the OT from moving downstream.

pressure with its lower temperature can cause evaporator icing (Figure 7-9).

7.2.1.2 Orifice Tubes   An orifice tube (OT) is a fixed-diameter orifice that the refrigerant must flow through; it is also called an *expansion tube* or *fixed orifice tube* (Figure 7-10). The diameter varies between systems and is about 1/16 inch (0.065 inch, 1.588 mm). It is much simpler and cheaper to produce than a TXV, but an OT cannot respond to evaporator temperature. At times of low cooling loads, it flows too much refrigerant, which floods the evaporator with liquid. An OT system must include a *low side accumulator* between the evaporator and compressor to catch and store liquid refrigerant. The accumulator is constructed so it retains the liquid and allows only gas to flow back to the compressor. The accumulator is usually attached to the evaporator outlet and connected to the compressor by the suction line (Figure 7-11). A **variable orifice valve (VOV)** has been developed. The VOV includes a valve that is sensitive to flow and pressure or temperature. Another style, the electronic OT, can also change orifice size. They are explained more completely in Section 8.4.3.

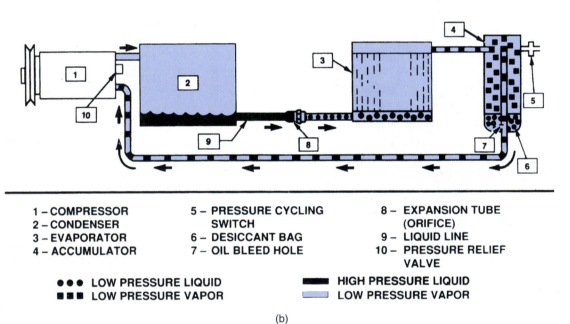

FIGURE 7-11 Two views of a typical OT system; *a* is somewhat realistic and *b* is schematic. Both show the arrangement of the components and the refrigerant flow. *(Courtesy of ACDelco)*

(a)

1 – COMPRESSOR
2 – CONDENSER
3 – EVAPORATOR
4 – ACCUMULATOR

5 – PRESSURE CYCLING SWITCH
6 – DESICCANT BAG
7 – OIL BLEED HOLE

8 – EXPANSION TUBE (ORIFICE)
9 – LIQUID LINE
10 – PRESSURE RELIEF VALVE

●●● LOW PRESSURE LIQUID
■■■ LOW PRESSURE VAPOR

▬▬▬ HIGH PRESSURE LIQUID
▭▭▭ LOW PRESSURE VAPOR

(b)

In some modern systems, the OT is mounted upstream, close to the condenser inside the liquid line. When the engine and the A/C system are shut off, high side pressure equalizes and bleeds off through the OT and makes a hissing sound, which might alarm some motorists; moving the OT upstream reduces this noise.

7.2.2 Evaporators

The refrigerant enters the evaporator as a spray or mist, leaving an area of a few hundred pounds per square inch (psi) and passing through a small orifice into an area of about 30 psi. Like most heat exchangers, a well-designed evaporator has a large amount of surface area in contact with the refrigerant and the air from the passenger compartment. The heat from the air causes the refrigerant to boil and turn into a vapor; the cooler air is returned to the passenger compartment (Figure 7-12).

In the evaporator of a TXV system, all of the refrigerant is vaporized and slightly superheated before reaching the evaporator outlet, also called a tailpipe. This is also the case in an OT system when there is a hot car, but as the car cools down some of the refrigerant is still in mist form at the tailpipe.

If liquid refrigerant enters the compressor, it can cause compressor damage. This is called **slugging.**

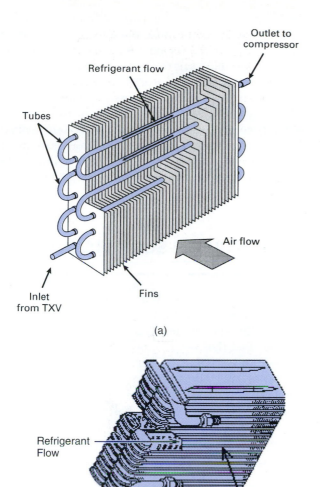

(a)

Outlet to compressor

Refrigerant flow

Tubes

Air flow

Inlet from TXV

Fins

(b)

Refrigerant Flow

Air Flow

FIGURE 7-12   A tube-and-fin (*a*) and a plate (*b*) evaporator. Each type has a large contact area for heat to leave the air and enter the refrigerant.

The design of a low side accumulator prevents compressor slugging.

7.2.3   Accumulator

The **accumulator** serves three major functions: (1) to prevent liquid refrigerant from passing to the compressor; (2) to hold the desiccant, which helps remove moisture from the system; and (3) to hold a reserve of refrigerant (Figure 7-13). The receiver–drier used in a TXV system serves the second two purposes and is mounted in the high side.

An accumulator is a container that holds about 1 quart (0.95 L) in volume. The inlet line from the evapo-

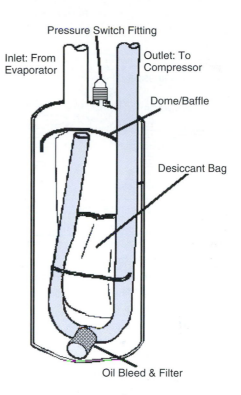

Pressure Switch Fitting

Inlet: From Evaporator

Outlet: To Compressor

Dome/Baffle

Desiccant Bag

Oil Bleed & Filter

FIGURE 7-13   Accumulators are designed so that vapor from the top leaves to the compressor. They contain desiccant to absorb water from the refrigerant and many include a fitting for low side pressure and the clutch cycling switch.

rator enters near the top. The outlet line to the compressor begins near the top, passes downward to the bottom, and then goes either out the bottom or back up to its exit. A small opening for oil bleed is at the lowermost point; this opening usually has a filter so debris will not block it. This routing of the outlet tube separates the refrigerant vapor at the top from the liquid at the bottom so that only vapor will leave the accumulator. A small amount of liquid refrigerant and oil also leaves through the bleed hole; the oil ensures that the compressor is lubricated. The small amount of liquid refrigerant helps cool the compressor.

The desiccant is a chemical drying agent called *molecular sieve* that removes all traces of water vapor from a system. Water can mix with refrigerant to form acids, which cause rust and corrosion of metal parts. Water can also freeze and form ice at the TXV or OT, which can block the flow of refrigerant into the evaporator. Desiccant is usually contained in a cloth bag inside the accumulator or **receiver–drier**. (Figure 7-14)

A desiccant variety referred to as XH-5 has commonly been used with R-12 in automotive systems.

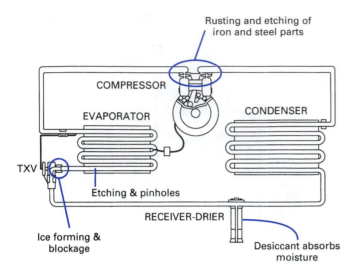

FIGURE 7-14 Water in an A/C system can combine with refrigerant to form acids. These acids can etch and dissolve components, cause rusting of metal parts, and cause ice blockage at the expansion device.

XH-5 has the ability to absorb about 1% of its weight in water, but this chemical suffers damage when it absorbs fluorine from R-134a, and it begins to decompose when it comes into contact with R-134a and PAG oil. Other desiccant types (XH-7 and XH-9) are compatible with R-134a and PAG. The receiver–drier or accumulator used in an R-134a system should use XH-7 or XH-9 desiccant. All new accumulators and receiver–driers contain either XH-7 or XH-9 desiccant. This desiccant is a little more expensive and requires a little more volume than XH-5. R-134a driers must have greater water absorption capacity because R-134a is more water soluble than R-12, so they are often slightly larger to hold the additional desiccant.

When off the vehicle, a new accumulator or receiver–drier must be kept closed as much as possible to keep it dry. Consider the desiccant a very dry sponge that is ready to absorb moisture. It has a magnet-like attraction that sucks moisture out of the refrigerant or air. Accumulators and receiver–driers are normally replaced when the system is serviced if the desiccant is suspected to contain water.

A refrigerant reserve is necessary because automotive A/C systems are subject to a wide variety of temperatures. This temperature variation causes the liquid refrigerant to change volume as it expands and contracts. An automotive A/C system also leaks a small amount of refrigerant through flexible hoses and the compressor shaft seal. Driving the compressor with an engine-driven belt requires a seal at the compressor drive shaft. Mounting the compressor on the engine re-

quires flexible hoses because the engine moves on its mounts. The volume in an accumulator (or receiver–drier) allows us to charge a slight excess of refrigerant into a system as a stored liquid that can change its volume to compensate for loss or volume change. Early A/C systems used rather large receiver–driers because refrigerant was cheap and the system leaked. Newer receiver–driers and accumulators are much smaller because barrier-type hoses have reduced the leak rate and refrigerant is more valuable (Figure 7-15).

◀ **PROBLEM SOLVING 7-1** ▶

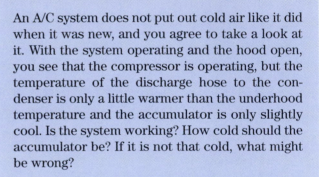

An A/C system does not put out cold air like it did when it was new, and you agree to take a look at it. With the system operating and the hood open, you see that the compressor is operating, but the temperature of the discharge hose to the condenser is only a little warmer than the underhood temperature and the accumulator is only slightly cool. Is the system working? How cold should the accumulator be? If it is not that cold, what might be wrong?

7.2.4 Refrigerant Charge Level

For an A/C system to work properly, a constant flow of liquid refrigerant must pass through the TXV or OT. While operating, the evaporator contains a refrigerant mist in the first two-thirds to three-fourths of its volume, with vapor in the remaining portion; the condenser contains a condensing vapor in the upper portion, with liquid in the bottom passages; and the line connecting the condenser to the expansion device is filled with liquid. The accumulator or receiver–drier is about half full of liquid (Figure 7-16).

Most newer A/C systems have improved efficiency and reduced the size of some components so they can operate with smaller charge volumes than in the past. At one time, the refrigerant capacity of many domestic systems was in the 3- to 4-lb range; today, most systems hold 1 1/2 to 2 1/2 lb of refrigerant. Some of the new systems have a capacity of 0.95 lb (0.43 kg). With this reduced volume, the actual charge amount is more critical.

If the volume of liquid drops so that vapor bubbles pass through the TXV or OT, the system is **undercharged** and its cooling effectiveness is reduced. If an excessive amount of refrigerant is put into a sys-

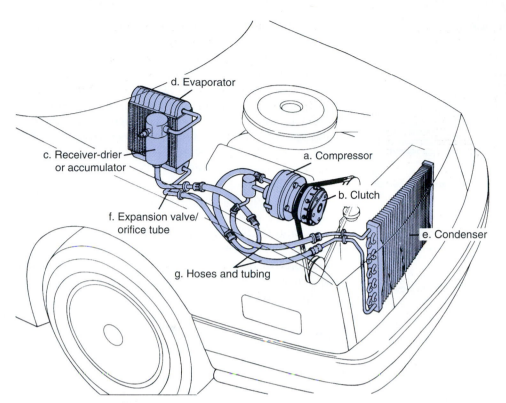

FIGURE 7-15 An automotive A/C system has the potential to lose refrigerant through hoses, the compressor shaft seal, and line fittings. *(Courtesy of Everco Industries)*

d. Evaporator

c. Receiver-drier or accumulator

a. Compressor

b. Clutch

f. Expansion valve/ orifice tube

g. Hoses and tubing

e. Condenser

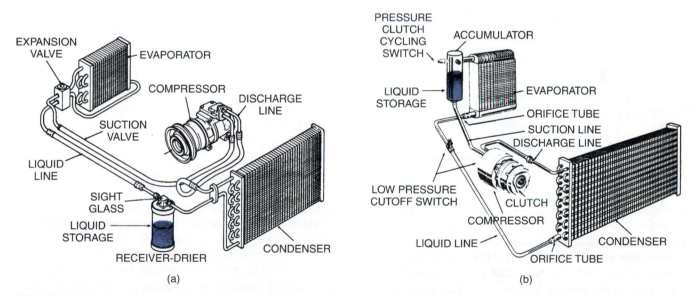

(a)

EXPANSION VALVE
EVAPORATOR
COMPRESSOR
DISCHARGE LINE
SUCTION VALVE
LIQUID LINE
SIGHT GLASS
LIQUID STORAGE
RECEIVER-DRIER
CONDENSER

(b)

PRESSURE CLUTCH CYCLING SWITCH
ACCUMULATOR
LIQUID STORAGE
EVAPORATOR
ORIFICE TUBE
SUCTION LINE
DISCHARGE LINE
LOW PRESSURE CUTOFF SWITCH
CLUTCH
COMPRESSOR
LIQUID LINE
ORIFICE TUBE
CONDENSER

FIGURE 7-16   A system with the proper charge has the receiver–drier *(a)* or the accumulator *(b)* about half full of liquid. *(Courtesy of Everco Industries)*

tem, the excess volume partially fills the condenser as a liquid and reduces its effective volume. This is called an **overcharge** and causes abnormally high pressures, especially in the high side, and poor cooling at the evaporator (Figure 7-17).

7.2.5 Evaporator Icing Controls

Most A/C systems operate at maximum capacity when it is necessary to cool the car. Compressor size (displacement) and the sizes of the evaporator and

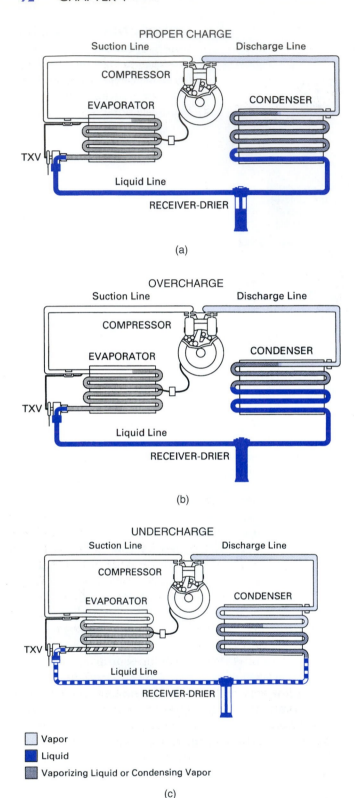

PROPER CHARGE

(a)

OVERCHARGE

(b)

UNDERCHARGE

(c)

☐ Vapor
■ Liquid
▨ Vaporizing Liquid or Condensing Vapor

FIGURE 7-17 A properly charged system has the condenser filled with condensing vapor and some liquid, a liquid line filled with liquid, a receiver–drier about half full of liquid, and an evaporator with vaporizing liquid (a). An overcharge with too much liquid causes liquid to partially fill the condenser (b). An undercharge has vapor in the liquid line and a starved evaporator (c).

condenser determine cooling power; these parts are normally designed to cool a particular car and its passengers at normal speeds on a hot day. Vehicle size and glass area, compressor displacement and operating speed, number of passengers, ambient temperature, and vehicle speed are all design parameters that are considered during the initial design of the A/C and heating systems. Some systems are designed to cool a car with the engine at idle speed and the compressor running at its slowest speed.

As the vehicle cools down, the cooling load on the evaporator drops, and its temperature also drops. As mentioned earlier, the minimum temperature for an evaporator is 32°F, the point at which water freezes and ice and frost form. There are several ways to prevent evaporator icing. These include *cycling the compressor clutch, controlling evaporator pressure* so it does not drop below 30 psi, and *reducing the displacement of the compressor.*

7.2.5.1 Cycling Clutch Systems

A **cycling clutch (CC) system** disengages the compressor and shuts the system off when the evaporator temperature or pressure drops below freezing. Most mobile A/C compressors are driven by a belt from the engine through a magnetic clutch (Figure 7-18). When the system is turned on, electricity is sent to energize the clutch. The current flow to the clutch is controlled by one or more switches; one of these is the on–off control at the heater–A/C control head.

Early A/C systems used a *temperature-controlled switch* mounted in the airstream from the evaporator. This thermal switch, also called an *icing* or *defrost switch*, is set to open and stop the current flow to the clutch when the temperature drops below 32°F and reclose when there is a temperature increase of about 5 to 15°F. This causes a pressure increase of about 10 to 20 psi that, in turn, produces temperature rise to melt any frost or ice on the fins. Some newer systems use a **temperature sensing thermistor.** A thermistor is a solid-state device that changes its electrical resistance in direct inverse relationship to its temperature; as the temperature goes up, the resistance is reduced and vice versa. It is used as an input to an electronic control module (ECM) to provide the actual evaporator temperature control.

Many OT systems use a **pressure switch** mounted in the accumulator or the **suction line** to the compressor. Remember that evaporator temperature and pressure are closely linked; they drop together. When the pressure switch senses the pressure dropping below a certain point (about 30 psi for R-12, slightly less for R-134a), this switch opens to stop the compressor. This is called the **cutout pressure;** depending on the particu-

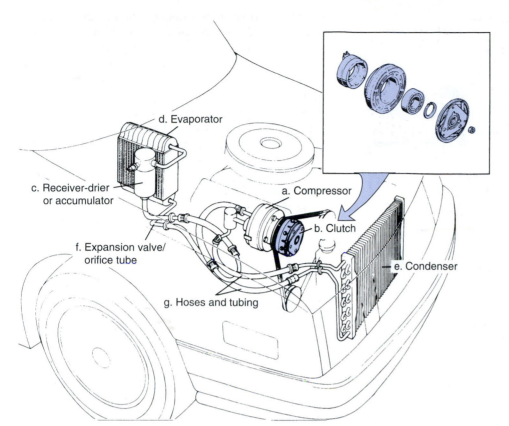

FIGURE 7-18 The compressor clutch allows us to cycle the compressor off and on to control evaporator temperature and to shut the system off. *(Courtesy of Everco Industries)*

d. Evaporator

c. Receiver-drier or accumulator

a. Compressor

b. Clutch

f. Expansion valve/ orifice tube

e. Condenser

g. Hoses and tubing

lar switch, this pressure is between 22 and 28 psi. Like the thermal switch, a pressure switch recloses when the pressure increases; the **cut-in pressure** is about 42 to 49 psi, again depending on the particular switch. With either of these systems, if ice and frost start to form because the evaporator gets too cold, the ice and frost melts during the off part of the cycle (Figure 7-19). Some vehicles use a **pressure sensor** in place of a pressure switch. The resistance of the sensor changes in direct relation to the pressure. It is an input to an ECM used for compressor clutch, cooling fan, and idle speed control as well as low-pressure and high-pressure protection.

7.2.5.2 Evaporator Pressure Controls If we can keep the evaporator pressure at 30 psi in an R-12 system or 28 psi in an R-134a system, the evaporator temperature will stay at 32°F. Lower pressures cause icing, and higher pressures cause a temperature increase. Two methods have been used in automotive systems to maintain the ideal evaporator pressure: *suction throttling* and *hot gas bypass.*

Many domestic A/C systems in the 1960s and 1970s used **suction throttling valves (STVs)—pilot-operated absolutes (POAs)** and **evaporator pressure regulators (EPRs)** were the most common. Some import vehicles used an EPR valve in the late

1990s. These valves are mounted at the evaporator outlet, the compressor inlet, or somewhere between. Most of them sense evaporator pressure; when the pressure starts to drop below a certain point, the valve closes down to restrict refrigerant flow to the compressor. When this occurs, the system has three basic pressures: low side evaporator pressure controlled to 30 psi (R-12), low side compressor inlet pressure below 30 psi, and high side pressure. A system that uses a suction throttling valve maintains an almost constant evaporator temperature of 32°F without cycling the clutch. It should be noted that the compressor drive load drops when the valve restricts the flow (Figure 7-20).

A few very early automotive systems (before 1960) used a valve that would sense evaporator pressure. When the pressure began to drop below 30 psi, the valve would allow hot gas from the high side to enter the evaporator. This valve was called a *hot gas bypass valve.* It worked, but now this system is considered crude (Figure 7-21).

7.2.5.3 Variable Displacement Compressors A **variable displacement compressor** provides smooth operation (no clutch cycling), a constant 32°F evaporator, and the most efficiency. This design includes a large compressor that can pump enough refrigerant to meet high cooling loads, and it reduces the displacement and

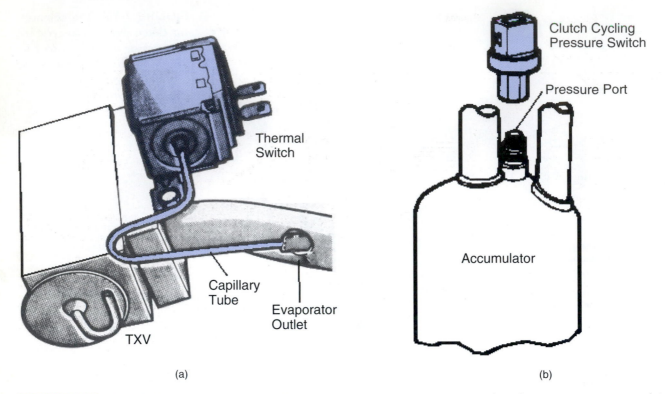

Thermal
Switch

Capillary
Tube

Evaporator
Outlet

TXV

(a)

Clutch Cycling
Pressure Switch

Pressure Port

Accumulator

(b)

FIGURE 7-19 Most TXV systems use a thermal switch to cycle the compressor out when the evaporator gets too cold (a). Most OT systems use a pressure switch to cycle the compressor out when the low side pressure drops too low (b).

FIGURE 7-20 A suction throttling valve (STV) stops evaporator pressure from dropping below 30 psi, and this keeps ice from forming on the evaporator.

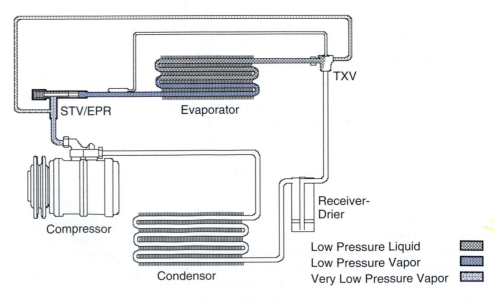

TXV

STV/EPR   Evaporator

Compressor

Receiver-
Drier

Condensor

Low Pressure Liquid
Low Pressure Vapor
Very Low Pressure Vapor

pumping capacity of the compressor to match the needs of the evaporator as the evaporator cools. At this time, variable displacement compressors are of the wobble plate type, vane type, and scroll-type compressor. These compressors are described in more detail in Chapter 8 (Figure 7-22).

7.3   HIGH SIDE OPERATION

The high side of an A/C system takes the low-pressure vapor from the evaporator and returns high-pressure liquid to the expansion device. To do this, the compressor must raise the pressure and concentrate the heat so

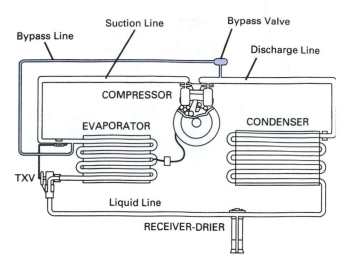

FIGURE 7-21 A hot gas bypass system diverts high side pressure into the evaporator to keep the pressure from dropping to the point at which icing can occur.

that the vapor temperature is above ambient. This causes heat to flow from the refrigerant to the air passing through the condenser. Removing the heat from the saturated vapor causes it to change state, to a liquid.

Major components in the high side are the compressor and the condenser. The condenser, like the evaporator, is a heat exchanger. The high side begins at the compressor and ends at the expansion device. The high side of a TXV system includes a receiver–drier.

7.3.1 Compressor

The compressor can be thought of as a pump that circulates refrigerant. It has to work against the restriction of the TXV or OT, and in doing this, it can increase the pressure about 10 times. The compression ratio normally varies from about 5:1 to 8:1, depending on ambient air temperature and refrigerant type. The pressure must be increased to the point where refrigerant temperature is above ambient air temperature and there is enough heat transfer at the condenser to get rid of all the heat absorbed in the evaporator.

At one time, most compressors used two pistons and a crankshaft. Because the pistons moved up and down in a cylinder, they are called **reciprocating piston** compressors. Other compressor designs use reciprocating pistons mounted in an **axial** position and operated by a **wobble plate** or a **swash plate** or **radial pistons** mounted on a **Scotch yoke.** There are two types of compressors that don't use pistons; these are **rotary vanes** and **scroll** designs (Figure 7-23).

A piston compressor uses reed valves to control refrigerant flow in and out of the cylinder. A reed is a thin,

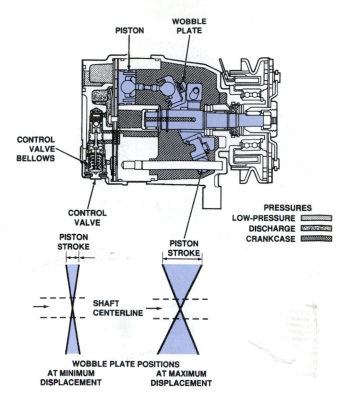

FIGURE 7-22 When the evaporator cools and low side pressure drops, the piston stroke of a variable displacement compressor is reduced so that compressor output matches the cooling load. *(Reprinted with permission of General Motors Corporation)*

flexible strip of metal that closes off one side of a hole in the metal valve plate or piston. Pressure from the reed side of the plate forces the reed tightly against the plate and keeps the hole closed. Pressure from the other side forces the reed open and causes refrigerant flow; the reed is a one-way check valve. When the piston moves downward, evaporator pressure forces refrigerant through the suction reed and fills the cylinder; this is called the *suction stroke.* The discharge reed is positioned so it blocks a back flow from the high side. During the upward or *discharge stroke,* piston action and cylinder pressure force the refrigerant through the discharge reeds and into the high side as cylinder pressure forces the suction reeds tightly closed (Figure 7-24).

7.3.1.1 Rotary Compressors Almost any style of air pump can be used as a refrigerant compressor. Several of these styles are used for stationary A/C units, but only two rotary styles are currently used in automotive systems.

Vane- and scroll-type compressors form chambers that enlarge to draw refrigerant into them at one location. This area is open to low side pressure. These

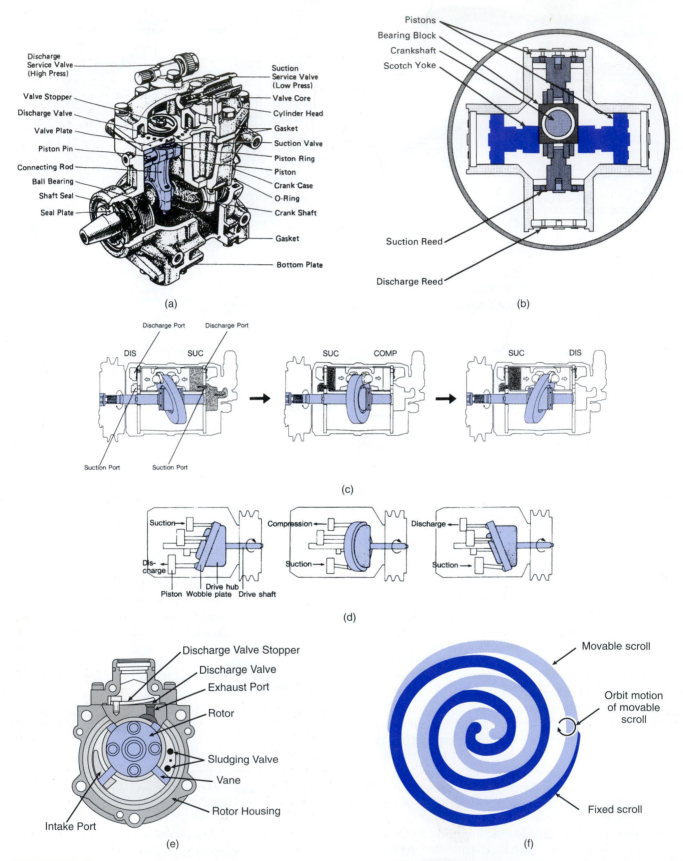

FIGURE 7-23   Piston compressors can drive the piston through a crankshaft *(a)*, Scotch yoke *(b)*, swash plate *(c)*, or wobble plate *(d)*. A rotary compressor can use vanes *(e)* or a pair of scrolls *(f)*. (a *and* e *are courtesy of Toyota Motor Sales USA, Inc.;* c *and* d *are courtesy of Zexel USA Corporation)*

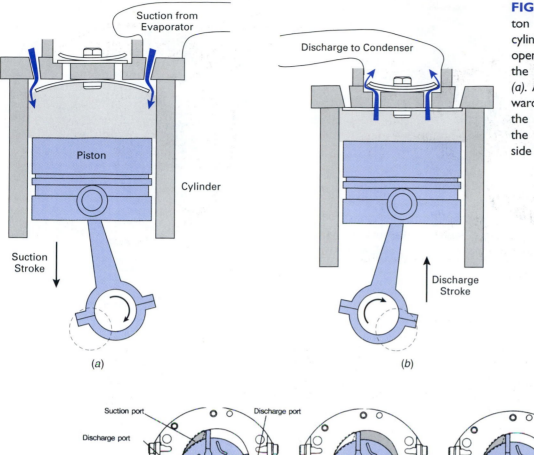

FIGURE 7-24 As the piston moves downward in the cylinder, evaporator pressure opens the suction reed and fills the cylinder with refrigerant (a). As the piston moves upward, piston pressure forces the discharge reed open and the refrigerant into the high side (b).

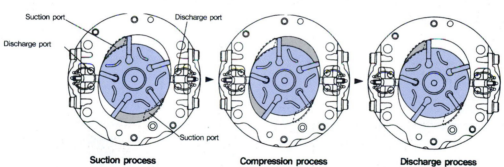

FIGURE 7-25 As the rotor turns in a clockwise direction, the vanes move in and out to follow the contour of the housing. This action forms chambers that get larger at the suction ports and smaller at the discharge ports. Evaporator pressure fills the chambers as they get bigger, and the reducing size forces the refrigerant into the high side. *(Courtesy of Zexel USA Corporation)*

chambers rotate to another location; then they contract to force the refrigerant into the high side (Figure 7-25).

7.3.1.1.1 Vane Compressors

The vanes of these compressors are mounted in a rotor that runs inside a round and eccentric, or a somewhat elliptical, chamber. The vanes slide in and out of the rotor as their outer end follows the shape of the chamber. Compressors with a round, eccentric chamber have one pumping action per vane per revolution (Figure 7-26). Compressors with elliptical housing have two pumping actions per vane per revolution; this type is sometimes called *balanced* because there is a pressure chamber on each side of the rotor. Early compressors used two vanes, and most newer compressors use five.

As the rotor turns, in one (or two) areas, the chamber behind the vane increases in size. This area has a port connected to the suction cavity. The following vane traps the refrigerant and forms a chamber as it passes by the suction port. The trapped refrigerant is carried around to the discharge port. In this location, the chamber size gets smaller; this increases gas pressure and forces it into the high side.

Vane compressors have been used on aftermarket systems and as OEM compressors. They have the advantage of being very compact and vibration free.

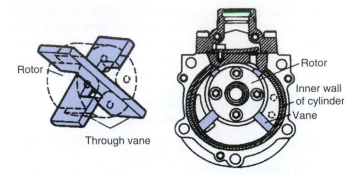

FIGURE 7-26 This through-vane compressor has vanes that contact the rotor housing at each end, and they slide to make a seal at each end as the rotor turns. The vanes form a pumping chamber that gets larger at the suction port and smaller at the discharge port. *(Courtesy of Toyota Motor Sales USA, Inc.)*

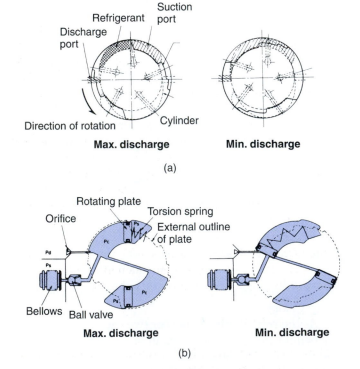

FIGURE 7-27 A variable displacement vane compressor can alter the location of the suction and discharge ports to reduce the amount of refrigerant that is pumped during each revolution *(a)*. The position of the control plate is controlled by a bellows that senses evaporator pressure *(b)*. *(Courtesy of Zexel USA Corporation)*

FIGURE 7-28 A cutaway view of a scroll compressor. Note that one scroll is secured to the housing and the other can be moved through its orbit by the drive-shaft. *(Courtesy of Sanden International)*

Variable capacity vane compressors are under development. These compressors move the suction port location to change the starting time of the compression process. Moving the suction port in a direction opposite the rotor causes the suction port to be closed earlier and reduces its capacity (Figure 7-27).

7.3.1.1.2 Scroll Compressors Scroll compressors use two major components: a fixed and a movable scroll. Both scrolls have a spiral shape that forms one side of the pumping chamber. The fixed scroll is attached to the compressor housing; the movable scroll is mounted over an eccentric bushing and counterweight on the crankshaft. It does not rotate, but it moves in an orbit relative to the stationary scroll—some class the scroll compressor as an *orbiting piston compressor* (Figure 7-28).

As the scroll orbits, it forms a pumping chamber that is open at the outer end. This chamber is moved to the center by the scroll's action as the pressure is increased. Two or three chambers are present at the same time. The outer ends of the scrolls are open to the suction port, and the inner ends connect to the discharge port (Figure 7-29).

A scroll compressor has the advantage of having very smooth operation and low engagement torque that allows the use of a small clutch. A scroll compressor can also be driven at higher revolutions per minute (rpm) than other designs, so that a smaller drive pulley is used.

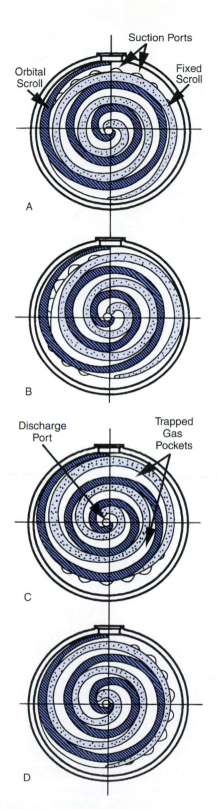

FIGURE 7-29 As the orbital scroll moves, it forms pumping chambers/gas pockets that start at the suction ports and force the refrigerant to the discharge port at the center. *(Courtesy of DaimlerChrysler Corporation)*

This compressor design is also much more efficient than the other compressor styles when it is operated at the design speed; this is a definite advantage for vehicles that tend to run most of the time at cruising speed. A scroll compressor is more expensive to manufacture.

◀   **PROBLEM SOLVING 7-2**   ▶

An A/C system does not put out cold air like it did when the car was purchased, and you agree to take a look at it. With the system turned on and the hood open, you see that the compressor is not running. What could cause this? What should you do next?

7.3.1.2 Electric Compressors   Electric vehicles do not have an engine, and hybrid vehicles do not usually run the engine continuously during vehicle operation.

An electric vehicle can use an electric compressor that operates from the battery pack. An electric compressor combines a scroll compressor with a DC electric motor (Figure 7-30). The motor is cycled on and off to produce the desired cooling. This unit can be mounted at any convenient place on the vehicle since it does not need to be connected to an engine. Some electric vehicles use a heat pump for A/C and heat; this unit is a smaller version of heat pumps used in homes. Heat pumps, much like an A/C system, move heat from one location to another. The heat pump operates off the vehicle battery pack.

Hybrid vehicles use an engine to charge the battery pack, and it is also used to drive the vehicle when needed. Most hybrid vehicles shut the engine off when the vehicle is cruising, operating at slow speeds, or stopped. One 2005 hybrid has a 4.6 cu. in. (75 cc) belt driven compressor that will stop when the engine stops; it also has a smaller 0.9 cu. in. (15 cc) electric compressor that runs during Idle-Auto-Stop to keep the A/C operating. Some hybrid vehicles use an A/C system much like other vehicles but run the engine constantly when the A/C is turned on.

7.3.2   Condensers

The **condenser** is the heat exchanger that passes the heat from the refrigerant to the air passing through it. Since this is where the heat leaves the A/C system, the condenser becomes the major component in determining the overall efficiency of a system. Refrigerant enters the top of the condenser as a hot vapor and leaves from the bottom as a cooler liquid with a few degrees of **subcooling** (Figure 7-31).

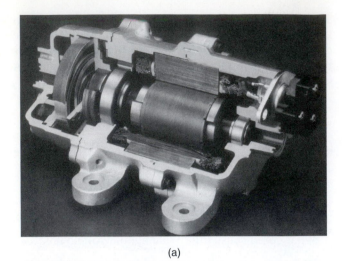

(a)

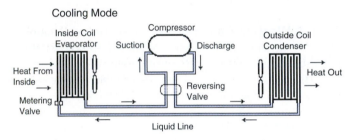

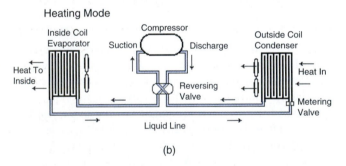

(b)

FIGURE 7-30 This electric scroll compressor *(a)* is operated by a DC electric motor operating off batteries. A similar compressor can be used in a heat pump *(b)*. Note that the heat pump is very similar to an A/C system that includes a reversing valve that can swap the high and low sides. *(a is courtesy of Sanden International)*

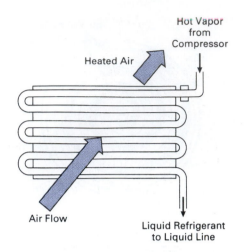

FIGURE 7-31 A condenser is a heat exchanger that transfers heat from the refrigerant to the air flowing through it.

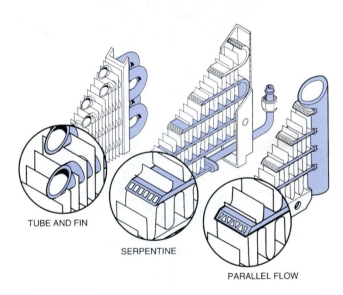

FIGURE 7-32 A tube-and-fin condenser is made up of a series of fins with the tubes passing through them. An extruded tube condenser uses flat tubes with the fins attached between them. Flat tube condensers can use either parallel or serpentine flow. *(Courtesy of Four Seasons)*

Early automotive condensers are of the **fin and tube** type and use a round tube that passes through the fins. Some condensers use a **flattened tube** with fins between the tubes (Figure 7-32). Many newer condensers use a flattened, extruded aluminum tube that is divided into several small refrigerant passages. The numerous fins provide the large amount of contact area needed with the airstream. The tubing is formed in either a **serpentine** or **parallel flow** arrangement

(Figure 7-33). Newer flat tube, parallel-flow condensers are more efficient and transfer heat much better, and this allows for a smaller and lighter component.

One way to think of condenser action is to consider the size of the inlet fitting and the line leading to it and compare it with the outlet fitting and line. The size of the suction hose for the low-pressure vapor (about 0.750-inch inside diameter) can also be compared with the size of the orifice in the expansion de-

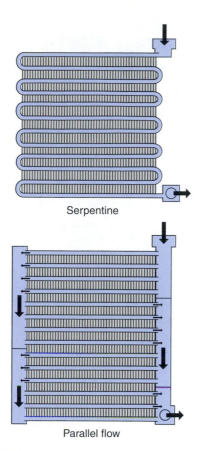

Serpentine

Parallel flow

FIGURE 7-33 The refrigerant follows a winding path through a serpentine condenser *(top)*; it follows a back-and-forth path through a parallel flow condenser *(bottom)*.

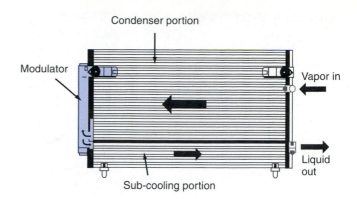

FIGURE 7-35 A dual condenser: the refrigerant flows from the condenser portion through the modulator/receiver–drier portion and then through the sub-cooling portion.

Some vehicles use a *dual condenser*, also called a *secondary condenser* or *subcondenser*, to provide additional capacity (Figure 7-35). In some cases, the receiver, called a modulator by one manufacturer, is positioned between the two condensers.

◄   **PROBLEM SOLVING 7-3**   ►

An A/C system does not put out cold air like it did when the car was purchased, and you agree to take a look at it. With the system operating and the hood open, you see that the compressor is operating, but the temperature of the discharge hose to the condenser is very hot and the receiver–drier is quite warm. Are these indications that the system is working correctly or incorrectly? Do you have enough information to determine what might be wrong?

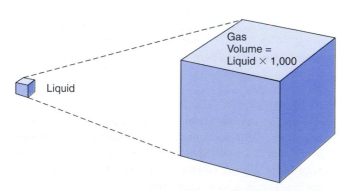

FIGURE 7-34 The volume of gas that enters a condenser is about 1,000 times the volume of liquid leaving it.

vice (about 0.060 inch). The gas must condense into a liquid or its volume will not fit through the TXV or OT. Remember that a gas has about 1,000 times the volume of the same liquid. As the latent heat of condensation is transferred to the airstream, the refrigerant vapor makes the necessary change into a liquid (Figure 7-34).

7.3.3   Receiver–Drier

A receiver–drier is used in the high side of a TXV system and, like an accumulator used in OT systems, contains a desiccant to remove moisture and provides a storage chamber for liquid refrigerant. Most receiver–driers also contain a filter to trap debris that might plug the TXV.

A receiver–drier has different internal line routing than an accumulator. Because it must pass liquid on to the TXV, the outlet line begins near the bottom; a filter screen is usually placed over the line opening. Many receiver–driers have a sight glass in the outlet line so

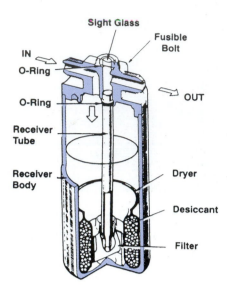

FIGURE 7-36 The outlet of a receiver–drier is close to the bottom so liquid flows on to the TXV. Many units include a sight glass so we can look at this flow. *(Courtesy of Toyota Motor Sales USA, Inc.)*

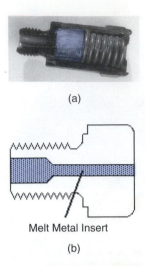

FIGURE 7-37 A high pressure relief valve *(a)* contains a strong spring that keeps the valve closed unless high side pressure (from the left) forces it open; the valve can close when the pressure drops. The fusible plug *(b)* contains a melt metal insert that will blow out if pressure gets too high.

the refrigerant flow can be checked to see if it is all liquid or contains bubbles. A receiver–drier should be about half full of liquid, so vapor bubbles are an indication of an undercharge (Figure 7-36). A sight glass is not used in most R-134a systems because the refrigerant has a cloudy appearance in a properly charged system.

7.3.4 High Pressure Control

Excessive high side pressure can produce compressor damage and a potential safety hazard if the system should rupture. Many systems contain a *high pressure relief* or *release valve*, and this is mounted on the compressor or at some location in the high side (Figure 7-37). R-12 relief valves are set to release pressure at 440 to 550 psi (3,034 to 3,792 kPa), and R-134a are a little higher at 500 to 600 psi (3,448 to 4,137 kPa). A few systems include a *low pressure relief valve* that is mounted in the low side. A relief valve is spring-loaded so excessive pressure will open the valve, and as soon as the excess pressure is released, the valve will reclose.

Many older and some modern systems include a *fusible plug*, also called a *fusible bolt* or *melting plug*. This small plug has a center of low-melting-point solder. Excessive high side pressure or temperature (about 400 psi/2,758 kPa or 220°F/110°C) will melt the center of the plug, and this will allow all of the refrigerant to escape from the system.

Releasing refrigerant from a system is not good. Modern systems include a **high pressure cutoff (HPCO) switch,** and this will cycle the compressor off before the pressure gets high enough to cause release.

7.4 LINES AND HOSES

The various system components must be interconnected so that refrigerant can circulate through the system. In modern vehicles, the majority of the lines are metal; hose is used only where necessary. Both flexible rubber and rigid metal hoses are used to link the components. The connections to the compressor must be flexible to allow for engine and compressor movement. Early R-12 hoses were solid rubber or rubber with one or two layers of reinforcing material, and refrigerants could permeate most of these flexible hose materials and escape from the system. Modern refrigerant hose is made with one or two nonpermeable inner layers with internal reinforcement and an outer layer for protection. The nonpermeable nylon layer forms a leakproof barrier; these hoses are commonly called **barrier hoses.** The materials for the various layers are developed to hold refrigerant loss to a minimum (Figure 7-38).

Metal tubing is used in many systems to connect stationary components such as a condenser to the receiver–drier or OT. Although metal aluminum tubing does not have permeation problems, corrosion caused

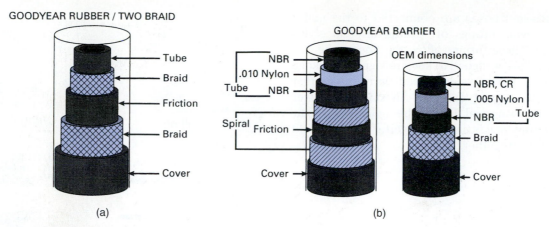

GOODYEAR RUBBER / TWO BRAID

Tube
Braid
Friction
Braid
Cover

(a)

GOODYEAR BARRIER

NBR
.010 Nylon
Tube   NBR
Spiral Friction
Cover

OEM dimensions

NBR, CR
.005 Nylon
NBR   Tube
Braid
Cover

(b)

FIGURE 7-38   A refrigerant hose contains one or two reinforcing braid layers around the rubber tube (a). A barrier hose includes an impervious nylon layer to reduce leakage (b). (Courtesy of Goodyear Tire & Rubber Company)

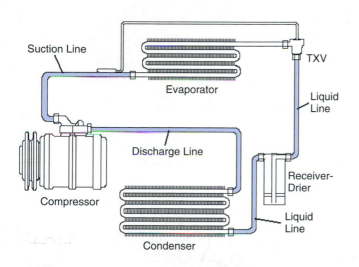

FIGURE 7-39   The three major hoses/lines are the discharge, liquid, and suction lines. Many systems have two liquid lines.

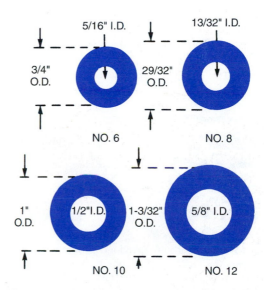

FIGURE 7-40   Most systems use three of these four refrigerant hose sizes. (Courtesy of Four Seasons)

by battery spillage or water can make holes in the tubing and produce leakage.

The lines in a system are named for their function or what they contain. Starting at the compressor, the **discharge line,** sometimes called the *hot gas line,* connects the compressor to the condenser. The **liquid line** connects the condenser to the receiver–drier and TXV or OT. A TXV system can have two liquid lines, one on each side of the receiver–drier. The suction line connects the evaporator to the compressor; it has the largest diameter because it transfers a low-pressure vapor (Figure 7-39). Theoretically, when the OT is mounted upstream in the liquid line, the line between the condenser and the evaporator should have two

names for the segments above and below the OT. In the A/C trade, it is simply called the liquid line, and a liquid line repair kit is required if you have to cut the line to replace the OT.

Four sizes of refrigerant hose are commonly used: #6, #8, #10, and #12. At one time, the numbers indicated the approximate size in 1/16 inch; a #6 hose has an inside diameter (ID) of about 6/16 or 3/8 inch. In modern practice, the sizes have changed, as shown in Figure 7-40. The suction line has an ID of 1/2 or 5/8 inch (12.7 to 15.9 mm) (a #10 or #12 hose). The liquid line has the smallest diameter, usually an ID of 5/16 inch (7.9 mm) (#6 hose). The discharge line has an ID of 13/32 or 1/2 inch (10.3 or 12.7 mm) (#8 hose). Metric sizes are also used.

The lines and hoses are connected to the major components using fittings of several different styles (Figure 7-41). These fittings allow the lines to be disconnected and are designed to keep refrigerant leakage to a minimum. Early systems used flare fittings that were very difficult to repair if they did leak. Most newer fittings use an O-ring seal that can be replaced to repair them. The spring-lock fitting uses a garter spring to hold the two portions together.

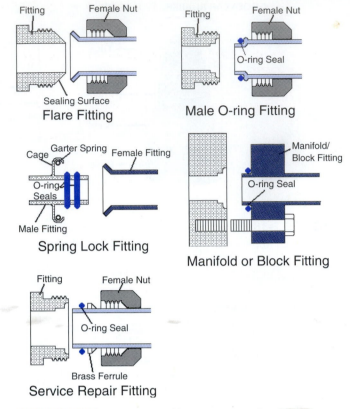

FIGURE 7-41   A variety of fittings are used to seal the refrigerant line connections. The service fitting is used for metal line repairs or to insert an inline filter.

REVIEW QUESTIONS

The following questions are provided to help you study as you read the chapter.

1. Automotive A/C systems use either a(n) _FOT_ _____ or a(n) _T_ _X_ _____ for the expansion device.

2. The refrigerant, _boils_ or _EVAPS_ in the low side and _condews_ in the high side.

3. When it is operating, the high side will have a high _pres_ and _Temp_.

4. An accumulator is used with an OT system because of the probability of a(n) _flooded_ evaporator.

5. In a TXV system, the refrigerant will have a few degrees of _Sup Heat_ as it leaves the evaporator.

6. The job of the _des_ _____ in the _Accum_ or _Rec Dryer_ is to remove all traces of water from the refrigerant.

7. A(n) _Acc_ _____ is used with OT systems and a _Rec Dryer_ _____ is used with TXV to hold a small refrigerant reserve.

8. A CC system _cycles_ the compressor _on/off_ to prevent _flood_ of the evaporator.

9. The major styles of compressors use _PISTON_, _____, or a pair of _pistons_ for pumping members.

10. Reed valves control the refrigerant flow in and out of the _cyl_ of a(n) _pis_ compressor.

11. In a(n) _serp_ condenser, the refrigerant follows a single, winding path from the top to the bottom; a _parrell flow_ condenser has manifolds at the sides to control the cross-flow.

12. The refrigerant line leaving a compressor is called the _dis_ _line_; the line from the condenser to the evaporator is called the _liq_ _line_; and the line from the evaporator back to the compressor is called the _suction line_.

CHAPTER QUIZ

The following questions will help you check the facts you have learned. Select the answer that completes each statement correctly.

1. Which of the following best describes the low side of a system?
   a. High pressure and high temperature
   b. High pressure and low temperature
   c. Low pressure and high temperature
   d. Low pressure and low temperature

2. Which of the following best describes the high side of a system?
   a. High pressure and high temperature
   b. High pressure and low temperature
   c. Low pressure and high temperature
   d. Low pressure and low temperature

3. In a properly operating system, the evaporator temperature is about _____.
   a. 25°F   c. 32°F
   b. 30°F   d. 35°F

4. The TXV is located at the _____.
   a. evaporator outlet   c. condenser outlet
   b. evaporator inlet   d. condenser inlet

5. The refrigerant inside an evaporator is a _____.
   a. gas   c. liquid changing to a gas
   b. liquid   d. gas changing to a liquid

6. An accumulator is very similar to a(n) _____.
   a. receiver–drier   c. condenser
   b. evaporator   d. orifice tube

7. Two technicians are discussing orifice tubes. Technician A says the OT is always placed close to the evaporator inlet. Technician B says the OT is placed close to the condenser in some vehicles. Who is correct?
   a. A only   c. Both A and B
   b. B only   d. Neither A nor B

8. Two technicians are discussing an A/C problem. Technician A says that an overcharge of refrigerant will cause a higher-than-normal high side pressure. Technician B says that a refrigerant overcharge will cause poor cooling. Who is correct?
   a. A only   c. Both A and B
   b. B only   d. Neither A nor B

9. Most A/C systems cycle the compressor clutch in regular intervals to control _____.
   a. condenser temperature
   b. compressor pressure
   c. evaporator temperature
   d. None of these

10. In a noncycling clutch system, evaporator freeze-up is prevented by controlling _____.
    a. TXV pressure
    b. evaporator pressure
    c. condenser pressure
    d. condenser temperature

11. Two technicians are discussing variable displacement compressors. Technician A says they are designed to control evaporator temperature. Technician B says they are designed to control evaporator pressure. Who is correct?
    a. A only   c. Both A and B
    b. B only   d. Neither A nor B

12. An automotive A/C compressor is of the _____ type.
    a. reciprocating piston
    b. scroll
    c. rotary vane
    d. Any of these

13. Two technicians are discussing the lines used to connect the A/C components. Technician A says they are usually rubber hoses with metal ends. Technician B says that metal tubing is often used. Who is correct?
    a. A only   c. Both A and B
    b. B only   d. Neither A nor B

◀ Chapter 8 ▶

AIR CONDITIONING SYSTEM COMPONENTS

LEARNING OBJECTIVES

After completing this chapter, you should:

1. Know how the components used in automotive A/C systems operate.
2. Be familiar with the variety of components used in today's A/C systems.
3. Be familiar with the variety of controls used in an automotive A/C system.

TERMS TO LEARN

barrier hose
captive O-ring
coaxial
compression ratio
condenser seals
crankshaft
discharge stroke
displacement
drive plate
ester
extruded tubes
inline filters
flux pole
hang-on
hygroscopic
lip seal
mineral oil

muffler
outgassing
polyalkylene glycol (PAG)
polyol ester (POE)
pressure relief valve
    pulley
reciprocating piston
reed valves
roof pack
rotary compressor
rotating field
rotor
Scotch yoke
scroll compressor
seal cartridge
seal seat
short cycle

sight glass
stationary field
suction stroke
suction throttling valve
    (STV)
superheat
swash plate
thermal fuse

thermistor
transducer
valves in receiver (VIR)
vane compressor
variable orifice valve
    (VOV)
wobble plate

8.1 INTRODUCTION

Automotive A/C components have been evolving steadily since the introduction of A/C in vehicles in 1940. From the early days, when A/C was a very expensive option in luxury cars, to today, when it is standard equipment in many models, many different types of systems have been used. This chapter describes this variety of components, concentrating on the newest and most commonly encountered (Figure 8-1).

8.2 COMPRESSORS

Most automotive compressors are of the **reciprocating piston** type. Compressors are steadily being downsized, made smaller to fit into tighter locations to reduce the overall vehicle weight. Piston compressors have disadvantages, chief among them the high inertial loads that result from moving a piston at a rather high speed, bringing it to a stop, moving it at a high speed in the opposite direction, bringing it to a stop, and so on.

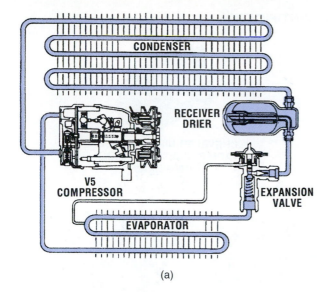

(a)

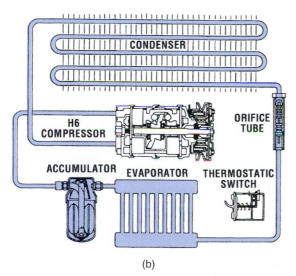

(b)

FIGURE 8-1   Both TXV (*a*) and OT (*b*) A/C systems have five major components. *(Courtesey of ACDelco)*

This movement produces vibrations and severe stress on moving parts. **Rotary compressors** merely spin the pumping member (in the case of vane compressors) or cause a member to move in an eccentric orbit (in the case of scroll compressors) (Figure 8-2).

Vane and **scroll** compressors also have potential problems, chiefly wear of the vane tips and outer chamber (which the vanes have to seal against) and wear between the vanes and the rotor (as the vanes slide in and out). Scroll compressors require rather complex machining to achieve constant sealing between the fixed and movable scrolls.

Currently, about 60 different makes and models of automotive compressors are manufactured. Many of these are versions of a particular model and use differ-

ent pulleys, switches, mounting flanges, and port configurations (Figure 8-3).

8.2.1 Piston Compressors

With one exception, all of the automotive compressors were of the piston type until the early 1980s (a rotary compressor was used on some General Motors [GM] models in the early 1950s). A piston compressor moves the pistons up and down in a cylinder to produce pumping action and controls the refrigerant flow with two sets of **reed valves.** The downward, or **suction, stroke** of the piston causes refrigerant to flow from the compressor suction cavity to push the suction reed open and fill the cylinder. The suction cavity is connected to the evaporator so it contains refrigerant vapor at evaporator pressure. An upward, or **discharge, stroke** of the piston generates pressure to force the refrigerant through the discharge reed into the discharge chamber and on to the condenser (Figure 8-4).

Pistons can be driven by a **crankshaft, swash plate, wobble plate,** or **Scotch yoke** and can be arranged *in line,* in a *V shape, coaxially,* or *radially.* Most early compressors were of the rather bulky in-line design. Most modern compressors use the more compact coaxial design.

Piston and cylinder diameters and length of stroke determine the internal size or **displacement** of the compressor in cubic inches (cu. in.) or cubic centimeters (cc). This is the volume of gas pumped with each revolution of the shaft. The displacement of the compressor is sized to meet the cooling load of the vehicle and the size of the engine (Figure 8-5). A larger compressor has the ability to cool a larger vehicle faster, but it also places a greater power draw on the engine. With some compact vehicles, compressor load places a significant power draw on the engine, and the cycling of the compressor clutch is quite noticeable and can be annoying. Many vehicles with small engines either disconnect the compressor clutch at idle speed or increase the idle speed when the compressor is operating to compensate for the load.

Most compressors have the ability to significantly increase gas pressure, depending on the needs of the system. With an engine, compression ratio is determined by the size of the cylinder and combustion chamber. With an A/C compressor, compression ratio is determined by the system's ability to condense refrigerant in the high side. In a system that is working properly, the **compression ratio** is about 5:1 to 7:1. Pressure ratios above 8:1 place added loads on the pistons and bearings in the compressor, as well as very high temperatures that can cause oil breakdown and lacquer and varnish deposits. The compression ratio of a system can be determined by simply

COMPRESSOR IDENTIFICATION

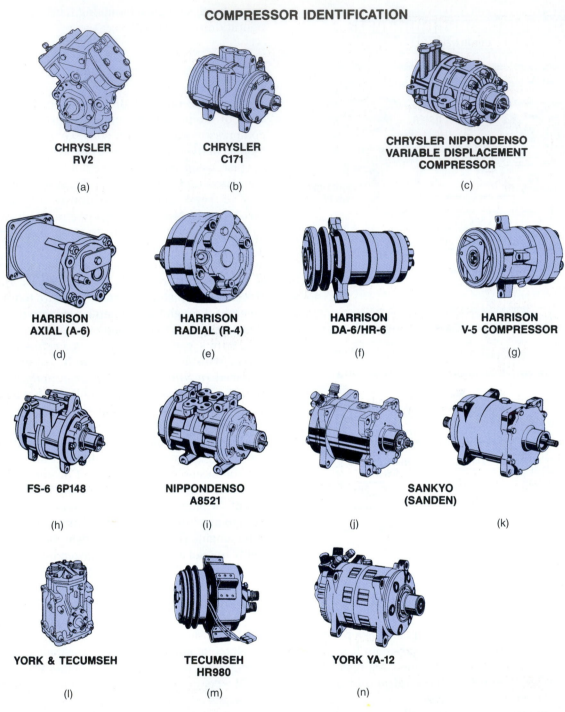

CHRYSLER
RV2

(a)

CHRYSLER
C171

(b)

CHRYSLER NIPPONDENSO
VARIABLE DISPLACEMENT
COMPRESSOR

(c)

HARRISON
AXIAL (A-6)

(d)

HARRISON
RADIAL (R-4)

(e)

HARRISON
DA-6/HR-6

(f)

HARRISON
V-5 COMPRESSOR

(g)

FS-6 6P148

(h)

NIPPONDENSO
A8521

(i)

SANKYO
(SANDEN)

(j)

(k)

YORK & TECUMSEH

(l)

TECUMSEH
HR980

(m)

YORK YA-12

(n)

FIGURE 8-2 Some of the variety of compressors. *a* and *l* use a crankshaft; *b, d, e, f, h,* and *i* use a swash plate; *c* and *g* use a wobble plate with a variable stroke; *e* and *m* use a Scotch yoke; *j* and *k* use a plain wobble plate; and *n* is a vane compressor. *(Courtesy of Everco Industries)*

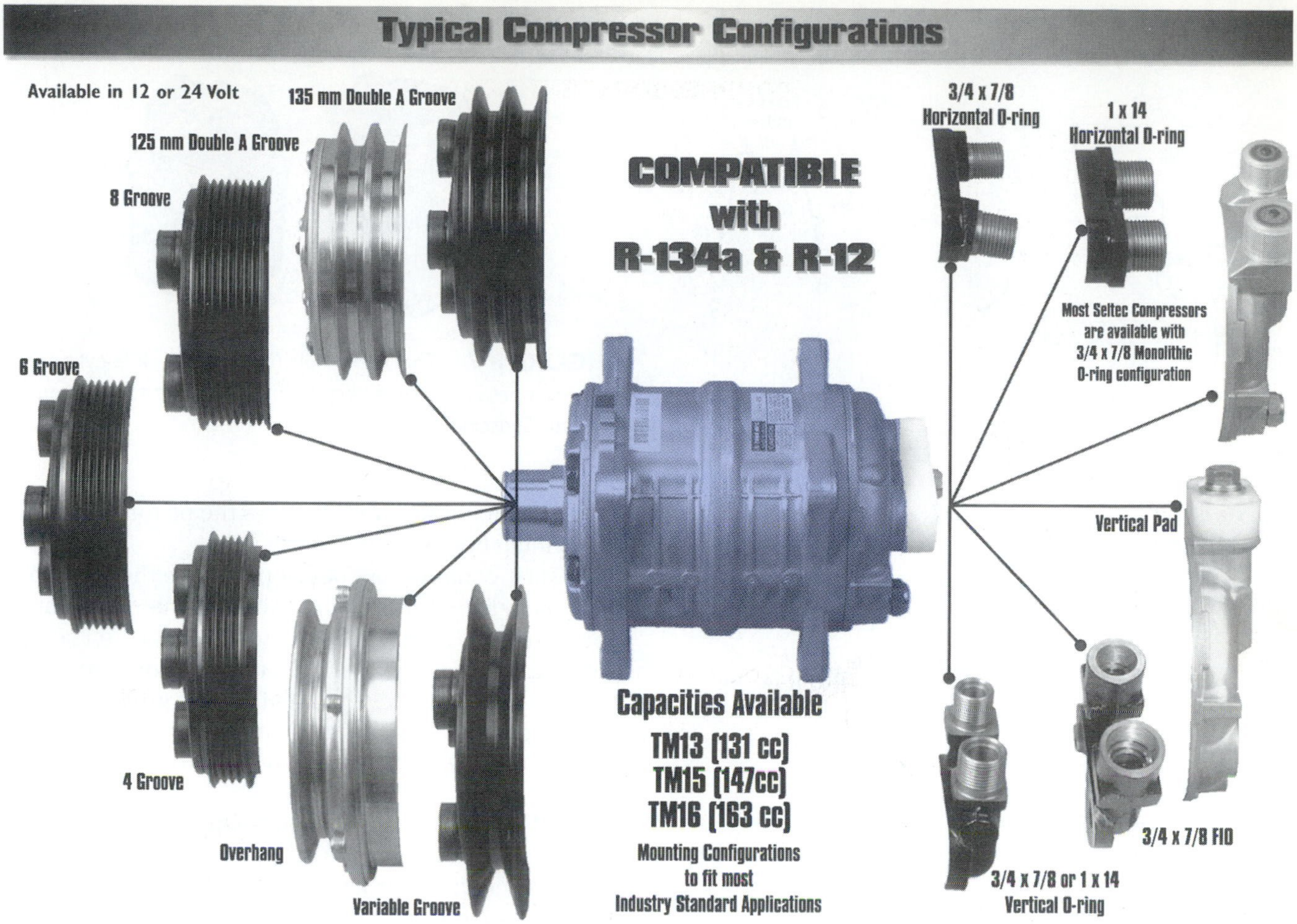

Available in 12 or 24 Volt

135 mm Double A Groove

125 mm Double A Groove

8 Groove

6 Groove

4 Groove

Overhang

Variable Groove

3/4 x 7/8
Horizontal O-ring

1 x 14
Horizontal O-ring

**COMPATIBLE
with
R-134a & R-12**

Most Seltec Compressors
are available with
3/4 x 7/8 Monolithic
O-ring configuration

Vertical Pad

**Capacities Available
TM13 (131 cc)
TM15 (147cc)
TM16 (163 cc)**

Mounting Configurations
to fit most
Industry Standard Applications

3/4 x 7/8 FIO

3/4 x 7/8 or 1 x 14
Vertical O-ring

FIGURE 8-3   This compressor is compatible with both R-134a and R-12 and is available in three different capacities or displacements, with one of seven different clutch configurations of either 12 or 24 volts, and with one of seven different rear head and line port configurations. *(Courtesy of Seltec)*

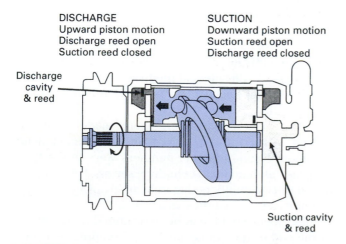

DISCHARGE
Upward piston motion
Discharge reed open
Suction reed closed

SUCTION
Downward piston motion
Suction reed open
Discharge reed closed

Discharge
cavity
& reed

Suction cavity
& reed

FIGURE 8-4   Rotation of the swash plate causes these double pistons to move through the suction and discharge strokes. Evaporator pressure fills the cylinders with refrigerant during the suction stroke. This refrigerant is pumped into the high side during the discharge stroke.

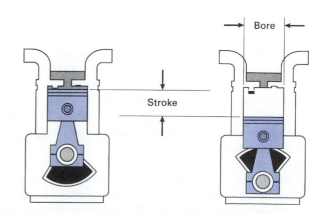

Bore

Stroke

FIGURE 8-5   The displacement of a compressor is determined by the length of the stroke, diameter of the cylinders (bore), and number of cylinders.

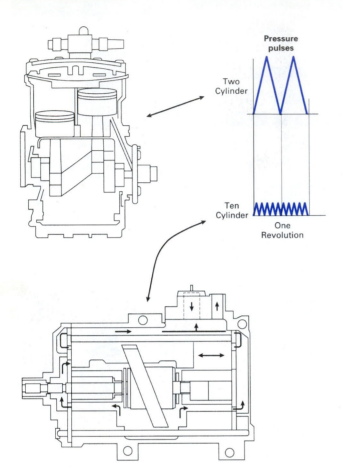

FIGURE 8-6 A 2-cylinder compressor creates 2 large pumping pulses per revolution. A 10-cylinder compressor (same displacement) creates 10 smaller pulses; its operation is much smoother.

dividing the absolute high side pressure by the absolute low side pressure. This formula can be used:

$$\text{Compression ratio} = \frac{\text{High side pressure} + 15}{\text{Low side pressure} + 15}$$

Each piston stroke causes a pressure pulsation in the high- and low-pressure lines at the compressor that can cause a slight vibration and drumming noise. A compressor with more cylinders has the advantage of running smoother and quieter. A 1-cylinder compressor causes 1 rather large pulsation per revolution; a 10-cylinder compressor causes 10 smaller pulsations (Figure 8-6).

Early compressors were built very much like small engines. Pistons with cast-iron rings operated in cast-iron cylinders; they included oil pumps to circulate oil to lubricate metal parts and prevent wear. Modern compressors use a Teflon band around the pistons, which serves to seal the bore and support the piston. This al-

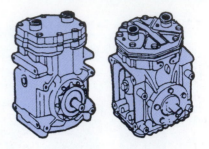

FIGURE 8-7 The Tecumseh (left) and York 2-cylinder, in-line compressors were very common at one time. *(Courtesy of Four Seasons)*

most frictionless material allows the piston to run in an aluminum bore with very little wear.

Most compressors developed since the 1960s have not included an oil pump. They use the refrigerant to bring the oil to the cylinders and route the oil scraped off the cylinders to lubricate the rotating parts in the crankcase. Such developments have greatly reduced the size and weight of the compressor and have also changed some of the service procedures.

8.2.1.1 Inline Piston Compressors Most of the systems in the 1960s and 1970s, except for those of General Motors and the Chrysler Corporation, used inline piston compressors. Two cylinders, one behind the other, were operated by a crankshaft. This was the primary compressor used by the Ford Motor Company and American Motors and in all of the aftermarket, dealer-installed, and hang-on installations. Two major manufacturers were the York Division of Borg Warner and Tecumseh. Determination of the particular compressor was made by model number, appearance, and whether the cylinder block and head were made from cast iron or aluminum. Compressors from these two manufacturers could be interchanged. They had similar mounting holes on each side and the base, and they could be mounted on the engine in an upright, left-hand, or right-hand position (Figure 8-7).

Most York compressors were made from aluminum with reinforcing webs on the cylinder head. The most common model numbers were in the DA 2 (die-cast aluminum, 2-cylinder) series. DA 2 is followed by two numbers that indicate displacement (for example, a DA 209 indicates a 9 cu. in. [147 cc] model). Displacement could also be determined by the shape of the end of the crankshaft. This compressor is currently used on heavy trucks, mobile industrial equipment, and farm equipment, and it is produced by Climate Control, Inc. A compact, 1-cylinder version of this compressor with a smaller overall size was manufactured (Figure 8-8).

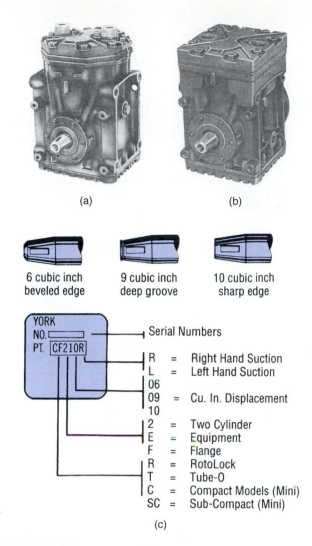

6 cubic inch beveled edge   9 cubic inch deep groove   10 cubic inch sharp edge

(c)

FIGURE 8-8   A York 209 compressor (a) and a more compact mini series (b). York compressors can be identified by part number and crankshaft appearance (c). (Courtesy of Four Seasons)

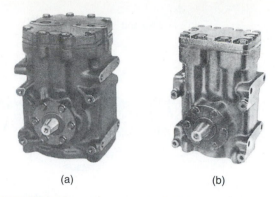

(a)   (b)

FIGURE 8-9   A Tecumseh HG 850 or HG 1000 (a) is identified by part number. The HG 500 (b) is a single-cylinder compressor. (Courtesy of Four Seasons)

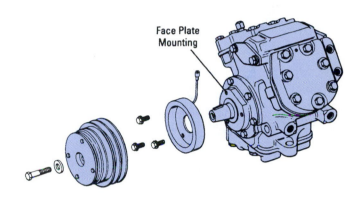

FIGURE 8-10   The two pistons in a Chrysler V compressor are arranged in a V shape. (Courtesy of ACDelco)

Tecumseh compressors were made from cast iron and were usually painted black. The most common model numbers were in the HG series. These letters were followed by three or four numbers that indicated displacement. Most of these compressors were HG 850 (for an 8.5 cu. in. [139 cc]) and HG 1000 (for a 10 cu. in. [164 cc]). An HG 500 model was also offered; it was a 5 cu. in. (82 cc) single-cylinder unit (Figure 8-9).

Several Japanese manufacturers produced 2-cylinder in-line compressors of various sizes. These compressors were used primarily on Japanese vehicles.

8.2.1.2 Two-Cylinder V Compressor   Through the 1960s and 1970s, Chrysler Corporation manufactured a 2-cylinder compressor with the cylinders in a V config-uration. These compressors were made from cast iron and were used as OEM installation on Chrysler vehicles (Figure 8-10).

8.2.1.3 Radial Compressors   Most radial compressors were made by GM for use on GM vehicles; Tecumseh produced a version for OEM use on Ford vehicles. Radial compressors use two double-ended pistons that cross at a rotating block and Scotch yoke crankshaft. Radial compressors are fairly compact and are much shorter than inline compressors (Figure 8-11).

The GM version of this compressor was produced from the mid 1970s to the late 1980s and is called the R-4 (radial 4-cylinder). It has a displacement of either 10 cu. in. (164 cc) or 11 cu. in. (180 cc). A number 10 or 11 is cast onto the rear of the compressor to indicate the size.

The Tecumseh version was produced from the mid to late 1980s and is called the HR 980. It has a displacement of 9.8 cu. in. (160 cc).

A version of the radial compressor was also produced by Keihin in Japan for use on Honda automobiles.

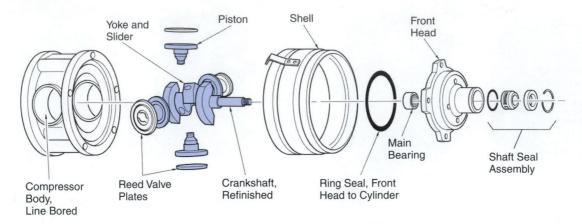

FIGURE 8-11   An R-4 compressor has two pairs of pistons that are driven by a Scotch yoke. *(Courtesy of Visteon)*

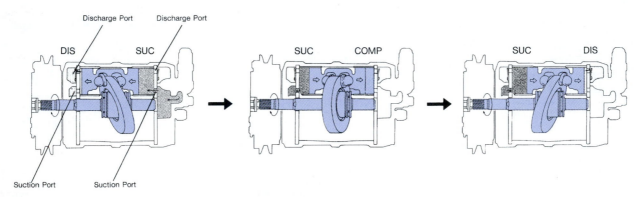

FIGURE 8-12   Note how rotation of the swash plate causes the pistons to slide through their strokes. Balls and shoes act as bearings between the swash plate and pistons. *(Courtesy of Zexel USA Corporation)*

8.2.1.4 Coaxial Swash-Plate Compressors   Coaxial swash-plate compressors drive the pistons through a swash plate, which is attached to the drive shaft. The swash plate is mounted at an angle so it will wobble and cause the reciprocating action of the pistons. The swash plate revolves with the shaft; each piston has a pair of bearings that can pivot as the swash plate slides through them. Each piston is double ended so that each end can pump, and the pistons are arranged parallel to and around the driveshaft. This is called a **coaxial** arrangement. One driveshaft revolution causes each piston end to move through a complete pumping cycle. The most common arrangement is three double pistons making a 6-cylinder compressor and a 10-cylinder using five pistons (Figure 8-12).

A swash-plate compressor must have passages to transfer refrigerant between the suction and discharge chambers at each end of the compressor. The suction crossover passage is usually designed so that it can provide lubrication to internal moving parts (Figure 8-13).

General Motors produced a 6-cylinder compressor called the A-6 from 1962 through the mid-1980s. Most A-6 compressors had a displacement of 12.6 cu. in. (206 cc), but some used dished pistons, which reduced the displacement to 10.8 cu. in. (177 cc). A-6 compressors used a cast-iron cylinder block, cast-iron piston rings, and an oil pump. Most were built with a clockwise (when viewed from the front) crankshaft rotation. Some were built to operate in the opposite direction for use in the Corvair (Figure 8-14).

In 1982, GM started production of a more modern version of this compressor, called the DA-6. The DA-6 cylinder block is made from die-cast aluminum and is slightly smaller and much lighter than the A-6. Its weight has been reduced from 33.25 lb (15.1 kg) to 12.5 lb (5.7 kg). The DA-6 uses Teflon piston seals, a lip-type shaft seal, and no oil pump. The DA-6 was superseded by the HR-6 and then by the HR6HE (Figure 8-15). General Motors uses these compressor designations: Delco

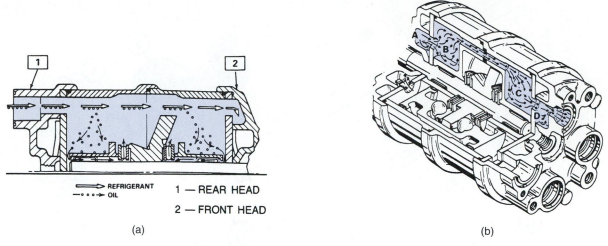

REFRIGERANT
OIL

1 — REAR HEAD
2 — FRONT HEAD

(a)

(b)

FIGURE 8-13 The suction (a) and discharge (b) crossover circuits of a swash-plate compressor transfer refrigerant to and from the cylinders at the other end. Note how oil from the suction crossover lubricates the internal parts. *(Reprinted with permission of General Motors Corporation)*

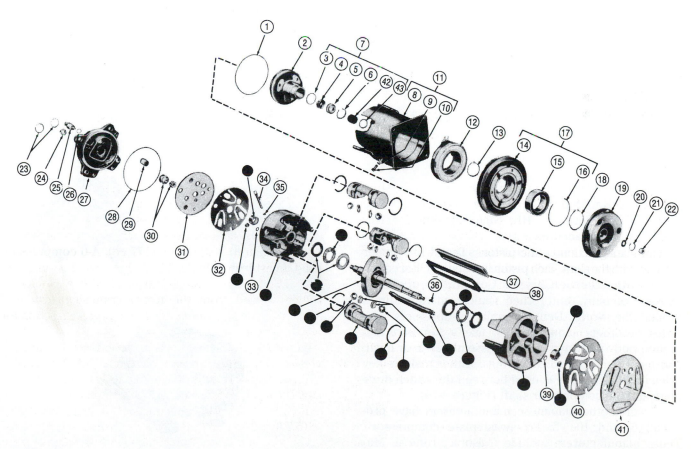

FIGURE 8-14 A disassembled view of an A-6 compressor; this compressor was very popular during the 1960s, 1970s, and early 1980s. *(Courtesy of ACDelco)*

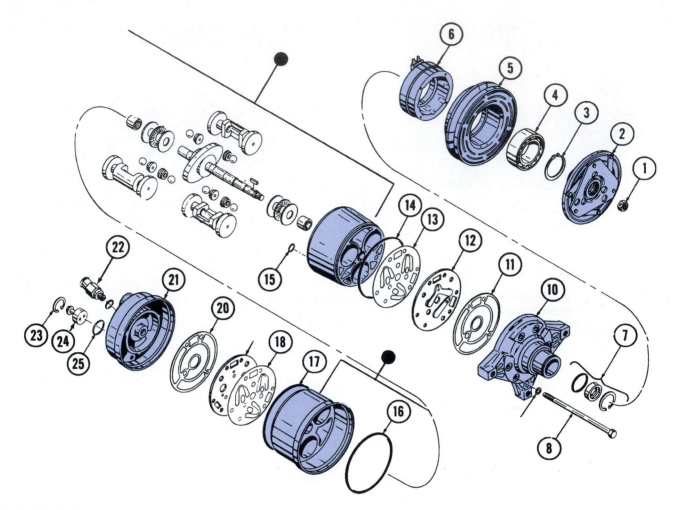

FIGURE 8-15 A disassembled view of a DA-6 compressor; this compressor replaced the A-6. *(Courtesy of ACDelco)*

Air = DA, Harrison = H, Harrison Radiator = HA, Harrison Redesigned = HR, High Efficiency = HE, Truck = HT, Upgraded HT = HU.

Nippondenso also manufactures 6- and 10-cylinder coaxial compressors. This design is used as OEM equipment by the DaimlerChrysler Corporation, the Ford Motor Company, and other vehicle manufacturers around the world. Denso coaxial compressors, like those of other manufacturers, use a four-part aluminum body with two cylinder assemblies, rear head, and front head sealed by O-rings. Either a single-key drive or splined drive is used between the clutch drive plate and the compressor shaft (Figure 8-16).

Several other Japanese manufacturers have produced 6- and 10-cylinder swash-plate compressors. These manufacturers include Calsonic, Hitachi, Mitsubishi, Nihon Radiator, Seltec, and Zexel (formerly Diesel Kiki) (Figure 8-17).

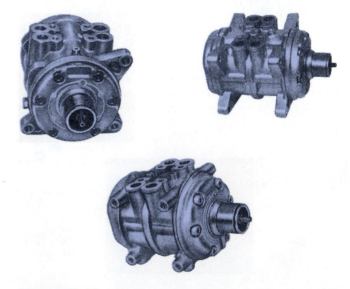

FIGURE 8-16 Three versions of Denso compressors; note the different mounting bosses. *(Courtesy of Four Seasons)*

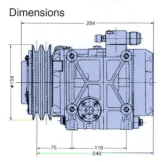 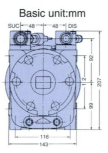

FIGURE 8-17 This Zexel compressor uses a swash-plate design. *(Courtesy of Zexel USA Corporation)*

8.2.1.5 Coaxial Wobble-Plate Compressors

Wobble-plate compressors drive the pistons through an angle plate that looks somewhat like a swash plate, but the wobble plate does not rotate and drives single pistons through piston rods. Bearings are used between the rotating drive plate and the wobble plate. Wobble-plate compressors commonly use five or seven cylinders (Figure 8-18).

General Motors used a 5-cylinder wobble-plate compressor from 1955 to 1961. This compressor was rather large and quite heavy and was replaced by the A-6. Compressors have evolved steadily through the years, becoming smaller, lighter units. GM is currently producing a variable displacement, 5-cylinder wobble-plate compressor, the V-5.

Sanden Corporation has produced compressors of this type since the mid-1970s, also under the names Abacus and Sankyo. The SD-505, 5.3 cu. in. (87 cc); SD-507, 6.59 cu. in. (108 cc); and SD-508, 8.4 cu. in. (138 cc) are all 5-cylinder units designed for automotive use. The SD 508-HD, 8.4 cu. in. (138 cc), and SD 510-HD, 9.8 cu. in. (161 cc), are 5-cylinder units designed for trucks and agricultural and industrial equipment. The SD-708, 7.8 cu. in. (129 cc), and SD-709, 9.4 cu. in. (155 cc), are 7-cylinder units designed for automotive use. Sanden compressors, like those of other manufacturers, are manufactured with a variety of mounting points, clutches, and cylinder heads to suit particular installations. Varieties of these compressors have been used for OEM installation by domestic and import vehicle manufacturers and in aftermarket installations.

8.2.1.6 Variable Displacement Wobble-Plate Compressors

Modern wobble-plate designs can be variable displacement compressors. When there is a low cooling load at the evaporator, the wobble plate is moved to a less angled position. This feature makes the compressor more efficient by reducing the drive load when it is not needed; it also eliminates the need to cycle the compressor off and on. Compressor displacement is the major control for preventing evaporator icing (Figure 8-19).

Wobble-plate angle is determined by the relative pressures at each end of the pistons; the exact angle is controlled by changing the pressure in the crankcase. When cooling load calls for high output and maximum displacement, crankcase pressure is kept low, and the wobble plate is at its maximum angle. The control valve bleeds crankcase pressure into the compressor suction cavity to lower the pressure. When cooling demand lessens, the control valve closes the bleed to the suction cavity and opens a passage between the discharge cavity and the crankcase, raising the pressure. Increasing

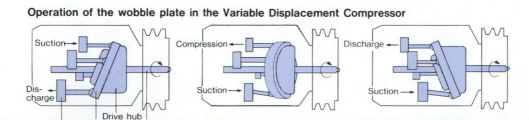

Operation of the wobble plate in the Variable Displacement Compressor

FIGURE 8-18 Rotation of the drive hub causes the wobble action of the wobble plate and forces the single pistons to move through their strokes. *(Courtesy of Zexel USA Corporation)*

FIGURE 8-19 A variable displacement compressor can change the angle of the wobble plate and piston stroke. This angle is changed by a control valve that senses evaporator pressure, which, in turn, changes wobble chamber pressure. (Courtesy of Zexel USA Corporation)

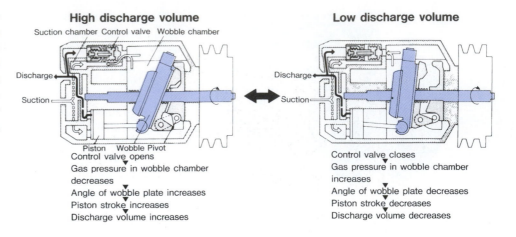

High discharge volume

Suction chamber Control valve Wobble chamber

Discharge

Suction

Piston   Wobble Pivot

Control valve opens
Gas pressure in wobble chamber decreases
Angle of wobble plate increases
Piston stroke increases
Discharge volume increases

Low discharge volume

Discharge

Suction

Control valve closes
Gas pressure in wobble chamber increases
Angle of wobble plate decreases
Piston stroke decreases
Discharge volume decreases

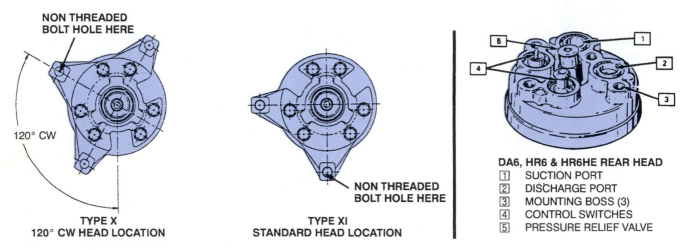

NON THREADED BOLT HOLE HERE

120° CW

TYPE X
120° CW HEAD LOCATION

NON THREADED BOLT HOLE HERE

TYPE XI
STANDARD HEAD LOCATION

DA6, HR6 & HR6HE REAR HEAD

1 SUCTION PORT
2 DISCHARGE PORT
3 MOUNTING BOSS (3)
4 CONTROL SWITCHES
5 PRESSURE RELIEF VALVE

FIGURE 8-20   Two of the DA6 and HR6 versions of the front head (left and center) and a view of the rear head (right). (Courtesy of AC Delco)

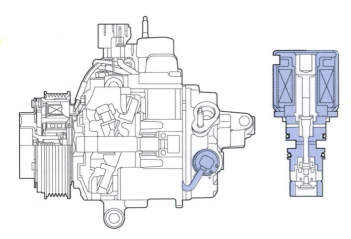

FIGURE 8-21   The piston stroke of this variable displacement compressor is controlled by crankcase pressure, which is adjusted using an electric solenoid (right). (Courtesy of Toyota Motor Sales USA, Inc.)

crankcase pressure raises the pressure on the bottom side of the pistons and causes the wobble plate to move to low angle, reducing displacement (Figure 8-20).

Crankcase pressure can also be changed using an electric solenoid that is controlled by an electronic control unit, or ECU (Figure 8-21). When cooling load is large, the ECU causes the solenoid to decrease compressor crankcase pressure for full compressor displacement. The ECU causes the solenoid to increase crankcase pressure and reduce displacement as the vehicle cools down.

Compact versions of the variable displacement compressor connect the pistons to the wobble plate using a spherical bearing similar to what is used in a swash-plate compressor (Figure 8-22).

In 1985, GM began installing a variable displacement compressor called the V-5 on certain vehicle models. This compressor is lightweight, at 12 lb (5.4 kg) (the 5-cylinder of the 1950s weighed 58 lb), and has a displacement of 0.6

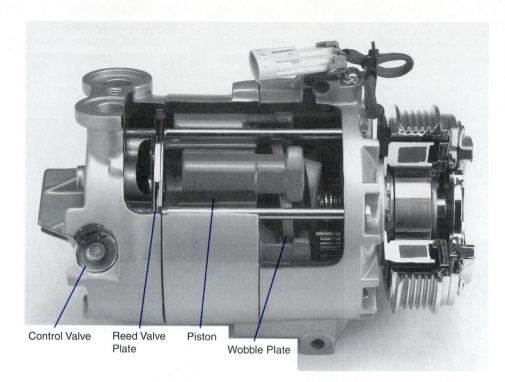

Control Valve   Reed Valve   Piston
                  Plate
                                  Wobble Plate

to 9.2 cu. in. (10 to 151 cc) (Figure 8-23). Compact variable compressors (CVC) are currently available in 6- and 7-cylinder versions in maximum displacement sizes from 7.6 to 11.2 cu. in. (125 to 185 cc). The GM compact variable compressor, CVC, uses a variable-angle swash plate and single-ended pistons. Some versions use electronic control of compressor output.

Other manufacturers, including Calsonic, Denso, Sanden, and Zexel, are currently producing variable displacement, coaxial wobble-plate compressors.

◀ SERVICE TIP ▶

A technician becomes concerned with the compressor make and model when he or she needs to obtain a replacement for a failed compressor. Replacement compressors are available as new or rebuilt units, and proper identification is made from the vehicle make, model, and engine size. Then, if needed, proper identification is made by the old compressor make and model (Figure 8-24). At times, a failed compressor is replaced with a different compressor make and model if the mounting points, clutch diameter and belt position, and line fittings are the same.

8.2.2   Compressor Clutches

An important part of almost every automotive compressor is the clutch, which allows us to easily turn it on or off. Magnetic clutches are used; they have a clutch coil where a magnetic field is generated when electricity is sent through it. The magnetic field pulls the drive plate against the rotating pulley to drive the compressor (Figure 8-25).

The clutch on most 2-cylinder inline and V compressors is a unit with both the pulley and the drive plate mounted on the compressor shaft. On a few early clutches, called **rotating field,** the field coil was built into the pulley, and brushes were used to conduct electricity to the coil. Most units are **stationary field** clutches, with the pulley and field coil mounted on the front of the compressor. A cavity in the pulley fits over the coil closely so it attracts the magnetic lines of flux (Figure 8-26).

Most modern clutches are three-piece units. The clutch coil and pulley are both mounted on an extension from the front of the compressor housing; the **drive plate** is attached to the compressor shaft. The drive plate is also called an *armature* or *disc,* and the **pulley** is also called a **rotor.** The pulley is mounted on a bearing on an extension of the front head. This placement allows the side load of the drive belt to be absorbed by the pulley bearing and compressor housing. It also allows easier servicing of individual clutch parts (Figure 8-27).

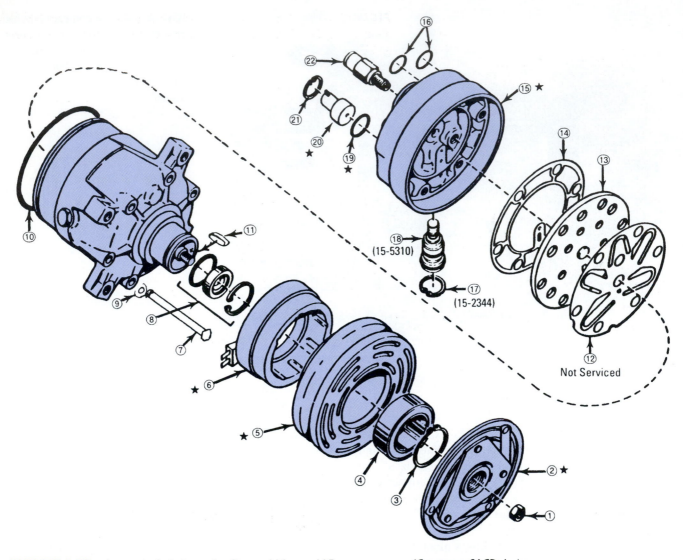

FIGURE 8-23   An exploded view of a General Motors V-5 compressor. *(Courtesy of ACDelco)*

FIGURE 8-24   The decal on this compressor identifies the type (SDB709) and the serial number. Note also that it uses a seven-groove, multi-V clutch, four mounting bolts, and vertical-pad service ports at the side.

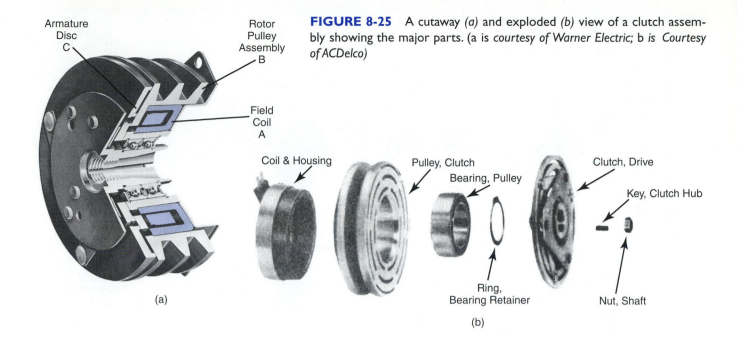

Armature Disc
C

Rotor Pulley Assembly
B

Field Coil
A

(a)

Coil & Housing

Pulley, Clutch

Bearing, Pulley

Clutch, Drive

Key, Clutch Hub

Ring, Bearing Retainer

Nut, Shaft

(b)

FIGURE 8-25 A cutaway (a) and exploded (b) view of a clutch assembly showing the major parts. (a is *courtesy of Warner Electric;* b is *Courtesy of ACDelco*)

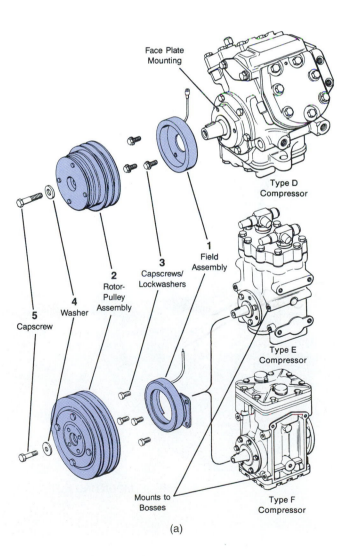

Face Plate Mounting

Type D Compressor

Type E Compressor

Type F Compressor

Mounts to Bosses

1 Field Assembly

2 Rotor-Pulley Assembly

3 Capscrews/Lockwashers

4 Washer

5 Capscrew

(a)

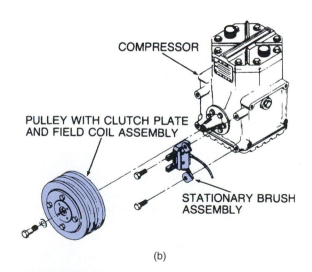

COMPRESSOR

PULLEY WITH CLUTCH PLATE AND FIELD COIL ASSEMBLY

STATIONARY BRUSH ASSEMBLY

(b)

FIGURE 8-26 In most clutches, the coil is stationary, secured to the compressor (a). In a rotating field clutch, the coil is built into the rotor, and a brush assembly is used to conduct electricity into and out of the coil (b). (*Courtesy of Warner Electric*)

119

FIGURE 8-27 Most compressors use three-piece clutches as shown here *(a)*. The rotor is driven by a belt, the hub drives the compressor shaft, and the coil is secured to the compressor *(b)*. *(Courtesy of Warner Electric)*

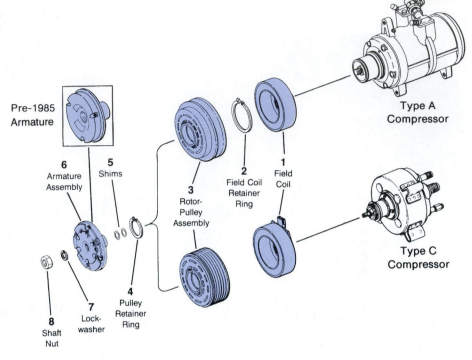

Pre-1985 Armature

6 Armature Assembly

5 Shims

3 Rotor-Pulley Assembly

2 Field Coil Retainer Ring

1 Field Coil

Type A Compressor

Type C Compressor

4 Pulley Retainer Ring

7 Lockwasher

8 Shaft Nut

(a)

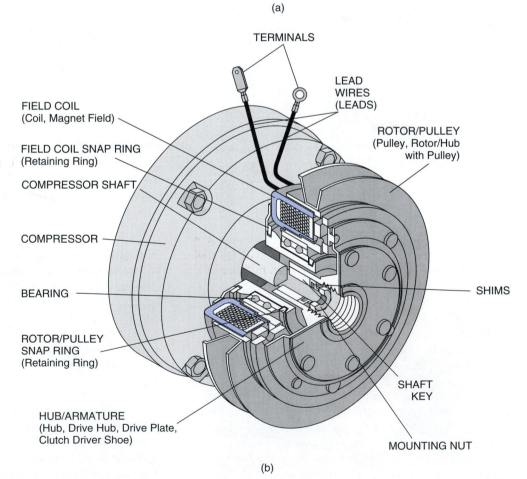

TERMINALS

LEAD WIRES (LEADS)

FIELD COIL (Coil, Magnet Field)

FIELD COIL SNAP RING (Retaining Ring)

COMPRESSOR SHAFT

COMPRESSOR

BEARING

ROTOR/PULLEY SNAP RING (Retaining Ring)

HUB/ARMATURE (Hub, Drive Hub, Drive Plate, Clutch Driver Shoe)

ROTOR/PULLEY (Pulley, Rotor/Hub with Pulley)

SHIMS

SHAFT KEY

MOUNTING NUT

(b)

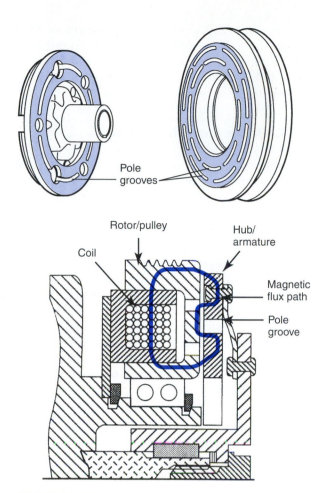

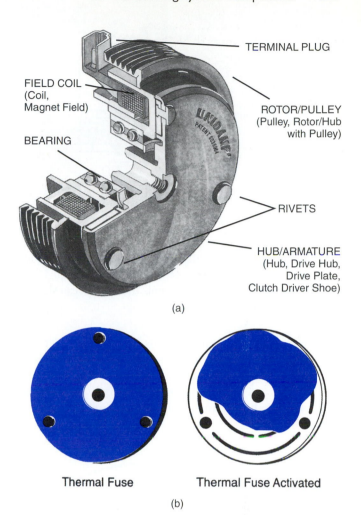

(a)

Thermal Fuse   Thermal Fuse Activated

(b)

FIGURE 8-28 The magnetic flux path is from the coil and through the metal of the rotor and clutch hub. When it meets a pole groove, it travels from the hub to the rotor or vice versa, which increases the clutch holding power.

FIGURE 8-29 The plastic shield on the front of this clutch hub (a) is a thermal fuse; if it gets too hot, it will melt and cause the clutch to fail before compressor damage occurs (b). (Courtesy of Warner Electric)

A variety of pulleys can be used on a compressor model. Important details to note when replacing a clutch assembly, pulley, or compressor are the type of drive belt (V or V ribbed), pulley diameter, number of V grooves, and position of V grooves.

Clutches used in some of the more modern systems have been redesigned to develop greater holding power, or torque capacity, to help prevent slipping. Modern clutches can transfer about 100 ft lb of torque, double that of early clutches. This is more necessary with R-134a because of the higher head pressure encountered.

Some design factors used to increase holding power are the number of **flux poles** (slots in the face of the clutch armature), the diameter of the rotor and armature, the use of copper or aluminum in the clutch coil (copper produces about 20% greater torque capacity), and the current draw of the coil (Figure 8-28).

Some modern clutches are designed to act as a sort of fuse to protect the compressor. When system problems cause increased compressor pressure loads to the point where damage might occur, the clutch slips for a longer period of time during engagement. This slippage generates heat, and in some designs, the added heat melts the **thermal fuse** in the drive plate (Figure 8-29). In clutches that do not use the thermal fuse, this added heat often causes bearing failure.

8.2.2.1 Damper Drives Some compressors do not use a clutch and are driven by a damper assembly.

The variable displacement compressor used on the new C-class Mercedes Benz does not use a clutch. The compressor is electronically controlled to go to minimum displacement of 2% output when A/C is not

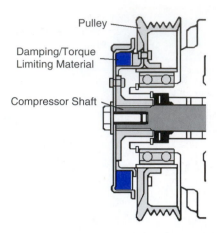

FIGURE 8-30 This pulley and hub are a one-piece assembly. Torque is transferred from the pulley through the rubber damping material to the hub; the rubber can shear if the compressor should lock up.

used; this displacement requires very little power and is enough to circulate oil through the moving parts. The pulley drive plate includes a rubber shear portion that can break to protect the drive belt in case the compressor should fail and lock up (Figure 8-30).

Another installation drives the compressor by a shaft from the back of a fuel injector pump though a rubber coupling. The rubber coupling dampens vibrations and also serves as a shear point to stop power transfer in case the compressor freezes up.

8.2.3 Compressor Shaft Seal

Another important part of every compressor is the seal that keeps refrigerant from escaping through the opening where the drive shaft enters. Many compressors use a rotating **seal cartridge** attached to the drive shaft and a stationary **seal seat** attached to the front of the compressor housing. Many compressors have one or two flats on the shaft so that the cartridge is positively driven (Figure 8-31).

A gasket or rubber O-ring is used so that the seal seat makes a gas-tight seal at the housing, and the seat has an extremely smooth sealing face. The carbon-material sealing member is spring loaded so that its smooth face makes tight contact with the seal seat. The cartridge also uses a rubber O-ring or molded rubber unit to seal the carbon to the driveshaft. Another important part of the seal is the compressor oil, which

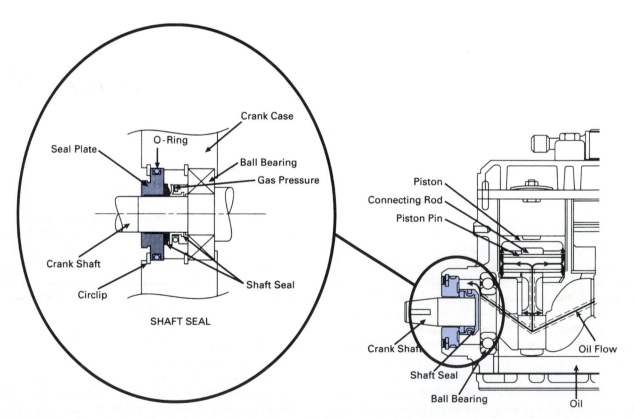

FIGURE 8-31 The shaft seal must keep refrigerant from escaping out the front of the compressor. Most compressors have an oil flow routed to them to reduce wear and improve the sealing action. *(Courtesy of Toyota Motor Sales USA, Inc.)*

CURRENT MODEL

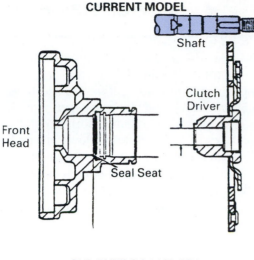

Shaft

Front Head

Clutch Driver

Seal Seat

LIP SEAL MODEL

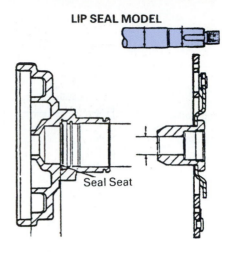

Seal Seat

OLD TYPE DA6 LIP SEAL

Ceramic Retainer

Ceramic Seal

Ceramic O-Ring

Carbon Seal

**2 PIECE
SEAL ASSEMBLY**

FIGURE 8-32 Many compressors use a two-piece seal with a rotating carbon seal and a stationary seal. *(Courtesy of ACDelco)*

NEW TYPE LIP SEAL

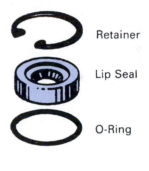

Retainer

Lip Seal

O-Ring

**1 PIECE
LIP SEAL**

FIGURE 8-33 Some newer compressors use a stationary lip seal that seals against the rotating shaft. *(Courtesy ACDelco)*

lubricates the surfaces and forms the final seal between the sealing surfaces (Figure 8-32).

A ceramic material has replaced cast iron for the seal seat in some compressors. Ceramic is not affected by water or acids, which can cause rust, corrosion, or etching of the iron seats. Ceramic seats are easy to identify because they are white instead of gray.

Modern compressor designs use a **lip seal.** The lip of the seal is made from Teflon and rides against a smooth portion of the driveshaft. Some shaft seals use double seating lips. The outer shell of the seal fits into a recess in the compressor housing and is sealed using a rubber O-ring. Gas pressure in the compressor ensures a tight fit between the seal lip and the shaft (Figure 8-33).

8.2.4 Compressor Lubrication

Refrigerant oil serves several purposes, the most important being to *lubricate* the moving parts of the compressor to reduce friction and prevent wear. Refrigerant oil also helps *seal* the compressor shaft seal, the insides of the hoses, and various connections between the parts to reduce refrigerant leakage. In addition, it lubricates the TXV and coats the metal parts inside the system to reduce corrosion (Figure 8-34).

The oil used in a system must be completely compatible with all the materials in the system. It also must be *miscible* or *soluble* with the refrigerant so that it will be circulated throughout the system (Figure 8-35). There are essentially three types of oil: **mineral oil** is used in R-12 systems, **PAG** (**polyalkylene glycol**) oils are used in most OEM R-134a systems, **POE** (**polyol ester**)(**ester**) oils are used in a few OEM R-134a systems,

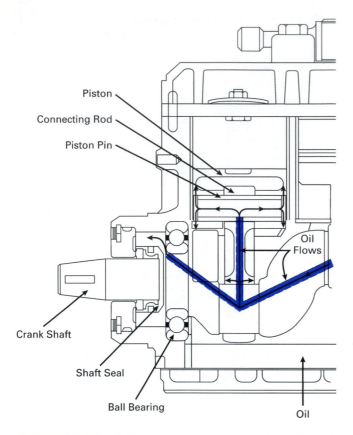

Piston

Connecting Rod

Piston Pin

Oil Flows

Crank Shaft

Shaft Seal

Ball Bearing

Oil

FIGURE 8-34   Older compressors pumped oil through passages in the crankshaft to lubricate moving parts. *(Courtesy of Toyota Motor Sales USA, Inc.)*

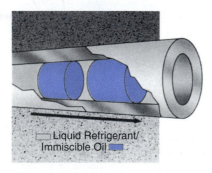

Liquid Refrigerant/ Immiscible Oil

FIGURE 8-35   If the oil is immiscible with the refrigerant, as shown here, it can separate out of the refrigerant. Poor lubrication will result. *(Courtesy of Castrol North America)*

and either ester or PAG oils are used in R-12 systems retrofitted to R-134a. PAG and POE are synthetic, human-made oils. Neither PAG nor POE are soluble in R-134a, but they are easily moved by the refrigerant flow so they travel through the entire A/C system. Most compressor remanufacturers consider PAG oil a better lubricant than ester oil.

◄   **SERVICE TIP**   ►

It is important to keep oil containers closed so that the oil does not absorb water from the atmosphere. A mineral oil can absorb about 0.005% water by weight. A PAG or ester oil is very **hygroscopic** and can absorb about 2 to 6% water (Figure 8-36). Some synthetic oils undergo hydrolysis if exposed to too much water and revert back to their original components: acid and alcohol.

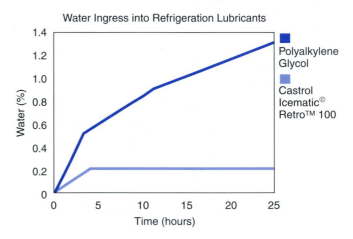

Water Ingress into Refrigeration Lubricants

■ Polyalkylene Glycol

Castrol Icematic© Retro™ 100

FIGURE 8-36   Some refrigerants and PAG oils are very hygroscopic and absorb moisture more rapidly than other oils, such as the polyol ester Icematic. *(Courtesy of Castrol North America)*

As mentioned earlier, mineral oils are not compatible with R-134a, and PAG oil is not compatible with R-12. Since R-12 and mineral oil are completely compatible, another important retrofitting step is a thorough system evacuation to ensure that all of the R-12 has a chance to boil out of the oil; this is called **outgassing.** Ester oil is more chlorine tolerant than PAG, which many people believe makes it more suitable for retrofitting R-12 systems.

Manufacturers designate specific blends of oil for R-12 and R-134a systems. There are over 30 varieties of refrigerant oil whose use depends on the requirements of a particular compressor or system. Piston, scroll, and vane compressors often require a different oil viscosity because of the different operating characteristics.

Most early compressor designs had a sump where oil was stored and used an oil pump to circulate oil to

FIGURE 8-37 This compressor separates oil from the refrigerant leaving the compressor to improve compressor lubrication. *(Courtesy of Toyota Motor Sales USA, Inc.)*

critical areas. Checking the oil level was a normal service operation on these compressors. A dipstick was usually used when systems had service valves, or the oil-level plug could be opened slightly on A-6 compressors to check the level. Newer compressors use internal pressures to circulate the oil. Some new compressor designs route the refrigerant flow so that it is forced to make a sharp U-turn. This will throw oil out and into a catch basin that directs the oil to lubrication passages (Figure 8-37). These compressors do not have a sump, but they normally contain a certain amount of oil (about 6 to 13 oz). The oil level on newer compressors can only be checked by removing the compressor and draining all of the oil, then measuring how much oil came out. This is normally done when a compressor is replaced or when major service is performed on the system.

Refrigerant oils are commonly available in several different viscosities: 46, 100, and 150 (Figure 8-38).

These are International Standards Organization (ISO) viscosities, measured at 40°C. Viscosity of the mineral oil used in early A/C systems was measured using a different scale: Saybolt Universal Seconds (SUS), and the most common refrigerant oil was 525 SUS. The most popular PAG oil used today is ISO 100. These oils are quite similar. Viscosity is a measurement of how thick the oil is and how easily it flows. The oil must be thick enough so that moving parts float on an oil film; wear occurs when moving parts rub against stationary parts. Oil must also be fluid enough to flow into the tiny spaces between parts. Compressor manufacturers normally specify the oil type and viscosity for each type of compressor.

When a system operates, oil is either absorbed or pushed by the refrigerant and migrates through the system. It does not stay in any particular component, but (as shown in Figure 8-39) a certain amount of oil can be expected in each component. Oil can also migrate while a system is shut off because of temperature changes of its various parts. Consequently, it is good practice, if conditions permit, to operate a system until normal conditions occur before checking oil levels.

◀ **PROBLEM SOLVING 8-1** ▶

A friend is concerned that something is wrong with her A/C system. It cools well, but she has found some oily dirt on the hoses. When you check it, you find two different spring-lock fittings with oily dirt on them. What is this telling you? Is it a good or bad sign?

Refrigerant Oil Types		Refrigerant Type	Viscosities
Mineral	Mineral Oil	R-12	300, 500/525 (SUS) (about 68 and 100 cSt)
PAG, Polyalkylene glycol	Synthetic	R-134a	46, 100, 150 @ 40°C (ISO)
POE, Polyolester	Synthetic	R-134a	100, 150 @ 100°C (ISO)
PolyAlpha + (ROC 68)	Synthetic	R-12/R-134a	68.2 @ 40°C (cSt)

Note: Most vehicle and compressor manufacturers recommend the use of PAG oil of the proper viscosity.

Note: Oil viscosity is measured using different methods; SUS: Saybolt Universal Seconds, ISO: International Standards Organization, cSt: Centistokes.

FIGURE 8-38 The major types of refrigerant oil, the refrigerant it is used with, and the viscosities in which it is commonly available.

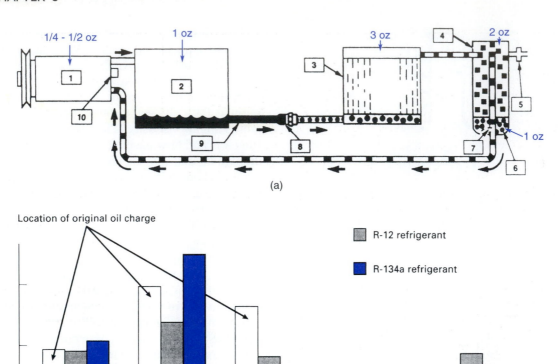

(a)

(b)

FIGURE 8-39 The oil in a system migrates when the system is operated *(a)*, and the migration is slightly different in R-12 and R-134a systems *(b)*. *(a Courtesy of ACDelco)*

8.2.5 Compressor Switches and Relief Valves

Many compressors contain one or more of the following: a **pressure relief valve,** a low- or high-pressure switch, and/or a low- or high-pressure sensor. The pressure relief valve is installed at the discharge port or into the discharge cavity. This valve opens to release excess refrigerant if high side pressure gets too high (Figure 8-40).

◀   **SERVICE TIP**   ▶

A relief valve discharging pressure produces a loud, popping noise, and the oil cloud that escapes with the refrigerant often looks like smoke. Most relief valves reclose after excess pressure has been released.

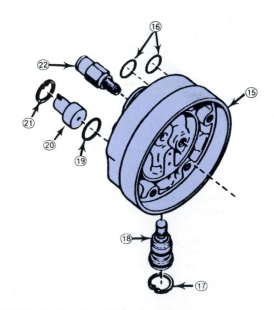

FIGURE 8-40 This V-5 20 compressor has a control valve (18), a control switch (22), and a pressure relief valve mounted in the near head. *(Courtesy of ACDelco)*

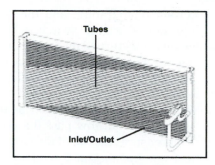

Compact Tube and Center Condenser (CTC)

The CTC is designed for applications where a very compact package is needed.

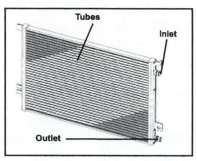

Headered Tube and Center Condenser (HTC)

The HTC is designed for high vehicle condensing performance needs.

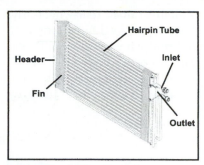

Tube and Fin Condenser (TFC)

The TFC is the lowest weight condenser in the Delphi Thermal line.

(a)

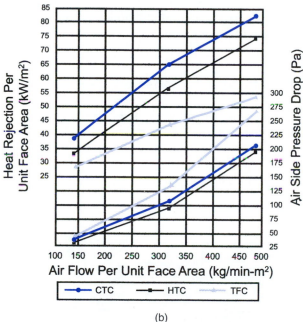

(b)

FIGURE 8-41   Three major types of condensers (*a*). The heat rejection and air side pressure drop are shown in *b*. *(Courtesy of Delphi Corp., all rights reserved)*

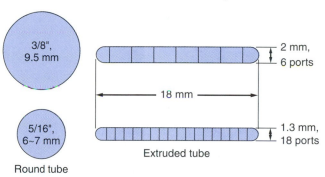

FIGURE 8-42   The common condenser tube sizes. Modern extruded tube condensers have up to 18 small ports or passages through the tube. Actual size is less than one-half of the drawing size.

Newer systems are designed to shut the system off if pressures get too high to avoid venting refrigerant into the atmosphere.

Switches can be connected to ports, leading to either the suction or discharge cavities in the compressor. These switches are usually used in circuits either to protect the compressor or system from damage or as sensors for the engine control module. They are described in more detail in Section 8.8.

8.3   CONDENSERS

The condenser has to get rid of the heat that is moved from the passenger compartment. Automotive condensers are simple devices, older tube-and-fin con-

densers are merely a tube bent back and forth into a serpentine shape with fins attached. After the tubes are pressed through the fins, return bends or manifolds are used to connect the tubes to give the desired flow pattern. Many modern condensers use a more efficient parallel flow with a manifold at each side (Figure 8-41). When flattened, **extruded tubes** are used, corrugated fins are often attached between two tubes. Parallel flow, flat tube condensers are much more efficient than the earlier design (Figure 8-42). This design allows a smaller, lighter condenser, and this can reduce high side pressure and compressor load.

The condenser of most vehicles is mounted in front of the radiator; ram air is forced through it by the vehicle's forward motion. This airflow is enhanced by the engine's cooling fan and shroud between the fan and radiator. Most rear-wheel-drive (RWD) vehicles use a fan driven by a fan clutch mounted on the water pump. Front-wheel-drive (FWD) cars normally use an electric motor to drive the fan. This motor is controlled by two or more switches: the engine coolant temperature switch, which turns the fan on when the coolant reaches a certain temperature, and the A/C control switch or high side pressure switch, which turns the fan on when the A/C is turned on or when the high side pressure reaches a certain point. Fan operation is described in more detail in Chapters 14 and 17 (Figure 8-43).

Many modern vehicles use foam **condenser seals** around the condenser to block airflow past the condenser (Figure 8-44). This ensures that all of the airflow entering through the front opening is forced to go through the condenser.

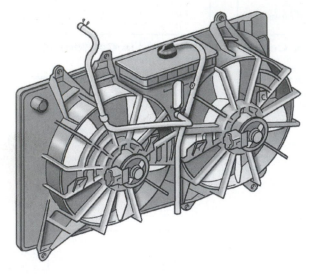

FIGURE 8-43 A pair of electric fans is used to pull air through the radiator and condenser. *(Courtesy of Toyota Motor Sales USA, Inc.)*

8.4 EXPANSION DEVICES

All early A/C systems used a TXV to control refrigerant flow into the evaporator. Many modern systems use an OT to meter this same flow.

8.4.1 Thermal Expansion Valves

A TXV is designed to allow a maximum flow of refrigerant, but this flow must have a few degrees of **superheat** at the evaporator tailpipe. The superheat ensures that all of the liquid has boiled. A TXV modulates the flow into the evaporator to match the heat load.

FIGURE 8-44 The foam seals at the front sides of this condenser force all of the air to flow through the condenser and prevent any airflow around or past it.

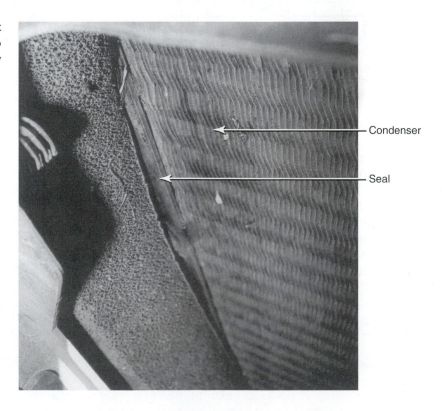

A TXV senses both temperature and pressure (Figure 8-45). Temperature is sensed by using a refrigerant charge sealed in a *sensing bulb* and a *capillary tube*, a very thin metal tube connected to a metal diaphragm. The metal diaphragm is arranged so that it can push against a group of three pins that, in turn, push on the valve plate to open it. Some valves use a single pin that becomes the valve stem with a ball valve at the end. The valve plate or ball also has pressure on it from the superheat spring that pushes to close the valve.

There is also a passage that allows evaporator pressure to act on the bottom of the diaphragm in opposition to thermal bulb pressure. In an *internally balanced* TXV, this passage is open to evaporator inlet pressure. In an *externally balanced* TXV, this passage connects to a length of small tubing that connects to the evaporator tailpipe. Externally balanced valves are used on some larger evaporators and give better response (Figure 8-46).

At room temperature, a TXV is open because the gas pressure in the capillary tube exerts a rather high pressure, greater than the spring. As the system cools, the temperature of the sensing bulb and capillary tube drops, and the pressure on the diaphragm drops with it. When the pressure at the diaphragm drops below the spring pressure, the valve closes. Also, if an excess amount of refrigerant enters the evaporator, high refrigerant pressure can act through the balance passage to close the TXV.

TXVs come in many forms. Most of the early valves threaded onto the evaporator inlet, and the liquid line threaded onto the valve. The thermal bulb, or end of the capillary tube, was clamped onto the evaporator tailpipe or inserted into a well in it. It was important that the thermal bulb be clamped tightly and be well insulated so that it transmitted an accurate temperature signal. If used, the external equalizer line threaded onto a fitting on the tailpipe.

Many newer valves are of the block or H type. These valves are connected with both the liquid and suction lines and the evaporator inlet and outlet. Some block valves use threaded fittings, and some are bolted between manifolds and are sealed using O-rings. Block valves use all of the features of other TXVs in a much more compact unit (Figure 8-47).

A TXV can also be a capsule inserted into a larger assembly. GM (between 1973 and 1975), Audi, and Volvo used a **valves in receiver (VIR)**, a receiver-drier with the TXV and the suction throttling valves built into it. The TXV capsule was mounted so that it controlled the refrigerant flow from the receiver portion to the evaporator port (Figure 8-48).

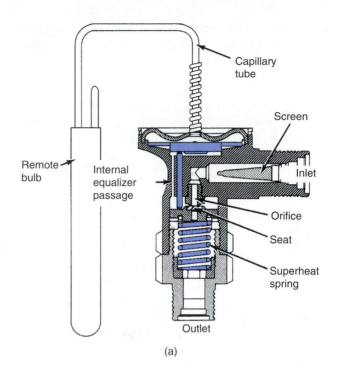

(a)

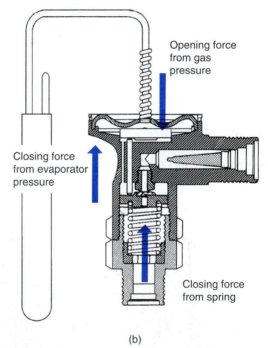

(b)

FIGURE 8-45 An internal equalized TXV. Note the internal passage to bring evaporator inlet pressure to the bottom of the diaphragm and the screen, which stops debris that might plug the valve (a). The valve is opened by gas pressure on top of the diaphragm and closed by pressure from the evaporator and the superheat spring (b). (*Reprinted with permission of General Motors Corporation*)

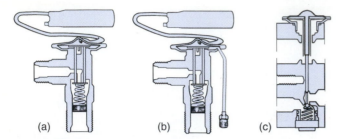

FIGURE 8-46   An internal equalized TXV has two large connectors for the liquid line and evaporator *(a)*; an external equalized TXV has an additional smaller line to connect to the evaporator outlet *(b)*; and a block-type TXV has four openings which connect to the evaporator, liquid line, and suction line.

FIGURE 8-48   Depending on available parts, a VIR assembly can be taken apart and repaired. *(Courtesy of ACDelco)*

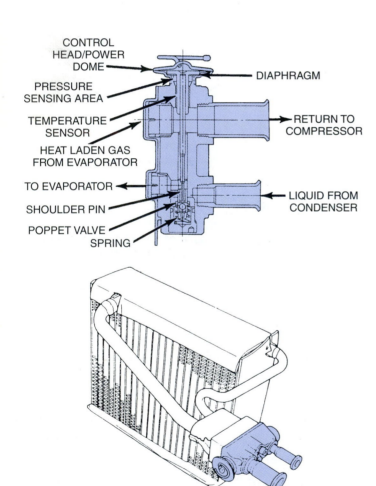

CONTROL HEAD/POWER DOME
DIAPHRAGM
PRESSURE SENSING AREA
TEMPERATURE SENSOR
RETURN TO COMPRESSOR
HEAT LADEN GAS FROM EVAPORATOR
TO EVAPORATOR
SHOULDER PIN
LIQUID FROM CONDENSER
POPPET VALVE
SPRING

FIGURE 8-47   A block TXV has the control head next to where the cooled gas is leaving the evaporator, eliminating the need for a thermal bulb and capillary tube. Note that this valve uses spring-lock fittings. *(Courtesy of DaimlerChrysler Corporation)*

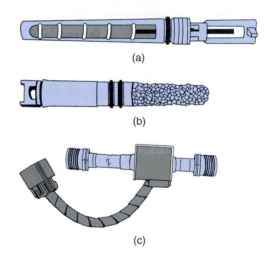

FIGURE 8-49   Most OTs are small brass tubes with a filter screen at each end *(a)*; some use a group of plastic beads *(b)*; and an electronic OT has a solenoid so it can change orifice size. *(Courtesy of ACDelco)*

Most TXVs have a small, very fine screen at their inlet. This screen traps debris that can plug the valve, and it can be removed for cleaning or to install a replacement.

8.4.2   Orifice Tubes

When first used in GM pickups, trucks, and some cars, the first orifice tubes (OTs) were porous brass units that looked somewhat like fuel filters. They are also called *fixed orifice tubes* (FOTs). Newer OTs are longer, more slender plastic units used on GM vehicles since the mid-1970s and on most Ford cars since 1980 (Figure 8-49).

Manufacturers color-code OTs to identify the car make and model for which a tube is used. There are at least eight different sizes of OTs that have a similar appearance but a size range from 0.047 to 0.072 inch (1.19 to 1.8 mm).

Most OTs are a thin brass tube that is a couple of inches long and has a plastic filter screen around it. This tube is sized to flow the proper amount of refrigerant into the evaporator for maximum cooling loads. Some modern OTs use a filter made up of many small plastic beads in place of the screen. As mentioned earlier, the OT floods the evaporator during light cooling loads, so a low side accumulator is always used with an OT. One expert states that under typical operating conditions, the evaporator might contain about 10 to 20% liquid, 70 to 80% saturated vapor, and 10 to 20% superheated vapor. The flow through an OT is also affected by pressure, and excessive high side pressure can cause evaporator pressure and temperature to become too high.

The OT in most early systems was placed into the evaporator inlet tube. An O-ring was used around it to stop refrigerant from flowing past the outside of the OT. Several small indentations, or dimples, were put in the tubing wall to keep the OT from moving too far into the evaporator. Many newer vehicles place the OT in the liquid line farther away from the evaporator, close to the condenser outlet. This is done because of complaints of hissing noises that occur after the vehicle is shut off and high side pressure bleeds down through the OT.

◄ SERVICE TIP ►

In an operating system, the OT position can be located by finding the point where the liquid line changes temperature from hot to cold. If the system is not operating, the dimples in the line show the OT location.

8.4.3 Variable Orifice Valves (VOVs)

Most OTs have a fixed-size orifice that is sized for the proper refrigerant flow to produce maximum A/C performance during 50- to 60-mph operation. At lower engine speeds, the orifice size is too large. Remember that the orifice size should produce the high side pressure for proper condenser action and the pressure drop into the low side to produce proper evaporator pressure and temperature. Vehicles that spend considerable time idling commonly have poor A/C performance and experience short compressor life (Figure 8-50).

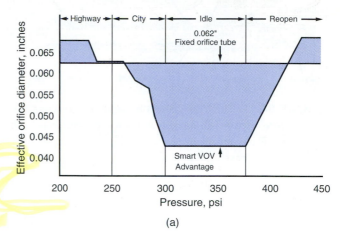

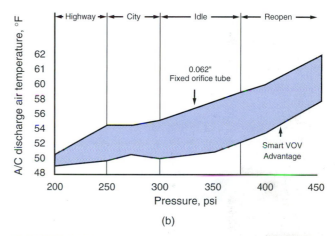

FIGURE 8-50 A flow rate of a VOV as compared to a fixed orifice tube. Note how the VOV is either larger or smaller under certain conditions (a) and produces cooler discharge air (b). *(Courtesy of Nartron Corporation)*

One vehicle manufacturer uses a **variable orifice valve (VOV)** that senses temperature to change the size of the orifice (Figure 8-51). A bimetal coil spring senses the temperature of the liquid refrigerant, and when the temperature increases, the spring moves the variable port to a closed position. This increases the restriction at the VOV and reduces the flow to the evaporator.

The VOV is the same external size and configuration as a fixed OT, and it contains an internal valve (Figure 8-52). The valve is calibrated to reduce the orifice size under conditions of high head pressure and low refrigerant flow rate. Installation of the VOV is simply a matter of removing the OT and installing the VOV plus an additional ounce of oil and an additional ounce

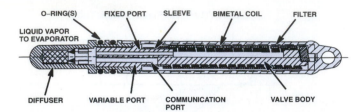

FIGURE 8-51   This VOV uses a bimetal coil to sense the temperature of the refrigerant. A higher temperature will cause the coil to expand and partially close the variable port to increase the restriction. *(Courtesy of DaimlerChrysler)*

(a)

HIGHWAY
High Freon Flow—Low Compressor Pressure—Large Orifice Area

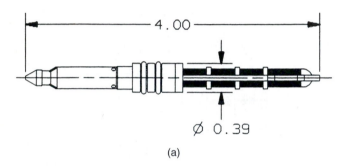

CITY
Medium-Low Freon Flow—Moderate Compressor Pressure—
Reduced Orifice Area

(b)

FIGURE 8-52   In a VOV *(a)*, the valve is inside the tubular portion at the left; it has the ability to reduce the flow rate as head pressure increases *(b)*. *(Courtesy of Nartron Corporation)*

or two of refrigerant. This device is becoming popular with law enforcement agencies. A VOV is also said to increase the performance of dual systems.

Some General Motors vehicles use an electronic orifice tube; it uses a solenoid to change orifice diameter. It has an orifice diameter of 0.062″ (1.57 mm) when turned off, and this increases to 0.080″ (2.03 mm) when the solenoid is energized. The solenoid is controlled by an ECM, or electronic control module, that uses primar-

ily three inputs: vehicle speed/VSS, engine rpm, and high side pressure. Energizing the solenoid increases the orifice size to reduce high side pressure.

◀   **PROBLEM SOLVING 8-2**   ▶

A friend is concerned that something is wrong with her A/C system. It cools well, but when the engine and the system are turned off, she hears a hissing noise. You also hear this noise when you check it. What could be causing this? Is this a sign of a problem?

8.5   EVAPORATORS

An evaporator, like a condenser, is a simple heat exchanger device. Some evaporators are merely groups of tubes with fins attached. Most evaporators are a series of plates sandwiched together to form both the refrigerant and air passages. A plate-type evaporator is the most efficient of these two styles (Figure 8-53).

Evaporators have at least two line connections. The smaller line connects to the TXV or OT, and the larger one connects to the suction line and to the compressor. Some evaporators have a third, very small line. This is an oil bleed line and is used in a system with a **suction throttling valve (STV).** This line allows oil to be pulled from the bottom of the evaporator to ensure compressor lubrication when the STV is throttling (Figure 8-54).

Many modern evaporators have a chemical coating to prevent bacterial growth that can cause bad odors.

8.6   RECEIVER–DRIERS AND ACCUMULATORS

Receiver–driers and accumulators serve two functions: (1) They store a supply of liquid refrigerant and (2) they contain desiccant. The purpose of refrigerant storage is to compensate for volume change due to temperature change or refrigerant loss. Desiccant is needed to remove moisture or water, which can cause rusting or corrosion.

As previously mentioned, the receiver–drier or accumulator used in an R-134a system should use XH-7 or XH-9 desiccant. New units contain either of these desiccants, so they are compatible with either R-12 or R-134a. These desiccants are a little more expensive and require a little more volume than XH-5, which was used in R-12 units.

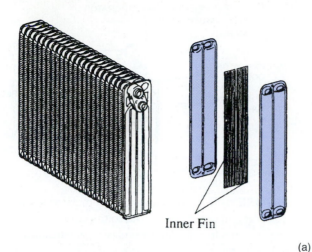
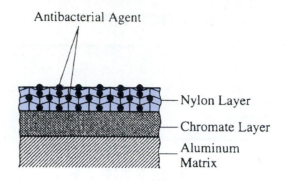

Inner Fin

(a)

FIGURE 8-53 A plate-type evaporator *(a)* is made from a group of plates that form the passages for the gas flow. Note that this one has an antibacterial agent to help prevent foul odors. A fin-and-tube evaporator *(b)* routes the refrigerant flow through one or more tubes. *(a courtesy of Toyota Motor Sales USA, Inc.; b courtesy of Four Seasons)*

Oil Bleed Line

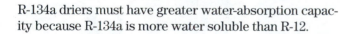

FIGURE 8-54 The evaporator used with a POA value has a small-diameter tube to carry oil from the bottom of the evaporator to the POA outlet. *(Courtesy of ACDelco)*

(b)

R-134a driers must have greater water-absorption capacity because R-134a is more water soluble than R-12.

8.6.1 Accumulators

The accumulator inlet on many vehicles is connected directly to the evaporator tailpipe. On other vehicles it is mounted separately, and a metal tube or rubber hose is used to connect it to the evaporator. The outlet of the accumulator is connected to the compressor inlet through the flexible suction line (Figure 8-55).

The inlet simply dumps the incoming refrigerant vapor and liquid into the container. The outlet begins near the top, runs downward to the oil bleed hole at the bottom, and then exits out of either the top or the bottom. As mentioned earlier, a fine mesh filter screen is used at the oil bleed hole to prevent plugging and compressor oil starvation. Most accumulators have an internal baffle to prevent incoming liquid refrigerant from passing directly into the outlet tube. The accumulator of a properly operating system normally holds liquid refrigerant at the bottom, and it supplies the compressor with refrigerant vapor from the top (Figure 8-56). Remember that this liquid refrigerant is at evaporator pressure, so it is at the same temperature as the evaporator.

In addition to the inlet and the outlet, accumulators are often equipped with one or two smaller ports. These traditionally have been 1/4-inch male flare fittings (the same size as a standard R-12 service fitting). These small fittings are for the low side service fitting and low side pressure switches (Figure 8-57). Replacement accumulators should have the same service and/or switch ports as the original accumulator.

◄ SERVICE TIP ►

The accumulator of some R-134a systems has an insulating jacket to help reduce the heat absorption and lower the air temperature at the discharge ducts.

◄ SERVICE TIP ►

The accumulator is normally replaced if a system has been opened to atmosphere for a period of time because the desiccant is probably saturated with moisture. It is also standard practice to replace the accumulator whenever major service work is done on a system, especially if the compressor is replaced.

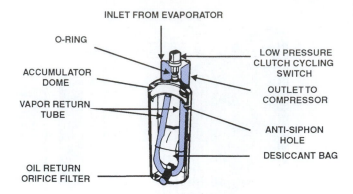

FIGURE 8-56   This cutaway accumulator shows the vapor inlet and outlet connected to the compressor, a baffle to keep liquid out of the inlet, the desiccant bag, and an oil bleed hole with filter screen. *(Courtesy of DaimlerChryster)*

FIGURE 8-57   This accumulator has large inlet and outlet fittings and two smaller ports, one for a pressure switch and the other for low side service. *(Courtesy of ACDelco)*

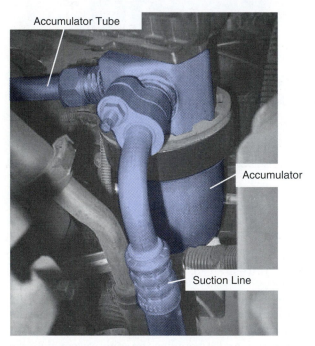

FIGURE 8-55   This accumulator has an accumulator tube that connects the evaporator outlet and a suction hose that connects to the compressor inlet.

8.6.2 Receiver–Drier

The receiver–drier is normally found in the high side liquid line, somewhere between the condenser and the TXV. Factory-installed systems use threaded fittings or block-type fittings with O-rings at the line connections. Receiver–driers for some dealer-installed and

FIGURE 8-58   Receiver–driers use threaded line connections *(a)*, block-type connections *(b)*, and spring-lock connections *(c)*. *(Courtesy of Four Seasons)*

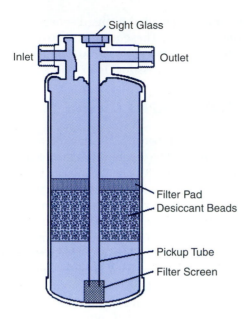

FIGURE 8-59 This cutaway receiver–drier shows the filter pads and desiccant; many units include a filter at the opening of the pickup tube. Note the sight glass at the top of the pickup tube.

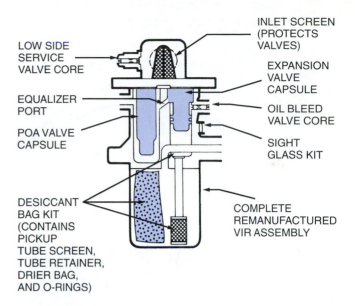

FIGURE 8-60 An exploded view of a VIR assembly; note the two valves and the receiver–drier portions. *(Courtesy of Four Seasons)*

aftermarket installations use push-on, barb-type fittings. On these, the hose is slid onto the fitting and secured with a clamp. The shapes and sizes of receiver–driers vary greatly (Figure 8-58).

The receiver–drier inlet dumps incoming refrigerant into the container. The outlet, often called a *pickup tube*, begins near the bottom and usually exits at the top. A fine-mesh filter screen is used at the inner opening to stop debris from passing out of the receiver–drier and on to the TXV. The receiver–drier is usually about half full of liquid refrigerant (Figure 8-59).

A receiver–drier can contain a sight glass, pressure release plug or valve, or switch. The **sight glass** allows observation of the refrigerant flow as it leaves the receiver–drier. The flow of R-12 should be invisible; remember that R-12 is clear, and the oil is dissolved in the liquid refrigerant. Bubbles or foam in the sight glass can indicate abnormal operation. R-134a would appear cloudy in a sight glass, so sight glasses are not commonly used in R-134a systems. The pressure relief device is described in Section 7.3.4. The switch is used to sense high side pressure. It can be used to prevent compressor operation if the pressure is either too low or too high.

As with an accumulator, a receiver–drier is normally replaced if the system is left open or if major service work is done, especially if the compressor is replaced.

The VIR assembly is a serviceable unit: Almost every one of its individual components can be replaced. A kit that contains a desiccant bag, pickup tube filter, and O-rings is available (Figure 8-60).

◀ **SERVICE TIP** ▶

When servicing a VIR, removal of the assembly is recommended to get better access to the screws, which tend to seize in the aluminum housing; also, index marks should be placed on the housing parts to ensure proper reassembly.

8.6.3 Filters and Mufflers

Inline filters are available from aftermarket sources for installation in the liquid line. These are designed to filter the refrigerant to stop debris from plugging the OT or TXV.

◀ **SERVICE TIP** ▶

Service problems have occurred because scale and other debris from the condenser and compressor have plugged the OT. Normally if this happens the OT is cleaned or replaced. To prevent recurrence of this problem, a technician has a choice: thoroughly clean and flush out the system or install a filter. If the system is still working well, it can be much simpler and cheaper to add a filter than to flush the system (Figure 8-61).

SERVICE FILTER

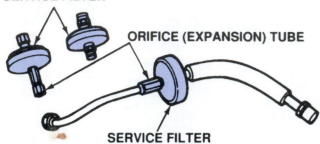

ORIFICE (EXPANSION) TUBE

SERVICE FILTER

FIGURE 8-61   Aftermarket inline filters can be added to a system to trap debris. Some include a replacement OT.

FIGURE 8-62   This muffler is a simple expansion or pulsation chamber; Some mufflers have internal buffles to help smooth compressor pressure pulses.

Mufflers are installed in the discharge or suction line of some systems. These mufflers are usually a simple baffled cylinder and are used to dampen the pumping noise of the compressor (Figure 8-62).

8.7   HOSES AND LINES

As mentioned earlier, because the suction and discharge lines in a system must be flexible, they are usually made of reinforced rubber hose. The liquid line can be made from metal because the parts it connects are rigidly mounted, but many systems use hose for this function also.

Various end fittings of different sizes are used for the connections. These fittings include female and male flare fittings, female and male O-ring fittings, block, pad, or manifold fittings with O-rings, spring-lock fittings, and simple push-on hose-to-barb connections (Figure 8-63). Early systems traditionally used flare fittings, but a leaky flare fitting is often expensive and difficult to repair. O-ring fittings are much easier to repair, simply by replacing the O-ring.

Block, pad, or manifold fittings are held together by a bolt or nut and are sealed by either a crimped metal gasket or O-rings (Figure 8-64). A newer style of fitting, called a P-nut fitting, uses a single O-ring.

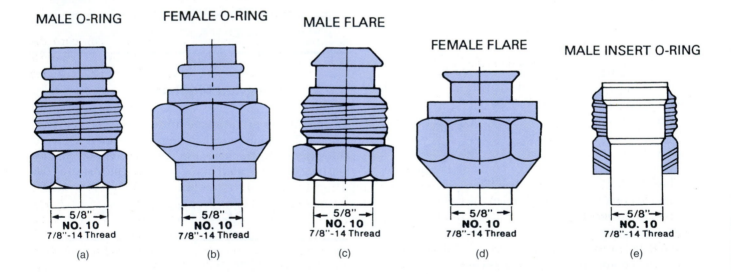

MALE O-RING   FEMALE O-RING   MALE FLARE   FEMALE FLARE   MALE INSERT O-RING

5/8"	5/8"	5/8"	5/8"	5/8"
NO. 10	NO. 10	NO. 10	NO. 10	NO. 10
7/8"-14 Thread	7/8"-14 Thread	7/8"-14 Thread	7/8"-14 Thread	7/8"-14 Thread
(a)	(b)	(c)	(d)	(e)

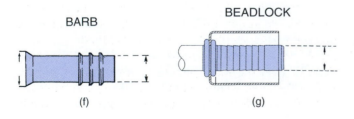

BARB   BEADLOCK

(f)   (g)

FIGURE 8-63   A/C fitting types include male O-ring (a), female O-ring (b), male flare (c), female flare (d), male insert O-ring (e), push-on barb (f), and beadlock (g). (Courtesy of Four Seasons)

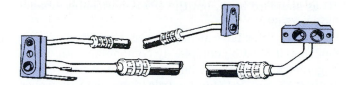

FIGURE 8-64 This suction and liquid hose has block fittings for the connections to the receiver–drier, TXV, and compressor; they are sealed by gaskets or O-rings. *(Courtesy of Four Seasons)*

◀ **SERVICE TIP** ▶

When making block connections, use a torque wrench. Overtightened connections damage the O-ring or distort the block and cause leaks.

O-ring fittings squeeze a rubber O-ring between the two parts being connected to make the seal. In most cases, the O-ring is slid over the end of the metal tube and is located by a raised metal ring or bead. Some manufacturers use a **captive,** also called a *captured,* **O-ring,** which locates the O-ring more positively in a shallow groove. Captive O-rings use a larger-diameter cross section than standard O-rings (Figure 8-65). Some designs use two O-rings for a better seal.

O-rings made from Buna or nitrile are commonly used in R-12 systems, but these materials are not compatible with R-134a. High-grade neoprene O-rings (HSN or HNBR), often tinted blue or green, are used in R-134a systems; these also can be used in R-12 systems. There is no color standard for O-rings; some manufacturers use red, yellow, and tan colors. Most manufacturers use the following color designations:

- Black indicates nitrile or neoprene
- Blue indicates neoprene or nitrile
- Green indicates HNBR

Because of this confusion, when you order O-rings, you should purchase them from a reputable source, specify the desired material, and then specify the color.

A spring-lock fitting is a type of quick-disconnect fitting. The female portion of this fitting has a flarelike ridge at the end; this ridge is gripped by a garter spring when connected. One or two O-rings form the seal between the two fitting parts. These O-rings must be resilient enough to compensate for slight movement between the two

Standard O-Ring

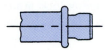
Captured O-Ring

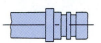
Dual O-Ring

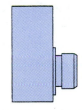
Male Block Fitting

FIGURE 8-65 Standard O-rings merely slide onto the line; captive O-rings are positioned in a groove, dual O-rings have a groove for each O-ring; and block Fitting has a groove for the O-ring. *(Courtesy of ACDelco)*

parts. Spring-lock fittings are connected by pushing one line over the other until the garter spring moves into position. A special tool is inserted into the fitting to expand the garter spring and release the fitting. Refrigerant leakage was a fairly common problem with early spring-lock fittings; newly designed O-rings have improved sealing ability (Figure 8-66). Another quick-connect fitting is held together by a hinged plastic cage. A special tool is used to release the cage (Figure 8-67).

Metal tubing is sized by its outside diameter (OD). Pipe and hose are sized by the inside diameter (ID); these sizes are often nominal (approximate) sizes. A number sizing is often used for refrigerant hose and fittings, with the most popular sizes being #4, #6, #8, #10, and #12: #4 equals 1/4 inch (4.4 mm), #6 equals 3/8 inch (8 mm), #8 equals 1/2 inch (11.1 mm), #10 equals

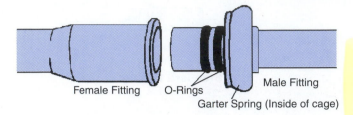

FIGURE 8-66 A spring lock fitting is a type of quick-disconnect fitting that is sealed by two O-rings and held together by a garter spring. A special tool is required to expand the garter spring to release the fitting.

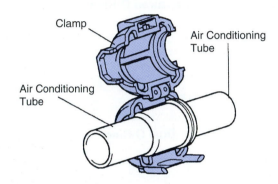

FIGURE 8-67 A plastic clamp latches over the Quick Joint of the two tubes and locks them together. *(Courtesy of Toyota Motor Sales USA, Inc.)*

5/8 inch (12.4 mm), and #12 equals 3/4 inch (15.5 mm) (Figure 8-68). A new reduced-diameter, lightweight hose is currently being used for some OEM and replacement usage. Reduced-diameter hose has the same ID as standard hose, but the OD is noticeably smaller (Figure 8-69).

A hose must have an impervious inner liner so it can seal, and it must be completely compatible with the refrigerant and oil. Some inner liners are effective with both R-12 and R-134a; a nitrile inner liner, however, works well with R-12 and has a high leak rate with R-134a. The inner layer is usually surrounded by rayon, another reinforcing layer, and the outer, protective layer of rubber. Some older hoses are made from nylon with a single protective layer. Nylon hoses have a smaller OD and are much more rigid. Modern hoses use a thin nylon layer, which is quite effective in containing R-134a; these are called **barrier hoses** (Figure 8-70).

Most OEM hose uses a captive ferrule to swage the hose onto the end fitting. Grooves or raised rings (barbs) at the fitting and the clamping action of the ferrule hold the hose securely in place (Figure 8-71). Repair of hoses and the fittings used for this repair are described in Chapter 16.

8.8 ELECTRICAL SWITCHES AND EVAPORATOR TEMPERATURE CONTROLS

A variety of electrical switches are used in A/C systems to prevent evaporator icing, protect the compressor, and control fan motors. In addition to electrical controls, some systems use a suction throttling valve (STV) to control evaporator pressure and prevent icing. An STV can be located anywhere between the evaporator tailpipe and the compressor inlet. Control switches can

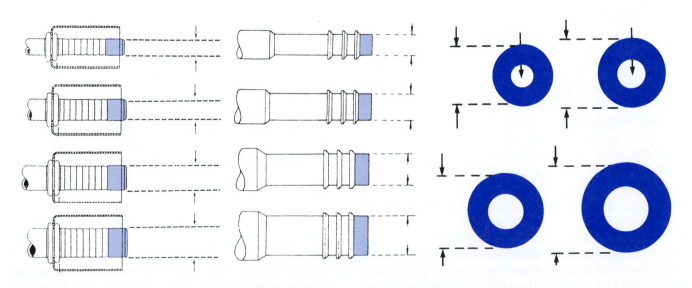

FIGURE 8-68 The outside diameter of the fitting and inside diameter of the hose determine the size. *(Courtesy of Four Seasons)*

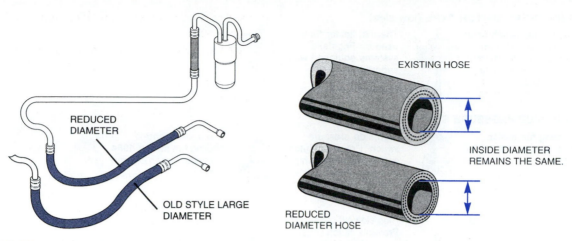

FIGURE 8-69   A reduced-diameter hose has the same inside diameter with a smaller outside diameter and lighter weight, making it more suitable for congested underhood spaces of fuel-efficient vehicles. *(Courtesy of Four Seasons)*

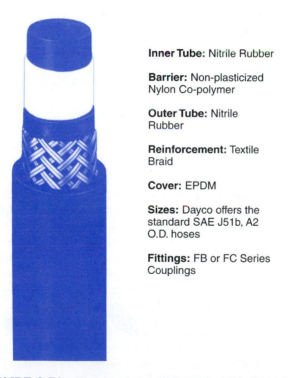

Inner Tube: Nitrile Rubber

Barrier: Non-plasticized Nylon Co-polymer

Outer Tube: Nitrile Rubber

Reinforcement: Textile Braid

Cover: EPDM

Sizes: Dayco offers the standard SAE J51b, A2 O.D. hoses

Fittings: FB or FC Series Couplings

FIGURE 8-70   This barrier-type hose is made from five layers of different materials. *(Courtesy of Dayco Products, Inc.)*

be located anywhere in the system; the most common locations are the compressor discharge or suction cavities, the receiver–drier, and the accumulator.

Some modern systems use a variable displacement compressor to prevent icing. As described in Sections 8.2.1.5 and 8.2.2.1, a valve that senses evaporator pressure is used in the compressor, and compressor displacement is reduced in response to that pressure (Figure 8-72).

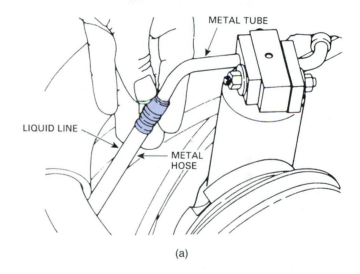

(a)

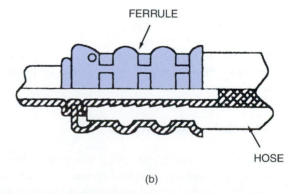

(b)

FIGURE 8-71   Most OEM hoses use a captive ferrule *(a)* that greatly increases the holding power; the ferrule is connected to the metal tubing (b). *(a courtesy of DaimlerChrysler Corporation; b courtesy of ACDelco)*

SUPERHEAT SWITCH TYPE (low side)

Superheat switch used on Harrison systems equipped with thermal limiter fuse. Metallic appearance.

Thermal limiter fuse used on Frigidaire systems equipped with superheat switch.

HIGH SIDE PRESSURE SWITCH TYPE

Cooling fan switch closes approx. 300 P.S.I. Natural colored plastic.

High side pressure switch. Prevents clutch engagement when high side pressure is below 40 P.S.I. Natural colored plastic.

Idle speed control/ cooling fan switch. 1984 Corvette. Green colored plastic.

High side cut-out switch. Prevents clutch engagement when high side pressure exceeds 430 P.S.I. Red colored plastic. Use with 90° connector.

High side cut-out switch. Prevents clutch engagement when high side pressure exceeds 430 P.S.I. Red colored plastic. Use with straight connector.

CHRYSLER SWITCH TYPE

Clutch cycling pressure switch located on back of compressor.

GM TWO-TERMINAL SWITCH TYPE

LOW PRESSURE
Cut-out switch.
Green colored plastic.
Blue colored plastic.
Yellow colored plastic.

HIGH PRESSURE
Cut out-switch.
Red colored plastic.
White colored plastic.

FAN SWITCH
Gray colored plastic.

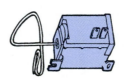

THERMOSTATIC CLUTCH CYCLING SWITCH

FIGURE 8-72 Some of the switches used in A/C electrical circuits. *(Courtesy of Everco Industries)*

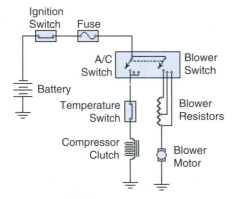

FIGURE 8-73 Many early A/C systems use a simple electrical circuit as shown.

8.8.1 Switches and Relays

At one time, the A/C electrical circuit was rather simple. As shown in Figure 8-73, a typical circuit connects the evaporator blower motor and compressor clutch at one master switch. The power to the clutch passes through a temperature switch that opens to cycle the clutch when the evaporator gets too cold. The power to the blower motor passes through a speed control switch so that the blower speed can be changed.

Today various switches, sensors, and relays are used. A sensor is usually an input to an electronic control module (ECM), and many sensors provide a variable signal so the ECM will know the actual temperature or pressure at certain points. A relay is essentially a magnetic switch that is controlled by another switch; a relay is used to control a greater amount of current than a switch can handle. Relays also allow computer control modules to control electrical circuits (Figure 8-74). Control switches and relays that you may encounter are as follows:

- *Ambient sensor or switch:* Senses outside temperature and is designed to prevent compressor operation when ambient temperature is below a certain point, about 35 to 40°F

- *Compressor high-pressure sensor or switch:* Mounted in compressor discharge cavity; senses high side pressure and is used to cut out the compressor clutch if pressure is too high or too low or provides a signal to another device that pressure is too high

- *Compressor low-pressure sensor or switch:* Mounted in compressor suction cavity; senses low side pressure and is often used to cut out the compressor clutch if pressure is too low

- *Compressor rpm sensor:* Provides input to the ECM that the compressor is running; ECM will cut out

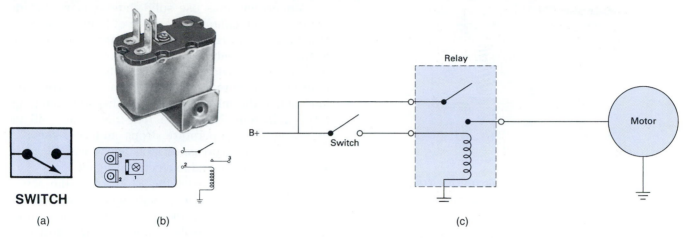

SWITCH

(a)   (b)   (c)

FIGURE 8-74   A switch *(a)* can open or close a circuit. A relay *(b)* does the same thing but can control more current. Most relays are controlled through switches *(c)*. *(a courtesy of Everco Industries;* b *courtesy of Four Seasons)*

compressor if rpm is low (possible belt slippage or impending compressor lockup)

- *Compressor superheat sensor or switch:* Function is similar to compressor low-pressure switch
- *Compressor high temperature switch:* Mounted on the compressor and shuts off the compressor if it gets too hot.
- *Compressor cutoff switch:* Mounted at power steering gear or transmission; senses pressure in that system and is used to stop the compressor under certain external conditions
- *Coolant temperature sensor, also called the engine coolant temperature (ECT):* Mounted near the engine thermostat; senses engine temperature for power-train control module and is also used to turn on cooling fan
- *Evaporator pressure sensor:* Provides input to the ECM as to the operating pressure in the evaporator
- *Evaporator temperature sensor:* Mounted at the evaporator; senses temperature and is used to cycle compressor clutch to prevent icing
- *High-pressure cutout switch:* Mounted at receiver–drier or liquid line; senses high side pressure and is used to cut out the compressor clutch if high side pressure is too high
- *High-temperature cutoff sensor or switch:* Mounted at the condenser outlet; senses condenser temperature and is used to cut out the compressor clutch if the temperature is too high
- *Low-pressure cutout sensor or switch:* Mounted in receiver–drier or liquid line; senses low pressure and is used to cut out the compressor clutch with low refrigerant charge
- *Master switch:* Mounted at control head; turns system on and off

- *Pressure cycling switch:* Mounted at accumulator; senses low pressure and cycles the compressor clutch to prevent evaporator icing
- *Radiator fan switch:* Mounted at engine thermostat cover or upper radiator hose; senses engine coolant temperature and operates radiator fan motor to prevent overheating
- *Thermostatic cycling switch:* Mounted at evaporator; senses air temperature and cycles the compressor clutch to prevent evaporator icing
- *Trinary pressure switch:* Mounted at receiver–drier; senses high side pressures and cuts out compressor clutch if pressure is too high or too low; can also be used to control radiator shutters or fan motor
- *Blower relay:* Can be used to turn blower on or off; most common usage is to provide high blower speed
- *Clutch cutoff relay:* Can be used to interrupt compressor clutch
- *Condenser fan relay:* Used to turn condenser fan motor on or off
- *Radiator fan relay:* Used to turn radiator fan motor on or off

Evaporator temperature in a cycling clutch system is usually controlled by either a thermostatic (thermal) or pressure switch. Both bellows and bimetal thermal switches are used. The bellows switch uses a capillary tube inserted into the evaporator fins. As with a TXV, the gas pressure in the capillary tube is exerted on a bellows. In a thermal switch, the bellows acts on a set of contact points. A warm evaporator produces a higher bellows pressure, which keeps the points closed; a cold evaporator reduces the pressure, which causes the points to open. A bimetal switch has a contact arm that is laminated from two metals with greatly different thermal expansion

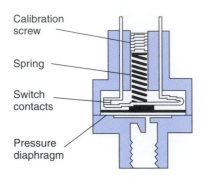

Calibration screw

Spring

Switch contacts

Pressure diaphragm

FIGURE 8-75 A pressure switch. The contacts are closed by gas pressure on the diaphragm; they are opened by the spring.

rates. When the switch is warm, the metals expand to close the contact points; as the switch cools, the metals in the arm contract to open the contacts. Both of these switch styles are calibrated so they are closed at temperatures above 32A°F and open at temperatures below 32A°F. When the switch opens, the compressor clutch cycles out. This causes the evaporator to begin warming, and after a few degrees of temperature increase, the switch closes to cycle the compressor in again.

A pressure cycling switch is mounted to sense low side pressure. Ice begins to form when evaporator pressure drops below 30 psi in an R-12 system or slightly less in an R-134a system. When evaporator pressure is above 30 psi, the switch contacts close so the compressor will operate. When the pressure drops below 30 psi, the switch opens and cycles the compressor out. After the compressor stops, evaporator pressure will increase; after an increase of about 10 to 20 psi, the pressure switch contacts close to cycle the compressor in again. This switch also prevents the compressor from operating if the pressure is too low from a refrigerant loss (Figure 8-75).

Many systems include a low-pressure switch to prevent compressor operation if there is a loss of refrigerant. Remember that damage will occur if the compressor is operated without refrigerant or the oil that refrigerant circulates through it.

◄ SERVICE TIP ►

If the system is low on refrigerant, it will **short cycle,** or rapidly cycle out and back in. This is the result of the compressor pulling the refrigerant out of the low side quickly to open either the cycling switch or the low-pressure switch. With the compressor off, the flow into the evaporator raises the pressure enough to reclose the switch and restart the compressor.

Modern systems use solid-state sensors that do not use switch contacts, a source of failure. The most common are **thermistors** and **transducers.** A thermistor is commonly used to sense temperatures. It is basically an electrical resistor that changes resistance in direct inverse relationship to its temperature. Most automotive thermistors are of the negative temperature coefficient, NTC, type. The resistance will increase as the temperature drops and vice versa. A transducer senses pressure; it changes a variable pressure signal into a variable electrical signal.

A transducer can let the ECM know the actual pressure in the low and/or high side of the system. Sensors provide an electrical signal to a control module that, in turn, controls compressor clutch or condenser fan operation. A/C system, blower motor, and radiator fan motor switches, sensors, and relays are described in more detail in Chapters 10 and 14.

◄ PROBLEM SOLVING 8-3 ►

A friend mentions that her A/C system is not working at all. With the system turned on and the hood open, you see that the compressor short cycles; it runs for a few seconds and then turns off for a while. What could be causing this? What will you need to do to confirm this opinion?

8.8.2 Suction Throttling Valves

An STV, also called a *control valve, evaporator pressure regulator valve,* or a *pressure regulator,* is used in the low side of some systems. STVs were common on domestic systems manufactured in the 1960s and 1970s. STVs are still used in some imported vehicles. Placed somewhere between the evaporator outlet and the compressor inlet, an STV is sensitive to evaporator pressure and, in one case, temperature. An STV is wide open when evaporator pressure is above 30 psi. When the evaporator cools and the pressure begins to drop below 30 psi, the valve closes to keep the pressure from dropping further. Most valve types modulate and close just enough to maintain correct evaporator pressure. Some valves close almost completely and cycle between open and closed to maintain the correct pressure. A system with an STV does not cycle the clutch except when the system is turned on or off (Figure 8-76).

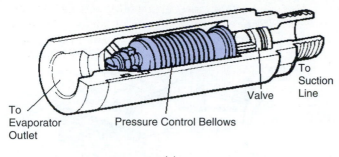

To Evaporator Outlet

Pressure Control Bellows

Valve

To Suction Line

(a)

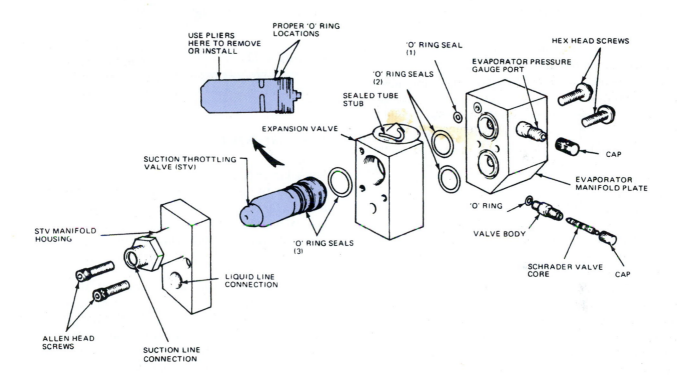

USE PLIERS HERE TO REMOVE OR INSTALL

PROPER 'O' RING LOCATIONS

'O' RING SEAL (1)

'O' RING SEALS (2)

SEALED TUBE STUB

EVAPORATOR PRESSURE GAUGE PORT

HEX HEAD SCREWS

CAP

EVAPORATOR MANIFOLD PLATE

EXPANSION VALVE

SUCTION THROTTLING VALVE (STV)

STV MANIFOLD HOUSING

'O' RING SEALS (3)

LIQUID LINE CONNECTION

'O' RING

VALVE BODY

SCHRADER VALVE CORE

CAP

ALLEN HEAD SCREWS

SUCTION LINE CONNECTION

(b)

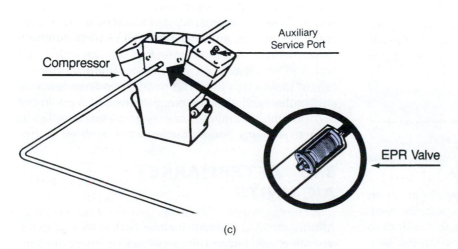

Compressor

Auxiliary Service Port

EPR Valve

(c)

FIGURE 8-76 Some STVs are connected into the suction line *(a)*, some are combined with the TXV*(b)*, and some are mounted in the compressor inlet *(c)*. (b *courtesy of ACDelco*; c *Courtesy of Everco Industries*)

These valves have gone by different names, depending on manufacturer and year. Major models are as follows:

- Robotrol: Early 1960s; aftermarket
- Selectrol: Early 1960s; aftermarket
- EPR: Chrysler Corporation, 1961 to 1979; mounted in compressor inlet
- EPRV: Toyota and Lexus; mounted in suction line of ATC systems
- ETR: Chrysler Corporation; mounted in compressor inlet
- POA: GM, 1965 to 1975; mounted at the evaporator outlet
- POA (capsule form): GM, 1973 to 1978 (Audi and Volvo); mounted in the VIR
- STV (early types): GM, 1962 to 1966; mounted at evaporator outlet; allows driver control of temperature through mechanical cable or vacuum control
- STV (modern types): Ford Motor Company, 1972 to 1979; mounted at evaporator outlet or suction line
- STV (capsule): Ford Motor Company, 1976 to 1981; combined with TXV in a unit called the combination valve

EPR, POA, and other STVs contain an internal bellows that expands or contracts in response to evaporator pressure. When pressure begins to drop, the expansion of the bellows closes the passageway to trap the pressure upstream in the evaporator (Figure 8-77). Downstream pressure in the suction line will be quite low, and frost and ice will often form on the suction line of a properly operating system.

◄ PROBLEM SOLVING 8-4 ►

> You have been driving your friend's 1976 Oldsmobile at freeway speeds for about an hour, and the day is hot so you have had the A/C on. You stop for gasoline. When you open the hood to check the oil, you notice that the A/C suction hose is covered with frost, from the compressor inlet to a valve at the rear of the engine compartment. Is this a good sign or something to be concerned about?

Some STVs use a diaphragm for pressure to act on instead of a bellows. The evaporator temperature regulator (ETR) valve uses an internal electric solenoid to open or close the valve; its operation is controlled by a thermal switch at the evaporator.

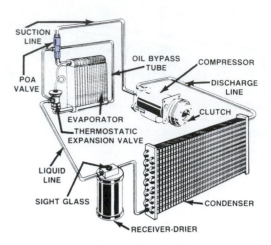

FIGURE 8-77 The POA valve in this system closes when evaporator pressure begins to drop too low. Evaporator temperature is kept just above icing. *(Courtesy of Everco Industries)*

8.9 REAR A/C SYSTEMS

Some larger vehicles (vans and small buses) have dual heat and A/C assemblies, with the rear unit mounted in a rear side panel or in the roof. The rear A/C unit consists of an evaporator and TXV that operates in parallel flow with the front unit (Figure 8-78). Tee fittings are placed in the liquid and suction lines so that refrigerant can flow through both units, with the flow through the rear unit dependent on the cooling load. Many dual systems use an OT to control the refrigerant flow into the front evaporator and a TXV with the rear evaporator. The rear evaporator is normally mounted in an assembly that includes a blower, heater core, and doors to control the air temperature and where the air returns to the passenger compartment.

The rear TXV shuts off the flow through the rear evaporator when the rear system is shut off, but a potential problem is created. A TXV does not ensure a complete shutoff, and refrigerant can leak through the valve. Because the blower is shut off, the evaporator will chill, and liquid refrigerant can puddle in this portion of the suction line. The puddle can flow down the suction line and slug the compressor causing a knock and possible damage. Some systems use a solenoid valve to stop any flow through the rear system.

8.10 AFTERMARKET A/C UNITS

Aftermarket A/C units are installed in a vehicle after it is assembled and leaves the assembly line. These units are designed for cars, trucks, vans, recreational vehicles

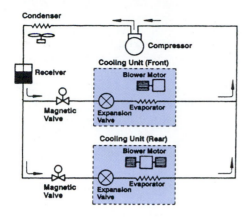

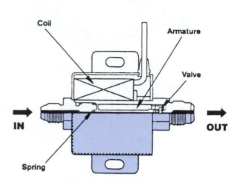

FIGURE 8-78   This dual A/C system uses a TXV at both the front and rear cooling units. A magnetic valve is used to positively shut off the flow to either unit. Note how the liquid and suction lines split to the two units. *(Courtesy of Toyota Motor Sales USA, Inc.)*

(a)

(b)

(c)

(d)

FIGURE 8-79   Aftermarket A/C systems are available that fit the evaporator under the dash of cars and pickups *(a)*, under the seats *(b)*, in the side panels *(c)*, or in the roofs of vans *(d)*. *(Courtesy of Acme Radiator & Air Conditioning)*

(RVs) and motor homes, ambulances, and tractors and farm equipment. Some units are packages with the entire system, including all of the A/C parts. Many units for vans, RVs, and ambulances include just the evaporator, blower, and air ducts to supplement the A/C unit already in the vehicle. Some of these include a supplementary heater (Figure 8-79).

The evaporator in some aftermarket units is in an assembly that includes a blower, air registers, and con-

trols. This unit is mounted under the dash and is often called a **hang-on** unit. The evaporator unit for van conversions mounts in the rear, with air discharge registers running forward or overhead. On some units, the evaporator case is incorporated into the factory heater system and uses the original blower and controls.

The evaporator case for trucks and farm equipment is often a **roof pack,** located in the vehicle's roof. The evaporator and its blower are positioned to

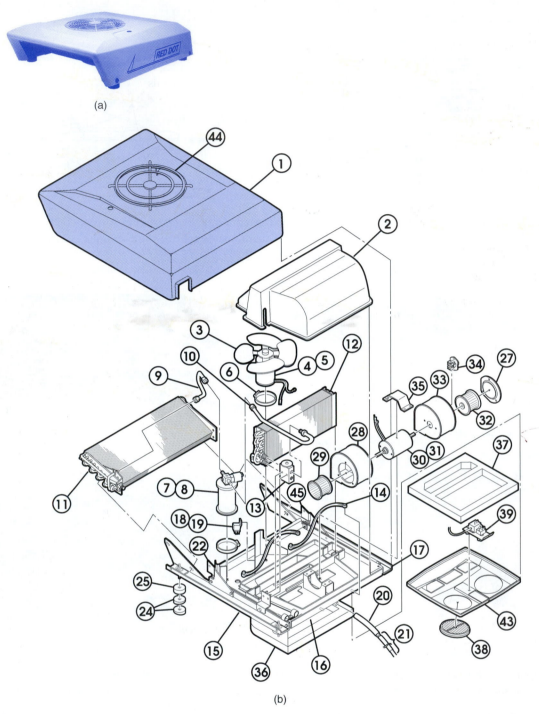

(a)

(b)

FIGURE 8-80   Rooftop A/C units that contain most of the A/C system are used in trucks, tractors, and various other vehicles. Assembled *(a)* and exploded *(b)* are shown. *(Courtesy of Red Dot Corporation)*

circulate air through the roof, and the condenser and its fans are located outside (Figure 8-80). The compressor is mounted on the engine in a normal manner and connected to the roof unit by long suction and discharge lines.

Complete units include a compressor with a mounting kit that includes mounts and drive pulleys, hoses, receiver–driers, and all other necessary parts. Supplementary units use tee fittings to connect into the existing liquid and suction lines.

443 570 2859

REVIEW QUESTIONS

The following questions are provided to help you study as you read the chapter.

1. A swash-plate compressor uses _dual piston Recip_ pistons, and a wobble-plate compressor uses _single live_ pistons.

2. _Suction Stroke_ moves the refrigerant through the suction reed as the piston moves _Down_, and piston pressure moves the refrigerant through the _dis reed_ during the upward stroke.

3. The wobble plate will move to a low-angle position when the _cooly load_ gets _low_.

4. For pumping members, a scroll compressor uses a(n) _Fixed Scroll_ and a(n) _movable scroll_ that travels in a small orbit.

5. Vane and scroll compressors are more _compact_, which makes them more suitable for modern vehicles with tight engine compartments.

6. The three major parts of a compressor clutch are the _clutch coil_, _hub_, and _Rotor_.

7. A simple way for the manufacturer to increase the strength of a clutch is to make slots called _Flux poles_ in the amature disc.

8. Oil is transported by the refrigerant because it is _Soluble_ with the refrigerant.

9. _Min_ oil is used with R-12, and _Pab_ or _ESoo_ is used with R-134a.

10. Refrigerant oils are _Hydro_ so the oil container should be kept _closed_ except when removing oil.

11. Most RWD vehicle condensers use _Ram Air_ flow to move air through the condenser.

12. A TXV is opened by _pressure_ on the _Recfrg_ coming from a warm _sence bulb_.

13. An OT is mounted at the _line ulet_ or in the _liquid line_ close to the condenser outlet.

14. A(n) _plate_-_Type_ evaporator is made from a series of stamped aluminum plates.

15. A TXV system will have a(n) _Rec_-_Drier_ mounted in the liquid line, and an OT system will use a(n) _Accum_ mounted in the suction line.

16. A(n) _spring lock_ fitting has the most potential for leaks, and a(n) _Flare fitting_ is the most difficult type to repair if leaking.

17. The hose type with an impervious inner layer is called a(n) _Barrier Hose_.

18. The minimum temperature of an evaporator is controlled by _cycling_ the _compress_ off and on, by _____ the _____ compressor, or by _stoppin_ the flow back to the compressor with a _S T V_.

CHAPTER QUIZ

The following questions will help you check the facts you have learned. Select the answer that completes each statement correctly.

1. In a reciprocating piston compressor, the pistons are driven by a _____. P 106
   a. crankshaft   c. wobble plate
   b. swash plate   d. All of these

2. Most York compressors use cylinders made from _____. P 110
   A. cast iron   B. aluminum

   Which is correct?
   a. A only   c. Both A and B
   b. B only   d. Neither A nor B

3. The reciprocating piston compressor used on many older General Motors vehicles is designated by which of the following? P 112
   a. R-6   c. DA-6
   b. D-6   d. A-6

4. Two technicians are discussing variable displacement piston compressors. Technician A says that the wobble plate is moved to the high-angle position for maximum output when the cooling load is high. Technician B says that the wobble plate angle is controlled by the pressure in the crankcase. Who is correct?
   a. Technician A   c. Both A and B
   b. Technician B   d. Neither A nor B

5. The General Motors variable displacement compressor has _____ cylinders.   114-116
   a. 4 or 6   c. 6
   b. 5 or 7   d. 8

6. Which of the following is an advantage offered by a scroll-type compressor?
   a. Smooth engagement
   b. Low engagement torque
   c. Ability to use a small clutch
   d. All of these

7. A _____ is used to seal the opening for the compressor driveshaft.

   A. carbon seal cartridge   **B.** lip seal

   Which is correct?

   a. A only   **c.** Both A and B
   b. B only   **d.** Neither A nor B

8. Two technicians are discussing refrigerant oils. Technician A says that the mineral oil used in R-12 systems is completely compatible with R-134a. Technician B says a synthetic oil should be used with R-134a. Who is correct?

   a. Technician A   **c.** Both A and B
   b. Technician B   **d.** Neither A nor B

9. Two technicians are discussing TXVs. Technician A says that the TXV senses evaporator temperature to control the valve opening. Technician B says that the TXV senses evaporator pressure to control the valve opening. Who is correct?

   a. Technician A   **c.** Both A and B
   b. Technician B   **d.** Neither A nor B

10. Two technicians are discussing A/C systems. Technician A says that the TXV systems always use a receiver–drier mounted in the suction line. Technician B says that the OT systems always use an accumulator in the suction line. Who is correct?

   a. Technician A   **c.** Both A and B
   b. Technician B   **d.** Neither A nor B

11. The fitting found on an accumulator is for which of the following?

   a. High side service   **c.** Flushing
   b. Leak detection   **d.** Low side service

12. A filter can be installed in the liquid line for which of the following?

   a. When the system is contaminated
   b. When extra moisture removal is needed
   c. Instead of flushing the evaporator
   d. All of these

13. The pressure cycling switch does which of the following?

   a. Closes the TXV
   b. Senses condenser temperature
   c. Senses high side pressure
   d. Senses low side pressure

14. Two technicians are discussing line fittings. Technician A says that many early A/C systems used flare fittings. Technician B says that modern systems commonly use O-rings to seal the fittings, and these are much easier to repair than flare fittings. Who is correct?

   a. Technician A   **c.** Both A and B
   b. Technician B   **d.** Neither A nor B

15. The hose that connects the compressor to the evaporator is commonly called the _____.

   a. discharge line   **c.** suction line
   b. liquid line   **d.** cold gas line

Chapter 9

HEATING SYSTEMS

LEARNING OBJECTIVES

After completing this chapter, you should:

1. Understand how the common automotive heating system works.
2. Know what parts make up the heating system.
3. Understand how heater temperature is controlled.

TERMS TO LEARN

Bowden cable	outlet hose
cellular	quick-connect coupling
control valve	thermal cycling
heater core	three-way design
hoses	thermostat
inlet hose	vacuum motor

9.1 INTRODUCTION

As previously mentioned, the heating system resembles a small version of the engine's cooling system. Some people consider the heater the most efficient part of the vehicle because it uses waste heat to warm the interior (Figure 9-1). The heating system is made up of the **heater core, hoses,** and, in some systems, a **control valve.**

It should be noted that Federal Motor Vehicle Safety Standard (FMVSS) 103 requires that every vehicle sold in the United States must be able to defrost or defog certain areas of the windshield in a specified amount of time. It also requires that this system must remain operable. The defrost/defog system in most vehicles uses the heater and diverts the airflow to the base of the windshield.

9.2 OPERATION

The **inlet hose** to the heater core connects to an outlet near the engine thermostat, or an area of the engine with the hottest coolant. The **outlet hose** from the heater core runs to a connection near the inlet of the engine's water pump, the area with the lowest coolant pressure. When the engine runs, coolant flows through the engine's water jackets and heater core. The heated coolant warms the heater core and the air passing through it (Figure 9-2). A **three-way-design thermostat** is used in a few engines to shut off coolant flow to the heater core when the engine gets very hot (see Chapter 17).

Some vehicles have a valve in the heater inlet hose that allows coolant flow to be shut off and keeps the core from heating up. Some vehicles use a heater valve to control the heat of the core and therefore the temperature of the air entering the passenger compartment (Figure 9-3). Most newer cars do not use a control valve, so the core is always the same temperature as the coolant. With these systems, the temperature of the air to the passenger compartment is controlled by an air temperature-blend door in the heater plenum. The operation of this door is described in Chapter 10.

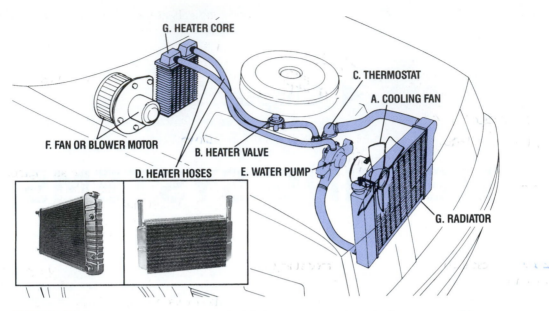

FIGURE 9-1 The main parts of a vehicle's heating system are the heater core, blower, heater hoses, and, in some cases, heater valve. *(Courtesy of Everco Industries)*

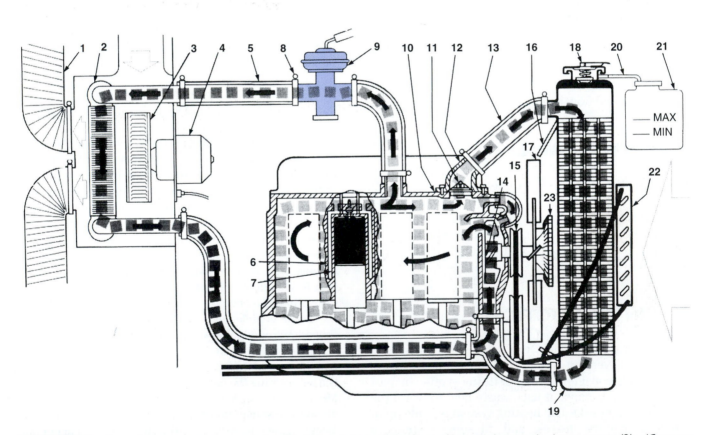

FIGURE 9-2 Some heater systems use a valve (9) that can shut off the flow of hot coolant to the heater core (2). *(Courtesy of Stant Manufacturing)*

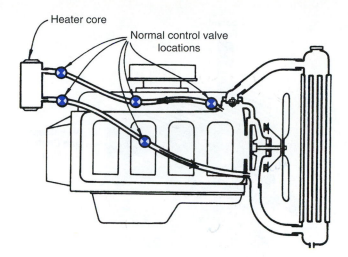

FIGURE 9-3 A heater control valve can be located at any of the locations shown.

9.2.1 Engine-Off Heater Operation

Some vehicles have a feature that allows the heater to keep operating when the engine is turned off. In cold climates, this keeps the vehicle warm while the operator is performing errands. The main component is an electric pump along with a bypass valve (Figure 9-4).

When the heater is on and engine is off, the bypass valve closes, and the pump operates to maintain a hot coolant flow through the heater core. When the heater is on with the engine running, the pump is shut off and the bypass valve is open to allow normal heater operation.

9.2.2 Electric and Hybrid Vehicle Heating Systems

Electric vehicles do not have an engine, and hybrid vehicles use an engine that does not run long enough to produce enough heat in the coolant for a heater. Some ultra-low emission vehicles do not produce enough waste heat to supply a heater. The Toyota Prius hybrid has two PTC (positive temperature coefficient) heater elements built into the heater core (Figure 9-5).

Electric vehicles that use a heat pump for A/C include a valve that switches the flow between the condenser and evaporator. This switches heat transfer from the condenser to the evaporator (see Figure 7-30). This is similar to what happens when a heat pump used in a home is asked to heat the residence. Some electric and hybrid vehicles supplement the heater with an electrical resistance heater. This greatly increased electrical draw from the batteries reduces the operating range significantly.

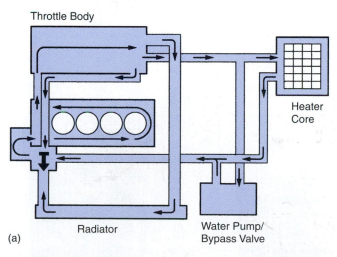

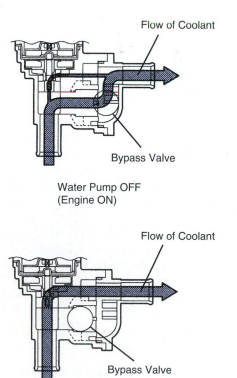

FIGURE 9-4 This hybrid vehicle has a pump/bypass that can pump hot coolant through the heater core (b, bottom) when the engine is shut off. During engine operation, the bypass valve (b, top) allows normal circulation. (Courtesy of Toyota Motor Sales USA, Inc.)

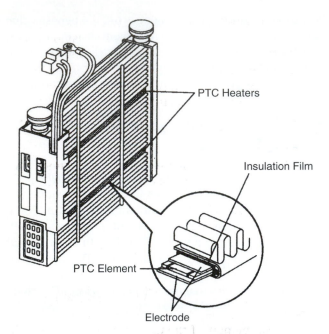

FIGURE 9-5   The two PTC, positive temperature coefficient, heater elements help warm up the heater core of this hybrid vehicle. *(Courtesy of Toyota Motor Sales USA, Inc.)*

9.3   HEATER CORE

The heater core is a heat exchanger much like the condenser, evaporator, and radiator. Heat transfers from the coolant, to the fins, and to the air passing through the core. As with other heat exchangers, there is a large area of fin-to-air contact to allow sufficient heat transfer and airflow (Figure 9-6).

Most heater cores use a **cellular** form of construction that is somewhat like a plate-type evaporator. The tubes are made by joining two corrugated brass or aluminum plates, and the corrugated fins are attached between pairs of tubes. In most cores, the tanks at the ends of the core serve as manifolds to direct the flow back and forth through the core.

A core is usually designed to fit a particular car model. The critical dimensions needed to ensure correct replacement are the depth, height, and width of the core and the diameters and shapes of the inlet and outlet tubes (Figures 9-7 and 9-8).

9.4   HOSES

Most heater hoses are made of reinforced rubber, which allows the flexibility needed to connect to a movable engine (Figure 9-9). Common hose sizes are 1/2, 5/8, and 3/4 inch (12.7, 15.8, and 19 mm). Some systems connect the hose to a metal tube that can be connected to the engine using either a threaded connector or a short hose section.

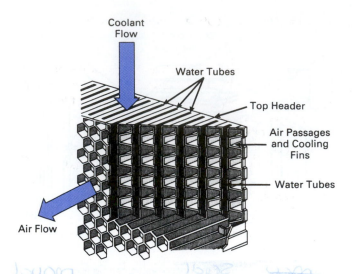

FIGURE 9-6   Heat is transferred from the hot coolant flowing through the water tubes to warm the air flowing through the fins of the core.

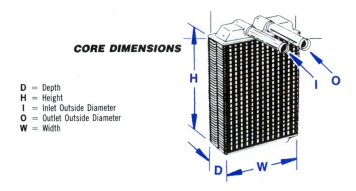

CORE DIMENSIONS

D = Depth
H = Height
I = Inlet Outside Diameter
O = Outlet Outside Diameter
W = Width

FIGURE 9-7   The critical dimensions needed when replacing a heater core. *(Courtesy of Four Seasons)*

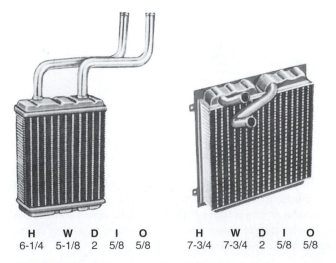

H	W	D	I	O		H	W	D	I	O
6-1/4	5-1/8	2	5/8	5/8		7-3/4	7-3/4	2	5/8	5/8

FIGURE 9-8   Two examples of the many shapes and sizes of heater cores. *(Courtesy of Four Seasons)*

This allows easier routing through congested or very hot areas around the engine that might cause hose failures.

Many systems use a smaller hose diameter for the heater inlet than for the outlet. This allows an easier exit of the coolant and reduces the pressure inside the core, which in turn reduces the possibility of leaks.

A hose is usually clamped to the connector using one of several styles of clamps. The screw-type or Whittek-type clamp is considered by many to be the most reliable and the easiest to install and remove. Some clamp styles tend to cut the hose or do not provide even clamping pressure all the way around the hose. The clamp should always be positioned so it is right next to the raised area of the connection. This

gives the most effective holding power and reduces one area where corrosion can form. Another clamping problem is caused by **thermal cycling** that causes the hose, fitting, and clamp to expand and contract each time the engine heats and cools. Spring-type clamps provide automatic retensioning. The hose tends to seize onto the connector so the technician needs to be careful when disconnecting a heater hose to prevent damaging the rather fragile heater core or its connectors.

Some newer vehicles use a **quick-connect coupling** at the hose-to-heater-core connections. Care and a suitable tool are required to disconnect these couplings to prevent damage to the very expensive hose assemblies (Figure 9-10).

9.4.1 Restrictors

Some systems include a restrictor to slow the coolant velocity as it passes through the heater core. The restrictor can be part of the manifold fitting or the inlet heater hose assembly. The major purpose of the restrictor is to slow the flow rate in order to reduce internal heater core erosion.

9.5 CONTROL VALVES

Most heater control valves are on–off valves and are used to make the core either hot or cold. Some valves are designed to modulate and adjust the flow so the core temperature can be controlled to all points between hot and cold. Some valves allow a return flow, so the coolant still circulates, bypassing the core when the valve is shut off.

The control for most valves is through a **vacuum diaphragm** or **motor.** These systems use a vacuum

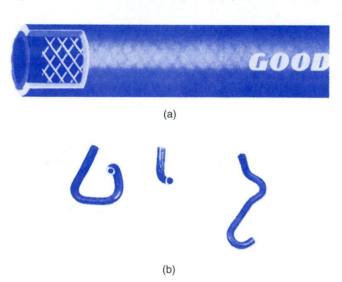

(a)

(b)

FIGURE 9-9 Heater hose uses reinforced rubber construction *(a)* and is available in straight or molded *(b)* shapes. *(Courtesy of Goodyear Tire & Rubber Company)*

FIGURE 9-10 Some vehicles use quick-connect couplings for the heater hose connections. The hose is merely slid firmly onto the connector to make the connection. It should be disconnected carefully using a suitable tool. *(Courtesy of Four Seasons)*

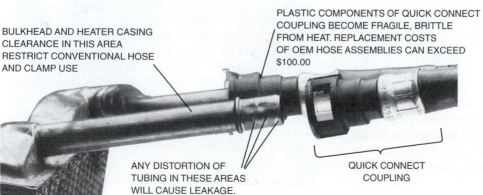

SPECIAL COUPLING TOOL

BULKHEAD AND HEATER CASING CLEARANCE IN THIS AREA RESTRICT CONVENTIONAL HOSE AND CLAMP USE

PLASTIC COMPONENTS OF QUICK CONNECT COUPLING BECOME FRAGILE, BRITTLE FROM HEAT. REPLACEMENT COSTS OF OEM HOSE ASSEMBLIES CAN EXCEED $100.00

ANY DISTORTION OF TUBING IN THESE AREAS WILL CAUSE LEAKAGE.

QUICK CONNECT COUPLING

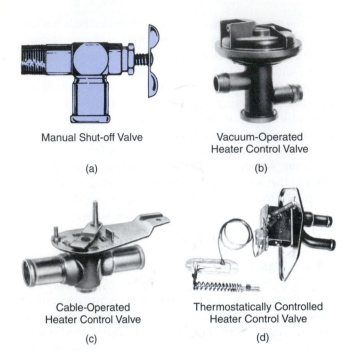

Manual Shut-off Valve   (a)

Vacuum-Operated Heater Control Valve   (b)

Cable-Operated Heater Control Valve   (c)

Thermostatically Controlled Heater Control Valve   (d)

FIGURE 9-11 A heater control valve can be operated manually *(a)*, by vacuum control *(b)*, through a mechanical cable *(c)*, or by a thermostatic element *(d)*. *(a courtesy of Four Seasons; b, c, and d are courtesy of Stant Manufacturing)*

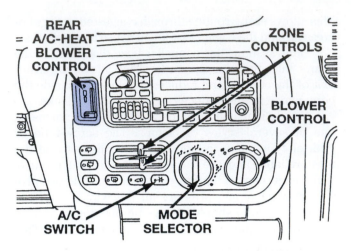

FIGURE 9-12 The control panels for a vehicle with front and rear climate control systems. *(Courtesy of Daimler-Chrysler Corporation)*

signal from the HVAC control head to close the valve and shut off the heater. This feature, using a normally open valve, allows heater and defroster operation if the valve or vacuum control system fails. Some valves are operated mechanically through a **Bowden cable,** a steel wire that slides through a housing. Bowden cables are commonly used for hood release mechanisms and in the past were used for carburetor choke control. A few older cars use manual control valves, which require someone to turn the valve stem to open or close the valve (Figure 9-11).

9.6   DUAL HEATING SYSTEMS

Many vehicles with rear A/C systems include a heater in the rear unit. These rear units include a heater core and temperature-blend door (Figure 9-12). The heater hoses include a tee fitting in each hose so heated coolant can flow through either or both heater cores. Some manufacturers include a water valve in the rear heater core so that hot coolant can be kept out of the core during A/C operation to improve A/C efficiency. The heater operation on these units is the same as that for a front unit.

9.7   AFTERMARKET HEATING SYSTEMS

Before heaters became standard equipment, aftermarket heating systems were installed in many cars. Today, these units are primarily designed for RVs, vans, and motor homes. They are normally installed after the vehicle has been built, by shops that specialize in heating and A/C service or RV van conversion and repair (Figure 9-13).

The units are basically a heater core in a case with a blower. After locating and mounting the case, the heater hoses are connected to the engine connectors or to tee fittings installed in the existing heater hoses. The blower switch is mounted at a convenient location and the power supply is connected to a source of B+ (battery positive). In some units, the heater is combined with an A/C unit, as described in Section 8.9.

◄   **PROBLEM SOLVING 9–1**   ►

You are riding with a friend on a cold winter day, and you notice that the air coming from the heater is only slightly warm. You mention this to him, and he tells you that it takes a long time for the heater output to become hot. What do you think might be wrong? What checks can you make to confirm your suspicions?

Imagine that the heater output stays cold and does not warm up at all. What do you think could cause this problem? What checks would you make to confirm your suspicions?

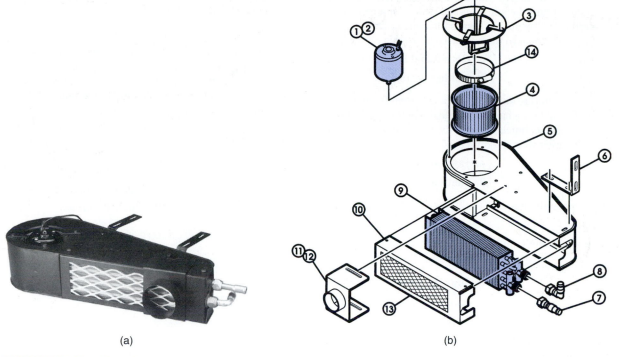

(a)   (b)

FIGURE 9-13   This aftermarket heater assembly *(a)* contains a heater core (9) and blower (1–4). An exploded view is shown in *(b)*. *(Courtesy of Ted Dot)*

REVIEW QUESTIONS

The following questions are provided to help you study as you read the chapter.

1. The heater core inlet hose connects to the engine close to the ___*therme*___, and the outlet hose is connected close to the water pump ___*inlet*___.

2. The heat from a vehicle's heater comes from the engine ___*coolant*___.

3. A(n) ___*plate type*___ *Cellular* heater core is made from a set of stamped metal plates.

4. Critical dimensions of a heater core include the ___*heighi*___, ___*width*___, and ___*depth*___ of the core plus the ___*diam*___ and ___*shape*___ of the tubes.

5. A hose clamp of good design will not ___*damage*___ the hose, clamp completely ___*around*___ the hose, and compensate for ___*cdius*___ and ___*tension*___.

6. Some modern heater hoses use ___*quick-connect*___ couplings at the heater core.

7. Temperature of the air leaving the heater ducts is controlled by a(n) ___*valve*___ that regulates the coolant flow through the core or by a(n) ___*temp-blend*___ door.

8. Some vans will use ___*after market*___ systems to help warm up the rear compartment.

CHAPTER QUIZ

The following questions will help you check the facts you have learned. Select the answer that completes each statement correctly.

1. Two technicians are discussing the coolant flow through a heater core. Technician A says that heated coolant en-

ters the heater inlet hose close to the engine thermostat. Technician B says the coolant from the heater core returns to the water pump outlet. Who is correct?

   a. A only   **c.** Both A and B

   b. B only   **d.** Neither A nor B

2. Two technicians are discussing the heater core. Technician A says that a heater core is a heat exchanger much like a radiator. Technician B says the coolant from the engine brings the heat to the heater core. Who is correct?

   a. A only   **c.** Both A and B

   b. B only   **d.** Neither A nor B

3. Two technicians are discussing heater hoses. Technician A says that most hoses have an inside diameter of about one inch or larger. Technician B says the heater core inlet hose is usually larger than the outlet. Who is correct?

   a. A only   **c.** Both A and B

   b. B only   **d.** Neither A nor B

4. Heater hoses are attached to the core using _____.

   A. clamps

   B. quick-connect couplings

   Which is correct?

   a. A only   **c.** Both A and B

   b. B only   **d.** Neither A nor B

5. Two technicians are discussing the heater output temperature. Technician A says that a valve is used to reduce coolant flow through the core when less heat is desired. Technician B says that most modern systems use a blend air door to control the coolant flow. Who is correct?

   a. A only   **c.** Both A and B

   b. B only   **d.** Neither A nor B

6. The control for most heater control valves is either a Bowden cable or mechanical.

   a. True   **b.** False

7. Two technicians are discussing heater temperature control. Technician A says that a control valve will be wide open when full heat is desired. Technician B says the coolant control valve should go wide open if the vacuum line is disconnected. Who is correct?

   a. A only   **c.** Both A and B

   b. B only   **d.** Neither A nor B

8. An aftermarket heater system consists of _____.

   a. a core   **c.** control switches

   b. a blower   **d.** All of these

Chapter 10

AIR MANAGEMENT SYSTEM

LEARNING OBJECTIVES

After completing this chapter, you should:

1. Understand the function of the air control doors in the A/C and heating duct system.
2. Understand how the temperature of the air entering the car is controlled.
3. Be familiar with the methods used to control the blower speed.
4. Be familiar with manual, semiautomatic temperature control (SATC) and automatic temperature control (ATC) systems.
5. Be familiar with the sensors and controls used with ATC and SATC systems and their function in controlling air temperature and flow.

TERMS TO LEARN

air distribution	ducts
air doors	dual-zone
air inlet	flap doors (flap valves)
air management system	HVAC air filter
ambient sensor	in-car sensor
aspirator	manual system
automatic temperature control system (ATC)	mode door
	multiposition switch
bleeds	plenum
blower motor	potentiometer
cabin air filter	pressure transducer
pulse width modulation (PWM)	semiautomatic temperature control system (SATC)
ram air pressure	sensor
recirculation	sliding mode door
resistor	temperature-blend door
restrictor	thermistor
rotary door	vacuum actuator

10.1 INTRODUCTION

A system that contains the HVAC plenum, ducts, and **air doors,** called the air management system or *air distribution system*, controls the airflow to the passenger compartment. Air flows into the case that contains the evaporator and heater core from two possible inlets. From the case, the air can travel to one or more of three possible outlets. Proper temperature control to enhance passenger comfort during heating should maintain an air temperature in the footwell about 7 to 14°F (4 to 8°C) above that around the upper body. This is accomplished by directing the heated airflow to the floor. During A/C operation, the upper body should be cooler, so the airflow is directed to the instrument panel registers. Airflow is usually controlled by three or more doors, which are called **flap doors** or **valves** by some manufacturers (Figure 10-1).

A multispeed blower is included in this system to force air through the ductwork when the vehicle is moving at low speeds or to increase the airflow at any speed. At freeway speeds, most systems have a natural airflow from **ram air pressure.** This is the pressure generated at the base of the windshield by the speed of the vehicle. This airflow is improved in some vehicles by exhaust registers placed in low-pressure areas toward the rear of the vehicle (Figure 10-2).

The HVAC control head or panel is mounted in the instrument cluster. The control system provides the

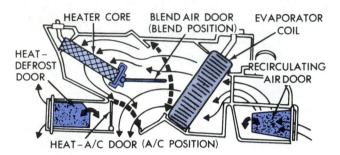

FIGURE 10-1   A heater and A/C system includes an evaporator, a heater core, a blower motor, and a series of doors to control airflow. *(Courtesy of DaimlerChrysler Corporation)*

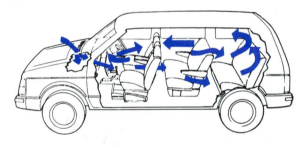

FIGURE 10-2   Fresh air enters through the grill below the front of the windshield; it becomes a high-pressure area when the car is moving forward. *(Courtesy of Daimler-Chrysler Corporation)*

switches and levers needed to control the different aspects of the heating and A/C system, which include

- System on and off
- Fresh or recirculated air
- A/C, defrost, or heating function
- Temperature desired
- Blower speed

The control head is connected to various parts through electrical connections, vacuum connections, mechanical Bowden cables, or a combination of these (Figure 10-3).

In vehicles using a **manual system,** the driver moves the temperature lever or dial to change the temperature setting, selects the air inlet and discharge locations, selects the blower speed, and turns the A/C compressor on or off. With a **semiautomatic temperature control system (SATC),** the driver selects the desired temperature using buttons or a dial; in some systems, the automatic controls adjust the temperature door and blower speed while the driver selects the air inlet and discharge locations. Different SATC systems allow different types of control for the driver to override certain automatic functions. With an **automatic temperature control system (ATC),** the driver can turn the automatic controls on or off and select the desired temperature. The ATC will adjust the blower speed, temperature door, air inlet door, and mode door to achieve the proper temperature.

A vehicle with an ATC system uses many of the same parts as a manual system. Automatic features include two or more temperature sensors, an electronic control module (ECM), and either a group of switches and relays or vacuum valves to control the vacuum or electric motors that operate the air control doors.

FIGURE 10-3   Most HVAC control heads include a control for turning things on and setting the mode of operation, a control for adjusting the temperature, and a control for the fan speed.

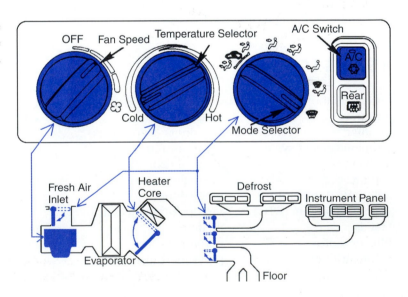

In this text, vehicles equipped with both heaters and A/C are described. A vehicle with a heater only is essentially the same in all respects except for not having an evaporator and the rest of the A/C components and the upper-level air discharge registers in the instrument panel.

10.1.1   Controlling Airflow

The amount or volume of HVAC air is controlled by blower speed. Higher speeds move more air. The inlet and outlet directions of the airflow and the discharge air temperature are controlled by swinging, sliding, or rotating valves. Most systems use a flap door that swings about 45 to 90 degrees (Figure 10-4). Swinging doors are very simple and require very little maintenance. Most flap doors are set to one end or the other of their travel. A temperature blend door is positioned at any place between the stops, wherever needed to produce the proper air temperature.

The space under the instrument panel is very congested, and some vehicles have developed a smaller HVAC case in order to allow more room. Reducing the HVAC assembly size usually reduces the weight, and this is also desirable. One of the more compact designs uses

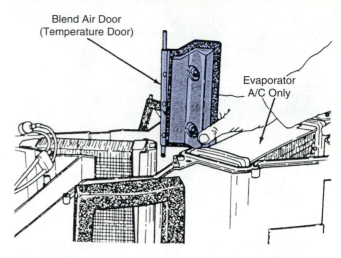

FIGURE 10-4   Many air control doors swing on their upper and lower pivots. *(Courtesy of DaimlerChrysler Corporation)*

a **sliding mode door** (Figure 10-5). This is also called a rolling door. Some of these door designs roll up, somewhat like a window shade, and unroll to block a passage.

Another design uses a **rotary door.** This pan-shaped door has openings at the side and edge, and

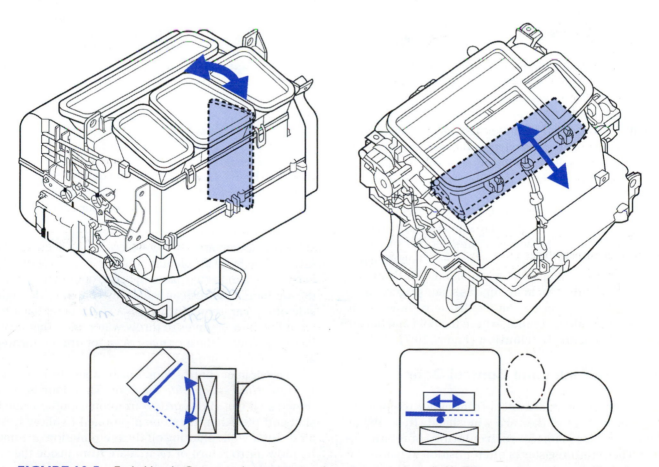

FIGURE 10-5   Early Honda Civics used a conventional temperature door (left). This was changed to a rolling design in the 2001 Civic. *(Courtesy of American Honda Motor Co., Inc.)*

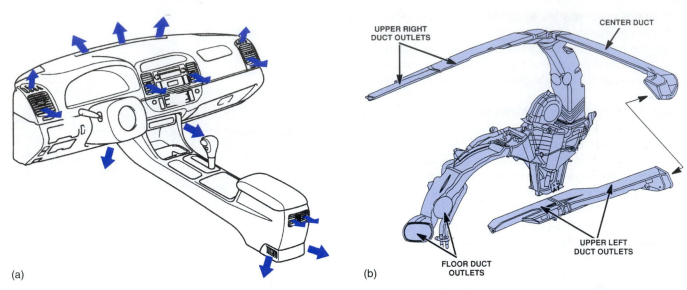

(a)   (b)

FIGURE 10-6   Many systems include ducts to move heated or cooled air to the rear seat area *(a)*. A rear system in a van can have ducts to move air forward *(b)*. *(a Courtesy of Toyota Motor Sales USA, Inc.; b Courtesy of DaimlerChrysler Corporation)*

the door rotates about 100 degrees to one of four different positions. Each position directs airflow to the desired outlet(s).

10.2   CASES AND DUCTS

The evaporator and heater plenum is molded from reinforced plastic or stamped sheet metal and contains the evaporator, heater core, and most of the air control doors. Sometimes the evaporator is in a case separate from the heater core, and these cases are connected by a duct. The plenum is connected to the air inlets and outlets using formed plastic or sheet-metal **ducts.** These often use portions of the body bulkhead and instrument panel sheet metal for mounting points, as well as parts of the ducts. Some cars use round, wire-reinforced, flexible ducts. These parts are required to contain and direct airflow, be quiet, keep outside water and debris from entering, and isolate engine fumes and noises. Their design is complicated by the limited space allotted to them and competition with other items for this space (Figure 10-6).

The duct system can be divided into three major sections: **air inlet, plenum,** where the cold and hot air are mixed, and **air distribution** (Figure 10-7).

10.2.1   Air Inlet and Control Door

Air can enter the duct system from either the plenum chamber in front of the car's windshield (fresh air) or from the **recirc** (short for **recirculation**) or return register. The return register is often positioned below the right end of the instrument panel. (The right and left

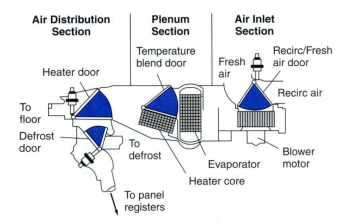

FIGURE 10-7   The three major portions of the A/C and heat system are air inlet, plenum, and air distribution. The shaded portions show the paths of the four control doors.

sides of the car are always described as seen by the driver.) The fresh air plenum often includes a screen to keep leaves and other large debris from entering with the air. Incoming fresh air is usually routed to the right side of the car, then downward; a sharp bend back toward the blower serves to throw water and other heavier objects out of the airstream. A water drain is located at this point (Figure 10-8).

The air inlet control door is also called the *fresh air, recirculation,* or *outside* air door. This door is positioned so it can allow airflow from one source while it shuts off the other. It can be positioned to allow fresh air to enter while shutting off the recirculation opening; to allow air to return or recirculate from inside the vehicle while shutting off fresh air; or, in some vehicles, to

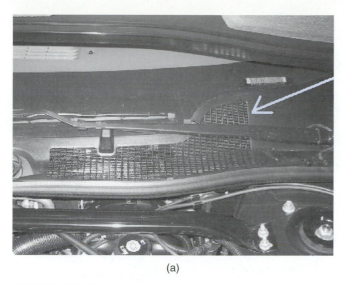

(a)

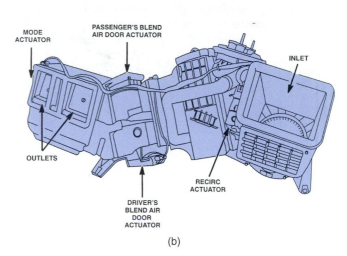

(b)

FIGURE 10-8 The fresh air inlet for most vehicles is at the base of the windshield *(a)*. On this car, it is under the hood *(arrow)*. Ductwork brings the fresh air to the HVAC case inlet *(b)*. (b *Courtesy of DaimlerChrysler Corporation*)

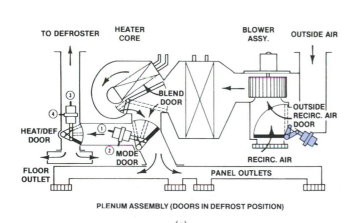

(a)

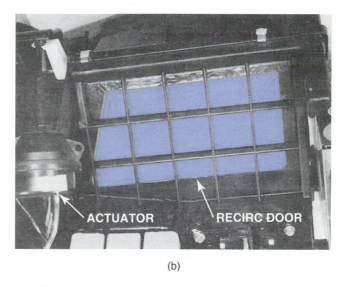

(b)

FIGURE 10-9 This outside-recirculation (air inlet) door is moved from one position to the other by a vacuum actuator (motor); here, it is in the fresh air position *(a)*. The actual unit is shown in *(b)*. *(Courtesy of DaimlerChrysler Corporation)*

allow a mix of fresh air and return air. In many modern vehicles, the door is set to the fresh air position in all function lever positions except off, max heat, and max A/C; max A/C and max heat positions the door to recirculate in-vehicle air (Figure 10-9).

10.2.1.1 Air Filtration Many modern systems include an **HVAC air filter** in the air distribution system. This filter, also called a **cabin,** *interior ventilation, micron, particulate,* or *pollen filter,* removes small dust or pollen particles from the incoming airstream (Figure 10-10). These filters require periodic replace-

ment; if they are not serviced properly, they will cause an airflow reduction when they become plugged.

There are two types of filter media: *particle filters* and *adsorption filters.* Particle filters remove solid particles like dust, soot, spores, and pollen using a special paper or nonwoven fleece material; these particles are about 3 micron or larger. Adsorption filters remove noxious gases and odors using an activated charcoal media with the charcoal layer between layers of filter media. These two filter types can be combined into a combination or two-stage filter. The filter media can have an electrostatic charge to make it more efficient.

FIGURE 10-10 This cabin/clean air filter can be removed through the glove compartment. Some filters have a charcoal center layer to remove odors. *(Courtesy of Toyota Motor Sales USA, Inc.)*

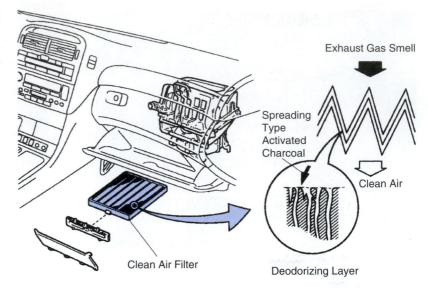

Exhaust Gas Smell

Spreading Type Activated Charcoal

Clean Air

Clean Air Filter

Deodorizing Layer

10.2.2 Plenum and Control Door

Most systems position the evaporator so all air must pass through it. This allows removal of moisture and dust particles by the evaporator's cold temperature. (Many systems operate the A/C when defrost is selected to dry the air.) The heater core is placed downstream so that air can be routed either through or around it; one or two doors are used to control this airflow. This door is called the **temperature-blend door;** some of its other names are *air mix door, temperature door, blend door, diverter door,* and *bypass door.*

The temperature-blend door is connected to the temperature lever at the control head using a mechanical Bowden cable; in some modern vehicles, the temperature-blend door position is adjusted through an electric servomotor. When the temperature lever is set to the coldest setting, the temperature-blend door routes all air so it bypasses the heater core; air entering the passenger compartment is at its coldest, coming straight from the evaporator. When the temperature lever is set to the hottest setting, the temperature-blend door routes all air through the heater core, and heated air goes to the passenger compartment. Setting the control lever to somewhere between cold and hot will mix or temper cold and hot air, allowing the driver to adjust the temperature to whatever is desired.

In the past in some vehicles, the evaporator was placed or stacked right next to the heater core. These systems controlled the air temperature by regulating the amount of reheat at the heater core. A few modern vehicles are using a stacked heater and evapora-tor and reheating the heater core to adjust outlet temperature. The dual-zone version uses a two-part heater core to allow temperature control of each zone (Figure 10-11).

10.2.3 Air Distribution, Control Doors, and Outlets

Air from the plenum can flow into one or two of three outlet paths: (1) the A/C registers in the face of the instrument panel, (2) the defroster registers at the base of the windshield, and (3) the heater outlets at the floor under the instrument panel. Some vehicles include ducts to transfer air to the rear seat area, and some vehicles include ducts to demist the vehicle's side windows with warm air.

Airflow to these ducts is controlled by one or more **mode doors** controlled by the function lever or buttons. Mode doors are also called *function, floor–defrost,* and *panel–defrost* doors. Mode/function control sets the doors as follows:

A/C: in-dash registers with fresh air inlet
Max A/C: in-dash registers with recirculation
Heat: floor level with fresh air inlet
Max Heat: floor level with recirculation
Bi-level: both in-dash and floor discharge
Defrost: windshield registers

Many control heads also provide for in-between settings, which combine these operations. In many systems, a small amount of air is directed to the defroster

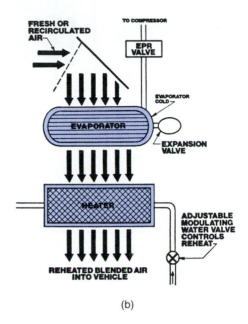

FIGURE 10-11   In a blend air system, all the air is cooled. Then some of it is reheated and blended with the cool air to get the right temperature *(a)*. In a reheat system, all of the air is cooled and then reheated to the correct temperature *(b)*. *(Courtesy of Everco Industries)*

ducts when in the heat mode, and while in defrost mode a small amount of air goes to the floor level.

10.2.4   Dual-Zone Air Distribution

Dual-zone air distribution allows the driver and passenger to select different temperature settings. The temperature choices can be as much as 30°F different. Dual-zone systems split the duct and airflow past the heater core and use two air mix valves or doors; each air mix valve is controlled by a separate actuator (Figure 10-12).

10.2.5   Horizontal-Split Airflow

One vehicle manufacturer has introduced a two-layer, split airflow system. This system allows fresh air to be sent through the case and to the defrosters while recirculated air is also brought through for heating. Fresh, outside air is drier during severely cold weather so there will be much less window fogging.

For heating purposes, recirculated air conserves heat that is inside the vehicle. The split airflow comes from a blower that has two fan chambers; one of them has a slightly larger fan wheel (Figure 10-13). Each fan inlet has a door that allows selection of fresh or recirculated air. The ductwork from the blower to the registers also has a divider.

10.3   CONTROL HEAD

Many types of control heads are used on today's vehicles. These control heads can vary greatly between manufacturers and even between vehicle models from a single manufacturer. All control heads do essentially the same thing, but they use different methods to do it.

Mechanical systems are the least expensive. Most early control heads used purely mechanical operation for the doors, and one or more Bowden cables connected the function lever to the air inlet and mode doors. The temperature lever was also connected to the temperature blend door by a Bowden cable. These

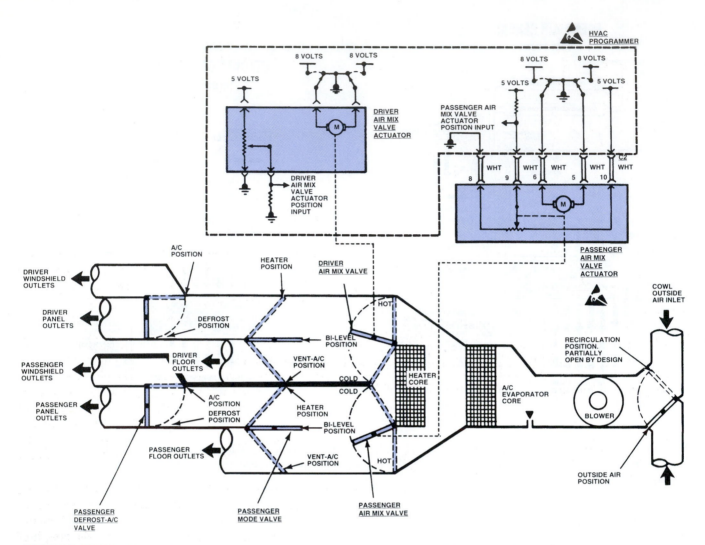

FIGURE 10-12 This dual-zone air distribution system has two temperature-blend–air mix doors and air distribution sections, one for the driver and one for the passenger. *(Reprinted with permission of General Motors Corporation)*

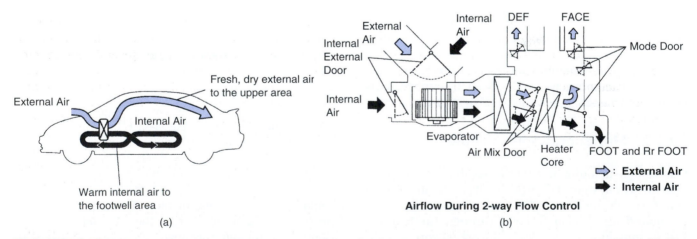

FIGURE 10-13 This split/two-way airflow system can deliver fresh air at face level and recirculated air at floor level *(a)*. The HVAC case and blower is divided as shown *(b)*. *(Courtesy of Toyota Motor Sales USA, Inc.)*

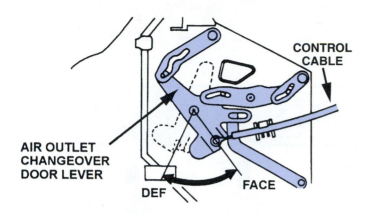

FIGURE 10-14 This unit uses mechanical cables to change the air door position. *(Courtesy of DaimlerChrysler Corporation)*

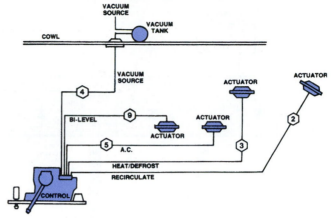

FIGURE 10-15 A typical vacuum control circuit starts at the vacuum source (engine), is controlled by a valve at the control head, and ends at the vacuum actuators or motors. *(Courtesy of Everco Industries)*

mechanical levers were rather simple and usually trouble free, but they had some disadvantages. They tended to bind and could require a good deal of effort to operate. A cable length adjustment was usually required to ensure complete door operation; modern systems can use automatic cable adjustments (Figure 10-14).

Many vehicles use **vacuum actuators,** sometimes called *vacuum motors,* to operate the air inlet and mode doors. These are controlled by a vacuum valve that is operated by the control head. Vacuum controls operate more easily than Bowden cables, and vacuum hoses are much easier to route through congested areas than cables. A Bowden cable is used for the temperature-blend door in most of these systems because of its ability to move the door to the exact position desired. When vacuum actuators operate, they alter the air–fuel mixture in the engine. Because vacuum controls affect engine operation and therefore emissions, modern vehicles are being designed to use electric control systems (Figure 10-15).

Some modern vehicles use electrical function switches at the HVAC control head. These are often called *electromechanical controls.* These switches operate a group of solenoid valves that control the vacuum flow to the vacuum motors at the doors. The vacuum actuators are the same as those just described, but the vacuum switches have been changed (Figure 10-16).

Many modern vehicles use electric motors to operate the air distribution and temperature-blend doors. The temperature lever at the HVAC control head for these systems is an electrical **potentiometer.** The potentiometer is a type of variable resistor; the electric motor responds to the electric signal by turning a portion of a revolution. This system is similar to a TV antenna direction motor (Figure 10-17). Proper control

motor position is determined using a feedback circuit or a control module that counts commutator bar movement. A feedback circuit is shown in Figure 10-37.

Blower speed control in many of these systems is through a multiposition electrical switch and a group of resistors or electronic controls. The position of the switch determines the amount of resistance in the blower circuit and therefore the speed of the motor (Figure 10-18). Electronically controlled systems use a **pulse width–modulated (PWM) blower motor,** which is described in Section 10.5. Blower speed is controlled by electronically switching the motor off and on, up to 40,000 times per second. Increasing the length of the on time produces higher speeds.

10.3.1 Vacuum Control Circuit

The vacuum control circuit begins at the engine, passes through small hoses, is controlled by one or more valves, and ends at one of several vacuum motors (actuators). The vacuum source is the intake manifold of the engine. Remember that a vacuum is really very low atmospheric pressure, and a vacuum is generated in the intake manifold of a gasoline engine operating with the throttle partially closed. Most systems use a one-way check valve and vacuum reservoir in the hose from the engine to maintain a supply of vacuum for operation during wide-open throttle conditions (Figure 10-19).

Early systems used rubber hose with a 3/16- or 1/4 inch (4.7- or 6.3-mm) ID. This material often became hard and brittle and then broke. Newer systems use

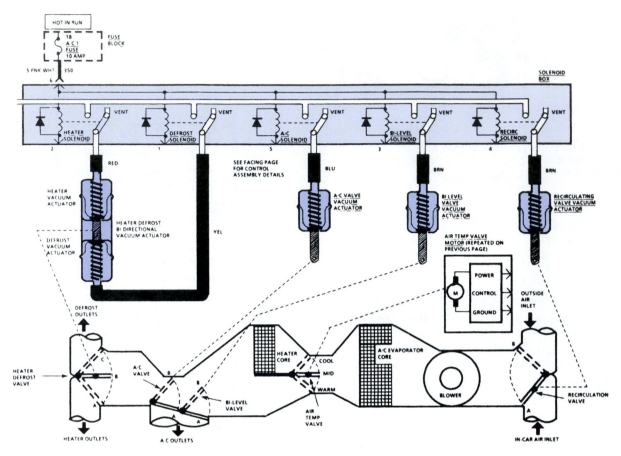

FIGURE 10-16   This system controls the vacuum actuators with a series of solenoid valves, one valve and control solenoid for each actuator operation. *(Reprinted with permission of General Motors Corporation)*

1/8 inch (3.1-mm) plastic hose, which is much more durable. To make a connection, rubber hose is slipped over the tight-fitting connector; a pliable end is attached to plastic hoses to make the connection. Many vehicles combine the hoses at a multiport connector at the control valve and bulkhead connection. The hoses are coded with a color stripe so that, with the aid of a vacuum diagram, they can be easily identified.

Control valves normally have two major positions: The closed position vents the vacuum motor hose to atmosphere and allows the spring to move the motor to the off position; the open position connects the source vacuum to the motor. Many systems control all of the vacuum motors with a single valve, which has a position for each control function. Other systems use a valve block with a separate valve for each circuit. Some newer systems use an electric solenoid to function as the valve.

A vacuum motor consists of a flexible diaphragm in a metal canister. One side of the canister is sealed and connected to the vacuum source; this side usually in-

cludes a spring capable of pushing the diaphragm toward the other chamber. The other chamber has the diaphragm stem passing through it; this side is usually vented to atmosphere (Figure 10-20).

When the control valve connects the sealed chamber to the source vacuum, air pressure is pulled out of that chamber. Atmospheric pressure on the vented side pushes on the diaphragm to move the motor to the on position. When the sealed chamber is vented to atmosphere by the valve, the spring moves the motor to the off position. Air has to enter this chamber for the diaphragm to move (Figure 10-21).

Some vacuum motors use two sealed chambers. These dual-chamber motors have three operating positions.

A vacuum circuit can also include **bleeds** and **restrictors.** Bleeds are calibrated leaks into the circuit and are used to release a motor at a very slow rate. Restrictors are very small orifices that slow down the rate that a motor can apply.

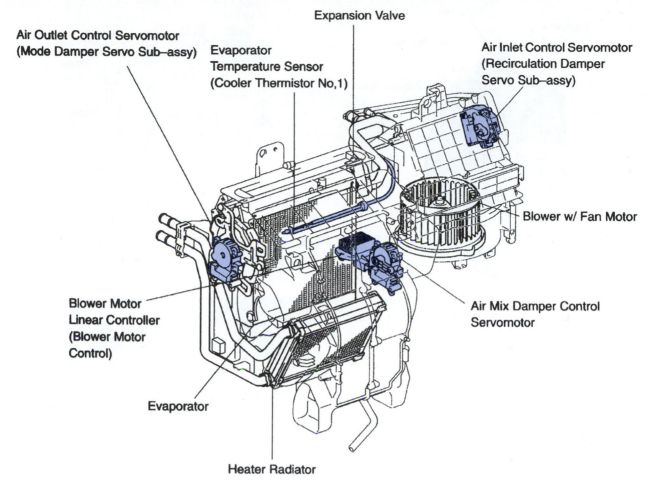

Air Outlet Control Servomotor (Mode Damper Servo Sub–assy)

Evaporator Temperature Sensor (Cooler Thermistor No,1)

Expansion Valve

Air Inlet Control Servomotor (Recirculation Damper Servo Sub–assy)

Blower w/ Fan Motor

Air Mix Damper Control Servomotor

Blower Motor Linear Controller (Blower Motor Control)

Evaporator

Heater Radiator

FIGURE 10-17 This HVAC system uses electric servomotors to operate the doors. The electronic blower motor control and evaporator temperature sensor are also shown. *(Courtesy of Toyota Motor Sales USA, Inc.)*

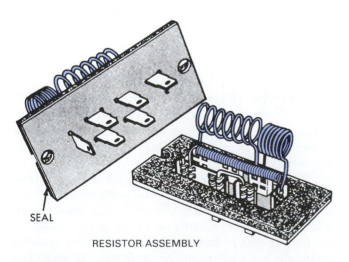

SEAL

RESISTOR ASSEMBLY

FIGURE 10-18 Most systems route blower electrical feed through one or more resistors to obtain the slower speeds. *(Courtesy of DaimlerChrysler Corporation)*

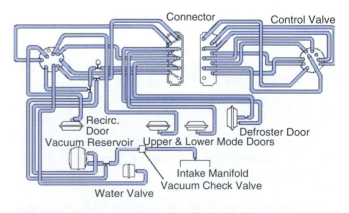

Connector

Control Valve

Recirc. Door

Defroster Door

Vacuum Reservoir

Upper & Lower Mode Doors

Intake Manifold Vacuum Check Valve

Water Valve

FIGURE 10-19 This vacuum control circuit includes a check valve and reservoir to maintain constant vacuum during acceleration. Most vacuum harnesses are color-coded to help in locating a particular hose during repair procedures.

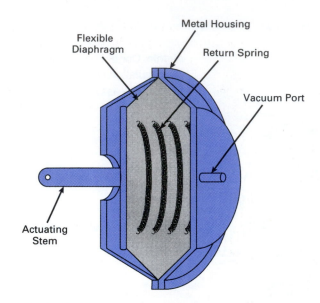

FIGURE 10-20   A vacuum actuator. This unit uses an internal spring to return the diaphragm when there is no vacuum signal.

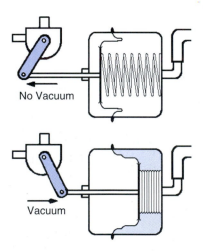

FIGURE 10-21   With no vacuum signal, the spring extends the actuator shaft to place the door in a certain position (*top*). A vacuum signal pulls the shaft inward and moves the door to the other position (*bottom*).

10.3.2   Electrical Control Circuits and Blower Motors

Automotive electrical circuits begin at the battery or alternator. This connection is often called B+, for battery positive. The electricity passes through wires, and the flow is controlled by switches or relays. In the HVAC system, the actuators that do the work are either solenoid valve(s), a blower motor, servomotor(s), or a compressor clutch (described in Section 8.2.3).

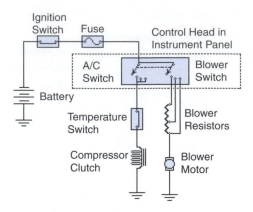

FIGURE 10-22   Most early HVAC systems had simple electrical circuits and placed the blower and A/C switch in the control head as they do today.

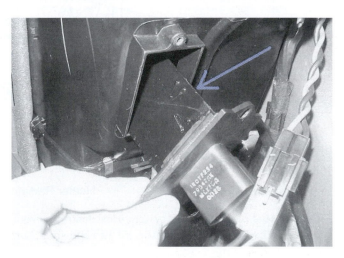

FIGURE 10-23   This blower resistor is just slightly larger than a credit card. (*Courtesy of James Halderman*)

In most systems, the heat and A/C circuit begins at B+, connects to a fuse or circuit breaker, passes to the master on–off switch at the HVAC control head, and then branches off to the various parallel circuits. The master switch in many systems is operated by the function lever (Figure 10-22).

One of these circuits is through the **multiposition switch** to the blower. The low and intermediate switch positions route the electrical path through one or more **resistors.** The resistors cause a drop in the voltage at the blower and reduce blower speed. Older systems commonly use wire-wound resistors (see Figure 10-18); modern resistors are slightly larger than a credit card (Figure 10-23).

In a typical system, the lowest speed might have a resistance of 1.5 to 2 ohms and a blower voltage of about 4 volts. The medium-low speed might have a re-

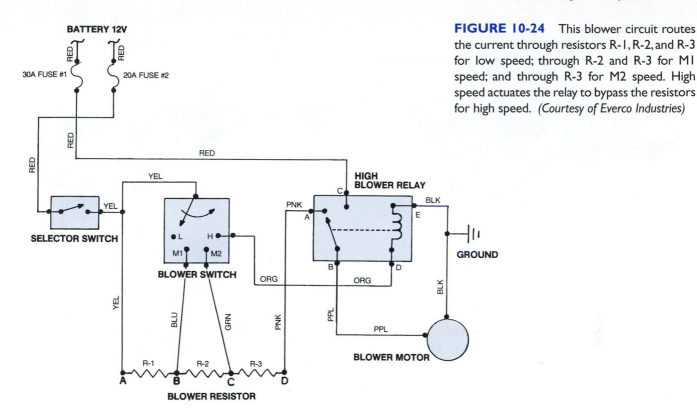

FIGURE 10-24 This blower circuit routes the current through resistors R-1, R-2, and R-3 for low speed; through R-2 and R-3 for M1 speed; and through R-3 for M2 speed. High speed actuates the relay to bypass the resistors for high speed. *(Courtesy of Everco Industries)*

sistance of 1 ohm and a blower voltage of about 6 volts. The medium-high speed might have a resistance of 0.3 ohm and a blower voltage of 8 or 9 volts.

High speed will have no resistance and a blower voltage of 12 to 14 volts (Figure 10-24). A typical blower motor at full speed will draw about 20 amps of current. The high blower speed in some systems operates a relay, so full battery voltage goes from a separate B+ connection to the blower.

Another variation is that while most systems control the B+ voltage to the motor, which is mounted with a ground connection, some systems are *ground-side switched*. The blower motor is connected directly to B+ through the fuse or circuit breaker, with the speed switch and resistors in the ground circuit. Some systems use electronic blower speed control, described in Section 10.5.3.

Most blower motors drive a squirrel-cage–type blower wheel, which is much quieter and more efficient than a fan. There are many types of blower motors, some of them fitting only one make or model of vehicle. The mounting method and any flanges, length and diameter of the motor, length and diameter of the shaft, and direction of rotation are all important when trying to locate a replacement motor. Blower motors are not serviceable and are replaced if they become faulty (Figure 10-25).

Electrical theory, trouble diagnosing, and service are described more completely in Chapter 14.

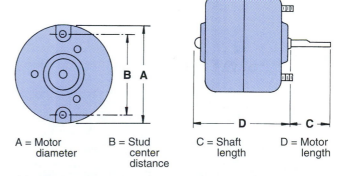

A = Motor diameter   B = Stud center distance   C = Shaft length   D = Motor length

FIGURE 10-25 The critical dimensions needed when replacing a blower motor are shown here. *(Courtesy of Four Seasons)*

10.4 REAR AIR DISTRIBUTION SYSTEMS

Some larger vehicles (vans and small buses) have dual heat and A/C units with an air distribution system that is completely separate from the front heat–A/C unit (Figure 10-26). The unit is usually mounted in a rear side panel or in the roof. It normally contains its own evaporator, heater core, blower, and doors to control temperature and airflow. With the exceptions that there is no

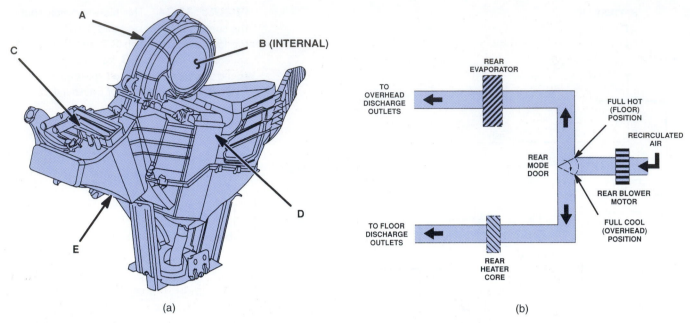

(a)   (b)

FIGURE 10-26   This rear HVAC assembly fits into the vehicle's rear side panel *(a)*. The simpler airflow is shown in *b*. *(Courtesy of DaimlerChrysler Corporation)*

fresh air intake so it can only recirculate and that there is no defog or defrost, most rear units perform just like front units. Depending on the vehicle's usage, the controls can be mounted in the instrument panel, the rear, or both.

◀   **PROBLEM SOLVING 10–1**   ▶

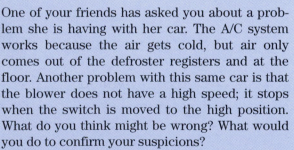

One of your friends has asked you about a problem she is having with her car. The A/C system works because the air gets cold, but air only comes out of the defroster registers and at the floor. Another problem with this same car is that the blower does not have a high speed; it stops when the switch is moved to the high position. What do you think might be wrong? What would you do to confirm your suspicions?

Another friend has an odd problem when he tows a trailer with his pickup. His A/C system usually works quite well, but when he has to drive up a long, uphill grade, the cold air discharge moves from the panel registers to the floor level. What might be wrong? What would you do to find the cause of this problem?

10.5   AUTOMATIC TEMPERATURE CONTROL AND SEMIAUTOMATIC TEMPERATURE CONTROL

ATC is essentially a system of sensors and controls that allows the driver to set a desired temperature at the HVAC control head and let the system take care of maintaining that temperature and selecting the proper air discharge location and blower speed. A semiautomatic temperature control (SATC) system is similar, but the driver selects the air discharge location and/or blower speed. These systems are basically manual heat and A/C systems with automatic controls. These controls can move the temperature-blend door, adjust the blower speed, and change the function and inlet door settings (Figure 10-27).

There are a variety of ATC systems, but they have some things in common. All use a group of sensors, a control device, and a set of actuators (Figure 10-28). The **sensors** determine the temperature inside and outside the car and the temperature the driver wants. The control device, usually an electronic control module (ECM) or electronic control assembly (ECA), compares these temperatures and resets the actuators as necessary to reach the desired temperature.

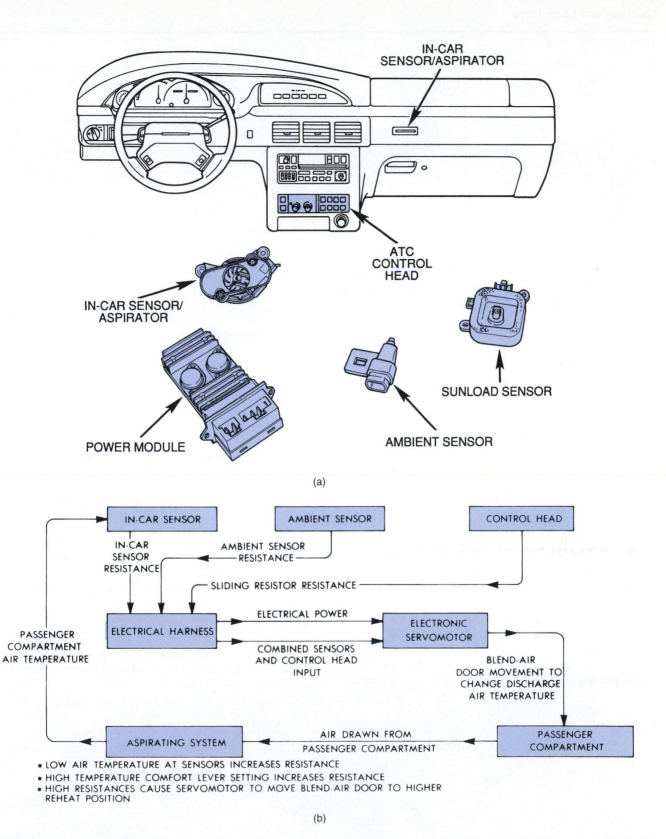

(a)

(b)

- LOW AIR TEMPERATURE AT SENSORS INCREASES RESISTANCE
- HIGH TEMPERATURE COMFORT LEVER SETTING INCREASES RESISTANCE
- HIGH RESISTANCES CAUSE SERVOMOTOR TO MOVE BLEND-AIR DOOR TO HIGHER REHEAT POSITION

FIGURE 10-27 Many ATC systems are a standard system plus these components *(a)*. They are combined as shown in *(b)*. *(Courtesy of DaimlerChrysler Corporation)*

Component Locations

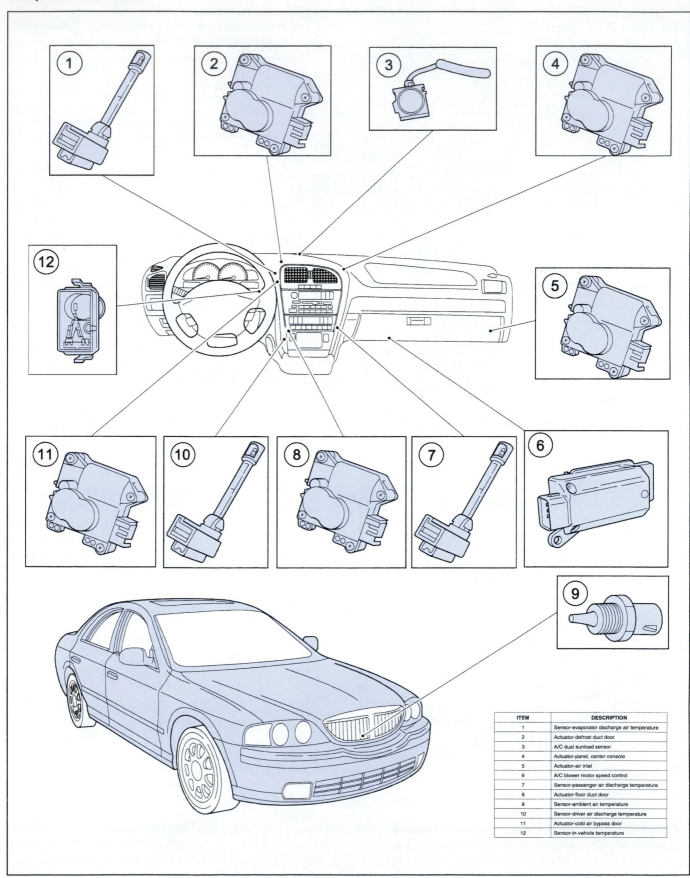

ITEM	DESCRIPTION
1	Sensor-evaporator discharge air temperature
2	Actuator-defrost duct door
3	A/C dual sunload sensor
4	Actuator-panel, center console
5	Actuator-air inlet
6	A/C blower motor speed control
7	Sensor-passenger air discharge temperature
8	Actuator-floor duct door
9	Sensor-ambient air temperature
10	Sensor-driver air discharge temperature
11	Actuator-cold air bypass door
12	Sensor-in-vehicle temperature

FIGURE 10-28 This ATC system uses 12 major components, in addition to the control head, at various locations. (*Courtesy of Visteon*)

10.5.1   ATC Sensors

Most systems use electrical temperature sensors called **thermistors.** An NTC, negative temperature coefficient, thermistor is a resistor that changes resistance value inversely to temperature changes; as the temperature increases, resistance decreases. As shown in Figure 10-29, these values change at a precise rate, and the two sensors have different temperature-to-resistance curves. One new system uses infrared temperature sensing. This dual-zone system uses infrared sensing, similar to a modern, handheld, noncontact thermometer, to monitor the surface temperature of and around the driver and passenger.

The **ambient sensor** measures outside temperature and is often mounted in the fresh-air portion of the duct. On some cars, it is mounted at the radiator shroud or in the area behind the front grill (Figure 10-30). On many older vehicles, the **in-car sensor** is mounted behind the instrument panel, and a set of holes or a small grill allows air to pass by it. Many newer cars place the in-car sensor in an **aspirator** connected to the blower case. Blower operation produces airflow through the aspirator and past the sensor (Figure 10-31). Some vehicles use an in-car sensor with a small, integrated fan so it can be mounted in any location like the vehicle's head liner (Figure 10-32).

In older systems, the driver selected a particular temperature by turning a temperature dial or sliding a lever. This operation adjusted a potentiometer. Modern electronic systems use push buttons or touch pads for temperature selection and give an electronic digital readout of the temperature setting. In the early systems, the ambient sensor, in-car sensor, and temperature potentiometer were connected in series between B+ and the electrical amplifier. In the newer systems, these have become parallel input circuits to the ECM (Figure 10-33).

Many modern systems also use an engine temperature sensor. This sensor keeps the system from turning on the heater before the coolant is warmed up and is often called *cold engine lockout.* Some systems also include a sunload sensor mounted on top of the instrument panel that measures radiant heat load that might cause an increase in in-vehicle temperature (Figure 10-34).

Some modern vehicles use an A/C compressor speed sensor so the ECM will know if the compressor is running, and by comparing the compressor and engine speed signals, the ECM can determine if the compressor clutch is slipping excessively. This system is often called a *belt lock* or *belt protection system.* It prevents the possibility of a locked-up compressor

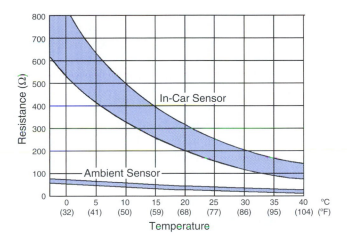

FIGURE 10-29   The resistance of ambient and in-car sensors varies directly with temperature.

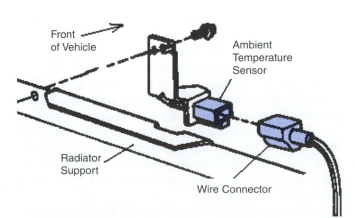

FIGURE 10-30   This ambient sensor is mounted onto the front of the radiator support; others are mounted at other locations under the hood or in the fresh air inlet section of the HVAC case.

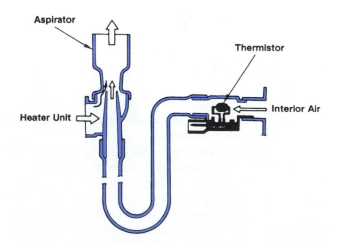

FIGURE 10-31   The aspirator causes an airflow past the thermistor (in-car sensor) when the blower motor operates. *(Courtesy of Toyota Motor Sales USA, Inc.)*

FIGURE 10-32 This sensor group includes three DAT (discharge air temperature) or in-vehicle sensors (one with a fan to move air) (*top left*), an OAT (outside air temperature) (*top right*), and an evaporator outlet temperature sensor (*bottom*). *(Courtesy of Delphi Corp., all rights reserved)*

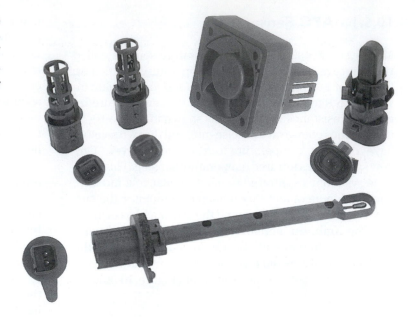

from destroying the engine drive belt, which, in turn, can cause engine overheating or loss of power steering. If the ECM detects an excessive speed differential for more than a few seconds, it will turn the compressor off.

A **pressure transducer** can be used in the low- and/or high-pressure line. The transducer converts the system pressure into an electrical signal that allows the ECM to monitor pressure. The pressure signal can be used to cycle the compressor to prevent evaporator freezeup, change orifice tube size or compressor displacement, or shut off the compressor or speed up cooling fan operation because of high pressures.

Some systems use an *air quality sensor*; this sensor detects hydrocarbons, HC. HC can come from vehicle engines or decaying animal material and often produces offensive odors. A few vehicles use a *relative humidity sensor*, RH, to determine the level of in-vehicle humidity. High RH increases the cooling load.

A few vehicles that are equipped with global position sensor (GPS) for navigation have a sun position strategy. Cooler in-vehicle temperatures are required if the vehicle is positioned so sunlight enters through the windshield or side windows.

Some early systems use a mechanical vacuum sensor that uses a bimetallic strip to measure temperature. This strip bends in response to temperature change; this bending action is used to control a vacuum valve. In one system, the bimetal sensor is positioned in a unit with both ambient and in-vehicle air passing by it. The driver control is attached so it acts on a pivot bar of the bimetal sensor. This unit provides a variable vacuum signal that is sensitive to ambient temperature, in-car temperature, and the driver's temperature setting. The signal is zero vacuum when heat is called for, engine vacuum when full A/C is called for, or somewhere between.

Most systems are designed so they return to a full heat position when turned off. This way, if they fail, they will fail to that position. A person in the southern United States would probably be uncomfortable if the A/C and heat system failed, but in the northern states a heat and defrost system failure could be life threatening in the winter.

10.5.2 Control Device

The ECM, which is a microcomputer, acts on signals from the sensors to produce the desired action at the actuators. The ECM has an output to each item that is controlled, which can include the compressor clutch, blower speed, temperature-blend door, inlet air door, and mode doors. Some of these—the temperature-blend door, for example—have a feedback circuit that tells the ECM what position the door is in. This allows the ECM to move a door to any position within its operating range. Some actuators are two position: on–off or open–closed.

ECM strategy places a high priority on immediate responses to the in-vehicle and ambient temperatures and the temperature request from the control head. Information from the other sensors is used to fine-tune and adjust the response.

One modern system has the ability to count the actuator motor commutator segments so it is able to determine how far the motor revolves. A small current-flow reduction occurs as the space between the commutator bars passes under the brushes of a DC motor. This system needs no feedback circuit, but a calibration procedure must be performed if a motor is replaced.

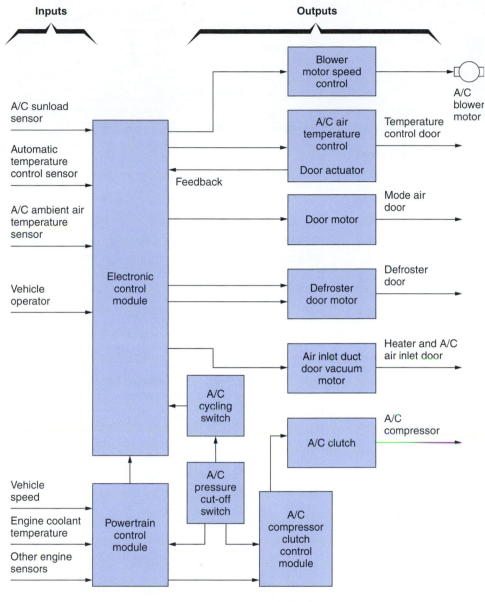

FIGURE 10-33 A block diagram showing the inputs to the electronic control assembly and the outputs; note that some of the outputs have feedback to the ECM.

ATC System Block Diagram

Modern systems have an output from the ECM to each of the controlled actuators or outputs. If vacuum motors are used for the recirculation and mode doors, the vacuum control solenoids and vacuum valve are often combined into a single assembly.

Older systems use an electronic amplifier that generates a signal to drive an electric servomotor or vacuum servomotor to the proper position (Figure 10-35). Systems that use vacuum servomotors also need a transducer to change the electrical signal from the amplifier into a vacuum signal for the servomotor. Both styles of servomotors provide a linear motion. They are positioned at one location for full heat, another position for full A/C, or anywhere in between. The servomotor is connected to electric switches, vacuum valves, and the temperature blend door.

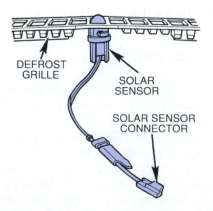

FIGURE 10-34 The solar sensor provides a signal to the control module when the sun shines on it. *(Courtesy of DaimlerChrysler Corporation)*

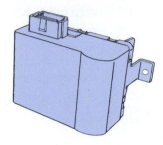

FIGURE 10-35 This electronic servomotor converts the signal from the sensors and control head and moves to adjust the temperature-blend door, mode doors, and blower speed. *(Courtesy of DaimlerChrysler Corporation)*

OPERATION

Air Inlet Door	Recirc		Fresh Air
Heater Water Valve	Closed		Open
Mode Door	A/C Mode	Bi–Level	Heater Mode
Temperature Door	Max Cold	Blend	Max Heat
Blower Speed	High – I3 – I2 – Slow – I2 – I3 – High		
Temperature Control Setting	Coolest		Warmest

← With high temperatures, system will start here.

→ With cold temperatures, system will start at this end.

FIGURE 10-36 When the system is cold, the servomotor produces the operations on the right; when the system is hot, servomotor movement changes to produce the operations on the left.

When the sensors indicate cold in-vehicle conditions, below the driver's settings, the servomotor moves to its full heat position. Here the A/C compressor is turned off; the temperature blend door is at the full heat position; the mode doors direct the heated air to floor level; the blower motor is at high speed; and, in some systems, the air inlet door is set to recirculate. When the sensors indicate an in-vehicle temperature that is too high, the servomotor moves to its full A/C position; the compressor is turned on; the temperature-blend door is set to full cold; the mode doors are set to the instrument panel registers; the blower is set to high speed; and, in some systems, the air inlet door is set to recirculate. When the sensors indicate moderate temperatures, the servomotor moves to a mid position. Depending on the temperature, the compressor may operate, the temperature-blend door will be in the middle, the mode doors may be mixing between floor and instrument panel, the air inlet door is at fresh air, and the blower operates at low speed (Figure 10-36).

A system with a mechanical vacuum sensor connects the sensor directly to the vacuum servomotor. This servomotor is essentially the same as that in a system using electrical sensors.

10.5.3   Actuators

Some ECM-controlled ATC systems use vacuum motor door actuators and control them through solenoid valves; some use electric door actuators controlled directly from the ECM. The ECM sends an electric signal to a particular solenoid or door actuator, which causes either the solenoid to operate the vacuum valve (which in turn causes the vacuum motor to operate the door) or the electric door actuator to move the door. Electric door actuators can be either continuous-position or two-position units (open or closed). Continuous-position actuators can stop anywhere in their range and need a feedback circuit so the ECM will know their position. The temperature-blend door is operated by an electric servomotor (continuous-position actuator) that can move the door to any position called for to produce an air mix of the desired temperature (Figure 10-37).

Older ATC systems operate the air inlet and mode doors using vacuum motors, the same as a manual system. The temperature-blend door is connected to the servomotor through a connecting link. The servomotor also operates a slide valve to control the vacuum to the door motors and a switch for blower speed control.

The blower motor in some ECM-controlled systems operates through a set of different-value resistors with a high-speed relay, like most manual systems. Other systems operate through a PWM or duty-cycle process in which the controller turns the voltage on and off many times a second. If the on cycle and the off cycle are each one-half the time, there is a 50% duty cycle, and the motor runs at half speed. If the off portion is greater than the on portion (say 25% on and 75% off), there is a 25% duty cycle, and the motor runs slowly. As the on portion gets longer and the off portion shorter (say 75% on and 25% off for a 75% duty cycle), the motor runs at three-fourths speed (Figure 10-38). A system that uses resistors usually has four definite stepped speeds. The duty-cycle system has an infinite number of speeds with a gradual change between them (Figure 10-39).

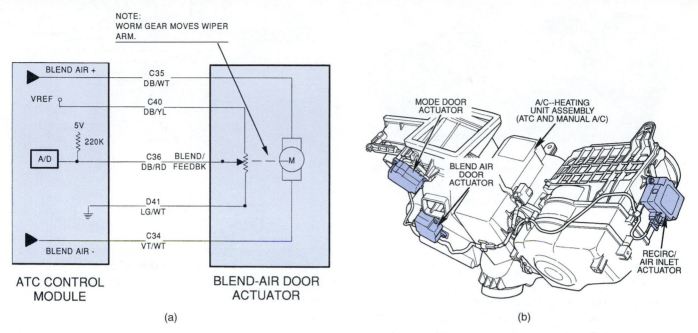

NOTE:
WORM GEAR MOVES WIPER ARM.

ATC CONTROL MODULE

BLEND AIR +

VREF

5V
220K

A/D

BLEND AIR -

C35
DB/WT

C40
DB/YL

C36   BLEND/
DB/RD FEEDBK

D41
LG/WT

C34
VT/WT

M

BLEND-AIR DOOR ACTUATOR

(a)

MODE DOOR ACTUATOR

A/C--HEATING UNIT ASSEMBLY (ATC AND MANUAL A/C)

BLEND AIR DOOR ACTUATOR

RECIRC/ AIR INLET ACTUATOR

(b)

FIGURE 10-37   These mode door, blend air door, and recirculation–air inlet actuators are electric motors (a). The circuit for the blend air door is shown in (b). (Courtesy of DaimlerChrysler Corporation)

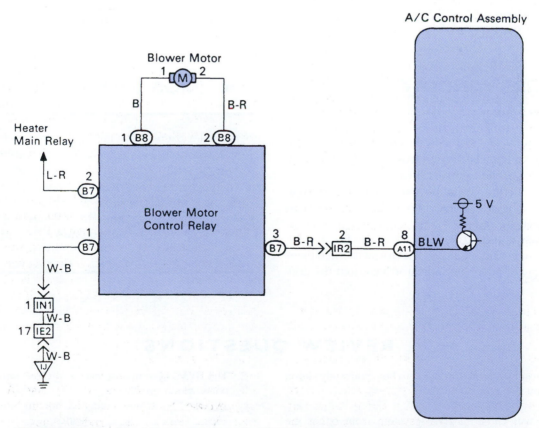

Blower Motor

1 M 2

B

B-R

Heater Main Relay

L-R

2 B7

1 B7

W-B

1 IN1

W-B

17 IE2

W-B

IJ

1 B8

2 B8

Blower Motor Control Relay

3 B7

B-R

2 IR2

B-R

8 A11

BLW

A/C Control Assembly

5 V

FIGURE 10-38   The blower motor wiring diagram shows the transistor in the A/C control assembly controlling the blower motor control relay. (Courtesy of Toyota Motor Sales USA, Inc.)

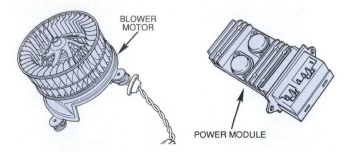

FIGURE 10-39 The power module is used to switch the current feed to the blower and produce infinite blower speeds. *(Courtesy of DaimlerChrysler Corporation)*

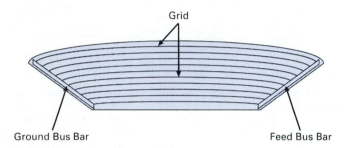

FIGURE 10-40 A rear window defroster routes electricity from the feed bus bar at one side through the grid to the ground bus bar to warm and defrost or de-ice the window.

10.6 REAR WINDOW DEFROSTER

The rear window defroster is an electrical resistance heater designed to clear fog and frost from the rear window. The wires of the electric grid are visible in the rear glass. When current from the car's electrical system flows through the grid, it heats up and warms the glass (Figure 10-40).

The system consists of the connection to B+ through a fusible link or circuit breaker, a control switch and timer at the instrument panel, an indicator light, and the grid.

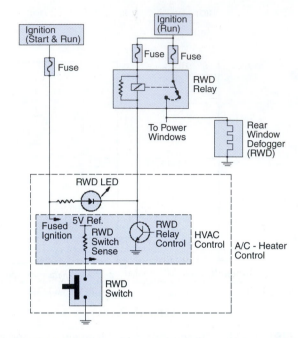

FIGURE 10-41 This circuit for a rear window defogger (RWD) includes an LED light in the instrument panel and three fuses.

When the switch is operated, the timer turns the system on and then shuts it off after 10 minutes. Most systems can be reactivated if necessary (Figure 10-41).

◄ **PROBLEM SOLVING 10–2** ►

An older friend has asked you about a problem he is having with his A/C system. It is a late-model vehicle with ATC. On a hot day, the air comes out of the panel registers with good air movement, but it is about the same as the outside temperature. What do you think might be wrong with this car? What checks can you make to confirm your suspicions?

REVIEW QUESTIONS

The following questions are provided to help you study as you read the chapter.

1. Airflow will enter an HVAC system from either the _ram - air pressure_ at the base of the windshield or through the _fresh registers_.

2. The HVAC system case can be divided into three major parts which are the _air inlet_ section, _plenum_ where cold and hot air are mixed, and _air distribution_ section.

ps 161

3. The air inlet door is normally set to recirculation when the mode controls are set to __max A/c__ or __max heat__.

4. When the temperature control is at full heat, the __Blend Door__ will direct all of the airflow through the __heater core__.

5. Many modern systems use a(n) __cabin filter__ to remove dust and pollen from the airstream.

6. A(n) __Dual Zone__ system requires two sets of temperature doors and mode doors.

7. Mode doors can be operated by a(n) __Bowden cable__, __vacuum Actuator__ or __electric Solenoids__.

8. Low blower operation routes the current flow through a __resistor__, and the current for high blower operation often comes directly from a(n) __12v source__.

9. Electric door control motors usually include a(n) __variable resistor__ so the controls will know what the motor position is.

10. The two major sensors used with ATC systems are the __ambient - sensor__ and __in car__ sensors; some systems also use a(n) __engine temp__ sensor.

11. Many ATC systems use a(n) __aspirator__ to bring an airflow across the __in - car__ sensor.

12. Some systems use __dry cycle system__ blower motor speed control to provide an infinite number of blower speeds.

CHAPTER QUIZ

The following questions will help you check the facts you have learned. Select the answer that completes each statement correctly.

1. Which of the following methods is used to connect the A/C control head to the airflow control doors?
   a. Electrical
   b. Vacuum
   c. Bowden cable
   d. All of these

2. Air can enter the duct system through which of the following?
   a. Fresh air plenum
   b. Recirculate return
   c. Defrost duct
   d. Both a and b

3. Two technicians are discussing A/C door operation. Technician A says that when the control head is set to heat, the mode door should direct air discharge from the instrument panel ducts. Technician B says the air discharge should be at floor level. Who is correct?
   a. A only
   b. B only
   c. Both A and B
   d. Neither A nor B

4. Most vacuum control valves have _____ operating position(s).
   a. one
   b. two
   c. three
   d. four

5. The _____ blower speed has the least electrical resistance.
   a. low
   b. high
   c. medium-low
   d. medium-high

6. Two technicians are discussing A/C blower operation. Technician A says that modern systems use a squirrel-cage–type blower. Technician B says that a plain fan-type unit is used with systems having cable type controls. Who is correct?
   a. A only
   b. B only
   c. Both A and B
   d. Neither A nor B

7. An ATC system has the ability to automatically _____.
   a. move the temperature-blend door
   b. adjust the blower speed
   c. change the function door setting
   d. All of these

8. Two technicians are discussing ATC sensors. Technician A says that an NTC thermistor has more resistance as it warms up. Technician B says an increase in temperature will cause an NTC thermistor to have lower resistance. Who is correct?
   a. A only
   b. B only
   c. Both A and B
   d. Neither A nor B

9. Many modern systems use an engine temperature sensor that _____.
   a. allows heater operation as soon as the engine is started
   b. turns on the A/C compressor after the engine has warmed up
   c. blocks A/C operation when the engine is cold
   d. prevents heater operation until the coolant is hot

10. An ATC system uses a(n) _____ sensor to determine the temperature of the incoming air.
   a. in-vehicle
   b. ambient
   c. anticipation
   d. sunload

◀ Chapter 11 ▶

HVAC SYSTEM INSPECTION AND TROUBLE DIAGNOSIS PROCEDURES

LEARNING OBJECTIVES

After completing this chapter, you should be able to:

1. Inspect an HVAC system to determine whether it is operating correctly, and if not to make further tests to locate the subsystem at fault and the cause of the problem.
2. Check system temperatures and determine if they are correct.
3. Follow a logical procedure to locate the cause of a problem in an HVAC system.
4. Complete the Automotive Service Excellence (ASE) tasks related to HVAC inspection and test procedures.

TERMS TO LEARN

after blow module   groundout
comeback   technical service bulletin
diagnostic trouble code   (TSB)
   (DTC)   trouble tree
functional test   visual inspection

11.1   INTRODUCTION

Except for preventative maintenance operations, vehicle service work should begin with a systematic procedure to determine exactly what is wrong. If trouble diagnosis is thorough and accurate, all problems can be located and repaired at the same time.

◀ SERVICE TIP ▶

Refrigerant must be recovered from an A/C system before repairs can be made; after the repairs are complete, the system must be recharged. An incomplete or inaccurate diagnosis usually leads to an incomplete repair, which may mean going through the recovery and recharge steps twice, wasting time and possibly some refrigerant.

A still bigger concern for technicians is the repair that fails after the vehicle has left the shop and the vehicle comes back. In the vehicle service field, **comebacks** are usually repaired at the expense of the shop and the technician. It is much better to fix the problem the first time a vehicle comes into the shop. A comeback can cause an immediate loss of time and money, but the biggest loss is often the shop's reputation.

Diagnosis procedures vary greatly . . . depending on the nature of the problem and the experience of the technician. If the vehicle shows a familiar set of symptoms, the experienced technician can often shortcut the procedure and go directly to the steps that confirm the cause for that particular problem. After technicians determine the probable cause, they often make other checks to verify or confirm their conclusion.

Chapter 12 describes the diagnosis procedure for all of the problems normally encountered in the A/C subsystem of the HVAC system. Diagnoses of the heater, air management, and control subsystems are described in Chapter 13. Electrical and electronic circuits and their diagnostic procedures are described in Chapter 14. Heater core and hose problems and cooling system problems and repair are described in Chapter 18.

An important step in the early part of the diagnostic procedure is to ensure that there is a problem and, if there is, to determine which HVAC subsystem is at fault. It is possible to get a complaint such as *insufficient cooling* from an A/C system on a very hot and humid day, and under these conditions, the cooling load often exceeds the capacity of the system. The system can be operating properly at full design capacity. In this case, the only thing a technician can do is to try to educate the customer about what is happening.

◄ SERVICE TIP ►

A competent technician normally makes several diagnosis checks of a system. Diagnosis usually begins with a thorough under-hood inspection using sight, sound, touch, and even smell. Under-hood checks usually begin with an inspection while the engine is off, and parts of this check are repeated with the engine running. The inspection procedure also includes a check of the HVAC system controls, blower, and air management doors both while the engine is off and while it is running. After these checks, the technician should know whether the system is operating properly or which subsystem has a problem.

11.2 HVAC SYSTEM INSPECTION

HVAC system inspection, often called a **visual inspection** or a **functional test,** is the quickest way to locate obvious problems (Figure 11-1). It also gives the technician a good idea of the overall condition of the system. During this step, the technician determines whether the A/C system is an R-12, retrofitted from R-12, or R-134a system; a TXV or OT system; or a cycling clutch, STV, or variable compressor system. Although this is called a visual inspection, the competent technician listens for things like clutch or idler bearing problems; feels for system temperatures and under hoses for damage, excessive vibration, and evidence of leaks; shakes parts such as compressor mounts while feeling for looseness;

and is aware of any unusual smells such as from an antifreeze leak or a moldy evaporator.

A technician often follows a service checklist like that shown in Figure 11-2 while doing a visual inspection. This list keeps important checks from being overlooked, and it also gives the customer an idea of what was done. Many motorists seldom open the hood, and of those who do, only a few understand what they are looking at.

11.2.1 A/C System Inspection

To inspect an HVAC system, you should:

With the engine off, the under-hood checks are as follows:

1. Check the condition of the belts. With a V-belt, roll the belt so you can see the sides. Cracked, frayed, highly glazed, or otherwise damaged belts should be replaced. On belts that show wear or damage, check the condition and alignment of the pulleys. Faulty belts should be replaced (Figure 11-3).
2. Check the tension of the belt by pushing against the center at a longer span. Any belts that seem loose should be readjusted. A belt tension gauge is the most accurate way of checking belt tightness. With serpentine belt systems, you should be able to see and feel the automatic tensioner operate as you push on the belt.
3. Inspect the refrigerant hoses and lines for oily residue and damage. Oil residue with caked-on dirt indicates a probable leak. Each of the A/C test ports should be capped.
4. While checking the hoses and lines, determine whether you are dealing with a TXV or OT system and whether an STV or a variable displacement compressor is used. The compressor shape and model number are used for identification.
5. Check the compressor mounting bolts to make sure they are tight.
6. Check to make sure there is an air gap at the compressor clutch. If there is good access, turn the clutch plate while you feel for smooth compressor operation (Figure 11-4).
7. Check the electrical wires to the clutch, blower motor, and any A/C switches for good, tight connections and possible damage.
8. Check the vacuum hoses between the intake manifold and bulkhead, looking for kinked, cracked, or loose hoses.
9. Check the condition of the radiator cooling fan, fan clutch or motor, and fan shroud.

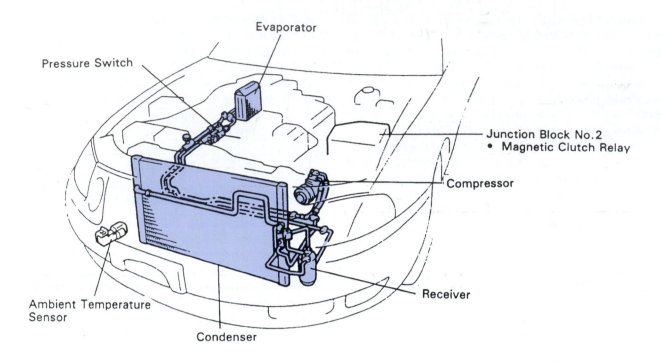

Evaporator

Pressure Switch

Junction Block No. 2
• Magnetic Clutch Relay

Compressor

Ambient Temperature
Sensor

Receiver

Condenser

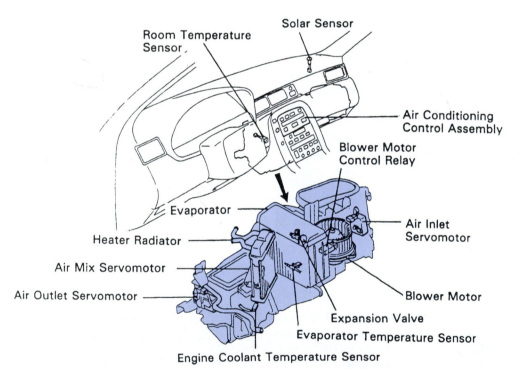

Solar Sensor

Room Temperature
Sensor

Air Conditioning
Control Assembly

Blower Motor
Control Relay

Air Inlet
Servomotor

Evaporator

Heater Radiator

Air Mix Servomotor

Air Outlet Servomotor

Blower Motor

Expansion Valve

Evaporator Temperature Sensor

Engine Coolant Temperature Sensor

FIGURE 11-1 A visual inspection checks all of the visible, under-hood components for possible wear or damage. The under-dash components are checked for noise and proper airflow. *(Courtesy of Toyota Motor Sales USA, Inc.)*

AIR CONDITIONING SERVICE CHECK LIST

Customer _____ Date _____

Address _____

City _____ State _____ Zip _____

Year _____ Make _____ Model _____

License No. _____ Engine _____ V.I.N. _____

Description of Problem _____

GAUGE READINGS				TEMPERATURE READINGS		
	INITIAL	FINAL			INITIAL	FINAL
High			Ambient			
Low			Duct			
Aux.						

COMPONENT CHECKS

COMPONENT	OK	REPAIR	COMPONENT	OK	REPAIR
1. Drive Belts: Proper Tension	☐	☐	15. Pressure Cycling Switch: Fitting/O Ring Leaks	☐	☐
Condition	☐	☐	On/Off Cycling Time	☐	☐
2. Charging System: Volts	☐	☐	Electrical Connection	☐	☐
Amps	☐	☐	16. Accumulator: Mounting Hardware	☐	☐
Volt Drop	☐	☐	Inlet/Outlet Temperature	☐	☐
3. Fan Clutch: Bearing	☐	☐	Fittings/Leaks	☐	☐
Leaks Front/Rear	☐	☐	17. Suction Line: Mounting and Routing	☐	☐
4. Idler Pulley: Bearing	☐	☐	Fittings/Leaks	☐	☐
Groove/Surface	☐	☐	Hose Condition	☐	☐
5. Compressor Clutch: Air Gap	☐	☐	Temperature	☐	☐
Bearing	☐	☐	18. Radiator: Leaks	☐	☐
Field Coil	☐	☐	Air Fins Clean	☐	☐
Electrical Connections	☐	☐	Hose and Clamps	☐	☐
Surge Diode	☐	☐	Pressure Cap	☐	☐
6. Compressor: Leaks-Shaft Seal/O Rings	☐	☐	Over Flow Tank and Hose	☐	☐
Mounting Hardware	☐	☐	19. Cooling System:		
Operation	☐	☐	Antifreeze 2 years or 30,000 miles	☐	☐
7. Discharge Line: Muffler	☐	☐	Freeze Protection (−20° minimum)	☐	☐
Hose	☐	☐	Heater Hoses, By-Pass Hose and Clamps	☐	☐
Fitttings	☐	☐	Heater Control Valve	☐	☐
8. Condenser: Fittings/Leaks	☐	☐	Thermostat	☐	☐
Fins Clean	☐	☐	20. Electric Cooling Fan: Bearings	☐	☐
Mounting Hardware	☐	☐	Fan Blade	☐	☐
Temperature Change	☐	☐	Electric Connection	☐	☐
9. Receiver/Drier: Mounting Hardware	☐	☐	Amp Draw	☐	☐
Fittings	☐	☐	Coolant Sensor	☐	☐
Even Temperature	☐	☐	Relays	☐	☐
Sight Glass	☐	☐	21. Blower Motor Circuit:		
High Pressure Valve	☐	☐	Blower Motor Amp Draw	☐	☐
10. Liquid Line: Routing/Mounting Hardware	☐	☐	Electrical Connections	☐	☐
Even Temperature	☐	☐	Harness Connections	☐	☐
Fittings	☐	☐	Blower Switch	☐	☐
11. Thermostatic Expansion Valve:			Blower Resistor	☐	☐
Leaks	☐	☐	22. Vacuum Control Circuit:		
Inlet/Outlet Temperature	☐	☐	Vacuum Canister	☐	☐
Sensing Bulb Clean/Tight	☐	☐	Vacuum Hoses	☐	☐
Insulation Tape	☐	☐	Vacuum Motors	☐	☐
11A. Orifice Tube:			Vacuum Control Switches	☐	☐
Fittings/Leaks	☐	☐	Vacuum Check Valve	☐	☐
Inlet/Outlet Temperature	☐	☐	23. Dash Control Switches:		
12. Evaporator: Leaks	☐	☐	Proper Mode Changes	☐	☐
Mounting Hardware	☐	☐	Temperature Control Cable	☐	☐
Air Flow	☐	☐	Duct Doors	☐	☐
Discharge Air Odors	☐	☐	24. System Control and Protection:		
Condensation Drain	☐	☐	Low Pressure Protection Switches	☐	☐
13. Suction Throttle Valve:			High Pressure Protection Switches	☐	☐
Leaks	☐	☐	Wide Open Throttle Switch or TPS	☐	☐
Inlet/Outlet Temperature	☐	☐	Power Steering Cutoff Switch	☐	☐
Operating Pressure	☐	☐	Coolant Temperature Switch	☐	☐
14. Thermostatic Clutch Cycling Switch:			Coolant Temperature Relay	☐	☐
Sensing Bulb—Clean/Tight	☐	☐	Power Brake Delay Relay	☐	☐
On/Off Cycling Times	☐	☐	Throttle Kick Solenoid	☐	☐
Insulation Tape	☐	☐	Isolation Relay	☐	☐
Electrical Connection	☐	☐	A/C Relay	☐	☐
			Time Delay Relay	☐	☐
			Constant Run Relay	☐	☐

Remarks _____

Repair Estimate _____

Part No. A9578   Copyright 1989 by Everco Industries, Inc.   Printed in U.S.A.

EVERCO®
A MOOG AUTOMOTIVE COMPANY

FIGURE 11-2 Many technicians use a checklist like the one shown here while inspecting a system. It provides a good record of the inspection to show the customer. *(Courtesy of Everco Industries)*

FIGURE 11-3 A drive belt should be replaced if it has any of the problems shown. *(Courtesy of Dayco Products, Inc.)*

Replace belts showing the following:

V-BELTS	V-RIBBED BELTS

V-BELTS

Wear on bandless V-belts is difficult to detect. That's why Gates reminds consumers to replace their belts every 4 years, no matter how they look.

Glazing
Slick sidewalls lose gripping power and the belt slips.

Cracks
Deep cracks indicate the undercord is stressed to the breaking point.

Missing chunks and separating layers
This damage causes the belt to slip and eventually break.

Streaked sidewalls
Foreign objects, or a rough pulley pit the sidewalls and the belt starts slipping.

Tensile break
Broken cords can lead to the belt breaking.

V-RIBBED BELTS

V-ribbed belts show distinct wear patterns. And when the belt on a serpentine drive breaks, the car is disabled.

Cracking
Use Gates "EARLY WARNING" gauge to check belts. If 3 or more rib cracks appear within 3 inches, 80% of belt life is gone. Replace it.

Chunking
When chunks break off the belt ribs, it can fail at any moment.

Pilling
Wear causes rubber build-up in the grooves and the belt runs unevenly.

---

10. Check the condition of the radiator and heater hoses, looking for swollen, soft, cracked, kinked, or leaky hoses (Figure 11-5).

11. If the engine and radiator are cool, remove the cap and check the appearance of the coolant, which should be clean and have a bright color. The coolant level should be level with the lower radiator cap seat.

12. Check the faces of the condenser and radiator core; they should be clean, with no restriction to airflow. There should be no apparent leaks.

◀ **SERVICE TIP** ▶

A missing A/C service cap can allow a refrigerant leak of up to 1 lb (2.2 kg) of refrigerant per year.

REAL WORLD FIX: The 1992 Dodge Caravan (140,000 miles) had a failure of the serpentine belt that unraveled and caused a failure of the A/C drive belt. The belts have been replaced, but now the A/C clutch will not engage. The fuses are okay, but there is no power to the clutch.

FIX

Following advice, the technician checked the pressure switch that is mounted on an A/C line below the radiator and found the flapping belt had disconnected the wire connections. Replacement of these wires onto their connectors fixed this problem.

With the engine off, the in-car checks are as follows:

1. Operate the blower switch through its various speeds while you listen to the fan and motor for unusual noises. Note that some systems do not have

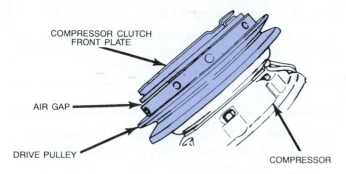

FIGURE 11-4 With the engine off, compressor clutch inspection includes a check for air gap between the clutch plate and pulley. The hub and compressor shaft should rotate smoothly, without runout of the clutch plate. *(Courtesy of DaimlerChrysler Corporation)*

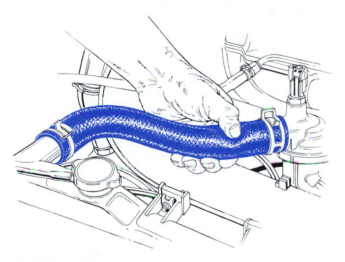

FIGURE 11-5 Hose inspection can be difficult in tight quarters. Check for cracks and cuts and squeeze the hose to check for hardening or excessive softness. Squeeze the hose close to the ends to check for softening. *(Courtesy of The Gates Rubber Company)*

blower operation unless the heat or A/C controls are on or unless the engine is running (Figure 11-6).

2. Move the temperature lever of mechanically operated doors to both ends of its travel. It should move smoothly and stop before making contact at the ends. A late stop indicates that adjustment is needed.

◄   **SERVICE TIP**   ►

On many cars, a "thunk" noise occurs as the temperature door contacts the stop. If you are in an area with cold winters, make sure it "thunks" at the full heat stop; if you are in an area with hot summers, make sure it "thunks" at the full cool stop.

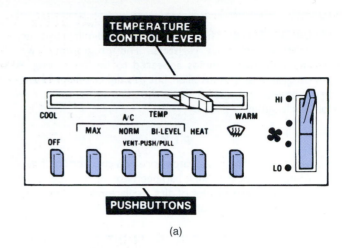

(a)

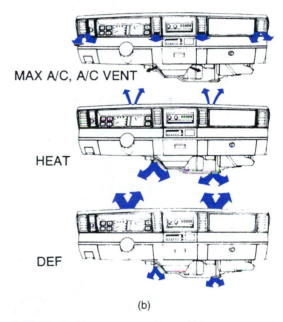

(b)

FIGURE 11-6 Inspection includes a check for proper blower operation through each of the speeds *(a)* and air discharge from each location for the different functions *(b)*. *(Courtesy of DaimlerChrysler Corporation)*

With the engine running, the in-car checks are as follows:

1. Note the alternator charge indicator; it should show a normal charge level or voltage after the engine runs a short while.

2. Set the blower speed to high, move the function control to all of its positions, and note the air discharge. The airflow should change to the various outlets and should be about the same from each outlet.

3. Turn on the A/C to determine whether the compressor clutch engages and the compressor operates.

REAL WORLD FIX: The 1988 Buick (73,000 miles) had very little airflow from the registers. The programmer was checked, and the solenoids appeared to be functioning. A new programmer was installed, but this did not help. Changing the operating mode produces the same amount of airflow from each outlet.

FIX

Following advice, the evaporator core was checked and found to be plugged almost solid. It had been leaking, and the refrigerant oil had collected a lot of dirt. Replacement of the evaporator core fixed this problem as well as an A/C problem.

AUTHOR'S NOTE

A good review of HVAC basics would have saved the unneeded replacement of the programmer.

◄ SERVICE TIP ►

Many modern HVAC systems include a cabin air filter, and many vehicle owners are not aware that these require periodic replacement. A plugged filter will cause a severe airflow reduction and also could be the source of a bad odor.

◄ SERVICE TIP ►

Reduced airflow can also be caused by a plugged evaporator core. This can be checked by measuring the blower motor current draw. Any restriction to the airflow will reduce the power requirement for the blower motor and the amount of current required. A more complete explanation can be found in Section 14.5.

REAL WORLD FIX: The 1996 Ford Explorer (50,000 miles) had a faulty blend door actuator motor. A new motor was installed, but it did not operate the door. The power supply and ground checked good, and the motor can be made to operate. After determining that the new motor was the wrong part for this vehicle, even though it looked the same, the correct motor was installed, but it still would not operate the door.

FIX

Closer inspection revealed that the blend door operating shaft had broken off. Installation of a new, updated heater box/blend door assembly fixed this problem.

REAL WORLD FIX: The 1986 Saab (170,000 miles) HVAC system has no temperature control; it stays at a constant, hot temperature. The stepper motor operates the arm attached to the blend door in what appears to be a normal manner.

FIX

Following advice from other technicians, the system was disassembled. The sealing foam from the blend door had disintegrated, and a large piece had fallen down and jammed the door. This caused the door operating arm to break. Replacement of the plenum section fixed this problem.

REAL WORLD FIX: The 1993 Pontiac Bonneville (120,000 miles) has a very poor airflow from the instrument panel registers. This is a manual system so there is no scan tool information. The technician is concerned about removing the instrument panel to locate the problem.

FIX

Following advice, the glove compartment seals were checked and found to be faulty. Another faulty seal was also found after the radio was removed. Repair of these two air leaks fixed this problem.

AUTHOR'S NOTE

Some vehicles route the instrument panel air through the glove compartment. Radios are often easy to remove, providing a way to check hidden areas.

◄ SERVICE TIP ►

With the hood and driver's door or window open, on most vehicles you can hear an audible click as the compressor clutch engages when you turn the A/C system on. Set the system to A/C, cold temperature, and high blower speed. With electronically controlled systems, the engine must be running for the A/C clutch to operate.

With the engine running, the under-hood checks are as follows:

1. Make sure the compressor clutch is engaged and the compressor is running. Listen for any signs of improper compressor operation. If there are any, feel the compressor for harsh, rough motions.

2. Disconnect the clutch to make sure it releases smoothly. With the clutch released, listen for proper clutch bearing operation. If there are unusual noises, carefully feel the compressor next to the clutch for harsh, rough operation. Reconnect the clutch and note the engagement (Figure 11-7).

3. Feel the temperature of the A/C lines and hoses. Be cautious on the high side because the lines should be warm to hot, with the temperature increasing. All the lines on the low side should be cool to cold, with the temperature getting colder (Figure 11-8).

4. Feel the temperature of the heater hoses. If the engine is at operating temperature, both hoses should feel hot. Expect a temperature difference on heater systems with a coolant flow control valve.

5. Check the drive belts. They should be running straight and smooth, with a slight rippling allowed in the belt section returning to the crankshaft pulley. Excess belt whip or slap indicates that adjustment is needed or the idler has failed.

6. Check the fan operation (if running). The fan should be turning smoothly, with good airflow. Depending on the temperature and type of fan clutch, a mechanical fan in an RWD car should deliver

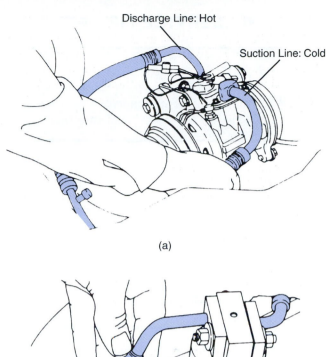

(a)

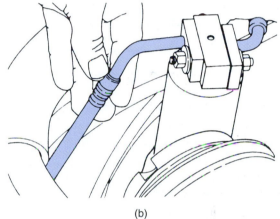

(b)

FIGURE 11-8 When a system is operating properly, the suction line to the compressor should be cool, and the discharge line should be hot to very hot *(a)*. The liquid lines should also be hot *(b)*. *(Courtesy of DaimlerChrysler Corporation)*

moderate to high airflow. An electric drive fan is probably operating to produce airflow.

7. Check the evaporator drain. By this time, there should be a small puddle of water under the evaporator area and drops of water coming from the drain. With some vehicles, the drain is routed through a frame member; check the vehicle service information if you cannot locate the drain. *Note:* In areas with very low humidity, water may not drain out.

◀ **SERVICE TIP** ▶

An infrared, noncontact thermometer is a fast and easy way to check system temperatures (see Figure 12-12).

FIGURE 11-7 With the engine running, compressor clutch inspection includes a rapid engagement as the clutch wire is connected, a clean disengagement with no drag as the wire is disconnected, smooth and quiet pulley operation, and very little runout of the pulley.

◀ **SERVICE TIP** ▶

To determine if there is adequate airflow through a condenser, many technicians place a sheet of paper or a dollar bill in front of the condenser; with the engine running at idle speed, it should stick there.

With the engine still running, check inside the vehicle for overall operation. By now the A/C system should be delivering cool to cold air from the instrument panel registers. Moving the temperature control should cause a temperature change. Changing the function control to heat should move the air discharge to floor level.

◀ **SERVICE TIP** ▶

Automatic operation of ATC can be checked by warming the in-vehicle sensor with a heat gun (it should shift to a colder operation), cooling the sensor with a quick-freeze aerosol (it should shift to a warmer operation), or bringing a lightbulb over the sunload sensor (it should shift to a colder operation).

◀ **SERVICE TIP** ▶

An in-car sensor must have an airflow past it in order to measure the temperature. This airflow is caused by the aspirator or an integrated fan. You can test the airflow by placing a piece of tissue paper next to the sensor; the paper should be held in place by the air pressure.

11.3 PROBLEM DIAGNOSIS

A visual inspection often locates the exact cause of a problem. It nearly always reveals the nature of the problem, showing in what area of the system the problem lies. If there is no blower motor operation along with no compressor clutch operation, for example, an experienced technician knows that in many vehicles these are branches of a single electrical circuit. Therefore, the most probable cause is a blown fuse; the second most probable cause is either a faulty switch at the control head or a bad connection to that switch. With modern vehicles, there can be a problem in the electrical control circuit or control modules.

The most important aspect of diagnosis is knowledge of how a system works. If we understand a system, we know what to expect from each part of that system, and we also know what to expect when that part does not work. Classroom instruction and information sources such as service manuals and this text can help you in this regard.

Also important in diagnosing problems is knowing where failure is most likely to occur. In an A/C system, refrigerant leaks are more common than compressor failures, and leaks are much more likely to occur at line connections than in metal tubing. Experience and troubleshooting charts can help you master diagnosis (Figure 11-9).

Complete diagnosis is concerned with locating the exact cause of a problem relatively quickly. For example, let's say that the cause of no blower motor and compressor operation was a blown fuse. A fuse might blow from old age or a high-voltage spike from the system, but it is more probable that excess current flow caused by a shorted or grounded circuit is the cause. If the only repair is to replace the fuse, the system will probably come back with another blown fuse.

Another example is a system with poor A/C operation that is caused by a low charge level. The low charge level was probably caused by a leak. The leak should be located and repaired to fix the cause of the problem rather than simply topping off or recharging the system.

REAL WORLD FIX: The 1988 Dodge Caravan (130,000 miles) had a complaint of no heat from the heater. The engine thermostat was working, and the engine coolant was getting hot. The heater hoses are hot, but the technician is concerned that there is no vacuum signal to the heater control valve.

FIX

A check of a vacuum diagram shows that a vacuum signal is only at the valve during A/C to close the valve. He was advised to check the temperature blend door, and it was found to be stuck. A small hole was drilled into the plenum case at the lower bearing for the door, and penetrating oil was sprayed into the hole. This freed the door and fixed the problem.

Diagnosis charts, also called **trouble trees**, help guide the technician through the procedure to locate the cause of a problem in the shortest time possible. In most cases, they use a logical, systematic series of tests and checks to isolate the area causing the problem. Charts are available from vehicle manufacturers and suppliers

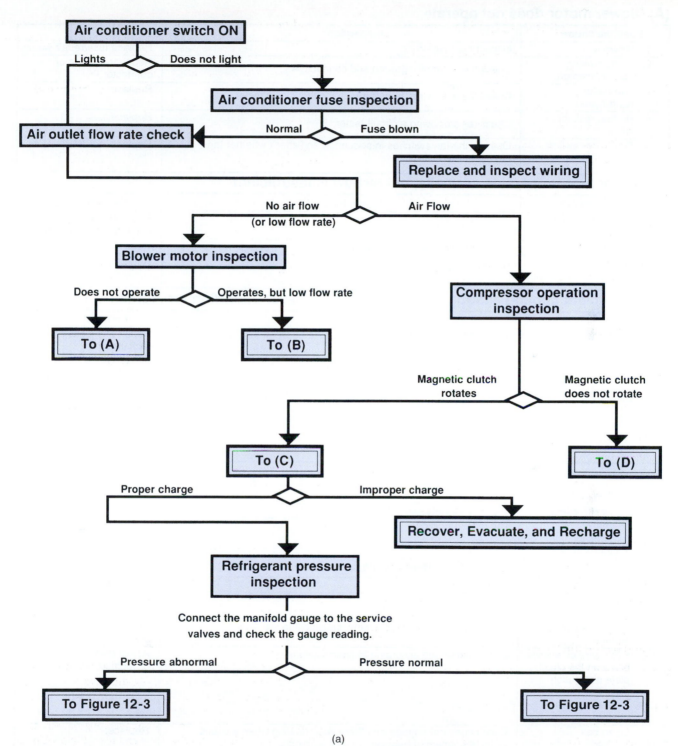

(a)

FIGURE 11-9 A trouble tree can be followed to determine the cause of the problem *(a)*. Note that some checks lead to further checks that are listed on the troubleshooting charts *(b)*. *(Courtesy of Zexel USA Corporation)*

(Continued)

TROUBLESHOOTING CHART

(A) Blower motor does not operate

Possible cause	Inspection	Remedy
1. Blown fuse.	Inspect the fuse/wiring.	Replace fuse/repair wiring.
2. Broken wiring or bad connection.	Check the fan motor ground and connectors.	Repair the wiring or connector.
3. Fan motor malfunction.	Check the lead wires from the motor with a circuit tester.	Replace.
4. Broken resistor wiring.	Check resistor using a circuit tester.	Replace.
5. Fan motor switch malfuction.	Operate the fan switches in sequence and check whether the fan operates.	Replace.

(B) Blower motor operates normally, but airflow is insufficient

Possible cause	Inspection	Remedy
1. Evaporator inlet obstruction.	Check the inlet.	Remove the obstruction and clean.
2. Air leak.	Check the cooling unit case joints.	Repair or adjust.
3. Defective thermo switch (frozen evap.).	Check the switch using a circuit tester.	Replace.

(C) Insufficient cooling although airflow and compressor operation are normal

Possible cause	Inspection	Remedy
1. Insufficient refrigerant.	There will be little temperature difference between the low and high-pressure sides.	Repair any leaks and recharge the refrigerant to the correct level.
2. Excessive refrigerant.	Verify by gauge reading.	Utilize your refrigerant recovery equipment to capture excess refrigerant. Charge to the correct refrigerant level.

(D) The compressor does not operate at all, or operates improperly

Possible cause	Inspection	Remedy
1. Loose drive belt.	The belt oscillates considerably.	Adjust the tension.
2. Internal compressor malfunction.	The drive belt slips.	Replace compressor.
• Magnetic clutch related		
3. Low battery voltage.	Clutch slips.	Recharge the battery.
4. Faulty coil.	Clutch slips.	Replace the magnetic clutch.
5. Oil on the clutch surface.	The magnetic clutch face is dirty, causing it to slip.	Replace, or clean the clutch surface.
6. Excessive clearance between the clutch plate and clutch disk. The clutch plate clings when pushed.	Check clutch gap according to specifications.	Adjust the clearance, or replace the clutch.
7. Open coil.	Clutch does not engage and there is no reading when a circuit tester is connected between the coil terminals.	Replace.
8. Broken wiring or poor ground.	Clutch will not engage at all. Inspect the ground and connections.	Repair.
9. Wiring harness components.	Test the conductance of the pressure switch, thermoswitch, relay, etc.	Check operation, referring to the wiring diagram, and replace defective parts.

(b)

FIGURE 11-9 Continued.

of A/C parts. Most vehicle manufacturers develop charts for the features of a particular system. For example, as you will find out, the normal low side pressure of a cycling clutch system is different from that of a system that uses an STV or variable displacement compressor, and the diagnostic procedure for each of these systems is slightly different. The diagnostic chart helps eliminate those portions of a system that are working properly so we can concentrate our tests and further checks on those portions where the problem might be.

With a common problem, such as *no or insufficient cooling*, an experienced technician knows the problem can be caused by a number of faults in the A/C system, faulty door or blower operation in the air management system, or faulty compressor switching by the controls. Most vehicle manufacturers recommend that problem-solving or troubleshooting procedures be done in an organized manner (Figure 11-10).

Step 1: Verify the Complaint
Verifying the complaint ensures that the technician understands the nature of the problem. If possible, the customer should explain or demonstrate the problem. It is

Diagnostic Test Procedure

1. Verify Complaint
   — Operate HVAC
2. Determine Related Symptoms
   — Under-Hood Checks
   — In-Car Checks
3. Analyze System
   — Pressure Tests
   — Temperature Checks
   — Check DTCs
   — Review Service Information
4. Isolate Concern
   — Review Checklist
   — Review Service Information
5. Determine Problem
6. Repair Problem

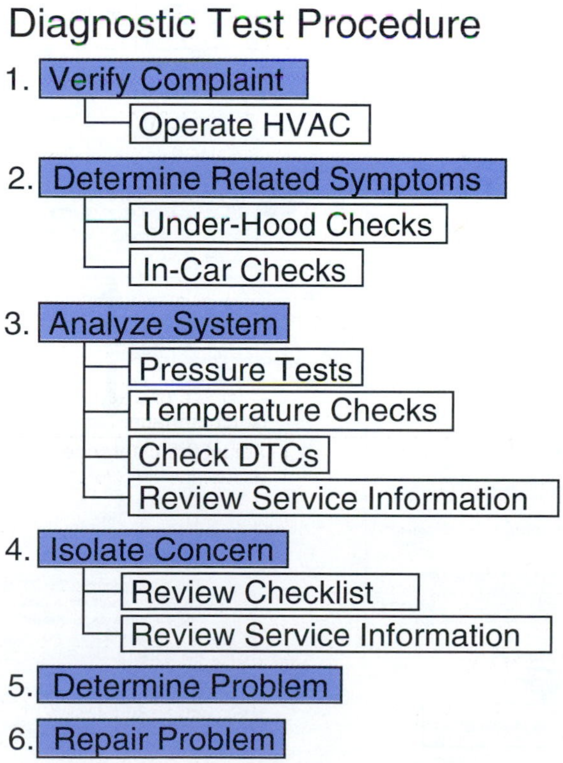

FIGURE 11-10 A thorough diagnostic procedure follows steps like these to locate and repair problems the first time a vehicle is worked on.

also helpful to determine the vehicle's history, for example, if there have been any previous HVAC repairs. In many cases, this can be done in the service bay; in others, a road test is required to duplicate the conditions under which the fault occurs. This step requires that the technician be familiar with the system and how it should perform. It is sometimes necessary for the technician to learn the exact nature or operating conditions; this is especially important with intermittent problems that happen only once in a while.

Step 2: Determine Related Symptoms
Some problems require preliminary checking to determine which avenue to take. This stage usually includes visual inspections along with feeling for system temperatures and listening for abnormal sounds. For example, one of the early checks for a *no cooling* complaint is to see whether the compressor operates. If it does, the problem is probably caused by a fault in the A/C system; if it does not operate, the problem can be caused by a fault in the air distribution system or the controls.

Step 3: Analyze Symptoms
With our modern and complex systems, more things can go wrong, and some of these are design or component problems. When these occur often enough on a particular make or model, the manufacturer develops a **technical service bulletin (TSB)** that describes the problem symptoms and the recommended repair procedure. Technicians in independent shops use service manuals, in printed and computer versions, including TSBs. Many new-car dealerships have on-line, dealership-to-factory computer connections for up-to-date service bulletins and diagnostic information.

Step 4: Isolate the Concern
Many information sources, both printed and electronic, include a checking procedure to isolate the causes of various problems. This information can be in the form of charts showing the probable and possible faults or in the form of flowcharts (Figure 11-11). Flowcharts are often called

(a)

X — Most Probable Cause(s)
● — Possible Causes
COMPLAINT–CONDITION

COMPLAINT–CONDITION	Sec. HVAC Controls	Damage Temp. Cable	Damage Mode Cable	HVAC Module Temp. Door	HVAC Module Mode Door	HVAC Module Linkage	Cable(s) Disconnected	Damage Air Ducts	Case Drain Plugged	Mode Cable Adjust	Temp. Cable Adjust	Damage Air Outlets	Debris in Evap. Housing
Mode Lever Binds/Sticks			X		●	X							
Temp. Lever Binds/Sticks	X		●			X						●	
No Mode Change			●			●	X			●			
No Temp. Change		●				●	X						
Unequal Air Distribution								X	X			●	
Odor from Air Outlets									X				X

(a)

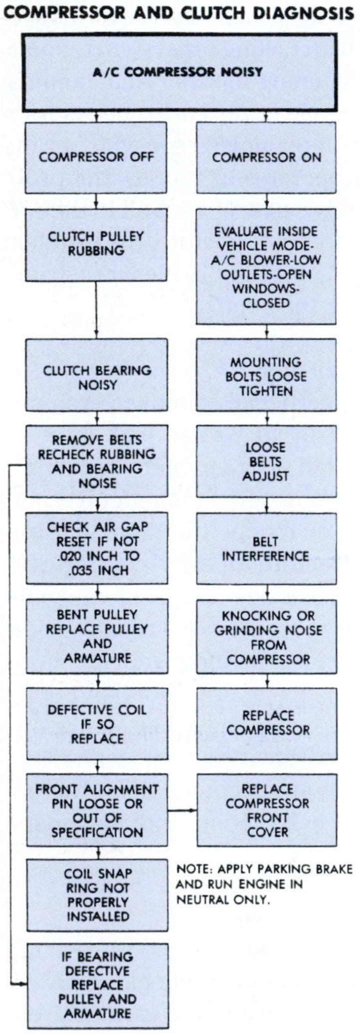

COMPRESSOR AND CLUTCH DIAGNOSIS

A/C COMPRESSOR NOISY

COMPRESSOR OFF
- CLUTCH PULLEY RUBBING
- CLUTCH BEARING NOISY
- REMOVE BELTS RECHECK RUBBING AND BEARING NOISE
- CHECK AIR GAP RESET IF NOT .020 INCH TO .035 INCH
- BENT PULLEY REPLACE PULLEY AND ARMATURE
- DEFECTIVE COIL IF SO REPLACE
- FRONT ALIGNMENT PIN LOOSE OR OUT OF SPECIFICATION
- COIL SNAP RING NOT PROPERLY INSTALLED
- IF BEARING DEFECTIVE REPLACE PULLEY AND ARMATURE

COMPRESSOR ON
- EVALUATE INSIDE VEHICLE MODE-A/C BLOWER-LOW OUTLETS-OPEN WINDOWS-CLOSED
- MOUNTING BOLTS LOOSE TIGHTEN
- LOOSE BELTS ADJUST
- BELT INTERFERENCE
- KNOCKING OR GRINDING NOISE FROM COMPRESSOR
- REPLACE COMPRESSOR
- REPLACE COMPRESSOR FRONT COVER

NOTE: APPLY PARKING BRAKE AND RUN ENGINE IN NEUTRAL ONLY.

(b)

ATC DIAGNOSTIC FLOWCHART

Start car, allow engine to warm up. Turn off instrument panel lights. Select panel mode operation by momentarily pushing the panel button.

Does the ATC Control light up? — NO → Are the fuses and wiring OK? Refer to Electrical Service Manual.
- YES → Replace the ATC Control.
- NO → Repair the wiring or replace fuse.
- START THE RETEST

YES

Momentarily push the DEF., FLOOR and BI-LEV buttons together to start the self-diagnostics test.

The control will flash an:

This means the computer is busy testing.

3) Check the following items when the display is flashing.

Note: Engine must be running.

QUESTIONS

A) Do **all** the symbols flash as above?

B) Is the blower motor running at a high speed?

C) Does the air blow out of the panel outlets?

D) Does discharge air become hot then cold?

A NO ANSWER

See the ATC Diagnostic Chart

1) The blower will stop and the control will flash an error code number from 1 to 16. Record this number and push the PANEL button to resume test.

Note: No codes found. Retest to verify.

The Control will do one of two things

2) Display

This display means the test is over. If no error codes occurred and the answers to questions A, B, C and D were yes, then the system is OK. Refer to the Fault Code Section if the display indicated any error code or if the answer to any of the questions was no.

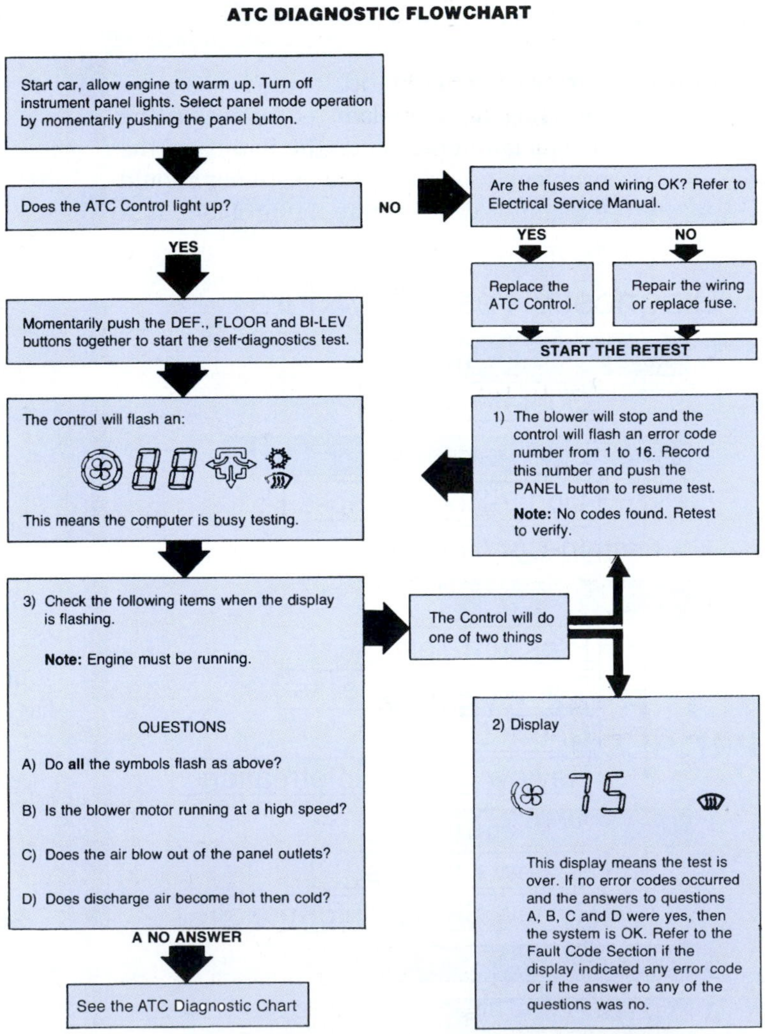

(c)

FIGURE 11-11 Three problem diagnosis charts. Chart *a* shows the most probable and possible causes of a group of problems. Chart *b* shows the procedure for locating a noisy compressor problem. Chart *c* is a flowchart for locating an ATC problem. *(a is courtesy of Saturn Corporation; b and c are courtesy of DaimlerChrysler Corporation)*

trouble trees because of the way they branch off to check other possible causes.

This step includes checking for electronic **diagnostic trouble codes (DTCs).** DTCs for older vehicles are specific to the vehicle make and model, making service information necessary to determine the procedure as well as the meaning of the codes. DTCs are described more completely in Chapter 14.

Step 5:   Determine Problem

While making checks, you often have to make decisions. Is the operation right or wrong or good or bad? Does your answer lead you to the need for additional checks? You might have to return to step 3 or 4 for more information. At the end of this step, you should have determined one of the following options:

- There is nothing wrong, and the system is operating normally.
- The system is almost operating properly, but some part of it needs adjustment or reprogramming.
- A faulty part needs to be repaired or replaced.

Step 6:   Repair Problem

Verify the repair. The HVAC system should operate properly and should not reset any DTCs. Repair operations for the HVAC subsystems are described in Chapters 14, 15, 16, and 17. They are also covered in vehicle service manuals.

11.4   HVAC SYSTEM PROBLEMS

As a technician diagnoses a system problem, it is usually very easy to determine the faulty subsystem. For example, a *no cooling from A/C* complaint is often diagnosed with a check to ensure compressor operation and then a check of system temperatures and pressures. If there is no pressure, the system probably has a leak that needs to be fixed; this would be an A/C system problem. If the compressor does not operate, then the technician checks for a voltage signal at the clutch. If there is a signal, the clutch must be faulty; this is also an A/C system problem. If there is no volt-

age, there must be an open switch, relay, or fuse interrupting the signal, and this could be a problem in the control circuit.

Some problems cross the line between HVAC subsystems or do not fit neatly with a subsystem.

◄   **SERVICE TIP**   ►

A complaint of uneven air discharge temperature from the instrument panel registers (cold on one side and warm on the other) can be caused by a low charge level. This will cause some parts of the evaporator to be cold while others are warm. It is possible for the air from the cold side to flow to a single register.

REAL WORLD FIX: The 1995 Chevrolet Lumina (60,000 miles) came in with a complaint of no A/C. The system appeared to be low on refrigerant so it was leak tested, the refrigerant recovered and recycled, and the system evacuated and recharged. The high and low side pressures were now okay, but the air coming from the ducts was not cold. An under-dash check shows vacuum at the proper location, and the blend door seems to be working.

FIX

A closer under-dash inspection revealed an ink pen blocking complete movement of the blend door lever; removal of the ink pen fixed this problem.

REAL WORLD FIX: The 1999 GMC Yukon (24,000 miles) has a wet floor on the passenger side. The A/C is not draining to the outside, and the technician cannot find the drain.

FIX

Following advice, the technician checked the proper location and found that the drain hose was missing and that the drain was plugged. Cleaning the drain and installing a new drain hose fixed this problem.

AUTHOR'S NOTE

Some vehicles have drains that are very difficult to locate; for example, one vehicle drains the HVAC case to the inside of a body frame member.

11.4.1   System Odors

Some systems develop a musty, moldy smell, which is not really a fault of the system. Some sources classify these odors into two types:

- "Dirty socks/gym locker" odor, which has an organic cause
- "Refrigerator, cement, or dusty room" odor, which is caused by chemicals

The organic odor problem is most common in areas with high relative humidity, and it is caused by mildew-type fungus growth on the evaporator and in the evaporator plenum. Modern evaporators have more fins that are closer together, and they tend to trap more moisture and bacterial growth. The cool surface of the evaporator collects moisture as it dehumidifies the air, and most of this moisture runs out of the bottom of the case. After a vehicle is shut off, the moist surface of the evaporator warms up, and this warm, wet area becomes an ideal environment for fungus and bacteria growth. A coating is applied to many evaporators to speed up water runoff; this coating helps dry the evaporator and reduce bacterial growth. Airborne bacteria also collect on this surface, and if the surface stays moist, these bacteria will live and grow, creating the unpleasant smell. When we turn on the air conditioning or even the ventilation, we blow that smell into the car.

Several companies market chemicals, essentially fungicides, to kill the bacterial growth, or detergents to clean the evaporator core. Some of these chemicals and a procedure to use them have been approved by vehicle manufacturers. These chemicals are sprayed into the ductwork or onto the evaporator fins.

◄ SERVICE TIP ►

In some systems, spraying a liquid into the inlet of ductwork simply wets the blower fan and does very little good. It is much better to spray the material onto the evaporator fins. With some systems, fairly good access can be obtained by removing the blower motor resistor; other systems require drilling a properly placed hole, which must be covered when you are finished. Be sure to follow the manufacturer's procedure and wear the required safety gear; most require a face shield or goggles, and some require a respirator (Figure 11-12).

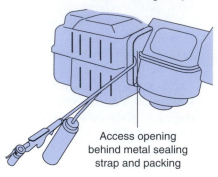

Metal Sealing Strap

Access opening behind metal sealing strap and packing

FIGURE 11-12 A foul smell from the A/C can be cured by spraying a cleaning solution or fungicide onto the evaporator to either clean it thoroughly or kill the bacteria. *(Courtesy of Airsept, Inc.)*

◄ SERVICE TIP ►

Bacterial growth can be prevented by regularly drying off the evaporator. Running the system on vent or heat with the A/C off is a good way, but most people do not want to do this on a hot day. Sometimes just turning the A/C off shortly before the car is parked will let the high side pressure bleed off, so the evaporator will warm up slightly and dry off faster.

◄ SERVICE TIP ►

Bacterial-growth odor can be prevented by operating the A/C in fresh air mode rather than recirculation. The moisture from the outside air collects on the evaporator core and can wash the growth off the core.

Some manufacturers install an **after blow module**, also called an *electronic evaporator dryer module*. In some vehicles, the A/C control module is programmed to operate the blower for a drying cycle after the car is shut off. This device turns on the blower (with the ignition switched off for 30 to 50 minutes) and lets it run long enough to dry off the evaporator after the vehicle

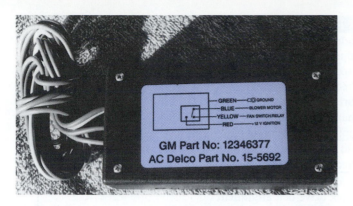

FIGURE 11-13   An afterblow module can be connected into the blower motor circuit. It will operate the blower motor after the system is shut off to dry the evaporator and prevent bacterial growth. *(Courtesy of Airsept, Inc.)*

has been shut off. One system waits 10 minutes, runs the blower on high for 10 seconds, shuts down for another 10 minutes, and then repeats the 10-second operation and 10-minute pause for 10 cycles. The object is to blow the moist air out of the evaporator without discharging the battery. After blow modules are available for vehicles with both ground or B+ side blower switch systems (Figure 11-13).

11.4.2   Noise Problems

The A/C system is the potential source for several noise problems, and the compressor and clutch are the main culprits. When diagnosing noise problems, it helps to remember that noise pitch is related to the frequency of the item that is producing the noise. A moaning or growling noise is a relatively low-frequency noise caused by something moving slowly; a whine or squeal is a high pitch and frequency noise produced by something moving rapidly.

Another problem can be **groundout,** in which a vibrating metal A/C line contacts another surface (flat surfaces produce the most noise). Groundout problems also occur when the exhaust pipes make metal-to-metal contact with the vehicle body.

◄ **SERVICE TIP** ►

Groundout problems are cured by either separating the A/C lines from the other surface or clamping them together.

◄ **SERVICE TIP** ►

When there is a suspected noise problem with a compressor, the first check is to note the noise change with the clutch engaged and disengaged. If the noise stops with the clutch disengaged, the problem must be caused by the compressor; if the noise continues, it could be the clutch bearing. The second check is to (1) feel for a vibration by touching the area next to the clutch (a noisy part vibrates at a frequency that matches the noise frequency) or (2) remove the drive belt (if the noise stops, one of the items driven by that belt was making the noise).

◄ **SERVICE TIP** ►

A high pitched noise from the area of the compressor clutch that occurs during engagement can indicate a weak clutch. Check for proper voltage at the clutch, an excessive clutch air gap, or excessive high side pressure. This noise can also be caused by a loose or misaligned drive belt. With serpentine belts, check to make sure the automatic tensioner is operating correctly.

Figure 11-14 can help you locate the cause of other noise problems.

NOISE	SOURCE	CURE
Moan, growl	Compressor	Tighten mounting brackets
		Adjust drive belt
		Check for internal damage
		Check for excessive high side pressure
	A/C lines	Cure groundouts
		Change hose length or material
	Blower motor	Replace blower motor
Chatter (at idle)	Compressor	Add ½ lb. R-134a & 3 oz PAG oil to check effect
		Check for internal damage
Whine, squeal	Compressor	Check for faulty bearings, interference with rotating parts
	P/S pump	Check drive belt alignment
	Alternator	Check drive belt for edge wear
	Belt idler	
Hiss, gurgle	Orifice tube	Normal if occurs at A/C shut down
	TXV	Isolate or insulate liquid line
	Heater core	Bleed air from heater core
Chirp, thump	Compressor clutch	Click is normal at clutch engagement
		Chirp indicates slippage
Knock	Compressor	Tighten mounting brackets
Rattle of constant frequency	Blower fan	Remove interference with blower wheel

FIGURE 11-14 The causes of most HVAC noises are shown here.

REVIEW QUESTIONS

The following questions are provided to help you study as you read the chapter.

1. The goal of automotive technicians is to fix vehicle problems ~~correctly~~ the _first_ _time_ .

2. HVAC system inspection normally begins _under_ the hood with the _engine_ _off_ .

3. During the under-hood inspection, the technician should determine what _type_ of _refrig_ the vehicle has.

4. _Oiled_ _Dirt_ on a refrigerant hose or fitting can indicate a leak.

5. With the system off, there should be a(n) _air_ _gap_ at the compressor clutch plate.

6. The in-vehicle HVAC system checks include operation of the _Blower_ and _Control Head_ for airflow control.

7. Compressor engagement is usually indicated by an audible _click_ .

8. An early step in determining how to make a repair is to check for _D T C_ .

9. _Trouble Trees_ will often lead the technician to the cause of many HVAC problems.

10. Many stinky HVAC system problems are caused by _mold_ _growth_ on the evaporator.

CHAPTER QUIZ

The following questions will help you check the facts you have learned. Select the answer that completes each statement correctly.

1. Technician A says that you should begin HVAC problem diagnosis with a thorough inspection. Technician B says that you can determine from the inspection what type of system you are dealing with. Who is correct?
   a. A only
   b. B only
   c. Both A and B
   d. Neither A nor B

2. Technician A says that sometimes nothing is wrong with a system when there is a complaint of insufficient cooling. Technician B says that you should begin diagnosing this complaint by checking the A/C system pressures. Who is correct?
   a. A only
   b. B only
   c. Both A and B
   d. Neither A nor B

3. Technician A says that while the compressor clutch is off, it's OK if the pulley and clutch plate touch. Technician B says that too much air gap can cause clutch slippage during engagement. Who is correct?
   a. A only
   b. B only
   c. Both A and B
   d. Neither A nor B

4. Technician A says that oily residue on a hose can indicate a refrigerant leak. Technician B says that this residue is normal for most connections. Who is correct?
   a. A only
   b. B only
   c. Both A and B
   d. Neither A nor B

5. Technician A says that a quick check of A/C system operation is to feel the temperature of the suction and discharge lines. Technician B says that the suction line should be cold and the discharge line hot after a minute of system operation. Who is correct?
   a. A only
   b. B only
   c. Both A and B
   d. Neither A nor B

6. Technician A says that replacement of the fuse is the only repair necessary for a blown fuse. Technician B says that a blown fuse is caused by a system fault such as high resistance. Who is correct?
   a. A only
   b. B only
   c. Both A and B
   d. Neither A nor B

7. Technician A says that the first step in diagnosing a problem is to verify what the complaint is. Technician B says that a TSB can tell you the cure for some problems. Who is correct?
   a. A only
   b. B only
   c. Both A and B
   d. Neither A nor B

8. Technician A says that a misadjusted blend door can cause poor A/C operation. Technician B says that you can check this by clamping off a heater hose. Who is correct?
   a. A only
   b. B only
   c. Both A and B
   d. Neither A nor B

9. Technician A says that foul-smelling air from the A/C ducts is caused by bacteria growing on the evaporator fins. Technician B says that this problem can be cured by installing a control that operates the blower motor after the vehicle is shut off. Who is correct?
   a. A only
   b. B only
   c. Both A and B
   d. Neither A nor B

10. Technician A says that a refrigerant line groundout problem makes a whining noise at moderate speeds. Technician B says that knocking noises are a sure sign that the compressor has failed. Who is correct?
    a. A only
    b. B only
    c. Both A and B
    d. Neither A nor B

Chapter 12

A/C SYSTEM INSPECTION AND DIAGNOSIS

LEARNING OBJECTIVES

After completing this chapter, you should be able to:

1. Inspect an A/C system to determine whether it is operating correctly, and if not make further tests to locate the cause of the problem.
2. Connect a manifold gauge set to a system and check system pressures.
3. Determine whether system pressures are normal, and if abnormal determine the cause of the fault.
4. Check a TXV and determine whether it is operating properly.
5. Locate the source of a refrigerant leak.
6. Complete the ASE tasks related to A/C system diagnosis.

TERMS TO LEARN

back seat	service hose
compound gauge	service unit
Delta T	shutoff valve
electronic leak detectors	ultrasonic leak
front seat	detector
hand valves	vacuum pump
manifold gauge set	valve core
mid seat	depressor
rub-through	

12.1   INTRODUCTION

If the HVAC inspection (as outlined in Section 11.2) has determined a fault in the A/C system, further checks can be made to determine the exact cause of the problem. This further evaluation usually consists of a check of system pressures and temperatures while also checking for unusual noises, vibrations, and smells (Figure 12-1).

◀ SERVICE TIP ▶

Remember that the purpose of the A/C system is to make the evaporator cold, slightly above 32°F (0°C). We determine its temperature by feeling the suction line where it reenters the engine compartment; it should be cold to touch (Figure 12-2). The suction line warms up as it goes to the compressor, but it still should be cool to touch. The discharge line leaving the compressor should be hot to very hot; use caution when you feel this line. Remember that the condenser must give up heat to the ambient air, so it must be hotter than ambient temperature.

System pressures are closely linked to temperatures. The hot part of the system is the high side, and the pressure is about 150 to 350 psi, rather high. High side pressure is directly linked to ambient temperature and the airflow

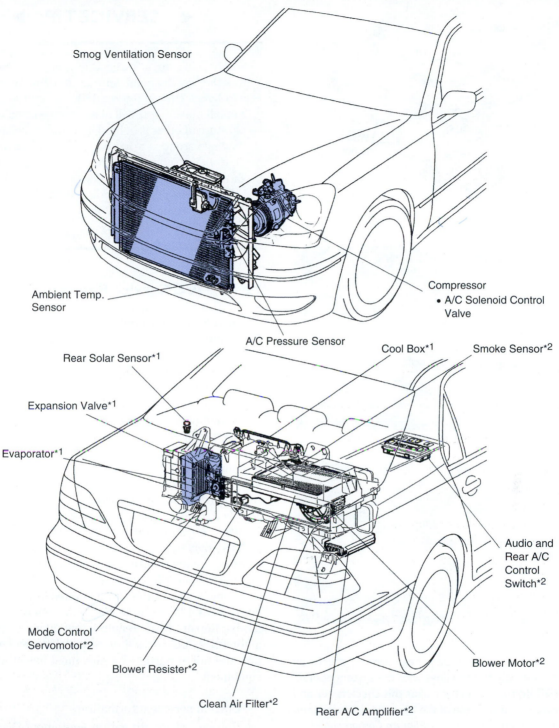

Smog Ventilation Sensor

Ambient Temp.
Sensor

A/C Pressure Sensor

Compressor
• A/C Solenoid Control
  Valve

Rear Solar Sensor*1

Expansion Valve*1

Evaporator*1

Cool Box*1

Smoke Sensor*2

Audio and
Rear A/C
Control
Switch*2

Mode Control
Servomotor*2

Blower Resister*2

Clean Air Filter*2

Rear A/C Amplifier*2

Blower Motor*2

*1: Only for Rear A/C
*2: With Rear A/C and Air Purifier

FIGURE 12-1 Possible A/C problems include refrigerant leaks and flow restrictions along with compressor and drive belt failure. *(Courtesy of Toyota Motor Sales USA, Inc.)*

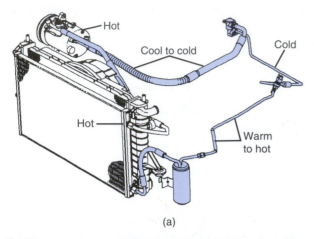

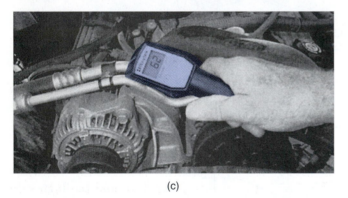

FIGURE 12-2 Many technicians begin system checks by feeling the temperature of the lines with the system operating *(a)*; an infrared thermometer makes this check faster and more accurate *(b and c)*. Some of the lines should be hot, and some should be cold. (a *courtesy of Saturn Corporation*)

through the condenser. The cold part of the system is the low side, where the pressure is lower, about 30 psi.

Leak checks to find the location of refrigerant loss are another important test that the A/C technician performs. Refrigerant loss allows refrigerant to enter our environment, which it may harm, and it also hinders the performance of the A/C system.

◀ **SERVICE TIP** ▶

When using an infrared thermometer, remember that the sensing beam spreads out and increases in width as it travels outward. If you are too far from a small object, you will also be measuring the temperature of objects behind it. Infrared thermometer readings are also affected by the emissivity of the item being checked. Shiny, light-colored items should be marked with a dark marker or covered by a single layer of dark-colored tape. See Worktext Appendix D for a more complete description of infrared thermometer usage.

12.1.1 A/C Service Regulations

At one time, anyone could service or repair A/C systems for remuneration or profit. Since the passage of the Clean Air Act in 1992, American A/C technicians must be certified and certain pieces of service equipment must meet required specifications. The federal EPA has the power to enforce the technician certification and shop equipment requirements.

As specified by the Clean Air Act, since January 1992, automotive A/C technicians must complete an approved training program and use approved equipment. Approved training programs are offered by the *International Mobile Air Conditioning Association Foundation (IMACA), the Mobile Air Conditioning Society (MACS),* the *National Institute for Automotive Service Excellence (ASE),* as well as private and public sources. Technicians who successfully complete a training program receive a certificate bearing their certificate number.

Some states in the United States have additional requirements. For example, the California Bureau of Automotive Repair (BAR) requires that all shops performing automotive A/C service or repair that involves evacuation and full or partial charging must have the following equipment:

- Current service information
- Refrigerant identification equipment that meets or exceeds SAE standard J1771
- Refrigerant leak detection equipment that meets or exceeds SAE standard J1627
- Refrigerant recovery equipment that meets or exceeds SAE standards J1732, J1770, J1990, and J2209
- Low- and high-pressure A/C system gauges (The low-pressure gauge must be capable of measuring from 0 to 30″ Hg and from 0 to 250 psi. The high-

pressure gauge must be capable of measuring from 0 to 500 psi.)

- A/C system vacuum pump that is capable of reducing system pressure to a minimum of 29.5″ Hg
- Thermometer that is capable of measuring air temperatures from 20 to 100°F

If the shop claims to inspect, service, diagnose, or otherwise lead the customer to believe that it repairs A/C systems, the repair procedure must include checking at least 13 items for such problems as damage, leaks, missing parts, and so forth. The checked items must include the hoses, tubing, and connections; compressor and clutch; compressor drive plate rotation; service ports and caps; condenser; expansion device; accumulator, receiver–drier, and/or inline filter; drive belt(s) and tensioner; fan clutch; cooling fan; all accessible electrical connections; and the refrigerant to ensure that it is not contaminated. The system must be checked for leakage while it has an internal pressure of 50 psi or greater; the compressor clutch, blower, and air control doors must operate properly; and the low and high side pressures along with the center duct temperature must be recorded on the final invoice.

12.2 A/C PRESSURE CHECKS

The pressures in the high and low sides of a system are normally a factor of the refrigerant type and the temperature of the evaporator and the condenser. The temperature of a saturated vapor is tied to the pressure and vice versa (Figure 12-3).

Pressure tests are made using either a portable manifold gauge set or a service unit. Self-contained service units go by various names, such as *charging station, refrigerant handling systems, refrigerant management center*, or *recovery/recyling/recharging units*. They usually include a pressure gauge set, **vacuum pump,** and refrigerant supply for recharging; some include refrigerant recovery and recycling capability along with computer controls. Newer versions include refrigerant identifiers and the ability to perform refrigerant calculations like superheat and to analyze the pressure and temperatures to provide diagnostic information for problem solving (Figure 12-4).

The introduction of R-134a and the incompatibility between R-12 and R-134a and their respective oils have made different service equipment for each of these systems necessary (Figure 12-5). R-12 and its oil can contaminate an R-134a system and vice versa. The gauge sets and other equipment are quite similar, but different sets must be used to prevent mixing. To prevent cross-

contamination, the equipment must be dedicated to either R-12 or R-134a, but not both. The service fittings for R-134a systems are different, so R-12 equipment cannot be connected to them (Figures 12-6 and 12-7). Some service units are dual-gas units with R-12 and R-134a units side by side (Figure 12-8).

When R-12 and R-134a mix, they act like a single compound; the mix becomes physically and chemically different from both R-12 and R-134a. The mixture of R-12 and R-134a exhibits higher pressures (almost 10%), and there will be much greater corrosion and deterioration in the system (Figure 12-9). Mixing a blend or flammable refrigerant into R-12 is equally problematic. A/C service technicians must always be aware that someone may have charged R-22, R-134a, or a blend into an R-12 system.

Refrigerant that is cross-contaminated cannot be recycled; it must be disposed of and not reused. The price of refrigerant has increased to the point where it is too valuable to waste R-12 or R-134a by contaminating it, and cross-contaminated refrigerant creates a disposal problem.

12.2.1 Gauge Set

A **manifold gauge set** is a unit with two pressure gauges mounted on a manifold that has two hand valves and usually three hoses. Two of these hoses connect to the low and high side service ports of a system to allow the pressures to be read on the low and high side gauges. The low side gauge and service hose are color-coded blue, and the high side gauge and service hose are color-coded red. The third, center hose is coded yellow, white, or green. Yellow and white are the preferred colors for R-12, and solid yellow with a black stripe is preferred for R-134a. One of the **hand valves** controls the flow between the low side hose and the center hose, and the other hand valve controls the flow between the center hose and the high side hose (Figure 12-10).

Gauges are printed to give pressure readings in pounds per square inch, kilopascals, BAR, or a combination of these, with pounds-per-square-inch readings being the most popular in the United States. The pressure readings are normally printed in black. Most gauges are also printed with red scales that show the corresponding refrigerant temperature (Figure 12-11).

The low side gauge is a **compound gauge**; it can read pressures into a vacuum as well as pressures above atmospheric. The readings start at 0 (atmospheric pressure); they go downward to 30″ Hg (a vacuum) and upward to about 150 psi (pressure). The high side gauge is a pressure gauge that reads from

GAUGE PRESSURE RELATED TROUBLESHOOTING

Normal compressor suction and discharge pressures at an atmospheric temperature of 30–38°C {86–96°F} and engine speed of approx. 1,500 r/min are:

High-pressure side pressure: 1.5–1.7 MPa {15–17 kgf/cm², 213–242 psi}
Low-pressure side pressure: 0.13–0.2 MPa {1.3–2.0 kgf/cm², 18–28 psi}

Possible cause	Inspection	Remedy
Low-pressure side too high.	The low-pressure side pressure normally becomes too high when the high-pressure side pressure is too high. As this is explained below, the following inspection is only used when the low-pressure side pressure is too high.	
1. Defective thermoswitch.	The magnetic clutch switch turns off before the outlet air temperature is sufficiently low.	Replace the thermoswitch.
2. Defective compressor gasket.	The high- and low-pressure side gauge pressures equalize when the magnetic clutch is turned off.	Replace the compressor.
3. Poor expansion valve temperature sensor contact.	Frost has adhered to the suction hose/pipe.	Install the temperature sensor against the low-pressure pipe.
4. The expansion valve opens too far.	Same as above.	Replace.
5. Clogged compressor suction filter.	The compressor fitting is cool but the low-pressure hose is not.	Remove and clean the filter.
Low-pressure side too low.		
1. Insufficient refrigerant.	There will be little temperature difference between the low- and high-pressure sides.	
2. Clogged liquid tank.	Considerable temperature difference between the inlet and outlet sides, or the tank is frosted.	Replace the liquid tank.
3. Clogged expansion valve.	The expansion valve's inlet side is frosted.	Replace the expansion valve.
4. Expansion valve temperature sensor gas leak (damaged capillary tube, etc.).	The expansion valve's outlet side is chilled, and low pressure gauge indicates low pressure.	Clean or replace the expansion valve.
5. Clogged or blocked piping.	When the piping is clogged or blocked, the low-pressure gauge reading will decrease, or a negative reading may be shown. A frost spot may be present at the point of the restriction.	Clean or replace piping.
6. Defective thermoswitch.	The evaporator is frozen.	Adjust or replace the thermoswitch.
High-pressure side too high.		
1. Poor condenser cooling.	Dirty or clogged condenser fins. Cooling fans do not operate correctly.	Clean, and/or repair the fan.
2. Excessive refrigerant.	Verify by gauge reading.	
3. Air in the system.	Pressure is high on both high and low sides.	Evacuate and recharge with refrigerant.
High-pressure side too low.		
1. Insufficient refrigerant.	Refer to "1. Insufficient refrigerant," above.	

FIGURE 12-3 This troubleshooting chart relates possible system problems to abnormal gauge pressures. *(Courtesy of Zexel USA Corporation)*

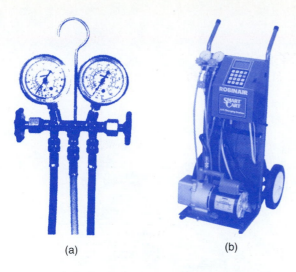

FIGURE 12-4 System pressure checks can be made using a simple manifold gauge set *(a)* or a charging station *(b)*. *(Courtesy of Robinair, SPX Corporation)*

(a) (b)

R-134A				R-12			
Temperature °C (°F)	Pressure kPa (Psi)	Temperature °C (°F)	Pressure kPa (Psi)	Temperature °C (°F)	Pressure kPa (Psi)	Temperature °C (°F)	Pressure kPa (Psi)
–9 (16)	106 (15)	38 (100)	857 (124)	–9 (16)	127 (18)	38 (100)	808 (117)
–8 (18)	115 (17)	39 (102)	887 (129)	–8 (18)	136 (20)	39 (102)	893 (121)
–7 (20)	124 (18)	40 (104)	917 (133)	–7 (20)	145 (21)	40 (104)	859 (125)
–6 (22)	134 (19)	41 (106)	948 (137)	–6 (22)	155 (22)	41 (106)	893 (129)
–4 (24)	144 (21)	42 (108)	980 (142)	–4 (24)	165 (24)	42 (108)	917 (133)
–3 (26)	155 (22)	43 (110)	1,012 (147)	–3 (26)	175 (25)	43 (110)	940 (136)
–2 (28)	166 (24)	44 (112)	1,045 (152)	–2 (28)	185 (27)	44 (112)	969 (140)
–1 (30)	177 (26)	46 (114)	1,079 (157)	–1 (30)	196 (28)	46 (114)	997 (145)
0 (32)	188 (27)	47 (116)	1,114 (162)	0 (32)	207 (30)	47 (116)	1,027 (149)
1 (34)	200 (29)	48 (118)	1,149 (167)	1 (34)	219 (32)	48 (118)	1,057 (153)
2 (36)	212 (31)	49 (120)	1,185 (172)	2 (36)	230 (33)	49 (120)	1,087 (158)
3 (38)	225 (33)	50 (122)	1,222 (177)	3 (38)	249 (36)	50 (122)	1,118 (162)
4 (40)	238 (35)	51 (124)	1,260 (183)	4 (40)	255 (37)	51 (124)	1,150 (167)
7 (45)	272 (40)	52 (126)	1,298 (188)	7 (45)	287 (42)	52 (126)	1,182 (171)
10 (50)	310 (45)	53 (128)	1,337 (194)	10 (50)	322 (47)	53 (128)	1,215 (176)
13 (55)	350 (51)	54 (130)	1,377 (200)	13 (55)	359 (52)	54 (130)	1,248 (181)
16 (60)	392 (57)	57 (135)	1,481 (215)	16 (60)	398 (58)	57 (135)	1,334 (194)
18 (65)	438 (64)	60 (140)	1,590 (231)	18 (65)	440 (64)	60 (140)	1,425 (207)
21 (70)	487 (71)	63 (145)	1,704 (247)	21 (70)	484 (70)	63 (145)	1,519 (220)
24 (75)	540 (78)	66 (150)	1,823 (264)	24 (75)	531 (77)	66 (150)	1,618 (235)
27 (80)	609 (88)	68 (155)	1,948 (283)	27 (80)	580 (84)	68 (155)	1,721 (250)
30 (85)	655 (95)	71 (160)	2,079 (301)	30 (85)	633 (92)	71 (160)	1,828 (265)
32 (90)	718 (104)	74 (165)	2,215 (321)	32 (90)	688 (100)	74 (165)	1,940 (281)
35 (95)	786 (114)	77 (170)	2,358 (342)	35 (95)	746 (108)	77 (170)	2,057 (298)

(The left portion of the R-134A column is bracketed "Evaporator Range" and the right portion "Condenser Range"; the same brackets appear for the R-12 columns.)

Note: Evaporator pressure represents gas temperatures inside the coil and not at the coil surfaces. Add to temperature for coil and air-off temperatures (4 to 6°C or 8 to 10°F). Condenser temperatures are not ambient temperatures. Add to ambient (19 to 22°C or 35 to 40°F) for proper heat transfer; then refer to chart.

Example:

$$\begin{array}{r} 32°\text{C} \\ +\ 22° \\ \hline 54°\text{C} \end{array}$$

54°C condenser temperature = 1,377 kPa (R-134) or 1,248 kPa (R-12), based on 30-mph airflow.

Conditions vary for different system configurations. Refer to the manufacturer's specifications.

FIGURE 12-5 System temperatures and pressures for R-134a and R-12. Note that the low side (evaporator range) pressures are close to each other, with a wider difference on the high side (condenser range), especially at higher temperatures. *(Reprinted with permission of General Motors Corporation)*

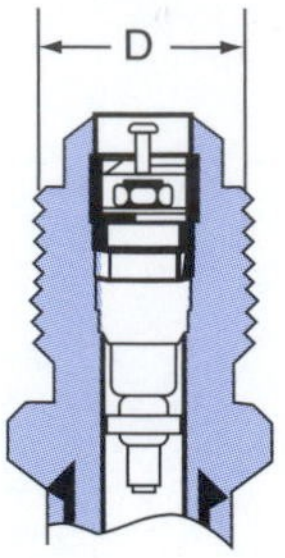

Low side: D = 7/16" (20 TPI)

High side: D = 3/8" (24 TPI)

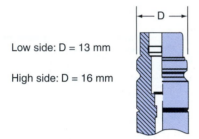

FIGURE 12-6 R-12 service ports use male flare fittings with two different sizes sealed by a Shrader valve. The low side fitting is larger.

Low side: D = 13 mm

High side: D = 16 mm

FIGURE 12-7 R-134a service ports use quick-disconnect–type fittings, and the high side fitting is larger.

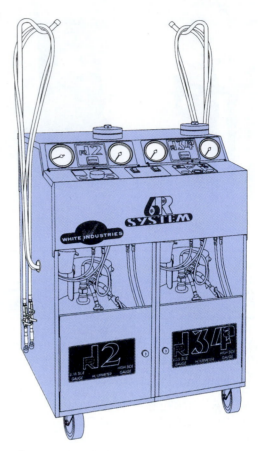

FIGURE 12-8 A dual A/C service unit that can be used on both R-12 and R-134a systems. Note that it is essentially two side-by-side units. *(Courtesy of White Industries)*

0 to about 500 psi (Figure 12-12). Many high side gauges have a restricting orifice in the passage leading to the gauge. This orifice dampens pressure pulsations from the compressor, which can cause very rapid needle movements. The manifold is drilled so a gauge will always read the pressure in its respective hose. Many gauges include a *calibration adjustment*. This screw is turned to adjust the gauge needle to 0 (when there is atmospheric pressure at the gauge) (Figure 12-13).

The center hose is the **service hose.** Depending on the service operation, it can be connected to a recovery unit, vacuum pump, or refrigerant supply. As mentioned, the two hand valves allow the technician to control the operation and the flow to or from the low side, high side, or both hoses (Figure 12-14). Some gauge sets have two center hoses so the manifold can be connected for two operations at the same time—a vacuum pump and refrigerant supply, for example. Some gauge sets include a sight glass at the center hose port so that the technician can observe the refrigerant flow through the manifold. Many manifolds include a hook so the manifold and gauges can be hung up, and many also have hose holders for the service ends of the hoses. Hose holders keep the hose ends clean and neat (Figure 12-15).

Hoses are available in different lengths: 36, 48, 60, and 72 inches (90, 120, 150, and 180 cm) are common.

Do not release refrigerants into the air

FIGURE 12-9 Different types of refrigerants should not be mixed. The resulting contamination can cause excessive pressures and damage the system. *(Courtesy of Zexel USA Corporation)*

With gauge sets, many technicians prefer the shorter length for the low and high side hoses and either a 48- or 60-inch length for the center hose. A manifold set is often hung from the car's hood or placed on a fender cover; long low and high side hoses become cumbersome and can get into the moving parts of the

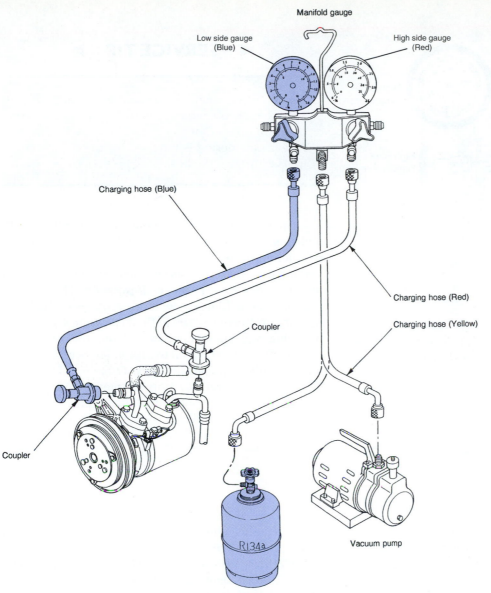

Manifold gauge

Low side gauge
(Blue)

High side gauge
(Red)

Charging hose (Blue)

Coupler

Charging hose (Red)

Charging hose (Yellow)

Coupler

Coupler

R134a

Vacuum pump

Refrigerant container

FIGURE 12-10 The blue, low side hose is connected to the low side of the system; the red, high side hose is connected to the high side of the system; and the center hose(s) is connected to a refrigerant container, vacuum pump, or recovery unit (not shown). *(Courtesy of Zexel USA Corporation)*

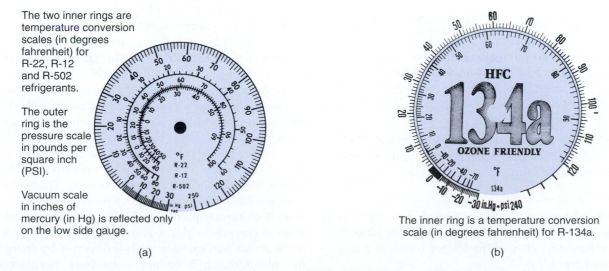

The two inner rings are temperature conversion scales (in degrees fahrenheit) for R-22, R-12 and R-502 refrigerants.

The outer ring is the pressure scale in pounds per square inch (PSI).

Vacuum scale in inches of mercury (in Hg) is reflected only on the low side gauge.

(a)

The inner ring is a temperature conversion scale (in degrees fahrenheit) for R-134a.

(b)

FIGURE 12-11 The faces of a low side gauge for R-12, R-22, and R-502 *(a)* and for R-134a *(b)*. The outer ring shows the pressure; the inner rings are temperature–pressure relationships. *(Courtesy of TIF Instruments)*

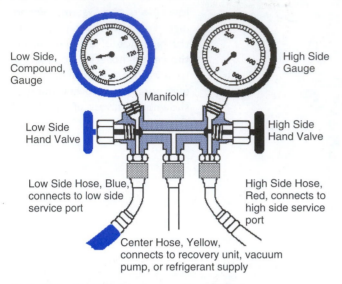

FIGURE 12-12 The low and high side gauges are mounted onto the manifold so they always read the pressure in their respective hoses. The manifold hand valves control the flow to and from the center hose.

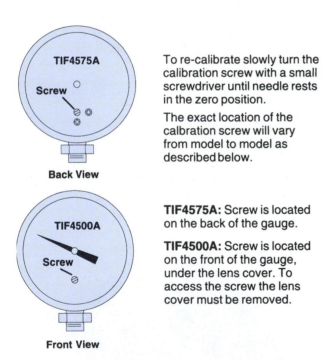

To re-calibrate slowly turn the calibration screw with a small screwdriver until needle rests in the zero position.

The exact location of the calbration screw will vary from model to model as described below.

TIF4575A: Screw is located on the back of the gauge.

TIF4500A: Screw is located on the front of the gauge, under the lens cover. To access the screw the lens cover must be removed.

FIGURE 12-13 Many gauges include a calibration screw, which is used to adjust the needle position to 0 (no pressure). *(Courtesy of TIF Instruments)*

engine. The longer center hose is needed to reach to the floor, where the vacuum pump is usually placed. Most charging stations use the longer hoses to reach the service fittings.

◀   SERVICE TIP   ▶

Longer hoses can hold a substantial amount of refrigerant when charging a system. As much as an ounce of refrigerant can be lost because of this. A longer time period is required for the refrigerant to pass through the hose.

The manifold end of the hose is normally straight and close coupled. The system end of the hose usually uses a longer, bent-metal section to allow easier connection to the system's service fittings. The system end also includes a **valve core depressor**. The knurled nut on some R-12 hoses includes grooves in the internal threads to control the path of escaping refrigerant, directing any sprayback away from the technician (Figure 12-16). SAE standard J2196 requires a **shutoff valve** within 12 inches (30 cm) of the end of the hose. This valve is closed to trap refrigerant in the hose when it is disconnected. Some hose brands use a seal feature that automatically closes as the hose is disconnected to prevent refrigerant loss and sprayback. A service hose for R-134a must have a black stripe along its length and be marked with "SAE J2196/ R-134a" (Figure 12-17).

In the past, all R-12 hose connections used 1/4-inch flare fittings, with normal 7/16-20 threads. Male fittings are used at the manifold and the system service fittings, and female fittings are used at each end of the hose. These fittings are sealed by a rubber ring in the hose end as the fitting is tightened. Knurled nuts are used at the hose ends and tightened by hand. Some high side R-12 service fittings are a quick-coupler style or a 3/16- or 1/8-inch flare fitting. A hose adapter is required to make these high side connections (Figure 12-18).

Systems that use R-134a require a metric service fitting with a $0.500 \times 16\text{-}2\text{G}$ Acme thread. This completely different fitting is used to prevent technicians from connecting equipment used for R-12 service. The system end of the hose uses a quick coupler to make the hose connection and can include a hand knob to depress and open the internal valve (Figure 12-19).

As mentioned earlier, a service fitting that uses unique threads to prevent improper connections is required for each of the different blends. These fitting sizes are shown in Appendix D. EPA regulations do not allow using an adapter so an R-12 or R-134a hose can be hooked onto these ports. However, the regulations do allow a standard gauge set to be converted by changing the hoses. Each hose set must have permanently

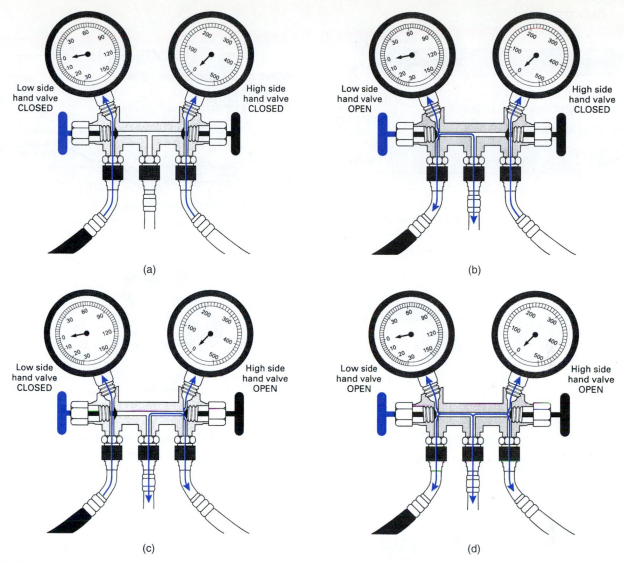

(a)

Low side hand valve CLOSED

High side hand valve CLOSED

(b)

Low side hand valve OPEN

High side hand valve CLOSED

(c)

Low side hand valve CLOSED

High side hand valve OPEN

(d)

Low side hand valve OPEN

High side hand valve OPEN

FIGURE 12-14 The low and high side manifold valves are used to control flow through the manifold. (*a*) is used when pressure checking a system; *(b)*, *(c)*, and *(d)* are used for various service operations.

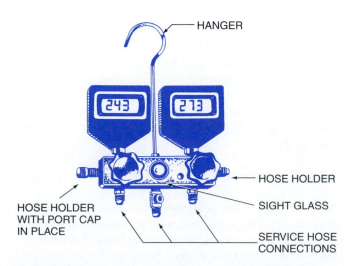

HANGER

HOSE HOLDER

SIGHT GLASS

SERVICE HOSE CONNECTIONS

HOSE HOLDER WITH PORT CAP IN PLACE

FIGURE 12-15 This gauge set has a hanging hook for suspending the gauge set and hose holders to keep the working ends of the hoses clean and neat when out of use. Note the electronic digital gauges. *(Courtesy of TIF Instruments)*

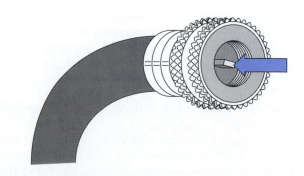

FIGURE 12-16 The working, system end of a hose for R-12 systems should have a gasket and Schrader valve depressor *(arrow)* in it; the manifold end should have only a gasket. The working end has a slight bend; the manifold end is straight.

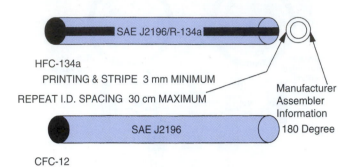

FIGURE 12-17   SAE-approved service hoses should have the markings shown. *(Reprinted with permission from SAE Document M-106, © 1992, Society of Automotive Engineers, Inc.)*

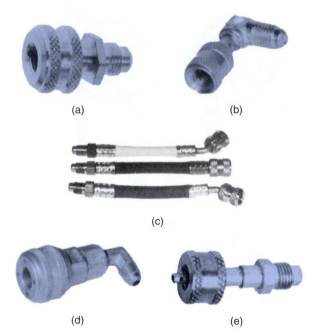

FIGURE 12-18   R-12 system service hose adapters include quick seal (stops backflow out of the hose when disconnected) *(a)*, 90° (shown) and 45° *(b)*, flexible *(c)*, quick disconnect *(d)*, and straight *(e)*. Adapter e is designed to fit GM Positive Seal valves. The female side is made in different sizes to fit the different high side ports. *(a,b,c, and d courtesy of Robinair, SPX Corporation; e courtesy of Kent-Moore)*

attached fittings for each refrigerant being checked (Figure 12-20).

Some systems that use an STV have a second low side service port to allow the use of a third gauge. A third gauge is a single, compound gauge, similar to the low side gauge, and is often attached directly to a service hose. The third gauge is usually attached to the third service port, which is downstream from the STV, closer to the compressor. Comparison of the low side

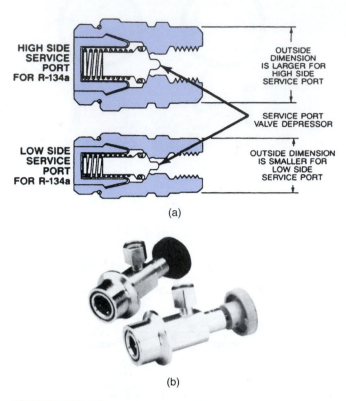

FIGURE 12-19   A cutaway view of R-134a service ports *(a)*. These service hose couplers use a quick-connect attachment to the fitting and a knob that is turned inward to depress the valve *(b)*. *(a courtesy of DaimlerChrysler Corporation; b courtesy of Robinair, SPX Corporation)*

pressure with that of the third gauge allows the technician to determine whether the STV is open or closed (Figure 12-21).

12.2.1.1 Electronic Gauge Sets Some modern gauge sets use electronic gauges and pressure transducers in place of hoses (Figure 12-22). One set has inputs for low side pressure, high side pressure, temperature, and vacuum sensing in microns. This allows the gauge to display both low and high side pressures, temperature from selected points, and vacuum in microns; it will also calculate and display refrigerant superheating and subcooling.

12.2.2   Service Ports and Valves

An R-12 system has a service port, which is simply a male flare fitting equipped with a Schrader-type valve core. This valve core is like the ones used in tire valves; the actual valve core is one designed for refrigerant. The suction service port uses a 1/4-inch flare fitting with 7/16-20 threads; the discharge port is usually a 3/16-inch

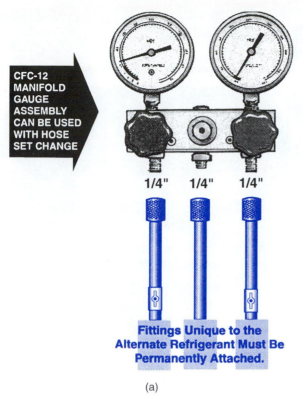

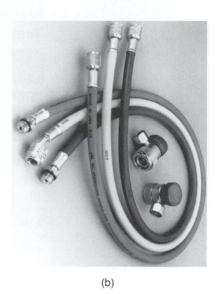

(a)   (b)

FIGURE 12-20 A gauge set may be used with different refrigerants by changing the hoses (a). Each hose set must have unique fittings, permanently attached, for that refrigerant. Hose set b connects R-134a service fittings to an R-12 manifold. (a *courtesy of the International Mobile Air Conditioning Association [IMACA];* b *courtesy of Mastercool*)

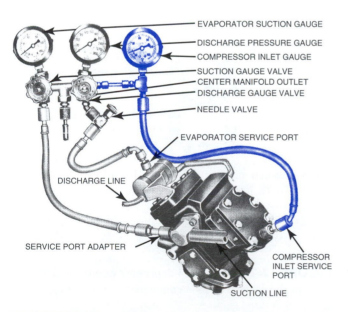

FIGURE 12-21 A third gauge (compressor inlet gauge) is being used to check the operation of the EPR valve located inside the suction line port. Many technicians do not use the solid bar holding the third gauge to the manifold and keep it separate. (*Courtesy of DaimlerChrysler Corporation*)

flare fitting with 3/8-24 threads. The service port should be covered with a protective cap that also serves as a secondary seal (Figure 12-23).

◀ **SERVICE TIP** ▶

If the protective cap is missing, dirt will enter the port and valve core, being attracted and trapped by the oil film. When the system is serviced, this dirt will enter either the gauge set or the system. Dirt particles can damage the valves and the gauges in the gauge set, damage the compressor, or plug small orifices if they enter the system. An unprotected port should be cleaned before connecting a hose to it.

The port is normally closed by the spring in the valve core. This is sometimes called a **back-seat** position, a term held over from stem-type service valves.

FIGURE 12-22 An electronic gauge set can measure low and high side pressures, vacuum (in microns), and temperature. It can also calculate superheating and subcooling. *(Courtesy of Robinair, SPX Corporation)*

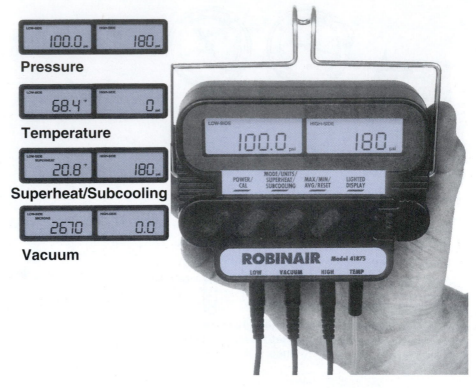

Pressure

Temperature

Superheat/Subcooling

Vacuum

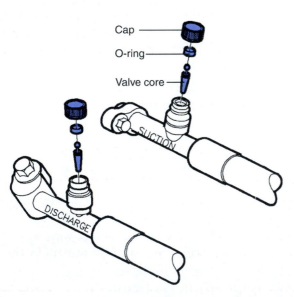

FIGURE 12-23 Each service port should have a cap to keep out dirt with a sealing O-ring to help prevent refrigerant loss. The valve core is the primary seal, and the cap and O-ring are the secondary seal. *(Courtesy of Saturn Corporation)*

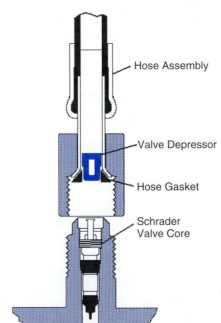

FIGURE 12-24 The valve depressor opens the Schrader valve as the service hose is connected to the fitting.

When an R-12 service hose is connected to the port, the depressor in the end of the hose pushes inward on the valve stem to open the valve (Figure 12-24).

Service ports for R-134a systems use a unique configuration; the low side service port is smaller than the high side port (13 and 16 mm [0.51 and 0.63 inch] OD). R-134a service hoses use color-coded quick couplers. These couplers automatically close the hose end when they are disconnected to prevent refrigerant loss. The valve in the service port is opened and closed as the coupler is connected and disconnected (Figure 12-25).

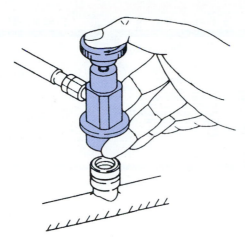

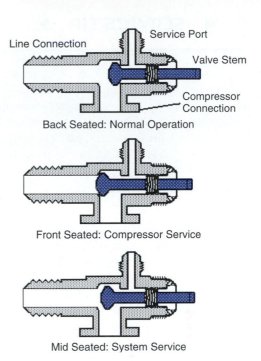

FIGURE 12-25 The locking ring is lifted as the R-134a service coupler is connected, and the coupler is pushed firmly inward until locked. Next, on some couplers, the knob is turned to depress the valve. *(Courtesy of Zexel USA Corporation)*

FIGURE 12-26 A service valve is normally kept in its back-seated position (*top*). Turning the valve stem completely inward, using a special wrench, will front seat the valve to shut off the hose connection (*center*). Turning the valve a turn or two inward will mid seat the valve (*bottom*); this opens the service port so system pressure can be read on a gauge set.

◄ SERVICE TIP ►

Some modern systems have only one service port, and some of these use an electronic transducer to sense the internal pressure. With these systems, the pressure can be read using a scan tool. If necessary, a service port can be installed using a saddle clamp (see Figure 15-50).

◄ SERVICE TIP ►

With both service valves front seated, the compressor can be disconnected from the service valves and removed from the system with the refrigerant trapped in the rest of the system by the service valves.

Some early A/C systems (R-12) use service valves at the service ports. A service valve has a stem that can be rotated using a 1/4-inch square socket or box wrench. This valve is set to one of three positions: back seat, **mid seat**, or **front seat**. During normal operation the valve is kept in the back-seat position: This closes the service port while the compressor port is left open. During service operations the valve is mid seated: This opens both the compressor port and the service port. During some special operations the valve is front seated: This closes the compressor port while the service port is left open. A service valve is fitted with protective caps for both the service port and the valve stem (Figure 12-26). While working with service valves, open-end wrenches, adjustable wrenches, and pliers should never be used on the valve stem. These tools will ruin the 1/4-inch square stem and prevent the use of the proper wrench.

12.2.3 Connecting and Disconnecting Gauges to a System

A **service unit** or gauge set is connected to a system so that diagnostic pressure checks can be made, to allow recovery of the refrigerant, and so a system can be evacuated and recharged. The first step in this procedure is to locate and identify the service ports.

On older systems, the low side service port is usually located between the evaporator outlet and the compressor inlet. With OT systems this was often on the accumulator. On many newer systems, the low side service port is located just downstream from the orifice tube, and this can be close to the condenser outlet.

In some vehicles, the low side service port is located just downstream from the OT. Some systems have two low side ports, one on each side of the STV. The low side hose is connected to the upstream service port (to read the evaporator pressure), and the third gauge is connected to the downstream service port if needed. Some OT systems do not have a separate low side service port. These systems require the removal of the low side pressure switch from the accumulator and the installation of a tee fitting. A Schrader valve is often used at the accumulator port, so there should be only a very small amount of refrigerant loss.

The high side service port is located between the compressor outlet and the expansion device, TXV or OT (Figure 12-27). Inspection of these ports tells the technician whether it is an R-12 or R-134a system and, on R-12 systems, whether an adapter is needed to connect the high side hose. All ports should be covered with a cap.

As the R-12 style service hose is being connected to a Schrader valve port, refrigerant often escapes because the valve depressor usually makes contact with the valve stem before the seal ring contacts the seat. This leak can be reduced by using the following procedure: Thread the knurled nut on the port one or two turns, grip the hose and push it quickly and firmly against the port, and tighten the nut to hold the hose in place. The knurled nut should be tightened only finger tight. The seal and seat can be damaged if pliers are used. If the seal leaks while finger tight, the sealing ring in the hose end should be replaced (Figure 12-28).

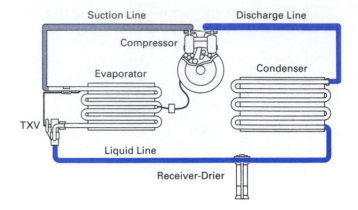

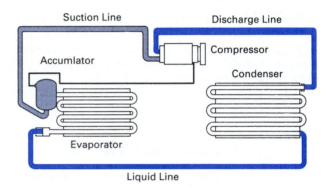

High side fitting location

Low side fitting location

FIGURE 12-27 The low side service port is normally located between the evaporator outlet and the compressor inlet. The high side service port is between the compressor outlet and the evaporator inlet.

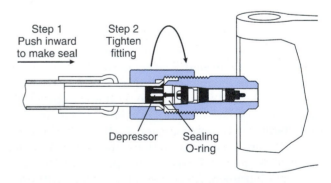

FIGURE 12-28 To reduce leakage when connecting a hose to an R-12 service port, push the hose firmly against the fitting and then finger tighten the fitting nut.

It was once common practice to purge the air from the hoses by making refrigerant flow through them for a few seconds. This vented refrigerant to the atmosphere, which is no longer an approved practice. With zero-loss hoses, refrigerant remains in the hoses while they are disconnected: There is no longer any need to purge the air from them. If using older-style hoses (which are no longer approved), a vacuum pump should be used to evacuate the air from the hoses as they are connected.

◄ CAUTION ►

Eyes and skin should always be protected when you are performing operations during which refrigerant might escape.

◄ CAUTION ►

With the increased possibilities of contaminated refrigerant, some experts recommend using a refrigerant identifier before connecting a gauge set to a system to determine the purity of the refrigerant in that system. Refrigerant identification is described in Section 15.3.2.

To connect a gauge set to a system, you should:

1. Make sure all of the valves on the manifold and hoses are closed. Also check R-12 hoses to ensure that the sealing ring and depressor are in the service ends of the hoses.

2. Remove the low side protective cap and connect the low side hose to the low side service port. In many cases, one or both of the caps can be stored on the manifold's hose holder (Figure 12-29).

3. Remove the high side protective cap. Connect the high side service hose to the port or adapter and store the protective cap. On R-12 systems determine whether an adapter is needed. If needed, many adapters have a valve core so they can be connected to the system; then the hose is connected to the adapter.

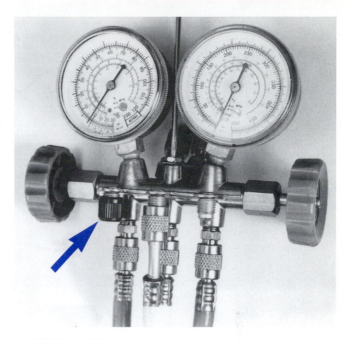

FIGURE 12-29 An R-12 service port cap can be stored on the manifold's hose holder.

4. Open the valve in each hose (leave the manifold valves closed) and read the system pressure on the gauges (Figure 12-30).

5. On systems equipped with service valves, mid seat the valve by turning the stem inward one or two turns using a service valve wrench. This valve must be back seated before disconnecting the hose.

When some hoses are disconnected, refrigerant and oil trapped in the hose may spray back and blow outward. The hand valve in the hose end should be closed or the hose equipped with an antiblowback check valve to trap this pressure. Some technicians wrap a shop cloth around the hose and fitting during removal to catch any oil and liquid refrigerant that is blown out.

◄ SERVICE TIP ►

Before connecting the hoses to R-134a service ports, check for a sharp edge or burr at the edge of the port: This burr can cut the seal in your hose connector. A sharp edge or burr can be removed with a file, sharp knife, or special tool.

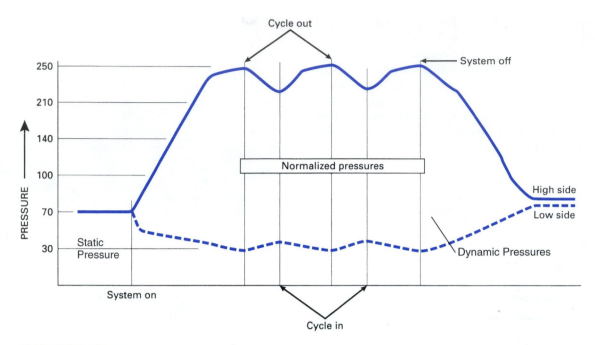

FIGURE 12-30 When the gauges are connected, they should both show the same pressure, which is dependent on the temperature. When the system is turned on the pressures will change, depending on evaporator temperature (low side) and ambient temperature (high side). Pressures will equalize again after the system is shut off.

To disconnect a gauge set from a system, you should:

1. Close the hand valves at the hose ends, if equipped; the manifold valves should also be closed.
2. Disconnect the low side service hose and replace the protective cap. Most protective caps include a sealing ring or O-ring. These should be threaded onto the port until the O-ring makes contact and then tightened finger tight. Replace the hose end on the hose holder.
3. Disconnect the high side hose, replace the protective cap, and replace the hose end on the hose holder.

◄ SERVICE TIP ►

After closing the service hose valve, some technicians will open both manifold valves. This allows the high side hose pressure to bleed into the low side. After the low side pressure drops back down, the manifold valves are closed and the hoses removed with a low pressure in both hoses.

◄ PROBLEM SOLVING 12–1 ►

The technician has connected a gauge set to a system, and both gauges show a pressure of about 10 psi. Is this the correct pressure for a system that is not running? If not, what might be wrong?

12.3 PERFORMANCE TEST

A performance test is used to determine whether the A/C system is operating properly and to indicate what is wrong if the system is not operating normally. The inspection checklist and report recommended by IMACA is shown in Figure 12-31.

Performance tests begin with a reading of the static system pressure with the engine off. The low and high sides of the system should be equal, and the pressure should be about the same as the pressure–temperature (PT) relationship for that refrigerant. For example, the pressure in an R-12 system at 70°F should be about 70 psi. An R-134a system should have a slightly higher pressure of about 71 psi. A lower pressure indicates a possible leak; a higher pressure indicates possible refrigerant contamination. A refrigerant identifier should be used to confirm the contaminants.

International Mobile Air Conditioning Association

CODE OF PROFESSIONAL PRACTICE

This Inspection Checklist is a summary of the steps detailed in the IMACA Code of Professional Practice manual. For detailed information, consult the manual.

VISUAL INSPECTION - Engine Compartment

1) Hoses, tubing and connections (Suction, Discharge & Liquid lines)
A. Examine exterior for deterioration, blistering, bubbling refrigerant, oil stains and battery acid damage or burns. Oil stains could indicate leakage.
B. Check for incorrect routing, rubbing, missing hardware or loose hoses, bent or collapsed tubing.

2) Compressor
A. Examine exterior for damaged or missing bolts / hardware, broken housing, oil stains.
B. Internal - rotate compressor 2 complete turns by hand to determine if seized or locked up.

3) Clutch
A. Examine for broken springs, burnt face, damaged grooves, oil stains from seal leak.

4) Service Ports
A. Check size and thread to determine type of refrigerant - confirm with engine compartment label.
B. Examine ports for missing caps, damaged threads and leaking Schrader valves.

5) Condenser
A. Check for loose or damaged connections, loose or missing hardware or air dams.
B. Examine coil for bent or damaged fins, restriction due to debris or dirt, oil stains.

6) Expansion Device (if possible)
A. Examine for physical damage or oil stains.

7) Evaporator Pressure Regulator (early models)
A. Check POA, EPR, STV (if equipped) for physical damage or oil stains.

8) Cabin Air (Evaporator) Filter (if equipped)
A. Check for physical damage, oil stains and for proper installation.

9) Accumulator or Receiver/Drier
A. Check for physical damage, loose or missing hardware, loose connections or oil stains.
B. Examine sight glass (Receiver/Drier only) for stains.

10) Drive Belts
A. Check for missing or damaged pulleys and tensioners; routing, tension and alignment.
B. Examine condition of belts for cracking, checking and excessive wear.

11) O-Rings, Gaskets, Spring Locks (if equipped)
A. Examine all connections not previously inspected for loose or missing parts and oil stains.

12) Inline Filter
A. Check for physical damage or oil stains.

13) Fan Clutch & Blade
A. Examine for fluid leakage or excessive bearing wear.
B. Check for damaged or bent blades on fan.

14) Electrical Components
A. Examine connectors for loose, burnt, broken parts or corrosion.
B. Examine wiring harness for burns, cracks or rubbing on insulation.

VISUAL INSPECTION - Passenger Compartment

1) Air Flow
A. Check all louvers for directional movement and air flow.

2) Control Head
A. Check all blower speeds.
B. Check controls for proper movement and function.
C. Check operation for heater, defrost and A/C.

3) Interior Condition
A. Check evaporator / heater case for water leakage.
B. Check carpet for water damage.

LEAK CHECK

1) Preparation (Engine Off)
A. A refrigerant identification check is recommended to verify the refrigerant in use or to detect flammables, unknown or contaminated refrigerant.
B. Connect manifold gauge - refrigerant pressure must read 50 psig or more. (Add refrigerant to increase the pressure if necessary).
C. Clean all connections using a clean dry rag.

2) Leak Check (Engine Off)
A. Start at the compressor discharge port and follow the flow of refrigerant through the system. Move the detector sensor completely around each connection.
B. Refrigerant is heavier than air; leak-check the underside of the hoses, clean and leak-check the condensate drain tube(s).
C. Leak check the compressor shaft seal.
D. Leak check evaporator through dash vents.

REPAIR SYSTEM PER CUSTOMER APPROVAL

FINAL PERFORMANCE EVALUATION

1) Functional Inspection (Engine On)
A. Check the compressor clutch for proper operation.
B. Check evaporator blower at all speeds
C. Check operation of function control doors for fresh air/recirculate (A/C - Max A/C), Dash louvers, Floor outlets, Defroster outlets
D. Check operation of heater flow control (if equipped).
E. Check fan clutch (if equipped). Once engine has reached normal operating temperature, turn off engine and "soak" fan clutch for 2 minutes. Restart engine, fan clutch should be engaged. With engine OFF, spin fan, should rotate maximum of 2 turns.
F. Check electrically driven condenser/radiator fan(s) (if equipped).

2) System Checkout (1,200 rpm's, condenser air flow = 35 mph)
A. Measure and record (on Inspection Report) temperature 2" in front of center of radiator. (Ambient temperature.)
B. Set A/C controls to OEM specs. Allow system to stabilize 5-10 minutes.
C. Record the high- and low-side pressure.
D. Record the center louver temperature and interior temperature.
E. Check operation of temperature controls.

3) Post Service Inspection
A. A final refrigerant check is optional to verify purity of refrigerant and absence of air.
B. Install service port caps and perform final leak check.
C. Perform final visual inspection. Check for tools and loose components.
D. Record results on Inspection Report.

CAUTION: Safety Glasses must be worn during any A/C diagnosis or repair procedure. Refrigerant may cause blindness if it comes in contact with eyes.

FIGURE 12-31 An A/C system checklist and inspection report. (*Courtesy of the International Mobile Air Conditioning Association [IMACA]*)

International Mobile Air Conditioning Association

Inspection Report

Code of Professional Practice

Customer Name: _____ License No.: _____
Automobile Year/Make: _____ Model: _____ Engine Size: _____
Inspection Performed By: _____ Date: _____

Procedure	Recommendations	Estimated Cost of Repairs	
		Parts	Labor
VISUAL INSPECTION - Engine Compartment			
1) Hoses, tubing and connections (Suction, Discharge & Liquid Lines)			
2) Compressor			
3) Compressor Clutch			
4) Service Ports			
5) Condenser			
6) Expansion Valve/Orifice Tube			
7) Evaporator Pressure Regulator (POA, STV, or VIR)			
8) Cabin Air (Evaporator) Filter (if equipped)			
9) Accumulator/Drier			
10) Drive Belts, Pulleys, and Tensioners			
11) O-rings, Gaskets, Seals, and Spring Locks			
12) Inline Filter			
13) Electric Fan, Fan Clutch, & Fan Blade			
14) Electrical Components			
VISUAL INSPECTION - Passenger Compartment			
1) Air ducts, louvers, sensors, control knobs, and cables			
2) Control Head			
3) Interior Condition			
LEAK CHECK - Engine Compartment (NOTE: Engine must be off during this procedure)			
1) Refrigerant Check			
2) Results of Leak Check			
Subtotal of Estimated Repair Costs			

Total Estimated Cost of Repairs Based on This Inspection: ☐

The above inspection was done in accordance with the IMACA Code Of Professional Practice procedures manual. If repairs are recommended you will be provided an estimate and only the repairs authorized by you (the customer) will be made. If further repairs are necessary you will be informed of and approve the additional parts and labor costs before the repairs are performed.
Thank You for your business!

Manager: _____
Date: _____

INITIAL PERFORMANCE EVALUATION
Type of Refrigerant: _____ Purity ☐Yes ___% ☐No High-Side Press.: _____ Low-Side Press.: _____
Louver Temperature: _____ Interior Temperature: _____ Ambient Temperature: _____
Amount of Refrigerant Added to System: _____ Amount of Refrigerant Recovered from System: _____

FINAL PERFORMANCE EVALUATION
Type of Refrigerant: _____ Purity ☐Yes ___% ☐No High-Side Press.: _____ Low-Side Press.: _____
Louver Temperature: _____ Interior Temperature: _____ Ambient Temperature: _____
Amount of Refrigerant Added to System: _____

FIGURE 12-31 Continued.

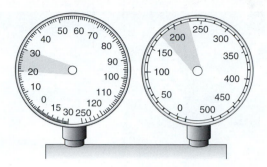

FIGURE 12-32 During normal operation, most systems will have a low side pressure around 20 to 30 psi and a high side pressure that is dependent on ambient temperature. Service information should be checked to determine the pressure for a specific system.

The pressures should become dynamic and change as the system is operated. The low side pressure drops and the high side pressure increases. After a rather quick pressure change as the compressor starts, the pressures change more slowly as the temperatures of the evaporator and condenser change. The low side pressure reflects the evaporator temperature; the high side pressure reflects the temperature of the liquid refrigerant leaving the condenser. The pressures normalize or stabilize when system temperatures reach normal operating points (Figure 12-32).

Most technicians try to simulate real-world operating conditions during a performance test. This is hard to do with the vehicle empty and sitting in a shop. The engine speed is adjusted to cruising speeds, about 1,500 to 2,000 rpm. The windows and doors are usually closed to reduce the heat load, but if a high heat load is desired, they are opened. Some manufacturers recommend closing the hood as far as possible to get close-to-normal airflow through the condenser.

A performance test should be run long enough to thoroughly chill the evaporator so the low-temperature de-icing control is activated. At this point the clutch cycles, the STV throttles, or the compressor reduces displacement. This time can be shortened by reducing the heat load, closing the doors and windows, and adjusting the blower speed to slow. Some manufacturers recommend measuring the clutch cycle rate and timing. Charts are then used to determine whether the cycle rate is wrong, and if so what problem is indicated.

Cold air from the discharge ducts usually indicates good performance. Some manufacturers specify duct discharge temperatures for their various systems.

Many technicians use this rule of thumb: Any system should be able to drop the air temperature at least 20°F as the air passes through the evaporator. In other words, if 75°F air enters the ductwork, 55°F or cooler air should leave the discharge registers.

To test system performance you should:

1. Connect the gauge set to the system, hang the gauge set from the hood or some convenient location or place it on a fender cover, and make sure the hoses are routed away from the moving engine parts and exhaust manifold.

2. Place a thermometer at the center of the radiator grill to record ambient temperature and one in the center A/C register to record system temperature (Figure 12-33).

3. Start the engine, turn the A/C on to full cold, open the registers, and adjust the blower speed to medium or medium-high. Adjust the engine speed to 1,500 to 2,000 rpm. On most vehicles, a small screwdriver can be inserted at some point in the throttle linkage to hold the throttle open.

4. Run the system for 5 to 10 minutes, or until the pressure readings stabilize.

5. Record the low and high side pressure readings and the ambient and system temperature readings. Check the evaporator outlet tube temperature; it should be cold. If the clutch is cycling, note the length of the on and off times (Figure 12-34). If the system uses an STV, check for a temperature drop between the STV inlet and outlet. In some systems, a frost line forms from the middle of the STV to some point on the suction hose when it is modulating pressure. If low side pressure or STV operation seems abnormal and the system has a third port, install a third gauge and record the pressure.

An infrared thermometer with a flexible probe can be used to measure the temperature of an item that is difficult to get to (Figure 12-35).

(a)

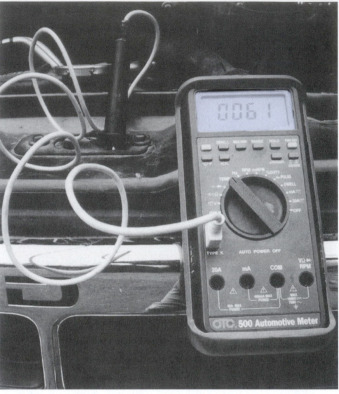

(c)

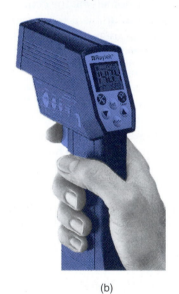

(b)

FIGURE 12-33 Proper high side pressure can only be determined from the temperature of ambient air entering the condenser. A dial pocket thermometer *(a)*, an infrared, non-contact thermometer *(b)*, or a digital thermometer *(c)* can be used. *(b courtesy of Raytek Corporation)*

6. If the system has a TXV and receiver–drier with a sight glass, note the condition of the refrigerant flowing past the sight glass. Cycle the clutch as you watch the sight glass. Shortly after cycle in, a flash of bubbles should flow past, and then the refrigerant should run clear. About 30 to 60 seconds after cycle out, another bubble flash should appear (Figure 12-36). With systems that have been retrofitted to R-134a, the sight glass normally has a cloudy or milky appearance and shows bubbles in a fully charged system. OT systems do not have sight glasses. On OT systems, feel the temperatures of the OT outlet and the bottom of the accumulator. They should be equal.

7. Reduce the engine speed to normal idle speed for 5 to 10 seconds before shutting the engine off.

8. Compare the readings of this test with those for a normal system.

◄ **SERVICE TIP** ►

On very humid days, the clutch may not cycle, even with the blower on low. To make sure the system will cycle, you might need to disconnect the blower or spray water on the condenser to force the evaporator temperature low enough to cycle the clutch.

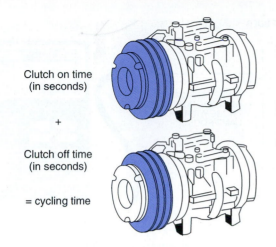

Clutch on time
(in seconds)

+

Clutch off time
(in seconds)

= cycling time

FIGURE 12-34 Clutch cycle time is determined by adding the time that the clutch runs to the time that it is stopped.

1. Clear

A clear sight glass can indicate one of the following conditions: a full system, an overfull system, or a near empty system.

2. Bubbles

Bubbles, whether large or small, indicate air or moisture is trapped in the system.

(Occasional bubbles during clutch cycling is normal.)

(Cool temperatures may require restricting airflow through the condenser to bring up system pressure for proper diagnosis (refer to service manual for additional information).

3. Oil Streaks

Oil streaks across the glass indicate there is no liquid R-12 in the system.

4. Foam

Foam indicates a low charge

FIGURE 12-36 A sight glass can be used to determine the condition of the refrigerant passing through the liquid line. *(Courtesy of DaimlerChrysler Corporation)*

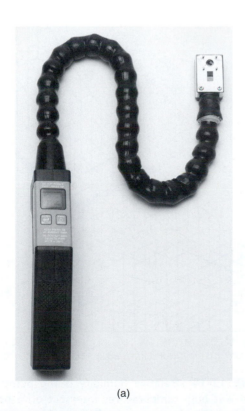

(a)

(b)

FIGURE 12-35 The FlexTemp is an IR thermometer with a flexible probe that can be used to take temperature readings in areas that are difficult to reach. *(Courtesy of Neutronics, Inc.)*

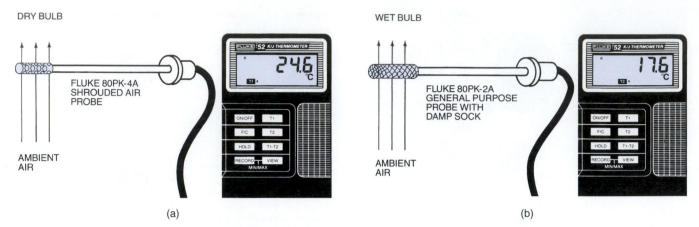

DRY BULB

FLUKE 80PK-4A
SHROUDED AIR
PROBE

AMBIENT
AIR

WET BULB

FLUKE 80PK-2A
GENERAL PURPOSE
PROBE WITH
DAMP SOCK

AMBIENT
AIR

(a)

(b)

FIGURE 12-37 Relative humidity is determined by measuring dry and wet bulb temperatures. Dry bulb temperature is measured using a plain thermometer *(a)*; wet bulb temperature is measured with a damp sock over the thermometer *(b)*. *(Courtesy of Fluke; reproduced with permission)*

12.3.1 Measuring Relative Humidity

Some manufacturers compare system pressures with relative humidity because the system must work harder when relative humidity is high. Relative humidity is measured by taking two temperature measurements, a dry bulb and a wet bulb temperature, and referencing these to a chart. A wet bulb is the same thermometer or electronic temperature probe with a damp sock on it. If the humidity is low, water evaporates from the wet bulb, and the cooling effect causes a lower temperature reading (Figure 12-37).

To measure relative humidity, you should:

1. Measure the ambient temperature using a dry thermometer or temperature probe and record this temperature.

2. Measure the ambient temperature using a wet bulb. Clean water is used to wet the bulb. Fan air across the wet bulb or move the bulb through air. Take several wet bulb readings until the temperature stabilizes at its lowest reading and then record this temperature.

3. Locate the dry and wet bulb readings on a psychrometric chart: The relative humidity is where these two lines intersect (Figure 12-38).

◀ **SERVICE TIP** ▶

With some thin electronic temperature probes, a shoelace can be cut and used as a sock over the probe. Wet the sock and you have a wet bulb.

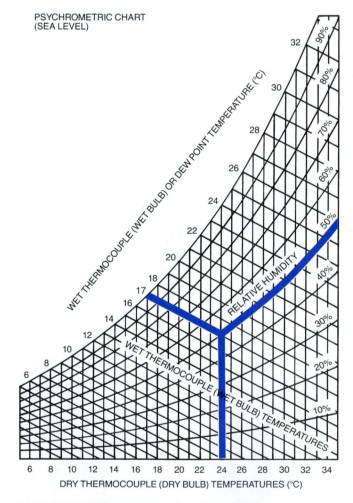

PSYCHROMETRIC CHART
(SEA LEVEL)

DRY THERMOCOUPLE (DRY BULB) TEMPERATURES (°C)

FIGURE 12-38 Relative humidity is the point where dry and wet bulb temperatures intersect on a psychrometric chart. In this example, a 17°C wet bulb and a 24°C dry bulb indicate 50% RH. *(Courtesy of Fluke; reproduced with permission)*

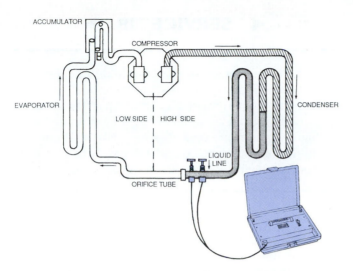

FIGURE 12-39 An electronic sight glass connected to a system. Bubble indicator lights light up and a beep sounds to indicate liquid or gas passing through the liquid line. *(Courtesy of TIF Instruments)*

12.3.2 Interpreting Sight Glasses

Most experienced technicians realize that a sight glass can give false readings. Depending on the design of the pickup location in the receiver–drier and the temperature, a sight glass can show bubbles in a system that is fully charged. It is also normal for an STV system to pass bubbles in the sight glass while the STV is operating to control evaporator pressure. The sight glass of an R-134a system normally has a milky appearance.

An electronic sight glass can be connected to the liquid line of a system without a sight glass (Figure 12-39). This unit sends an ultrasonic signal through the refrigerant and indicates whether bubbles pass through.

Bubbles can be expected to appear in the sight glass of a fully charged system

- Slightly after the clutch cycles in
- Slightly after the clutch cycles out
- At temperatures below 70°F
- When an STV is throttling

Therefore, a technician uses system pressures and temperatures to indicate correct charge level; the condition of the sight glass or output of an electronic sight glass should be considered just supplementary, helpful information.

12.3.3 Interpreting Performance Test Readings

For most drivers, the most important indicator of A/C performance is the discharge air temperature at the center A/C register. For a technician, the most important indicators are the low and high side pressures and temperatures. Many vehicles with borderline A/C performance can produce cool air with the vehicle parked in the shade, the windows closed, and the passenger compartment empty. The temperature range for the center register air discharge temperature is specified by most manufacturers; it is about 35 to 55°F, depending on ambient temperature and humidity.

◀ **SERVICE TIP** ▶

If no specifications are available, some technicians note the drop in air temperature as it passes through the evaporator; this drop should be at least 20°F. A technician can check this temperature by placing the back of his or her hand in front of the register; the air should have a cold, sharp feel to it.

Low side pressure, also called *suction pressure*, should tell evaporator temperature. The actual pressure varies slightly between R-12 and R-134a systems and the style of evaporator icing control. With cycling clutch systems, the low side pressure should drop to the point at which the clutch cycles out; then the pressure increases to the point at which the clutch cycles in again. This pressure range should be about 15 to 30 psi. At these pressures, the evaporator should be cold with a temperature in the mid 30s.

On systems that use an STV, the low side pressure should drop to the point at which the STV starts controlling it; from this point, the pressure should vary only a few psi. Normal low side pressure for most STV systems is about 30 to 35 psi. For an older Chrysler EPR system, evaporator pressure should be about 22 psi (152 kPa); with a Toyota EPR system, the evaporator pressure should be 27 psi (186 kPa). With a variable displacement compressor, the low side pressure should also drop to the control point, and then it should remain fairly constant. The exact pressure varies somewhat between system designs, but it should be within a range of 32 to 55 psi. The clutch does not cycle in either an STV or variable displacement compressor system (Figure 12-40).

Remember that the orifice in an OT system is merely a restriction between the low and high sides. Increased high side pressure can cause the pressure in the evaporator to increase, which in turn causes higher evaporator temperatures. Also, the accumulator is an extension of the evaporator and has the same pressure and temperature as the evaporator.

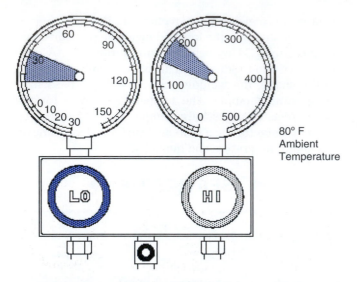

80° F
Ambient
Temperature

FIGURE 12-40 The low and high side pressures for a TXV system at 80°F. Note that they will vary about 10 to 15 psi on the low side and about 50 psi on the high side. High side pressures are also dependent on ambient temperature.

High side pressure, also called *discharge* or *head pressure*, should tell us condenser temperature; this pressure varies directly with ambient temperature and condenser airflow. After noting the ambient temperature on the thermometer at the vehicle's radiator grill, a technician often consults a chart to determine the pressure range for normal high side pressure (Figure 12-41).

◄ **SERVICE TIP** ►

Some technicians use a rough rule of thumb that high side pressure for an R-12 system should equal ambient temperature (°F) plus 100 psi. The range is ± 20 psi from this point. Using this method, the high side pressure on a 70°F day should be 170 ± 20 psi, or between 150 and 190 psi. With R-134a systems, high side pressure is slightly higher.

System pressure in modern vehicles is affected more by design variables than it was in earlier cars. Increasing engine speed usually increases pressure, and with many RWD cars, discharge pressure drops when a fan clutch engages to pull more air through the condenser. Discharge pressures are often higher in FWD cars because of their fan types and sizes. Condenser design and size also affect this pressure. With a modern system, the vehicle manufacturer's pressure chart for that particular make and model should be used for reference. High side pressures should produce a hot condenser and compressor discharge line.

A technician places both temperature and pressure readings into one of three categories: *normal, low,* or *high*. Normal readings indicate that the system is operating within design limits, and it is okay. Low or high readings indicate a fault.

FIGURE 12-41 Vent temperatures will vary with ambient temperature and relative humidity.

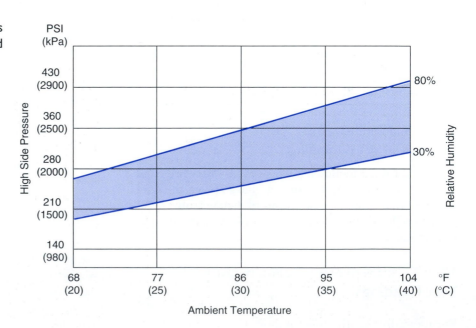

A cycling clutch system meets the following conditions if it is operating correctly:

Low side pressure: Normal: 15 to 35 psi with the clutch cycling; it will be on for about 45 to 90 seconds and off for about 15 to 30 seconds.
High side pressure: Normal: within the range of pressure for that ambient temperature.
Center register discharge temperature: Normal: between 35 and 55°F (in-vehicle temperature minus 20°F); cold and sharp feel.
Evaporator outlet: Cold, often with dew or sweat forming.
Sight glass: Clear, no foam, very few bubbles; the sight glass in an R-134a system has a milky appearance.
OT and accumulator comparison: Bottom of accumulator is as cold as OT, with dew or sweat forming on both.

Normal System Performance, Cycling Clutch

Ambient Temperature	Suction Pressure	Discharge Pressure	Center Outlet Temperature
80°F	15–35 psi	145–190 psi	35–55 psi

A good STV system has most of the same conditions except the following:

Low side pressure: Normal for that type of pressure control (usually 28 to 32 psi); no clutch cycling; dew, sweat, or possibly frost forming on the valve and extending on the suction hose toward the compressor; a third gauge shows a pressure drop from low side pressure (Figure 12-42).

Normal System Performance, STV System

Ambient Temperature	Suction Pressure	Discharge Pressure	Center Outlet Temperature
80°F	28–32 psi	145–190 psi	35–55 psi

A system that uses a variable displacement compressor should have the same conditions, except the following:

Low side pressure: Normal for that type of compressor; low side pressure drops as the evaporator cools but levels off and does not drop below a certain point; no clutch cycling.

System type	Normal low side pressure
Cycling clutch	
Thermal switch	15 – 30
Pressure switch	20 – 45
Suction throttling valve	28 – 32
EPR or ETR valve	22 – 30
Variable displacement comp.	30 – 40

(a)

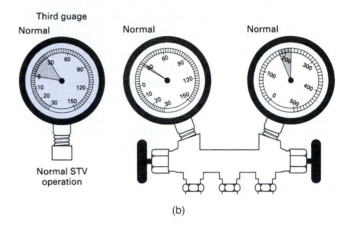

(b)

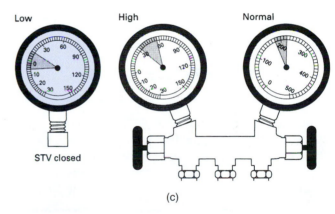

(c)

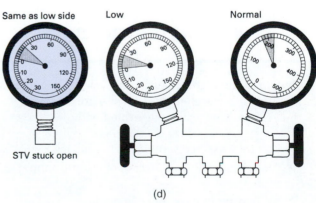

(d)

FIGURE 12-42 The low side pressures of various systems (a). If a third gauge is used on a properly operating STV system, it will show a pressure drop across the STV (b). An STV that is stuck closed (c), and an STV that is stuck open (d).

◀ **SERVICE TIP** ▶

Remember that the low end of low side pressure is controlled by the system controls, clutch cycling switch, or reduced compressor displacement.

If conditions are not normal, faults usually occur in certain combinations that indicate the nature of the problem. An experienced technician often recognizes a problem from a few of these clues. Most vehicle manufacturers and larger aftermarket suppliers publish diagnostic charts to aid in interpreting the cause of a problem. Remember that the A/C system can only make the evaporator cold, and problems in the air management system can cause warm air discharge (Figure 12-43).

Many technicians perform extra steps to confirm the exact nature of a problem. These steps are usually visual inspection of a part or feeling certain areas to determine the temperature. The goal is to locate all of the faulty parts so that they can be repaired using the simplest and quickest process.

◀ **SERVICE TIP** ▶

If the compressor clutch either does not engage or engages and then quickly releases, there could be excessive clutch clearance, an A/C system problem, or a problem in the electrical controls. These problems are described in Chapters 13 and 15.

◀ **SERVICE TIP** ▶

One prominent aftermarket A/C parts supplier recommends a system stress test before releasing the vehicle. This test is performed with:

- The vehicle placed outside in full sun if possible
- The engine idling at normal operating temperature
- System set to max A/C, max cold
- Blower on high
- Vehicle doors open

To perform a stress test, you should:

1. Measure and record the condenser inlet and outlet line temperature (within 4 inches or 100 mm of the condenser). The outlet line temperature should be cooler with a difference of 20 to 60°F (11 to 33°C). Less than 20°F difference indicates inadequate condenser performance.

2. Measure and record the ambient air temperature in front of the condenser and the discharge air temperature at the center registers in the instrument panel. The discharge temperature should be at least 30°F (17°C) colder if the system is working properly.

3. Measure and record the evaporator inlet (after the OT) and outlet (before the accumulator) line temperatures. The outlet line temperatures should be within 5°F (3°C). An excessive temperature difference indicates a possible charge level, OT, blend door, or condenser problem.

12.3.4 Abnormal Conditions

All of the following combinations of symptoms can cause poor A/C performance. Poor performance is most often the result of an evaporator that is not cold enough, but it can also be caused by an evaporator that is too cold and is frosty.

Abnormal System Performance, Low Charge Level or OT/TXV Blockage

Ambient Temperature	Suction Pressure	Discharge Pressure	Center Outlet
70 to 100°F	Low	Low	Cool to warm

Possible cause: Low refrigerant charge level.
Confirmation: Warm evaporator tailpipe; very little temperature drop across TXV or OT; bubbles or foam in sight glass; bottom of accumulator is warmer than OT; slightly low refrigerant on OT systems causes discharge air temperature to go cool to warm to cool with engine at higher speeds; air discharge temperature can be cool at one register and warm at another; with an under-

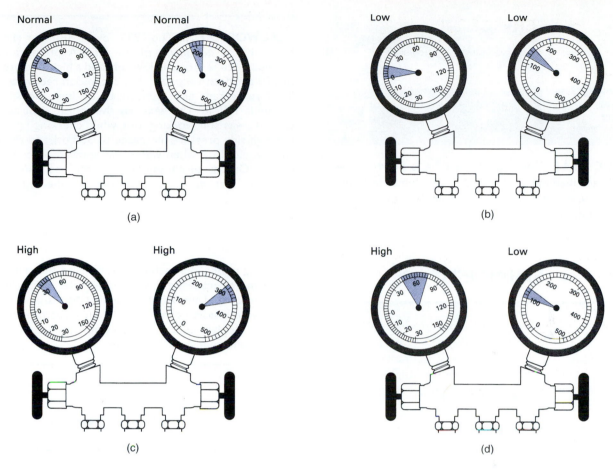

FIGURE 12-43 Typical gauge readings for a normal system (a) and faulty systems (b, c, and d).

change, the refrigerant recovery process is quite short.
Cure: Locate leak, repair leak, and recharge.

REAL WORLD FIX: The 2000 Cadillac Deville (41,000 miles) with dual comfort control had a problem of warm air coming from the driver's side outlet while cold air comes from the passenger side. Scan tool checks showed no electrical faults.

FIX

Following advice, the technician recovered the refrigerant charge, and determined that the system was undercharged. The system was recharged with the specified amount of refrigerant and began working properly.

Possible cause: Blocked TXV or OT.
Confirmation: Warm evaporator tailpipe; noticeable temperature drop across TXV or OT; usually shows frost; clear sight glass; low side pressure drops very fast when the clutch cycles in; low side may go into a vacuum; normal length of refrigerant recovery time and amount of refrigerant.
Cure: Remove and clean or replace TXV screen; check for TXV stuck closed; remove and replace (R&R) OT.

REAL WORLD FIX: The 1996 Ford van (115,000 miles) had warm air from the A/C ducts. The pressures were almost normal at 60 psi on the low side and 250 psi on the high side. The refrigerant was recovered and the system evacuated and recharged, but this did not help.

FIGURE 12-44 The top orifice tube is nearly plugged with a black material; the lower one has some small metal flakes on the screen that probably came from the compressor. *(Courtesy of James Halderman)*

◄ **SERVICE TIP** ►

If a restriction is suspected, on some vehicles (depending on how accessible the orifice tube is), it is a good practice to recover the refrigerant and inspect the OT. The nature of debris caught by the OT can indicate faults like a failed compressor (Figure 12-44).

◄ **SERVICE TIP** ►

A compressor is cooled by the incoming refrigerant so a properly operating system will have a compressor with a case temperature of about 130 to 150°F (54 to 66°C) in a much hotter engine compartment. Compressor case temperature can be easily checked using an infrared thermometer: an excessive operating temperature indicates a low charge level or internal friction from a low oil charge. Some compressors include a temperature switch to shut the compressor off if an overheat condition should occur.

FIX

A temperature check using an infrared thermometer showed a small temperature drop across the OT, so it was removed for inspection. Some shavings partially plugged it; since such parts are inexpensive, it was replaced using a new one. Replacement of the OT fixed this system; after recharging, there was a temperature drop across the OT of 35°F.

REAL WORLD FIX: The 1995 Toyota 4Runner (172,000 miles) had a complaint of no A/C. A pressure check showed − 20″ Hg on the low side and a high side pressure of 120 psi, both very low. The technician recovered 0.75 lb of refrigerant and found it to be low; the specified charge is 1.75 lb. The next day the vehicle returned, and the A/C was still working. But, while checking pressures, the high side pressure increased to 350 psi, and the pressure would drop when water was sprayed onto the condenser. On day three, the vehicle returned with system pressures that were about the same as the beginning of this repair.

FIX

Following advice, the technician recovered the refrigerant. He then replaced the TXV and receiver–drier; he also flushed the liquid line. After recharging the system, the pressures were almost normal, but the high side pressure was too high. Replacement of the fan clutch corrected this last problem and completed the repair.

◄ **SERVICE TIP** ►

If a blocked TXV or OT problem is intermittent and only occurs after the system has been run for awhile, the probable cause is ice forming at the TXV or OT. This can be confirmed by shutting the system off for a few minutes. If the system returns to normal for awhile, the ice has probably melted. In this case, the refrigerant should be recovered, the receiver–drier or accumulator should be replaced, and the system should be recharged with new or recycled refrigerant.

REAL WORLD FIX: The A/C in the 1997 Pontiac Grand Am (73,000 miles) is not working. The car came in with no refrigerant, and the system was recharged. The system pressures are normal—25 psi low side and 125 psi high side—but there is no cool air from the registers, and both high and low side lines are the same temperature.

FIX

Following advice that this system uses a variable displacement compressor that will try to maintain a 27 psi low side pressure, the technician checked the orifice tube and found it plugged. Replacement of the OT along with the accumulator fixed this system.

Abnormal System Performance, Thermal Switch

Suction Pressure	Discharge Pressure	Center Outlet
Low	Normal	Cool to warm

Possible cause: Faulty thermostatic or pressure switch.
Confirmation: Frost on evaporator tailpipe with evaporator icing and continuous compressor operation indicates a shorted or closed switch.
Cure: R&R switch.

Abnormal System Performance, Line Restriction

Suction Pressure	Discharge Pressure	Center Outlet
Low	Low to normal	Cool to warm

Possible cause: Restriction in liquid line.
Confirmation: Noticeable temperature drop in liquid line or receiver–drier; can have frost at this location.
Cure: R&R restricted item.

◄ **SERVICE TIP** ►

Many systems place the high side service port in the liquid line, downstream from the condenser. A plugged condenser in these systems will show up as low high side pressure while the compressor is showing signs of excessive pressure, noise, and very high temperatures.

REAL WORLD FIX: The 1993 Acura (107,000 miles) had a low side pressure of 10″ Hg. The expansion valve was replaced, but the pressure stayed low. If the TXV temperature bulb is warmed up, the pressure increases. The suction line is very cold.

FIX

After talking to the customer, the technician was told about an earlier accident. With this knowledge, a more thorough inspection was performed that revealed a crimped suction line under the air cleaner.

Replacement of this damaged line fixed this problem.

AUTHOR'S NOTE

A more thorough under-hood inspection should have revealed this fault.

◄ **SERVICE TIP** ►

A low side restriction *usually* causes low high side pressure while a high side restriction *usually* causes excessive high side pressure. Remember that an A/C system is a closed loop, and a compressor can only pump the refrigerant that returns to it. System pressures will depend on the location of the restriction, amount of restriction, and the location of the service ports relative to the restriction.

◄ **SERVICE TIP** ►

If the A/C air discharge is not cold but the suction line is cold, suspect plugged evaporator fins or faulty temperature door operation (Figure 12-45). Restricted airflow through the evaporator will usually cause reduced blower current draw; see Section 14.8.3.

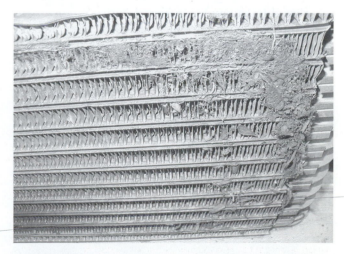

FIGURE 12-45 Part of this evaporator face is plugged by an oily mud and leaf debris. This reduces heat transfer and airflow. *(Courtesy of James Halderman)*

REAL WORLD FIX: The 1997 Taurus (80,000 miles) that came into the shop has no A/C. The O-rings in the liquid line and evaporator connections had been recently replaced to repair leaks. Both the high and low side pressures are 25 psi with the compressor shutting off after a few seconds. The compressor and orifice tube were replaced and the system was flushed, but this did not help. With a jumper wire across the low pressure switch, the pressure will drop to 10" of vacuum on both sides. The various components were tested by blowing air through them, and they could not blow through the condenser. The condenser was replaced, but this did not help.

FIX

Closer inspection revealed that the discharge hose was kinked so the flow was pinched off. Loosening the hose connections allowed better hose alignment and fixed this problem.

AUTHOR'S NOTE

When interpreting gauge readings, remember when high side service ports are downstream from the condenser, they do not give true compressor discharge pressures. Service operations must be done properly even though cramped engine compartments make proper inspection and service operations difficult.

Abnormal System Performance, Overcharge

Suction Pressure	Discharge Pressure	Center Outlet
High	High	Cool to warm

Possible cause: System overcharge.
Confirmation: Pressures become normal after some refrigerant has been removed; an excessive amount of refrigerant is recovered.
Cure: Recover refrigerant, evacuate, and recharge with correct amount.

Abnormal System Performance, Contaminated Refrigerant or Condenser Blockage

Suction Pressure	Discharge Pressure	Center Outlet
High	High	Cool to warm

Possible cause: Contaminated system: air or foreign refrigerant in system.

Confirmation: Use an identifier to determine the type and purity of the refrigerant. With air contamination, the problem is corrected by cure: recover, recycle, recharge, and check for leaks.
Cure: With contaminated refrigerant, recover refrigerant and send off for disposal. With air contamination, recover and recycle refrigerant, evacuate, and recharge.
Possible cause: Poor airflow through condenser.
Confirmation: Inspect front and back of condenser and radiator for debris; cool the condenser with water and watch for a pressure drop; check for proper fan and fan clutch operation and airflow.
Cure: Clean condenser and restricted surfaces; repair fan as needed. Make sure the condenser seals are properly installed.

◀ SERVICE TIP ▶

On RWD vehicles, faulty fan clutches are a major cause of excessive head pressure and compressor failure.

◀ SERVICE TIP ▶

Modern flat-tube, multipass condensers cannot be flushed effectively.

◀ SERVICE TIP ▶

If you suspect poor condenser airflow is the cause of poor cooling from the A/C, place a box fan in front of the condenser/radiator. If the A/C improves, check the condenser and fans for the source of the problem.

Possible cause: Plugged condenser (internal).
Confirmation: Measure temperature at condenser inlet and outlet; 40 to 50°F or greater differential indicates blockage.
Cure: Flush or R&R condenser.

REAL WORLD FIX: The high-pressure relief valve of the 1996 Mazda (37,000 miles) pops off. The low side pressure is 25–40 psi, but the high side pressure steadily increases until the valve pops off. The compressor, condenser, TXV, receiver–drier, and evaporator have all been replaced, and air has been blown through the lines to show no restriction. None of this has helped. Both cooling fans operate.

FIX

Following advice, the cooling fan airflow was checked, and it was found that one of the fans was running backward. Reversing the wires in the connector to this fan corrected the rotation and fixed this problem.

AUTHOR'S NOTE

If the technician had remembered the basic principles of A/C, this fault would have been found much quicker.

REAL WORLD FIX: The 1992 Honda Civic (173,000 miles) came in with an empty A/C system. The receiver–drier was replaced, the TXV and system were flushed, and the system was recharged with the proper amount of R-12. The system worked great, and the car was released to the customer. Several days later, the customer used the system, and after about 4 minutes, the engine began bogging down and the pressure relief valve popped off. The compressor was replaced, the system was flushed, and then recharged. After 30 minutes of operation, the high pressure problem returned.

FIX

A condenser temperature check showed only a 20°F difference from the top to the bottom, indicating an internal restriction. A new condenser was installed, and the temperature difference was now 50°F.

AUTHOR'S NOTE

The reason for replacing the compressor is unknown.

◀ SERVICE TIP ▶

Check for a plugged condenser by measuring the temperature drop from the inlet to the outlet using an infrared thermometer. A properly operating condenser will have a temperature drop of 11 to 33°C (20 to 60°F) between the inlet and the outlet. Check condenser temperature from top to bottom and from one side to the other. The temperature should drop evenly and gradually.

◀ SERVICE TIP ▶

If diagnosing a problem of excessive high side pressure on a system using multispeed electric fans, be sure that the fans will operate at their high speeds. Insufficient fan speed will cause excess high side pressure.

Abnormal System Performance, Faulty Compressor, OT, or TXV

Suction Pressure	Discharge Pressure	Center Outlet
High	Low	Cool to warm

Possible cause: Faulty compressor.
Confirmation: Feel compressor suction and discharge hoses for temperature change. Rotate the compressor drive plate and feel for the amount of internal resistance and damage.
Cure: R&R compressor and receiver–drier or accumulator.

◀ SERVICE TIP ▶

When a modern compressor fails, it will often produce black, sludgelike material that is commonly called *black death*. An inspection of the OT will usually show this material. System repair will require compressor, accumulator, and OT replacement, plus a thorough cleaning of the high side between the compressor and OT.

REAL WORLD FIX: The 1990 Lexus (165,000 miles) A/C does not work. Both the low and high side pressures are 70 psi with the compressor clutch engaged. The technician questioned whether this problem could be caused by a faulty TXV.

FIX

Further checking showed that the compressor shaft had broken. Replacement of the compressor and receiver–drier fixed this problem.

REAL WORLD FIX: A 1992 Saturn has a low side pressure of 60 psi and a high side pressure of 70 psi. It looks like the vane compressor has failed.

FIX

With the engine running at 2,000 rpm, the technician disconnected and reconnected the clutch about six times, and the internal vanes became free. The compressor started normal operation with good pressures and cooling.

Abnormal System Performance, Faulty TXV or OT

Suction Pressure	Discharge Pressure	Center Outlet
High	Low to normal	Warm

Possible cause: TXV stuck open, missing OT or faulty OT seal rings.

Confirmation: With TXV the suction line will be colder than expected for this pressure; TXV does not respond to TXV test; no or very little temperature drop across OT.

Cure: R&R TXV or OT seal rings.

◀ SERVICE TIP ▶

A quick check for poor evaporator airflow is to disconnect the blower. In a normally operating system, stopping the airflow should cause the evaporator temperature and low side pressure to drop.

REAL WORLD FIX: The customer had replaced the condenser in the 1988 Plymouth Horizon (174,000 miles) with a used one, and the shop evacuated and recharged the system. The low side pressure was 25″ Hg, with a high side pressure of 100 psi.

FIX

Checking revealed a faulty H-valve (TXV). Replacement of the H-valve and receiver–drier fixed this problem.

AUTHOR'S NOTE

It is not known why the condenser needed replacement or if the H-valve was plugged up with debris.

REAL WORLD FIX: The 1997 Mercury Mountaineer SUV (54,000 miles) came into the shop for a cooling problem caused by a faulty fan clutch. The A/C system was also checked, and the low side was 70 psi with a high side pressure of 180–200 psi. A faulty compressor was suspected, but the customer said that the A/C worked properly at highway speeds.

FIX

Further checking revealed that another shop had replaced the evaporator core. Someone had forgotten to install the OT into the new evaporator. Installation of the OT fixed this problem.

AUTHOR'S NOTE

It often helps to get the history of any previous vehicle repairs.

At this point, the technician usually makes further checks or begins the repair. Further checks can be rather simple or much more involved. For example, if the diagnosis indicates poor compressor operation, you can shut off the engine and rotate the compressor clutch by hand. A very low turning resistance confirms a faulty compressor. The diagnosis of a TXV being stuck open is harder to confirm because it must be removed from the system. An on-vehicle check for TXV operation can be made on most TXV systems. Several methods can be used to locate refrigerant leaks.

12.3.5 Verifying Refrigerant Charge Level

Three different checks, two of them quite accurate, can be made to verify whether a system has the correct amount of refrigerant. The simplest is to feel the temperature of the accumulator and OT using your hand. The other checks include measuring the difference in temperature, called the **Delta T** (ΔT), across the evaporator and measuring the amount of sub-cooling of the liquid leaving the condenser. If using system pressure, either static or dynamic, as a guide to charge level, remember that temperature has a definite role in the pressure of pure refrigerants and that contaminants—air or foreign refrigerants—greatly affect the pressure.

The Delta T method is preferred for OT–accumulator systems. The accumulator should contain some liquid refrigerant at the same pressure and temperature as the evaporator. Also, in a properly charged system, liquid leaves the OT, boils, and absorbs heat as it passes through the evaporator, so the evaporator outlet should be the same temperature or slightly cooler than the OT. This method requires two electronic thermometers or a digital voltmeter–ohmmeter with thermocouples to provide the needed accuracy. An accurate infrared thermometer can be used.

The sub-cooling method is preferred for TXV systems. The refrigerant leaving the condenser should be sub-cooled, or about 10 to 25°F cooler than its condensing point. This method requires an electronic thermometer and high side gauge pressure to determine sub-cooling.

The recommended service procedure for improper charge level is to recover the refrigerant, service (an undercharge indicates a leak), evacuate, and recharge.

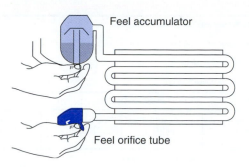

FIGURE 12-46 In a fully to slightly undercharged OT system, the bottom of the accumulator is as cold as the line just downstream from the OT. A warmer accumulator indicates an undercharge.

To make a hands-on check, you should:

1. Start the engine and run it at normal idle speed.
2. Open the hood and doors.
3. Set the selector to normal A/C, full cold, and high blower.
4. Feel the temperature of the evaporator inlet tube and accumulator surface (Figure 12-46). (a) If both are the same temperature, the charge level is okay; (b) if inlet is cooler, the system is undercharged; (c) if inlet is warmer, the system is overcharged.

To measure Delta T, you should:

1. Connect a gauge set to the system, as described in Section 12.2.3.
2. Connect an electronic thermometer pickup to the evaporator inlet and outlet lines (Figure 12-47).

3. Place a jumper wire across the connector to the clutch cycling switch so the compressor will run continuously.
4. Start the engine, turn the system on to high blower and normal A/C, and adjust the engine speed to 1,000 rpm.
5. Measure the temperatures, record them, and reduce the engine speed to idle.
6. Compare the temperatures to the chart in Figure 12-48. Note that this chart is for a specific vehicle make and model, and the amount of refrigerant that needs to be added is not necessarily the same for all vehicles. Another source says that the temperature difference should be 0°F, plus or minus 5°F.

To measure sub-cooling, you should:

1. Connect a gauge set to the system as described in Section 12.2.3.
2. Connect an electronic thermometer pickup to the liquid line near the condenser (Figure 12-49).
3. Start the engine, turn the system on to high blower and normal A/C, and adjust the engine speed to 1,000 rpm.
4. Block off the airflow into the condenser using cardboard or shop cloths so that the high side pressure increases to 260 psi. Do not allow the pressure to increase much above this level.
5. Measure the high side pressure and the liquid line temperature and record them. Remove the blocking material from the condenser and reduce the engine speed to idle.
6. Compare the pressure and temperature with the chart in Figure 12-50 to determine charge level.

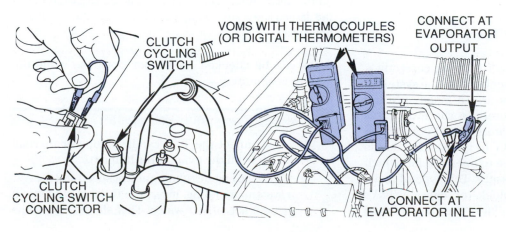

FIGURE 12-47 When measuring the Delta T across the evaporator, one electronic thermometer is attached to the inlet and another to the outlet. The temperature difference is the Delta T. The jumper wire at the clutch cycling switch keeps the compressor operating. (*Courtesy of Daimler-Chrysler Corporation*)

FIGURE 12-48 This chart indicates the amount of refrigerant that should be added to this particular system, depending on the Delta T. With any system, a Delta T of −3 to −10°F indicates a full charge of refrigerant. *(Courtesy of DaimlerChrysler Corporation)*

Evaporator Outlet and Inlet Temperature Differential

- If Outlet is WARMER than Inlet, temperature differential is plus (+).
- If Outlet is COLDER than Inlet, temperature differential is minus (-).

See the example in the Refrigerant Charge Check (Alternative Method).

Added Amount of R134a to Properly Charge A/C System	Ambient Temperature				
	21°C (70°F)	27°C (80°F)	32°C (90°F)	38°C (100°F)	43°C (110°F)
	Differential Temperature				
0.90 lbs. (14 oz.)	+22°C (+40°F)	+23°C (+42°F)	+24°C (+43°F)	+25°C (+45°F)	+26°C (+47°F)
0.75 lbs. (12 oz.)	+12°C (+22°F)	+12°C (+23°F)	+13°C (+24°F)	+15°C (+26°F)	+16°C (+28°F)
0.60 lbs. (10 oz.)	+4°C (+8°F)	+5°C (+9°F)	+6°C (+10°F)	+7°C (+12°F)	+8°C (+13°F)
0.50 lbs. (8 oz.)	0°C (0°F)	+0°C (+1°F)	+1°C (+2°F)	+2°C (+3°F)	+3°C (+4°F)
0.40 lbs. (6 oz.)	-1°C (-2°F)	-1°C (-1°F)	+0°C (-0°F)	0°C (0°F)	0°C (0°F)
Recommended Charge	-2 to -6°C (-3 to -10°F)				

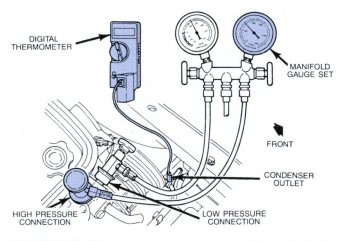

FIGURE 12-49 Sub-cooling is determined from the high side pressure and an accurate measurement of the condenser outlet. *(Courtesy of DaimlerChrysler Corporation)*

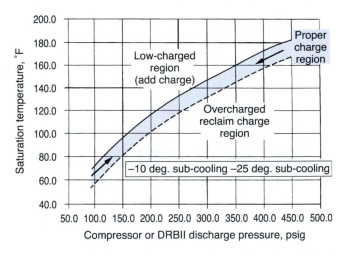

FIGURE 12-50 The point of intersection between the temperature and pressure indicates the relative charge level on this chart. Above the solid line is an undercharge; below the dashed line is an overcharge. *(Courtesy of DaimlerChrysler Corporation)*

12.3.6 On-Vehicle TXV Tests

If tests indicate that a TXV is not working correctly, a technician can make further checks while the system is still together. The first checks are to make sure the thermal bulb is attached securely to the evaporator tailpipe and well wrapped with insulation. Poor contact or insulation can cause the TXV to get a signal that is too warm. This causes the valve to open too far, which produces high evaporator pressure. This type of problem cannot occur with H, block, or capsule TXVs (Figure 12-51). TXVs with capillary tubes and thermal

bulbs can be checked for proper response while the system is operating.

To check TXV operation, you should:

1. Disconnect the TXV capillary tube or thermal bulb from the evaporator tailpipe.
2. With the engine running at test speed and the A/C system operating, insert the thermal bulb into a container of ice water. This should cause the

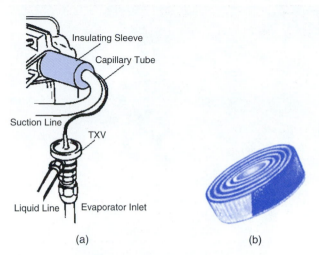

(a)   (b)

FIGURE 12-51   The thermal bulb of the TXV should be clamped tightly to the evaporator tailpipe and insulated with a foam sleeve *(a)* or wrapped with insulating tape, a thick, pliable tape *(b)*. *(b courtesy of Four Seasons)*

TXV to close down, and a noticeable drop in low side pressure should occur (Figure 12-52).

3. Remove the thermal bulb from the ice water and warm it in your hand or warm water. This should cause the TXV to open up, and a noticeable increase in low side pressure should occur.

With block-type TXVs, CO_2 can be sprayed onto the diaphragm portion to cool it. This should cause the valve to close.

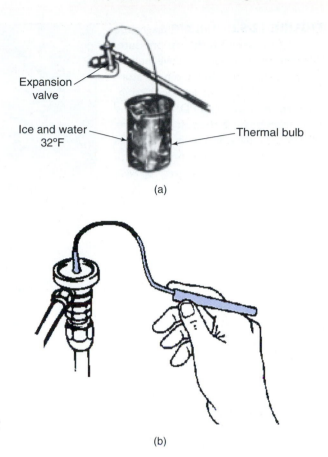

(a)

(b)

FIGURE 12-52   Chilling the thermal bulb with ice water *(a)* or CO_2 should cause the valve to close and the low side pressure to drop. Warming the bulb with your hand *(b)* should cause the valve to open and the low side pressure to increase. *(a courtesy of DaimlerChrysler Corporation)*

◀ **PROBLEM SOLVING 12-2** ▶

While checking for the cause of a system with a low side pressure that is too high, you make the checks for a faulty TXV, but cooling or heating the thermal bulb does not change the pressure readings. Does this system have a faulty TXV? What else could cause this problem?

12.3.7 Electronic Diagnostic Tool

A/C diagnostic tools has been developed by several companies to aid technicians in testing A/C sysems (Figure 12-53). One tool is based on a small handheld PDA (personal digital assistant) computer, and it compares the high and low side pressures to ambient temperature and relative humidity. The technician also inputs the temperature of various components, such as the condenser, evaporator, and hoses, using a flexible temperature probe.

After being connected to the A/C service ports, the diagnostic tool uses the software in the PDA to guide the technician through the test procedure. It prompts the technician to input needed component temperatures at the inlet and outlet of key components using the completely flexible temperature probe. It will determine good or bad A/C performance. It does this by recognizing proper operating pressures relative to ambient temperature, relative humidity, and component temperature and the clutch cycling rate. The tool also recognizes improper operating patterns for the most common A/C system problems. It will indicate the nature of about 24 different problems. It also has the ability to print out a detailed copy of the data that were logged during its operation.

FIGURE 12-53 This A/C diagnostic tool uses low and high side pressure, ambient temperature, relative humidity, and A/C component temperature readings from various locations to input into the PDA. The PDA guides the technician through the test procedure, analyzes the data, and then determines if the system is operating properly or, if not, what is wrong. *(Courtesy of Neutronics, Inc.)*

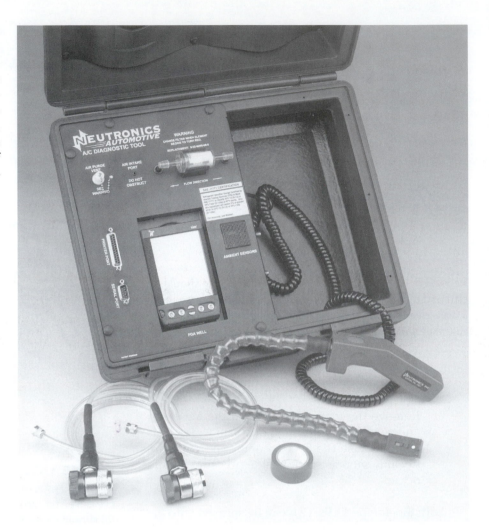

◀ **SERVICE TIP** ▶

The electronic portion of some service units and gauge sets have the ability to calculate the amount of sub-cooling.

12.4 A/C SYSTEM REFRIGERANT LEAK TESTS

There are several ways to locate refrigerant leaks. Those commonly used for automotive systems range from very simple soapy water to flame-type detectors and electronic units. Dye or trace solutions are used when trying to locate very difficult or slow R-12 leaks. A fluorescent tracer solution has become a popular method of leak location in both R-12 and R-134a systems. These methods have different abilities to find a leak (Figure 12-54).

◀ **SERVICE TIP** ▶

Many R-12 leaks are easy to locate because refrigerant oil tends to escape with the refrigerant. This oil leaves a telltale spill that collects dust. The PAG and POE oils used with R-134a tend to dissipate or be washed away and don't leave this telltale trace.

An experienced technician begins leak detection with a visual inspection for this oil residue at line connections and other points and for oil throw-off from the compressor clutch. A compressor shaft seal leak often carries oil to the clutch plate, and centrifugal force throws the oil outward and onto the hood or other parts next to the clutch. The most probable leak locations are any line connection (especially spring lock connections), the compressor seal, any other compressor seal-

Leak Detection Method	LEAK RATE			
	Fast	Med. Fast	Med. Slow	Slow
Vacuum Check	Good	Fair	Not Effective	Not Effective
Bubbles	Good	Good	Poor	Not Effective
Electronic	Excellent	Excellent	Excellent	Excellent
Fluorescent Dye	Excellent	Excellent	Excellent	Excellent*

*Fluorescent dye is the only method that will locate a passive leak

FIGURE 12-54   These four leak detection methods have various amounts of success depending on the leak rate.

ing surfaces, the service ports, any place where a refrigerant hose or tube rubs against something, both ends of a hose where it joins a metal fitting, and any kink or dent in a metal refrigerant line. Also check for leaks at the evaporator and condenser.

◄   **SERVICE TIP**   ►

To determine if a compressor shaft seal is leaking, slip a 3 × 5 card into the clutch gap and, with the engine off, cycle the clutch on and off several times. If there is oil on the card when you remove it, the shaft seal is leaking.

There are many **electronic leak detectors;** these are the most popular style of leak detector. Most are rather expensive, very accurate, and completely safe to use. Many electronic leak detectors can be used for both R-12 and R-134a systems.

Early electronic leak detectors were quite effective in locating R-12 leaks, but they did not have enough sensitivity to locate comparable leaks in R-134a systems. Some types of detectors are triggered by other chemicals like brake cleaner or antifreeze so they will give false alarm signals. There are several different types of electronic detectors. The heated diode sensor was the first type approved by SAE standard J1627. Newer styles using heated anode sensors and corona discharge sensors are also approved and available. It is recommended that if you are considering a purchase, choose a unit that meets the SAE standard and is made by a reputable manufacturer that supports its product. Average sensor life is about 100 to 200 hours, and sensor replacement can be expensive. Also, most units have tips with filters that must be cleaned or replaced (Figure 12-55).

Infrared sensing is used in the new INFICON D-Tek Select (Figure 12-56). This sensor is more sensitive and said to be able to detect a leak of 0.10 oz (3 gm) per year.

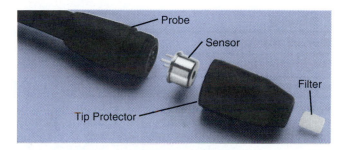

FIGURE 12-55   Removing the tip protector from the electronic leak detector probe allows the filter or sensor to be replaced. *(Courtesy of INFICON)*

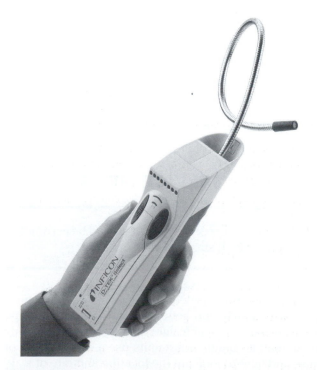

FIGURE 12-56   This electronic leak detector uses infrared sensing. A leak is indicated by a variable intensity audible/sound signal and a flashing LED. *(Courtesy of INFICON)*

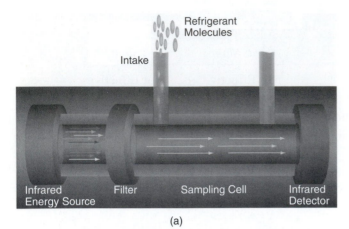

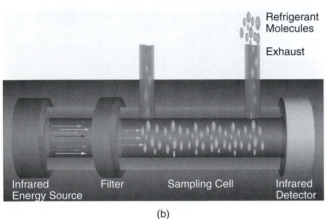

FIGURE 12-57 Infrared energy is sent through a filter that removes all the energy that is not in the range of refrigerants. Any refrigerant passing through the sampling cell will remove more of the energy and cause the leak detector to respond. *(Courtesy of INFICON)*

The sensor is not overloaded or poisoned by exposure to too much refrigerant, is not affected by smoke or humidity, and should also last longer, by up to 800 hours of use (Figure 12-57).

◀ **SERVICE TIP** ▶

When buying a leak detector, it should be certified as meeting SAE standard J1667.

Most electronic leak detectors emit a clicking noise that starts slowly and gets faster as it detects a leak. Some units use a flashing light that flashes more quickly as the leak is found. Some units use a combination of noise and light to indicate the location and rate of leakage. These leak detectors use a search probe where air and any leakage are drawn into the unit; this probe must be kept clean.

FIGURE 12-58 An ultrasonic leak detector converts the sound of a gas leaking through a small opening into a sound that we can hear using a set of headphones. It also displays the leak rate on a scale. *(Courtesy of Robinair, SPX Corporation)*

Another tester type based on electronics is the **ultrasonic leak detector** (Figure 12-58). This tester "listens" for the sound of gas escaping. This sound is at a frequency higher than the human ear is capable of hearing. The tester converts that sound to an audible frequency. The unit is pointed at the suspected leak location, and the technician listens for the noise on a headset or watches the indicator scale. It can pick up sound from a distance, and the sound level will grow louder as the detector is moved closer to the leak.

◀ **SERVICE TIP** ▶

Some technicians charge the system with nitrogen to a pressure of 150 to 200 psi (1,034 to 1,379 kPa). The higher pressure will increase the leak rate. Pressures above 200 psi can damage the system.

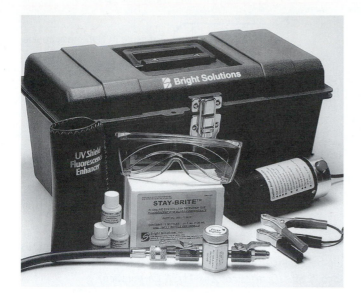

FIGURE 12-59 A tracer solution leak detection kit. Tracer solutions are charged into the system; a color stain visible under an ultraviolet light indicates the leak area. *(Courtesy of Bright Solutions)*

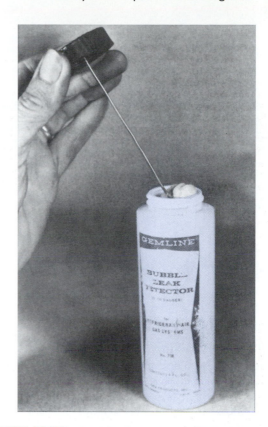

FIGURE 12-60 Bubble leak detector. This is like a liquid soap mixture.

Dyes and tracer leak detectors are usually charged into the system with the refrigerant. Dye was once sold in small cans of R-12 but is not used any more; the dye leaves a visible stain when it leaks out. The red dyes can ruin interior carpeting and upholstery if they come into contact with the vehicle's interior. Fluorescent trace solutions are commonly used now; these solutions are available in small containers and special capsules. They are propelled into a system by either a refrigerant charge, system pressure, or a hand-powered pump. The fluorescent tracers or dyes glow under ultraviolet light so that they show up more easily. These solutions can pinpoint the location of small leaks relatively quickly (Figure 12-59). Some vehicle manufacturers dislike trace solutions because they may contaminate a system. Other manufacturers add fluorescent tracer dye with the original refrigerant charge.

The simplest and least expensive leak detector is soapy water. Commercial liquid solutions are available, or you can make a mixture of about one-half water and one-half liquid dish soap. The liquid solution is applied to a suspected area with a dauber, small brush, or spray bottle; leaks make bubbles or foam. Liquid solutions have the advantage of showing the exact location to pinpoint a leak at a service port or line connection, but this method only finds leaks of about 40 oz per year and it is too slow to use it on large areas (Figure 12-60). A leak of 1/4 oz (7 g) per year will form a bubble in about 10 minutes.

Flame-type leak detectors *are not* recommended by most experts. These are also called a halide torch. They use a small propane bottle (usually 1 lb) and a burner to

heat a copper reaction plate or wires. Gas flow to the burner passes through a venturi, where the search hose is attached. This creates a vacuum that pulls air through the search hose. If a CFC comes in contact with red-hot copper, it changes the flame color. A flame-type leak detector has a sensitivity capable of finding a leak as small as 8 to 10 oz (227 to 284 g) per year.

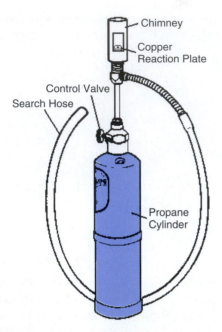

FIGURE 12-61 A flame leak detector (no longer recommended) heats the copper reaction plate to red-hot. The flame color will change if a CFC touches this plate.

◀ **CAUTION** ▶

If using a flame-type leak detector, make absolutely certain that there is not a flammable refrigerant, hold the unit at arm's length away from your face so you will not breathe the fumes, and be aware of the location of the flame at all times (Figure 12-61).

◀ **SERVICE TIP** ▶

When you need to locate a refrigerant leak, you should remember the following guidelines:

- Make sure there is enough refrigerant in the system to produce normal pressures (at least 50 psi). (With an empty system, this will be about 7 to 10% of the total charge.)
- Conduct leakage tests in an area free of wind and drafts.
- If the area is contaminated with refrigerant, use a fan to blow the excess away.

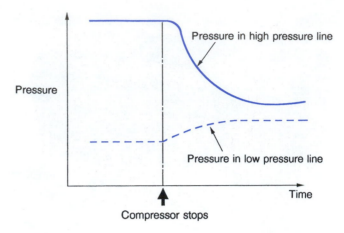

FIGURE 12-62 A leak in the high side of a system shows up best right after the system is shut off, before the pressure drops off. *(Courtesy of Zexel USA Corporation)*

- Operate the system long enough to circulate the refrigerant and produce normal pressures (Figure 12-62).
- Shut the engine off while searching for leaks.
- Clean oily spots with a dry shop cloth; solvents may leave a residue that could confuse the leak tester.
- Hold the leak detector probe under the point being checked, because refrigerant is heavier than air (Figure 12-63).
- Move the probe about 1 inch (2.5 cm) per second while checking along a line or hose at a distance of 1/4 inch or less from the item being checked.
- Make sure the probe of an electronic leak detector does not touch the item being checked.
- When checking a specific location, hold the probe stationary for about 5 seconds.
- If a leak is indicated, move the probe away, blow out the area with shop air, and then return to verify the problem.

◀ **SERVICE TIP** ▶

Check the high side for leaks right after shutting the engine and system off while the pressure is the highest.

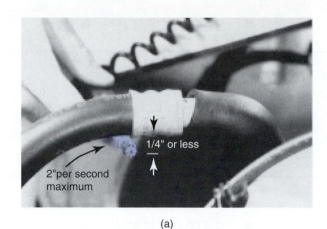

(a)

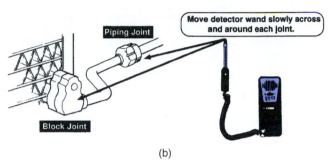

(b)

FIGURE 12-63 The leak detector probe should be kept under the line or component, within 1/4 inch, and when checking a hose, moved along at a rate of 2 inches per second (a). Move the probe around each line fitting and service port (b). (b Courtesy of Toyota Motor Sales USA, Inc.)

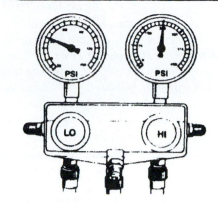

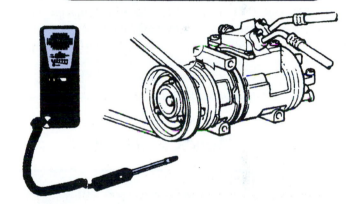

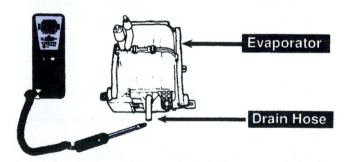

◄ **SERVICE TIP** ►

To increase system pressure for leak checking, heat the accumulator or receiver–drier. A heat gun can be used or you can wrap the unit with a small heating pad.

◄ **SERVICE TIP** ►

A faulty Schrader valve can be removed by unscrewing it just like a tire valve; in many cases, a tire valve service tool can be used. A special service tool is used in very tight locations. A new A/C Schrader valve should be installed; tire valves will not work properly.

◄ **SERVICE TIP** ►

A leaking high-pressure relief valve can be replaced using a new valve and gasket.

◄ **SERVICE TIP** ►

At least one vehicle manufacturer uses a painted steel accumulator with a foam insulating wrap. The foam retains condensed water next to the accumulator, which promotes rust; after a few years it can rust through, producing a refrigerant leak. Although accumulator leaks are fairly rare, a painted accumulator is probably steel, and these should be checked for rust and leaks.

◄ **SERVICE TIP** ►

A leak in an R-134a system is generally harder to locate and requires more patience and care than a leak in an R-12 system. Many technicians search using an electronic detector and following the recommended SAE J1628 procedure, and if they cannot locate the leak, they use fluorescent dye, which tends to locate the smaller leaks.

◄ **SERVICE TIP** ►

A leak that occurs at the service port fitting may be temporarily sealed if you connect a gauge set and hoses to it. Disconnect the hoses and check the exposed port and valve.

Other possible leak locations that are often overlooked are the pressure switches; unplug the electrical connectors so you can check the entire switch body.

◄ **SERVICE TIP** ►

At the completion of a job, when the hoses are disconnected, one technician puts a few drops of mineral-type refrigerant oil in each service port. Bubbles forming in the oil indicate a leaking Schrader valve.

◄ **SERVICE TIP** ►

During a hot soak period on a hot day, evaporator pressure can reach 250 to 400 psi, much higher than the pressure normally found during leak checks. Fluorescent dye is the most effective leak checking process for very small evaporator leaks, but inspection is very difficult.

◄ **SERVICE TIP** ►

If you think a compressor shaft seal is leaking but the leak does not show up using your detector, rotate the compressor drive plate by hand to another position. Sometimes corrosion or a small pit in the shaft sealing surface will produce a leak with the shaft in certain positions but not others.

◄ **SERVICE TIP** ►

If you feel a leak might be caused by the compressor shaft seal and you have good access to the compressor, remove the clutch hub and check the shaft area.

To locate a refrigerant leak using an electronic leak detector or soap solution, you should:

1. Wipe away any oil and dirt from line connections, hoses, and so forth with a shop cloth.
2. Check to make sure the leak detector probe tip and filter are clean.
3. Turn on the electronic leak detector and adjust or calibrate it according to the unit's instructions (Figure 12-64).
4. Begin at a convenient location. Some technicians prefer to follow the normal path through a system and move the probe under each of these points of possible leakage, staying within 1/4 inch of the part being checked.

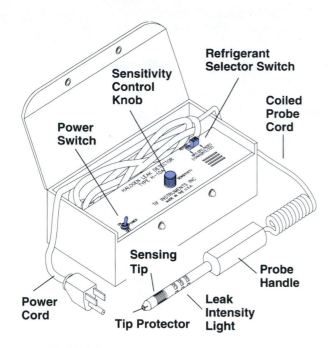

FIGURE 12-64 Some electronic leak detectors have a sensitivity adjustment that is usually adjusted to give a slow noise or light response. *(Courtesy of TIF Instruments)*

a. *Compressor:* Line connections, surfaces where parts are joined, any switches and valves, the clutch and pulley (Figure 12-65)

b. *Condenser:* Line connections, all welded joints, any visible damage

c. *Receiver–drier:* Line connections; sight glass; any switches, plugs, or relief valves

d. *TXV or OT:* Line connections

e. *Evaporator:* Line connections, at the evaporator drain tube and instrument panel outlet with the blower at the lowest speed setting

f. *Accumulator:* Line connections, switches, or service port

g. *Hoses:* Line connections, where the hose end meets the metal connector, any area that shows damage or rubbing contact

h. *Service ports:* Valve core, remove cap or disconnect gauge hose

5. If the electronic leak detector indicates a probable leak at a point such as a line connection or joint in the compressor shell, dab a wet film of soap solution over the point. Observe for bubbles, which confirm the point of leakage (Figure 12-66).

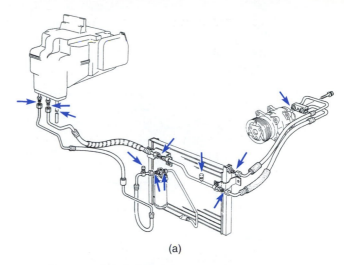

(a)

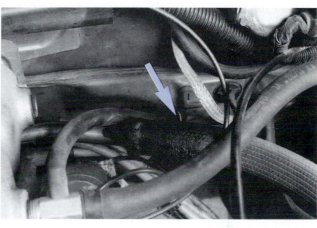

(b)

FIGURE 12-65 The most probable leak areas are indicated by arrows, but leaks can occur anywhere along a hose and at the compressor *(a)*. The oily, dirty coating *(arrow)* on this hose indicates a probable leak *(b)*. *(a courtesy of Zexel USA Corporation)*

◀ **SERVICE TIP** ▶

If an evaporator leak is suspected, run the system long enough for the engine and HVAC system to warm up to normal operating temperatures. With the engine and system off, run the blower motor for about 10 minutes to warm up the evaporator and increase the temperature and low side pressure. Shut off the blower motor, wait for 10 to 15 minutes, and check for a refrigerant leak at the evaporator drain.

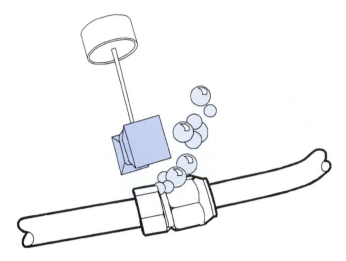

FIGURE 12-66 Refrigerant leaks cause bubbles to form when liquid leak detector is spread over the area. This pinpoints the leak location. *(Courtesy of Saturn Corporation)*

◀ **SERVICE TIP** ▶

If you need to check for a leak in the area between the condenser and radiator, place a length of plastic hose over the tester probe. This extension will let you extend the reach through small areas.

◀ **SERVICE TIP** ▶

When checking hoses, pay special attention at places where the hose contacts other objects that might cause a **rub-through**.

◀ **SERVICE TIP** ▶

When checking for leaks at the evaporator drain, place a clear plastic hose over the probe of the tester to help ensure that you do not contaminate the probe with water.

To locate a leak using fluorescent tracers, you should:

1. Add the proper amount of fluorescent additive into the dye injector tool and, *if using a handpowered injector system*, connect the injector

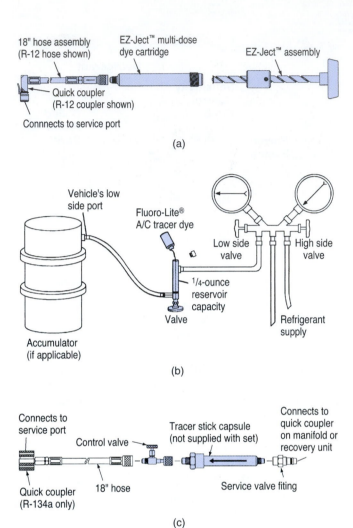

FIGURE 12-67 Tracer solutions can be injected into a system that is shut off using a hand-powered injector *(a)* or added into an operating system by using a dye injector *(b)* or Tracer-Stick capsule *(c)*. *(Courtesy of Tracer Products, a division of Spectronics Corporation)*

to a service port, operate the injector to inject the proper amount of dye, and disconnect the injector tool (Figure 12-67). *If using a system with dye capsules or containers:*

a. Connect the tool in series in the low side service hose *or* connect the disposable Glo-Stick capsule into the low side service hose (Figure 12-68).

b. If the system is low on refrigerant, connect a refrigerant source to the center hose, open the low side handwheel, and allow refrigerant pressure to force the dye into the system. If the system has normal pressure, start the engine, turn on the A/C, open both low and high side service valves, and allow high side pressure to force the additive into the system.

(a)

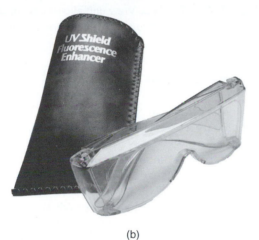

(b)

FIGURE 12-68 A refrigerant leak shows up as a yellow-green glow under ultraviolet light *(a)*. A leak shows up easier if yellow fluorescent enhancer glasses are worn *(b)*. *(a courtesy of Robinair, SPX Corporation; b courtesy of Bright Solutions)*

◀ **SERVICE TIP** ▶

The rule of thumb is 1/4 oz (7 g) of dye per system with a limit of 1/2 oz (14 g). Excessive dye can cause problems. There is also a recommendation that different brands of dye should not be mixed.

2. Run the system for a few minutes to circulate the fluorescent dye; then shut off the system and engine.
3. Shine a high-intensity ultraviolet light over the system as you carefully search for a glowing fluorescent trail or puddle, which indicates a leak. Wearing yellow goggles enhances the vis-

ibility of the leak, making it easier to find. Follow the trail to the exact location of the leak.

◀ **SERVICE TIP** ▶

Some technicians will shine the UV light into a system's service port to check for dye. If they see a glow, no additional dye should be added.

◀ **SAFETY TIP** ▶

UV rays are harmful to your eyes. Do not look into the lamp. The special yellow goggles will also help protect your eyes from these harmful rays.

◀ **SERVICE TIP** ▶

In tight locations where you need to check behind a fittting or line or underneath a compressor, position a mirror so you can reflect the UV light and examine these hidden areas. Another helpful trick is to wipe these hidden areas with a clean cloth, and then shine the light onto the cloth. A fluorescence stain on the cloth indicates that it picked up dye from a leak.

◀ **SERVICE TIP** ▶

In cases where the leak is very slow, the fluorescent dye is injected into the system and the vehicle is given back to the customer to give the leak time to show up. After a few days, the vehicle is returned for leak checking.

The leakage location determines the needed repair. Occasionally a leaky connection can be corrected simply by tightening the fitting. But the fitting should not be overtightened—that can damage the O-ring or seal seat, making the repair more serious than necessary. If the fitting still leaks when tightened to the correct torque, replace the O-ring (Figure 12-69).

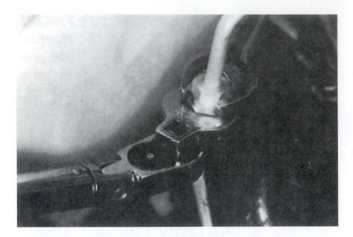

FIGURE 12-69 Line connections must be tightened to the correct torque. A crow's-foot adapter is being used on the torque wrench as a backup wrench keeps the other half of the fitting stationary. *(Courtesy of Nissan Motor Corporation in USA)*

REAL WORLD FIX: The 1993 Dodge Colt (128,000 miles) has no A/C. The system was found to have no refrigerant. The system would hold a vacuum, so the system was recharged after evacuating it and dye was added. System pressures were normal, so the car was given back to the customer. The car came back the next day with an empty system. A check using a blacklight showed no sign of the dye. The system was recharged, but a check with an electronic tester showed no leak. The system was charged again, and the next day, all of the refrigerant had leaked out. The evaporator core was removed and inspected, but no sign of a leak was found.

FIX

While checking for a leak again, a soft spot on the discharge hose was found. When the bubble was cut open, dye was found inside the bubble. Cutting the hose open revealed that the hose inner liner had failed. Replacement of this hose fixed the leak problem.

◀ **SERVICE TIP** ▶

A fluorescent dye must be circulated to the leak, and it is transported by refrigerant oil. Water will wash it away along with the dye. This helps cleanup after the repair has been made, but it also can remove the ability of finding a leak if the vehicle is operated where water can splash on portions of the A/C system.

FIGURE 12-70 The Flex-View unit allows a technician to inspect the evaporator through a 1/2-in. hole. *(Courtesy of Robinair, SPX Corporation)*

12.4.1 Evaporator Inspection

The evaporator must be checked visually if you are using dye to locate a possible leak, and this can be very difficult when you can't see the evaporator. A borescope–like tool is available that allows you to inspect the evaporator (Figure 12-70). The tip of the tool can be inserted through a small, 1/2-in. (13 mm) hole in the HVAC case, and the technician looks through the eye piece. Sometimes removal of the blower resistor provides access. If drilling is necessary, the hole can be closed using a shop-made patch.

12.4.2 Vacuum Pump Leak Tests

During the evacuation and recharging stage of system service, it is a common practice to determine whether the system holds a vacuum as a final check for leaks. This process takes only a few minutes: Simply shut off the service valves after the system is down to a full vacuum (almost 30″ Hg), wait 5 minutes, and recheck the vacuum. If the vacuum stays at 30″ Hg, the system does not have a leak.

◀ **SERVICE TIP** ▶

Checking the vacuum of a system may indicate a leak that does not exist. The O-rings and compressor shaft seal are designed to keep pressure in, not out. They can allow a slight leakage into the system and still seal perfectly under pressure. If the system's refrigerant has just been recovered, a pressure rise can be caused by refrigerant outgassing or boiling out of the oil. When experienced technicians check the vacuum of a system, they interpret a slight pressure rise as an indicator of normal conditions. A continuous pressure increase indicates a small leak.

Adapters can be fitted to the compressor or evaporator, so these parts can be individually checked for leaks. These adapters can be commercial fittings or can be made in the shop by connecting the proper line fitting to a 1/4-inch male flare adapter. The check is usually a quality control check for a compressor that has been repaired or a final check before removing an evaporator suspected to be leaking. Evaporator replacement is a difficult, time-consuming job that should not be done unless absolutely necessary (Figure 12-71).

To vacuum test a single A/C component for leaks; you should:

1. Recover any remaining refrigerant from the system and disconnect the lines to that component. (Refrigerant recovery is described in Section 15.3.1.)

2. Attach an adapter to each line connection; connect the low and high side service hoses to these adapters.

3. Connect the center service hose to a vacuum pump, open both manifold valves, and operate the vacuum pump until there is an almost 30" Hg vacuum for 2 minutes.

4. Shut off both hand valves, wait 5 minutes, and recheck the vacuum. If it has not lost vacuum, the component is good. If it has lost vacuum or if the vacuum will not go this deep, check the line fittings and pump. If they are okay, a leak is indicated.

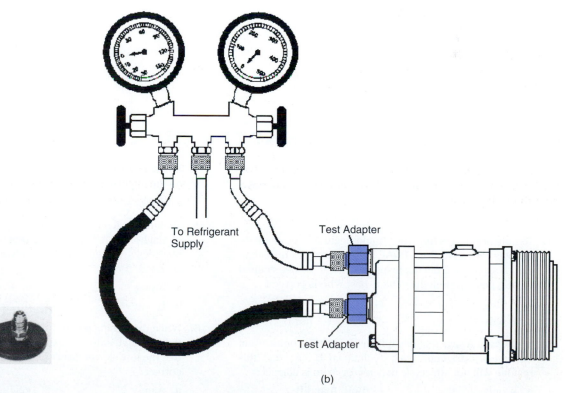

To Refrigerant Supply

Test Adapter

Test Adapter

(a)

(b)

FIGURE 12-71 Special adapters *(a)* are available to allow connection of a gauge set to a compressor *(b)* or portions of a system. The compressor can then be pressure or vacuum checked for leaks. *(a courtesy of Robinair, SPX Corporation)*

REVIEW QUESTIONS

The following questions are provided to help you study as you read the chapter.

1. An A/C gauge set contains a(n) _____ _____ and a(n) _____ _____ pressure gauge, at least two hand valves, and _____ _____.

2. An A/C service unit will include _____ _____, a(n) _____ _____, and a(n) _____ _____.

3. An A/C service unit can also include equipment to _____ and _____ refrigerant.

4. A low side, R-12 service port is the same as a 1/4-inch _____ _____.

5. A high side, R-134a service port is _____ than the low side port, and both ports use a(n) _____-_____ style coupler.

6. The low side gauge and hose are colored _____, and the high side gauge and hose are colored _____.

7. When the hoses are connected to an R-12 system on a 70°F day, both gauges should read about _____ _____.

8. In an R-134a system with normal operation, the low side pressure should be about _____ psi, and the suction line should be _____.

9. In an R-134a system with normal operation, the discharge line should be _____, and the high side pressure will _____ as ambient temperature increases.

10. Bubbles are expected to appear in the sight glass during _____ _____.

11. High relative humidity can cause _____ high side _____.

12. Low pressure on the low and high sides is commonly caused by _____ _____.

13. A faulty compressor can cause _____ low side pressure and _____ high side pressure.

14. The refrigerant charge level can be verified by checking the _____ and _____ of the refrigerant at the condenser outlet.

15. The most popular refrigerant leak detectors used today are _____ _____ and _____ _____.

16. A system should have a pressure of at least _____ _____ when checking for a leak.

17. The leak detector probe should be moved along about _____ _____ from the location being checked at a maximum rate of _____ inch(es) per second.

18. A fluorescent trace will show up better if you wear _____ _____.

CHAPTER QUIZ

The following questions will help you check the facts you have learned. Select the answer that completes each statement correctly.

1. Technician A says that you should begin A/C problem diagnosis with a thorough HVAC system inspection. Technician B says that from the inspection it can be determined what type of system the vehicle has. Who is correct?
   a. A only
   b. B only
   c. Both A and B
   d. Neither A nor B

2. Technician A says that oily residue on a fitting or hose can indicate a refrigerant leak. Technician B says that this residue will not affect a leak detector. Who is correct?
   a. A only
   b. B only
   c. Both A and B
   d. Neither A nor B

3. When a system is operating correctly, the lines and hoses on the high side should be cool to the touch.
   a. True
   b. False

4. Technician A says that pressure checks are one method of diagnosing A/C problems. Technician B says that trouble trees are used only for mechanical problems. Who is correct?
   a. A only
   b. B only
   c. Both A and B
   d. Neither A nor B

5. While discussing a manifold gauge set, technician A says that the high side service hose is blue. Technician B says that the low side pressure gauge goes up to 750 psi. Who is correct?
   a. A only
   b. B only
   c. Both A and B
   d. Neither A nor B

6. Technician A says that the manifold gauge set for R-12 can be used on all systems. Technician B says that R-134a systems use service ports with metric flare threads. Who is correct?

   a. A only   **c.** Both A and B

   b. B only   **d.** Neither A nor B

7. On a system that uses service valves, the valve is kept in the _____ seated position for normal operation.

   a. front   **c.** mid

   b. back   **d.** None of these

8. An R-12 system is shut off, and the ambient temperature is 70°F. The evaporator pressure should be about _____.

   a. 50 psi   **c.** 83 psi

   b. 70 psi   **d.** 100 psi

9. In most R-12 systems that use an STV, the normal low side pressure should be about _____.

   a. 15 to 20 psi   **c.** 28 to 30 psi

   b. 15 to 30 psi   **d.** over 35 psi

10. High side pressure is affected by _____.

    a. ambient temperature   **c.** refrigerant charge level

    b. fan clutch operation   **d.** All of these

11. A faulty A/C system has a high low side pressure and a high high side pressure. Technician A says that the system is probably starved. Technician B says that the system has a bad thermostatic switch. Who is correct?

    a. A only   **c.** Both A and B

    b. B only   **d.** Neither A nor B

12. _____ can be used to locate refrigerant leaks.

    a. Soap and water   **c.** Electronic testers

    b. Flame-type testers   **d.** Any of these

13. The engine should be running while the technician checks for leaks.

    a. True   **b.** False

14. Technician A says that the system should be operated after injecting fluorescent dye into it. Technician B says that wearing yellow-tinted goggles can help you find the dye traces, and this also protects your eyes. Who is correct?

    a. A only   **c.** Both A and B

    b. B only   **d.** Neither A nor B

Chapter 13

HEATING AND AIR MANAGEMENT SYSTEMS INSPECTION AND DIAGNOSIS

LEARNING OBJECTIVES

After completing this chapter, you should be able to:

1. Inspect a heater system to determine whether there is proper coolant flow through the core.
2. Inspect a heater system to determine whether there are any coolant leaks.
3. Check the operation of mechanical and vacuum controls and determine whether there are any faults.
4. Complete the ASE tasks related to heater system diagnosis.
5. Complete the ASE tasks related to air management system diagnosis.

TERMS TO LEARN

air bleeds	electrolysis
cable adjustment	erosion
corrosion	on-board diagnostics
cycling	(OBD)
diagnostic trouble code	quick-connect coupling
(DTC)	

13.1   INTRODUCTION

Problems in the heater system or air management system can show up with improper operation of the components or during the HVAC system inspection (see Section 11.2). Further tests can be done to determine the exact causes of these problems.

13.1.1   Heater Inspection

Most heater complaints are of insufficient heat, wet carpet, excessive window fogging, or air discharge from the wrong location. Occasionally a few other problems can occur; most of these problems are listed in Figure 13-1. The most commonly encountered problems are not enough heat output and leaks. Not enough heat output is usually caused by either poor coolant circulation through the heater core or coolant that is not hot enough.

With copper or brass heater cores, leaks are often the result of **cycling;** this is the expansion and contraction of the core that takes place between a cold start with zero coolant pressure and operating temperatures and pressures. The most common causes of failure with aluminum heater cores are **corrosion** and **erosion.** Corrosion is caused by chemical action and

PROBLEM	CAUSE	CURE
Insufficient heat	Plugged heater core	Replace heater core
	Closed water valve	Repair or adjust valve control
		Repair or replace valve
	Kinked heater hose	Realign or replace hose
	Faulty blend door position	Repair or adjust door control
	Faulty heater core seals	R&R core seals
	Low coolant level	Correct coolant level & repair leak
	Open engine thermostat	Replace thermostat
Excess heat	Faulty blend door position	Repair or adjust door control
	Open water valve	Repair or adjust valve control
		Repair or replace valve
Wet carpet/window fogging	Leaky core	Replace heater core
	Hose leaks	Repair hose connections
Noisy operation	Air trapped in core	Bleed air out

FIGURE 13-1   Most heater system problems can be placed in one or more of these categories.

electrolysis. The chemicals eat away the metals; **electrolysis** speeds up this chemical change if the coolant becomes acidic. Erosion is wear from the coolant flowing past the metal until the metal is too thin to function properly, and erosion increases if the coolant becomes contaminated with abrasive materials. Having clean coolant with an effective inhibitor package is extremely important in systems with aluminum components; coolant maintenance is covered more completely in Chapters 17 and 18.

REAL WORLD FIX: The heater core in the 1994 Pontiac Bonneville (109,000 miles) was leaking, and the core had been replaced four different times at another shop. The cooling system was checked for combustion leaks and none were found. A new, top-quality core was installed, but the vehicle returned in two and a half months with the same problem, a leaking core.

FIX

Following advice from a technical service bulletin (TSB), the technician thoroughly flushed the cooling system to remove abrasive silicates from the old antifreeze. A new heater core was installed, and the system was filled with new antifreeze and water coolant. This repair fixed the problem.

In all modern engines, coolant temperature is controlled by the engine thermostat, and the thermostat is designed to bring the engine temperature quickly up to the operating point for proper emission control. An engine that is too cold does not operate efficiently, and besides losing power and wasting fuel, the exhaust contains more pollutants than if it is at the proper temperature. Some modern vehicles with **on-board diagnostics (OBD)** turn on the check engine lamp, also called the *malfunction indicator light (MIL)*, if the engine stays cool too long after start-up; this also sets a **diagnostic trouble code (DTC)**. Thermostat tests are described in Section 18.3.4.

Heater output is dependent on vehicle HVAC design and ambient temperature, but with most vehicles, a properly operating heater should provide discharge air that is at least 60°F (33°C) warmer than ambient air (Figure 13-2).

13.1.2   Coolant Circulation Checks

Most technicians begin checking the insufficient heat complaint by feeling the heater hoses to check for coolant circulation. With the engine at operating temperature, they both should be too hot to hold comfortably. If the hoses seem too cool, feel the upper radiator hose; it should be hot (as hot as the thermostat opening temperature), about 190 to 200°F (88 to 94°C). If the upper hose is too hot to hold, the thermostat is probably working properly. If the heater hoses are not hot, something is blocking circulation through the heater system.

With the heater operating, the outlet hose should be about 20°F (11°C) cooler than the inlet because of the heat transfer at the heater core.

Ambient Temperature		Minimum Output Temperature		Ambient Temperature		Minimum Output Temperature	
°F	°C	°F	°C	°F	°C	°F	°C
0	−18	114	42	50	15	141	60
10	−12	120	49	70	21	144	62
20	−6	126	52	80	27	150	64
40	4	132	56	90	32	153	67
50	10	137	59				

FIGURE 13-2 Heater output, measured at the floor outlet, should be at or above the temperatures shown.

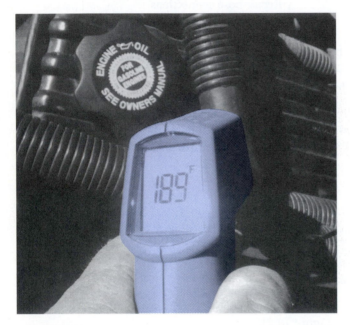

FIGURE 13-3 Heater hose temperature can be checked quickly with an infrared thermometer. This return hose is 189°F, which indicates good flow through the heater core.

◀ **SERVICE TIP** ▶

Make sure that the system is full of coolant. A low coolant level might not supply a full flow to the heater core.

If the problem is poor circulation, check to see whether there is a water valve in the system; if there is, make sure it is open. Most water valves are vacuum operated and are normally open. A vacuum signal closes the valve. Vacuum control system checks are described in Section 13.4.3.

If you do not find a restricted water valve, you should disconnect the heater hoses to check for blockage. Use caution and allow the system to cool to comfortable temperatures before removing the radiator cap or disconnecting a hose. The reasons for these cautions are described in Chapter 18.

◀ **SERVICE TIP** ▶

An infrared thermometer makes coolant circulation checks easier, safer, and more accurate. Simply point the unit at the heater hoses and read their temperature (Figure 13-3).

◀ **SERVICE TIP** ▶

Some vehicles have a coolant restrictor at one of the heater core connectors. This restrictor orifice can become plugged.

◀ **SERVICE TIP** ▶

Use care when removing a hose from a heater core connection; do not force hoses on or off a connector. The hose will probably stick to the connector, and the twisting and pulling to try to remove it can easily damage the connector. On systems that use **quick-connect couplings,** use the proper tool to release the coupling and then pull the coupling straight off the heater core connector (Figure 13-4). Damage to the coupling or connector can necessitate expensive repairs. Proper hose removal methods are described in Section 18.2.5.

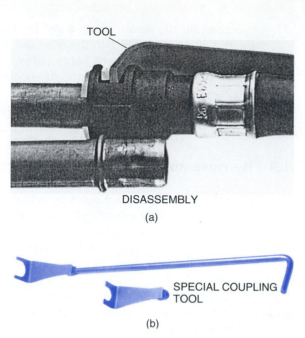

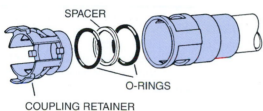

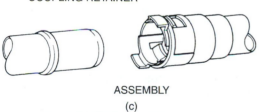

FIGURE 13-4 A special tool (*a* and *b*) is required to release the lock on quick-connect heater hose couplers. The O-rings (*c*) must be in good condition and lubricated with silicone to prevent leaks. (*Courtesy of Four Seasons*)

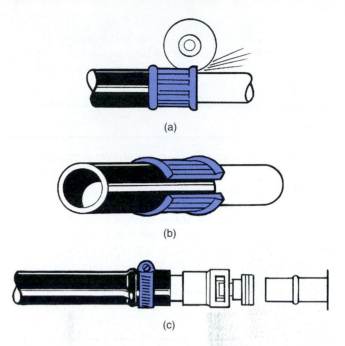

FIGURE 13-5 An alternate repair method for damaged heater hoses using quick-connect couplers is to cut off the ferrule (*a*), remove the damaged hose from the quick-connect nipple (*b*), and clamp a new hose onto the nipple (*c*). (*Courtesy of The Gates Rubber Company*)

To check heater core coolant circulation, you should:

1. Place a drain pan to catch the escaping coolant and disconnect the engine ends of both heater hoses.
2. Blow into one of the hoses; air along with coolant should come from the other hose.
3. *If you cannot blow through the system*, disconnect the other end of one of the hoses and blow through it. The hose is faulty if you cannot blow through it.
4. Repeat step 3 on the other hose.
5. With the hoses removed, blow into one of the heater core connections; *if you cannot blow through it*, the core is plugged and should be replaced.

◄ **SERVICE TIP** ►

A less expensive option to repair a leaky heater hose using quick connectors is to remove the damaged hose from the connector by cutting the ferrule. If using an abrasive wheel, wear eye protection. Be careful not to cut too deeply and damage the nipple (Figure 13-5). Carefully remove the ferrule and old hose and clamp a new hose to the connector.

◄ **SERVICE TIP** ►

Heater core flushing is described in Section 18.4, but flushing is not effective if the core is completely plugged. Some sources suggest filling a plugged core with ammonia, but this is not recommended because ammonia can eat away some heater cores very rapidly. The best repair is to replace the core, and many heater cores are mounted inside of the evaporator–heater case.

REAL WORLD FIX: The 1985 BMW 535i (237,000 miles) has a strange problem. The heater works great at idle speeds, but there is no heat while driving down the road. The coolant was changed, and the system was refilled using an Air Lift to ensure no air locks. The heater control valve was checked. The screen is clean, and the plunger moves in and out.

FIX

Following advice, the technician rebuilt the mono valve using the proper repair kit. This 10-minute job fixed this problem.

13.1.3   Heater Core Leak Check

A leaky heater core usually shows up as coolant dripping from the A/C–heater case and a wet carpet or an oily mist or fog coming from the defroster ducts. This leak can be confirmed by pressure loss during a system pressure test.

◄   SERVICE TIP   ►

It is possible for the leak to be located at the heater hose connection that allows coolant to run along the connector and into the case. For this reason, and also because heater core replacement is usually difficult and expensive, it is recommended that an additional check be made to confirm that the core is bad. This test can be made with the core still in place or on the bench. If bench testing, the core can be placed underwater and the air bubbles from a leak will show the exact location of the leak.

To test a heater core for leaks, you should:

1. Partially drain the coolant and disconnect both the hoses from the heater core.
2. Plug one of the connections and connect a vacuum pump or a hand pressure tester to the other connector (Figure 13-6).

3. Depending on the tester, pump a 28″ Hg vacuum or a 30 psi pressure into the core and observe the gauge. If the core holds either the vacuum or pressure for at least 20 seconds (some sources recommend 3 minutes), it is good. If the vacuum or pressure does not hold, the core should be replaced.

13.1.4   Remove and Replace Heater Core

A leaking or restricted heater core must be replaced. The heater core is normally contained inside of the HVAC case, and with most vehicles, the HVAC case must be removed to allow heater core replacement (Figure 13-7). A few vehicles have an HVAC case with removable panels that allow easy heater core removal. Before starting a replacement procedure, it is highly recommended to consult the replacement procedure for that particular vehicle model.

REAL WORLD FIX: The 1995 Pontiac Grand Am had a leaking heater core so it was replaced. The problem reoccurred three more times; each time an OEM or ACDelco core was used. A heater core ground wire was added during the third replacement, but this did not help.

FIX

Following advice, the technician checked the engine electrical grounds. One of the grounds was found to be missing the star washer and was not completely tight. Installing the star washer and properly tightening the mounting bolt fixed this expensive problem.

◄   SERVICE TIP   ►

When replacing a heater core, check the coolant and if the coolant is dirty or old, change it. Many heater core leaks are caused by dirty or worn-out coolant.

13.1.5   Bleeding Air from Core

As a cooling system is filled, air can get trapped in some places inside the system. Some systems are equipped with air bleed valves that are opened during the filling process to let the air escape. The manufacturer's coolant fill process should be consulted.

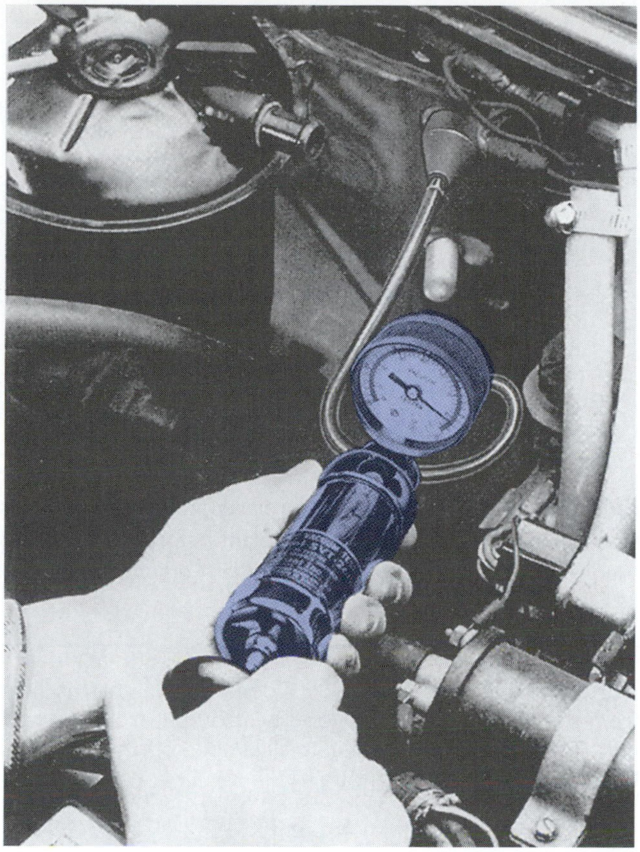

FIGURE 13-6 One heater core connector is plugged as the vacuum tester pumps the core into a vacuum to test for leaks. A pressure tester can also be used in the same way. *(Courtesy of Stant Manufacturing)*

◀ SERVICE TIP ▶

After filling a cooling system, it is a good practice to run the engine until the thermostat opens and add additional coolant as it becomes necessary. Thermostat opening is indicated by the upper radiator hose becoming warm. During the waiting period, turn on the heater to full heat or defrost, which should open any water valves, and feel for a warm air discharge, which indicates that the core is full of coolant. If the air does not warm up, bleed the air from the core by loosening the uppermost heater hose at the core. A "burp" of air indicates the release of an air lock. When coolant starts coming from the loosened hose, replace the hose and retighten the connection (Figure 13-8).

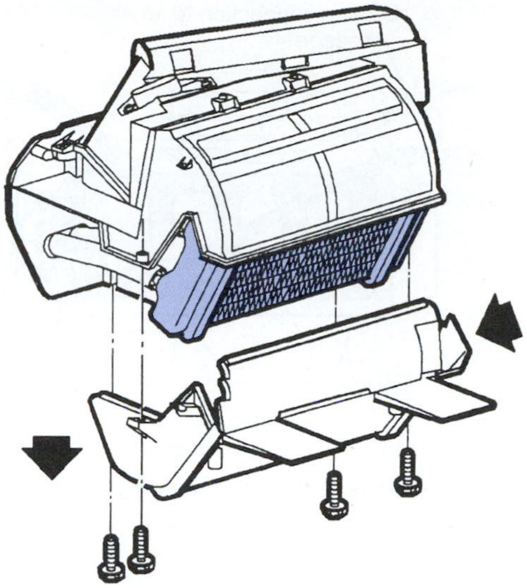

(a)

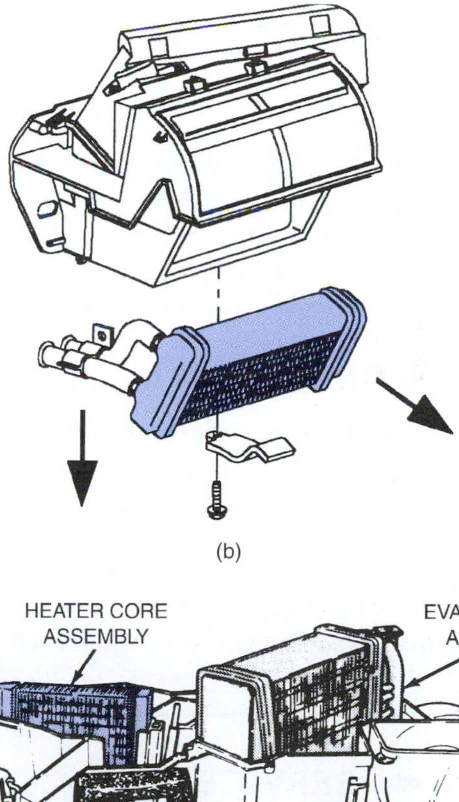

(b)

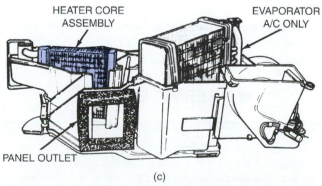

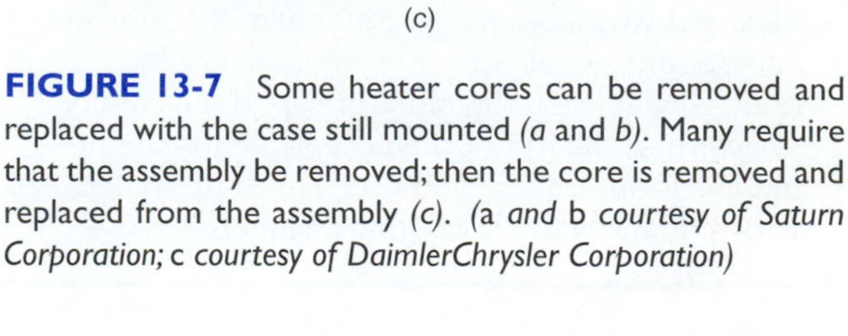
HEATER CORE
ASSEMBLY
EVAPORATOR
A/C ONLY
PANEL OUTLET

(c)

FIGURE 13-7 Some heater cores can be removed and replaced with the case still mounted *(a* and *b)*. Many require that the assembly be removed; then the core is removed and replaced from the assembly *(c)*. *(a and b courtesy of Saturn Corporation; c courtesy of DaimlerChrysler Corporation)*

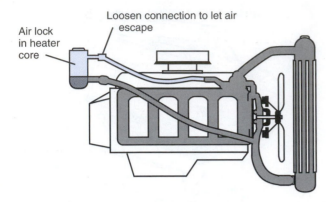

FIGURE 13-8 In many systems the heater core or its hoses are above the engine's water jackets. Loosening the upper heater hose allows the air lock to leave and coolant to enter the core.

◄ SERVICE TIP ►

Gurgling noises can be caused by an air lock in the heater core. One method of removing the air lock is to remove the coolant recovery reservoir from the radiator filler neck, attach a vacuum pump to the filler neck, and pull a vacuum on the coolant. Other methods of preventing or removing air locks are described in Chapter 18.

◄ SERVICE TIP ►

Some technicians prefer to cut the heater hose and install a flushing tee when changing coolant. The tee fitting allows the attachment of a garden hose to the system for flushing, and the cap on the tee allows complete filling of the system. Other technicians dislike the tee because it alters the system and can cause problems.

◄ SERVICE TIP ►

When replacing a rear-mounted heater core, the length of the hoses and the placement of the core make it difficult to bleed the air out of the core and lines. Some heater cores are mounted in a location that is higher than the radiator cap. If the connections are at the top of the core, which is the normal location, it is a good practice to fill the core with coolant before installing it (Figure 13-9).

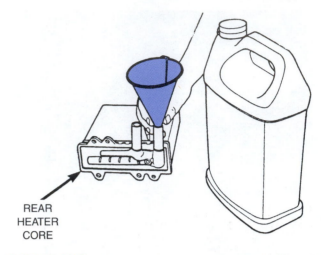

REAR
HEATER
CORE

FIGURE 13-9 This manufacturer recommends filling this rear-mounted heater core with coolant before installing it in the vehicle. *(Courtesy of DaimlerChrysler Corporation)*

REAL WORLD FIX: The 1989 Dodge Caravan has no heat from the front heater with good heat output from the rear unit. If the hose to the rear unit is clamped off, there is good heat output from the front unit.

FIX

It was discovered that a restrictor should be located in the hose to the rear unit. Installation of a restrictor fixed this problem.

◄ SERVICE TIP ►

Some cooling system service machines evacuate all the air out of a cooling system using a vacuum pump. A check is then made to see if the system is leak-free and will hold the vacuum. A valve is then turned so coolant is pulled in to fill the cooling system. The entire procedure takes about 5 or 6 minutes. (See Section 18.2.4.1.)

13.2 HVAC AIR FILTER REPLACEMENT

In many vehicles filter replacement is a simple matter of opening the access and removing and replacing the filter element (Figure 13-10). With some vehicles, parts such as a portion of the instrument panel or the center console must be removed (Figure 13-11). The exact procedure is described in the service information. The cabin filter is located either under the instrument panel or under the hood in the fresh air plenum.

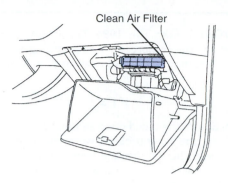

Clean Air Filter

FIGURE 13-10 This cabin/clean air filter is replaced by lowering the glove box door and removing a cover panel. *(Provided courtesy of Toyota Motor Sales USA, Inc.)*

(a)

(b)

FIGURE 13-11 A slightly dirty filter is being removed from the fresh-air chamber *(a)* (under hood), and a new filter is being slid into the opening *(b)*.

◀ **SERVICE TIP** ▶

A dirty cabin filter can cause reduced HVAC airflow. Failure to replace a charcoal-media filter at the proper interval can cause odor problems. A "wet sock" odor during wet weather is an indication of a dirty charcoal filter.

13.3 AIR MANAGEMENT SYSTEM CHECKS

Most air management system problems are related to the blower motor operation and the air doors not moving to the proper position. The basic styles of door control are as follows:

- Manual, using levers and mechanical cables
- Vacuum switches, hoses, and motors
- Electronic actuators and ATC or SATC using electric-solenoid–operated vacuum motors or electronic actuators

Some systems use a combination of cable, vacuum, and electronic actuators.

The biggest obstacle that a technician normally encounters when troubleshooting the air management system is access to the components. The under-dash area is very cramped and congested, often filled with wires, braces, and ductwork.

REAL WORLD FIX: The 1988 Buick has poor airflow coming from the ducts. The blower sounds normal at all speeds, but the airflow is not correct for the different speeds. The vacuum servos all seem to be working properly, and the temperature cable and its door are moving.

FIX

Inspection showed that the evaporator core was covered with oily debris. Replacement of the leaking evaporator core fixed this problem.

REAL WORLD FIX: The 1993 BMW 525i (213,000 miles) had a problem of poor air discharge. The blower motor and air control doors seem to be working properly. The technician's information does not indicate that this vehicle has a cabin filter.

FIX

Following advice, the technician checked and located a very plugged cabin filter. A filter replacement fixed this problem.

◀ **SERVICE TIP** ▶

Caution should be exercised when pulling, pushing, or probing wires to prevent the unexpected. At least one case of a technician accidentally triggering the air bags has been reported. On many cars, the control head can be partially disconnected and moved out far enough from the instrument panel to get to the cables or vacuum selector valve and hose connections behind it (Figure 13-12).

Electric or electronic circuit checks for blower motor, switches, solenoids, and electronic actuators are described in Chapter 14.

13.3.1 Blend Door Operation

If the temperature-blend air door does not close off completely to the full cool position, some heated air will mix in the plenum and the air discharge will be warmer than it should be. With older, mechanical cable-operated doors, it is fairly easy to look at the stop position or to listen for the "thunk" noise as you move the temperature lever rapidly from full hot to full cold.

With many modern, electric-actuator–operated doors, we can no longer feel the door movement, and many of them operate almost silently. Also, most modern under-dash areas are so filled up that we cannot see or reach into the door area to feel its operation.

FIGURE 13-12 After removing the fascia panel and two retaining screws, this control head was pulled outward to gain access to the mechanical, electrical, and vacuum connections.

REAL WORLD FIX: The 1994 Taurus A/C system was recharged, and the compressor was operating normally with good pressures, but it would not switch from heat to A/C.

FIX

On inspection of the blend door and motor, signs of an earlier repair for the same problem were found. Someone had cut a hole into the housing and manually moved the blend door to full heat. At the customer's request, the technician moved the door to full cold.

AUTHOR'S NOTE

It is expected that this vehicle will have a temperature control problem when the weather turns cool.

◀ **SERVICE TIP** ▶

A fairly accurate test for whether the blend door is operating properly is to clamp off the heater hose. If the air register discharge temperature drops more than a few degrees (some technicians use 5°F or 3°C as the cutoff point), you know the heated air is mixing in, probably from faulty door operation.

REAL WORLD FIX: The 1996 Ford Explorer (58,000 miles) stays on full heat all the time. The rest of the system seems to operate okay. Following advice and working through the glove compartment, the technician removed the blend door motor and determined that the operating shaft of the blend door was broken.

FIX

This blend door was replaced from under the hood by recovering the refrigerant, removing the evaporator, and removing the blend door from a new plenum assembly. The operating shaft had to be altered slightly in order to install it into the old plenum, but it performed satisfactorily after installation.

AUTHOR'S NOTE

Experienced technicians often develop shortcuts to certain jobs. These usually speed the job and save the customer money.

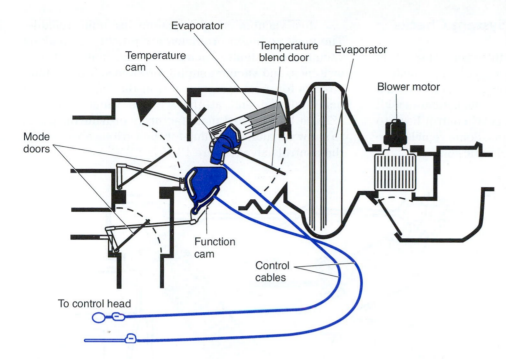

◄ **SERVICE TIP** ►

It is also a good idea to check OEM TSBs; at least one vehicle model's manufacturing process left plastic material that blocked complete door movement.

13.3.2 Cable Control System Checks and Adjustments

Cable systems are the simplest and most trouble free of all air management systems. The most common problems are (1) the need for adjustment so door travel matches the movement of the control lever and (2) sticky, binding cables that do not move easily. Some cable systems include a slotted bellcrank that operates two doors at the same time, and some of these can be freed up by lubricating them (Figure 13-13). Replacement of a faulty cable varies between vehicle makes and models. The manufacturer's recommended procedure is usually the quickest and easiest method.

Cable adjustment is checked by moving the temperature control lever to the hot and cold ends and either feeling or listening for the temperature-blend door to stop before the lever. The control lever should not reach its stop at either end (Figure 13-14). The adjustment on many early systems was at the attachment point for either the cable or the housing. Some newer systems use a self-adjusting clip that slips along the cable to the correct location. This clip must be preset to the proper position as the cable is connected.

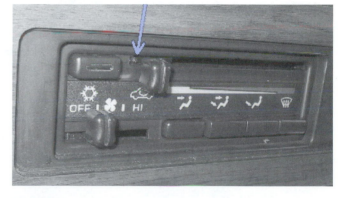

FIGURE 13-14 A small gap (*arrow*) should be between the temperature lever (full cold position) and the end of its slot if the cable is adjusted properly.

◄ **SERVICE TIP** ►

Many technicians give priority of the door adjustment relative to their geographic location and climate. In areas that have cold winters, make sure the door "thunks" when moved to full heat; customers in these areas are more sensitive to lack of heat output. In areas that have hot summers, make sure the door "thunks" when moved to full cool; customers in these areas are more sensitive to lack of A/C.

13.3.3 Vacuum Control System Checks

If the problem complaint and the visual inspection show fresh air door or mode door problems, a fault in the vacuum control system is indicated. As mentioned earlier, most older systems use vacuum actuators with a vacuum selector valve at the HVAC control head to control the operation of these doors. Some vehicles use vacuum actuators controlled by electric solenoids.

Most vacuum control systems are quite reliable. The most common problems are pinched or leaking vacuum lines, faulty vacuum motors, faulty selector switches, and vacuum supply problems. The vacuum circuits for most systems start at the engine's intake manifold and end at the various vacuum motors (Figure 13-15). Most manufacturers provide diagrams to show vacuum switching for the various positions of the control valve (Figure 13-16).

FIGURE 13-15 Most of the components of this vacuum control circuit are under the instrument panel.

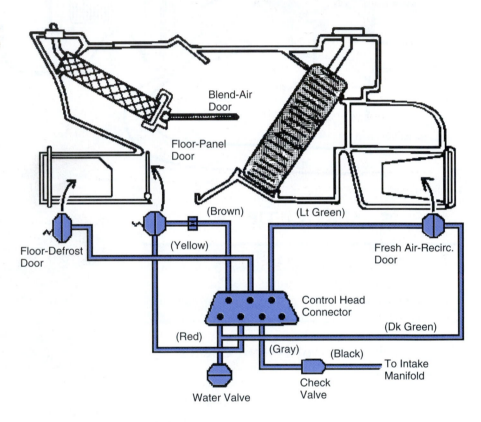

FIGURE 13-16 This diagram shows the vacuum circuit during the recirculating–panel control head vacuum switch position. *(Courtesy of DaimlerChrysler Corporation)*

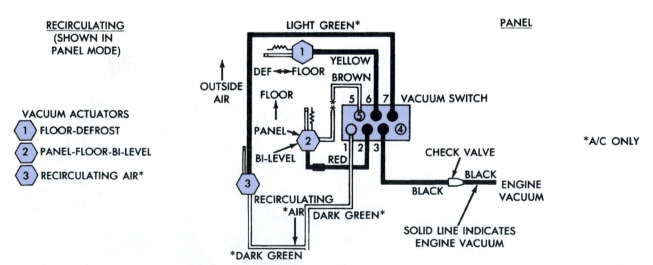

Troubleshooting a vacuum system usually begins by ensuring that the manifold vacuum is present at the selector valve. Hose color-coding, connections, and any **air bleeds** or restrictors are shown in vacuum diagrams. The system shown in Figure 13-15 uses a black hose to connect the selector valve or vacuum switch to the engine vacuum source, a small reservoir, check valve, and the manifold connection. This hose should have normal engine vacuum, about 18 to 20″ Hg, whenever the engine is running and for a few minutes after the engine is shut off. The basic test tools are a vacuum gauge and a hand vacuum pump, and these are connected into the system to measure the amount of vacuum (Figure 13-17). Occasionally a leak can be located by holding one end of a 3/8- or 1/2-inch hose next to your ear as you pass the other end along the expected leak area (Figure 13-18). A hissing noise indicates the leak.

REAL WORLD FIX: The 1992 Pontiac Bonneville (109,000 miles) HVAC system stays on floor/defrost no matter where the controls are set. The technician is not sure how the doors operate, but he does not hear a vacuum leak.

FIX

Following advice from other technicians, the under-hood vacuum lines were inspected, and the plastic vacuum storage canister was found to be cracked. Replacement of this item fixed this problem.

◄ **SERVICE TIP** ►

A tight-fitting piece of rubber hose can be used to splice plastic lines.

◄ **SERVICE TIP** ►

In the past, with rubber hoses it was possible to kink or pinch a line closed to shut off vacuum flow. This practice should be avoided with modern, hard plastic lines because the kink can cause a break and later failure. Hard plastic hoses should be isolated by disconnecting them and plugging the opening. Rubber vacuum hoses can be squeezed closed using pliers.

REAL WORLD FIX: The 1987 Ford LTD (115,000 miles) A/C system worked properly until you accelerated; it would then switch to full heat and low blower speed. It switches back when you let up on the gas. The ATC temperature sensor has been replaced, but this did not help. The system works properly if a manual vacuum pump is attached to the system.

FIX

Following advice, the technician reinspected the vacuum check valve, and found it to be faulty. Replacement of the check valve fixed this problem.

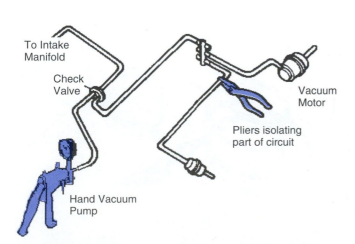

FIGURE 13-17 Vacuum leaks can be located using a hand vacuum pump and gauge while isolating portions of the circuit using plugs or pliers.

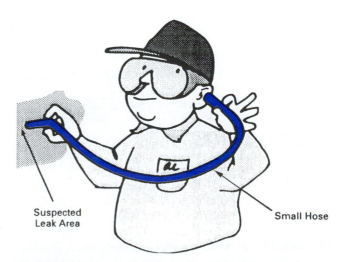

FIGURE 13-18 Vacuum leaks can be located by using a hand vacuum pump with a gauge while isolating portions of the circuit.

To troubleshoot a vacuum control system, you should:

1. Gain access to the vacuum selector valve, disconnect the vacuum hose harness from the selector valve, and identify the various hoses.

2. Connect a vacuum gauge to the hose coming from the vacuum source and start the engine. There should be at least 15 inches of vacuum. If the vacuum is less than 15 inches, repeat this check at the source vacuum locations, the intake manifold, check valve, and tank. The problem is located between the areas of adequate vacuum and inadequate vacuum. If the vacuum is 15 inches or greater at the control head, shut off the engine and note the reading. It should hold for a short period (Figure 13-19). Vacuum drop-off in-

dicates a leak at the hose connections, tank, or check valve.

3. Connect the hand vacuum pump to the vacuum hose, either for each of the vacuum actuators or just for the door actuator that is not working right, depending on the nature of the problem. Operate the pump to generate 15 to 20 inches of vacuum and, if possible, observe and listen for operation of the door actuator (Figure 13-20).

4. Reconnect the vacuum harness to the selector valve with the hand vacuum pump connected in place of the source vacuum hose. Move the selector valve to each of its control positions and operate the pump to determine whether a vac-

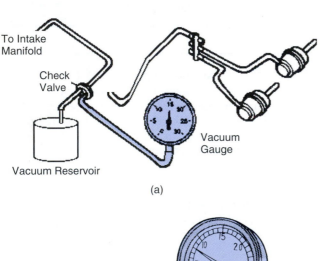

(a)

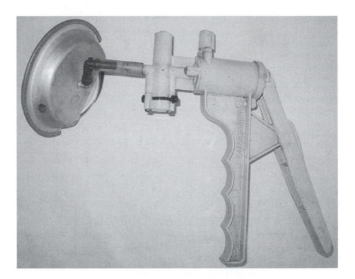

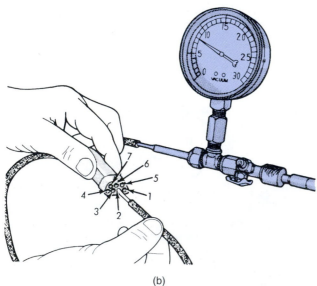

(b)

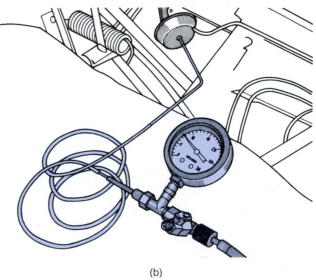

(b)

FIGURE 13-19 With the engine running, there should be at least 15 inches of supply vacuum at the control head *(a)*. Vacuum can be measured by probing the connector with a vacuum gauge *(b)*. A vacuum actuator circuit should also hold the vacuum. *(b courtesy of DaimlerChrysler Corporation)*

FIGURE 13-20 An actuator can be tested to see whether it operates and holds a vacuum using either a hand or motorized vacuum pump. *(b courtesy of DaimlerChrysler Corporation)*

uum can be generated. A faulty selector valve is indicated if a circuit operates during the check in step 3 but not in this step.

◀ SERVICE TIP ▶

Vacuum leaks can also be detected using an ultrasonic leak detector or smoke machine. The ultrasonic tester (see Figure 12-57) can "hear" a vacuum leak and indicate its location. The smoke machine pumps machine-made smoke into the vacuum circuit so you can see the smoke escaping through the leak.

◀ SERVICE TIP ▶

If a vacuum is generated but it bleeds off rapidly, a small leak is indicated. Check the diagram to determine whether a vacuum bleed is contained in that part of the circuit; if so, this might be a normal condition.

If a vacuum cannot be generated, a leak in the hose or actuator is indicated.

If a vacuum is generated but the actuator does not operate, a kinked or plugged hose or faulty motor is indicated. In either case, move the vacuum pump directly to the actuator connection and retest.

REAL WORLD FIX: While driving the 1993 Dodge Caravan at cruise speeds with the A/C on, the system will start discharging all of the air out of the defroster ducts. It also does this under a hard acceleration. The vacuum storage tank and all of the vacuum lines under the hood have been checked and are okay. The vacuum check valve and control head have been replaced, but this did not help.

F I X

Following advice, the mode door actuator was tested and found to have an internal leak. Replacement of this vacuum motor fixed this problem.

REVIEW QUESTIONS

The following questions are provided to help you study as you read the chapter.

1. Wet carpet and excessive window fogging are signs of a heater _____ _____ .
2. Early heater core failure can be caused by _____ or _____ resulting from _____ coolant.
3. Poor heater output can be caused by _____ engine _____ or _____ through the heater core.
4. When a vehicle is operating, _____ heater hoses should be _____ .
5. The hose connections at the heater core of some modern vehicles use _____ connectors

that can require a(n) _____ to disconnect them.
6. A heater core can be checked for leakage by testing it to see if it will hold either a(n) _____ or _____.
7. A(n) _____ can prevent a heater core from filling with coolant.
8. An improper blend door adjustment can cause reduced _____ or _____ from the HVAC system.
9. When a control cable is replaced, the _____ should be checked.
10. A(n) _____ _____ is indicated if an actuator will not hold a vacuum.

CHAPTER QUIZ

The following questions will help you check the facts you have learned. Select the answer that completes each statement correctly.

1. Technician A says that faulty heater operation can be caused by a faulty engine cooling system. Technician B says that a complaint of insufficient heat can be caused by someone not filling a cooling system properly. Who is correct?

    a. A only
    b. B only
    c. Both A and B
    d. Neither A nor B

2. Technician A says that a heater core leak can be the result of the coolant wearing a hole through the core. Technician B says that a core leak can be caused by chemical action eating a hole through the core. Who is correct?

    a. A only
    b. B only
    c. Both A and B
    d. Neither A nor B

3. Technician A says that the heater core inlet hose is connected to the water pump inlet. Technician B says that the heater inlet hose is often bigger than the outlet hose. Who is correct?

    a. A only
    b. B only
    c. Both A and B
    d. Neither A nor B

4. Insufficient heat output from a heater can be caused by a(n) _____.

    a. plugged core
    b. faulty thermostat
    c. air lock
    d. Any of these

5. Technician A says that faulty cable adjustments can cause improper heat and A/C operation. Technician B says that a broken vacuum hose can do the same thing. Who is correct?

    a. A only
    b. B only
    c. Both A and B
    d. Neither A nor B

6. A vacuum motor should _____.

    a. move when vacuum is applied to the port
    b. hold a vacuum

    Which is correct?

    a. A only
    b. B only
    c. Both A and B
    d. Neither A nor B

◀ Chapter 14 ▶

HVAC SYSTEM ELECTRICAL OR ELECTRONIC CONTROLS: THEORY, INSPECTION, DIAGNOSIS, AND REPAIR

LEARNING OBJECTIVES

After completing this chapter, you should:

1. Understand the relationship between volts, amperes, and ohms.
2. Understand the circuits required for electrical units to operate.
3. Be aware of the types of HVAC circuit problems that may be encountered.
4. Be familiar with the procedure used to locate and repair HVAC problems.
5. Complete the ASE tasks related to electrical or electronics diagnosis and repair.

TERMS TO LEARN

alternating current (AC)
ampere (amp)
ampere-turns
belt-lock strategy
body control module (BCM)
circuit breaker
complete circuit
conductor

diagnostic trouble code (DTC)
diode
direct current (DC)
electronic control module (ECM)
electrostatic discharge (ESD)
fuse

fusible link
ground
ground circuit
high-resistance circuit
malfunction indicator light (MIL)
multiplex
ohm (Ω)
open circuit
parallel circuit
positive temperature coefficient (PTC)

pulse width modulation (PWM)
relay
scan tool
schematic
series circuit
smart control heads
smart motors
volt (V)
watt
wiring diagram

14.1   INTRODUCTION

At one time, the electrical control circuit for the heat and A/C system was rather simple; a few checks with a test light located most problems. Today's systems have evolved into complex electronic circuits with connections to the **electronic control module (ECM)** and/or **body control module (BCM).** The HVAC control head on some vehicles features touch panel operation and a digital readout of in-car and outside temperature and can call up **diagnostic trouble codes (DTCs).**

These features have made it necessary for the HVAC technician to have a working knowledge of automotive electricity and basic electronics. Instruction in basic automotive electronics is required; this chapter provides a brief review.

14.2 BASIC ELECTRICITY

Three measurable aspects of electricity concern a technician: **volts (V), amperes (amps),** and **ohms (Ω).**

Voltage is electrical force, comparable to the pressure and suction generated by the A/C compressor: Voltage forces electrical flow much like pressure forces refrigerant flow. In a car, the source of this voltage is the battery or alternator.

An ampere is the amount of *current* flowing through a circuit. It can be compared with the amount of refrigerant that flows through an A/C circuit.

An ohm is a unit of electrical *resistance*. Ohms are used to control the amount of current flow, much like an OT or TXV restricts refrigerant flow. The symbol Ω (omega) is commonly used to indicate ohm. Zero, or a very few, ohms of resistance allow a large current flow; a high amount of resistance reduces or stops current flow (Figure 14-1).

Electrical power is measured in **watts;** this is the product of volts multiplied by amps, V × A = W.

Like an A/C system, electricity requires a **complete circuit** from the energy source, through the appliance or component doing the work, and back to the energy source (Figure 14-2). This circuit is made up of the battery or alternator, protection devices, wires, switches, and electrical components—all electrical **conductors.** A modern vehicle has many different electrical circuits, with about a mile (1.6 km) of wire completing them. Each

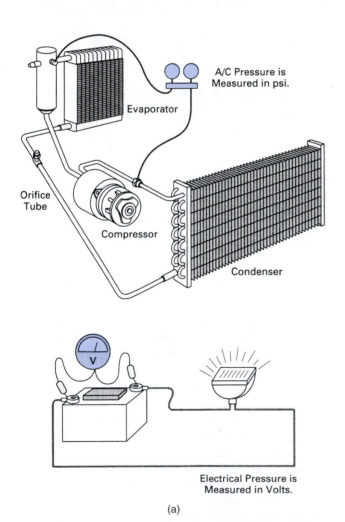

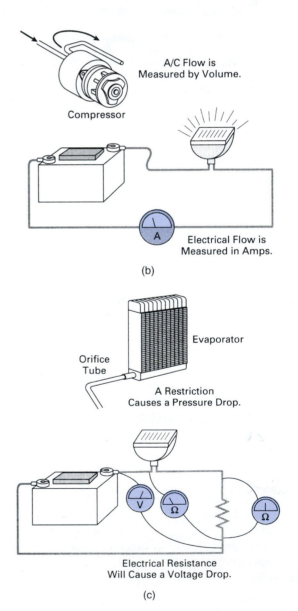

FIGURE 14-1 Electrical pressure is measured in volts; refrigerant pressure is measured in pounds per square inch (*a*). Electrical current flow is measured in amps; refrigerant flow is measured by volume (*b*). Electrical resistance causes a voltage drop; resistance in an A/C system causes a pressure drop (*c*).

circuit begins at a positive battery or alternator (B+) connection and ends at a battery or alternator **ground** connection (B−). Many are simple, one-component circuits; some use a **series circuit** with several components connected in a string, and some use a **parallel circuit** with branches that allow current flow through separate paths

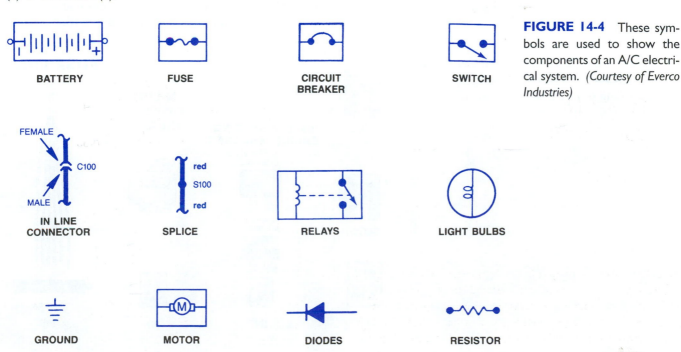

FIGURE 14-2 An electric circuit must be complete for current to flow. Circuits are shown in the form of a diagram (*a*) or schematic (*b*).

(Figure 14-3). Vehicle manufacturers provide **wiring diagrams** that are maps of these circuits. These wiring diagrams or **schematics** often use symbols for the components to help simplify the drawings (Figure 14-4).

Most vehicle circuits use **direct current (DC)**. DC always travels in one direction; the direction of electron flow is thought to be from negative to positive. Most commercial and household electricity is **alternating current (AC)**; AC switches direction many times a second. Most vehicles use 12-volt circuits, and most household and commercial circuits are either 110 (really 117) or 220 volts. Automotive electrical circuits will probably increase to 42 volts in the near future. Some hybrid vehicles have 150- to 200-volt electric drive systems.

Many technicians see a strong similarity between electrical circuits and A/C systems or the vacuum control circuits used to control the air ducts. Voltage can be compared with either compressor pressure or the pressure differential in a vacuum motor. These forces produce movements, such as amperage and refrigerant or

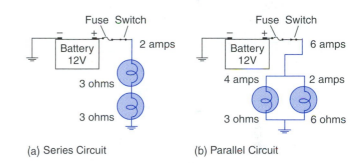

(a) Series Circuit   (b) Parallel Circuit

FIGURE 14-3 A series circuit (*a*) and a parallel circuit (*b*).

FIGURE 14-4 These symbols are used to show the components of an A/C electrical system. (*Courtesy of Everco Industries*)

BATTERY   FUSE   CIRCUIT BREAKER   SWITCH

IN LINE CONNECTOR   SPLICE   RELAYS   LIGHT BULBS

GROUND   MOTOR   DIODES   RESISTOR

vacuum flow (movements created by pressure differences). Electrical circuits and vacuum circuits are both paths of that movement. A switch and a vacuum valve can start or stop flow, an electrical resistor and an OT can restrict or reduce flow, a variable resistor and a TXV can adjust the amount of flow, and a diode and a vacuum check valve allow flow in one direction only.

14.2.1 System Components

Most electrical systems have five major components (Figure 14-5):

1. Power source
2. Protection devices

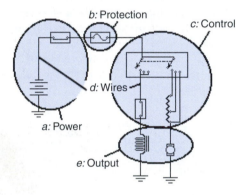

FIGURE 14-5 This A/C electrical circuit has a power source (*a*); fuses to protect the circuit (*b*); switches to control the circuit (*c*); wires connecting each of the components (*d*); and two outputs: the blower motor and the compressor clutch (*e*).

FIGURE 14-6 Circuit protection can be fuses with tubular or flat blade connections (*a*), a circuit breaker (*b* and *c*), or a fusible line (*d*). *(Courtesy of DaimlerChrysler Corporation.)*

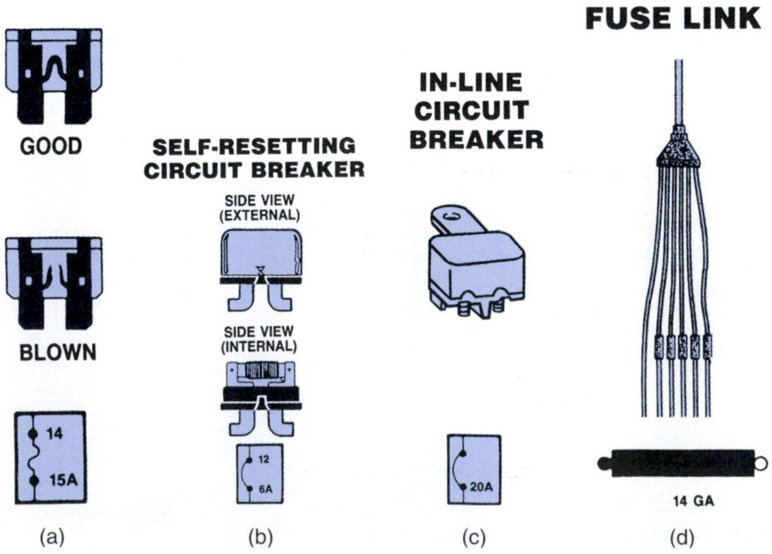

3. Control devices
4. Connecting wires
5. Output devices

As mentioned, the power source for vehicle systems is either the battery or the alternator. The battery is used primarily when the engine is not running or when the electrical demands exceed the rating of the alternator. When fully charged, battery voltage is a little more than 13 V. If electricity is used without the engine running, the voltage drops. Before vehicles had computers, most circuits would not work properly with a battery voltage of less than 9 V; vehicles using computers require at least 10.5 V. With the engine running, the alternator raises the voltage applied to the circuit to a regulated voltage between 13.5 and 15.5 V.

If too much current flows through a circuit, it can cause serious overheating of the wires and increase the likelihood of burnout or fire. Protection devices allow enough current flow through a circuit for normal operation, but if a short or ground circuit occurs, excessive current flow causes the protection device to open the circuit. These protection devices are *fuses, fusible links, PTCs,* or *circuit breakers* (Figure 14-6).

- A **fuse** is a device that melts at a certain current flow. Fuses are designed to be easily replaced if they melt or blow out.
- A **fusible link** is a one-time protection device. It is a short piece of wire, about four wire gauge sizes smaller than the wire used in that circuit. A current overload causes the fusible link to burn out.
- A **PTC, positive temperature coefficient,** is a thermistor that acts like a self-resetting circuit

GOOD

BLOWN

14
15A

(a)

SELF-RESETTING CIRCUIT BREAKER

SIDE VIEW (EXTERNAL)

SIDE VIEW (INTERNAL)

12
6A

(b)

IN-LINE CIRCUIT BREAKER

20A

(c)

FUSE LINK

14 GA

(d)

breaker. The circuit is opened by the temperature increase as the current reaches the maximum value. The circuit will reclose when the cause of the excess current flow is corrected.

- A **circuit breaker** senses current flow. If amperage becomes excessive, a set of contacts cycles open to protect the circuit. Some circuit breakers reclose after cooling down; some must be reclosed mechanically by pushing a button or lever.

The switch is a common control unit used to break (open) a circuit to stop current flow or to make (close) a circuit to allow current flow. Most switches offer no resistance ($0\ \Omega$) when they are closed and infinite resistance ($\infty\ \Omega$) when they are open. Some switches are combined with rheostats or variable resistors so that the amount of resistance can be changed. These switches can be used to control the brightness of instrument panel lights or the speed of a motor. A switch can control a unit directly, like the pressure switch in a compressor clutch circuit, or indirectly through a relay.

A **relay** is essentially an electromagnet and a set of switch contacts. The electromagnet is controlled by another switch and requires only a small current flow. When the magnetic coil is energized by its control circuit, the magnetic pull closes the switch contacts, which, in turn, control a larger current flow. These are called *normally open (NO) relays*. Some relays are *normally closed (NC)*; they are opened by the control circuit (Figure 14-7).

The wires used to complete an electrical circuit are normally composed of a copper conductor surrounded by a plastic insulator. Copper is a good electrical conductor and offers a relatively small amount of resist-ance. The amount of metal in the wire portion determines the gauge of the wire and the amount of current it can safely carry (Figure 14-8). Plastic is a poor conductor, which makes it a very good electrical insulator; this insulation contains the current flow in the wire. Insulation allows two or more wires to be placed next to each other or alongside ground without having the current bypass the desired electrical path.

In most vehicles, the metal body, frame, transmission, and engine provide part of the electrical circuit called the **ground circuit** (Figure 14-9). The negative side of the battery and alternator are connected to ground, called earth in some countries. Each electrical component is also connected to ground, normally by the metal case or frame of the component being bolted in place. Some components use a separate ground wire fastened to a ground connection to complete a circuit. At one time, some cars used a positive ground.

Output devices in most HVAC circuits are the *compressor clutch* and the *blower motor*. These are often called the *load*. The compressor clutch is essentially an electromagnet. A magnetic field is created when electric current travels through a coil of wire. The strength

WIRE SIZE CONVERSION TABLE			
Metric Size mm²	AWG Size	Metric Size mm²	AWG Size
.22	24	5.0	10
.5	20	8.0	8
.8	18	13.0	6
1.0	16	19.0	4
2.0	14	32.0	2
3.0	12	52.0	0

(a)

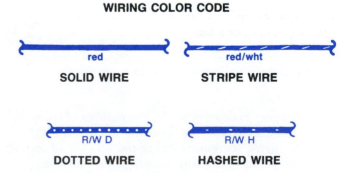

(b)

FIGURE 14-8 Electrical wire is sized by gauge sizes, American wire gauge (AWG) (*a*). Wire colors with stripes, dots, or hash marks are used to identify particular wires (*b*). *(Courtesy of Everco Industries)*

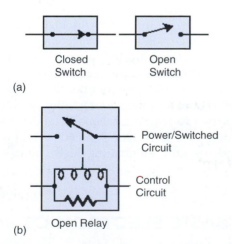

FIGURE 14-7 A simple switch can be normally open or normally closed (*a*). Relays use a magnetic coil to close or open switch contacts (*b*).

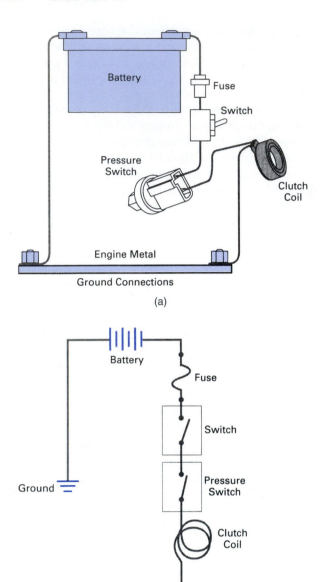

FIGURE 14-9 Insulated wires are used to conduct electricity to the clutch coil. The metal of the engine forms the ground circuit to complete the circuit back to the battery. A circuit is shown in a diagram (*a*) and a schematic (*b*).

of this magnet is determined by the number of turns of wire in the coil and the amount of current, called **ampere-turns.** Increasing either the number of turns or the amperage increases the magnetic pull. Current flow is determined by the resistance in the wire of the coil (Figure 14-10).

When current flows through the wire coil of an electromagnetic device such as a relay or clutch coil, it creates a magnetic field. When the current stops flowing in the coil, the magnetic field collapses, possibly

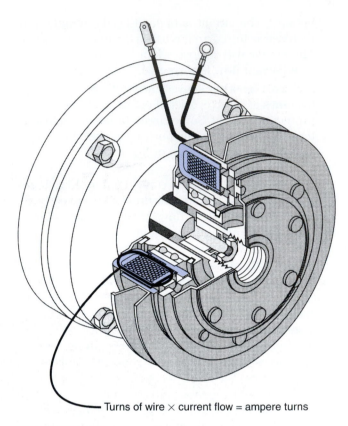

Turns of wire × current flow = ampere turns

FIGURE 14-10 The strength of a magnetic coil is determined by multiplying the number of wire turns by the current flow. *(Courtesy of Warner Electric)*

creating problems in computer-controlled circuits. When a magnetic field collapses over a coil of wires, high voltage is induced in the coil. This is the operating principle of an ignition coil or transformer: Whenever the current flow to an A/C clutch or relay is shut off, the magnetic field collapses, inducing voltage in the circuit. This voltage can spike to a very high voltage, high enough to damage solid-state electronic controls. To prevent this damage, a **diode** is included in the circuit. Connected to each end of the coil, a diode allows current to pass in one direction but not the other. During normal operation, the diode does nothing but block unwanted current flow past the coil. When the system is shut off, the diode allows the induced current to bleed off around the coil, eliminating high voltage spikes (Figure 14-11).

14.3 BASIC ELECTRONICS

Solid-state electronics is the basis of modern computers and automotive control modules. Solid-state electrical devices are units in which nothing moves except

(a)

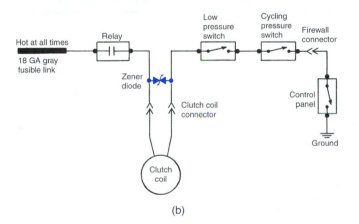

(b)

FIGURE 14-11 The zener diode at the clutch coil connector prevents a high voltage spike when the clutch releases. *(b courtesy of Everco Industries)*

electrons. They include diodes, transistors, and integrated microchips. These units are quite reliable because nothing in them wears out. They can, however, be easily damaged by rough handling and vibration, high temperatures, high current flow, and high voltage spikes from the circuit or **electrostatic discharge (ESD).** Electronic devices are usually used for sensing and control circuits.

Automatic temperature control (ATC) lends itself to electronic control circuits (Figure 14-12). These systems can be divided into *sensors*, the *control panel and module*, and *actuators*.

14.3.1 Sensors

As mentioned in Chapter 10, sensors monitor ambient temperature, in-car temperature, driver input, and, maybe, engine coolant temperature, compressor rpm, compressor temperature and sun load. In some vehicles, A/C low side and high side switches or pressure transducers are also inputs to the control module. These can be a switch that is made to open or close at certain pressures, a transducer that senses pressure, or a thermistor that senses temperature.

Some vehicles with a single accessory drive belt use a **belt-lock strategy** to prevent the possibility of a seized compressor stopping the drive belt. A compressor rpm sensor generates a signal that lets the ECM know how fast the compressor shaft is turning. This speed is compared to the engine rpm signal, and if there is 30% or greater difference, the ECM will disengage the compressor clutch. Excessive belt slippage or compressor lockup could cause total belt failure that could result in stopping the power steering pump and the engine's water pump and causing an overheated engine with a hard-to-steer vehicle.

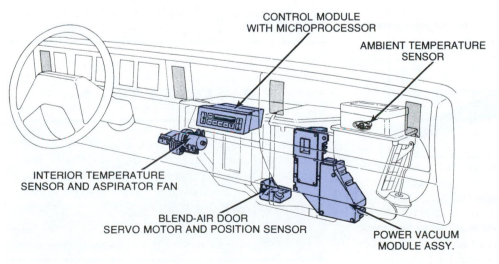

FIGURE 14-12 Most of the control components of an ATC system are solid-state electronic devices—diodes, thermistors, and transistors. *(Courtesy of DaimlerChrysler Corporation)*

Temperature sensors are *thermistors*, units that change electrical resistance relative to temperature. One new system uses infrared temperature sensing. A *transducer* produces a variable electrical signal that is relative to pressure, allowing the control module to monitor actual pressure in that part of the system (Figure 14-13). A pressure signal allows the ECM to monitor system operation, determine whether the compressor is operating, and turn on the radiator or condenser fan when necessary.

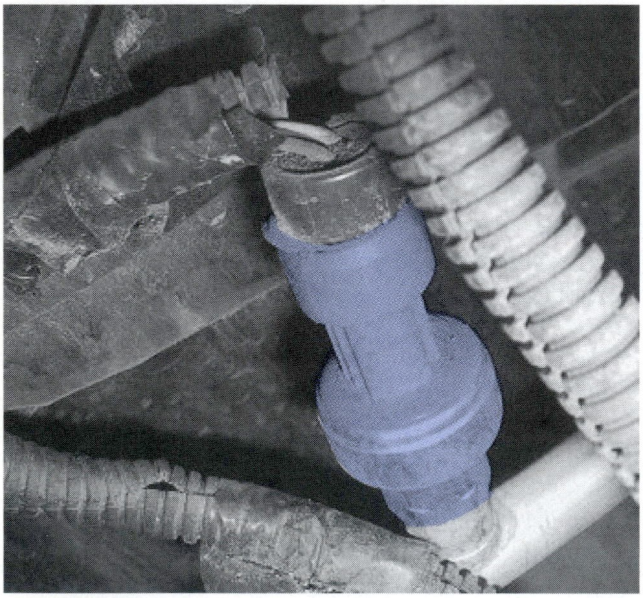

The control module sends a low-voltage (about 5 V) signal to some sensors; the sensor returns a voltage that is relative to the condition of the system. For example, a particular ambient sensor has a resistance of 7.2 k (7,200) Ω at 32°F and 3.4 k (3,400) Ω at 100°F (Figure 14-14): Because sensor resistance has more than doubled, the voltage returning from the sensor to the control module will be much lower at 32°F than at 100°F.

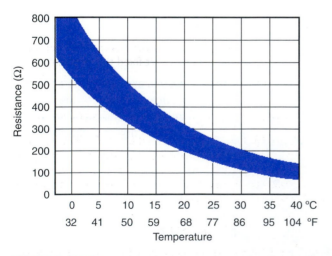

FIGURE 14-13 This pressure sensor is a transducer that changes high side pressure into an electrical signal for an ECM input.

FIGURE 14-14 The resistance value of the in-car sensor or ambient sensor is inversely related to the temperature. As the temperature increases, the resistance decreases.

◀ **SERVICE TIP** ▶

Suspect an rpm sensor problem if the compressor starts but disconnects after a short or very short operation. With a relay or switch circuit fault, the compressor will not start at all.

◀ **SERVICE TIP** ▶

Air must pass across the in-vehicle sensor. A quick check for this is to hold a strip of thin tissue paper in front of the sensor grill. The paper should be pulled against the grill openings.

◀ **SERVICE TIP** ▶

An open or shorted ambient sensor is bad and must be replaced. One that is out-of-range can often be cleaned using alcohol and a Q-tip.

◀ **SERVICE TIP** ▶

If you need to replace an ambient or in-car sensor, the best replacement is from the OEM dealer. But if none is available, remember that most temperature sensors are common NTC resistors. If you know the specified resistance value, a replacement can often be purchased at an electronic supply house.

REAL WORLD FIX: Under hard acceleration, the 1992 Mercedes (95,000 miles) A/C compressor shuts off, and it will not restart until the engine is cycled off and then on. This problem does not occur during normal acceleration. The compressor rpm sensor was checked, and it is good. Voltage supply to A/C components is good.

FIX

A closer check of the rpm sensor revealed that it lost connection when the engine lifted due to torque reaction. Repair of this wire connection fixed the problem.

REAL WORLD FIX: The 1989 Honda (80,000 miles) compressor was replaced, and the system was recharged. The system operates, but the compressor shuts off after 5 seconds. If the A/C is turned off and then on, the compressor will operate for another 5 seconds.

FIX

Following advice, the technician checked the rpm sensor using an ohmmeter, and this sensor had an open circuit. Replacement of the rpm sensor fixed this problem.

14.3.2   Control Module

An ECM, BCM, or HVAC control module is programmed to open or close circuits to the actuators based on the values of the various sensors. Although it is unable to handle the electric current for devices such as the compressor clutch or blower motor, the control module can operate relays. These relays in turn control the electric devices. Units that use small current flows, such as a light-emitting diode (LED) or digital display, operate directly from the control module (Figure 14-15).

An ECM is programmed with various strategies to suit the requirements of the particular vehicle. For example, when A/C is requested by the driver of a vehicle with a relatively small engine, the ECM will probably increase the idle rpm. On this same vehicle, the ECM will probably shut off the compressor clutch during wide-open throttle (WOT). On other vehicles, the ECM might shut off the compressor clutch at very high speeds to prevent the compressor from spinning too fast. In some cases, part of the A/C and heat operating strategy is built into the control head; these are called **smart control heads.** In some cases, door operating strategy is built into the door operating motors, and these are called **smart motors.**

With some modern control modules, various calibration values can be reprogrammed by technicians in the field. These calibration values include the high side pressure at which the cooling or condenser fan operates or the coolant temperature at which the cooling fan operates. Improper fan operation can lead to engine overheating, poor performance from the A/C or heating system, or a control module that denies the driver's request for A/C.

Many control modules are programmed to run a test sequence at start-up (when the ignition key is turned on); if improper electrical values are found, the ECM indicates a failure by turning on the **malfunction indicator light (MIL),** often the A/C indicator light at the control head. Some ECMs also monitor the system during operation and indicate a failure or stop the compressor if there is a problem. One system, for example, notes the frequency of clutch cycling; remember that short cycling indicates a low refrigerant charge level. If there are too many clutch cycles during a certain time period, the control module will shut off the compressor and set a DTC. A technician can read the DTC, also called an *error code*, by following a certain procedure. Looking up codes in a manual shows where the problem is and what tests are needed to determine its exact cause (Figure 14-16).

Wire connections at the sensors and control module must be clean and tight to prevent any change in value. A small amount of corrosion can produce enough resistance to cause a significant value change in these low-voltage, low-current circuits. Most manufacturers use mechanical-locking, weather-tight connectors (Figure 14-17). Many also use waterproof conductive compound (dielectric silicon) on these connections to help protect them.

REAL WORLD FIX: The 1991 Acura (126,000 miles) has a problem of intermittent A/C operation. The voltage to the A/C compressor relay checks good. An A/C leak has been repaired and the system recharged.

FIX

Following advice, the timer fan control was checked and found to be bad. Replacement of this part fixed this problem.

REAL WORLD FIX: The 1995 Ford Explorer (90,000 miles) has a problem of the A/C cutting out after the vehicle runs for a while and when sitting still at stoplights. A **scan tool** check indicates the ECM is sending a wide-open throttle (WOT) signal to the A/C relay.

FIX

On a test drive, the technician noticed that this problem occurs when the temperature gauge is close to hot. Replacement of the engine thermostat fixed this A/C problem.

1991 AUTOMATIC TEMPERATURE CONTROL

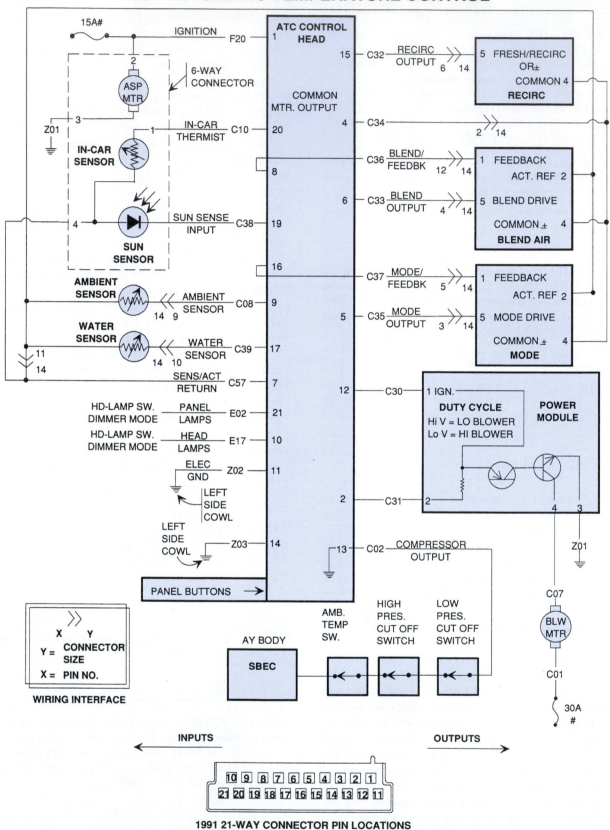

FIGURE 14-15 This electronic control head receives B+ power through terminal 1 and input through the other terminals shown at the left. It controls the components shown at the right. *(Courtesy of DaimlerChrysler Corporation)*

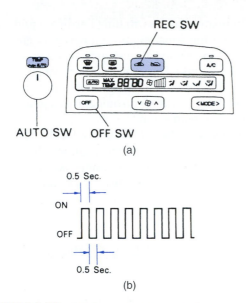

(a)

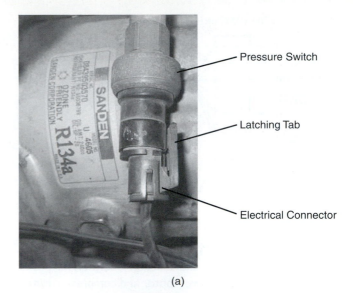

(a)

(b)

FIGURE 14-16 With the ignition switch on, pressing the AUTO and REC switch at the same time will enter a DTC check on this vehicle (*a*). A blink code (*b*) will be indicated by flashes of the indicator lights. (*Provided courtesy of Toyota Motor Sales USA, Inc.*)

REAL WORLD FIX: The 1991 Camry (130,000 miles) A/C system shuts off the compressor after driving for about 30 minutes. The engine cooling fans run properly and continue to run after the compressor shuts off. The A/C indicator light in the instrument panel stays on. The A/C system pressures check out normal.

FIX

A check of the wiring diagram showed that the A/C circuit included an engine temperature sensor, and this sensor was found in the upper radiator hose. The radiator core was checked, and about half the tubes were plugged up. Replacing the radiator and backflushing the engine fixed this problem.

14.3.3   Actuators

The *actuators* for a system are the relays, motors, and lights operated by the control module. Lights are the display at the A/C control head and trouble indicators. The relays in an ATC system can control the blower speed, compressor clutch, radiator fan motor, condenser fan motor, and motors for the temperature-blend door, fresh air door, and mode doors. Modern systems operate the air inlet, mode, and temperature doors using bidirectional (reversible) electric motors. These motors run one direction to open a door and the opposite direction to close the door. The ECM chooses the direction and operates relays or transistors to provide current flow in the proper direction.

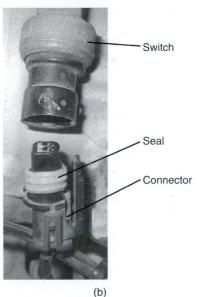

(b)

FIGURE 14-17 Modern electrical components use weather-tight connectors with locks to keep the contacts clean and tight (*a*). Releasing the latching tab allows the connector to be removed (*b*).

With the air doors, operation is usually in a complete motion, from one door stop to the other, but the temperature door is placed in any position to suit the desired output temperature. There are three basic styles of motors: two wire, three wire, and five wire. Each of these has a pair of wires that provide DC power to the motor. Five-wire motors have three wires for the feedback circuit, and three-wire motors use the third wire to indicate door position. The feedback circuit tells the ECM where the door is positioned. Door position motors also include a feedback (sensor) circuit to the control module to inform it of actual door position

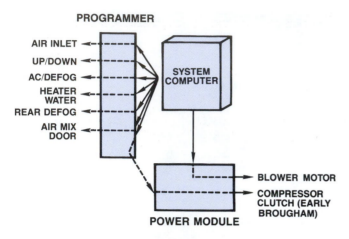

PROGRAMMER

AIR INLET
UP/DOWN
AC/DEFOG
HEATER WATER
REAR DEFOG
AIR MIX DOOR

SYSTEM COMPUTER

BLOWER MOTOR
COMPRESSOR CLUTCH (EARLY BROUGHAM)

POWER MODULE

FIGURE 14-18 This ATC system uses a programmer to control the temperature and function doors and a power module to control the blower motor and compressor clutch. *(Reprinted with permission of General Motors Corporation)*

(Figure 14-18). The feedback circuit starts at a potentiometer (variable resistor) that is rotated by the motor. Motor operation changes the amount of resistance. A voltage signal from the ECM will be reduced by the amount of this resistance (see Figure 10-12). A smart motor will include part of this door positioning strategy.

The position of some door operating motors is controlled by a different strategy. DC motors use a segmented commutator to conduct electricity into the armature. When these commutator bars pass the brushes, there is a brief change in the current flow to the motor. The ECM notes these small pulses and can count them. The number of pulses relate to revolutions of the motor and can tell the ECM the position of the motor and door.

Most systems require a calibration process so the ECM can learn where the doors and operating motors are.

14.3.4 Multiplex

Multiplex allows one wire to work for more than one circuit; in most cases, every vehicle circuit uses a separate wire or circuit board part to complete the circuits. **Multiplex** switches a pair of wires so they complete multiple circuits, which greatly reduces the number of wires in a car. Multiplexing is usually done between two control modules, such as the power train control module (PCM) and the BCM. The two modules use some of the same sensors, and the output of one often affects the output of the other (Figure 14-19). For example, when the driver turns on the A/C, this becomes an A/C request signal to the PCM, which might actually turn on the A/C and use this signal as a value for when to begin cooling fan operation or what the engine idle speed should be.

Multiplex is also called a *bus information system*, and besides reducing the amount of wire connections,

it also eliminates some switching hardware and current flow through the sensors and improves diagnostics. It requires a chip or microprocessor in each control module and Bus+ and Bus− wires between the control modules. The Bus+ and Bus− wires are twisted together to prevent stray electromagnetic signals from altering signal transmission.

The biggest impact of multiplex for the HVAC technician is probably that more and stranger things can affect the operation of the A/C compressor clutch and cooling fan if either the PCM or BCM do not operate properly. A technician has to be more aware of the circuit for that particular vehicle.

14.4 A/C CLUTCH CIRCUITS

Older systems, before electronic control, used rather simple compressor clutch circuits like those illustrated in Figures 14-5 and 14-9. Besides the control switch, there was a thermal or pressure switch to cycle the clutch to prevent evaporator icing and probably a low- or high-pressure protection switch to block the compressor from operating when conditions in the system were not right. These switches are normally connected in a series circuit so that the opening of any of the switches will stop compressor operation.

Many modern vehicles use a relay to supply power to the clutch (Figure 14-20). Power input to this relay is normally from ignition run (B+ voltage or hot when the ignition is in the run position) and passes through a fuse for circuit protection. The ECM or PCM provides the ground for the control circuit through the relay so that the compressor is turned on when the ECM or PCM provides the ground connection. The A/C request signal to turn on A/C comes to the ECM or PCM from the instrument panel control switch, and this request circuit can pass through the same type of switches used on older systems. More modern sensors, thermistors, or pressure transducers are used in some vehicles to replace switches.

◀ SERVICE TIP ▶

Operating voltage at a clutch should be almost the same as battery voltage (within 0.2 V). If it is lower, perform a voltage drop check: connect the + voltmeter lead to the + battery post and the − lead to the B+ connector at the clutch. The reading should be 0.2 V or less. Next connect the − voltmeter to the − battery post and the + lead to the ground connection at the compressor. Again, the reading should be 0.2 V or less. Excessive voltage drop indicates a problem in that part of the circuit.

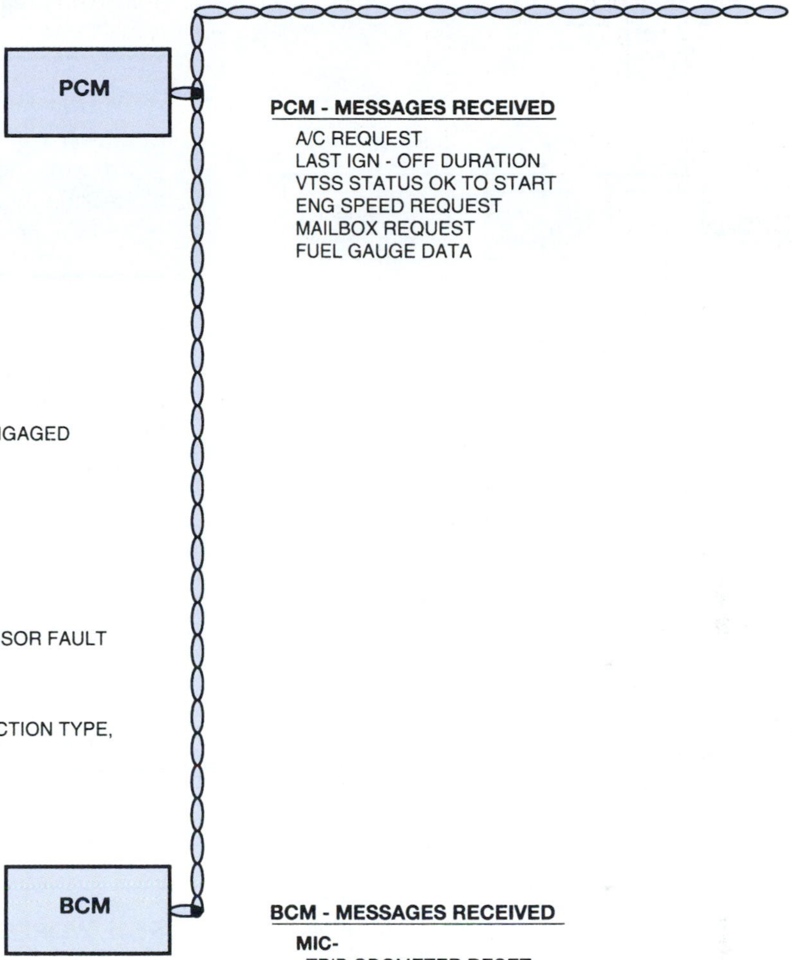

PCM - MESSAGES TRANSMITTED

ENG RPM
MAP VALUE
INJECTOR ONTIME
DISTANCE PULSES
VEHICLE SPEED
THROTTLE POSITION VALUE
SYSTEM VOLTAGE
ACCUMULATED MILEAGE
TARGET IDLE SPEED
MANUAL OR AUTO TRANS
PARK/NEUTRAL POSITION
CHECK ENGINE LEVEL ON/OFF
UPSHIFT LEVEL ON/OFF
AUTO TRANS TCC ENGAGED OR DISENGAGED
A/C CLUTCH STATUS ON/OFF
BRAKE APPLIED/ NOT APPLIED
OK TO LOCK DOORS
CRUISE ENGAGED/DISENGAGED
ENGINE COOLANT TEMPERATURE
BATTERY TEMPERATURE
BAROMETER
A/C PRESSURE
ENGINE COOLANT TEMPERATURE SENSOR FAULT
THROTTLE POSITION SENSOR FAULT
CHARGING SYSTEM FAULT
SYSTEM VOLTAGE HIGH WARNING
ENGINE MODEL (DISPLACEMENT, INJECTION TYPE,
  ENG. TYPE, BODY STYLE)
TORQUE REDUCTION EXECUTED

PCM

PCM - MESSAGES RECEIVED

A/C REQUEST
LAST IGN - OFF DURATION
VTSS STATUS OK TO START
ENG SPEED REQUEST
MAILBOX REQUEST
FUEL GAUGE DATA

BCM - MESSAGES TRANSMITTED

PCM-
  A/C REQUEST
  LAST IGN - OFF
  VTA STATUS OK TO START
MIC-
  GAUGE POSITION
  FUEL GAUGE
  TEMPERATURE GAUGE
  SPEEDOMETER
  TACHOMETER
  LAMPS ON/OFF
    LOW FUEL
    DOOR AJAR
    UPSHIFT
    CRUISE
    PRNO3L (EACH POSITION AND ALL POSITIONS)
    SEATBELT
    CHARGING SYSTEM
    HIGH BEAM
    CALIFORNIA EMISSIONS
    ENGINE TEMPERATURE
    CHECK ENGINE
    CATALYST WARM-UP
  VEHICLE ODOMETER
  TRIP ODOMETER
  DISPLAY DIMMING
  IGNITION ON
  BCM REPLACED (ORIGINAL/REPLACED)

BCM

BCM - MESSAGES RECEIVED

MIC-
  TRIP ODOMETER RESET
  US/METRIC DISPLAY
TCM-
  PRN03L POSITION
PCM-
  ENGINE RPM AND MAP
  INJECTOR ON-TIME
  DISTANCE PULSES
  MANUAL OR AUTO TRANS
  PARK/ NEUTRAL POSITION
  CHECK ENGINE LAMP ON/OFF
  UPSHIFT LAMP ON/OFF
  OK TO LOCK DOORS
  CRUISE ON/OFF
  ENGINE COOLANT TEMPERATURE
  CHARGING SYSTEM FAULT
  SYSTEM VOLTAGE HIGH WARNING

FIGURE 14-19 The multiplex between the BCM and PCM is the path for each to send messages or signals to each other as well as the transaxle control module (TCM), electromechanical instrument cluster (*MIC*), air bag control module (ACM), and data link connector (DLC). *(Courtesy of DaimlerChrysler Corporation)*

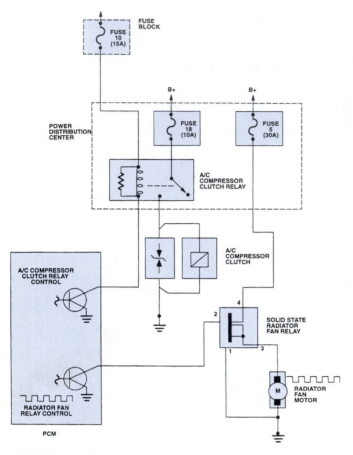

FIGURE 14-20 This A/C compressor clutch relay is controlled by the PCM. Note that the radiator fan motor uses a solid-state relay that is also controlled by the PCM. *(Courtesy of DaimlerChrysler Corporation)*

◄ **SERVICE TIP** ►

It is also a good practice to repeat voltage tests with the engine running. Actual voltage should increase from about 12 V to about 14 V.

Clutches in modern vehicles still need battery voltage and a current flow just like the older systems. The relay must be energized to turn the clutch on and deenergized to turn it off; this function is taken care of by the fuse providing B+ and the ECM or PCM providing ground. The ECM or PCM receives the request for turning on the clutch, receives operating conditions, and contains the strategies for turning the clutch on or off. The ECM or PCM can also receive input from other control modules such as the BCM or electronic ATC modules.

◄ **SERVICE TIP** ►

With at least one vehicle manufacturer, the A/C clutch will not turn on unless all blower speeds are working. If you have a problem of no clutch activation, check to make sure that the vehicle has all blower speeds.

REAL WORLD FIX: The 1984 Mercedes-Benz A/C fails when the driver forces a downshift from the transmission. This action causes the A/C fuse to blow. The A/C and transmission work normally during all other driving operations. An inspection of the wiring and fuse box shows no problem.

FIX

Replacement of a shorted transmission downshift solenoid fixed this problem.

AUTHOR'S NOTE

Apparently, the transmission downshift solenoid shares the same fuse as the A/C compressor, and the faulty downshift solenoid drew excessive current.

REAL WORLD FIX: The 1991 Mitsubishi (89,000 kilometers) came in for a stereo radio installation, and the owner complained that the A/C comes on every time the ignition is switched on, even when the A/C controls are off.

FIX

The A/C circuit was traced on a wiring diagram, and it was found that the A/C circuit is dependent on the vehicle's interior light. The interior light operation is often not noticed during daylight, and this circuit had a blown fuse. Replacement of the interior light fuse fixed this A/C problem.

REAL WORLD FIX: The 1988 Corvette (123,000 miles) has no A/C; the compressor clutch does not engage. The clutch operates if the technician connects a jumper wire for ground to the green wire at the clutch connector. The technician does not have a schematic of this clutch circuit.

FIX

Advice from fellow technicians directed the technician to the blower control module that was the cause of the problem. Replacement of this module fixed this problem.

REAL WORLD FIX: The 1994 Volkswagen Jetta (75,000 miles) came in with a request to check the A/C. A low charge level was found, so the refrigerant was recovered from the system and then evacuated and recharged. But, when the system was to be checked, the compressor clutch would not engage; there was no voltage to it. Using a jumper wire engaged the clutch, and the system worked normally. The fuses are good, but the technician did not have a wiring diagram for this system.

FIX

Given a wiring diagram, the technician learned that this system has a high-temperature switch mounted in the compressor, and this switch was open. Replacement of the high-temperature switch fixed this system.

REAL WORLD FIX: The 2001 Chevrolet Malibu (5,000 miles) came from a body shop after a front-end accident repair. The compressor and discharge hose had been replaced by the body shop. The A/C clutch would not engage because of no signal to the A/C clutch relay. A scan tool would not activate the relay so the BCM and control head were replaced, but this did not help. The relay and compressor clutch will operate if the proper pin on the relay or BCM is grounded.

FIX

Following advice, the technician double-checked the refrigerant pressure sensor and found that jumping the sensor would activate the clutch. The sensor was replaced, but this did not help. Further checking revealed that the pressure port in the new hose was not drilled completely through. Carefully drilling the hole completely allowed the sensor to receive a pressure signal and fixed this problem.

14.5 BLOWER MOTOR CIRCUITS

As partially described in Chapter 10, the blower motor that moves air through the air distribution system can have three or four fixed speeds through a set of resistors or an infinite number of speeds through **pulse width modulation (PWM).** Blower motors are fairly powerful so they can move the air volume needed; during high blower operation they will draw about 20 amps.

Older systems used a multiposition rotary or slide switch with a position for "off" plus each of the speeds. Each of the output positions is connected to a resistor or the relay for high blower speed. Using a high blower

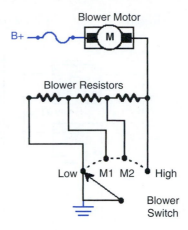

FIGURE 14-21   This blower uses ground-side switching. Note that the blower switch and resistors are between the blower motor and the ground connection.

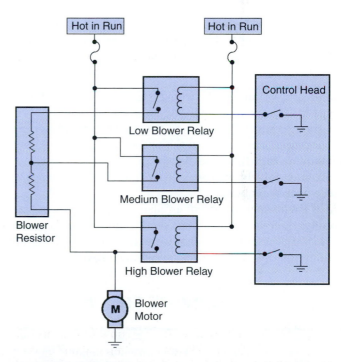

FIGURE 14-22   Three relays (*at right center*) control the current flow for the three blower speeds. Note that the flow for low and medium speeds pass through a resistor.

relay reduced the current flow through the blower speed switch. A variation of this circuit was to use ground-side switching. B+ was sent directly to the motor, and the resistors for speed selection were in the circuit between the motor and ground (Figure 14-21).

Another variation is to use a relay to complete the circuit through each of the resistors (Figure 14-22). This reduces the current flow through the switching device

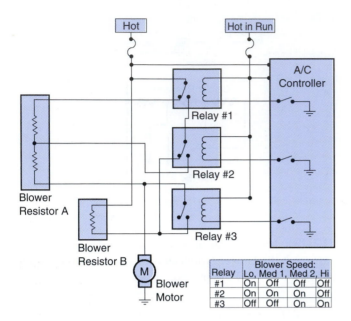

Relay	Blower Speed: Lo, Med 1, Med 2, Hi			
	Lo	Med 1	Med 2	Hi
#1	On	Off	Off	Off
#2	On	On	On	Off
#3	Off	Off	On	On

FIGURE 14-23 This system uses three relays to provide four blower speeds. Note that the relays are energized by A/C controller in the proper order to provide those speeds.

and allows an ECM strategy to control the blower speed. These circuits will vary; one circuit uses three relays to control four blower speeds (Figure 14-23). By operating these relays in the proper sequence, off, low, medium, and high speeds are produced. Three relays produce four blower speeds by operating the relays in the proper sequence.

PWM speed control is also controlled electronically; the control head can send a pulsed signal to the blower power module that turns the blower on and off to match the signal pulses (see Figure 10-39).

◀ SERVICE TIP ▶

A blower motor works the hardest when it is moving the most air. A current draw of under 18 amps (at 14 V) on high blower indicates an airflow restriction. You can prove this by measuring the current draw with the blower motor assembly off the car and mounted in a vise with no restriction to the inlet and outlet. Use a controlled voltage of 14 V. The current draw will be about 20 amps or greater. Next place a section of cardboard over the inlet and/or the outlet, and note the change in current draw.

REAL WORLD FIX: The blower on the 1997 Taurus (48,000 miles) would not operate at any speed. The fuses were good, but there was no B+ power to the motor, resistors, or switches. The A/C compressor comes on, indicating that there is an A/C request signal.

FIX

Following advice, the technician checked the wires in a plastic holder above the parking brake pedal. He found a connector pulled apart, and reconnecting these wires fixed this blower problem.

REAL WORLD FIX: The 1994 Mercury Grand Marquis (89,000 miles) SATC system blower did not work when floor output was selected. Heat and blower operation was normal in all other mode positions. It also had an intermittent blower operation, and this was fixed by replacing the blower motor.

FIX

Following advice to check the cold engine lock out switch, the technician found that the blower would operate with a jumper across the switch. Replacement of this switch fixed this problem.

REAL WORLD FIX: The blower motor along with the filter on the 1999 Mercedes S420 were replaced last year, and it returned with the same complaint. It showed water damage with white corrosion on the electrical connectors and aluminum parts along with a very damp filter. The hood and blower area seals appear normal.

FIX

It was determined that the customer washes the vehicle daily at an automatic car wash. A recommendation to the customer to have the vehicle washed by hand cured this problem.

14.6 COOLING FAN CIRCUITS

The engine cooling fan(s) of most modern FWD vehicles are also controlled through one or two relays using circuits much like the compressor clutch. The relays are

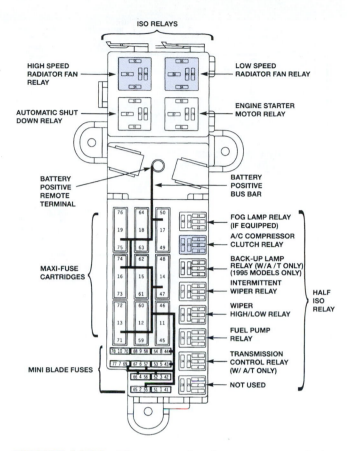

FIGURE 14-24 This power distribution center includes two radiator fan relays and the compressor clutch relay, as well as fuses to protect their operation. *(Courtesy of DaimlerChrysler Corporation)*

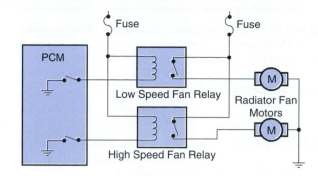

FIGURE 14-25 The current for this two-fan circuit is controlled by two relays, which are in turn controlled by the PCM.

ECM or PCM fan operation strategy on some modern vehicles can be reprogrammed in the field; this allows the technician to change the point at which the fan is switched on. Changing the program strategy of an ECM or PCM requires a compatible scan tester with the proper internal capability, and the procedure is very specific to the vehicle model.

often mounted at the power distribution center with the other relays and fuses for the vehicle (Figure 14-24). Some vehicles use a pair of relays, one for high speed and one for low speed. Some vehicles use two separate fans. In some vehicles one or both of these relays are connected directly to B+, so fan operation can occur with the engine shut off.

Relay operation is controlled by the ECM or PCM with a strategy based on both engine coolant temperature and A/C high side pressure (Figure 14-25). The cooling fan must begin operation when the engine reaches a specified temperature (about 212°F) to prevent overheating. Two-speed systems turn the fan on first at low speeds and then high speeds as engine temperature increases. A PWM fan circuit is shown in Figure 14-20. Some systems start fan operation whenever the A/C is switched on; others switch the fan on when the high side pressure reaches a certain pressure.

REAL WORLD FIX: The 1990 Cadillac (60,000 miles) control head displays a message of "A/C Overheating" while driving around town. On the highway, the engine temperature reached 253°F, and an A/C pressure check shows 400 psi and rising. The pressure drops to about 200 to 275 psi when water is sprayed on the condenser. The refrigerant was recovered, and it was determined that it was overcharged about 1 pound. The system was evacuated and recharged, but with the engine at idle speed, the compressor locked up. A new compressor was installed, but the pressures were still too high. The electrical connector to the cooling fan had been replaced some time ago.

FIX

A check of the cooling fan showed that it was running backward. Reversing the wires at the connector fixed this problem.

◀ **SERVICE TIP** ▶

Airflow direction from a fan can be easily checked by holding a piece of string or paper into the airstream and seeing which way it is blown.

REAL WORLD FIX: The cooling fans on the 1994 Dodge Intrepid (175,000 km) run constantly as soon as the engine is started. Both fan relays and their circuits check good. A scan tool reads that the relays are OFF, but with the engine running, they are switched ON.

FIX

A further check using the scan tool shows an A/C pressure of 400 psi, and this revealed a pressure transducer fault. Replacing the transducer fixed this problem.

REAL WORLD FIX: The A/C on the 1997 Subaru Legacy (119,000 miles) stopped after driving a short distance. This problem occurred each time the vehicle was operated. All of the wiring, switches, and relays check out good. ECM power and ground circuits are good, and the ECM was replaced but the same problem occurs.

FIX

A further scan tool check showed that the A/C would shut off at a 232°F coolant temperature. This indicated a cooling system problem so the cooling system was flushed and the coolant replaced. This fixed the A/C problem.

14.7 ELECTRICAL CIRCUIT PROBLEMS

Most electrical problems fall into one of four categories: open, high resistance or weak, shorted, or grounded. These problems can occur in either a continuous or intermittent manner; intermittent problems are usually much harder to locate and are often the result of the vehicle's movement, vibration, and changes in temperature. With the proper equipment and knowledge, most electrical components can be easily checked to determine whether any of these problems are present.

14.7.1 Open Circuits

An unwanted **open circuit** is an incomplete, broken circuit in which no current can flow and is usually caused by a broken or disconnected wire, a blown fuse or fusible link (probably caused by a short or ground), or a broken filament in a lightbulb. Source voltage is present up to the faulty point. A weak circuit has excessive resistance that causes a voltage drop. An open circuit causes a complete loss in voltage and current.

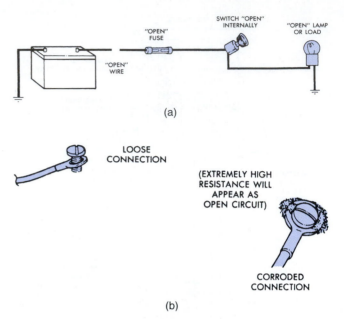

(a)

(b)

FIGURE 14-26 An open circuit is a break in the circuit that will stop the current flow (*a*). Corroded or loose connections will cause high resistance that will reduce the current flow (*b*). *(Courtesy of DaimlerChrysler Corporation.)*

An open or weak circuit can occur at any point between the B+ and ground connections (Figure 14-26).

REAL WORLD FIX: The 1998 Jeep Cherokee (37,000 miles) has an intermittent problem of the HVAC blower, speedometer, and tachometer all shutting off at the same time. The new car dealer replaced the low pressure cycling switch and PCM and cleaned the electrical connectors, but this did not help.

FIX

Following advice, the technician checked the instrument panel electrical ground stud and found that the nut was missing. Cleaning the terminals and installing a nut on this stud provided the proper ground connection and fixed this problem.

14.7.2 High-Resistance Circuits

A **high-resistance circuit** is similar to an open circuit, except a reduced amount of current (not enough to do the job) flows. This circuit is often caused by a corroded, loose, or dirty connection. A high-resistance circuit causes reduced voltage; this is called a *wasted voltage drop*. Excess voltage drop in turn reduces the current flow.

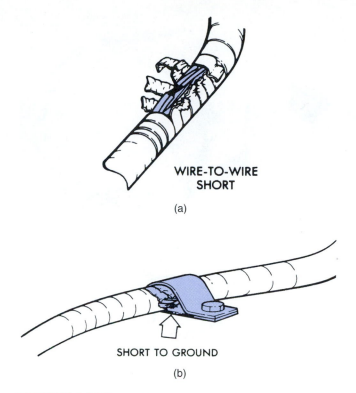

FIGURE 14-27 A short circuit is often a wire-to-wire connection that can reduce magnetic coil strength or allow current to flow to the wrong circuit (*a*). It can also be a short to ground (*b*). *(Courtesy of DaimlerChrysler Corporation)*

14.7.3 Shorted Circuits

Although some people use the term *shorted circuit* to describe any electrical problem, a short circuit is most often found in a wire bundle or harness. If the wires lose their insulation and the metals of the wires touch, current flows on the shortest path with the least resistance and bypasses part of the circuit. The effect of the short is a lower coil resistance because of the shortened path, allowing an increase in current flow. The strength of the magnet is also reduced because of fewer ampere-turns. A short can also occur between the wires of two separate circuits if their insulation is damaged and will cause an unwanted current flow between the circuits (Figure 14-27). Some people call a short a *copper-to-copper connection*.

14.7.4 Grounded Circuits

A grounded circuit is similar to a short except the bare wire touches ground. This is sometimes called a *short-to-ground* or *copper-to-iron* connection. The grounded circuit completes a path directly back to battery ground (B−), so the rest of the circuit is bypassed. Again, cur-

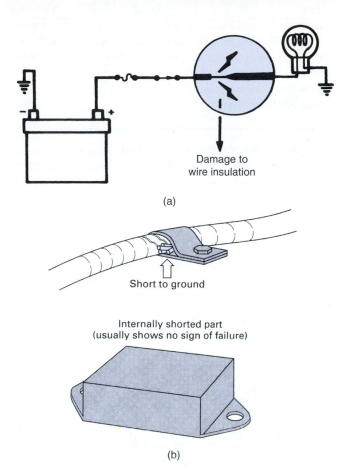

FIGURE 14-28 A ground or short-to-ground circuit occurs when damage to the insulation allows an electrical path to the metal of the vehicle (*a*). It can occur at a wire or inside a component (*b*). *(Courtesy of DaimlerChrysler Corporation)*

rent follows the path of least resistance. Depending on where the connection occurs, a grounded circuit can have zero resistance, and the current flow will instantly increase to the limit of the fuse, wire, or battery. This usually causes rapid burnout, and the resulting smoke or burned-out wire is often easy to locate (Figure 14-28).

14.7.5 EMI, RFI

Electronic circuits can be influenced by electromagnetic induction (EMI) and radio frequency interference (RFI). RFI, a form of EMI, is the interaction between ferrous metal objects and the magnetic field around a current-carrying wire. Vehicle manufacturers twist electrical wires together, use shielded coaxial cable, and install metal shielding to protect some circuits from EMI interference.

EMI can cause strange electronic circuit malfunctions and an ECM to set a DTC when there is no real fault. If this is encountered, first check the vehicle for improperly installed aftermarket electronic accessories. These include a cellular telephone, radar detector, remote starter system, radio, or any other non-OEM electrical accessory. Discarded shields or misrouted wires from an improperly performed repair can also cause EMI problems.

REAL WORLD FIX: The customer had replaced the blower motor in the 1995 Cadillac (72,000 miles) with a new OEM part, and this motor failed. The blower available voltage and ground were checked and found to be good. A new blower motor was installed, but it soon failed also.

FIX

Following advice, the engine spark plug wires were replaced and repositioned as far away from the blower motor and wiring as possible. Another new blower motor was installed, and this one has not failed.

14.8 MEASURING ELECTRICAL VALUES

At one time, technicians used a test light, jumper wire, and analog voltmeter–ohmmeter or multimeter (a combination ammeter, ohmmeter, and voltmeter) for troubleshooting automotive electrical problems. Today, the weather-tight connectors on modern cars make the use of a jumper wire very difficult (Figure 14-29). The common test light and analog meter should not be used on solid-state circuits because they cause the circuit to draw too much amperage from the ECM. This amperage overload can cause faulty sensor meter readings or damage. The meter must have an internal resistance of 10 megohms (10,000,000 Ω) or greater. LED test lights and most digital multimeters (DMMs) can be safely used on any automotive circuit.

Most test lights are simple, cheap, durable, and easy to use. They have one wire, which is normally connected to ground, and when the probe contacts B+, the bulb lights up. Some test lights are self-powered by an internal battery. Self-powered lights can be used to check *continuity* (a continuous, complete circuit) through a component such as a clutch coil. Most test lights indicate either a pass or fail; because they cannot make measurements, they do not tell us how faulty the component is (Figure 14-30).

Meters make measurements and come in two types: *analog* (a needle sweeps across a scale) and *digital* (actual value is displayed in a series of digits). As mentioned earlier, analog meters should not be used on electronic circuits because they draw too much power and can

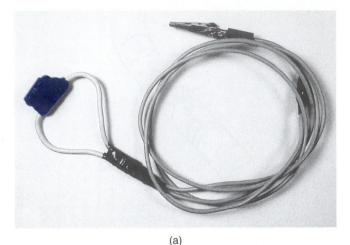

(a)

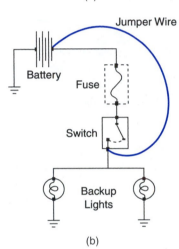

(b)

FIGURE 14-29 Jumper wires can often be used to bypass portions of a circuit to determine where the problem is located. This jumper wire has a fuse to limit the current flow (*a*). If the lights illuminate with the jumper wire installed, the problem is the fuse, switch, or wires to the battery (*b*).

damage a circuit. The modern DMM is more accurate, easier to read, and can be used on all modern computer circuits. On circuits with changing values, however, the sweep of an analog needle is much faster and much easier to follow than the rapidly changing display of digits. For that reason, some digital multimeters include a bar graph for a quicker response to value changes.

Multimeters have a selector switch that must be set to the desired function. Some meters also have a range switch set to the area where the readings are expected to fall. The range selector should always be set above the highest reading expected and then reset downward until readings occur (Figure 14-31).

Computer-controlled circuits also require care because of possible damage through electrostatic discharge (ESD). ESD is the shock you feel or the spark

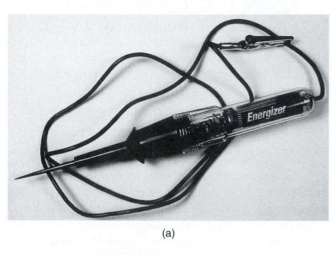

(a)

(a)

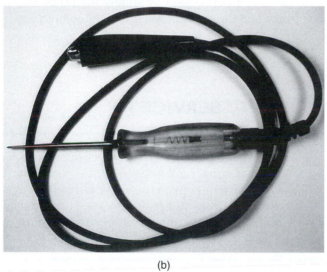

(b)

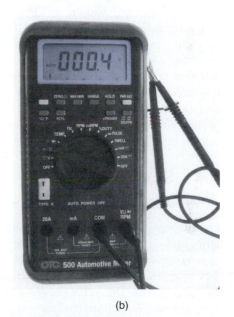

(b)

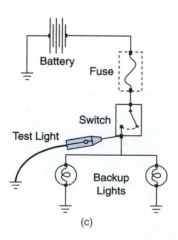

(c)

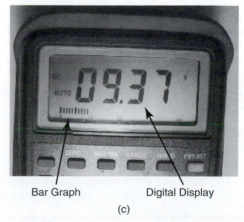

Bar Graph   Digital Display

(c)

FIGURE 14-30   A self-powered test light includes a battery and can be used to check for continuity (a). An ordinary nonpowered test light (b) can be used to determine if a point in a circuit has voltage (c).

FIGURE 14-31   An analog (a) and a digital (b) multimeter. The digital display and bar graph are both displaying 9.37 volts (c). (b courtesy of OTC Division, SPX Corporation)

FIGURE 14-32 Extreme care should be used when testing components that display this ESD symbol.

V (Volts) = C X R
C (Current) = V ÷ R
R (Resistance) = V ÷ C

FIGURE 14-33 This modernized version of Ohm's law shows the relationship between volts, current (amps), and resistance.

you see sometimes when you touch metal after walking across carpet or sliding across a seat covering. The electrostatic charge of electricity felt is several hundred volts; such an ESD can easily damage solid-state electronic devices. The symbol shown in Figure 14-32 is placed on some components and wiring diagrams to indicate components that can be damaged by ESD. Unless you are connected electrically to the vehicle's ground, do not touch that component or its electrical connections. Do not make electrical measurements or checks on these components unless instructed to do so, and always follow directions exactly. If directed to make voltage checks, connect the negative probe to ground first.

Modern weather-tight connectors present a difficult problem when probing for electrical values. You can disconnect a connector and probe the ends, but sometimes this is an inaccurate reading without normal circuit load. Thin probes are available that allow back-probing a connection by sliding the probe into a connector and through the weather-tight connectors.

◀ **SERVICE TIP** ▶

Ohm's law includes a formula that compares the relationship of the three major electrical values. A modernized version of Ohm's law is shown in Figure 14-33. If you know two of the values, you can easily calculate the third. This becomes handy if one value, resistance, is hard to measure but two other values, volts and current, can be measured easily.

◀ **SERVICE TIP** ▶

It is recommended that the vehicle's air bags be deactivated before making any checks under the instrument panel. Accidental shorting of the air-bag circuit wires can cause the air bags to deploy. This can cause possible injury to the technician and bystanders and will require expensive repairs.

◀ **SERVICE TIP** ▶

Corrosion can enter a wire that has the insulation pierced. Fingernail polish or battery sealant spray can be safely used to seal wire insulation so that water does not leak into the connector or component and cause future corrosion and resistance.

◀ **SERVICE TIP** ▶

Many modern compressor clutch coils include a clamping diode to suppress a high-voltage spike and protect the ECM. If this diode fails, the high-voltage spike can cause the radio to turn off and then back on. A quick diode check is to tune the radio to a weak AM station near 1400 Hz and cycle the compressor off and on; a "pop" from the radio speakers indicates a faulty diode.

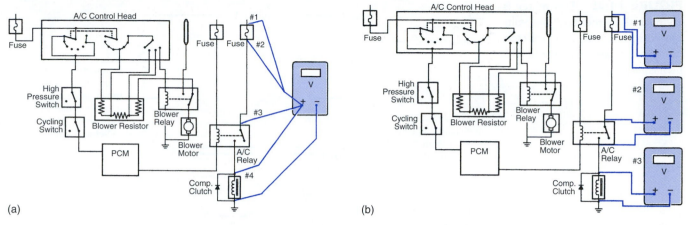

FIGURE 14-34   Voltage is measured by connecting one voltmeter lead (normally the negative) to ground and probing the wire connections with the other lead (a); different readings indicate a voltage drop. Voltage drop can also be checked at each component (b).

REAL WORLD FIX: The 1996 Dodge Caravan (134,000 miles) with a dual-zone system has temperature control only on the left side. The control unit was replaced with a unit known to be good, but this did not help. The door actuator was replaced, but this did not help. The temperature door can be easily moved by hand so it is not binding. A wire insulation rub-through from contacting a sharp piece of metal was found and repaired, but this did not help. The system was recalibrated and returned to the owner, but after several weeks it returned with intermittent good operation along with fluctuating temperature, switching from cool to hot.

FIX

A closer inspection of the wiring revealed two more places where the insulation and wiring had rubbed through. Replacement of the harness and padding of the sharp edges fixed this problem.

AUTHOR'S NOTE

Rub-throughs occur at places where the wiring harness contacts sharp edges of the instrument panel.

14.8.1   Measuring Voltage

A voltmeter is used to measure voltage and voltage drop by connecting the negative lead to ground and probing various points along the circuit with the positive lead. The meter displays the actual voltage for that point in the circuit; depending on the circuit and its components, this reading should be B+ (around 12 V) or some lesser value. A 0 reading indicates an open circuit between the probe and B+. A reading less than B+ indicates a voltage drop; this can be good or bad. If you have full battery voltage to the component and a full battery voltage drop across the component, the component is either using all the electric power or has an open circuit.

Voltage can also be measured by connecting the negative lead to the ground side of a component and the positive lead to the B+ side. The reading will be the amount of voltage dropped across that component. It should be noted that voltage drop only occurs while the circuit is on and under load. The *total voltage drop in any circuit is always equal to the sum of each voltage drop*, and this is *equal to the source voltage*. Usually, all of the voltage drop occurs across the actuator or output device. A 12-V drop across an element may be okay if it is an open switch, *or* it may indicate that the element is open (Figure 14-34).

To measure voltage, you should:

1. Adjust the voltmeter control to select V or DC V.
2. Connect the negative, black, or − lead of the voltmeter to a good, clean ground.
3. Determine the point where you want to measure, and touch or connect the positive, red, or + lead to the connector.
4. Read the voltage on the meter.

In a simple, old-fashioned A/C compressor clutch circuit, there should be B+ voltage right up to the insulated clutch connection and a 12-V drop across the

FIGURE 14-35 This meter is connected to measure the voltage drop across the resistor. *(Courtesy of Fluke; reproduced with permission)*

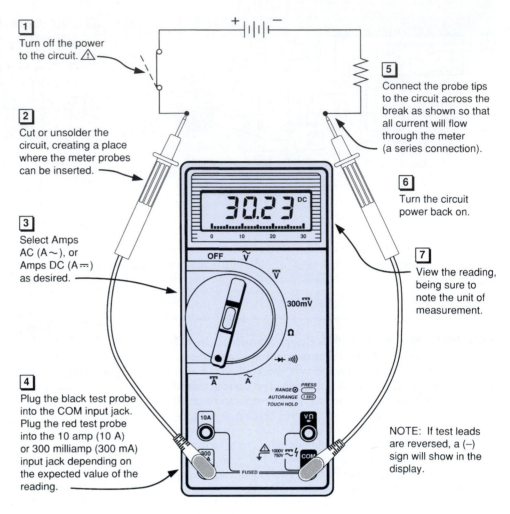

1 Turn off the power to the circuit. ⚠

2 Cut or unsolder the circuit, creating a place where the meter probes can be inserted.

3 Select Amps AC (A∼), or Amps DC (A⎓) as desired.

4 Plug the black test probe into the COM input jack. Plug the red test probe into the 10 amp (10 A) or 300 milliamp (300 mA) input jack depending on the expected value of the reading.

5 Connect the probe tips to the circuit across the break as shown so that all current will flow through the meter (a series connection).

6 Turn the circuit power back on.

7 View the reading, being sure to note the unit of measurement.

NOTE: If test leads are reversed, a (−) sign will show in the display.

FIGURE 14-36 Voltage drops across resistors can be measured indirectly (*a*) or directly (*b*). Source voltage at the input side minus the indirect measurement will equal the direct measurement.

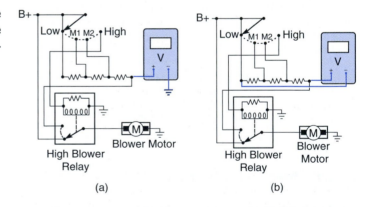

(a)   (b)

clutch. A small drop across a connection or switch is allowed, but this is usually limited to about 0.2 or 0.3 V per connection. Any greater drop indicates a high-resistance problem that will cause a circuit to function below normal and should be corrected (Figure 14-35).

A heating and A/C blower fan circuit is a different example in which we expect a significant drop across the blower speed resistors. Voltage readings at the blower motor connection should be about 12 V on high, 9 V on medium-high, 6 V on medium-low, and 4 V on low. This tells us that 0 V was dropped before the motor on high, 3 V (12 − 9 = 3) were dropped on medium-high, 6 V were dropped on medium-low, and 8 V were dropped on low (Figure 14-36).

To measure total voltage drop, you should:

1. Select V or DC V.

B+ side voltage drop:

2. Connect the positive, red, or + lead of the voltmeter to the positive, +, battery post.
3. Touch or connect the negative, black, or − lead to the B+ side of the component.
4. Read the voltage drop on the meter.

Ground side voltage drop:

5. Touch or connect the positive, red, or + lead of the voltmeter to the ground side of the component.
6. Touch or connect the negative, black, or − lead to the negative, −, battery post.
7. Read the voltage drop on the meter.

Component voltage drop:

8. Touch or connect the positive, red, or + lead of the voltmeter to the B+ side of the component.
9. Touch or connect the negative, black, or − lead to the ground side of the component.
10. Read the voltage drop on the meter.

◄ SERVICE TIP ►

A star lock washer is often used between the ground terminal and the mounting point. The twisted shape of the washer arms cut through surface dirt and paint to make good electrical contact.

14.8.1.1 Voltage Source

HVAC system voltage usually begins at the vehicle's electrical power distribution center (see Figure 14-24). Some vehicles will use a relay that is energized by the ignition switch or through the ECM; other vehicles will use a fuse for the HVAC circuit. A separate fuse or relay is often used for the A/C clutch, HVAC blower motor, and engine cooling fan.

A wise technician begins voltage checks at the fuse or relay to ensure that there is proper system voltage at the beginning, at least 12 V, and this should be higher (about 14 V) when the engine is running (Figure 14-37).

14.8.2 Measuring Resistance

An ohmmeter is used to measure the resistance of electrical components. The two ohmmeter leads are con-

FIGURE 14-37 This fuse check shows a good voltage reading; the reading should be the same at both fuse contact points. The negative (−) voltmeter is connected to a good ground.

nected to the two ends of a wire or connections of a component, and the meter displays the resistance value of that component. Ohmmeters are self-powered by an internal battery. *They must never be connected to a circuit that has power* because the usually higher voltage from the circuit will damage the ohmmeter. Some meters have a protective fuse that will burn out to save the meter. Always turn the system power off or disconnect the power lead when checking a circuit with an ohmmeter to prevent damage to the meter. Disconnecting the circuit will also keep the meter from reading other parts of the circuit. When checking components with parallel circuits, remember that the meter does not know which path you wish to measure. It will include all possible paths. To be safe, disconnect one end of the component you are measuring. Many DMMs are designed not to affect solid-state components when measuring resistance.

Many DMMs are self-ranging and give a reading of any resistance value within their ability (Figure 14-38). Older analog meters require setting the meter to the range (1 k or 1,000 Ω, 10 k or 10,000 Ω, 1 m or 1,000,000 Ω) and recalibrating the meter for each range. An analog ohmmeter is calibrated by connecting the leads and rotating the calibration knob until the meter reads 0.

An ohmmeter is useful for checking an item such as a clutch coil when it is off the vehicle; connect the two ohmmeter leads to each end of the coil. If the resistance

FIGURE 14-38 A digital multimeter being used to measure resistance. Be sure to turn off or disconnect the electrical power to the circuit when using ohmmeter functions. *(Courtesy of Fluke; reproduced with permission)*

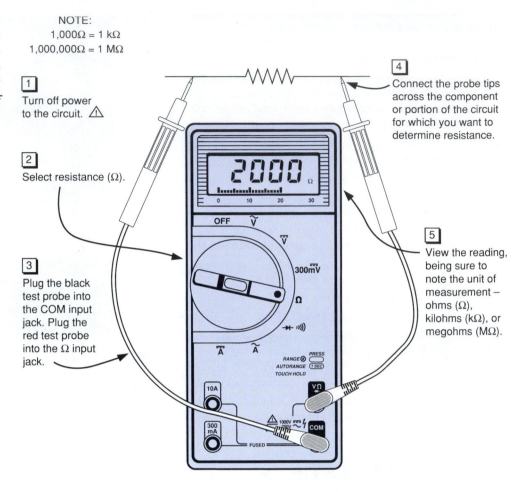

NOTE:
1,000Ω = 1 kΩ
1,000,000Ω = 1 MΩ

1 Turn off power to the circuit. ⚠

2 Select resistance (Ω).

3 Plug the black test probe into the COM input jack. Plug the red test probe into the Ω input jack.

4 Connect the probe tips across the component or portion of the circuit for which you want to determine resistance.

5 View the reading, being sure to note the unit of measurement – ohms (Ω), kilohms (kΩ), or megohms (MΩ).

⚠ Make sure power is off before making resistance measurements.

value matches the specifications (about 3 to 5 Ω), the unit does not have a short circuit and shows continuity. Moving one of the leads to the unit's mounting point checks for a grounded coil; at this time the reading should be infinite (∞ Ω) (Figure 14-39). A DMM displays *OL* for open leads to indicate infinite (out-of-limits) resistance.

To measure resistance, you should:

1. Disconnect at least one lead of the component, and make sure that all electrical power to the component is shut off.
2. Adjust the ohmmeter or DMM control to ohms, Ω.
3. Touch or connect the positive, red, or + lead to one side of the component.

4. Touch or connect the negative, black, or − lead to the other side of the component.
5. Read the amount of resistance on the meter.

Diode check:

6. Reverse the two connections, steps 3 and 4.
7. Read the amount of resistance on the meter. A change in resistance indicates that the diode has more resistance in one direction.

◄ **SERVICE TIP** ►

Dirty, slightly corroded switch contacts can be cleaned by rubbing them with a Pink Pearl eraser.

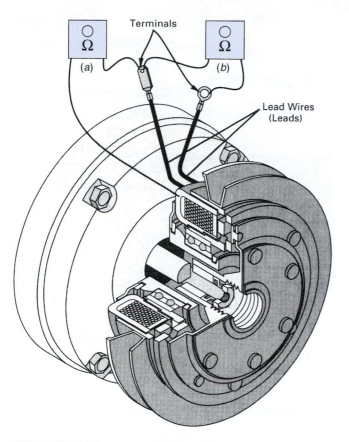

FIGURE 14-39 Attaching one of the ohmmeter leads to the coil housing checks for a ground (*a*). Connecting the two leads of the ohmmeter to the two leads of a clutch coil measures resistance and checks for shorts (*b*). The resistance reading should match the manufacturer's specification; the ground reading should be 0. *(Courtesy of Warner Electric)*

◀ **SERVICE TIP** ▶

It is possible for a clutch coil to have a weak internal connection and test out showing continuity and correct resistance with an ohmmeter. This weak connection causes reduced current flow, so many technicians prefer to check circuit resistance using an ammeter. If a circuit has the correct current flow with the correct input voltage, it has the proper resistance and therefore is good.

◀ **SERVICE TIP** ▶

A rule of thumb for most clutch coils is about 3 to 5 Ω of resistance and a 3- to 5-amp current flow.

14.8.3 Measuring Amperage

An ammeter is used to measure amperage, and it is often connected by breaking the circuit and connecting the ammeter in series with the circuit. Some ammeters use a transformer-type, inductive pickup, which is simply placed over or around the wire. Most technicians prefer the inductive pickup because it is much easier to connect, and it does not change the circuit in any way. If the current readings measured in the circuit are less than specifications, a weak circuit with excessive resistance is indicated. If the current readings are higher than specifications, a shorted or grounded circuit is indicated (Figure 14-40).

To measure amperage/current flow using an inductive pickup, you should:

1. Connect the inductive pickup to the DMM, and select DC Amps on the meter control.
2. Open the inductive pickup jaws and place them to surround the current-carrying wire.
3. Turn the component on, and read the amount of amperage on the meter.

To measure amperage/current flow using the meter leads, you should:

1. Select DC Amps on the meter control; make sure the meter is set to an amount larger than the expected current reading.
2. Disconnect one connector for the circuit being tested at a convenient location (Figure 14-41).
3. Connect the positive, red, or + lead to the wire or connector that is the most positive or closest to B+.
4. Connect the negative, black, or − lead to the other side (most negative) of your broken connection. The ammeter leads should be in series with the circuit being tested.
5. Turn the component on, and read the amount of amperage on the meter.

◀ **SERVICE TIP** ▶

Measuring the resistance of a clutch coil can be difficult, but measuring voltage and clutch current flow can be easy (see Figure 14-41). If the voltage measures at 13.9 V and there is a 3-amp current draw, solenoid resistance is 13.9 ÷ 3 = 4.6 Ω.

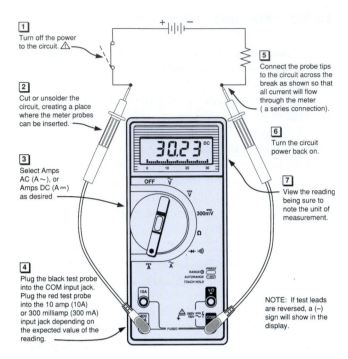

1 Turn off the power to the circuit. ⚠

2 Cut or unsolder the circuit, creating a place where the meter probes can be inserted.

3 Select Amps AC (A~), or Amps DC (A⎓) as desired

4 Plug the black test probe into the COM input jack. Plug the red test probe into the 10 amp (10A) or 300 milliamp (300 mA) input jack depending on the expected value of the reading.

5 Connect the probe tips to the circuit across the break as shown so that all current will flow through the meter (a series connection).

6 Turn the circuit power back on.

7 View the reading being sure to note the unit of measurement.

NOTE: If test leads are reversed, a (–) sign will show in the display.

⚠ Always make sure the power is off before cutting or unsoldering the circuit and inserting the DMM for current measurements. Even small amounts of current can be dangerous.

⚠ Never attempt a voltage measurement with the test probes in the current jacks. Meter damage or personal injury may result!

(a)

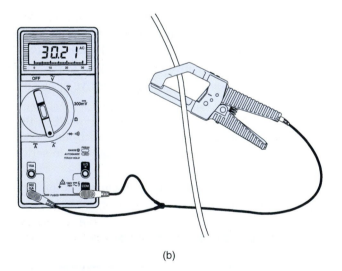

(b)

FIGURE 14-40 A digital multimeter being used to measure current flow (a). A transformer probe can be used to check current flow without breaking the circuit (b). *(Courtesy of Fluke; reproduced with permission)*

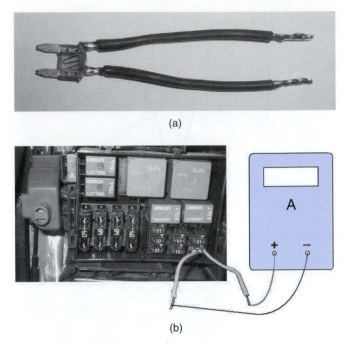

(a)

(b)

FIGURE 14-41 A blown fuse has been modified by soldering a short wire to each test point (a). Replacing a circuit fuse with the modified fuse allows an easy location to check the circuit's current flow (b).

REAL WORLD FIX: The Toyota Supra (56,000 miles) has no A/C, and a check shows a blown 10-amp fuse. The fuse was replaced. The technician tried to get a current reading, but the fuse blew before the reading could be read.

FIX

The technician measured the coil resistance using an ohmmeter, and the reading was 1.2 ohms, too low. Replacement of the clutch coil fixed this problem.

REAL WORLD FIX: The blower on the 1998 Dodge RAM van (90,000 miles) would only work on high speed. A faulty resistor block was found and replaced to fix the problem. The vehicle returned with the same problem and was repaired using the same fix. The vehicle returned again with the same problem and was repaired using the same fix.

FIX

Following advice, the technician checked the blower current draw, and the blower was drawing 21 amps. A new blower had a 12-amp current draw. Replacement of the blower motor and resistor block fixed this problem.

◀ **SERVICE TIP** ▶

Some technicians diagnose a circuit by measuring the current flowing through it. As components are switched on or off, the current flow should change to match the added or decreased load. For example, we know that a compressor clutch circuit is complete if the current flow increases by about 4 amps when the A/C is turned on.

◀ **SERVICE TIP** ▶

If using an inductive pickup and the current flow is very low, making current-flow reading difficult, and there is sufficient slack in the wire, make a loop in the wire and close the induction pickup over the doubled wire. This will double the current reading.

◀ **SERVICE TIP** ▶

Current flow is the same at all points through a simple circuit so current can be measured at any point. A convenient way of measuring current is at the fuse. Remove the clutch fuse and substitute a modified fuse. This is an old, burned-out fuse with a wire attached to each blade of the fuse (see Figure 14-41). Connect the ammeter leads to the two fuse connections to read current and operate the compressor using the normal controls or a scan tool. Current flow for clutch coil will be displayed when A/C is activated.

◀ **SERVICE TIP** ▶

Many current-flow checks are made with the engine off using B+ V. When troubleshooting problems caused by excessive current flow, make the critical current checks with the engine running using alternator voltage.

REAL WORLD FIX: The A/C fuse (10 amps) blows when the engine of the 1988 Camry is accelerated; it does not blow while the engine is idling. The wires were inspected, and they appear good.

FIX

The clutch coil was replaced, and this fixed the problem.

AUTHOR'S NOTE

Apparently the coil had a short, and when the engine speed was increased, the higher voltage from the alternator increased the current flow.

◀ **SERVICE TIP** ▶

Some technicians make extended time period current-flow checks using a fused jumper wire to supply current to the suspected component. This jumper is used to replace the current feed wire to that component using a fuse that matches the maximum current rating for it. The vehicle can then be driven for a period of time, and if the fuse burns out, you know that it used too much current.

REAL WORLD FIX: The compressor clutch on the 1995 Ford Windstar (112,000 miles) does not engage, and a voltage check shows no power to the clutch. Voltage checks at the integrated control module show good B+ power and grounds at the proper pins. Use of a scan tool shows normal system voltages, except there is a fluctuating WAC (wide-open throttle cutoff) voltage accompanied with a fluctuating idle speed, and if all the outputs are turned on using the scan tool, the voltage drops to 7 V.

FIX

Checking the current flow through the low-pressure switch shows 0.35 amps, but using a jumper around the switch increases the current flow to 3 amps, and this causes the clutch to engage. Replacement of the low-pressure switch fixed this problem.

AUTHOR'S NOTE

It is unknown why a voltage drop at the low-pressure switch showed only a 0.18 V drop.

◄ SERVICE TIP ►

A shorted clutch coil diode will cause the circuit to draw too much current, so the clutch circuit fuse will blow as soon as it is turned on. Diodes can be checked using an ohmmeter, but the easiest way to check this problem is to cut one of the leads to the diode. If the current flow is now okay, the diode is faulty and should be replaced. If the problem still exists, it is caused by a different fault.

◄ SERVICE TIP ►

A blower motor draws about 20 to 25 amps at high speed. If there is an inlet or outlet airflow restriction, current draw will drop to about 16 to 18 amps. If the rotation is reversed or the wrong blower cage/wheel is used, the current draw will be about 7 amps.

◄ SERVICE TIP ►

A generic replacement for the A/C clutch diode can be purchased from an electronics supply store, Part Number 1N4004. When installing it, make sure that the marked end, a silver band, of the diode is connected to the B+ wire.

◄ SERVICE TIP ►

Current draw can increase as a component reaches operating temperature. In one case, the current draw through a clutch coil was in the normal range, about 3 amps, but when warmed up using a heat gun, it increased to about 10 amps.

14.8.4 Interpreting Measurements

The technician must be familiar with the circuit and its components so he or she knows what to expect while measuring electrical values. Wiring diagrams can be used to follow the current flow through a circuit, much like a road map shows us how to get from one point to another. At one time these circuits were quite simple

and easy to follow; with many modern vehicles, the technician has to study the diagram and any information available on that particular circuit to identify what he or she is working with and what path the current follows.

◄ SERVICE TIP ►

Some students have difficulty reading wiring diagrams. The following tips should make this easier:

- Begin by locating the component (compressor clutch, blower, etc.) you are concerned with.
- Find the path to ground for the component, and note any switches, wire connectors, and wire splices in the ground path.
- Find the path to B+ from the component.
- Note any fuses, relays, switches, wire connectors, and splices in the B+ connection.
- Note how the relays are controlled, whether the relay is NO or NC, or if it is a double-contact relay, and note the path of the relay control circuit.
- If the circuit is complex, make a copy of it or cover it with a clear sheet of plastic; now, you can use a marker pen to clearly trace and identify its paths.

◄ SERVICE TIP ►

Exact specifications are often not available for many automotive circuits. The resistance value or current draw for a clutch or relay coil is not always given. When testing with a meter, the technician often has to guess what a usable range should be. In most circuits, B+ voltage should be found up to the major output device, except for an allowance for slight voltage drop at the connectors.

◄ SERVICE TIP ►

A possible cause for no blower operation is ice locking the blower wheel. It is possible for the HVAC case of a vehicle that is parked in the rain with a plugged evaporator drain to partially fill with water. If the temperature drops, the water can freeze. This problem can cause early and total failure of the blower.

REAL WORLD FIX: The 1993 Saab had a faulty blower replaced. Four months later it came back with intermittent blower operation and a buzzing noise from the blower during right turns. It was determined that water in the evaporator case was getting into the blower wheel, but checking showed that the evaporator drain was open.

FIX

On closer inspection, another drain, in a hard-to-see location, was found. This hose was twisted, causing it to block draining.

14.8.5   Advanced Testing Methods, Electronic Self-Diagnosis

Most modern electronic systems perform a trouble diagnosis on themselves, their sensors, and their output circuits each time they start up. If they locate an electrical problem, they will set and display a diagnostic trouble code, DTC. This can be either *soft* (temporary) or *hard* (semipermanent). A soft code is erased from the control module's memory when the ignition key is turned off; a hard code is erased by performing a special operation, pressing certain control head buttons, or removing the fuse for the control module. This is called *clearing codes.* Some systems can record and display the history of past failures. Self-diagnosis is very specific to the model of vehicle. Follow the exact directions given by the vehicle's manufacturer or, if using a portable scanner, the directions given by the manufacturer of that scanner (Figure 14-42).

In most systems, self-diagnosis is entered (started) by pushing a particular combination of buttons on the control head. The codes resulting from self-diagnosis are displayed (1) on the control head display, (2) on a handheld scanner unit, or (3) on a voltmeter or test light. A scanner is a tool used to enter self-diagnosis, display DTCs, and perform diagnostic checks (Figure 14-43). In most systems, the DTC is read as a one- or two-digit number or a combination of letters and numbers; some systems display the code by a pattern of pulses from a voltmeter or flashes of light. This is often called a blink code (Figure 14-44).

The DTC number indicates the nature of the problem. This number is keyed to a series of tests that must be performed to locate the exact fault. These tests usually involve measuring the voltage or resistance of particular portions of the circuit and are found in any good service manual.

After the fault is located and repaired, the codes must be cleared. With soft codes, this is easily done by turning off the key. Hard codes are cleared by pushing a particular combination of buttons on the control head,

performing certain operations with the scan tool, or removing the control module fuses.

◄ SERVICE TIP ►

Many electronic problems are caused by loose connections at wire connectors and inside of electrical components. These can often be located by twisting the wire connectors or tapping the component with the plastic handle of a screwdriver as the tests are being made.

◄ SERVICE TIP ►

A scan tool lets you erase codes without affecting any other electrical circuits. Disconnecting the battery erases all of the electronic memory of most vehicles, including clock settings and station presets for the radio, which may irritate the vehicle owner. Removing the control module fuses erases the memory of only that control module but can also cause problems. Some A/C systems are controlled through the ECM, and some of these have adaptive learning for the engine and transmission. On them, the ECM adjusts certain engine functions to particular geographic locations or driving styles; this takes up to 100 miles of driving. If you pull the fuse on these cars, it can take about 100 miles of driving before engine functions are switched from a normal setting to the owner's location and driving style. During this time the vehicle can run poorly.

REAL WORLD FIX: The A/C compressor on the Suzuki Sidekick (56,000 miles) does not operate. There is voltage at the A/C fuse but not at the compressor. The PCM increases the idle speed when the A/C is turned on, indicating that it is receiving the A/C request signal.

FIX

A check of the wiring using a wiring diagram revealed that someone had removed a stereo system, disconnected the B+ lead, and tucked the lead under other wires. Reconnecting the wires fixed this problem.

AUTHOR'S NOTE

It is a good practice to keep an eye out for previous repairs and modifications.

FIGURE 14-42 This diagnostic link connector (DLC) is at the bottom of the instrument panel (*a*). A scan tool can be connected to the DLC, which allows it to connect to the vehicle's controls (*b*). *(b courtesy of MACS)*

(a)

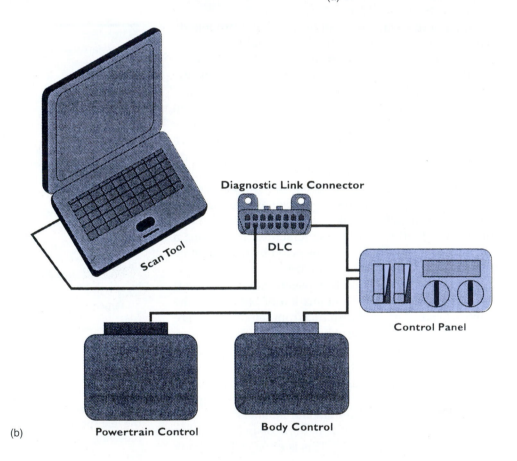

(b)

REAL WORLD FIX: The 1995 Lincoln Town Car (115,000 miles) has no A/C; the compressor clutch does not engage. This is an ATC system, and all the fuses are good. There is power to the control module but no power out. A jumper wire between the proper connections will produce clutch operation.

FIX

Following advice, the technician checked the WOT relay and found it to be good. He then back-probed the control module output using a test light as he tapped on the side of the module. Power came on, and this indicated a faulty module. Replacement of the control module fixed this problem.

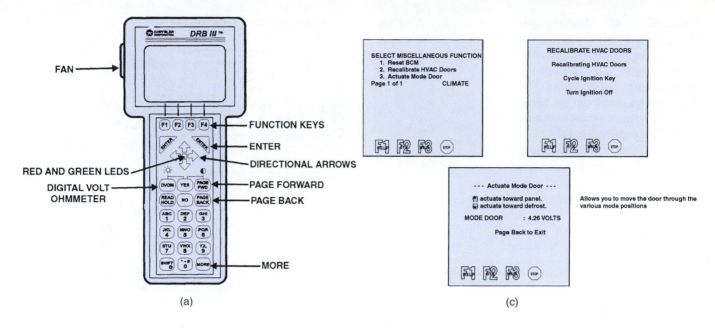

(a)

(b)

(c)

FIGURE 14-43 The DRB III is a scan tool that is dedicated to DaimlerChrysler vehicles (*a*). It can be used to read various functions (*b*) or perform various service operations. (*Courtesy of DaimlerChrysler Corporation*)

After the faults have been repaired and the codes erased, rerun the self-diagnosis to make sure that all of the faults have been corrected.

REAL WORLD FIX: The automatic transmission of the 1995 Oldsmobile 98 (85,000 miles) only has third gear when shifted to drive. The technician has found that a fuse blows, and this fuse is also for the A/C clutch. This transmission technician has a concern that this problem could be caused by the clutch clamping diode.

FIX

Following advice, the technician found the clamping diode and testing showed that it has a short. Replacement of the A/C clamping diode fixed this transmission problem.

◀ SERVICE TIP ▶

At least one system counts the time that the clutch cycles on and off; it determines if it cycles too fast or is off too long relative to the on time. This system is programmed to call this "low refrigerant" and will shut off the clutch. After the leak is repaired and the system recharged, some systems will not reenergize the clutch until certain fault-clearing operations are performed with the control head.

FIGURE 14-44 With the ignition switch on and the fan switch off, pressing on the recirculation control switch will cause this vehicle to enter self-diagnosis. The DTC can be read from the blinking of the recirculation indicator light. The pattern for DTC 2 is shown. *(Courtesy of American Honda Motor Co., Inc.)*

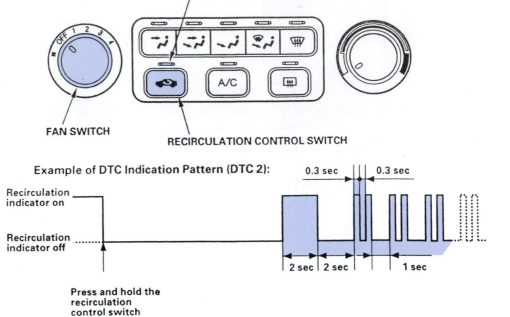

RECIRCULATION INDICATOR

FAN SWITCH

RECIRCULATION CONTROL SWITCH

Example of DTC Indication Pattern (DTC 2):

Recirculation indicator on

Recirculation indicator off

Press and hold the recirculation control switch

0.3 sec   0.3 sec

2 sec   2 sec   1 sec

REAL WORLD FIX: The 1993 Jeep Cherokee (123,000 miles) has a problem of constant heat at floor level. A scan tool check shows codes 21 and 23, "Mode and blend doors not moving." The doors operate if voltage is supplied to them, and the grounds at both motors are good. The controller was replaced, but this did not fix the problem.

FIX

Following advice, the technician checked the multipin connector below the glove box, and it was found to be partially plugged in. Making a complete connection at this connector fixed this problem.

14.8.5.1 Scan Tools. Scan tools are available from vehicle manufacturers and aftermarket sources. These units are connected to the vehicle's diagnostic connector and are bidirectional test units that can save considerable time in locating electrical faults. Scan tools allow the technician to:

- Read DTCs and, in some cases, serial data.
- Read signals from the sensors to the control module.
- Read signals from the control module to the actuators.
- Command the control module to operate the actuators.
- Record a snapshot of a problem occurrence showing both the input and output signals.
- Clear the DTCs.

Scan tools can display only electrical or electronic signals and can only indicate if a problem occurs in a particular circuit. Further checks are required to locate the exact cause of a problem.

REAL WORLD FIX: The 1994 Cadillac (96,000 miles) came in with no refrigerant. The leak was found and repaired. The system was recharged, but the compressor clutch would not engage. The battery was disconnected to clear any codes, but this did not help. A scan tool check shows the compressor relay is not getting a ground signal from the ECM.

FIX

A check revealed that the evaporator inlet sensor had been broken because someone had installed the OT backward. Replacement of the sensor and proper installation of the OT fixed this problem.

REAL WORLD FIX: The 1992 GMC pickup (115,000 miles) came in with the A/C light blinking on the control panel and indicating a low charge level. The faulty compressor front seal was replaced along with the accumulator, OT, and high-pressure cutoff switch. The system was recharged, and it worked well, except the A/C light was still blinking. Disconnecting the battery cable stopped the blinking light, but after a few days it began blinking again.

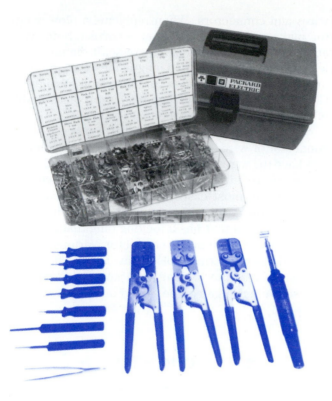

FIGURE 14-45   A terminal repair set. It includes replacement connectors and special pliers to install them, as well as a group of tools to remove terminals from weather-tight connectors. *(Courtesy of Kent-Moore)*

F I X

After checking TSB #92-1B-90, the technician disconnected the green wire from the control head, and this cured the blinking light.

REAL WORLD FIX: The 1992 Buick (101,000 miles) A/C system does not work; the compressor clutch does not engage. A jumper wire across the A/C relay causes the clutch to engage, and the system works normally. All three of the system switches check out as good, and the system has a full refrigerant charge.

F I X

A scan tool was connected to the system, and the DTCs were cleared. This fixed the system.

A U T H O R ' S   N O T E

The DTCs were probably set by an earlier fault that was repaired, but the trouble codes were not cleared.

REAL WORLD FIX: The compressor on the 1996 Chevrolet Monte Carlo will not engage; a jumper wire at the relay will cause engagement. A scan tool check shows that there is an A/C request signal from the control head. Another ECM was installed, but this did not help.

F I X

Further checks using the scan tool showed an IAT (inlet air temperature) of −38°; this indicated a faulty IAT sensor. An inspection revealed that the sensor was unplugged. Reconnecting the sensor fixed the problem.

REAL WORLD FIX: The 1990 Nissan Maxima (185,000) miles) came in to have a cooling fan replaced. Job completion check showed that the cooling fan and A/C operated, but both the A/C and fan would cut off and on at the same time. The relays checked good.

F I X

Further checks showed slightly odd A/C request voltages. All the normal grounds were checked, and these were okay. The technician noticed that the temperature gauge also fluctuated about 1/4 of its range when the compressor would come on, so he checked the engine ground. He found that the battery ground cable had been replaced, but during that replacement, the engine ground was cut. A proper engine ground was installed, and this fixed this problem.

REAL WORLD FIX: The 1996 Dodge Caravan (133,000 miles) had a problem of no heat. Tests showed a bad control head so the control head was replaced with a used one. This produced heat but only at the passenger side. Further checks show separate blend doors and possibly two mode door actuators (it was hard to tell because of the limited space). Using a stethoscope, the technician could hear that only one of the actuators operate when the controls are moved. He suspects that this is a dual HVAC system.

FIX

The VIN was taken to the dealership, and it was determined that this was a dual system in which someone had installed a single-system control head. Installing the proper control head fixed this problem.

REAL WORLD FIX: The 1999 Buick (48,000 miles) was hit hard in the rear end, and this accident deployed both air bags. The instrument panel had been partially disassembled to replace the air bags. The car was returned to the body shop that did the repairs, with a complaint of low heat output from the left registers (dual-zone system). After attempting repairs, the body shop sent the car to another repair shop. The repair shop checked and repaired all the DTCs, and these appeared to have been caused by the body shop's repair attempts. The two blend door motors were removed and bench checked, and they seem to be operating correctly. Supply and reference voltages at both motors are correct. Watching the door operation using a scan tool shows normal operation of the right blend door motor, but the left motor goes to mid-position and stays there. The technician attempted to reprogram the system but could not.

FIX

Following advice, the technician replaced the programmer, and this fixed the problem. The calibration procedure was to turn on the ignition for three minutes, and the programmer went through the procedure, operating the doors and fan motor.

14.8.5.2 Actuator Motor Calibration When the ECM or actuator motor has been replaced on some vehicles, a calibration procedure is often required. This procedure resets the ECM so that it will operate the compressor clutch and other actuators in the proper manner. It is sometimes required when the battery is disconnected. Calibration procedure varies between different vehicle makes and models and is described in the vehicle service information.

14.9 ELECTRICAL SYSTEM REPAIR

Normally a faulty electrical component such as a switch, relay, blower motor, or clutch is repaired by removing and replacing (R&R) it. The R&R operation is usually a relatively simple process of disconnecting the wires or connectors, removing the component, installing the new component, and reconnecting the wires and connectors. When replacing a blower motor, make sure the replacement is correct. Some variables and critical dimensions are shaft diameter and length, motor diameter and length, location, and spacing of mounting bolt holes, and direction of rotation. Clutch coil replacement requires partial disassembly of the compressor (described in Chapter 16).

Occasionally a technician must replace a faulty connector or wire by splicing the wire. A few connectors have the wires molded into them, so replacing the connector requires splicing the new connector to each wire. In most cases, however, individual wires can be removed from the connector. These wires have an end terminal that has a locking tang that expands to hold the terminal in the connector. Various special terminal disconnecting tools are available. The tool is pushed against the locking tang and depresses the tang so the terminal can be pulled out (Figures 14-45 and 14-46).

◄ SERVICE TIP ►

Be aware that it is possible to cause the vehicle's air bags to deploy if the wrong electrical wires are connected. This deployment can possibly cause injury to the technician or bystanders; it will cause an expensive repair. It is recommended that the air bags be deactivated using the manufacturer's recommended procedure before doing any testing or work under the instrument panel.

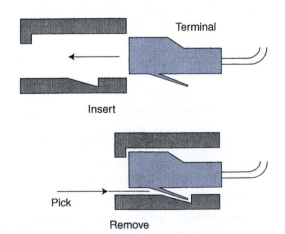

FIGURE 14-46 A terminal is usually pushed into a weather-tight connector until it locks into place (*a*). A pick tool is used to unlock the terminal for removal. (*Reprinted with permission of General Motors Corporation*)

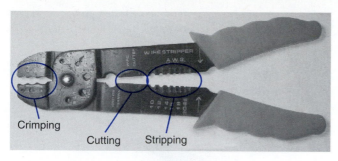

Crimping   Cutting   Stripping

(a)

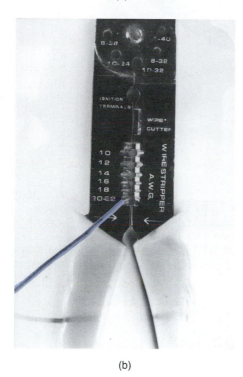

(b)

FIGURE 14-47 A wire stripping and crimping tool (*a*). The stripping area is used to cut the insulation and pull it off the wire (*b*).

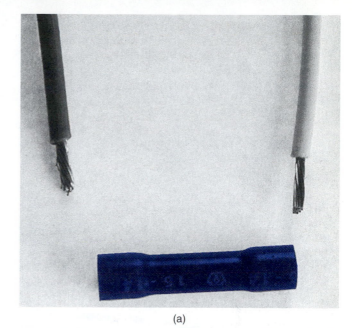

(a)

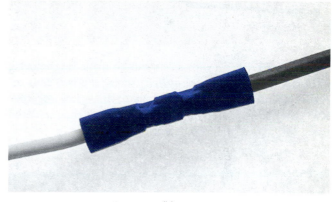

(b)

FIGURE 14-48 A splice can be made quickly by crimping a wire connector to the two wires.

To splice a wire, you should:

1. Make sure the new wire is the same size or larger than the original. Strip off an amount of insulation slightly longer than the splice clip, or about 3/8- to 1/2-inch (10 to 13 mm) long (Figure 14-47).

2. Push the two wire ends together so the bare wires overlap and place a splice clip over the connection (Figure 14-48).

3. Use a crimping tool to firmly squeeze the splice clip onto the connection. *Or*, if a splice clip is not being used, twist the connection so the wires are tight.

4. Use a soldering gun or iron to heat the wires enough to melt solder, and apply 60/40 rosin core

solder to the hot wires until the solder flows through the joint (Figure 14-49). Do not use acid core solder.

5. Insulate the splice by wrapping it with either plastic electrical tape or a shrink tube. A shrink tube is a plastic tube slid over the splice and heated with a match so it shrinks tightly in place.

◄   **SERVICE TIP**   ►

The wire stripper can be used as a gauge: The smallest opening that clearly strips the insulation without nicking or cutting the wire strands is the wire gauge.

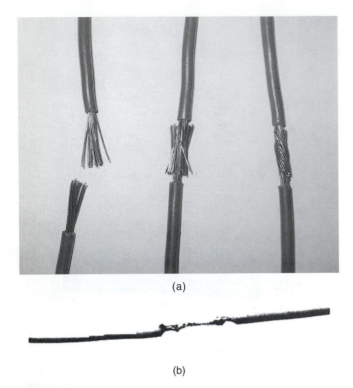

(a)

(b)

FIGURE 14-49 A wire splice can be made by removing insulation from the two wires (left); sliding the two ends together (center); and twisting them so they stay together while they are soldered (a). The connection is then soldered using rosin core solder for security (b).

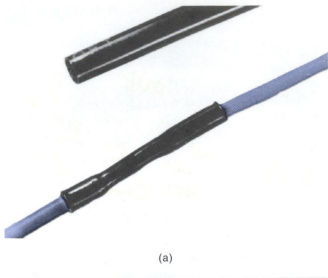

(a)

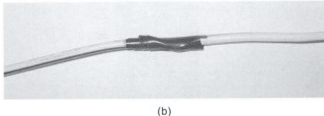

(b)

FIGURE 14-50 A wire splice should be insulated using shrink tubing (a) or by wrapping it tightly with plastic tape (b).

◀ **SERVICE TIP** ▶

If using a shrink tube, slide a piece of tube, about 1/2-inch longer than the splice, over the wire before connecting it in step 2. Slide the tube away from the connection while soldering it. After soldering the connection, slide the tube to the proper location and heat it to shrink the tube to lock it in place.

If using tape, make sure the tape is wrapped tightly and smooth and looks neat (Figure 14-50).

REAL WORLD FIX: The 1993 Honda Prelude came in with a complaint of the A/C shutting off and blowing hot air. This problem is intermittent, occurring as many as three times a day. The A/C relay was cycled many times with no malfunction. The A/C pressures are good, and the compressor clutch gap is 0.028 inch, within specifications.

FIX

Following advice from other technicians, the A/C switch control circuit board was inspected for bad solder joints; none were found, but tapping and twisting the board caused a momentary loss of compressor operation. All of the solder joints that looked suspect were resoldered, and this fixed the problem.

14.9.1 Electrical Component Replacement

Most faulty electrical components are simply removed by disconnecting the electrical connections and removing the mounting fasteners. They are replaced by reversing the procedure. The procedure to remove and replace a compressor clutch coil is described in Section 16.2.2.

A wise technician will always inspect the electrical connector and all of its terminals to make sure that they will make good contact and make sure that the connector latches lock securely.

REVIEW QUESTIONS

The following questions are provided to help you study as you read the chapter.

1. Electrical force is called _____ ~~watt~~ ; a(n) _____ ~~Amp~~ is the amount of electrical current flow; and _____ ~~Ohms~~ are the units of electrical resistance.

2. Most electrical circuits include a(n) _____ ~~power~~, _____ ~~cir~~, _____ ~~prot~~, _____ ~~cot~~, _____ ~~sour~~, _____ ~~switch~~, and _____ ~~to~~ _____ ~~load cond~~.

3. Electric wires transmit electricity through the _____ while the current flow is contained by the _____.

4. The strength of a compressor clutch coil is determined by the number of _____ _____ and the amount of _____ _____.

5. The diode at the clutch coil protects the electronic _____ _____ from voltage _____.

6. An in-vehicle sensor is a type of _____ that increases resistance when the temperature _____.

7. A(n) _____ converts a(n) _____ signal into an electrical signal.

8. If the ECM finds a problem in an electronic control system, it will turn on the _____ _____ _____ and set a(n) _____ _____ _____.

9. Most actuator motors contain a(n) _____ _____ so the ECM will know the motor position.

10. A smart control head contains _____ for motor _____.

11. _____ allows a pair of wires to be used for more than one _____.

12. A strategy that prevents potential compressor problems from damaging the accessory drive belt is called _____ _____ strategy, and it works when the compressor _____ _____ signal shows a slower speed than the engine.

13. A(n) _____ _____ is when electric current leaves the wire it is supposed to be in to go to another wire, and a(n) _____ _____ is when electric current leaves the wire it is supposed to be in and goes to ground.

14. A blown fuse is often an indication of _____ _____ flow.

15. An ECM can be damaged by _____ if you touch one of the terminals with your finger.

16. A clutch coil should have at least _____ _____ at the B+ terminal when the engine is running.

17. A _____ _____ allows you to read DTCs, the signals from the sensors to the ECM, and the signals from the ECM to the actuators.

18. The best way to clear a DTC without erasing memory of other electronic circuits is to use a(n) _____ _____.

CHAPTER QUIZ

The following questions will help you check the facts you have learned. Select the answer that completes each statement correctly.

1. Which of the following is the unit for electrical pressure?
   - a. Amp
   - b. Ohm
   - c. Volt
   - d. Watt

2. Most automotive electrical systems use AC current.
   - a. True
   - b. False

3. A fusible link is usually four wire sizes _____ than the wire used in that particular circuit.
   - a. larger
   - b. smaller
   - c. Either a or b
   - d. Neither a nor b

4. Which of the following is considered an output device in an ATC system?
   - a. Compressor clutch
   - b. Blower motor
   - c. Both a and b
   - d. Neither a nor b

5. Which of the following is monitored by a sensor in an ATC system?
   - a. Ambient temperature
   - b. In-vehicle temperature
   - c. Sunload
   - d. All of these

6. Electrical mode doors in an ATC system usually have a feedback sensor string connected to them.
   - a. True
   - b. False

7. Which of the following test instruments can be used on any automotive electrical circuit?
   - a. Test light
   - b. Ohmmeter
   - c. Analog multimeter
   - d. DMM

8. Modern electronic circuits can be damaged by _____.
   - a. electrostatic discharge
   - b. excess heat
   - c. rough handling
   - d. Any of these

9. Which of the following is true concerning ohmmeters?

   a. Ohmmeters are self-powered.

   b. Ohmmeters can be used on live circuits.

   c. Ohmmeters cannot be used to check continuity.

   d. None of these are true.

10. A rule of thumb for clutch coil resistance is _____.

    a. 10 ohms   **c.** about 5 amps

    b. 3 to 5 ohms   **d.** 5 to 10 ohms

11. A vehicle with an ATC system has heater and defroster operation, but the A/C is not working properly. To diagnose this problem, the technician should _____.

    A. check for trouble codes

    B. clear the trouble codes

    Which is correct?

    a. A only   **c.** Both A and B

    b. B only   **d.** Neither A nor B

12. An example of a short circuit is a _____.

    a. clutch coil with a resistance of 0.5 Ω

    b. burned-out lightbulb

    c. burned wire with bad insulation that touches ground

    d. Any of these

13. The blower motor runs on high speed only. This indicates a faulty _____.

    a. high blower relay   **c.** switch

    b. resistor bank   **d.** None of these

14. The vehicle overheats because the cooling fan does not operate. This could be caused by a _____.

    a. faulty fan relay

    b. bad blower motor ground connection

    c. faulty blower motor

    d. Any of these

Chapter 15

REFRIGERANT SERVICE OPERATIONS

LEARNING OBJECTIVES

After completing this chapter, you should:

1. Be familiar with the preventive maintenance operations and the adjustments necessary to keep a heating and A/C system operating properly.
2. Be able to perform basic A/C service operations, given the operating manual for the equipment.
3. Be familiar with how to retrofit R-134a into an R-12 system.
4. Be able to complete the ASE tasks related to refrigerant handling.

TERMS TO LEARN

black death	noncondensable gasses
charging cylinder	(NCG)
conversion fitting	out-gasses
cubic feet per minute	partial charge
(cfm)	pressure-temperature
electronic scales	(PT)
evacuate	recover
fingerprint	recycle
flush	retrofit
identifier	slugging
in-line filter	tank certification
live flushing	topping off
micron	vented

15.1 INTRODUCTION

The service and repair of heating and A/C systems consist of preventive maintenance operations; the adjustment, repair, overhaul, or replacement of system components; and standard A/C service operations. These standard operations include identifying the refrigerant in a system to determine what it is and if it is contaminated, recovery and recycling of good refrigerant, recovery and disposal of contaminated refrigerant, evacuation of a system, recharging a system with refrigerant, checking the oil level in a compressor or system, and retrofitting an R-12 system with an alternate refrigerant, preferably R-134a.

There are several important facts to keep in mind when servicing an A/C system:

- A/C systems are designed to operate using a specific amount of a particular refrigerant. This is never changed unless the system is retrofitted to use an approved refrigerant.
- A/C systems are designed to operate using a specific amount of a particular refrigerant oil. This is never changed unless the system is retrofitted to use an approved refrigerant, and a change of oil type is normally required at this time.
- Adding any other chemical into a system can create a chemical problem that can cause system damage or failure.

Most vehicle and A/C system parts suppliers have a statement similar to this: Use only approved products. A/C systems found to be contaminated with unapproved products void any warranty for the A/C system.

Service steps are often performed along with repair operations; for example, replacement of a faulty compressor begins with recovery of the refrigerant and ends with recharging the system. Normally, repair operations are necessary because of improper system operation or failure. The diagnostic checks described in Chapter 12 show the cause of the failure and what repair operations are needed. (These repair operations are described in Chapter 16.) Before proceeding with any service or repair procedures, be sure to protect your eyes and skin.

15.1.1 Gauge Pressures

Gauge pressures are normally referenced to sea level. Because most pressure gauges are affected by atmospheric pressure, the same pressure will read slightly different at different altitudes. This will usually have very little effect on A/C service other than the vacuum readings during system evacuation.

15.2 PREVENTIVE MAINTENANCE AND ADJUSTMENT OPERATIONS

An often neglected area, preventive maintenance and adjustment operations are comparable to the engine-off, under-hood checks described in Section 11.2. The purpose of preventive maintenance is to locate potential problems before they cause a failure.

The major wearing item in a heating and A/C system is the compressor drive belt and automatic tensioner; with many late-model vehicles, this belt also drives the alternator and water pump. Most vehicles will not operate for long if this belt fails, so it is usually replaced at the first signs of fatigue. Because the first indication of possible failure is often a broken belt, many service technicians recommend replacing the drive belts every 4 or 5 years. This might be sooner than really necessary, but the cost of belt failure is usually much greater in both time and money (Figure 15-1) (see also Figure 9-2). Belt inspection and replacement are described in more detail in Chapter 18.

Another preventive maintenance operation is to check for proper seals, debris, and bent fins at the condenser. Debris is usually cleaned off using an air nozzle or water spray. A stiff fiber brush, such as a denture brush, can also be used; brushing is in a direction parallel to the fins (Figure 15-2). Bent-over fins can be straightened using a small probe, fin comb, or fin straightener.

15.3 A/C SERVICE OPERATIONS

◄ CAUTION ►

Remember that there is a possibility of injury from refrigerant contact. Goggles or a face shield should be worn to keep liquid refrigerant from getting in the eyes, and gloves should be worn to protect the hands. Avoid breathing refrigerant vapors.

FIGURE 15-1 As you inspect a drive belt, roll the belt so you can check the sides and inner face. Any signs of possible failure mean the belt should be replaced.

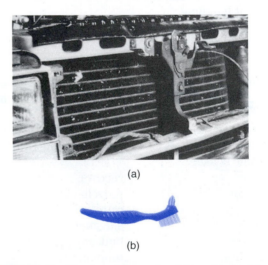

(a)

(b)

FIGURE 15-2 The condenser should be checked for debris at the front and rear of the core (*a*). Debris can be removed using a denture brush (*b*). (*a courtesy of Everco Industries*)

Before any repair operations can be done on an A/C system (except for electrical and some compressor clutch operations), the refrigerant must be **recovered** from the system. Refrigerants must not be released or vented into the atmosphere; a good technician performs the service and repair operations in such a way as to prevent refrigerant venting during or after the repair (Figure 15-3). At one time, refrigerant was simply **vented** or bled out, discharged, and released, the major concern being the amount of oil that was lost. Now venting is prohibited by the Clean Air Act. New, pure (or virgin) R-12 was charged back into the system. Today's A/C service usually begins with the recovery of

whatever refrigerant is left in the system. This refrigerant will be **recycled** into that or another A/C system; refrigerants have become too valuable to waste (Figures 15-4 and 15-5).

Refrigerant identification has become extremely important. R-12 is out of production and the existing stocks are gone or nearly gone. Bootleg R-12 is

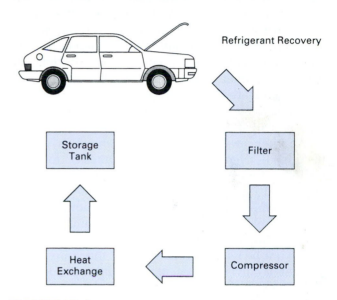

FIGURE 15-4 A recovery unit removes refrigerant vapor from the vehicle. It then filters the refrigerant before compressing it so it condenses and can be stored as a liquid in the storage tank.

Do not release refrigerants into the air

FIGURE 15-3 Refrigerant must not be released or vented into the atmosphere.

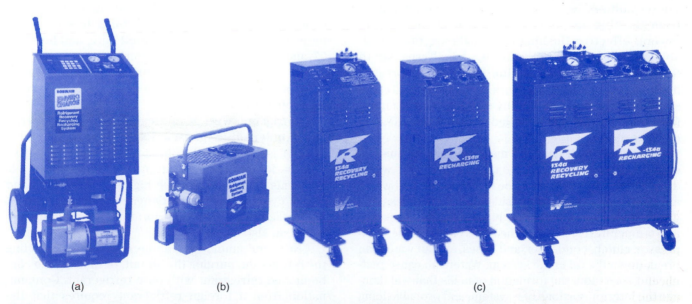

(a)   (b)   (c)

FIGURE 15-5 Recovery machines are available in full-service form (in combination with recycling, vacuum pump, and recharging functions) (*a*), recovery only units (*b*), and recovery and recycling combinations (*c*). This particular unit (*c*) can be "married" into a single unit or "divorced" into two separate units. (a *and* b *courtesy of Robinair, SPX Corporation;* c *courtesy of White Industries*)

available, but some of this is of a counterfeit and unknown composition. With R-134a available in small cans at many stores and quite a few blends available, a wise technician does not recover refrigerant unless he or she is sure of what is being recovered from the system. Imagine recovering a refrigerant contaminated by R-22 or a hydrocarbon into your recovery bottle that is half full of R-12. Even worse, imagine that you recycled this refrigerant, and you used it to charge another system. A recycling machine is designed to remove water, oil, solids, and air, not another refrigerant. The result of this action is that you have contaminated your recovery and recycling machine, contaminated and ruined the R-12 in the bottle, and contaminated the other system(s). Many compare contaminated refrigerant to a virus that can sometimes spread at a very rapid rate.

Another practice that has changed is system flushing. It used to be common practice to **flush** portions of an A/C system using a liquid to remove debris and foreign particles, usually the result of a failed compressor. The most common flushing agents were R-11, R-113, and petroleum solvents. Because the two refrigerants contain CFCs, they should not be used or released into the atmosphere. Petroleum solvents present a potential fire hazard, and it is extremely difficult to remove all of the solvent from the system when flushing is complete; the detrimental effects that solvents have on the system are now known. In early R-134a retrofit tests, more failures occurred in systems that were flushed with R-11 or R-113 than in systems that were not flushed. These failures were attributed to contamination from flushing agents that remained in the system. Several effective flushing chemicals are now available from commercial sources. An alternative to flushing is to install an **in-line filter** or compressor inlet screen to trap any debris in a system. Filter installation is recommended by several vehicle manufacturers. The filter is installed ahead of the TXV, OT, or compressor.

After the repair has been made, the system must be evacuated to remove all of the air and any water droplets or vapor that might be in it. Both air and water are contaminants. Air is considered a noncondensable gas, and it causes excessively high discharge pressures and temperatures. Besides the added load on the compressor, clutch, condenser, and hoses, air and water can break down the oil in the system. Water can cause rusting and corrosion, the formation of acids that will damage the interior portions of a system, and probable icing at the expansion device.

◀ **SERVICE TIP** ▶

Some experts emphasize that the best way to remove water from a system is to replace the desiccant (accumulator or receiver–drier) and that system evacuation removes the noncondensable gasses.

Recharging a system involves putting the right amount and type of refrigerant into a system. Recharging uses new or recycled refrigerant or a mixture of the two. (At one time, small cans [400 g or 1 lb] were commonly used, but now most shops use larger containers. Since November 1992, small containers [less than 20 lb] of R-12 have been available for purchase only by certified technicians.) Recharging equipment must accurately measure the quantity of refrigerant that is charged into a system.

15.3.1 Refrigerant Contamination

At one time, contamination of refrigerant was rare, and the majority of the problems were caused by air from improper service procedures. Today, with the variety of blends, hydrocarbons, and other refrigerants, along with recycled refrigerants, contamination is a much greater problem. The A/C industry defines contaminated refrigerant as anything less than 97% pure; 98% and better is considered pure, and between 97 and 98% is questionable. Purity standards (SAE J1991 and J2099 and ARI 700-88) permit a small amount of contamination with new (virgin) and recycled refrigerant.

Refrigerant with 2% or greater of another material (**noncondensable gasses [NCG]** or foreign refrigerant) is considered contaminated (SAE standard J1661). If the contamination is greater than 5%, problems such as excessive high side pressures and clutch cycling rate result. Other unseen problems of oil breakdown, seal deterioration, or compressor wear can also occur.

NCG contamination can be reduced by recycling the refrigerant, purging the air out, or diluting the contaminated refrigerant with pure refrigerant. Contamination from a foreign refrigerant requires that the refrigerant be sent off for reclaiming or disposal.

REAL WORLD FIX: The A/C system in the 1984 Chevrolet motorhome (58,000 miles) was recharged using 3 pounds of R-12. The TXV had been replaced because of suspected restriction. The system still does not cool very well, and the technician has asked for help.

F I X

Following advice, the refrigerant in the A/C service unit was checked and found to be contaminated with air. After purging the air from the refrigerant supply, the A/C system was recharged, and this fixed the problem.

15.3.1.1 Sealant Contamination
Another source of what many HVAC technicians consider a contamination is that coming from chemicals that are intended to seal refrigerant leaks. There are two general types of sealants:

- A chemical that promotes swelling of rubber O-rings and seals
- An epoxy/epoxy-like, one- or two-part, moisture-cure polymer

Some small cans of R-134a contain the first sealer style at a price that is slightly higher than plain R-134a. This type of sealant can cause problems.

The second sealant style is described in Section 15.5. Sealants of this type have cured and solidified in the hoses and solenoid valves of recovery machines, causing serious problems.

15.3.2 Refrigerant Identification

Two methods are used to identify the refrigerant in a system. One is to look at the service fittings and refrigerant label, which tells the technician what refrigerant *should* be in the system. The other is to use a refrigerant **identifier** to determine what is actually in the system—whether it is R-12 or R-134a, or whether it is contaminated with a foreign refrigerant or air. The second method is much better when we consider the problems that can be created if we recover a blend or hydrocarbon refrigerant.

◄ CAUTION ►

Recovering a hydrocarbon refrigerant using an electric-driven machine can cause an explosion inside the machine.

There are two types of refrigerant identifiers. One type, referred to as a *go-no-go identifier* (accuracy to about 90% or better), indicates the purity of the refrigerant with lights that indicate pass or fail. The other type, referred to as a *diagnostic identifier* (accuracy to 98% or better), displays the percentage by weight of R-12, R-134a, R-22, hydrocarbons, and air (displayed as NCG) (Figure 15-6). Knowing the nature of the contaminants lets you know what approach to take. If the contaminant is air, you can safely recover and recycle the refrigerant for reuse. If the contaminant is another refrigerant or a hydrocarbon, you must use a special recovery procedure and send off the recovered mixture for disposal or recycling. Recycling machines cannot remove a foreign refrigerant, only air, water, oil, or particulates. Newer identifiers include a printer port, so a hard-copy readout can be printed for the customer's use (Figure 15-7).

At times, slightly contaminated refrigerant can be saved. The standard for recovered R-12 purity is 98%.

◄ SERVICE TIP ►

The readout in Figure 15-7 shows R-12 contaminated with 3.8% R-134a. If this amount of contaminated refrigerant is diluted with two to three times as much pure R-12, the contamination would be less than 2%.

Some shops are using the diagnostic-style identifier as a quality-control check of new refrigerant they purchase. New R-12 that has been in storage is available through reputable suppliers. Badly contaminated new (virgin) refrigerant is also being found, some of which is bootleg and being imported illegally. Contaminated refrigerant should not be charged into a system. You will pay a high price to purchase the contaminated refrigerant and also to dispose of it.

To identify the refrigerant in a system, you should:

1. With the engine and the system shut off, connect the identifier to the low side service port using the correct hose assembly for the system's refrigerant type.

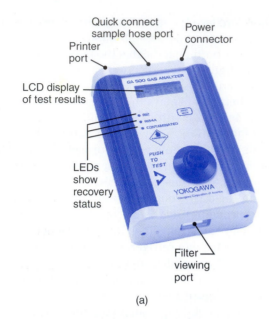

(a)

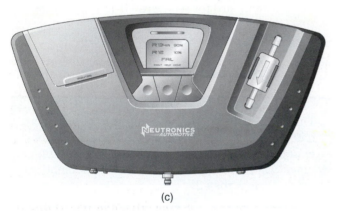

(c)

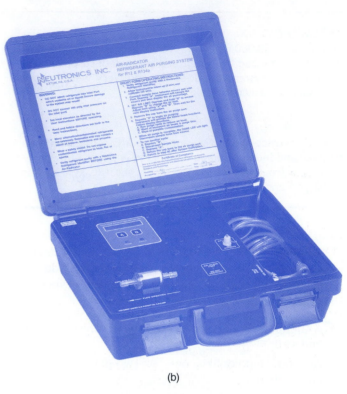

(b)

FIGURE 15-6 A refrigerant identifier uses a refrigerant sample to determine what it consists of (*a* and *b*). The results are displayed by a digital image or flashing lights. Some include a printer; this model (*c*) will also display what SNAP refrigerant is in the system. *(a reprinted by permission of Yokogawa Corporation of America; b and c coutesy of Neutronics Inc.)*

2. Check the filter for the incoming gas; it will show a color change if contaminated.

3. Allow a gas sample to enter the unit. Some units include a warning device to make sure liquid refrigerant does not enter it. Many units include a warning device to indicate a flammable refrigerant.

4. Read the display to determine the nature of the refrigerant. Some units allow printing of the results at this time. If the refrigerant is good or R-12 or R-134a contaminated with air, it can be safely recovered and recycled.

5. When the analysis is complete, some units display instructions to disconnect the sampling hose and then bleed out the gas that was sampled. If the hose is not disconnected when prompted, the identifier can bleed excess refrigerant from the system.

Refrigerant Analysis		
Refrigerant R-134a	=	3.8%
Refrigerant R-12	=	96.2%
Refrigerant R-22	=	0.0%
Hydrocarbons	=	0.0%
Conclusion:	>>>FAIL<<<	
Date: _____		
Technician: _____		
Car Model: _____		
VIN: _____		

FIGURE 15-7 This printout from an identifier shows that the R-12 in this system is cross-contaminated with 3.8% R-134a. This refrigerant is unusable.

◄   **SERVICE TIP**   ►

An identifier cannot identify a blend directly, but by looking at the combination on the display, you can sometimes tell what the refrigerant is. An identifier can only identify the refrigerants contained in the blend. This is referred to as a **fingerprint**; for example, one source says that FR-12, FRIGC, will appear as 2% HC, 26% R-12, 3% R-22, and 69% R-134a. It is recommended that you use your identifier on each of the blends that you encounter and record the readings (fingerprints) for later reference.

◄   **PROBLEM SOLVING 15-1**   ►

A vehicle came in with a complaint of a noisy compressor along with poor cooling. When you put gauges on and tested the system, you found high low side pressure and very high pressure on the high side. Your identifier indicates 12% R-134a, 80% R-12, and 8% NCG. Do you know what caused the customer's complaint? What should you do now?

15.3.2.1   Sealant Identification

A simple and relatively inexpensive identifier called the *Quick Detect* has been developed so technicians can tell if a system contains a sealant (Figure 15-8). Recovering refrigerant that contains a sealant might cause damage to the recovery unit. There have been cases where sealant has cured inside the machine, causing loss of the machine and expensive repairs.

To identify presence of a sealant in a system, you should:

1. Run the system for at least 2 minutes to circulate the refrigerant and possible sealant.
2. Select the proper coupler, R-12 or R-134a.
3. Wet the orifice of the sensing plug with water, shake out any excess water, and install the sensing plug into the tool's coupler.
4. Connect the sealant detector to the coupler, and attach the coupler to the system.
5. Note and record the flow rate; it should be 1.5 or greater.

6. Observe the flow rate for three minutes, and note any increases. A drop in flow rate of 30% or greater from the highest flow indicates that a sealant is present.

◄   **SERVICE TIP**   ►

A special filter called the *Recycle Guard* is available that can be attached to the inlet hose of the recovery machine (Figure 15-9). The Recycle Guard filter is designed to remove contaminants like sealants and dye before they can enter the recovery unit.

15.3.3   Refrigerant Recovery

Most recovery units are part of the service unit and have two service hoses and low and high side pressure gauges and are connected directly to both low and high side service ports. Other recovery units are connected to the center hose of a manifold gauge set. Remember that a recovery unit must be dedicated to either R-12 or R-134a; it cannot be used for both. Blends or contaminated mixtures should be recovered using a different, separate machine. The hoses should be equipped with shutoff valves within 12 inches of the ends and have end fittings to match the refrigerant used.

At this time, there is concern about recovering refrigerant from a system that has a refrigerant blend or the wrong refrigerant added to it. A wise technician is careful to check the service history of the vehicle. Many refuse to service a vehicle if there is a chance that it contains contaminated refrigerant. Identifiers should be used. If the correct machine is available, R-12 or R-134a can be recovered. Do not recover refrigerant that is cross-contaminated unless you are recovering it for disposal.

Most recovery units contain an oil separator, a compressor-like pump, and a condenser-like heat exchanger. They draw refrigerant vapor out of a system and, like the high side of an A/C system, convert it into liquid for storage. Recovery units weigh the amount of refrigerant that is recovered, which tells the technician if all the refrigerant from a fully charged system has been recovered or whether the system was fully charged. Oil removed and separated during the recovery process is usually drained into a measuring cup and noted so that this amount of new oil can be

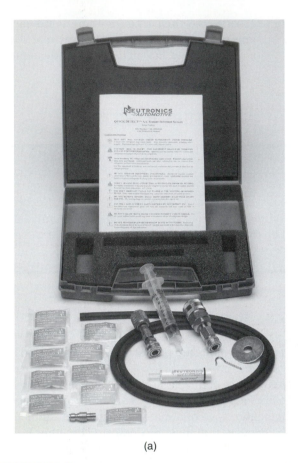

(a)

(b)

FIGURE 15-8 A sealant detector set (*a*) includes a flow meter, hose, two system couplers, and test plugs. A sealant in the system is indicated if the refrigerant flow drops during the 3-minute test period. *(Courtesy of Neutronics Inc.)*

replaced in the system as it is recharged (Figure 15-10). This feature is helpful during a retrofit, because it tells the technician how much of the mineral oil has been removed.

◄ **SERVICE TIP** ►

Oil recovery also gives an indication of the oil volume in the system; if no oil is recovered, the system is probably low on oil. If an excessive amount of oil is recovered, the system probably has too much oil.

Some refrigerant in a system is absorbed in the oil and does not leave the oil immediately when a system is emptied. This trapped refrigerant **out-gasses** or boils out of the oil later, after the pressure has been removed. Recovery units shut off automatically after the main refrigerant charge has been removed and the system

drops into a slight vacuum. To completely remove the refrigerant, run the normal recovery procedure and then recheck the pressure after a 5-minute wait. If the pressure has increased, restart the recovery process.

◄ **SERVICE TIP** ►

If recovery occurs too quickly, moisture can freeze and block the removal of all the refrigerant. A short while later, the ice from the moisture will thaw and release refrigerant. This can produce a "burp" of pressure that will blow oil out of any open line. This problem can be eliminated by either recovering the refrigerant at a slower pace, leaving the recovery equipment attached to the system for a longer time period, or by heating the accumulator or receiver–drier during the recovery process.

Filter Out Sealant, Dye, & Lubricant

FIGURE 15-9 A Recycle Guard can remove sealant, dye, and oil from the refrigerant as it is being recovered. *(Courtesy of Airsept)*

Output Valve
--Pure refrigerant exits to your recovery equipment

Input Valve
--Contaminated refrigerant enters filter

Control Knob allows filter bypass --Use for Recovery or Charging

Traps sealant, dye, and lubricant in canister

State-of-the-Art High Porosity Filter --Inexpensive filter can be replaced in under five minutes

Recycle Guard™

Easy cleanout contaminant drain

◀ SERVICE TIP ▶

Recovering refrigerant from a system that has a leak can cause serious air contamination in the recovered refrigerant. Most recovery units are designed to shut themselves off when the system develops a slight vacuum after all of the refrigerant has been recovered. If there is a loose hose connection or a leak in the system, it will not reach a vacuum, and the unit becomes an air pump that pulls in air through the leak and moves it into the recovery tank. The recovery process should be monitored so it can be stopped manually if the system pressure does not drop properly. It is very difficult to remove excess air from refrigerant that is overly saturated with air.

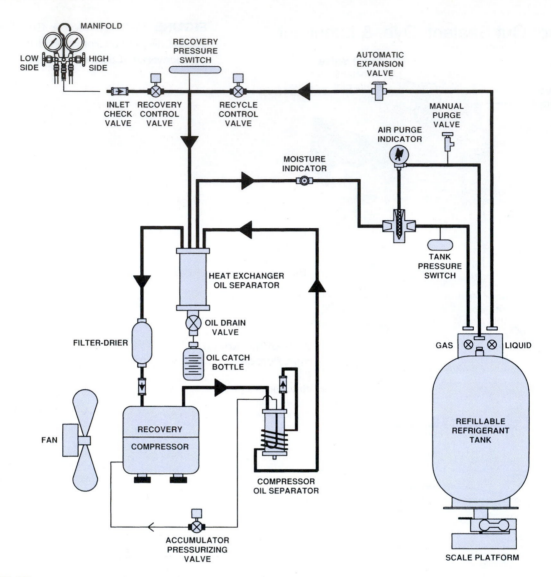

FIGURE 15-10 The flow diagram for a recovery-recycling machine showing the internal components and the path that refrigerant takes during recovery and recycling. *(Courtesy of Robinair, SPX Corporation)*

◄ **SAFETY NOTE** ►

Some vehicles with electronic fuel injection have a fuel pressure test port that uses a 1/4-inch flare fitting, the same as an R-12 service port. Make sure that the refrigerant recovery unit is connected into the A/C system and not the fuel system.

The storage container for recovered refrigerant must be approved by the Department of Transportation (DOT) and carry the letters *DOT* and the certification numbers. Also note the date of tank manufacture; as described in Section 5.3.2, recovery tanks must be inspected and certified to be in good condition every 5 years. The container in Figure 15-11 has two hand valves, a blue valve for liquid and a red valve for vapor.

Some rules to follow for refrigerant recovery are:

- Do not reuse disposable cylinders.
- Make sure that the recovery cylinder is labeled for the refrigerant being recovered.
- Make sure the **tank certification** is in order and the cylinder retest date has not expired.
- Inspect the cylinder for damage; do not fill a damaged cylinder.

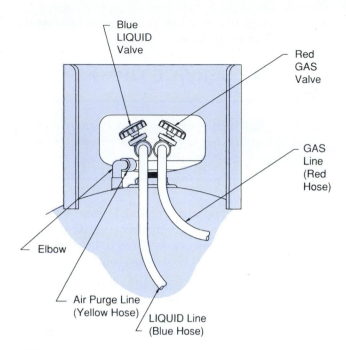

FIGURE 15-11 The container used for recovered refrigerant must be approved by the DOT; the connections to the recovery unit are shown here. *(Courtesy of Robinair, SPX Corporation)*

- Make sure the measuring scale is accurate.
- Make sure the cylinder is free-standing on the scale with no restriction of free movement.

To recover the refrigerant from a system, you should:

1. Identify the refrigerant in the system.
2. Make sure the hoses have the proper shutoff valves and are compatible with the refrigerant in the system. Check to make sure all valves are shut off.
3. Connect the recovery unit to the system or to the center hose of the manifold gauge set, following the directions of the manufacturer and the precautions in Section 12.2.3 (Figure 15-12).
4. Open the required valves and turn the machine on to start the recovery process, following the directions of the machine's manufacturer (Figure 15-13). Note the receiver–drier or accumulator; frost formation indicates that refrigerant is boiling out of the oil contained in the receiver–drier or accumulator.
5. Continue the recovery until the machine shuts off or the pressure reading has dropped into a

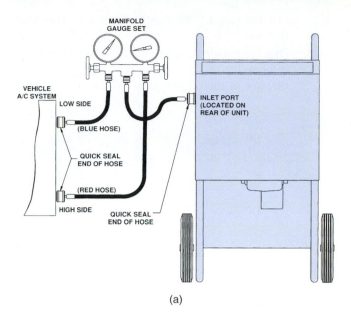

(a)

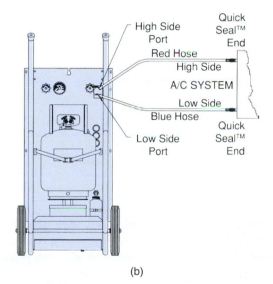

(b)

FIGURE 15-12 Some recovery units use a single hose connection for the center service hose of a manifold gauge set (*a*). A full-service unit has two service hose connections to the low and high sides of the A/C system (*b*). *(Courtesy of Robinair, SPX Corporation)*

vacuum. If the system does not drop into a vacuum, it probably has an air leak; manually stop the recovery process.

6. Verify complete recovery by shutting off all valves and watching the system pressure. If pressure rises above 0 psi within 5 minutes, repeat steps 4 and 5 to recover the remaining refrigerant.
7. With all of the valves shut off, disconnect the recovery unit. If the unit is also equipped to

evacuate and recharge the system, disregard this step.

8. Drain, measure, and record the amount of oil removed from the system with the refrigerant; dispose of the oil properly (Figure 15-14). This

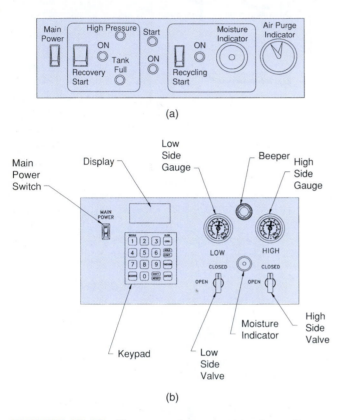

(a)

(b)

FIGURE 15-13 The control panels vary depending on the capabilities of a particular recovery-only, recovery and recycling (*a*), or full-service (*b*) machine. *(Courtesy of Robinair, SPX Corporation)*

FIGURE 15-14 During the recovery process, oil from the system is separated into a container so the technician will know how much oil was removed. *(Courtesy of Robinair, SPX Corporation)*

amount of new oil should be added during the recharging process.

◀ **SERVICE TIP** ▶

Recovery can be speeded up and made more complete by heating the accumulator or receiver–drier with a heat gun or hair dryer.

The system can now be repaired. Present standards and good work habits require that recovered refrigerant be recycled before reuse, even if it is to be returned to the system from which it was recovered.

15.3.3.1 Recovering Contaminated Refrigerant
Special procedures should be followed when you need to remove a contaminated or a blend refrigerant from a system. You should not use an R-12 or R-134a recovery machine to remove a contaminated or a blend refrigerant. As with a gauge set, an R-12 machine can be converted to recover blends, but this machine should be used only for blends unless it is decontaminated after each usage. If the mixture contains more than 4% hydrocarbon, it should be considered explosive, and this mixture should not be recovered using an electric-powered machine. Air-powered recovery machines are available and can be safely used for explosive mixtures.

Hydrocarbon refrigerants, blends, and unknown mixtures should be recovered into containers clearly labeled CONTAMINATED REFRIGERANT. The proper color for these containers is gray with a yellow top. Recovery of contaminated refrigerant using a recovery machine is essentially the same as recovering unconta-

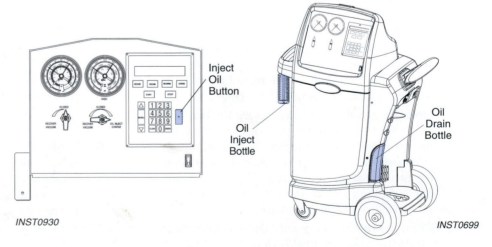

INST0930

Control Panel

INST0699

Diagram of the Oil Injection System

minated refrigerant except that the contaminated material must be sent off for disposal or off-site recycling.

Refrigerant recovery without a machine using the following procedure is *not* a truly effective process.

> *To recover contaminated refrigerant without using a recovery machine, you should:*

1. Connect a gauge set to the system.
2. Connect the container for the recovered mixture to the center hose and place the container in a larger, tublike container with ice to chill it as much as possible.
3. Open the high and low side gauge valves and allow the mixture to leave the system.
4. Start the engine, disconnect the compressor clutch wire, and turn on the system to high heat and high blower to warm it up as much as possible.
5. When recovery is completed as much as possible, close all valves, shut the system and engine off, and ship the recovered mixture to an approved refrigerant reclaimer.

15.3.4   Recycling Refrigerant

Most recycling units pump the recovered refrigerant through a very fine filter to remove foreign particles, past a desiccant to remove water, and through an oil separator to remove any excess oil. Air is removed by venting it, using the noncondensable purge, from the top of the liquid refrigerant. Remember that recycled refrigerant must meet the same purity standards as new (virgin) refrigerant: less than 15 ppm moisture, less than 4,000 ppm oil, and less than 330 ppm air. Some machines have a sight glass equipped with a moisture indicator so that the operator can tell when the moisture has been removed. Some are designed to stop operation if a filter or desiccant change is needed. Some can perform the recycling process in a single pass from the storage container through the cleaning process and back to the storage container; these machines often complete the recycling process while the system is being evacuated. Others require several passes, and the recovery process continues to circulate the refrigerant as long as necessary (Figure 15-15).

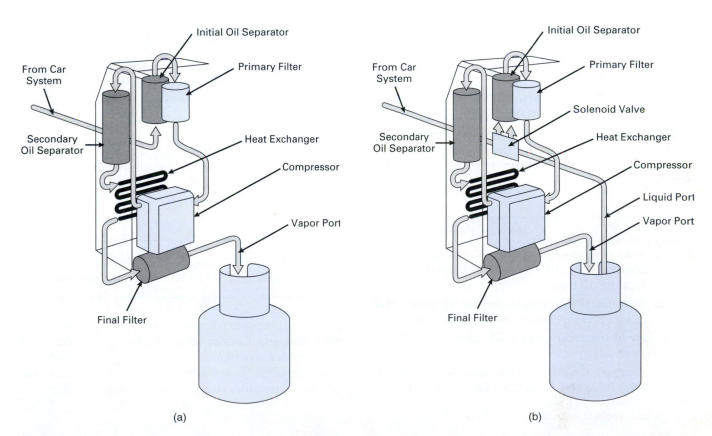

(a) (b)

FIGURE 15-15   A single-pass recycling machine (*a*) cleans and filters the refrigerant as it is being recovered. A multipass machine (*b*) recovers the refrigerant in one operation and then cycles the refrigerant through filters and separators in another operation.

The recycling machine is dedicated to a particular type of refrigerant, and a recycled blend can only be recharged back into the vehicle it came from or another vehicle from the same fleet.

To recycle refrigerant, you should:

1. Open the valves or perform the programming steps required by the machine manufacturer and turn on the machine.
2. The machine operates until excess foreign particles and water have been removed or for a programmed length of time and then shuts off. Check the moisture indicator to ensure that the refrigerant is dry. If the machine does not shut off in the proper amount of time, its internal filters or desiccant probably require service (Figure 15-16).

◀ SERVICE TIP ▶

Sometimes all of the air will not be removed in one recycling pass. Repeat the recycling as needed to remove all of the excess air.

15.3.4.1 Air Contamination Checks   After recovery is completed, you can check for excess air in the refrigerant by evaluating the **pressure–temperature** relationship (PT). This is best done after the temperature has stabilized through the liquid refrigerant; the start of the workday is an ideal time.

To check the PT relationship, you should:

1. Keep the storage container at a temperature above 65°F (21°C) and away from direct sunlight for 12 hours.
2. Read the pressure in the container using a calibrated pressure gauge with 1-psi increments.
3. Read the temperature of the air next to the container.
4. Compare the pressure and temperature readings with Table 15-1 for R-12 or Table 15-2 for R-134a.

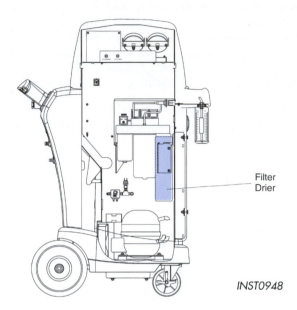

Filter
Drier

INST0948

Location of the Filter-Drier
(a)

(b)

FIGURE 15-16   Recycling machines have a filter and desiccant that must be replaced after a certain amount of use (*a*). These parts are available from various sources (*b*). *(Courtesy of Robinair, SPX Corporation)*

NOTE: All of the pressures are referenced for sea level. These pressures will be lower at higher elevations.

If the pressure for a particular temperature is less than that given in the table, the refrigerant does not contain an excess amount of air and is considered uncontaminated. If the pressure is greater than that given in the table, slowly vent or purge gas from the

TABLE 15-1   **If the pressure of a container of R-12 exceeds that shown here for a particular temperature, the refrigerant is contaminated, probably with air (SAE 1989).**

Temp. (°F)	psig	Temp. (°F)	psig	Temp. (°F)	psig	Temp. (°F)	psig	Temp. (°F)	psig
65	74	75	87	85	102	95	118	105	136
66	75	76	88	86	103	96	120	106	138
67	76	77	90	87	105	97	122	107	140
68	78	78	92	88	107	98	124	108	142
69	79	79	94	89	108	99	125	109	144
70	80	80	96	90	110	100	127	110	146
71	82	81	98	91	111	101	129	111	148
72	83	82	99	92	113	102	130	112	150
73	84	83	100	93	115	103	132	113	152
74	86	84	101	94	116	104	134	114	154

(Reprinted with permission from SAE Document M-106, © 1992, Society of Automotive Engineers, Inc.)

TABLE 15-2   **If the pressure of a container of R-134a exceeds that shown here for a particular temperature, the refrigerant is contaminated, probably with air (SAE J2211).**

Temp. (°F)	psig	Temp. (°F)	psig	Temp. (°F)	psig	Temp. (°F)	psig
65	69	79	90	93	115	107	144
66	70	80	91	94	117	108	146
67	71	81	93	95	118	109	149
68	73	82	95	96	120	110	151
69	74	83	96	97	122	111	153
70	76	84	98	98	125	112	156
71	77	85	100	99	127	113	158
72	79	86	102	100	129	114	160
73	80	87	103	101	131	115	163
74	82	88	105	102	133	116	165
75	83	89	107	103	135	117	168
76	85	90	109	104	137	118	171
77	86	91	111	105	139	119	173
78	88	92	113	106	142	120	176

(Reprinted with permission from SAE Document M-106, © 1992, Society of Automotive Engineers, Inc.)

top of the container (red valve) until the pressure drops below that given in the table. If the pressure does not drop, the refrigerant must be recycled or sent off for disposal or recovery. A recent development is a two-gauge unit that attaches onto the re-covery container. One gauge is a pressure gauge that shows the actual refrigerant pressure; the other gauge is a thermometer calibrated to show the ideal pressure. Excess air is indicated if the actual pressure is higher (Figure 15-17).

FIGURE 15-17 This dual-gauge set has a pressure gauge and a thermometer calibrated to read the pressure that should correspond to that temperature. A comparison of the two indicates refrigerant purity. *(Courtesy of Mastercool)*

An air purge is a manual or automatic operation that can take place during the recycle process of some recycling machines (see Figure 15-18). Air purge is an automatic operation in some machines that occurs during the evacuation cycle; shortcutting the evacuation time can cause an incomplete air purge. If recycling is attempted with contaminated refrigerants or some blends, the entire mix can be dumped as the machine attempts to purge air.

When the air purge operates, some refrigerant boils off as the pressure drops, and this boiling absorbs heat and lowers the liquid temperature, which in turn lowers the pressure. This drop in pressure can make you falsely believe that you have purged all of the air. With refrigerant that is severely contaminated with air, it is thought that some of the excess air is contained in the liquid, not just sitting on top of it, making it much more difficult to purge. If you encounter this, you should make a partial air purge and then let the PT relationship stabilize over a period of time. Then you can recheck the PT and purge again if necessary.

A new unit that monitors refrigerant optically automatically bleeds out excess air (Figure 15-18). One unit is designed to be used directly on an A/C system, a recovery–recycling machine, or a refrigerant container; some units are intended to be used only on containers. Air purge units bleed off or "burp" the air in short cycles

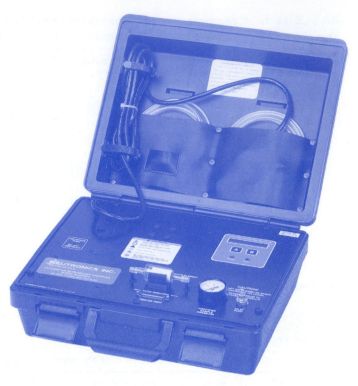

FIGURE 15-18 This automatic air purge tool can be connected to an A/C system or bottle of refrigerant. It checks for air contamination, automatically purges a small amount of gas, and repeats this process. *(Reprinted by permission of Neutronics Inc.)*

and then monitor the remaining gas, repeating the purge cycles as necessary.

15.3.5 Flushing an A/C System

When a compressor fails, it usually sends solid compressor particles into the high and possibly the low sides, and this material can plug the condenser passages and OT. It is always a good practice to check the OT or TXV filter screen for debris when there is a compressor failure and to flush the system, install a filter, or both before completing the job.

◄ **SERVICE TIP** ►

Debris from a failed compressor is often a fine, black material called *goo* or **black death** by many technicians. This mixture of small particles of aluminum and Teflon mixed with refrigerant oil will be trapped between the compressor discharge port and the orifice tube. It is very difficult to flush out, especially from a modern condenser.

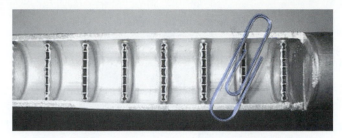

FIGURE 15-19 This condenser has been cut open to show how small the passages are when compared to an ordinary paper clip. Flushing is not an effective way to clean them.

◄ **SERVICE TIP** ►

No flushing operation will remove 100% of metal debris from a failed compressor. The very small metal particles can only be stopped by a filter.

Flushing is done by pumping a liquid material through the passages in a reverse or normal flow direction. A gas such as shop air or nitrogen is not really effective in removing solid material; remember that many condensers have very small passages that can be easily clogged and that air can bypass a clogged passage (Figure 15-19). Flushing agents can be a commercial flushing solution, liquid refrigerant, or very lightweight ester oil; ester oil has very little or no solvent action for solid particles, and remaining ester oil might be difficult to remove from the system. A compressor cannot be flushed. An accumulator or receiver–drier is usually not flushed; it is simply replaced. There is some question about whether an evaporator should be flushed; most experts believe that the OT or TXV screen will filter out larger debris. Most flushing is done on the high side, from the compressor connection of the discharge line to the OT or receiver–drier fitting of the liquid line or vice versa (Figure 15-20).

◄ **SERVICE TIP** ►

It is very difficult or impossible to flush a modern flat-tube condenser with its multiple, small passages. One or more of the small passages can be plugged so the flush material will pass through any open passages.

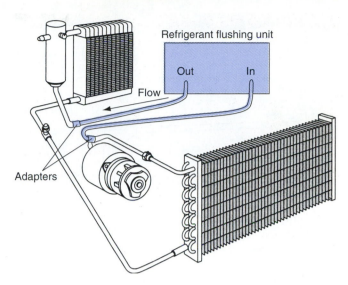

FIGURE 15-20 Portions of an A/C system can be flushed to remove debris and excess oil. Adapters are used to connect a flushing unit, which pumps the flushing material through the components.

◄ **SERVICE TIP** ►

If flushing a system using air pressure, the air must be clean. Shop air often contains oil and metal debris from the air lines, and these can contaminate the system being cleaned. Experienced technicians recommend using bottled nitrogen gas, which is clean and inert.

At this time, there are two schools of thought on how to flush. One is to use a solvent to clean the discharge line, condenser, and liquid line up to the OT or receiver–drier (Figure 15-21). A solvent is effective in dissolving foreign material, but contamination and later problems may result if all of the solvent is not removed from the system. The other procedure uses liquid refrigerant to flush the entire system (except for the compressor) from the suction line at the compressor inlet to the discharge line at the compressor outlet. A refrigerant flush removes most solid particles and oil, and it is fairly easy to remove all of the refrigerant from the system. Most recovery–recycling machines can be fitted with a flushing kit that allows them to pump liquid refrigerant into one line and recover that refrigerant from the other line (Figure 15-22).

The flushing process requires an adapter fitting at each of the connections; these fittings can be made in the shop or purchased (Figure 15-23). It also requires a

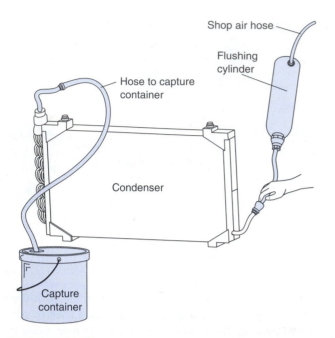

FIGURE 15-21 A/C components can also be flushed using a portable tool kit and special adapters. The flush is forced through the condenser using shop air pressure.

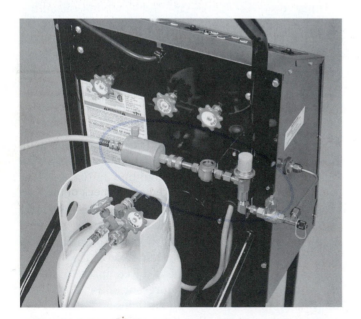

FIGURE 15-22 This recovery and recycling system has an optional flushing kit that uses recovered refrigerant to flush a system clean. The refrigerant is then recycled for reuse. *(Courtesy of Robinair, SPX Corporation)*

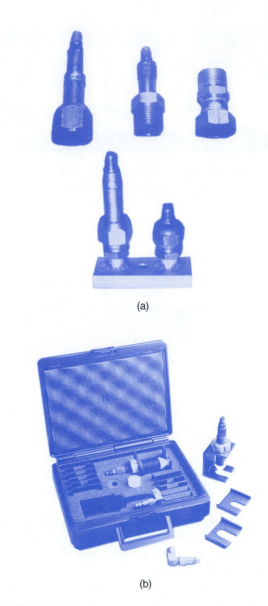

(a)

(b)

FIGURE 15-23 Adapters to connect the flushing unit into the system can be commercial fittings (*a*) or fittings made in the shop (*b*). *(a courtesy of MACS; b courtesy of Robinair, SPX Corporation)*

container for the flushing agent and a way to force it into the line; some systems use a pump, and others use shop air pressure (Figure 15-24). Because the flushing agent is either expensive or has ozone-depleting or greenhouse-effect gas restrictions, a catch container is connected to the outlet end to capture it. The liquid flushing agent is then forced through the condenser and lines until as much of the debris as possible is removed.

FIX

A check of the TXV showed that it was plugged again. Removal of the liquid line allowed a thorough cleaning, removed all of the desiccant particles, and fixed this problem.

AUTHOR'S NOTE

The liquid line could have been flushed or a filter installed earlier in this repair to prevent some of the problems from occurring. I'm not sure why the new TXV was replaced instead of being cleaned.

◄ **SERVICE TIP** ►

If you suspect that a system has too much oil in it, flush the system using liquid refrigerant, and add the specified amount of oil for the system.

◄ **SERVICE TIP** ►

Some technicians place a paper coffee filter to catch the debris in the flush material going to the catch container. This allows them to inspect the material being flushed from the system and to determine the effectiveness of the flushing process.

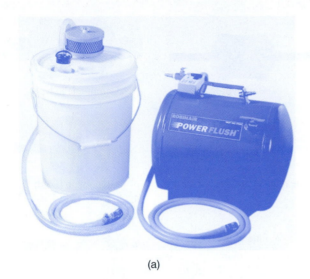

(a)

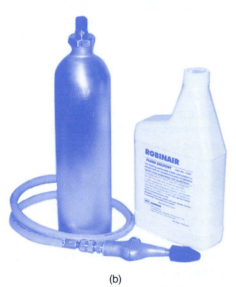

(b)

FIGURE 15-24 The power flush unit (with catch container at left) forces the flushing solvent through the lines in a pulsating manner (a); the operator of the flush gun (b) controls the flow at the nozzle. *(Courtesy of Robinair, SPX Corporation)*

REAL WORLD FIX: The 1990 Infiniti (87,000 miles) came in with no A/C because of a leaking evaporator. The system was recharged, but it still did not cool. The pressures were 25 psi on the low side and 110 psi on the high side. The compressor and TXV were replaced using OEM parts, but the pressures stayed the same and there was still no cooling. Checking the parts that were just installed showed the new TXV plugged with desiccant, so the TXV and receiver–drier were replaced. After recharging again, the same problem was found.

REAL WORLD FIX: The 1993 Jaguar (170,000 miles) came in with no A/C. The high side pressure was slightly low, and the low side pressure would drop into a vacuum. The pressures would equalize when the system was shut off. The refrigerant was recovered, and a check of the TXV showed desiccant pellets. The receiver–drier and the TXV were replaced, air was blown through the liquid line, and the system was evacuated and recharged. A retest of the system shows almost the same problem: The system cools well for a few minutes, and then the low side pressure drops into a vacuum.

FIX

Flushing the liquid line and installation of a filter along with evacuation and recharging the system fixed this problem.

◀ **SERVICE TIP** ▶

On vehicles with dual evaporators, remember to check the liquid line going to the rear evaporator and TXV for contaminants.

15.3.6 Installing an In-Line Filter

If a compressor fails, debris in the form of metal particles often travels downstream through the condenser and is trapped in the receiver–drier or OT, where it can cause plugging. Some compressor failures send debris into the suction line (see Section 16.2). A similar problem can occur because of scale from a poorly cleaned condenser or evaporator; evaporator scale can damage the compressor. The technician can install a supplementary in-line filter in either the high side or low side. This filter is sometimes changed after an hour of operation and is called **live flushing.** The high side filter is usually placed in the liquid line between the condenser and the receiver–drier or OT, and the low side filter is installed in the suction line to the compressor (see Figure 16-3). In-line filters are available with push-on, barb-type connections for rubber or nylon hoses or compression-type connections for metal tubing. They are available with connections to fit different line sizes. Some filters include a new OT (Figure 15-25).

To install an in-line filter, you should:

1. Recover the refrigerant from the system.
2. Select the location for the filter. The flexibility of hose allows a great deal of freedom. With metal tubing, you need to locate a straight section of tubing slightly longer than the filter's connections.
3. *With hose,* cut out a hose section with a hose cutter, very sharp knife, or sharp utility knife so a neat connection will be made; coat the filter connections with refrigerant oil; firmly push the filter into the hose; and secure the connection using either a screw-type clamp or a metal ferrule ring. (*Note: Push-on, barb-type fittings and screw-type clamps are not approved for R-134a systems.*)

To install an in-line filter in a metal line, you should:

1. Recover the refrigerant from the system.
2. Cut the metal tube using a tube cutter in two places to provide the proper amount of room for the filter.

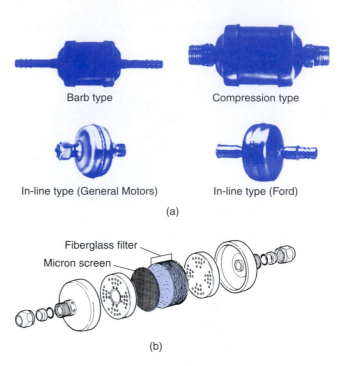

(a)

(b)

FIGURE 15-25 In-line filters are available in different forms, depending on how they will be connected into the system (*a*). An exploded view of an in-line filter is shown in *b*. (*a courtesy of Four Seasons*)

3. Debur the cut ends of the tube.
4. Clean the ends of the tube inside and out; the inside can be cleaned using a cotton swab dipped in mineral oil.
5. Place the filter, ferrules, and nut (without the O-rings) in position, and tighten the nuts to the correct torque to "set" the ferrules.
6. Remove the nuts, wet the O-rings with mineral oil, and slide them into place. Retighten the nuts to the correct torque to complete the installation.

Installation of a compressor suction screen is described in Section 16.2.1.

Hose and tubing connections are described in more detail in Section 16.3.

15.3.7 Checking and Correcting Oil Levels

Too little oil in a system can cause compressor wear and damage. Too much oil can cause excessive low and high side pressures. There is a tendency for some technicians in this industry to add oil when it is not needed, causing an overfill.

Early A/C systems used compressors with oil sumps, and it was relatively easy to check the oil level using a dipstick or the level plug in an A-6 compressor. Most modern compressors do not have an oil sump. The only way to check the amount of oil is to remove the compressor and drain it or to recover the refrigerant and note how much oil comes out. You should also note that it is almost impossible to drain all of the oil out of a compressor or evaporator because of the internal shape or out of an accumulator or receiver–drier because of the oil absorbed in the desiccant bag.

◀ **SERVICE TIP** ▶

An observant technician gets a good idea of the oil charge when he or she opens a line connection, like an orifice tube, and looks inside. It should always be damp with oil. A dry OT indicates low oil charge. One that is dripping with oil indicates too much oil.

◀ **SERVICE TIP** ▶

Some technicians drain the accumulator or receiver–drier and measure the amount of oil. If 6 or 8 ounces of oil come out when 3/4 ounce was expected to drain, the system has too much oil. If very little oil comes out, the system is oil starved.

The proper amount of oil can be kept in a system by adding oil to replace the amount of oil removed when a component is replaced. This is usually only a small amount as shown in Figure 16-61. Compressor replacement requires a slightly larger amount as described in Section 16.2.6.

There is a procedure to check the volume of oil charge in the refrigerant, and one manufacturer, Seltec, recommends a charge of 3 to 6% oil to properly lubricate its compressors. This procedure uses the weight of the refrigerant with its oil charge, and it requires a service port close to and upstream of the TXV or OT, an empty, generic oil charge container, and a scale that is accurate to a gram.

To determine oil charge, you should:

1. Attach the empty container and valve to a vacuum pump, and pull a deep vacuum. Close the valve, remove from the pump, and weigh the container and valve. Record this weight.

2. Run the A/C system and allow it to stabilize. Attach the container to the liquid line service port, and open the valve to allow the internal vacuum to pull in refrigerant from the system. Close the container, and disconnect it from the system.

3. Weigh the container of refrigerant with the oil it contains and record this weight.

4. Connect the container to a recovery unit and recover the refrigerant. This should remove the refrigerant but leave the oil.

5. Weigh the container and remaining oil and record this weight.

6. Subtract the weight of the container (step 1) from the weight of the container and refrigerant (step 3). The result is the weight of the refrigerant with oil. Record this weight.

7. Subtract the weight of the container (step 1) from the weight of the container with oil (step 5). The result is the weight of the oil that was contained in the refrigerant. Record this weight.

8. Divide the weight of the oil (step 7) by the weight of refrigerant (step 6). Multiply this by 100 to obtain the percentage of oil.

◀ **SERVICE TIP** ▶

Do not let PAG oil contact the vehicle's painted surfaces. PAG can damage paint.

◀ **SERVICE TIP** ▶

You can test the oil in a system by placing a few drops into water. Mineral and ester oils will react like normal oils and form floating beads. Some PAGS will dissolve into the water and disappear; other PAGS will form a film layer beneath the surface of the water.

15.3.8 Evacuating a System

Evacuating is also called *pumping the system down.* After a system has been repaired, all of the air and moisture that might have entered must be removed. Removing air is fairly easy; it is simply pumped out by the vacuum pump. Water removal is more difficult because it must be boiled and the water vapor pumped out with the vacuum pump. The water boils because of the reduced pressure in a vacuum; Figure 15-26 shows the

Temperature (°F)	Vacuum (inches)	Microns*	Pressure (psi)
212	0.00	759,968	14,696
205	4.92	535,000	12.279
194	9.23	525,526	10.162
176	15.94	355,092	6.866
158	20.72	233,680	4.519
140	24.04	149,352	2.888
122	26.28	92,456	1.788
104	27.75	55,118	1.066
86	28.67	31,750	0.614
80	28.92	25,400	0.491
76	29.02	22,860	0.442
72	29.12	20,320	0.393
69	29.22	17,780	0.344
64	29.32	15,240	0.295
59	29.42	12,700	0.246
53	29.52	10,160	0.196
45	29.62	7,620	0.147
32	29.74	4,572	0.088
21	29.82	2,540	0.049
6	29.87	1,270	0.0245
−24	29.91	254	0.0049
−35	29.915	127	0.00245
−60	29.919	25.4	0.00049
−70	29.9195	12.7	0.00024
−90	29.9199	2.54	0.000049

*Remaining pressure in systems in microns:
1.000 inch = 25,400 microns = 2.540 cm = 25.40 mm
0.100 inch = 2,540 microns = 0.254 cm = 2.54 mm
0.039 inch = 1,000 microns = 0.100 cm = 1.00 mm

FIGURE 15-26 The boiling point of water is reduced as a system is put into a vacuum. Microns provide a much more accurate way of measuring vacuum. *(Courtesy of Robinair, SPX Corporation)*

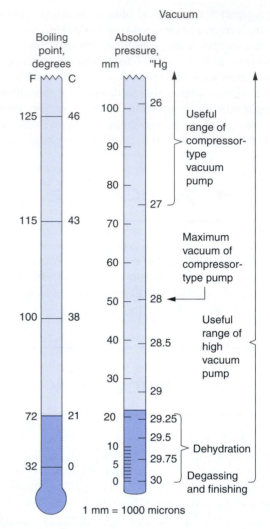

FIGURE 15-27 Vacuum pumps differ in their ability to remove all of the refrigerant and water from a system.

boiling points. Note that it takes a vacuum of 28″ Hg or lower to boil water at room temperature.

Vacuum pumps are rated by both **cubic feet per minute (cfm)** and **micron** ratings. The cfm rating tells us the volume it can pump; the micron rating tells us how deep a vacuum it can pull. An automotive A/C system requires about a 1.2- to 1.5-cfm rating, whereas a larger system used in a bus or truck needs about a 5- to 6-cfm vacuum pump. Using a vacuum pump that is too small requires a much longer evacuation time, which causes excess wear on the vacuum pump. A perfect vacuum is 29.92″ Hg, or 0 microns (a micron is equal to one-millionth of a meter). The micron rating of a vacuum pump tells us how deep a vacuum it can pull under field conditions—the lower the better. For example, a

vacuum pump that pulls down to only 27″ Hg (685,800 microns) is only effective on temperatures above 110°F (43°C). A good vacuum pump will pull a system down to under 500 microns (29.90″ Hg); this drops the boiling point of water to around 0°F (−18°C) (Figure 15-27).

◀ **SERVICE TIP** ▶

If your plan is to remove water from a system, remember that there is no way to reliably determine how much water is in a system. We only have indicators. Because of this, there is no accurate way to determine how long to evacuate a system. The best approach is to put new desiccant in the system by replacing the accumulator or receiver–drier, and

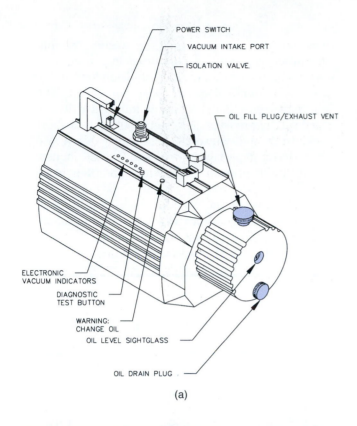

POWER SWITCH
VACUUM INTAKE PORT
ISOLATION VALVE.
OIL FILL PLUG/EXHAUST VENT
ELECTRONIC VACUUM INDICATORS
DIAGNOSTIC TEST BUTTON
WARNING: CHANGE OIL
OIL LEVEL SIGHTGLASS
OIL DRAIN PLUG

(a)

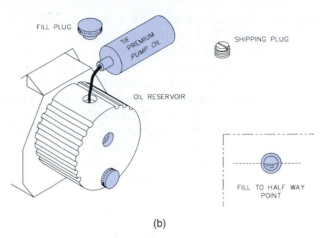

FILL PLUG
SHIPPING PLUG
TIF PREMIUM PUMP OIL
OIL RESERVOIR
FILL TO HALF WAY POINT

(b)

FIGURE 15-28 This vacuum pump includes an oil change warning light (*a*). Old oil is drained out, and new oil is added to the correct level (*b*). (*Courtesy of TIF Instruments*)

evacuate the system down to 500 microns to remove all noncondensables and any free moisture. Long evacuations do no harm to a system, but they take more time and probably add wear to the vacuum pump.

◀ SERVICE TIP ▶

One technician recommends comparing the reading in microns to the atmospheric pressure for that day. If the barometric atmospheric pressure is 29.99, a vacuum of 28.49″ Hg (95%) is good enough. At this point, there is no need to evacuate any longer and wear out the vacuum pump.

◀ SERVICE TIP ▶

If a system is evacuated to 500 microns, the boiling point of water will be 0°F. With the vacuum pump shut off and the valves closed, the pressure will possibly increase because any water in the system will boil and become vapor.

◀ SERVICE TIP ▶

A vacuum pump can be tested to see if it will boil water. Connect a service port to the lid of a glass jar (many 16- to 32-oz food jars will work), and connect this to the vacuum pump inlet. Add about an inch of water into the container, and connect the lid tightly. Start the vacuum pump, and observe the water. If it boils, the pump is good. It is recommended to change the oil because of the water that entered the pump. If the water does not boil, try changing the oil in the vacuum pump, and repeat the test to see if that fixes it.

A vacuum pump must be maintained with the proper oil level and periodic oil changes to ensure proper operation. If service is neglected, it will not pump to its design capabilities. Some modern electronic units flash a warning if the oil has not been changed at the proper interval (about 10 hours) (Figure 15-28).

New refrigerant service machines are equipped with oil-less vacuum pumps. These units eliminate the need to service the vacuum pump. One particular pump is a two-stage pump that is rated at 95% of barometric pressure; it will pull a 29″ vacuum in a 29.2 atmosphere. To run without lubricating oil, the pump uses two high-temperature plastic pistons operating in anodized aluminum cylinders with a Teflon-type cup seal. The piston and connecting rod are one piece. The crankshaft and connecting rod bearings use a lubricated and sealed ball bearing.

It is accepted practice to evacuate an automotive system for 20 to 30 minutes. This time can be shortened on a dry system and should be lengthened on a wet system. The longer evacuation helps ensure proper long-term system operation.

◀ SERVICE TIP ▶

Some compressors have the service ports mounted very low on the side of the compressor. This position allows the vacuum pump to draw the oil out of the compressor. When evacuating a system with this service port location, check to see if you have pulled out a significant amount of oil; if so, replace it with new oil.

If the system is contaminated with moisture, it is accepted trade practice to replace the accumulator or receiver–drier and, if there is metal or debris, to install an in-line filter.

◀ SERVICE TIP ▶

At the end of your selected time period for evacuation, shut off the vacuum pump, close the manifold valves, and after a few minutes check the low side gauge for a pressure rise. An increase in pressure indicates either something—refrigerant or water—is changing state to become a gas or that there is a leak.

◀ SERVICE TIP ▶

Experience can teach you how to tell a wet system from a dry system by watching the low side pressure drop during evacuation. This pressure drop depends on the rating of the vacuum pump,

size of the system, and any water (or oil-absorbed refrigerant) contained in the system. As water or refrigerant boils, it produces a much greater volume of gas to be pumped out. The more gas there is to pump, the longer it will take to drop the pressure. A system that takes a short time to drop down to 28″ Hg is fairly dry. A system that pumps right down to 20 to 26 inches, holds at this pressure for a while, and then drops to 28 inches probably contained a liquid that boiled out while the vacuum dropped from 20 to 28 inches. It is good practice to continue evacuation for at least 15 to 20 minutes after the pressure has dropped to its lowest reading.

◀ SERVICE TIP ▶

Vacuum readings are affected by altitude and the drop in atmospheric pressure that occurs. At 1,000 feet (305 m) above sea level, a complete vacuum is 28.92″ Hg, about 1″ Hg less than at sea level. This pressure will increase at a rate of about 1″ Hg per 1,000-foot elevation increase.

◀ SERVICE TIP ▶

If you suspect a low side restriction, open the low side manifold valve and evacuate through the low side with the high side valve closed. If the high side does not pull down into a vacuum along with the low side, there is a restriction. If the high side pulls down properly, open the high side manifold valve and complete the evacuation.

◀ SERVICE TIP ▶

Self-contained digital vacuum gauges, capable of indicating very low readings, are available (Figure 15-29). These gauges are normally connected directly to the system service port.

To evacuate a system using a manifold gauge set and portable vacuum pump, you should:

1. Connect the manifold service hoses to the system service ports if necessary; normally these are still connected from the recovery process. There should be no or very little pressure in the system. Connect the center service hose to the vacuum pump inlet (Figure 15-30).

2. Open both manifold valves completely (and the vacuum pump valve if there is one) and start the vacuum pump. You should notice an air discharge from the vacuum pump and a drop in gauge pressures.

3. Check the gauge pressures periodically. After about 5 minutes, the pressure should be lower than 20″ Hg. A leak is usually the cause if the pressure has not dropped this low. You can confirm a leak by closing all valves, shutting off the vacuum pump, and watching the pressure. If it steadily increases, there is a leak that must be located and repaired before continuing.

4. Continue evacuation for the desired length of time, close all valves, shut off the vacuum pump, and note the low side pressure (Figure 15-31).

5. After 5 minutes, recheck the low side pressure. If the vacuum held steady, the system is good and ready to be recharged. If the low side pressure increased, a possible leak is indicated; note the comments in Section 12.3.1.

When using an A/C service unit, evacuation is often simply a matter of flipping a switch, assuming the service hoses are still connected from the recovery operation. Some modern stations use electric solenoids to control the flow inside the machine, and starting the evacuation process opens the solenoids needed for this process. Some also include a microprocessor that can be programmed to run the vacuum pump for the desired length of time. Some older charging stations are purely mechanical; on these units, the proper valves must be opened as the vacuum pump is started (Figure 15-32).

Display

FIGURE 15-29 This digital, micron vacuum gauge can display a vacuum reading of 1 to 760,000 microns in 1-micron increments. It can also display vacuum in Pascal or millibar units. *(Courtesy of INFICON)*

FIGURE 15-30 This portable vacuum pump is connected to the center service hose. Both gauge valves are open during the evacuation process. *(Courtesy of Daimler-Chrysler Corporation)*

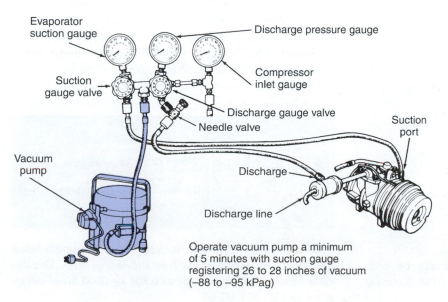

Evaporator suction gauge

Discharge pressure gauge

Suction gauge valve

Compressor inlet gauge

Discharge gauge valve

Needle valve

Suction port

Vacuum pump

Discharge

Discharge line

Operate vacuum pump a minimum of 5 minutes with suction gauge registering 26 to 28 inches of vacuum (−88 to −95 kPag)

FIGURE 15-31 After the proper amount of time at 28″ Hg of vacuum, the vacuum pump is shut off and the manifold valves are closed. A tight system holds this vacuum for at least 5 minutes. *(Courtesy of Nissan Motor Corporation in USA)*

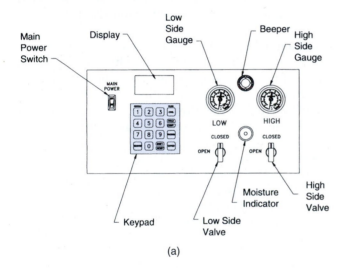

(a)

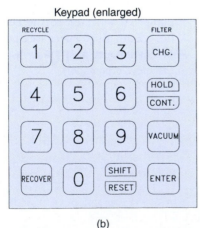

(b)

FIGURE 15-32 Some charging stations can be programmed to vacuum a system for a certain period. *(Courtesy of Robinair, SPX Corporation)*

15.3.9 Recharging a System

After the system has been evacuated, it can be recharged with the correct amount of new or recycled refrigerant. Charge level is system specific, and as the volume of HVAC systems has been downsized, the amount of refrigerant has become critical. The charge level is normally found on a specification decal fastened to some location under the hood; on many modern vehicles, this decal tells both the type and volume of refrigerant used. The decal is attached to the compressor on some older systems. If the decal is missing or illegible, charge specifications are also given in service manuals published by the vehicle manufacturer and aftermarket A/C component suppliers (Figure 15-33).

The best method to charge a system is to start with an empty system and charge in the specified amount as measured by accurate scales. When systems were larger, refrigerant was cheaper, and environmental concerns were not as great, **partial charging** or **topping off** was a common practice: Refrigerant was added to a system with a low charge level.

Partial charging is no longer a recommended practice for several reasons:

- The leak in the system should be located and repaired to stop refrigerant loss into the atmosphere.
- It is very easy to overcharge a system as the partial charge is added. Older systems with large receiver–driers and accumulators had a tolerance for slight overcharges that newer systems do not have.

FIGURE 15-33 Modern vehicles include an under-hood decal that shows refrigerant type and charge level. This decal indicates a factory charge of 0.907 kg (2.00 lb) of refrigerant and SP-20 PAG oil.

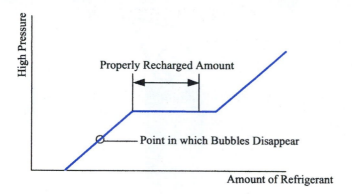

FIGURE 15-34 The bubbles in a sight glass will disappear at a point lower than the proper charge amount. High side pressure will increase at a point that the system is already overcharged. *(Courtesy of Toyota Motor Sales USA, Inc.)*

An overcharge causes excessively high pressures that can damage the system and cause refrigerant release through the pressure relief valve (Figure 15-34).

- A nonprofessional might have added the wrong refrigerant and contaminated the system.
- Topping off is illegal in some areas and countries.

Now that recovery and recycling equipment is common, it is relatively easy to remove and recycle the system's refrigerant, repair any leaks, and recharge the system with the specified amount of new or recycled refrigerant. This gives a much more reliable repair and removes the guesswork of partial charging.

REAL WORLD FIX: The front TXV (front and rear system) was replaced on the 1993 Dodge Caravan (95,000 miles) and the system was recharged, but the A/C does not cool. The high side pressure is excessive, over 450 psi; the low side pressure is normal. The technician questions if the charge specification is correct at 61 oz.

F I X

Following advice, the technician rechecked his math. He had interpreted the sticker reading of 3.13 to be 3 lbs and 13 oz, which equals 61 oz. It really means 3.13 lbs, or 3.13 × 16 or 50 oz. Recovering the refrigerant and recharging to the proper level of 50 oz fixed this problem.

15.3.9.1 Partial Charging Occasionally partial charging or topping off still has a place with R-12 vehicles if the vehicle owner cannot afford to **retrofit** the vehicle or the value of the vehicle is not worth the cost of a retrofit. Partial charging adds refrigerant into a partially filled system until it has a full charge. The technician usually determines the charge level by watching the sight glass or

watching the high side pressure. Remember from Chapter 12 that neither of these methods is completely reliable in determining charge level. Several things can cause bubbles in the sight glass or affect the high side pressure, and there are two better methods of determining charge level (as described in Section 12.3.5). Also remember that the reason for the low charge level is often a leak, and experienced technicians are very thorough in their attempts to prevent refrigerant leaks, especially of R-12, into the atmosphere.

When performing a partial charge, the following practices are recommended:

- Check the system for leaks; if a leak is found and the cause is located, repair the leak.
- Identify the refrigerant remaining in the system. If the refrigerant is contaminated with air or a foreign refrigerant, fix the system rather than simply charging it.
- Inject fluorescent dye during the partial charge, and call the vehicle back in a week or so to check for a leak. When the leak is located, you can recover the refrigerant, repair the leak, and evacuate and recharge the system.

Partial charging is a continuation of the performance test described in Section 12.3. At step 6, on a system with a low charge level, you will note bubbles or foam in the sight glass or an accumulator that is warmer than normal, system high side pressure that is lower than normal, and poor cooling at the A/C ducts. From this point, with the system operating, the technician slowly charges refrigerant into the low side until the sight glass clears up or the accumulator begins to feel cold at the bottom; then about 1/4 lb of additional refrigerant is added to complete the charge while carefully watching the high-pressure gauge to make sure that the pressure does not increase as the additional refrigerant is added. If the high side pressure or the level of cold air output does not become normal, something else is wrong with the system.

◄ SERVICE TIP ►

Professional service technicians prefer not to top off a system because the system probably has a leak that should be repaired. Also, the system contains an unknown amount of refrigerant, oil, and possible contaminants. It is a much better practice to recover the refrigerant and see how much refrigerant and oil come out. The refrigerant can now be recycled to remove any air that might have been present and then returned to the system along with additional refrigerant to fill the system with the specified amount of clean oil.

REAL WORLD FIX: The 1996 Explorer (95,000 miles) was brought in with a request to add more refrigerant because of poor cooling. The technician informed the customer that he felt it was already overcharged.

FIX

The refrigerant in the system was recovered, and there was 3.25 lbs. The system was recharged to the 1.5-lbs specification, and this fixed the poor cooling problem.

15.3.9.2 Charging from Large Containers

Most shops use larger refrigerant containers, in the 20- to 30-lb size, so the amount to be charged into the system must be measured. The units most commonly used are the **charging cylinder** and **electronic scales.** These can be either individual portable units or parts of a charging station.

The charging cylinder unit, dial-a-charge, uses a clear sight column where the volume of refrigerant is shown. A calibrated shroud around the outside of the unit is dialed or rotated until the graduated numbers for that refrigerant at that pressure (gauge at the top) are next to the sight column. The vertical graduations compensate for volume changes due to temperature. The technician normally adds refrigerant to the charging cylinder until it contains the amount needed for a system; this amount is then charged into the system (Figure 15-35).

Modern service units use electronic scales that can be programmed for the desired charge level. The refrigerant container is placed on the scale, and a hose is used to connect its valve to the scale. The operator then programs in the charge volume desired and starts the charge process. When the proper amount of refrigerant has left the container, an electric solenoid in the unit shuts off the refrigerant flow. These units can also be operated manually, with the operator holding down a button or switch until the desired amount of refrigerant has left the container (Figure 15-36).

Moving the refrigerant into the system requires that the charging container pressure be greater than the system pressure. Because the process begins with the system in a vacuum, the first portion goes rather quickly, but the first 1/2 lb or so fills the internal volume and starts generating pressure. As refrigerant boils and leaves the container, it cools the remaining refrigerant and causes a pressure drop. Many charging stations include heaters for the refrigerant container to raise its internal pressure to help force refrigerant into the system. When heaters are used, the system does not need to be operated. The pressure difference can also be increased by starting the A/C system so the low side pressure drops and then charging only into the low side.

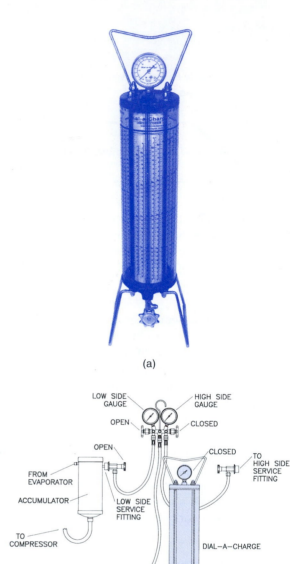

(a)

(b)

FIGURE 15-35 This charging cylinder has a calibrated shroud marked with the refrigerant volumes for different temperatures (*a*). Refrigerant is added to the cylinder from a large container; this amount of refrigerant is then charged into the system (*b*). *(Courtesy of Robinair, SPX Corporation)*

Remember that the high side service unit or manifold valve should never be open while the system is operating. Systems with low-pressure cutout will not operate, and older GM cars with thermal limiter fuses will burn out the fuse, when the charge level is very low. Jumper devices can be used to temporarily bypass these low-pressure protection devices (Figure 15-37).

Unit Controls

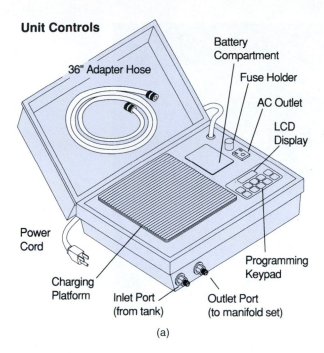

(a)

Hook-Up

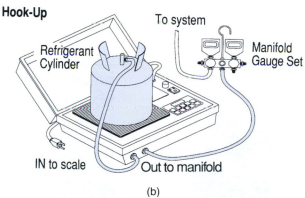

(b)

FIGURE 15-36 This charging scale includes a weighing platform and a shutoff solenoid valve (*a*). The container of refrigerant is placed on the scale, and the unit is programmed to allow the correct amount of refrigerant to enter the system (*b*). *(Courtesy of TIF Instruments)*

◀ **SERVICE TIP** ▶

Some technicians prefer to begin the charging process into the high side (system off). The high side pressure should increase immediately as the valve is opened. There should be a slight delay and a slower low side pressure increase as refrigerant bleeds through the TXV or OT. A pressure increase that is too rapid indicates a possible compressor internal leak; too slow an increase indicates a possible restriction of the TXV or OT (Figure 15-38).

(a)

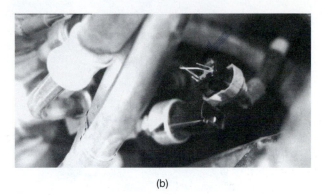

(b)

FIGURE 15-37 This tester and adapter is designed to test GM thermal fuse circuits and to allow bypass of the thermal fuse during charging operations (*a*). A bent paper clip can often be used as a jumper to bypass pressure switches (*b*). *(a courtesy of Four Seasons)*

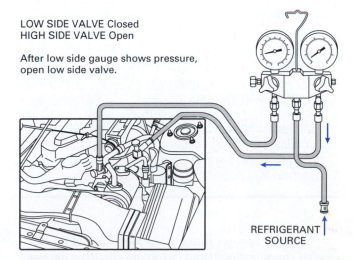

LOW SIDE VALVE Closed
HIGH SIDE VALVE Open

After low side gauge shows pressure, open low side valve.

REFRIGERANT SOURCE

FIGURE 15-38 Some technicians prefer to begin the charging procedure by adding pressure to the high side; a pressure increase in the low side should begin a few seconds later as the refrigerant passes through the expansion device.

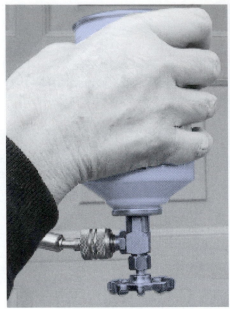 

Charging Liquid   **Charging Vapor**

(a)

FIGURE 15-39 Liquid or vapor can be charged into a system depending on whether the refrigerant container is held inverted or upright (*a*). The liquid is normally at the bottom of the container (*b*).

◀ **SERVICE TIP** ▶

Some technicians prefer to complete the charging process with the system operating so they can watch the gauge pressures and temperatures normalize, even though this is not necessary with most modern charging stations. Normal A/C system operation should occur about 1/4 to 1/2 lb before the system is completely charged. This last volume becomes reserve to be stored in the receiver–drier or accumulator. At this point, the sight glass should clear up or the bottom of the accumulator should become cold. The high side pressure should not increase as the remaining refrigerant is charged into the system.

With the system running, caution should be exercised if charging liquid into it to avoid **slugging** the compressor; letting liquid refrigerant enter a running compressor can cause severe damage. If the container is upright, gas will leave it; if the container is upside down, liquid will leave it. With approved recovery con-

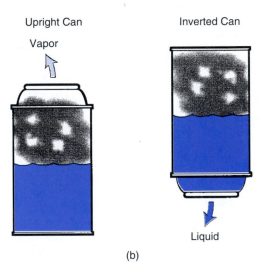

Upright Can — Vapor

Inverted Can — Liquid

(b)

tainers, either liquid or gas can be removed from an upright container, depending on which valve is opened. Putting 1 lb of liquid into a system is much faster than putting in 1 lb of gas because of a liquid's much smaller volume (Figure 15-39). Some blend refrigerants and small cans containing oil or fluorescent dye must be charged as liquid.

To charge a system using a charging station, you should:

1. Enter the specified amount of refrigerant into the charging scale or into the charging cylinder unit. This charge process begins with the sys-

FIGURE 15-40 Many A/C service units can be programmed to operate through a leak check and evacuation procedure. If the system passes the leak check, the service unit will be programmed to charge the proper amount of refrigerant into the system.

tem still under a vacuum, with the manifold valves closed (Figure 15-40).

2. Depending on the equipment being used, open the necessary valves and push the correct buttons to program the unit or fill the charging cylinder with the correct amount of refrigerant. Once the gauges show a pressure increase in the system, turn on the refrigerant heater (if so equipped).

3. When the charge volume has entered the system, close the necessary valves.

4. Start the A/C system, let it run until the pressures stabilize, and note system pressures as described in Section 12.2.4. They should be normal.

◄ **SERVICE TIP** ►

If liquid has been charged into a system, it is possible that liquid refrigerant has entered the compressor because of the location of the compressor and service ports. If you suspect this, rotate the compressor drive plate by hand at least one revolution to ensure that this has not occurred.

15.3.9.3 Charging from Small Cans When a system is to be charged from small cans, the technician needs to determine how many cans are needed. This is done by dividing the system's specification by the net weight of the cans. For example, the specification for a system might be 2 1/4 lb, 2.25 lb, or 2 lb 4 oz (all of these are the same); this amount needs to be converted so that the total weight is in ounces.

- There are 16 ounces in a pound. Multiply 2×16 to get 32, and $32 + 4 = 36$. This system holds 36 oz of refrigerant.

- Next, divide 36 by the weight in a small can, which in this case is 14 oz (some are 12 oz); $36 \div 14 = 2$ with 8 left over.

- To charge this 36-oz system using 14-oz cans, add two full cans plus 8 oz from a third can, leaving 6 oz in the third can.

Measuring the amount removed from the third can is done most accurately by weighing the can, tapper, and hose as the refrigerant is pulled out. For example, if this weight is 24 oz when we start, we stop when the weight has dropped to 16 oz, which is 8 oz less. The remaining refrigerant can be approximated by feeling the can temperature (the liquid level will be colder than the gas portion at the top) or by tipping the can (suction pressure will increase when liquid enters the hose) (Figure 15-41).

FIGURE 15-41 If using small cans, be sure to note the net weight of the can. The cans of R-12 (*a*) hold 14 and 15 oz of refrigerant; the cans of Freeze 12 and R-134a (*b*) hold 12 oz. *(b is courtesy of Technical Chemical Company [TCC])*

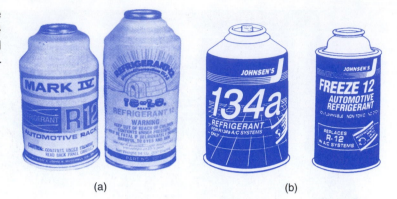

(a)   (b)

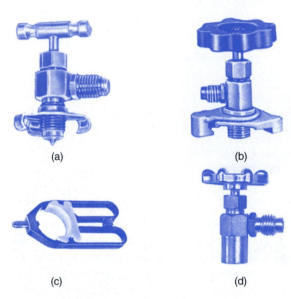

(a)   (b)

(c)   (d)

FIGURE 15-42 Three different can tappers can be used with small R-12 cans (*a–c*). Different adapters that thread onto the can are required for R-134a (*d*) and blends. *(Courtesy of Four Seasons)*

Small cans are sealed and must be tapped to get the refrigerant out. Older cans had a seam at the top, and the can tapper gripped this seam. Some can tappers fit around the can and pierce the side. These side tappers are faster to use: A quick squeezing action is all that is needed to attach the tapper and pierce the can, and it is removed using one quick motion. Can tappers for R-134a and some blends thread onto the top of the can (Figure 15-42).

To charge a system using small cans, you should:

1. Locate the specifications and determine the number of small cans needed. The charge process should begin with the system still under a vacuum, with the manifold valves closed.

2. Attach the can tapper to the center service hose, connect the can to the tapper, and pierce the first can of refrigerant.

3. Open the high side service valve, watch the low side pressure increase, and then open the low side service valve. The refrigerant can becomes cold as the refrigerant boils and transfers to the system. If the manifold is equipped with a sight glass, liquid refrigerant should be seen moving into the system. Shaking the can of refrigerant allows you to note the remaining liquid volume and also allows the whole can area to warm the remaining refrigerant.

4. When the charging action slows down, close the high side valve, make sure the hoses are clear of the soon-to-be-rotating engine parts, start the engine, and turn on the A/C system and blower to high speed.

5. When the first can empties, close the low side valve, remove the first can from the tapper, and install and pierce the next can. With some can tappers, air can enter, and the center hose will have to be evacuated or purged. If the charge level is less than 28 oz, stop charging before the second can empties.

6. Depending on system capacity, repeat step 5 until the last can is reached. Measure the amount of refrigerant you remove from the final can to ensure that the right amount of refrigerant enters the system.

7. Close both manifold valves. With the system operating, note the low and high side pressures; they both should be normal.

◀ **SERVICE TIP** ▶

When a can empties, allow the low side pressure to drop as low as it will go to pull as much refrigerant as possible from the can. It is easy to leave as much as an ounce in the can, and this can cause an undercharged system or one without any refrigerant reserve.

◄ **SERVICE TIP** ►

Tampering has become a major concern with many A/C service technicians; once a system has been serviced and put in proper operating condition, they want it to stay that way. A set of seals has been developed so it is easy to tell if a system has been opened. These seals are plastic sleeves that are placed over the service fittings and heated to shrink them to fit the fitting and cap (Figure 15-43). Another type of service port seal is similar to an electrical tie wrap, and installs without the need of a hot air gun. The seal must be cut in order to remove the service cap.

15.4 RETROFITTING R-134A INTO AN R-12 SYSTEM

Retrofitting is normally a repair-driven operation; it is not done until absolutely necessary. All experts agree that if a system was designed for R-12, R-12 should be used in it when it requires service, even though some systems cool better after changing to R-134a. We do know that new (virgin) R-12 will only be available for a limited time, so if a system requires service, consideration should be given to converting it to R-134a. This is especially true if major repairs, such as a compressor replacement, are needed. When R-12 is no longer available, the choice will be between retrofitting and not having A/C at all.

15.4.1 Refrigerant Choice for Retrofit

Any EPA SNAP-approved refrigerant, listed in Appendix D, can be used to replace R-12. Some of these are called "drop-in refrigerants"—but remember that there is no such thing. All of them require a similar retrofit procedure. Some of the things you should consider when choosing which refrigerant to use are the following:

- It must be EPA approved and have unique service fittings and label.
- R-134a is the refrigerant used in every new vehicle.
- Unique service, recovery, and charging equipment are required for each refrigerant; most shops have R-12 and R-134a equipment.
- Most major compressor manufacturers and builders will not warranty a compressor that failed if a blend refrigerant was used in it.
- Some of the blends cost three or four times as much as R-134a and must be sent off for disposal or recycling if a system needs future service.

(a)

(b)

(c)

FIGURE 15-43 System Guard seals are placed over the service ports and locked in place by shrinking them using a hot air gun. The system cannot be opened without cutting the seal. *(Courtesy of System Guard)*

- Blends that contain R-134a (some people call them dirty R-134a) share the same compressor problems as R-134a.
- Blends should be charged into a system as a liquid to reduce fractionation.
- Blends that contain R-22 must use barrier hoses and compatible inner seals (see Figure 5-15).
- Blends that contain HCFC (R-22) will be phased out when global-warming limits are enacted.
- More than 2% hydrocarbon content can produce a flammable mixture.
- The vehicle might travel to an area where the blend and its service equipment are not available.
- Blends are outlawed in some areas, including at least one Canadian province.
- Some blends do not work as well with leak detectors and fluorescent dyes.

All vehicle manufacturers, both international mobile air conditioning organizations (IMACA Foundation and MACS) and most service shops favor using R-134a for retrofits. It is relatively inexpensive, used in all new vehicles (so the service equipment is fairly common), readily available, and, because it is a single-compound refrigerant, can be recycled in service shops. Many shops are recovering any R-12 in systems to be retrofitted and saving that refrigerant for use in vehicles that are difficult or expensive to retrofit.

15.4.2 Possible Retrofit Problems

R-134a refrigerant works quite well in most R-12 systems. However, some areas of concern include:

- Oil degradation from chemical contamination, resulting in compressor damage.
- Incompatibility of compressor seal material, resulting in leakage. A compressor that contains Viton seals cannot be used with R-134a.
- Incompatibility of desiccant type, causing further contamination.
- Permeability of hoses, resulting in leakage.
- Increased high side pressure, causing pressure release through the relief valve, increased loss through hoses, and compressor damage.
- Systems with a pressure relief valve must have a *high-pressure cutoff switch*, also called a *refrigerant containment switch*, installed.
- Inability of compressor type or clutch to work reliably at higher high side pressures.

◄ **SERVICE TIP** ►

The Ford FX-15 compressor might not handle the higher pressure when a system is retrofitted to R-134a. It was replaced by the FS-10 compressor in mid-1993; the FS-10 is a much stronger version of the FX-15. Two ways to identify an FX-15 are (1) note the date on the back side of the rear mounting flange; if the date is 94 or later, it is an FS-10; and (2) pull the clutch plate, and count the number of splines; the FX-15 has 16 splines and the FS-10 has 21.

REAL WORLD FIX: The 1989 Honda (100,000 miles) has a bad compressor, and the vehicle owner would like to repair the system and retrofit it to use R-134a. The technician is concerned that a new or repaired version of this compressor will not stand up to the pressures of an R-134a system. The compressors that were received were longer than the original and would not fit.

F I X

Research found a supplier with a kit containing a new compressor with brackets, an accumulator, and hose sections that allowed a more durable compressor to be fitted to this system.

An R-134a molecule is smaller than an R-12 molecule. Consequently, a system with a very small R-12 leak will have a bigger, more rapid leak with R-134a. All leaks in a system to be retrofitted should be repaired (Figure 15-44).

Some of the compressors that have or might have problems with an R-134a retrofit are listed in Appendix E at the back of this book.

Some RWD vehicles are proving difficult to retrofit; this difficulty is related to condenser capacity and airflow through the condenser.

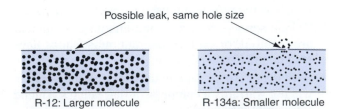

FIGURE 15-44 The R-134a molecule is smaller than an R-12 molecule, so the leak rate through the same hole is greater.

◀ **SERVICE TIP** ▶

IMACA has recommended the following guidelines: Check the high side pressure of the system operating with R-12 and compare the pressure to ambient temperature (AT) plus 40. If the high side pressure is less than AT + 40, the system should operate quite well with R-134a. If the pressure is above AT + 40, the pressure might become excessive with R-134a, and the best time to make improvements is during the retrofit process, after the R-12 has been recovered. In some cases, a more efficient or larger condenser is needed. In most cases, however, increased airflow from a higher-capacity fan, better fan shrouding, seals around the condenser to control the airflow, or recalibrated fan controls will solve this problem.

15.4.3 Retrofit Procedure

There are two types of retrofit procedures:

- *High performance*, also called *Type I*, is the most effective and follows the recommendations of the vehicle manufacturer and ensures that the performance will be equal to the original operation.
- *Economy*, also called *Type II*, is the least expensive and replaces only those parts necessary to comply with federal requirements. This procedure is the one used by most shops and is described in this section.

   The exact procedure used to retrofit R-134a varies depending on the design and materials in a particular system. For example, many late model R-12 systems are equipped with barrier-type hoses along with compressors and accumulators or receiver–driers that are completely compatible with R-134a, so there is no need to replace these parts. Older cars probably require replacement of both the compressor and hoses, especially if they show a lot of wear.

   Some odd things are turning up as a result of retrofit tests. Apparently, chlorine from R-12 seasons a compressor so that a used, good R-12 compressor would probably operate satisfactorily with R-134a. Some new R-12 compressors have a higher failure rate with R-134a than used R-12 compressors. Rebuilt compressors, compatible with R-134a, are available. Also, mineral oil apparently coats the inside of the hoses, so the leak rate through them is much lower than expected when retrofitting a system to R-134a.

   When retrofitting, at least 99% of the R-12 must be removed from the system and as much of the mineral oil as practical. Remember that more than 2% R-12 will

Castrol Retrofill Procedure

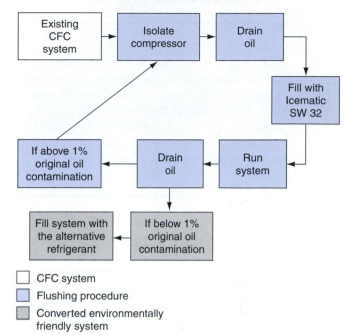

☐ CFC system
☐ Flushing procedure
☐ Converted environmentally friendly system

FIGURE 15-45   A procedure used to remove oil from an R-12 system before an R-134a retrofit. *(Courtesy of Castrol North America)*

cause excessive high side pressures and other problems and that the oil has absorbed R-12. A recovery unit removes the R-12 vapor and some of the oil and measures the amount of oil removed; some units measure the amount of R-12 also. Complete R-12 removal can be difficult because of the amount absorbed by any remaining oil. Remember that thorough oil removal also helps eliminate R-12 from the system.

   Oil removal is more difficult because it must be either drained out, flushed out, or pulled out with the R-12. Complete draining of some components requires removal of the component, which greatly increases the labor costs. As described in Section 15.3.5, liquid R-12 can flush oil out (Figure 15-45). Any remaining mineral oil will probably gel and settle in the bottom of the accumulator or evaporator. It is known that flushing the system with R-11 causes future problems.

◀ **SERVICE TIP** ▶

One way to partially identify the oil type in a system is to put a few drops of the oil into a container of water. PAG is very hygroscopic and will be dissolved into the water. An end-capped PAG will form an oil film. Ester and mineral oil will form a ball that floats on top of water.

◀ **SERVICE TIP** ▶

Most vehicle manufacturers recommend using R-12 in an R-12 system as long as this refrigerant is available, but most of them have also developed a TSB that describes the recommended retrofit procedure for those vehicles that can be retrofitted. These procedures should be used when R-12 is not easily available. Publications containing these OEM retrofit procedures are available from several sources.

◀ **SERVICE TIP** ▶

PAG oil is proving more durable than ester oil, and there are fewer compressor failures in systems where it is used in the retrofit, especially in cases with borderline lubrication.

In actual practice, shops are quite successful with Type II retrofits of both FWD and RWD vehicles. Most retrofits of FWD vehicles are quite easy (Figure 15-46).

R-134a is lighter than R-12, so a system should be charged to about 80 to 90% the amount of the R-12 capacity. Some aftermarket sources have made R-134a retrofit charge capacities available. If you need to figure the new charge level, simply multiply the R-12 charge level by 0.8. For example, if the R-12 charge is 2 lb

(32 oz), $32 \times 0.8 = 27$ oz. General Motors guidelines for retrofitting its vehicles recommend multiplying the R-12 charge level by 0.9 and subtracting 0.25 lb (4 oz). Using this procedure, $32 \times 0.9 = 29 - 4 = 25$, slightly less than the 27 oz (80% level). Refer to Section 12.2.5.2 for methods to get the proper charge in the system.

REAL WORLD FIX: The 1990 Plymouth Voyager (88,000 miles) had a leak in the high side and two faulty TXVs (rear air), so it was decided to retrofit to R-134a. The system was flushed, and both TXVs, the compressor, receiver–drier, discharge line, and all seals were replaced. Eight oz of PAG oil were added, and the system was evacuated for 90 minutes before charging it with 34.5 oz of R-134a. When tested, the system did not cool well, and the pressures were excessive: 75 psi low side and 225 psi high side. The heater hoses were clamped off, but this did not help.

FIX

The refrigerant was recovered, and the system was recharged with 30 oz of R-134a for a 70% charge level. This smaller refrigerant charge fixed this problem.

AUTHOR'S NOTE

The original charge specification for this vehicle is 43 oz, and DaimlerChrysler Corporation recommends a retrofit charge level of 32 oz of R-134a.

Both vehicle and aftermarket manufacturers produce kits that include the parts needed to convert particular systems (Figure 15-47). Vehicle manufacturer kits are for Type I retrofit, and most aftermarket sources provide Type II kits. Depending on the particular make and model, a kit can include the following:

- A sticker to identify that it is an R-134a system, along with the charge level (Figure 15-48)
- R-134a-type service fittings to be permanently installed over the existing service fittings
- Replacement hoses with the R-134a service fittings
- Replacement O-rings
- Ester or PAG oil
- Replacement receiver–drier or accumulator with XH-7 or XH-9 desiccant
- Replacement system switches calibrated for R-134a pressure
- Replacement TXV or OT calibrated for R-134a pressure
- High-pressure cutoff switch

Simpler kits cost less than $50.

IMACA R-134a Retrofit Flow Chart

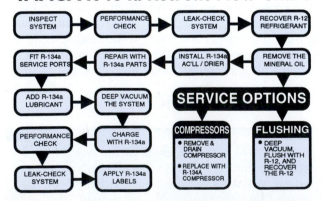

FIGURE 15-46 This flowchart shows the procedure to follow when retrofitting an R-12 system with R-134a. *(Courtesy of the International Mobile Air Conditioning Association [IMACA])*

(a)

(b)

FIGURE 15-47 A retrofit kit can be simple and inexpensive (*a*) or very complete, designed for a particular vehicle (*b*). (*a*) includes oil, R-134a service fittings, decals, and new O-rings. (*b*) contains all of these items plus a replacement condenser, control switch, hoses, receiver–drier, and TXV. (*a courtesy of Castrol North America; b courtesy of Wynn Oil Company*)

◄ **SERVICE TIP** ►

When retrofitting an OT system, it is a good practice to replace the orifice tube with one that is about 0.010″ (0.026 mm) smaller than the one used in the R-12 system. R-134a is lighter than R-12, and the R-12 orifice tube will allow too much R-134a to flow. This will drop high side pressure and increase low side pressure.

The R-12 service fittings must either be converted to R-134a service fittings or permanently capped to make them unusable. Normally, they are converted using a **conversion fitting** (Figure 15-49). A conversion fitting is threaded over the R-12 fitting, using the same Schrader valve, and a thread-lock adhesive locks it in place. It is a good practice to replace the old Schrader valves with ones that are compatible with R-134a. If an R-12 fitting is in a bad location or is unusable, it can be capped and a saddle clamp with the R-134a fitting can be installed. A saddle clamp is placed over a straight section of metal tubing and locked in place, and the tubing is pierced to provide an opening (Figure 15-50).

NOTICE: RETROFITTED TO R-134a

⚠ **CAUTION:** System to be serviced by qualified personnel. R-134a refrigerant under high pressure.

Retrofit procedure performed to SAE J1661.

134a Charge Amount:
134a Lubricant Type: Amount:
Retrofit Performed by:
Name:
Address:
City: State: Zip:
Date of Retrofit:

FIGURE 15-48 A label that shows retrofit information must be placed over the old R-12 information decal. (*Courtesy of Four Seasons*)

◄ **SERVICE TIP** ►

The most popular conversion fittings are either hollow or contain a pin extension to contact the valve stem. The hollow style is quite short and is simply threaded over the service port. Fittings with a pin extension ensure better valve opening as the service hose is connected, but the pin extension must be adjusted after installation. Turn the pin extension inward until it just contacts the valve stem and then turn it outward one half-turn.

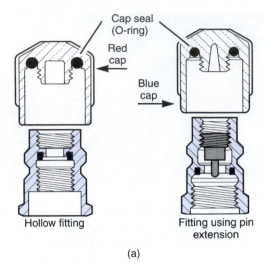

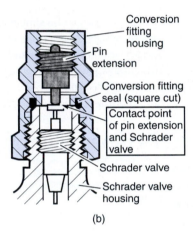

FIGURE 15-49 The two most popular conversion fittings thread directly onto the R-12 service ports (*a*). Fittings that use a pin extension should be adjusted after installation so there is slight clearance between the pin extension and the Schrader valve (*b*). *(Courtesy of Four Seasons)*

To retrofit a system, you should:

1. Visually inspect the system to ensure good condition, install a gauge set, and operate the system to bring it up to operating temperatures. Check for proper operation and note any needed repairs. Record the high side pressure for later comparison.

2. Recover the R-12 from the system, restarting the recovery procedure to remove as much oil-dissolved R-12 as possible.

3. Make any repairs to the system to cure problems that were found in step 1.

4. If the compressor failed, remove the failed compressor, flush the system and/or install a high side filter, and install the replacement compressor along with a new accumulator or receiver–drier.

5. Check the system to determine whether a high-pressure relief valve is used. If it has one, a high-pressure cutoff switch must be installed to stop the compressor before pressure relief valve release pressures occur (Figure 15-51). The switch is installed so it senses high side pressure and is wired into the clutch wire or relay so it can interrupt clutch operation.

6. If directed, R&R the receiver–drier or accumulator.

7. R&R any hoses that were leaking, or as directed. If a blend refrigerant that contains R-22 is to be used, check the hoses to make sure that they are barrier hoses. You should be able to find the identification name and number on the hose.

8. R&R any line-fitting O-rings on connections that were disturbed, or as directed.

9. R&R any switches and valves as directed.

FIGURE 15-50 This port is part of a saddle clamp that can be placed over a metal line; the line is then pierced and a Schrader valve is installed. *(Courtesy of ACDelco)*

FIGURE 15-51 This high-pressure cutoff switch can be installed in a high side port and is connected into the clutch wiring so the compressor will be shut off before it reaches pressures that must be released through the relief valve. *(Courtesy of ACDelco)*

10. Add the proper type and amount of oil—ester or PAG—into the compressor oil fill port or suction port. If the accumulator or receiver–driver is replaced, pour part of the oil into the inlet port.

11. Install the R-134a service fittings. Any old Schrader valves that remain in service should be replaced with new R-134a valves.

12. Fill out and install the identifying decal to properly identify the system. The old label must be rendered unreadable.

13. Connect a vacuum pump to the system and pull a minimum vacuum of 29″ Hg (500 microns) for at least 30 minutes to evacuate the system.

14. Recharge the system using R-134a. Charge the system with 80 to 90% of the specified amount of R-12. Proper charge level can be verified by any of the methods described in Section 12.2.5.2.

15. Operate the system and check for proper operation, paying careful attention to the high side pressure.

16. Test for leaks.

◄ SERVICE TIP ►

When retrofitting a cycling clutch system that uses a low side pressure switch, the switch can often be adjusted to allow lower evaporator temperatures. Turn the adjuster screw one-half turn at a time in a counterclockwise direction. Adjust the switch to obtain a cycle-out pressure of 22 psi (152 kPa) with an engine speed of 1,500 rpm.

◄ SERVICE TIP ►

If a system that you retrofitted does not cool sufficiently and has excess high side pressure, an auxiliary fan may solve your problem. These fans are available as pusher or puller fans, for mounting at either the front or the rear of the condenser, and in sizes from 9 to 16 inches across. It is recommended that you use the largest fan that you can fit into place. Several aftermarket sources supply the fans along with mounting kits, wiring harnesses, and installation directions.

15.5 USING AND INSTALLING SEALANTS AND STOP LEAKS

Many technicians dislike stop leaks as they are considered an inadequate or temporary repair method and the best repair is to actually fix the leak. Stop leaks also have a reputation of plugging up small orifices that might reduce the proper flow of refrigerant or oil; plus there is a question of whether the stop leak material will contaminate the rather delicate chemical balance within an A/C system. In spite of these misgivings, sealants are becoming more popular; some very good technicians use them as a less expensive way to either fix or reduce the leak rate of systems in which a very small leak cannot be found or is too expensive to repair by normal methods. Sealants are not considered a cure-all or first-resort repair, but as another way to cure particular leaks. Large leaks will not seal; the cause of the leak must be repaired using normal methods.

Modern sealants are single or two-part chemicals that are moisture activated; such a chemical remains fluid until it contacts moisture. The sealant is purchased as a kit that includes the sealant with a valve and short adapter hose (Figure 15-52). The absence of moisture

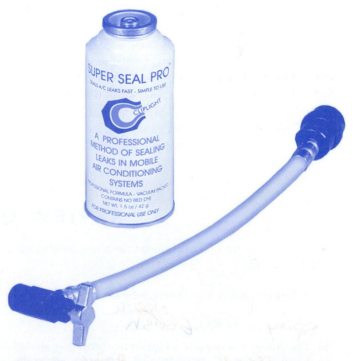

FIGURE 15-52 This kit contains a pressurized can of A/C sealant and a hose to attach it to the A/C system. The proper procedure should be followed when using a sealant. *(Courtesy of Cliplight)*

inside the A/C system along with the heat and pressure prevent the sealant from hardening inside the system.

To install a sealant, you should:

1. Recover the refrigerant from the system.
2. Evacuate the system for 5 minutes. The vacuum should drop to at least 25 inches, one source recommends 29 inches, and it should hold a 23-inch vacuum, one source says 25 inches, for at least 5 minutes.

NOTE: If the system will not pass this test, the leak is probably too large to be closed effectively using sealant.

3. Evacuate the system with a deep vacuum for at least 20 minutes to remove all traces of moisture from the system.

TIP: Heat the accumulator/receiver–drier to ensure that all moisture is driven out.

4. Attach the adapter hose to the sealant container and the low side service port. Pierce the sealant container if necessary.
5. With the sealant container inverted, open the valve and let the system vacuum pull the contents into the system. If used, immediately repeat this step with the second part of the sealant.
6. Remove the sealant adapter, reattach the service hoses and gauge set, and recharge the system. One source recommends waiting 5 minutes before starting the system.

7. Install a label close to the refrigerant charge decal indicating that a sealant has been installed.
8. Start the system and run it for at least 15 to 20 minutes to circulate the sealant.

◀ CAUTION ▶

Refrigerant service machines have experienced problems of lines plugging up and solenoids sticking after recovering refrigerant from systems containing sealants. One compressor manufacturer will not warranty compressors if sealant residue is found in them.

REAL WORLD FIX: The 1997 Volvo (97,000 miles) had a small leak in the evaporator core, and the customer insisted that a stop leak be installed. The stop leak did not effectively seal the leak. The system was thoroughly flushed as a new evaporator, accumulator, and orifice tube were installed. The system worked but did not get really cold. Three months later, the compressor failed so the system was flushed again, and the compressor, accumulator, and orifice tube were replaced. The system still does not work properly, and the evaporator has been removed and checked along with the air control doors in the HVAC case.

FIX

The system was flushed one more time and the accumulator and orifice tube were replaced for the third time. The system appears to be operating normally.

REVIEW QUESTIONS

The following questions are provided to help you study as you read the chapter.

1. A dirty condenser with debris at the front can be cleaned using _Air_ _NOZZU_, _wetur_ _sprey_, or a(n) _brush_
2. The first step in any refrigerant service procedure should be to _recover_ what type of _Refrig_ is in the system.
3. More than _2_ % air in the refrigerant of an A/C system is considered contaminated.
4. Refrigerant contaminated with air should be _purged_ and then _Recycld_
5. A shop that does full refrigerant service on both older and newer A/C systems must have _2_ sets of service _equip_.
6. A recycling machine has the ability to remove _oil_, _water_, _Air_, and solid _particl_ from the refrigerant.
7. Refrigerant that is contaminated with air will have a(n) _pressure_ that is _greater_ than normal for a particular temperature.

8. A(n) ~~Accum Comppre~~ or _Rec Drier_ should never be flushed, and it is doubtful that a flat-tube _Condense_ can be cleaned by flushing.

9. A(n) _Inline filter_ can be installed in the liquid line to trap debris that can plug the OT.

10. Water is removed from inside an A/C system by _____ the system to a(n) _____ lower than the boiling point of water.

11. The _oil_ in most vacuum pumps must be _changed_ periodically in order to keep the pump operating properly.

12. Partial charging of a system is not recommended because of the difficulty of adding the _correct amount_ of refrigerant.

13. The proper charge amount for a vehicle can be found on the _Label_ under the vehicle's _Hood_.

14. It will take _3_ small (12 oz) _cans_ of refrigerant to charge a system that holds 2 1/4 lbs of refrigerant.

15. If retrofitting an R-12 system to R-134a, a small refrigerant leak will become _larger_, and high side pressures will probably _increase_.

16. If retrofitting a system that contains a high-pressure relief valve, a(n) _high pres cut off such_ must be installed.

17. When retrofitting a system, new _Service ports_ must be permanently installed over the existing ones, and a(n) _new label_ must be filled out and placed over the old one.

16
16
4
__
36

36

CHAPTER QUIZ

The following questions will help you check the facts you have learned. Select the answer that completes each statement correctly.

1. Technician A says that eye protection should be worn when working with refrigerants. Technician B says to avoid skin contact with refrigerants and their oil. Who is correct?
   a. A only
   b. B only
   c. Both A and B
   d. Neither A nor B

2. Two technicians are discussing how to remove refrigerant from a system. Technician A says that you can vent it into the atmosphere as long as it has moisture in it. Technician B says that all refrigerant must be captured. Who is correct?
   a. A only
   b. B only
   c. Both A and B
   d. Neither A nor B

3. Technician A says that the same recovery unit can be used for R-12 and R-134a. Technician B says that the service hoses from an R-134a recovery unit must have shutoff valves within 18 inches of the end. Who is correct?
   a. A only
   b. B only
   c. Both A and B
   d. Neither A nor B

4. Technician A says that high pressure in recycled refrigerant is only caused by air contamination. Technician B says that recycled refrigerant should have the same purity standards as new refrigerant. Who is correct?
   a. A only
   b. B only
   c. Both A and B
   d. Neither A nor B

5. Technician A says that compressor failure sends metal and debris through the system, so it should be flushed using R-11. Technician B says that a good method to solve this problem is to replace the compressor and install an in-line filter. Who is correct?
   a. A only
   b. B only
   c. Both A and B
   d. Neither A nor B

6. A system contaminated with moisture should be evacuated for a minimum of 15 minutes.
   a. True
   b. False

7. Technician A says that checking the pressure–temperature relationship is a reliable way to check for contaminated refrigerant. Technician B says that refrigerant with more than 2% of a foreign refrigerant normally should be sent off for reclaiming or disposal. Who is correct?
   a. A only
   b. B only
   c. Both A and B
   d. Neither A nor B

306

8. Refrigerant can be contaminated with NCG if the _____ .
   a. recovery unit hose is not tight
   b. system is not thoroughly evacuated before recharging
   c. technician uses sloppy service procedures
   d. All of these

3

9. Technician A says that a system should be evacuated twice as long if the vacuum pump will only pull it down to 20″ Hg. Technician B says that the system might have a leak in it if it will not pull down into a deep vacuum. Who is correct?
   a. A only
   b. B only
   c. Both A and B
   d. Neither A nor B

10. Technician A says that refrigerant charge levels are given in service manuals. Technician B says that charge levels are printed on the under-hood decal. Who is correct?

    a. A only
    b. B only
    c. Both A and B
    d. Neither A nor B

11. Technician A says that an overcharge will cause excessively high system pressures. Technician B says that a small can of refrigerant holds 1 lb. Who is correct?

    a. A only
    b. B only
    c. Both A and B
    d. Neither A nor B

12. We normally charge refrigerant into the high side with the engine running.

    a. True
    b. False

13. Technician A says that retrofitting a system is simply a matter of recovering the R-12 and recharging it with a drop-in refrigerant. Technician B says that the charge level specification is the same with R-134a as with R-12. Who is correct?

    a. A only
    b. B only
    c. Both A and B
    d. Neither A nor B

14. Technician A says that SNAP approval indicates a good refrigerant that will have no problems in a system. Technician B says that using any refrigerant that contains R-22 requires the system to have barrier hoses. Who is correct?

    a. A only
    b. B only
    c. Both A and B
    d. Neither A nor B

◀ Chapter 16 ▶

A/C SYSTEM REPAIR

LEARNING OBJECTIVES

After completing this chapter, you should be able to:

1. R&R an A/C compressor.
2. Perform the standard bench repairs on a compressor and clutch, given the proper service manual and special tools.
3. R&R an A/C hose and make any necessary repairs to that hose.
4. R&R any A/C component, given the proper service manual.
5. Complete the A/C system repairs listed in the ASE Task List, Section B.

TERMS TO LEARN

barb fitting	finger-style crimp
beadlock ferrule	gut pack
beadlock fitting	lip-type seal
bubble-style crimp	Lokring fitting
compressor bench checks	seal protector
compressor leak checks	spring lock coupling
ferrule	two-part seal

16.1   INTRODUCTION

Much of A/C system repair consists of removing and replacing faulty components. Most repair operations recover the refrigerant, make the actual repair, and then evacuate and recharge the system. Most specific repair operations are described in vehicle manufacturers' service manuals; in printed and computer service information published by Alldata, Chilton Motors, and National Service Data; and in technical service bulletins (TSBs) published by vehicle and HVAC system manufacturers and MACS. These resources usually describe the fastest, easiest way to make a repair on a particular make and model of car. When a technician performs a repair for the first time on a specific car make and model, he or she should locate the repair in the service information and follow that procedure. *The descriptions given in this text are very general.*

◀ SERVICE TIP ▶

Before beginning any refrigerant service operations, protect your eyes and skin.

In a survey of its members, MACS determined that the most frequent A/C repairs involve (in order) the compressor (more than 20%), hoses, control devices, the evaporator, electrical circuits, the TXV or OT, the receiver–drier or accumulator, and the condenser (3%). These repairs were either to repair or replace a failed part or to correct a leak (Figure 16-1).

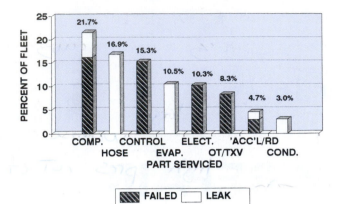

FAILED [ ] LEAK

FIGURE 16-1 The most common reasons for servicing automotive A/C systems are shown in this graph, the outgrowth of a survey by MACS of its members in the A/C service business. *(Courtesy of MACS)*

16.2   COMPRESSOR REPAIR

Normal compressor repair includes replacement of the entire unit or of the clutch and clutch coil, shaft seal, gaskets and O-rings, and, occasionally, the reed valve plate. The extent of repair depends on the particular compressor, the availability of repair parts, the special tools required to make the repair, and the skill of the technician. Many technicians prefer to repair the original compressor, if practical, to eliminate problems in obtaining the correct replacement. On many compressors, it is very easy to remove and replace the head, so the head, reed valve plate, and O-ring or gasket are often replaced. Compressors with severe internal damage or for which the repairs are difficult or time consuming will probably be replaced with new or rebuilt units. This is another case in which the repair description in a service manual can help the technician determine what course to take.

◄ SERVICE TIP ►

Compressor failure rate is increasing on modern vehicles. This increase has been attributed to:

- reduced refrigerant charge levels with less tolerance for leakage,
- smaller compressors with tighter tolerances, and
- smaller, tighter engine compartments with much higher under-hood temperatures.

FIGURE 16-2 This set contains the special tools needed to service the clutch and shaft seal of Ford FS-6 and Chrysler C-171 compressors. *(Courtesy of Kent-Moore)*

When a compressor is replaced, some of the variables that should be checked to verify their correct replacement are the following:

- Clutch pulley (see Section 16.2.2)
- Compressor make
- Mounting lug type, location, and spacing
- Switch location and types
- Clutch coil connector location
- Port location, size, and type
- Refrigerant type

Occasionally, the repair operation can be performed with the compressor still in place on the engine, but it is usually removed. Bench repairs usually allow for better cleanup and access to all portions of the compressor.

Special service tools are available through the vehicle manufacturer and from several aftermarket sources, some of which supply the manufacturer. Special tools are often required for clutch removal and replacement, seal removal and replacement, and internal compressor repairs. Special tool kits contain the specific tools for different compressor models and often include pressure test plates, which allow the compressor to be checked for leaks while still on the bench (Figure 16-2).

◄ SERVICE TIP ►

Before replacing a compressor that has a complaint of a grinding/buzzing noise, apply a prying pressure against the compressor. If the noise stops, check for compressor mounting problems like loose bolts or a broken mounting bracket.

◄ **SERVICE TIP** ►

Occasionally a vane compressor will appear to have failed if the vanes stick in the innermost position. Sometimes they can be freed up by adding oil through the low side port, running the engine at about 3,000 rpm, and cycling the clutch in and out.

REAL WORLD FIX: The 1990 Taurus came from the body shop after damage from an accident had been repaired. The condenser had been replaced and the system recharged, but it did not cool. The technician recovered the refrigerant, evacuated the system, and tried to recharge it, but it would not take the last 8 oz of the 2 lb, 12 oz charge specification. The compressor clutch operates, but both gauges show a pressure of 60 psi.

FIX

A more thorough check showed that the compressor shaft was broken. Replacement of the compressor along with a new accumulator fixed this problem.

16.2.1 Compressor R&R

Depending on access to the compressor and its mounting bolts, compressor R&R can be either fairly easy or very difficult. A compressor is often removed from the car to repair the clutch or to replace the seal, gaskets, or O-rings. Like most other operations, the exact procedure to follow on a particular car is given in the service manual. If a failed compressor is replaced, it is recommended that the receiver–drier or accumulator be replaced at the same time and the amount of oil in the system be checked and adjusted.

◄ **SERVICE TIP** ►

If the failed compressor sent debris into the discharge line, the line and the condenser should be replaced or flushed to remove the debris or a filter should be installed to keep it from traveling downstream. Many technicians install one or two in-line filters to ensure the system operates properly or to protect the new compressor.

◄ **SERVICE TIP** ►

When a compressor fails internally, it will often send metal particles into the suction line. The compressor must be replaced with a new or rebuilt unit, but this material can enter the new compressor and cause early failure. A suction filter screen has been developed to trap the debris in the suction line (Figure 16-3).

◄ **SERVICE TIP** ►

Many new and rebuilt compressors come with an oil charge for the whole system; some come with an oil charge for just the compressor. Some replacement R-12 compressors come with a mineral oil charge, an R-134a compressor comes with a PAG or POE oil charge, and some compressors intended for either refrigerant come empty of oil. Be sure to read the information that comes with the compressor.

◄ **SERVICE TIP** ►

The compressor housing can become distorted as it is tightened onto the mounts if the mounting pads do not align exactly with the brackets. This can cause a leak between the housing parts. To ensure that this does not occur:

- Snug the compressor bolts.
- If there are gaps between the compressor pads and the brackets, either loosen the brackets to allow them to align properly or shim the pads to eliminate the gaps.
- Tighten the compressor mounting bolts to the correct torque.
- Tighten the bracket bolts to the correct torque.

◄ **SERVICE TIP** ►

With most compressors, new oil is added by pouring it slowly into the suction port. With a GM V-5 compressor, the oil must be added through the drain plug at the bottom of the compressor.

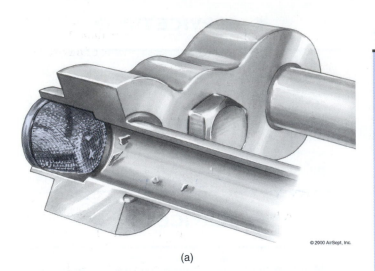

(a)

© 2000 AirSept, Inc.

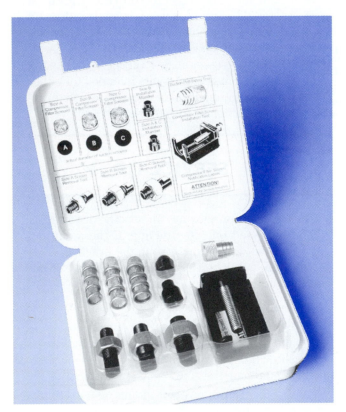

(b)

FIGURE 16-3 Compressor failure can send debris into the suction line. A filter screen (a) can be installed into the suction using a special tool set (b). *(Courtesy of Air Sept)*

◄ **SERVICE TIP** ►

Before replacing a failed compressor, it is wise to determine why the old compressor failed; if the cause of failure is not corrected, the new compressor will probably fail also. The most common cause of compressor failure is poor lubrication, excessive pressures and temperatures, or a burned-out clutch. Poor lubrication is usually the result of insufficient oil, insufficient refrigerant, the wrong type of oil, the wrong oil viscosity, oil breakdown from excessive heat, or acidic oil from water in the system. Excessive pressure and temperature are usually the result of internal or external condenser restrictions, poor airflow through the condenser, an overcharge, or contaminated refrigerant. Clutch burnout is usually the result of insufficient voltage at the clutch or excessive high side pressure.

◄ **SERVICE TIP** ►

When installing a new or rebuilt/remanufactured compressor, follow these guidelines:

- Return the system to as close to like-new condition as possible.
- Replace the accumulator or receiver–drier.
- If the compressor failure sent metal debris into the high or low side lines,

    Flush the lines and/or install liquid line filter or a suction-line filter screen.

    Replace the OT or clean the TXV filter screen.

    With modern flat-tube condensers, be aware of probable internal condenser plugging.

- Add the correct amount of the proper oil, and split the oil, half to the compressor and half to the accumulator/receiver–drier.
- Check the clutch air gap, and correct it if necessary.
- Check the clutch operating voltage; it should be 12 V or greater with the engine running.
- Tighten the compressor mounting bolts evenly to the correct torque.

- Evacuate the system a minimum of 500 microns or 30 minutes (some recommend 45 to 60 minutes).
- Charge the system with the proper amount of clean refrigerant.
- Rotate the compressor shaft by hand a few revolutions (some recommend 10 revolutions) to ensure that refrigerant oil has not filled a cylinder.

To remove a compressor, you should:

1. Recover the refrigerant from the system.
2. Disconnect the compressor clutch and any switch or sensor wires.
3. Disconnect the drive belt.
4. Disconnect the discharge and suction hoses and cap the hoses to prevent dirt and moisture from entering. On some vehicles, reverse steps 4 and 5 for different access to the hose connections.
5. Remove the compressor mounting bolts and remove the compressor (Figure 16-4).
6. With most newer systems, drain the oil from the compressor by placing it over a drain pan with

the discharge and suction ports downward; some compressors have a drain plug that must be removed. Measure the amount of oil drained out. Note the condition of this oil and discard it in the approved manner (Figure 16-5). Oil with metal particles indicates a failed compressor; brown or dark oil indicates overheating from excessive high side pressures.

To replace a compressor, you should:

1. Adjust the oil level in the compressor as instructed by the vehicle or compressor manufacturer.
2. Install the compressor on the engine and replace the mounting bolts.
3. Install the drive belt, adjust the belt tension, and tighten all mounting bolts to the correct torque.
4. Using new gaskets or O-rings, connect the discharge and suction lines.
5. Connect the clutch and switch or sensor wires.
6. Evacuate and recharge the system and check for leaks.

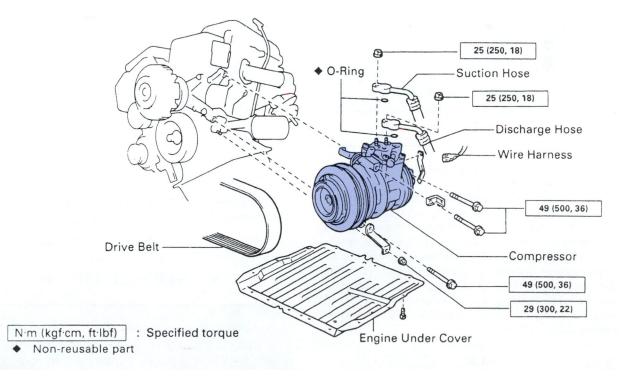

◆ O-Ring

25 (250, 18) — Suction Hose
25 (250, 18)
Discharge Hose
Wire Harness
49 (500, 36)
Compressor
49 (500, 36)
29 (300, 22)

Drive Belt

Engine Under Cover

| N·m (kgf·cm, ft·lbf) | : Specified torque
◆ Non-reusable part

FIGURE 16-4 The procedure for removing and replacing this compressor. Note the tightening torques and the parts that must be replaced. *(Courtesy of Toyota Motor Sales USA, Inc.)*

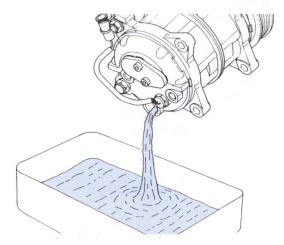

FIGURE 16-5 Oil is drained by pouring it out of the suction and discharge ports; it can also be drained out of the oil drain or oil level–checking plug opening, if so equipped. *(Courtesy of Zexel USA Corporation)*

◀ SERVICE TIP ▶

When installing a compressor with a cross-bolt type of mount, set the compressor in place and try to wiggle the compressor to determine if it is setting flat onto each of the mounting points. If the mounting points are warped, the compressor will be twisted and stressed as the bolts are tightened. This will probably result in a leak at the compressor case seals. The bolts should be carefully tightened by hand to the correct torque.

REAL WORLD FIX: The 1991 Ford Explorer (165,000 miles) came in with a bad compressor. The compressor, orifice tube, and accumulator were replaced, and the system was recharged. It worked well so the vehicle was returned to the customer. Thirty miles later, the vehicle returned with a shredded drive belt. The belt was replaced, and the vehicle was returned to the customer. Thirty-five miles later, the vehicle returned with another shredded drive belt. The compressor clutch appeared to be slipping, so the compressor and drive belt were replaced, and the vehicle was returned to the customer. Thirty miles later, the vehicle returned with another shredded drive belt.

FIX

Following advice, the technician double-checked the other pulleys and found that the power steering pulley was not installed completely onto the pump. Proper installation of the power steering pulley fixed this problem.

REAL WORLD FIX: The 1992 Nissan Pathfinder (110,000 kilometers) came in with a bad compressor. The clutch had overheated and welded itself together. The compressor and clutch were replaced along with the receiver–drier. The system was recharged, but it did not cool properly. The system pressures at idle were 85 psi on the low side and 105 psi on the high side; at 2,000 rpm, the pressures changed to 55 psi on the low side and 150 psi on the high side. The TXV was replaced twice, but this did not help.

FIX

It was determined that the rebuilt compressor was faulty. A second compressor replacement fixed this problem.

16.2.2 Clutch and Clutch Coil R&R

Most modern clutches are three-part assemblies with a separate drive hub (armature), rotor pulley, and coil. Many earlier clutches were two-part units that combined the hub and rotor pulley, and a few were single units with all three parts combined in a single assembly. When replacing these parts, the technician must use care to ensure the correct replacement. This checking procedure should include the following:

1. Determine shaft type (tapered or straight, key or splines) (Figure 16-6).
2. Determine pulley and belt size and type.
3. On one- or two-part units, determine whether a single- or double-row ball bearing is used.
4. Determine compressor make and model.
5. Measure pulley diameter.
6. Measure pulley groove placement.
7. With some units, determine clutch manufacturer (Figure 16-7).

◀ SERVICE TIP ▶

A slipping clutch will have a blue, overheated appearance. It can generate a temperature of 700 to 800°F (371–427°C) in 3 minutes or less. The clutch bearing lubricant melts at about 300°F (150°C) and can run out of the bearing. The bearing will fail shortly after this, possibly causing damage to the compressor snout.

Check pulley/belt size

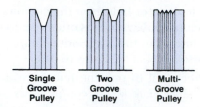

Single Groove Pulley   **Two Groove Pulley**   **Multi-Groove Pulley**

Count the number of belts needed to drive the clutch and determine their size. Belt size is given by dimensions "C" and "D" in the dimensional information section of this catalog.

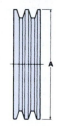

(a)

Measure diameter of pulley

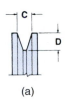

Measure the pulley from edge to edge across its face in the middle of the clutch. This diameter is listed in the dimension charts as "A."

(b)

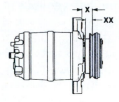

X = From the front surface of the mounting ear to first pulley groove midpoint.

(c)

FIGURE 16-6 When replacing a clutch or pulley, check the type and size of the pulley belt grooves (a), the pulley diameter (b), and groove spacing (c) to make sure the replacement part is correct. *(Courtesy of Warner Electric)*

FORD CLUTCH

HUB

ALIGNED SLOTS
PULLEY (FRONT)

STAKED BEARING (3 PLACES)
PULLEY (REAR)

FLAT ROUND MOUNTING PLATE
FIELD COIL (REAR)

WARNER ELECTRIC CLUTCH

HUB

STAGGERED SLOTS
PULLEY (FRONT)

STAKED BEARING (3 PLACES)
PULLEY (REAR)

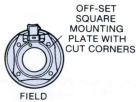
OFF-SET SQUARE MOUNTING PLATE WITH CUT CORNERS
FIELD COIL (REAR)

NIPPONDENSO CLUTCH

HUB

ALIGNED SLOTS
PULLEY (FRONT)

BEARING RETAINER RING (NOT STAKED)
PULLEY (REAR)

OFF-SET ROUND MOUNTING PLATE
FIELD COIL (REAR)

FIGURE 16-7 Some compressors use a clutch from one of several manufacturers; parts from one manufacturer should not be used with parts from another. *(Courtesy of Warner Electric)*

◄ **SERVICE TIP** ►

Some late model clutch assemblies have undergone changes to improve clutch holding power. Early and late versions of these units should not be combined because this can cause rubbing between the parts or clutch slippage. If one of these parts has to be replaced, all three portions should be replaced as a unit. Another point to remember on three-part assemblies is that the clearance, or air gap, between the hub and rotor pulley must be adjusted during replacement and that magnetic action pulls the coil into the rotor pulley as the clutch operates. These parts must be properly positioned as they are assembled (Figure 16-8).

In some cases, the clutch repairs can be made with the compressor in place on the engine. If compressor removal is necessary, follow the procedure described in Section 16.2.1.

◄ **SERVICE TIP** ►

If a slipping clutch is found, check to determine if the clutch surfaces were wet or dry. Wet surfaces indicate that a seal leak caused the problem. Dry surfaces indicate that excessive clearance, weak clutch coil magnetism, or excessive high side pressure caused the problem.

To remove a clutch assembly, you should:

1. Remove the locknut or bolt from the compressor shaft. A clutch hub wrench is often required to keep the hub from turning. Some compressors do not use a locknut (Figure 16-9).

2. Use the correct tool to pull the hub from the compressor shaft. On some compressors, a group of adjustment shims are under the clutch hub.

3. Remove the rotor pulley retaining ring and the rotor pulley. A special puller is required on most compressors; the rotor pulley can be slid off some compressors, such as the Nippondenso styles.

4. Mark the location of the clutch coil wire connector, remove the retainer ring, and remove the coil. Some compressors use a press fit to secure the coil in place. These coils are removed using a special puller.

If one or more clutch parts fail, inspect the parts to determine the cause of failure. If the parts are removed to gain access to the compressor seal, check them to make sure they are serviceable.

◄ **SERVICE TIP** ►

If the compressor is mounted with the drive belt in place, engage the clutch. The magnetic force will lock the hub and hold it from turning while you loosen the nut.

FIGURE 16-8 The correct pulley being used with the correct field coil (left and center). A weak mismatch with possible rubbing occurs if the parts are switched (right). *(Courtesy of Warner Electric)*

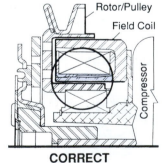

CORRECT
Straight Field Coil to
Straight Rotor/Pulley

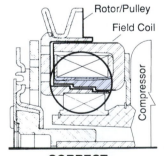

CORRECT
Stepped Field Coil to
Stepped Rotor/Pulley

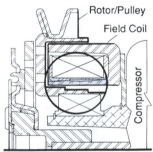

INCORRECT
Straight Field Coil to
Stepped Rotor/Pulley

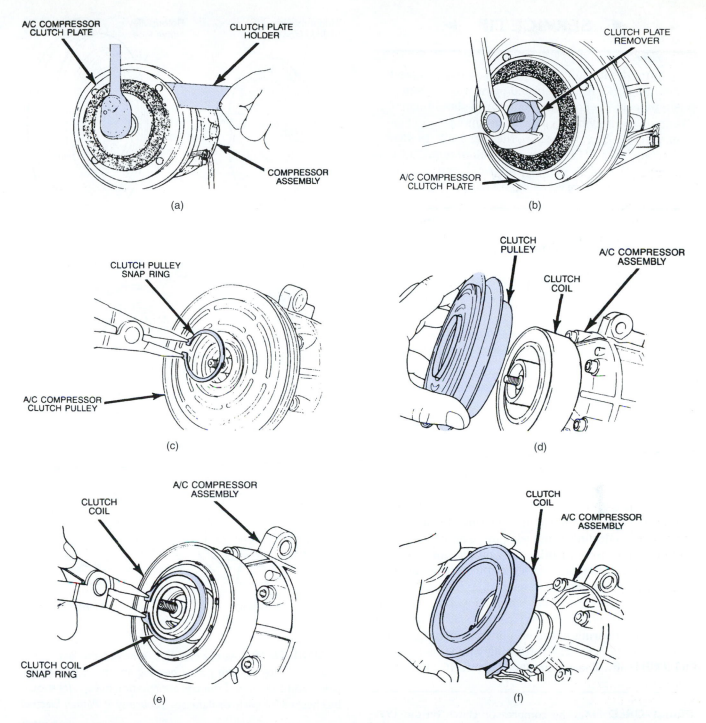

FIGURE 16-9 This clutch assembly is removed by removing the retaining nut *(a)*, pulling the clutch plate *(b)*, removing the pulley retaining ring *(c)*, removing the pulley *(d)*, and removing the coil retaining ring and the coil *(e)* and *(f)*. Special pullers are often required to remove the plate, pulley, or coil. *(Courtesy of DaimlerChrysler Corporation)*

◀ SERVICE TIP ▶

A burned-out clutch with blued, heavily scored contact surfaces and burned paint was obviously slipping and is not functioning. You should determine what may have caused the slippage and failure. In this case, make sure there are at least 10.8 V (some sources recommend a minimum of 12 V at the clutch connector) at the clutch and that the discharge pressure is not excessively high.

Other important points to check are the following:

- Contact faces for the hub and rotor pulley should be flat and fairly smooth, without excess scoring (Figure 16-10).
- Hub drive springs or rubber should not be broken.
- The pulley should rotate smoothly and quietly on its bearing.
- There should be no rubbing contact between the rotor pulley and coil.
- There should be no wear at the clutch coil antirotation locating hole or pin.

A faulty rotor pulley bearing can usually be removed and replaced. This is usually a simple process of driving or pressing the old bearing out and installing a new one. When installing a new bearing, it is important not to exert a driving or pressing force across the inner bearing parts; press or drive only on the outer bearing race, where it fits tightly with the rotor. On some units, the bearing is retained by a snap ring; on many newer units, the bearing is staked. Staking involves upsetting or deforming metal so it overlaps the bearing and bore. As a staked bearing is driven out, the staked metal is bent out of the way. The rotor pulley must be restaked to lock the new bearing in place (Figure 16-11).

REAL WORLD FIX: The compressor clutch on the 1991 Lincoln (87,000 miles) operates intermittently. There is B+ voltage through the A/C relay to the compressor, and the wiring looks good.

FIX

With the engine running, the technician carefully tapped the front of the clutch hub with a broom handle, and the clutch engaged. With the engine off, the clutch air gap was measured and found to be too wide, over 0.060". Adjusting the clutch air gap to the proper width, 0.020", fixed this problem.

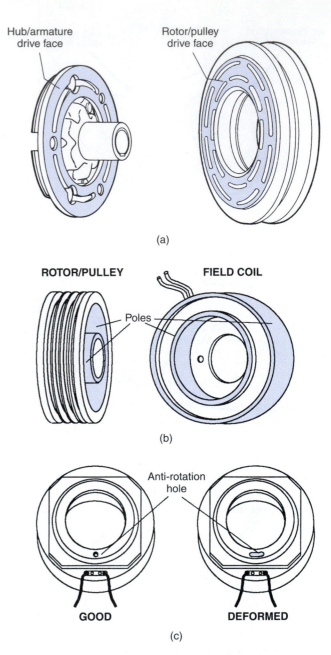

FIGURE 16-10 As the clutch is removed, the face of the hub and pulley (a), the pulley bearing and the poles of the pulley and coil (b), and the coil antirotation hole(s) (c) should be checked for wear or damage. *(Courtesy of Warner Electric)*

To replace a clutch assembly, you should:

1. Replace the coil, making sure that the antirotation pins and holes are aligned and the wire connector is in the correct position. The coil must be pressed in place on some compressors (Figure 16-12).
2. Replace the coil retaining ring. On some compressors, the retaining ring has an inner bevel;

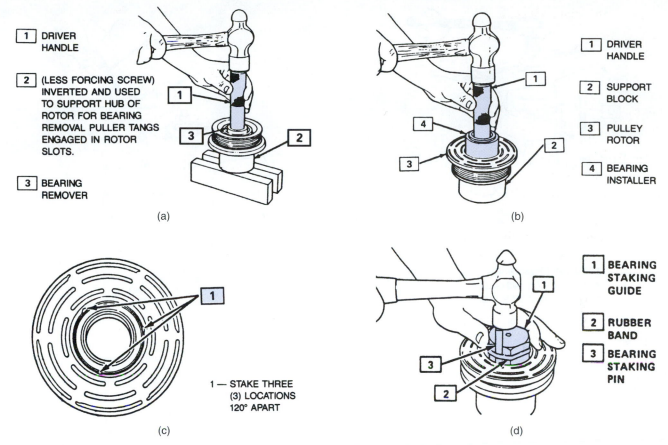

1 DRIVER HANDLE

2 (LESS FORCING SCREW) INVERTED AND USED TO SUPPORT HUB OF ROTOR FOR BEARING REMOVAL PULLER TANGS ENGAGED IN ROTOR SLOTS.

3 BEARING REMOVER

(a)

1 DRIVER HANDLE

2 SUPPORT BLOCK

3 PULLEY ROTOR

4 BEARING INSTALLER

(b)

1 — STAKE THREE (3) LOCATIONS 120° APART

(c)

1 BEARING STAKING GUIDE

2 RUBBER BAND

3 BEARING STAKING PIN

(d)

FIGURE 16-11 A faulty bearing being removed (a) and a new bearing being installed (b) into a pulley. Special tools are required to ensure that the pulley and bearing are not damaged. Another tool is required to stake the pulley (c) to lock the bearing in place (d). (Reprinted with permission of General Motors Corporation)

this bevel must face away from the coil. Be sure that the retaining ring enters its groove and fits tightly (Figure 16-13).

3. Install the rotor pulley and replace the retainer ring. Some retainer rings have a beveled face; this side must face away from the pulley. Test this installation by rotating the rotor pulley; it must rotate freely, with no interference.

4. On some compressors, install the adjusting shims onto the shaft, install the drive key, and align and install the hub. On many GM compressors, the hub must be pulled onto the shaft. It should be pulled on just far enough to get the correct air gap.

5. Install the shaft locknut or bolt and tighten it to the correct torque.

6. Check the clutch air gap at three locations around the clutch. The clearance should be within specifications at all three points. If it is too wide or too narrow, readjust the air gap. If it is too wide at one point and too narrow at another, replace the hub (Figure 16-14).

◀ **SERVICE TIP** ▶

Some manufacturers recommend measuring clutch gap using a dial indicator. Set up the dial indicator with the measuring stylus against the clutch plate (Figure 16-15). Turn on the A/C to energize the clutch, or using jumper wires connect the coil to a battery; the amount of clutch plate travel (air gap) will be shown on the dial indicator.

◀ **SERVICE TIP** ▶

A clutch used in an R-134a system will not tolerate an air gap that is too wide. It will slip when high pressures are encountered.

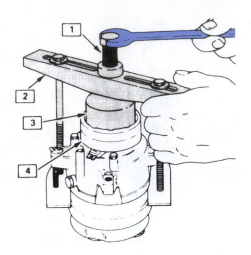

1 –SCREW
2 –PULLER CROSS BAR
3 –CLUTCH COIL INSTALLER
4 –CLUTCH COIL ASSEMBLY

(a)

1–CLUTCH COIL
2–DRIFT PUNCH
3–STAKE IN FRONT
   HEAD (3 PLACES)

(b)

1–FRONT HEAD SURFACE   3–CLUTCH
                                COIL
2–STAKE FRONT HEAD   HOUSING
   0.28-0.35mm DEEP (.010-.015")

(c)

FIGURE 16-12 On this compressor, the clutch coil must be pressed into place (a) and locked with three stake marks from a punch (b). The staking (c) upsets metal to firmly hold the coil in position. (*Reprinted with permission of General Motors Corporation*)

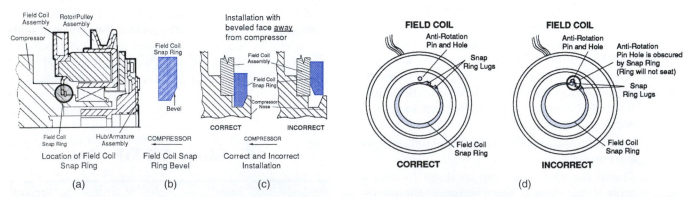

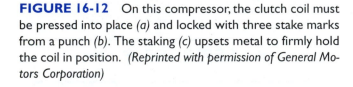

FIGURE 16-13 When parts are held in place using a snap ring (a), the bevel portion of the ring (b) should be positioned so it enters the groove to tighten against the part being retained (c). Placing the lugs of the snap ring so they are on the antirotation pin can keep the ring from properly entering its groove (d). (*Courtesy of Warner Electric*)

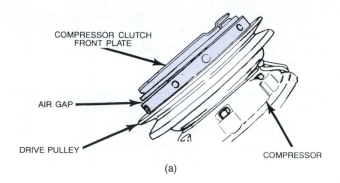

FIGURE 16-14 The air gap between the plate and pulley should be correct *(a)*; some compressors use a shim pack under the plate hub to adjust this air gap *(b)*. *(Courtesy of DaimlerChrysler Corporation)*

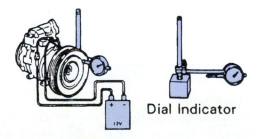

FIGURE 16-15 Clutch gap can be checked using a dial indicator to measure clutch plate movement. The clutch can be energized using a pair of jumper wires as shown. *(Courtesy of Toyota Motor Sales USA, Inc.)*

REAL WORLD FIX: The 1986 Mercedes (141,000 miles) came in with a complaint of no A/C. A bad A/C relay was found and replaced. The A/C would operate, but at 1,800 rpm the compressor would cut out. The compressor rpm sensor was replaced. This helped, but the compressor would still shut off intermittently.

FIX

The clutch air gap was checked and found to be too wide, 0.040 in. with a specification of 0.015 in. Removal of a few shims to get the correct gap fixed this problem.

◄ **SERVICE TIP** ►

Many clutch and seal snap rings have a slight bevel on one side, and the snap ring groove is also beveled. The beveled edge is placed away from the clutch coil or pulley bearing, which causes the snap ring to move toward the part it retains, holding it tighter.

◄ **SERVICE TIP** ►

When installing new clutch components, it is good practice to burnish the contact surfaces before putting the clutch in service. Do this by cycling the clutch on and off at a rate of 10 to 15 times a minute for a total of 10 to 15 cycles with the engine speed at 2,500 to 3,000 rpm. One manufacturer recommends 50 cycles. Burnishing wears the surfaces to perfectly match each other, increasing the holding power, before the clutch has to engage at full head pressures. Recheck the air gap after burnishing.

16.2.3 Compressor Shaft Seal R&R

With most compressors, the shaft seal is removed from the front of the compressor after the clutch plate has been removed. On some compressors, the seal is positioned inside the front head, and partial disassembly of the compressor is required to get to it. Two styles of seals are used: two-part seal assemblies and lip-type seals.

The **two-part seal** consists of a seal seat and a seal cartridge. The seal seat is stationary and is secured to the front of the compressor. An O-ring or gasket is used to prevent refrigerant from leaking between the compressor and the seal seat. The seal seat is made from either cast iron (gray) or ceramic (white) material and has a polished sealing face. The seal cartridge fits over the compressor shaft and rotates with the shaft. Many compressors have flat areas on the shaft where the cartridge fits for a positive drive connection. The actual sealing member is a disk of carbon with a highly polished face; this face is pushed against the seal seat by a

FIGURE 16-16 This shaft seal set includes (clockwise from top left) a dust shield, O-ring, seat cartridge, and seat. *(Courtesy of ACDelco)*

spring. A rubber bellows or O-ring is also included in the cartridge to seal the seat to the shaft and prevent a refrigerant leak in this area. A film of oil between the sealing faces of the seat and cartridge forms the final seal and prevents wear (Figure 16-16).

A **lip-type seal** uses a Teflon, TFE material seal lip that seals against the compressor shaft. The seal lip is bonded to a steel shell mounted in the front of the compressor. An O-ring is used to seal the shell to the compressor. Internal refrigerant pressure helps keep the sealing lip against the shaft to stop refrigerant from escaping. Compressor oil provides the final seal and also prevents seal lip and shaft wear (Figure 16-17).

Lip seals are being improved with newer designs (Figure 16-18).

◀ SERVICE TIP ▶

Some seal leaks are caused by pits in the compressor shaft in the area of the seal lip. A replacement seal is available that has two seal lips, and each one is offset from the original seal lip position.

Seals should not be reused; new seal parts should always be installed. These parts should be thoroughly lubricated with mineral-type refrigerant oil as they are installed.

◀ SERVICE TIP ▶

When handling the new seal parts, avoid touching the sealing surfaces with your fingers. These sealing surfaces can be damaged by acids from your skin.

Special tools are required for most seal replacements. These tools are designed to grip the seal cartridge or seat so they can be quickly pulled out or slid back into the proper position.

To remove a lip-type seal, you should:

1. Recover the refrigerant.
2. Remove the compressor clutch plate.
3. Remove the clutch hub drive key if it is still in the shaft.
4. Remove the seal retaining ring (Figure 16-19).
5. Attach the seal puller to the seal and, using a rotating motion, pull the seal from the compressor.
6. Thoroughly clean the area inside the compressor neck where the seal is located.
7. Use an O-ring pick tool to hook and remove the O-ring. Discard the O-ring and seal.
8. Clean the O-ring groove and compressor shaft.

◀ SERVICE TIP ▶

Use mineral refrigerant oil to lubricate the parts as they are assembled. It is less hygroscopic and safer for you to use, and the small amount that is used will not affect an R-134a system. Mineral oil is currently available in aerosol containers, making its use easier and faster (Figure 16-20).

To replace a lip-type seal, you should:

1. Check the sealing surface on the compressor shaft to make sure that it is smooth and clean. Oil the new O-ring, position it on the O-ring installer, and install the O-ring into its groove. Make sure that it is seated completely in its groove.
2. Place the **seal protector** over the compressor shaft to prevent damage to the seal lip as it is installed (Figure 16-21).
3. Place the new seal onto the installer, oil the seal lip, and install the seal using a rotating motion.
4. Install the new retaining ring with the flat side of the ring against the seal and the beveled side outward. Make sure the ring enters its groove all the way around.
5. Rotate the compressor shaft a few turns, pressurize the compressor, and check for leaks.

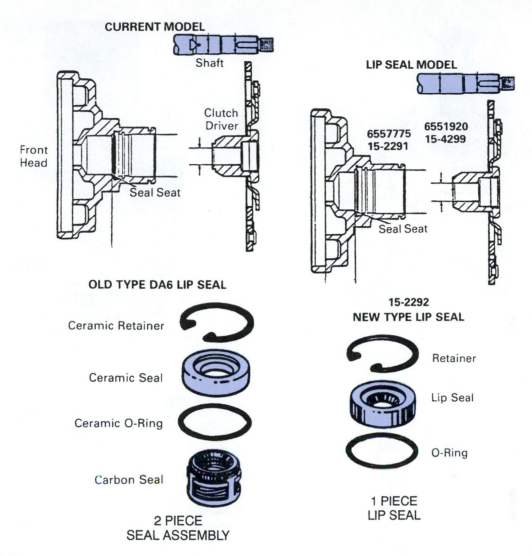

CURRENT MODEL

Shaft

Clutch Driver

Front Head

Seal Seat

LIP SEAL MODEL

6557775
15-2291

6551920
15-4299

Seal Seat

OLD TYPE DA6 LIP SEAL

Ceramic Retainer

Ceramic Seal

Ceramic O-Ring

Carbon Seal

**2 PIECE
SEAL ASSEMBLY**

15-2292
NEW TYPE LIP SEAL

Retainer

Lip Seal

O-Ring

**1 PIECE
LIP SEAL**

FIGURE 16-17 Older General Motors compressors use a two-piece seal assembly *(left)*. Newer compressors use the one-piece assembly *(right)*. *(Courtesy of ACDelco)*

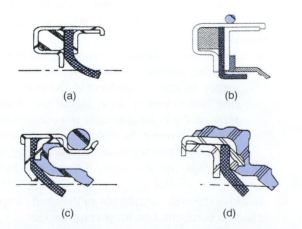

(a)

(b)

(c)

(d)

FIGURE 16-18 The compressor shaft lip seal has evolved over time from the early single-lip unit *(a)* to the modern double-lip seal *(d)*. *(Courtesy of Delphi Corp., all rights reserved)*

(Testing a compressor for leaks is described in Section 16.2.5.)

6. Evacuate and recharge the system and check for leaks.

To remove a two-part seal, you should:

1. Recover the refrigerant.
2. Remove the compressor clutch assembly.
3. Remove the clutch hub drive key from the shaft.
4. Remove the seal seat. On some compressors:
    a. The seal seat is retained by a group of bolts at the front of the compressor. Remove these bolts and remove the seat.
    b. The seal seat is held in the compressor neck by a retaining ring. Remove the retaining

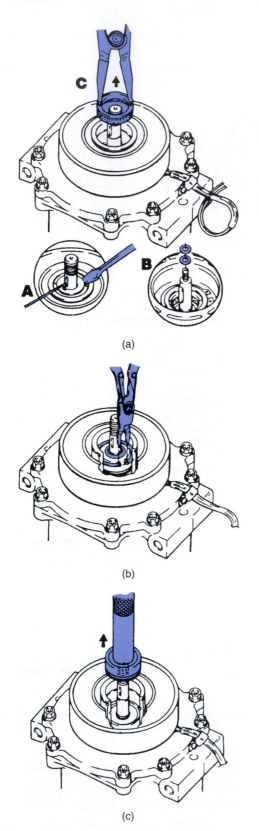

(a)

(b)

(c)

FIGURE 16-19 Replacement of this seal begins with removal of the dust cover (if used), shaft key, and shims *(a)*; then the seal retaining ring *(b)*; and then the seal cartridge *(c)*. *(Courtesy of Sanden International)*

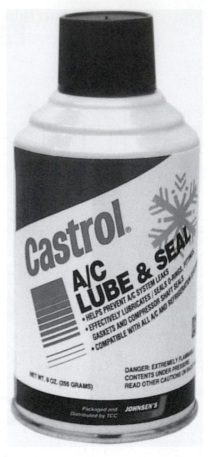

FIGURE 16-20 A/C Lube & Seal is a premium mineral lubricant in an aerosol container. It is a convenient method of lubricating parts, O-rings, and fittings as they are assembled. *(Courtesy of Technical Chemical Company, TCC)*

ring, attach a puller to the seal seat, and pull the seat out using a rotating motion (Figure 14-22).

    c. The front head must be removed; the center cylinder sections should be clamped together to prevent disturbing the center O-ring before this is done. Install the clamp, remove the bolts that hold the compressor together, remove the front head, remove the reed plate from the front head, and drive the seal seat out the rear of the front head (Figure 16-23).

5. Remove the seal cartridge from the shaft. A special tool is required on most compressors.

6. Remove the seal seat O-ring if it was not removed with the seal seat.

7. Thoroughly clean the seal and seal seat areas.

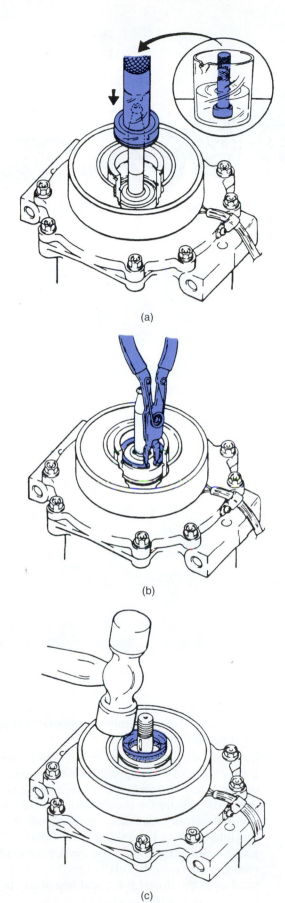

(a)

(b)

(c)

FIGURE 16-21 The seal is replaced by placing the seal on an installation tool, dipping it in clean refrigerant oil, and sliding it on to the compressor shaft *(a)*; the retaining ring is installed *(b)*; and then any other items taken out during the removal are replaced *(c)*. *(Courtesy of Sanden International)*

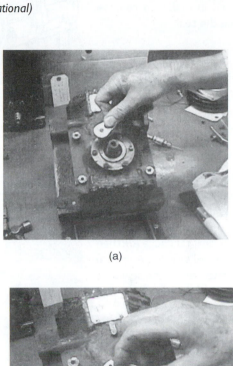

(a)

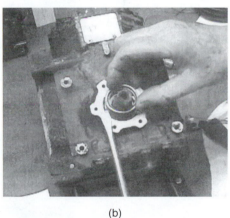

(b)

(c)

FIGURE 16-22 A two-piece seal is removed from the compressor by removing the seal seat *(a)*, and then the seal (*b* and *c*). Some seal cartridges will separate so some parts must be removed separately. *(Courtesy of Climate Control)*

FIGURE 16-23 The shaft seal of many Nippondenso-type compressors is inside the front head. The compressor must be partially disassembled in order to remove and replace the seal.

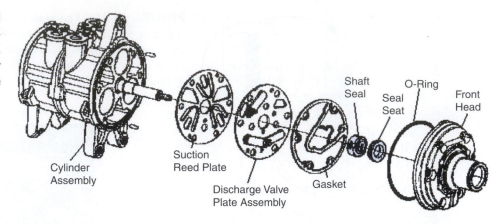

Shaft Seal

Seal Seat

O-Ring

Front Head

Cylinder Assembly

Suction Reed Plate

Discharge Valve Plate Assembly

Gasket

FIGURE 16-24 The two-piece seal is installed by coating the sealing surfaces and compressor shaft with clean refrigerant oil (*a* and *b*); installing the seal cartridge (*d*); then installing the seal seat (*d*). A special tool is used to center the seal seat to the shaft. (*Courtesy of Climate Control*)

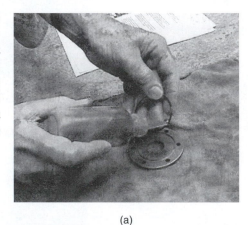

(a)

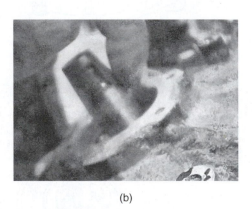

(b)

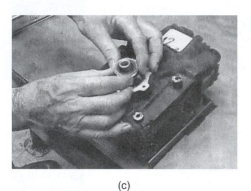

(c)

(d)

To replace a two-part seal, you should:

1. Install a seal protector over the compressor shaft.
2. On some compressors, oil the new O-ring and position it in its groove; a special tool is sometimes needed.
3. Oil the new seal and slide it over the compressor shaft. On some compressors, the seal must be rotated to engage the flat areas. You should feel the seal move in farther and the compressor shaft rotate as these flat areas are engaged.

Some compressors require a special installer for the seal (Figure 16-24).

4. Lubricate the seal seat and slide it into position. If a special tool was required to pull the seat, use the same tool to install it to ensure that it is positioned correctly. On compressors with the seal inside the front head, drive the seal seat and O-ring into the front head using the special tool, install a new O-ring in the front head, position the reed valve over the dowel pins, position the front head over the dowel pins, and install the bolts and tighten them to the correct torque.

5. Install the seal seat retainer. Remember that the seal cartridge should exert a forward pressure against the seat. *If bolts are used*, center the seal seat to the shaft and tighten the bolts to the correct torque. *If a retaining ring is used*, position the flat side of the retaining ring against the seat and, using a special tool, push inward on the ring until it enters its groove.

6. Rotate the compressor shaft a few turns, pressurize the compressor, and check for leaks.

7. Evacuate and recharge the system and check for leaks.

16.2.4 Compressor Repair

Compressor internal repair is limited by the availability of repair parts, service information, and the skill level of the technician. A noisy or roughly operating compressor that passes metal or plastic particles and shavings out the discharge is normally replaced with a new or rebuilt unit. If a system's high side pressure is too low and low side pressure too high, with these pressures within 30 to 50 psi of each other, the compressor is probably bad and should be either repaired or replaced. (This problem can be caused by faulty reed valves or an internal leak.) Another indication of a malfunctioning compressor is metal or plastic debris at the OT or TXV screen. When replacing a compressor, be sure that the replacement part is the right one and is compatible with the refrigerant used. Remember that if the compressor failed, the system is probably contaminated; the receiver–drier or accumulator is normally replaced also, and, in some cases, the condenser should be flushed or an in-line filter installed.

◀ **SERVICE TIP** ▶

At least one A/C system on a fairly popular vehicle has two low side service ports, and an inexperienced technician installed both service hoses to these low side ports (an adapter was needed to connect the high side hose). The gauges read the same pressure, indicating a bad compressor, but intuition and other indications suggested that the compressor was operating. Seeking advice from an experienced A/C technician produced a few laughs and advice about where to connect the high side service hose.

Internal gasket and O-ring, reed valve sets, and replacement heads are available for some compressors, and replacing a cylinder head and reed valve plate can be a relatively simple process. An internal assembly or **gut pack** is available for some compressors: This is an assembly that contains all of the internal wearing parts. Installing a gut pack allows the compressor shell, heads, and clutch to be reused. As mentioned earlier, the actual service procedure given in the manufacturer's service manual should be followed.

Many shops prefer to install a new or rebuilt compressor rather than make internal repairs on an old unit.

To remove a reed valve assembly, you should:

1. Recover the refrigerant from the system. If necessary, remove the compressor as described in Section 16.2.1.

2. Drain the oil out of the compressor and mount it in a holding fixture. Inspect the oil for debris and contamination.

3. Remove the head bolts and separate the head from the compressor.

4. Remove the reed valve assembly from the cylinder block or head (Figure 16-25).

5. Locate and remove the alignment dowel pins used on most compressors.

6. Remove the upper and lower gaskets or O-rings; there is usually one on each side of the reed valve plate.

7. Wash the cylinder head and top of the cylinder with clean solvent and air dry.

To replace a reed valve assembly, you should:

1. Install the alignment dowels into the holes in the cylinder assembly.

2. If a gasket is used between the reed valves and cylinders, wet the gasket with refrigerant oil and place it in the correct position.

3. Lubricate the reed valves with refrigerant oil and place them in the proper position, being sure to align the dowel pins and passages.

4. Wet the upper gasket or O-ring with refrigerant oil and position it.

5. Position the head, being sure to align the dowel pins.

6. Install the head bolts and tighten them to the specified torque using a diagonally opposite tightening sequence (Figure 16-26).

7. Rotate the compressor shaft to test the assembly, pressurize the compressor, and test for leaks.

8. Replace the compressor as described in Section 16.2.1.

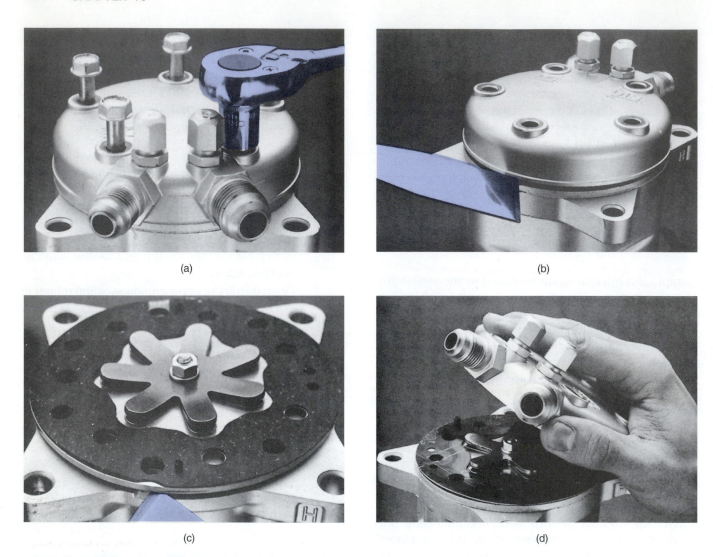

(a)

(b)

(c)

(d)

FIGURE 16-25 The valve plate of a Sankyo compressor can be replaced by removing the bolts (a) and the head (b), removing the valve plate (c) and old gasket, and installing a new valve plate with gaskets (d). Note that (c) is a 7-cylinder compressor while (a), (b), and (d) show a 5-cylinder compressor. (Courtesy of Sanden International)

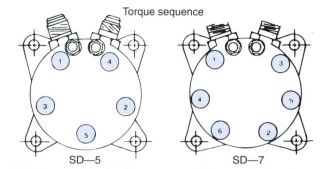

Torque sequence

SD—5   SD—7

FIGURE 16-26 When a compressor head is replaced, the bolts should be tightened to the correct torque and in the correct sequence. (Courtesy of Sanden International)

16.2.5 Compressor Bench Checks

Compressor bench checks consist of rotation checks of the compressor and clutch and leak checks. The rotation checks are for excessive drag, roughness, and excessive runout. These checks should always be made on a used compressor before installing it (Figure 16-27).

To make a rotating compressor check, you should:

1. Rotate the compressor drive hub and observe the air gap or clearance between the drive plate and rotor pulley. Hold the rotor pulley stationary during this check.

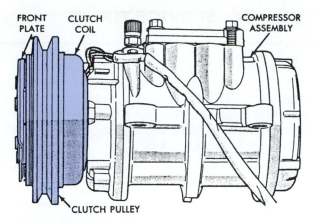

FRONT PLATE CLUTCH COIL COMPRESSOR ASSEMBLY

CLUTCH PULLEY

FIGURE 16-27 A compressor can be bench checked to ensure that the pulley turns smoothly without excessive runout and with no interference. The front plate (and compressor shaft) should also rotate smoothly without excessive runout. Excessive drag, noise, or clearance inside the compressor indicates a faulty compressor. *(Courtesy of DaimlerChrysler Corporation)*

◄ **SERVICE TIP** ►

A bent plate or compressor shaft is indicated if the runout is greater than the air gap specification range.

2. After rotating the shaft several turns, feel for roughness and excessive drag. One manufacturer gives a rotating torque specification of 7 lb-ft maximum.

◄ **SERVICE TIP** ►

Stop the rotation and quickly turn the shaft backward as you feel for excessive internal clearance. The shaft should rotate smoothly and fairly easily, with no internal free play.

3. Rotate the rotor pulley while holding the shaft stationary and observe the air gap. The pulley should rotate smoothly and quietly.

◄ **SERVICE TIP** ►

A bent rotor pulley is indicated if runout is greater than the air gap specification range.

Compressor leak checks require adapters that connect the discharge and suction ports to the service hoses of a manifold gauge set. Commercial adapters are available for most compressors, or they can be made in the shop by adapting the appropriate line fitting or block-off plate to the proper service valve fitting. Clean, oil-free, and water-free shop air can be used for these checks. An internal leak check looks for leaks from the discharge to the suction side in the compressor; an external leak check looks for leaks to atmosphere. While making an internal leak check, remember that reed valves do not make a perfect seal, and some leakage can be expected.

To make compressor leak checks, you should:

1. Install the pressure test adapters to the compressor ports.

2. Connect the service hoses of a manifold gauge set to the service valves and a 60-psi or greater pressure source (see Figure 12-71).

3. Open the high side hand valve and watch the pressure gauges. The high side pressure gauge should increase to source pressure immediately as the valve is opened. The low side pressure gauge should show a delayed and much slower pressure increase. An internal compressor leak is indicated if the low side pressure increases too rapidly.

4. Open both valves until both gauges show source pressure and then close both valves. Observe the gauge pressures—they both should hold steady. An external leak is indicated if they show a pressure loss.

5. Apply a soap solution to probable leak locations: the shaft seal, cylinder head, any other compressor body joint, any bolts, any switches or pressure relief valves, and the drain plug. A leak will produce bubbles.

16.2.6 Compressor Oil Level Checks

At one time, most compressors had an oil sump; the level was checked relatively quickly using a dipstick. With most modern compressors, there is no oil sump or way to use a dipstick. Checking the oil level is further complicated by the fact that the oil travels through the system with the refrigerant and can migrate while the system is shut off. To get a truly accurate check, the system should be operated for 10 to 20 minutes before checking levels. Too little oil in a system contributes to compressor wear or damage; too much can cause slugging in the compressor or excessive discharge pressures.

◀ **SERVICE TIP** ▶

Most systems have two specifications. One is for the amount in the system; on average, this is about 10 oz. The other is for the compressor; this is a specified amount somewhere between 3 and 6 oz.

Normally, an A/C system does not lose oil or contaminate that oil. Oil loss is usually the result of a refrigerant leak. Whenever a major system component is replaced, a certain amount of oil should be added to the new part to compensate for the oil removed. Oil contamination is usually caused by compressor failure, water or other chemicals, or system overheating. Contaminated oil points to a problem inside the system. If the proper equipment is available, the system should be flushed with liquid refrigerant, an in-line filter installed, the receiver–drier or accumulator replaced, and the system thoroughly evacuated. System oil level–checking procedure is described in Section 15.3.7.

◀ **SERVICE TIP** ▶

Improper system oil level has two probable results: If there is too little oil, compressor noise and eventual failure will occur. If there is too much oil, poor heat transfer with reduced in-vehicle cooling will occur.

◀ **SERVICE TIP** ▶

In an undercharged system, oil will tend to stay in the evaporator, and reduce compressor lubrication.

◀ **SERVICE TIP** ▶

Remember that refrigerant oil, especially PAG oil, is hygroscopic and will absorb water from the atmosphere if possible. Always keep the oil container capped; replace the cap immediately after pouring oil out of it. If you are working with PAG oils, also remember that you should wear nonpermeable gloves so the oil will not come into contact with your skin.

◀ **SERVICE TIP** ▶

If you add oil to a system into the suction port or line, the oil may become trapped on top of the pistons when it starts operation, and this can damage the compressor. Rotating the compressor shaft at least 10 turns by hand should pump any trapped oil out of the cylinders.

To check the oil level in a compressor with dipstick provision, you should:

1. Operate the system (if it can be operated) for 10 to 20 minutes to normalize the oil levels.
2. *If the system is equipped with service valves, isolate the compressor from the system (Figure 16-28). If the system is equipped with Schrader valves,* recover the refrigerant from the system.

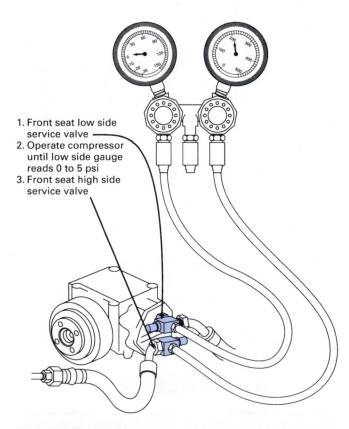

1. Front seat low side service valve
2. Operate compressor until low side gauge reads 0 to 5 psi
3. Front seat high side service valve

FIGURE 16-28 If the compressor is equipped with service valves, it can be isolated from the system following this procedure.

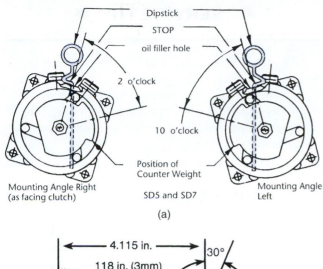

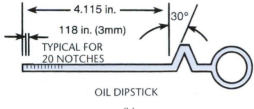

(a)

(b)

Mounting Angle (Degrees)	Acceptable Oil Level In Increments					
	505	507	508	510	708	709
0	4-6	3-5	4-6	2-4	4-6	3-5
10	6-8	5-7	6-8	4-5	5-7	4-6
20	8-10	6-8	7-9	5-6	6-8	5-7
30	10-11	7-9	8-10	6-7	7-9	6-8
40	11-12	8-10	9-11	7-9	8-10	7-9
50	12-13	8-10	9-11	9-10	9-11	8-10
60	12-13	9-11	9-12	10-12	10-12	9-11
90	15-16	9-11	9-12	12-13	11-13	10-13

(c)

FIGURE 16-29 A Sankyo compressor has an oil sump and provision to use a dipstick to check the oil level (*a*). The checking procedure and the acceptable levels are shown here (*b* and *c*). *(Courtesy of Sanden International)*

3. Remove the checking plug and insert the dipstick into the bottom of the compressor. The compressor shaft may have to be rotated to allow the dipstick to enter (Figure 16-29).
4. Remove the dipstick and measure the oil level.
5. Compare the oil level with the specification and adjust the level if necessary.
6. Replace the checking plug and tighten it to the correct torque.
7. Evacuate and recharge the system and test for leaks to return it to service. For service valve systems, back-seat the service valves to return it to service.

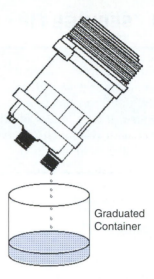

FIGURE 16-30 The oil level in this compressor is being checked by pouring the remaining oil into a graduated container.

◄ **SERVICE TIP** ►

Some compressor designs make it virtually impossible to drain all of the oil out of them.

To check the oil level in a compressor without dipstick provision, you should:

1. Operate the system (if it can be operated) for 10 to 20 minutes to normalize the oil levels.
2. Recover the refrigerant.
3. Remove the compressor as described in Section 16.2.1.
4. Drain the oil from either the drain opening or the service ports, measure the quantity drained out, and compare the amount drained out with the specifications. Check the condition of this oil and dispose of it in an approved manner (Figure 16-30).
5. Pour the specified amount of new oil of the proper type and viscosity into the compressor inlet and replace the compressor as described in Section 16.2.1.
6. Evacuate and recharge the system and check for leaks.

◀ **SERVICE TIP** ▶

If the amount of oil drained from the compressor is low, the compressor design is trapping oil or the system is low on oil; in the latter case, extra oil should be added. If the amount of oil is high, the system is wet with too much oil, and an undercharge of new oil should be added.

16.3   HOSE AND FITTING REPAIR

Most refrigerant leaks are through a faulty hose or hose connection, and, depending on the nature of the leak, several repair methods are possible. These can be as simple as tightening a loose fitting or as complex as making up a refrigerant hose.

◀ **SERVICE TIP** ▶

Early failure of hoses and fittings in a FWD vehicle can be the result of faulty engine mounts. The top of the engine in this type of vehicle rocks back and forth, from the front to the back, during vehicle operation; an excessive amount of rocking caused by faulty mounts can lead to premature hose failure.

◀ **SERVICE TIP** ▶

Early failure of hoses or fittings near the compressor can be caused by loose compressor mounting bolts. Compressor vibration can cause cracks and breakup of metal parts.

◀ **SERVICE TIP** ▶

Dual O-ring fittings can be difficult to separate; the preferred method is to use a special tool designed for that purpose. An alternate method if there is still pressure in the system is to loosen the fitting nut and operate the system; the internal pressure can loosen the fitting.

16.3.1   Fitting Repair

Leaky line fittings cannot be made to seal by over-tightening them, and the size of the fitting nuts and the wrenches used with them make overtightening easy. If the fitting is tight and still leaks, it must be taken apart and inspected for damage, and a new O-ring must be installed. Torque specifications for the various line fittings are provided by the vehicle manufacturer (Figure 16-31).

Most line fittings are sealed by one or two O-rings. At this time there are at least 5 different O-ring materials and 37 different sizes used in automotive A/C systems. Some of the sizes are very similar, the only difference being a slight change in thickness. O-rings are sized by internal diameter and cross-section; there are both fractional-inch and metric sizes. Most O-rings have a round cross-section; some are oval.

The chemical names for O-rings can be very confusing because of the seemingly conflicting use of chemical manufacturers' special names. O-rings must be chemically compatible with the refrigerant and oil used in the system (see Figure 5-15). The most commonly used references are *nitrile butadiene rubber (NBR)* and *hydrogenated nitrile butadiene rubber (HNBR)*. NBR, nitrile, or *Buna N* rubber is the standard O-ring material; this is a black material used in R-12 systems. Buna N is commonly used for *static installations* in which both parts are stationary, relative to each other. A different, more resilient material must be used in *dynamic installations* with movement (as in a

Typical Line Torque Specifications			
Metal Tube OD	Hose Size	Fitting Wrench Size	Torque: O-Ring Fitting
1/4"	No. 4		5-7 ft-lb, 14-20 N-m
3/8"	No. 6	3/4"	11-13 ft-lb, 15-18 N-m
1/2"	No. 8	7/8"	15-20 ft-lb, 20-27 N-m
5/8"	No. 10	11/16"	21-27 ft-lb, 28-37 N-m
3/4"	No. 12	1 1/4"	28-33 ft-lb, 38-45 N-m

FIGURE 16-31   This chart shows the tightening torque for the various sizes of hose and line fittings. It is easy to overtighten most of these because of the large wrenches.

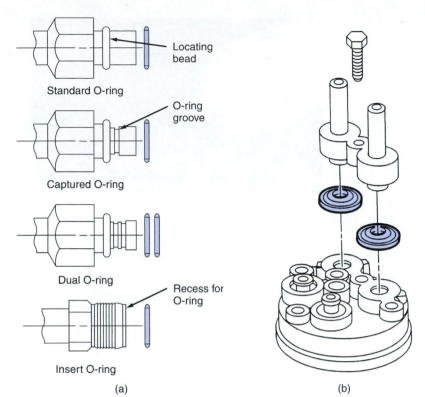

FIGURE 16-32 Some of the O-rings used to seal line connections. *(Courtesy of ACDelco)*

Standard O-ring — Locating bead

Captured O-ring — O-ring groove

Dual O-ring

Insert O-ring — Recess for O-ring

(a)

(b)

spring lock coupler), and this is also a black material. HNBR is commonly used with R-134a, and neoprene O-rings are used in OEM installations. HNBR is also a black material, but it has a blue tint. Some O-rings used with R-134a are made from *highly saturated nitrile (HSN)* and have a green color. Teflon O-rings are used with the service fittings on some early compressors; this material is white (Figure 16-32).

◄ **SERVICE TIP** ►

Do not trust the color of the O-ring to tell you the material it was made from. OEM O-rings can be black, green, brown, red, purple, tan, blue, or yellow. In most cases, an aftermarket green HNBR is an acceptable replacement. Purchase O-rings from a reputable source and specify their intended use.

◄ **SERVICE TIP** ►

HNBR and HSN O-rings work for both R-12 and R-134a installations. These O-rings should be used for all R-12 systems to help make such systems

ready for future retrofitting and also to reduce the need to stock NBR O-rings. All O-rings should be lubricated with standard mineral refrigerant oil as they are installed unless specified differently by the manufacturer.

To repair a leaky fitting with threaded connectors, you should:

1. Recover the refrigerant from the system.
2. Clean the fitting and disassemble it. Note that after the initial loosening, the nut should turn freely on the threads.
3. Remove the old O-ring and inspect both O-ring mating surfaces for damage. Nicked or deformed sealing surfaces require replacement.
4. Obtain the correct O-ring replacement and position it right next to the locating bead or, if a captive O-ring, in its groove (Figure 16-33).
5. Wet the O-ring with mineral type refrigerant oil (Figure 16-34). Wet the threads of the fitting with the same oil.
6. Carefully align the assembly and finger-tighten the nut.

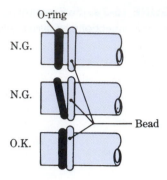

FIGURE 16-33 When an O-ring is installed, it should be placed in its proper position next to the locating bead or in its groove. *(Courtesy of Nissan Motor Corporation in USA)*

7. Use one wrench to keep the fitting from turning and, using a torque wrench, tighten the nut to the correct torque (Figure 16-35).

8. Evacuate and recharge the system and test for leaks.

◀ SERVICE TIP ▶

An iron fitting nut tends to seize onto the aluminum, male fitting of some components. If this occurs, heat the fitting nut using a hot air gun, and carefully work the nut back and forth until it is free. To prevent this problem from occurring, some technicians put never-seize compound or mineral refrigerant oil on these threads when assembling a component.

To repair a leaky fitting with a spring lock connector, you should:

1. Recover the refrigerant from the system.

2. Fit the spring lock coupling tool of the correct size over the line, close the tool, and push the tool into the cage opening to release the garter spring (Figure 16-36).

3. Pull the male and female fittings apart and remove the tool.

4. Clean the fitting parts, remove the old O-rings using a wood or plastic pick, and inspect the fittings for damaged sealing surfaces or garter spring. A damaged or bad garter spring should be replaced. Soft, silicon-impregnated brushes are available to clean the female fitting.

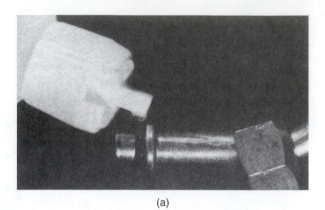

(a)

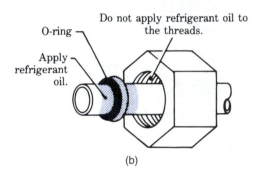

(b)

FIGURE 16-34 The O-ring must be wetted with ordinary refrigerant oil as it is installed. *(Courtesy of Nissan Motor Corporation in USA)*

5. Place the new O-rings in position and wet them with mineral-type refrigerant oil.

6. Assemble the fitting by simply pushing the two parts together with a slight twisting motion. Visually check your assembly; the flared end of the female fitting should have disappeared behind the garter spring (Figure 16-37). To assemble a newer Quick Connect fitting style, slide the two refrigerant lines together, place the plastic cage over the fitting, and close the cage (Figure 16-38).

7. Evacuate and recharge the system and test for leaks.

◀ SERVICE TIP ▶

Special clamps are available from aftermarket sources to help cure spring lock coupling leakage. These clamps secure the two coupling parts to eliminate the relative motion that causes the leak (Figure 16-39).

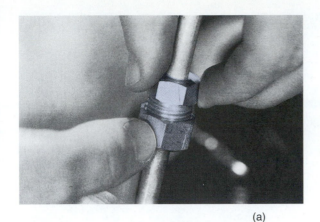

(a)

Torquing
A/C Lines
With
Adapter

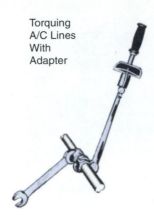

FIGURE 16-35 The fitting should be assembled finger-tight and then tightened using a torque wrench (*a*). A crows foot adapter can be attached to the torque wrench (*b*). (a *courtesy of Nissan Motor Corporation in USA*)

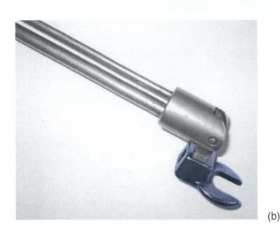

(b)

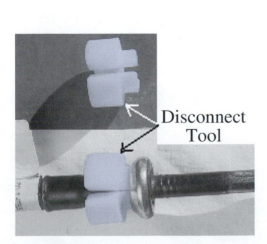

Disconnect Tool

FIGURE 16-36 A spring lock coupling is disconnected by placing a special tool over the line and pushing the tool into the coupling to release the spring so the coupling can be pulled apart.

Male Fitting:
Clean O-Ring Grooves
Lubricate &
 Replace O-Rings
Replace Garter Spring

Female Fitting:
Clean & Lubricate

Assembled Fitting:
Make sure Garter
 Spring is visible
 completely around
 fitting

FIGURE 16-37 A leaking spring lock coupling can often be repaired by cleaning the O-ring grooves and the male and female ends. After installing and lubricating new O-rings, the fitting is assembled, making sure the spring traps the flared end of the male fitting.

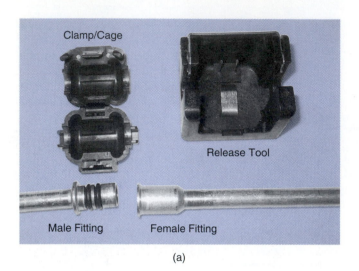

Clamp/Cage

Release Tool

Male Fitting

Female Fitting

(a)

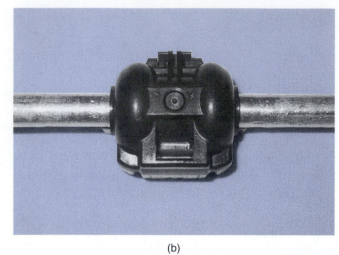

(b)

FIGURE 16-38 A disassembled quick-release fitting with the locking cage and the cage release tool (a). Two prongs of the release tool enter the assembled cage to release it so that the fitting can be taken apart (b).

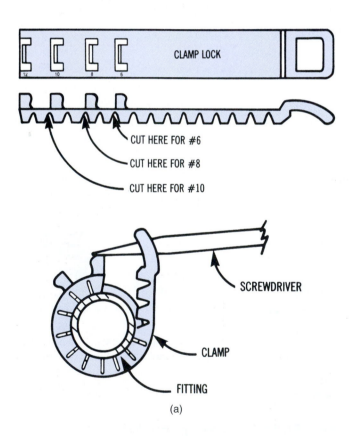

CLAMP LOCK

CUT HERE FOR #6

CUT HERE FOR #8

CUT HERE FOR #10

SCREWDRIVER

CLAMP

FITTING

(a)

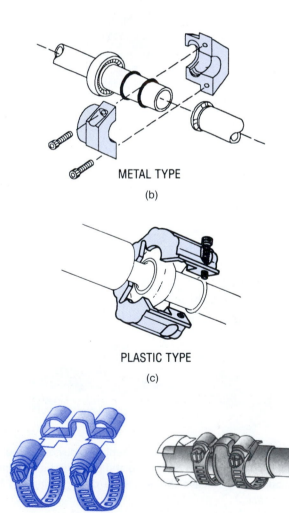

METAL TYPE

(b)

PLASTIC TYPE

(c)

(d)

FIGURE 16-39 Four different clamping systems are available to lock a spring lock coupling together to prevent future leakage. (a, b, and c courtesy of Four Seasons; d courtesy of T.D.R. Stabilizer Clamp Company)

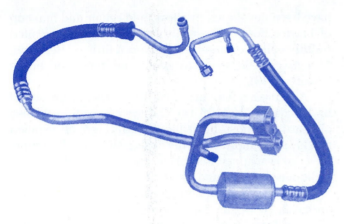

FIGURE 16-40 This OEM suction and discharge line assembly uses one manifold-type fitting at the compressor; this connection is usually sealed using a pair of O-rings. *(Courtesy of Four Seasons)*

16.3.2 Line Replacement

A faulty hose or metal line is often repaired by removing and replacing it with a new or repaired line. This normally involves disconnecting each end of the line at a fitting. Some hoses, like the suction and discharge, are combined with another line, making a double connection at the compressor, condenser, or evaporator. A manifold-type connector sealed with a pair of O-rings is commonly used at these connections (Figure 16-40).

> *To remove and replace a hose or metal line, you should:*

1. Recover the refrigerant from the system.
2. Clean the line connections and disconnect each end of the line.
3. Note how the line is routed, remove any line holding brackets and hose ties, and remove the line.
4. Clean and inspect the sealing surfaces for damage at each line connector.
5. Install new O-rings at each sealing connection, wetting the O-rings with refrigerant oil.
6. Assemble each connection and tighten each fitting nut or retaining bolt to the correct torque.
7. Replace all line brackets and hose ties.
8. Evacuate and recharge the system and test for leaks.

16.3.3 Hose Repair and Makeup

A hose can sometimes be repaired by replacing one of the ends or by cutting out a damaged section and splic-

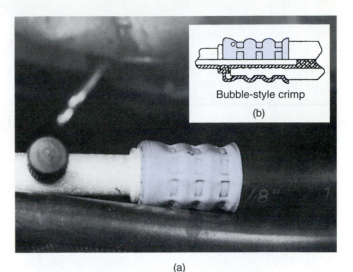

Bubble-style crimp
(b)

(a)

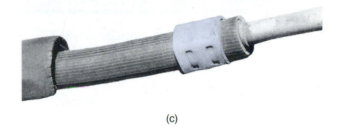

(c)

FIGURE 16-41 An OEM hose clamped in place using a captive, beadlock ferrule *(a)*; a beadlock fitting makes a very secure connection *(b)*. A fitting using a ring-type ferrule is shown in *(c)*. *(Courtesy of ACDelco)*

ing it back together. Many early systems used rather long hoses. Refrigerant hose is expensive; repairing a damaged hose can reduce repair costs. The fittings described here allow the technician to make up a replacement hose if a new hose is not available or is too expensive.

Most OEM hoses are connected to the line fitting with a captive, **beadlock ferrule** so the hose is gripped by both the line connector and the ferrule (Figure 16-41). These line connectors have grooves or very small barbs to grip the hose; they cannot be reused with the hose secured by a separate **ferrule** or clamp. Aftermarket R-12 repair fittings use three large, raised rings or barbs to grip the line securely. These fittings are connected to the hose with a metal shell.

◄ **SERVICE TIP** ►

Some A/C repair shops have tubing repair centers that allow them to duplicate almost any OEM A/C line. They can bend new tube to the desired shape;

form the proper beads at the end of the tube; attach a **beadlock fitting** or **barb fitting** at the end of the tube; secure a hose to the fitting; and pressure test the assembly to make sure there are no leaks.

◀ **SERVICE TIP** ▶

In the past, a screw or worm gear clamp was commonly used, but these clamps are no longer recommended because they will not pass the coupling integrity performance requirements. Some screw clamps are fitted with a locator extension that places the clamp directly over the barbs (Figure 16-42).

It should be noted that barb fittings may cut the inner liner of barrier hoses and that neither a screw clamp nor a noncaptive ferrule meets the new SAE leakage specifications for R-134a systems. New service fittings with a captive metal ferrule and a new clamping method

have been developed to allow field repair and makeup of barrier hoses. These fittings are commonly called **bubble crimp** or *one-piece beadlock* fittings. Beadlock fittings can be used to repair all types of hoses (Figure 16-43).

A recent innovation is the E-Z Clip system developed by Aeroquip (Figure 16-44). This system requires the use of a particular hose, but it allows the fitting to be installed quickly and simply. After the hose is slid onto the fitting, the cage is snapped into place, and then the clamps are positioned and secured using the special pliers.

Service fittings of both the barb and beadlock types are available in standard and jump sizes, with various styles of fitting types and bends. The standard size fitting matches the thread diameter of the connector with the diameter of the hose (Figure 16-45).

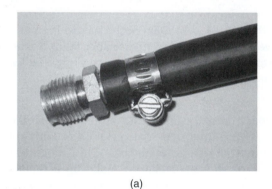

(a)

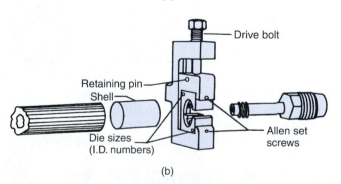

(b)

FIGURE 16-42 A hose for an R-12 system can be fastened to a fitting using a screw clamp *(a)* or a metal shell *(b)*, which is crimped using a special tool. A screw-type A/C hose clamp is no longer a recommended service procedure. *(b courtesy of Four Seasons)*

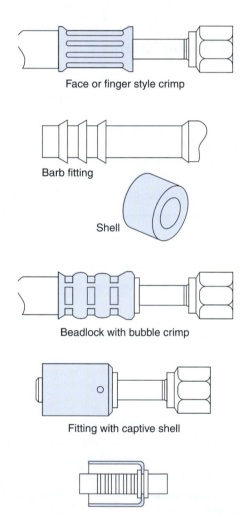

Face or finger style crimp

Barb fitting

Shell

Beadlock with bubble crimp

Fitting with captive shell

FIGURE 16-43 Barb-type service fittings are of two parts; the fitting and a shell that uses a **finger-style crimp** *(top)*. A beadlock fitting has a captive shell that is locked in place using a bubble crimp *(bottom)*. *(Courtesy of ACDelco)*

FIGURE 16-44 The E-Z Clip system consists of a special fitting and case *(top left)*, GH134 hose, and two clips. A hose cutter *(lower left)*, crimping pliers, and refrigerant oil are used during hose and fitting assembly. *(Courtesy of Eaton Corporation)*

◀ **SERVICE TIP** ▶

Remember that the fitting sizes are identified by the diameter where the hose is connected (the diameter is roughly in 1/16): 6 = 6/16 (3/8), 8 = 8/16 (1/2), 10 = 10/16 (5/8), and 12 = 12/16 (3/4) (Figure 16-46). For example, the connector nut for a #8 hose uses a 3/4-inch, 16 thread, and probably a 7/8-inch wrench. Jump sizes, also called step-up or step-down sizes, allow a different size hose to be fitted to a particular connector (e.g., a 3/4-inch fitting to a #8 or #12 hose).

FITTING SIZE (IN INCHES)			
Size	*Tube OD*	*Thread Diameter*	*Hose ID*
6	3/8 (0.375)	5/8	5/16
8	1/2 (0.500)	3/4	13/32
10	5/8 (0.625)	7/8	1/2
12	3/4 (0.750)	1 1/16	5/8

FIGURE 16-45 Most replacement hose fittings match the hose ID to a particular tube and nut diameter.

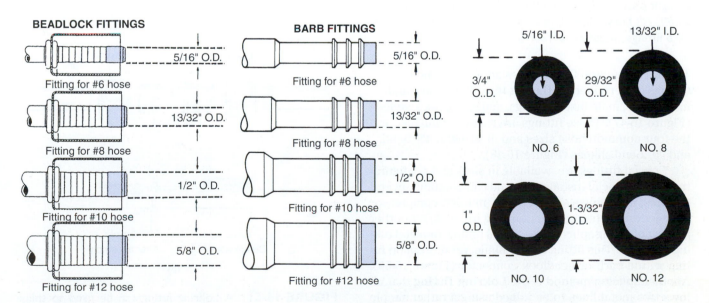

FIGURE 16-46 The stem section of beadlock and barb fittings matches the hose ID. *(Courtesy of Four Seasons)*

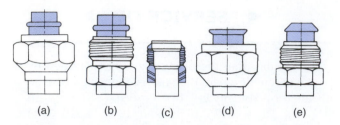

FIGURE 16-47 The threaded end of a replacement line fitting is available in female O-ring *(a)*, male O-ring *(b)*, male insert O-ring *(c)*, female flare *(d)*, and male flare *(e)* types. *(Courtesy of Four Seasons)*

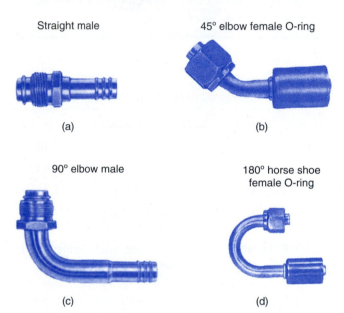

Straight male

45° elbow female O-ring

(a)

(b)

90° elbow male

180° horse shoe female O-ring

(c)

(d)

FIGURE 16-48 Replacement line fittings are available in straight *(a)*, and 45° *(b)* and 90° *(c)* bends and sometimes in a 180° *(d)* horseshoe bend; they can be either beadlock or barb fittings. *(Courtesy of Four Seasons)*

The most common fitting styles are female and male O-rings (determined by the nut threads), female and male flares, male insert fittings, and spring lock styles (Figure 16-47). These fittings are usually available for the four common hose sizes and in straight, 45° bend, and 90° bend shapes (Figure 16-48).

Special fittings are available in sizes and configurations to fit special installations and can combine several features, including a service valve, muffler, compressor connection, or tee connection (Figure 16-49). Another important fitting splices hose, metal tubing, or metal tubing to a hose. This fitting can combine a compression fitting with a barb or beadlock connector (Figure 16-50). Another splicing method is the **Lokring fitting** that allows two metal lines to be joined using a rather simple and quick procedure (Figure 16-51). It allows you to join a fitting to a metal line or to cut out a faulty part of a

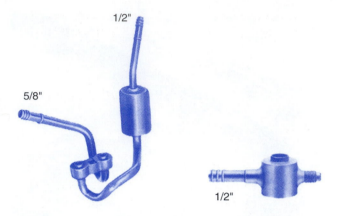

FIGURE 16-49 These two special fittings are used to connect a hose to a GM compressor. *(Courtesy of Four Seasons)*

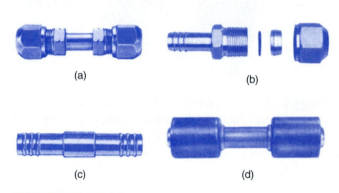

(a)

(b)

(c)

(d)

FIGURE 16-50 The fittings to splice two metal lines together *(a)*, a metal line to a hose *(b)*, or two hoses together *(c* and *d)*. *(Courtesy of Four Seasons)*

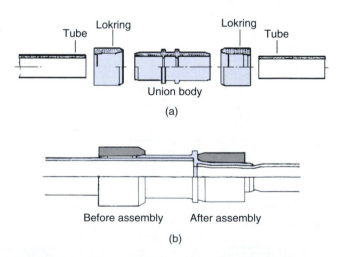

(a)

Before assembly   After assembly

(b)

FIGURE 16-51 A Lokring fitting can be used to splice two metal lines or a fitting to a line. *(Courtesy of American Lokring)*

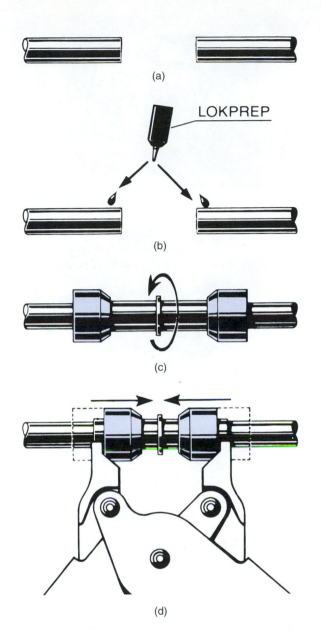

FIGURE 16-52 After cleaning the metal lines (a), a few drops of Lokprep are applied to the tubes (b), the tube ends are inserted into the union body (c), and Lokrings are squeezed over the union body using special pliers (d). (Courtesy of American Lokring)

metal line and rejoin the ends. This system requires a special handheld tool to compress the Lokrings (Figure 16-52).

It is also possible to reuse the original metal ends when replacing the hose portion. This is done by carefully slicing the metal shell on two sides, being very careful not to cut into the inner metal fitting. This allows spreading the metal shell and sliding the old hose off the fitting. Two special replacement shell designs are available. One design passes over the crimp for the

(a)   Remove factory collar.

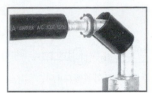

(b)   Assemble original fitting BLR ferrule and retainer.

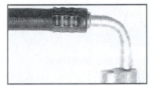

(c)   Bubble crimp to complete.

FIGURE 16-53 A damaged hose can be removed from the fitting by cutting the ferrule and prying it open (a). Then a special ferrule and retaining ring can be positioned on the fitting (b). The hose is then installed and the new ferrule is crimped to lock it in place (c). (Courtesy of BLR Enterprises)

original shell and a retainer ring fits into the groove in the crimp to retain the shell (Figure 16-53). The other design uses a large, offset hole in the shell; it is positioned into the fitting groove so the smaller portion of the hole fits into the groove. After placing either type of shell into position, the replacement hose is slid in place and the shell is crimped to lock the hose in place.

◀ SERVICE TIP ▶

A special repair fitting that is designed to save an OEM fitting is available (Figure 16-54). This fitting is the hose portion with a groove for a special ferrule design. The hose end of the OEM fitting is cut off, and the repair fitting is welded onto it. A new hose can then be attached to the original fitting.

Refrigerant hose is available in bulk lengths and in both double-braid and barrier-type hoses. Barrier hose has a thin, nonpermeable nylon layer to reduce leakage.

Fittings are secured onto a hose by crimping the metal shell with a special hose crimper; a different crimper is required for each crimp style.

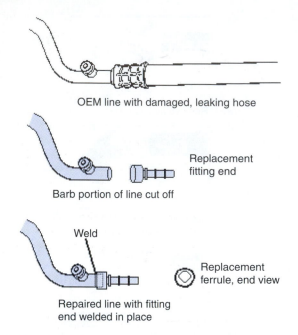

OEM line with damaged, leaking hose

Replacement fitting end

Barb portion of line cut off

Weld

Replacement ferrule, end view

Repaired line with fitting end welded in place

FIGURE 16-54 A line can be repaired by cutting the hose portion off and welding a new end fitting onto it. The replacement ferrule has an oversize, offset ferrule that can be slid into position to secure the new hose onto the fitting.

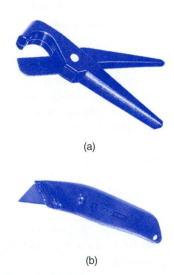

(a)

(b)

FIGURE 16-55 Refrigerant hose can be cut with a special cutter (a) or a sharp knife (b). (a courtesy of Four Seasons)

To attach a barb fitting to an R-12 nonbarrier hose using a finger-style crimp, you should:

1. Cut the hose to the proper length using either a hose cutter or a very sharp knife (Figure 16-55).
2. Wet the inside of the hose and the fitting barbs with refrigerant oil.

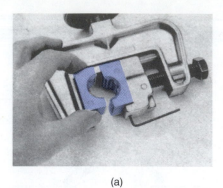

(a)

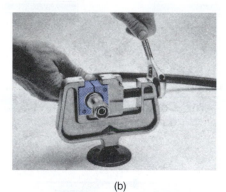

(b)

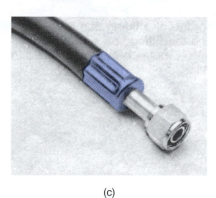

(c)

FIGURE 16-56 When making a finger-style crimp on the metal shell, dies of the correct size are installed in the tool (a) and the shell is crimped by tightening the tool drive bolt (b). A finished installation is shown in (c). *(Courtesy of Four Seasons)*

3. Place the shell of the proper size over the end of the hose and slide the fitting into the hose until the shell is snug between the hose end and the locating bead.
4. Make sure the dies are the proper size and place the fitting in the crimping tool with the shell centered in the dies (Figure 16-56).
5. Tighten the crimp tool bolt until the dies almost touch each other so the shell is completely crimped.

FIGURE 16-57 A beadlock crimping tool and a set of dies to make bubble-type crimps; the procedure is similar to that for making finger crimps. *(Courtesy of Four Seasons)*

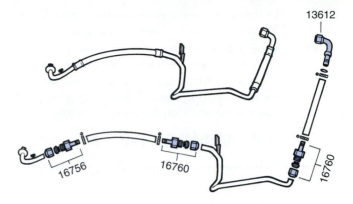

FIGURE 16-58 An OEM hose with three metal portions *(top)* can be replaced using two new hose sections, one line fitting (13612), and three connectors (16756 and 16760). *(Courtesy of Four Seasons)*

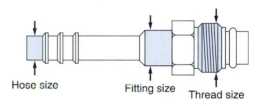

FIGURE 16-59 A fitting size is determined by measuring the tubing diameter next to the nut, the hose size is determined by measuring the diameter of the hose pilot (not the raised barbs), and the nut size is determined by measuring the diameter of the threads.

To attach a beadlock fitting to a hose using a bubble-style crimp, you should:

1. Cut the hose to the proper length using either a hose cutter or a very sharp knife.
2. Wet the inside of the hose and the fitting with refrigerant oil.
3. Insert the fitting into the hose until the cut end is visible in the hose-locating hole.
4. Make sure the dies are the proper size and place the fitting in the crimping tool with the shell centered in the dies (Figure 16-57).
5. Tighten the crimp tool bolt until the dies almost touch each other so the shell is completely crimped.

Refrigerant hose repair varies greatly depending on the affected hose, the damage to it, and the parts available. The following describes the replacement of a hose section between an accumulator and a compressor connection. Remember that the liner in a barrier hose can be damaged if used with a barb fitting. The procedures used to attach a fitting to a hose using either a finger- or bubble-style crimp are almost the same; the major difference is the crimping tool.

To repair this refrigerant hose, you should:

1. Recover the refrigerant and remove the hose as described in Section 16.3.2.
2. Determine the fitting type for each end. In this case, we will use a 90° female O-ring fitting at one

end and a compression-style fitting at the other (Figure 16-58). Two more compression-style fittings and another hose section are used at the other end of this line.

3. Determine the size of the fitting by measuring the tube OD size right next to the nut (Figure 16-59).
4. Determine the size of the hose by measuring the tube OD size at the hose end. Check the size charts to see if a jump size (step-up or step-down size) is needed.
5. Determine the best fitting angle.
6. Determine the length of hose needed; cut the hose using a hose cutter or sharp knife.
7. Determine the best location for the compression fitting. Cut the metal tube using a tubing cutter. If you use a hacksaw, be sure to file the rough end so it is smooth and clean out the resulting metal shavings. A compression fitting requires a straight section of metal tube about 1 inch long.
8. Clean the cut end and slide the nut and compression rings over the tube.

9. Wet the compression rings and tube end with refrigerant oil and slide the fitting in place.

10. Finger tighten the nut onto the compression fitting and, using two wrenches, tighten the nut to the correct torque. If O-rings are used, disconnect the nut(s), install the O-rings(s), and retighten the nut(s) to the correct torque.

◄ **SERVICE TIP** ►

The force needed to compress the ferrules onto the metal line can damage the O-ring if they are installed during the first assembly.

11. Crimp the shell, as previously described, to secure the hose to the fitting.

12. Repeat steps 10 and 11 to make the other hose connections.

13. Replace the hose using new O-rings.

14. Evacuate and recharge the system and check for leaks.

◄ **SERVICE TIP** ►

As mentioned, screw-type clamps are no longer a recommended hose-clamping method. If you must use them, place them over the hose and tighten the clamp to the proper torque. At this tightness, the outer rubber layer of the hose will be squeezed outward into the slots of the clamp.

◄ **SERVICE TIP** ►

Many A/C repair shops have the ability to pressure test hose assemblies that they have made up. This allows them to check the integrity of the new fittings.

16.4 A/C SYSTEM COMPONENT REPLACEMENT

If faulty, a major A/C component (the accumulator, condenser, evaporator, OT, receiver–drier, or TXV) is repaired by removing and replacing it with a new one.

Except for an OT, which requires a puller and some TXVs, the R&R operations are very similar. At one time, replacement of these components was relatively easy because there was rather good access, except when working with evaporators. In most cases, getting the evaporator case out of the vehicle is tedious and time consuming, sometimes requiring the vehicle or evaporator case to be cut. Many technicians will not change an evaporator without consulting a service manual. Today's vehicles with cramped engine compartments have made it increasingly difficult to get to underhood components.

◄ **SERVICE TIP** ►

When the compressor, evaporator, or TXV is replaced, the receiver–drier or accumulator should also be replaced. These failures were possibly caused by system contamination. This contamination will probably have loaded the desiccant capacity with moisture.

◄ **SERVICE TIP** ►

An outside-in failure can be caused by moisture and acids generated by decaying leaves in the bottom of the evaporator case. If this type of debris is found while replacing an evaporator, it is recommended that a screen be added to the fresh air intake to reduce chances of future problems.

◄ **SERVICE TIP** ►

It is good practice to keep the plastic caps in place on the new components until just before installation to keep as much moisture out of the system as possible. Remember, too, that removal of an accumulator, condenser, evaporator, or receiver–drier also removes a certain amount of oil from the system, and new oil should be added to the new part. The actual amount is usually specified in the service manual (Figure 16-60).

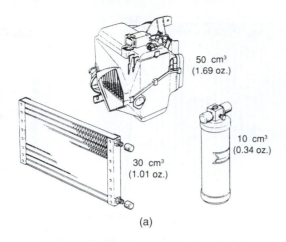

(a)

Component	Amount of oil cm³	(oz.)
Evaporator	50	(1.69)
Condenser	30	(1.01)
Liquid tank	10	(0.34)
Piping	10	(0.34)

(b)

FIGURE 16-60 When an A/C component is removed, a certain amount of oil is also removed. Typical amounts are shown here. *(Courtesy of Zexel USA Corporation)*

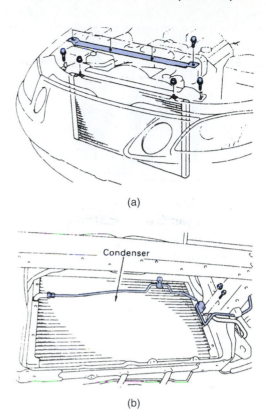

(a)

(b)

FIGURE 16-61 When an A/C component is replaced, the mounting brackets *(a)* and line fittings *(b)* should be replaced in the proper manner. *(Provided courtesy of Toyota Motor Sales USA, Inc.)*

◀ **SERVICE TIP** ▶

Be aware that it is possible to cause a vehicle's air bags to deploy if the wrong electrical wires are connected. This deployment can possibly cause injury to the technician or bystanders; it will cause an expensive repair. It is recommended that the air bags be deactivated using the manufacturer's recommended procedure before doing any work under the instrument panel.

To remove and replace a major A/C component, you should:

1. Locate and review the repair procedure in a service manual.
2. Recover the refrigerant from the system.

3. Disconnect and cap the refrigerant lines to the component.
4. Disconnect any mounting brackets and wires connected to the component and remove it (Figure 16-61).

◀ **SERVICE TIP** ▶

An experienced technician will often inspect failed components such as evaporators to determine if a leak was caused by an inside-out or outside-in failure. Inside-out failure is caused by acids inside of the system; the accumluator or receiver–drier must be replaced and the refrigerant recycled to remove the acids.

5. Install the new part and attach any mounting brackets and wires.

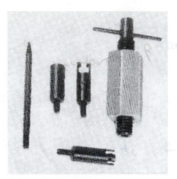

FIGURE 16-62 This orifice tube remover/installer kit has two tips to engage different orifice tubes, an extender for deep orifice tubes, and an extractor for broken tubes. *(Courtesy of Robinair, SPX Corporation)*

6. Remove the line caps, pour the proper amount of the correct refrigerant oil into the component or line, and connect the refrigerant lines.
7. Evacuate and recharge the system and test for leaks.

A special puller that attaches to the OT is normally used to pull the OT out of the tube. It is fairly easy to slide an OT in backwards, and if this happens the OT will be very difficult to remove. Use the removal tool to install the OT, and this will ensure it is installed in the right direction (Figure 16-62).

◀ **SERVICE TIP** ▶

There are two major OT variations: tab location and orifice size. The removal tabs are either at the OT inlet or outlet, and the orifice diameter can vary from 0.047″ to 0.072″. OTs are color-coded to show their diameter, but the color-code is not universal or completely reliable.

◀ **SERVICE TIP** ▶

Occasionally an OT sticks and breaks apart; special tools to pull broken OTs are available. A stuck OT can sometimes be loosened by heating (preferably with a heat gun) the evaporator inlet tube, but this requires great care. Another method that sometimes works is applying air pressure to the evaporator outlet in an attempt to blow the OT out of the inlet. (Before trying this, a shop cloth should be wrapped around the inlet tube to catch the flying OT.)

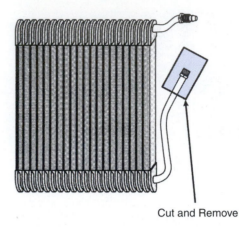

Cut and Remove

Repair Kit

FIGURE 16-63 If an OT cannot be removed or the evaporator inlet is damaged, the inlet tube can be cut off and a replacement kit can be installed. *(Courtesy of Four Seasons)*

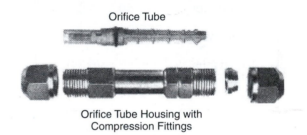

Orifice Tube

Orifice Tube Housing with Compression Fittings

FIGURE 16-64 Some orifice tubes are mounted into a section of the liquid line. This section must be cut out of the line, and a replacement housing section with the orifice tube is installed into the line.

◀ **SERVICE TIP** ▶

If the end of the OT breaks off, thread a long #8 or #10 drywall screw into the OT, heat the outer tube, and, using pliers or vise grips, pull outward on the screw to remove the OT.

If these methods fail, a service kit to replace the evaporator inlet tube is available. This kit is used by cutting off the evaporator inlet with the stuck OT still inside and installing a replacement tube and a new OT (Figure 16-63). A similar kit is used to replace an in-line OT. In this case, locate the indentations in the liquid line, which show where the OT is, and cut out that line section. The kit includes a new line section and OT and two compression fittings to connect it to the liquid line (Figure 16-64).

When replacing a TXV (other than a block-type TXV), the thermal bulb must be securely attached to the evaporator outlet tube. This area must be clean to en-

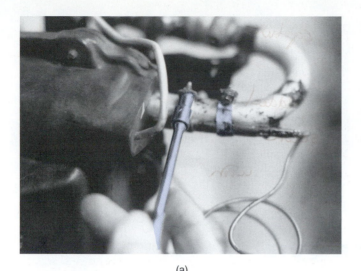

(a)

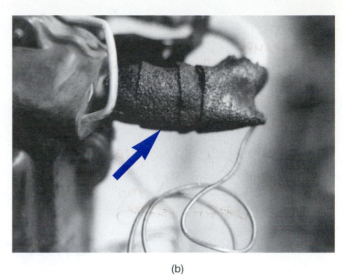

(b)

FIGURE 16-65   When a TXV is installed, the thermal bulb should be clamped securely to the evaporator outlet (a) and then wrapped with insulating tape (b).

sure good heat transfer. After attaching the thermal bulb, it must be wrapped with insulating refrigerant tape. This thick, pliable tape is used to keep outside heat from reaching the thermal bulb (Figure 16-65).

REAL WORLD FIX: The 1994 Jeep Grand Cherokee (103,000 miles) came in with no refrigerant because of a faulty hose. The hose and receiver–drier were replaced and the system recharged. It worked well but came back in a few days with a complaint of high engine temperature and poor A/C. The fan clutch was replaced, and this fixed the hot engine problem. The A/C was okay during normal driving but did not cool very well during stop-and-go conditions. The high side pressure was good, but the low side pressure was excessive.

FIX

The technician found out that the evaporator had been replaced a year ago, and an inspection of the evaporator revealed a poor-quality unit that was too small for the case.

Replacement of the evaporator core with an OEM comparable unit fixed this problem.

REAL WORLD FIX: The 1996 Cadillac DeVille (93,000 miles) came in with a locked-up compressor. The system was flushed, and the compressor, accumulator, and orifice tube were replaced. While the system was being recharged, the compressor cycled a few times and then stopped operating. The compressor will run with a jumper wire across the A/C relay. The control head display shows a malfunction, and a scan tool check shows a code for the evaporator inlet temperature sensor.

FIX

Following advice, the technician checked the inlet temperature sensor and found that the tip was bent; this was caused by installing the orifice tube too far into the line, bending the temperature sensor. Moving the orifice tube slightly outward and replacing the evaporator inlet temperature sensor fixed this problem.

REVIEW QUESTIONS

The following questions are provided to help you study as you read the chapter.

1. When installing a new or rebuilt compressor, it is a good practice to read the _____ _____ to determine the _____ and _____ of oil to put into the replacement compressor.

2. Always check the _____ _____ whenever a clutch is installed, and _____ it to the proper clearance if necessary.

3. When a clutch slips, it will _____ in a short period of time and probably _____ the bearing.

4. A lip-type compressor shaft seal must have a shaft surface that is _____ and not _____.

5. As you install a shaft seal cartridge, you should _____ _____ that the driving flats of the seal engage the _____ on the _____.

6. It is a good practice to test a used replacement compressor to determine there are no _____ *internal* or _____ leaks and the shaft _____ *rotates* smoothly with no excessive _____.

7. A replacement O-ring must have the correct _____ *dia* and _____ and be made from the proper _____ of _____.

8. When an A/C fitting is replaced, it must be tightened to the correct _____ of _____.

9. Leaks at a spring lock coupling can often be stopped by using a(n) _____ _____.

10. A replacement fitting for an R-134a hose should be of the _____ style and crimped using a(n) _____ style of crimp.

11. When a new component like an accumulator or evaporator is replaced, the proper amount of _____ should be _____ to that component.

12. When replacing an older-style TXV, be sure to _____ the thermal bulb to the evaporator tailpipe and wrap it _____ tape.

CHAPTER QUIZ

The following questions will help you check the facts you have learned. Select the answer that completes each statement correctly.

1. Normal compressor repairs include replacement of the _____.
   - **a.** shaft seal
   - **b.** clutch coil
   - **c.** reed valves
   - **d.** All of these

2. Technician A says that when the compressor is replaced, the oil levels should be checked. Technician B says that the oil from the old compressor can be reused. Who is correct?
   - **a.** A only
   - **b.** B only
   - **c.** Both A and B
   - **d.** Neither A nor B

3. Technician A says that as the clutch drive hub is replaced, the air gap should be checked at three different places. Technician B says that the air gap is not important as long as the clutch ohms are correct. Who is correct?
   - **a.** A only
   - **b.** B only
   - **c.** Both A and B
   - **d.** Neither A nor B

4. Technician A says that it is important to position snap rings correctly when replacing clutch parts on a compressor. Technician B says that the whole clutch assembly should be replaced if the pulley bearing fails. Who is correct?
   - **a.** A only
   - **b.** B only
   - **c.** Both A and B
   - **d.** Neither A nor B

5. The clutch must be removed and replaced to _____.
   - **a.** get access to the compressor shaft seal
   - **b.** remove and replace the compressor
   - **c.** Both a and b
   - **d.** Neither A nor B

6. Technician A says that shaft seal parts should be well lubricated as they are installed. Technician B says that special tools are often required when removing or replacing seal parts. Who is correct?
   - **a.** A only
   - **b.** B only
   - **c.** Both A and B
   - **d.** Neither A nor B

7. Oil level in an A/C compressor can be checked at any time.
   - **a.** True
   - **b.** False

8. When a compressor is replaced, it is a good practice to also replace the _____.
   - **a.** TXV
   - **b.** OT
   - **c.** Both A and B
   - **d.** receiver–drier or accumulator

9. Technician A says that you must install the compressor and charge the system to check for seal leaks. Technician B says that if you apply pressure to a compressor discharge port, pressure will show up immediately at the suction port. Who is correct?
   - **a.** A only
   - **b.** B only
   - **c.** Both A and B
   - **d.** Neither A nor B

10. Technician A says that most leaks at line fittings can be stopped by tightening the fitting nut a little tighter. Technician B says that line fitting O-rings should be properly positioned and lubricated with a drop of refrigerant oil as they are installed. Who is correct?
    - **a.** A only
    - **b.** B only
    - **c.** Both A and B
    - **d.** Neither A nor B

11. A new hose can be made up in the shop by installing the correct ends onto the right size, type, and length of hose.
    - **a.** True
    - **b.** False

12. Technician A says that new refrigerant oil should be added to new components such as accumulators or condensers as they are installed. Technician B says that two wrenches should be used when tightening most line fittings. Who is correct?
    - **a.** A only
    - **b.** B only
    - **c.** Both A and B
    - **d.** Neither A nor B

◀ Chapter 17 ▶

COOLING SYSTEM THEORY

LEARNING OBJECTIVES

After completing this chapter, you should:

1. Understand the cooling system's role in maintaining proper engine temperature.
2. Realize the effects that overcooling and overheating have on an engine.
3. Understand what the parts of the cooling system do and how they operate.
4. Understand what coolant is and what can happen if it is not properly maintained.

TERMS TO LEARN

coolant	fan clutch
coolant pump	fin-and-tube design
coolant recovery reservoir (CRR)	freeze plug
core	hoses
core hole plug	jiggle pin
corrosion-protection	organic acid (OA)
crossflow	pressure cap
downflow	propylene glycol (PG)
drive belt	relay
ethylene glycol (EG)	reverse coolant flow
expansion tank	serpentine V-ribbed belt
extended life antifreeze	shroud
fan belt	soft plug
	thermostat

thermosyphon	water jacket
V belt	water pump

17.1 INTRODUCTION

Automotive engines use a cooling system to remove excess combustion heat. Modern cooling systems are designed to maintain an even temperature of about 180 to 230°F (82 to 113°C); this is at or above the boiling point of water. A coolant mixture of water and antifreeze is used, and, because it is under pressure, the coolant has a still-higher boiling point.

An engine will be damaged if the operating temperature gets too high, above the coolant boiling point, which is about 260°F (125°C). This damage can appear as preignition and detonation, a warped or cracked cylinder head or block, or piston-to-cylinder-wall scuffing.

An engine performs poorly if it operates at too low a temperature, below the specified thermostat setting. Cold engine problems include poor oil flow, sludge formation in the oil, and poor fuel vaporization. Also, computer-controlled engines and transmissions will not go into normal operating modes if they are too cold; this causes poor performance and fuel mileage. Some vehicles set a diagnostic trouble code (DTC), and turn on the malfunction indicator lamp (MIL) if it takes too long to warm up to operating temperature.

Most modern automobiles are liquid cooled: Liquid coolant is used to transfer heat to the airstream. Many small gas engines and motorcycles are air cooled. Air is blown across fins attached to the cylinders and heads to

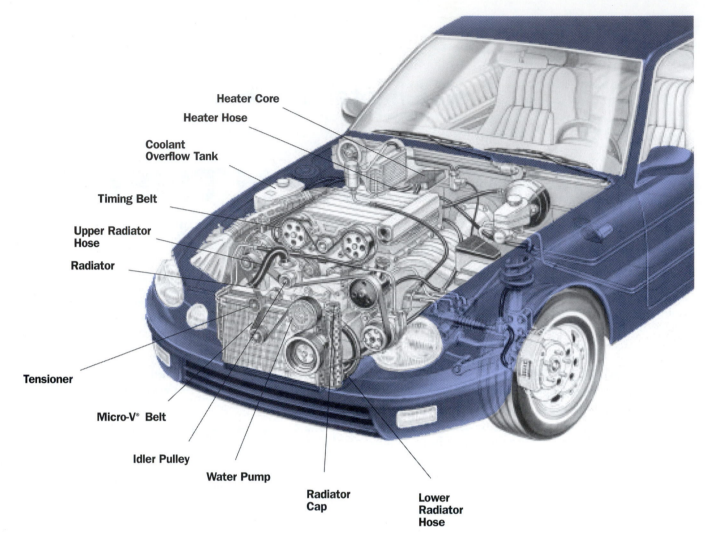

FIGURE 17-1 Most cooling systems contain these components. *(Courtesy of Gates Corporation)*

remove excess heat. Air-cooled engines are generally simpler and lighter weight, but liquid cooling provides much better temperature control over the cylinders and combustion chambers.

An automotive cooling system consists of the engine's water jackets, thermostat, water pump, radiator, fan, radiator hoses, and coolant (Figure 17-1). When an engine is at operating temperature on a warm day, the coolant circulates through the water jackets and radiator. The excess heat absorbed by the coolant in the water jackets is passed on to the air flowing through the radiator. When the engine is below operating temperature, the thermostat blocks the flow to the radiator, and the coolant circulates through the water jackets to raise the temperature evenly to an efficient temperature. On cool days when the engine is at operating temperature, the thermostat modulates the flow and allows just enough circulation through the radiator to remove

excess heat and maintain an efficient temperature in the engine. On warm days, the thermostat is probably wide open.

◀ **PROBLEM SOLVING 17-1** ▶

The engine in your friend's vehicle would not run so he pulled the cylinder head to see what was wrong. Two exhaust valves were badly burned, and the head was warped so coolant leaked into the combustion chambers. He has decided to install a rebuilt head. What do you think caused this problem? What checks should he make before he completes this job?

17.2 WATER JACKETS

When an engine cylinder block and head are cast, cavities called **water jackets** are formed around the cylinder walls and combustion chambers. These water jackets allow coolant to circulate around the very hot areas, including the exhaust valve seats, as well as the relatively cooler areas of the lower cylinders. The coolant absorbs heat from the hot areas and transfers this heat to the colder areas in the engine or radiator (Figure 17-2).

The engine block is cast by pouring molten iron or aluminum into a mold or form that is the shape of the outside and inside of the engine. The area for water jackets is filled with a sand core; projections or risers from the core extend to the outer mold to hold it in position. These risers leave a hole in the finished casting called a *core hole*. Core holes are normally filled with a cup-shaped metal plug or a threaded pipe plug. These cup plugs are commonly called **freeze plugs** or **soft plugs.** (Early motorists and mechanics thought that these plugs were put in the engine as safety plugs and that the plugs would pop out if the engine froze to protect the block from cracking. This idea is wrong; *soft plug* and **core hole plug** are better names.) The side of the engine block also includes a coolant drain plug that enters into the bottom of the water jacket (Figure 17-3).

17.3 THERMOSTAT

The **thermostat** is a temperature-controlled coolant valve. In most engines, it is located at the upper radiator hose connector, which forms the thermostat housing. In a few engines the thermostat is located at the lower radiator hose or inlet connection (Figure 17-4).

The two major functions of a thermostat are to speed up engine warm-up and to regulate operating temperature. The thermostat is closed when the coolant is cold; it opens when the coolant warms up to a specific temperature. Most modern vehicles use a 180, 190, or 195°F (82, 88, or 91°C) thermostat. A thermostat begins to open within a few degrees of the rating and should be fully open about 20°F (11°C) higher. The operating temperature point is often stamped on the thermostat.

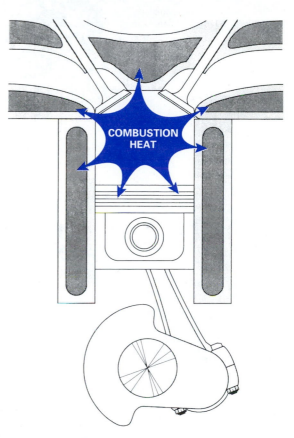

FIGURE 17-2 Water jackets are chambers that surround the cylinders and head of the combustion chamber.

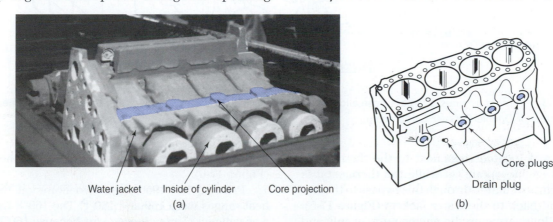

Water jacket   Inside of cylinder   Core projection
(a)

Core plugs
Drain plug
(b)

FIGURE 17-3 A cylinder block (a) is cast in a mold in which sand cores form the cylinders and water jackets (b). Molten cast iron fills the voids in the mold to form the outside of the block and the cylinder walls. (a *courtesy of Ashland Chemical*)

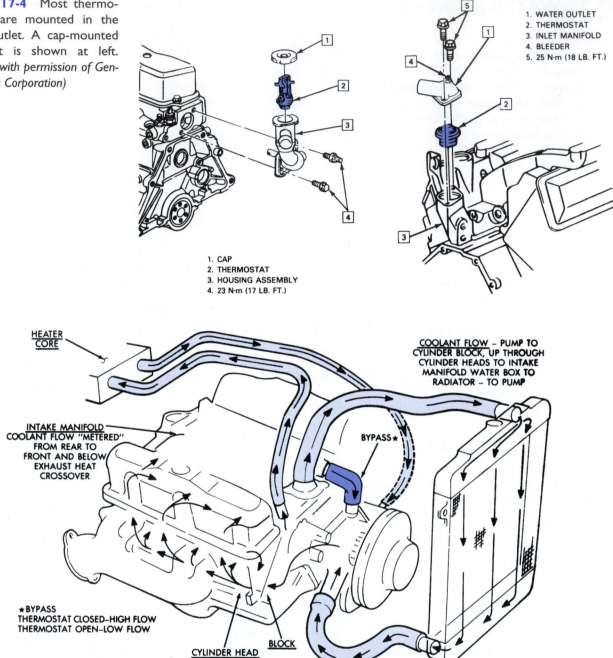

1. CAP
2. THERMOSTAT
3. HOUSING ASSEMBLY
4. 23 N·m (17 LB. FT.)

1. WATER OUTLET
2. THERMOSTAT
3. INLET MANIFOLD
4. BLEEDER
5. 25 N·m (18 LB. FT.)

HEATER CORE

COOLANT FLOW – PUMP TO CYLINDER BLOCK, UP THROUGH CYLINDER HEADS TO INTAKE MANIFOLD WATER BOX TO RADIATOR – TO PUMP

INTAKE MANIFOLD COOLANT FLOW "METERED" FROM REAR TO FRONT AND BELOW EXHAUST HEAT CROSSOVER

BYPASS ★

★BYPASS
THERMOSTAT CLOSED–HIGH FLOW
THERMOSTAT OPEN–LOW FLOW

CYLINDER HEAD   BLOCK

FIGURE 17-5 In most engines, a bypass hose allows coolant to circulate back to the water pump when the thermostat is closed. *(Courtesy of DaimlerChrysler Corporation)*

A bypass is located right next to the thermostat. During cold engine operation while the thermostat is closed, coolant circulates through this bypass to the water pump and back to the water jackets (Figure 17-5). This circulation warms up the engine parts evenly and also ensures that the thermostat is warmed up by the coolant. Some engines use a three-way thermostat; this design shuts off the bypass when the thermostat opens, and it directs all of the warm coolant to the radiator (Figure 17-6).

Prior to the 1950s, the two common thermostat heat ranges were 160 and 180°F. The 160°F thermostat was called a *winter thermostat* because 160°F was below the boiling point of the alcohol-based antifreeze used in those days. Alcohol antifreeze was called "temporary" because it was used only for winter operation;

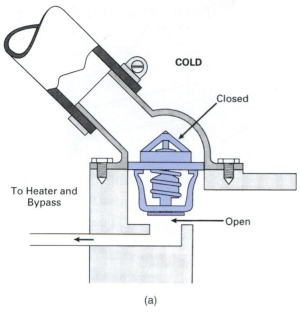

COLD

Closed

To Heater and
Bypass

Open

(a)

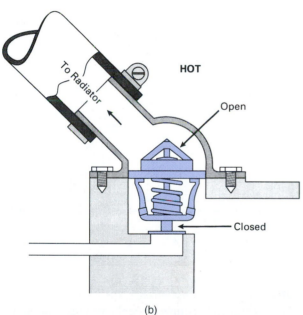

HOT

To Radiator

Open

Closed

(b)

FIGURE 17-6   Some systems use a three-way thermostat that closes off the bypass when the thermostat opens.

the alcohol would boil away if used in the summer. In the spring, when the days and nights warmed up, the motorist drained the antifreeze, changed to a 180°F *summer thermostat*, and refilled the system with water. Those days are long gone, but for some reason, the 160°F thermostat is still quite popular. A 160°F thermostat is too cold for modern engines.

The valve in most thermostats is closed by a spring and is opened by a wax motor or pellet. When the wax warms up and melts, it expands and compresses the rubber diaphragm to push away from the stemlike piston to

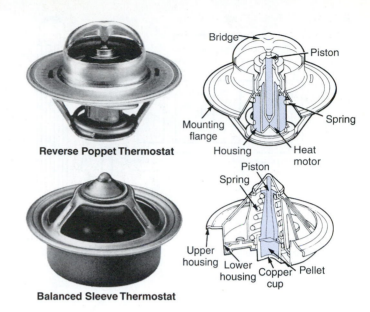

Reverse Poppet Thermostat

Balanced Sleeve Thermostat

Bridge — Piston
Mounting flange — Spring
Housing — Heat motor
Piston
Spring
Upper housing — Lower housing — Copper cup — Pellet

FIGURE 17-7   When the heat motor of the thermostat reaches the correct temperature, it pushes the piston outward and opens the thermostat. *(Courtesy of Stant Manufacturing)*

open the valve. The motor operates a valve of either reverse-poppet or balanced-sleeve design. This action is quite reliable and trouble free. However, a thermostat can fail, and if it fails, it will stick in either the open or closed position. If it sticks open, the engine will have a very long, slow warm-up period with delayed heater operation. If it sticks closed, the engine will overheat (Figure 17-7). On computer-controlled engines, replacement thermostats must have the same temperature rating as the original.

Many thermostats have a bleed notch or hole to help prevent air lock as the system is filled. A **jiggle pin** is often placed in the hole to prevent plugging.

In a few engines, the thermostat is located at the engine inlet to reduce thermal shock. When an engine operates on a cold day, the thermostat can open to allow cold coolant to enter and hot coolant to leave the engine. The thermostat recloses when the cold coolant reaches it but only after partial engine cooldown has occurred. Inlet thermostat systems prevent thermal shock that can cause warpage, especially with aluminum engine parts (Figure 17-8).

◄ **PROBLEM SOLVING 17-2** ►

The engine in a friend's vehicle overheats, and she has asked your advice. In trying to cure the problem, her father has removed the thermostat, but the car still overheats. Was this a wise move?

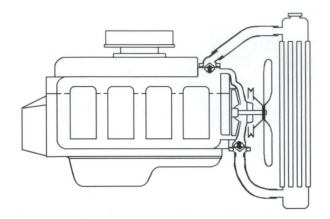

FIGURE 17-8 Most engines use a thermostat at the engine coolant outlet; a few place the thermostat at the coolant inlet.

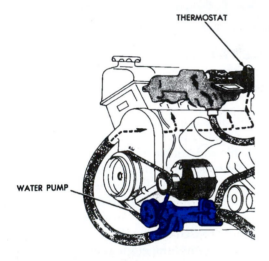

FIGURE 17-9 In most vehicles, the water pump is driven by the accesory drive belt. *(Courtesy of DaimlerChrysler Corporation)*

17.4 WATER PUMP

In most vehicles, the **water pump** is driven by the accessory drive belt, commonly called the **drive belt** or **fan belt,** at the front of the engine (Figure 17-9). In some modern engines, the water pump is gear driven. The water pump is a nonpositive displacement centrifugal pump. Coolant enters at the center of the pump, is caught by the impeller, and is spun outward to the outlet. The term **coolant pump** is used by some vehicle manufacturers (Figure 17-10).

In most engines the coolant is pumped into the lower water jackets, around the cylinders. It then flows toward the rear of the engine, upward to the cylinder head, and then to the outlet at the front of the head or intake manifold (Figure 17-11). On many transverse-mounted engines, the coolant flows into the engine at the

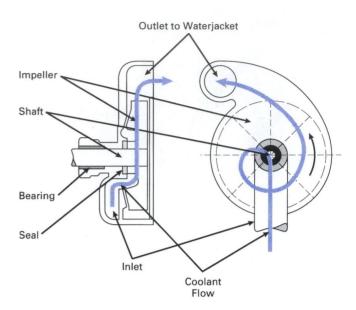

FIGURE 17-10 Coolant enters the water pump at the center of the impeller. From here, the impeller spins the coolant, and centrifugal force sends it through the outlet to the water jackets.

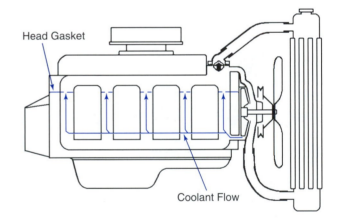

FIGURE 17-11 In most engines, the coolant flows into the block's water jackets, upward to the head(s), and out the passages at the front or rear of the head. The amount of flow is controlled by the holes in the head gasket.

water pump at the right end and outward at the thermostat housing at the other end. The placement and sizes of the passages in the head gasket control the flow to ensure adequate flow to all areas, especially the hottest.

A few engines use a **reverse coolant flow** so the coolant flows in at the cylinder head and out at the bottom of the block. Reverse flow brings the coolest coolant to the exhaust valve area, which is the hottest part of the engine. The cooler combustion chamber temperatures allowed Chevrolet engineers to increase the compression ratio of the LT1 engine, improving both horsepower

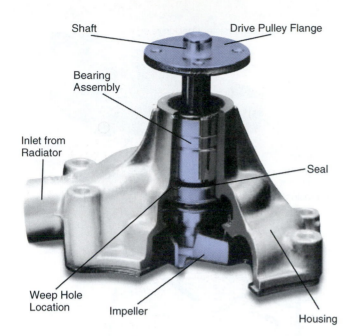

Shaft

Drive Pulley Flange

Bearing
Assembly

Inlet from
Radiator

Seal

Weep Hole
Location

Impeller

Housing

FIGURE 17-12 This cutaway view of a water pump shows the relationship of the shaft, bearing, seal, and impeller. A weep hole (not shown) allows any coolant that leaks past the seal to drain. *(Courtesy of Gates Corporation)*

and fuel mileage. Reverse flow also brings the heated coolant to the lower cylinder walls, which are the coolest. This results in more even temperatures throughout the engine and improved piston and ring wear.

Water pumps use a metal or plastic impeller with the curved pumping fins; the impeller is mounted on the end of the pump drive shaft. The shaft is usually supported by a permanently lubricated, double-row ball bearing. A carbon face seal is mounted where the shaft enters the pumping chamber, and a weep hole is placed between the seal and the bearing. The weep hole allows any coolant that has seeped through the seal to escape rather than pass into the bearing (Figure 17-12).

17.4.1 Drive Belt

In the past, most vehicles used one or more **V belts** to drive the water pump and other accessories. Many modern vehicles use a single, wide, **serpentine V-ribbed belt.** A V-ribbed belt is also called a *multi-V* or *poly-V belt* (Figure 17-13).

A V belt gets its name from the V shape of the belt and pulley groove. This belt is designed with a tensile member just under the top cover. This tensile member is a strong layer of cording, which prevents stretching (Figure 17-14). When the belt turns a corner around a pulley, the lower section must shorten, and the sides of the belt grip the pulley because of a slight thickening as

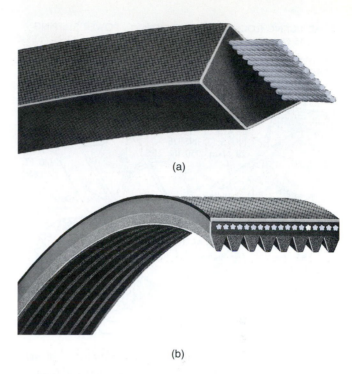

(a)

(b)

FIGURE 17-13 A V *(a)* and a V-ribbed belt *(b)*. The V-ribbed belt has smaller V sections. *(Courtesy of Goodyear Tire & Rubber Company)*

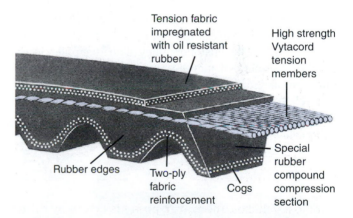

Tension fabric
impregnated
with oil resistant
rubber

High strength
Vytacord
tension
members

Rubber edges

Two-ply
fabric
reinforcement

Cogs

Special
rubber
compound
compression
section

FIGURE 17-14 A V belt is made from different compounds, each having a special purpose. *(Courtesy of Goodyear Tire & Rubber Company)*

the sides try to spread. A V belt can only transmit a certain amount of power, so in many cases three or four belts were needed to drive the A/C compressor, air pump, alternator, power steering pump, and water pump and fan. A loose belt will slip; it usually makes a squealing sound as it slips. This slippage generates heat, which can cause the belt to harden and glaze. One method of adjusting belt tension is to pivot one of the driven members or an idler pulley (Figure 17-15).

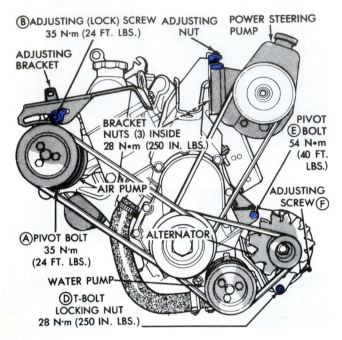

FIGURE 17-15 The tension of most V belts is adjusted by pivoting the driven component. *(Courtesy of Daimler-Chrysler Corporation)*

A serpentine V-ribbed belt drives through the friction of the belt on the pulley so the belt must wrap further around the pulley. A serpentine belt bends in both directions so that the back of the belt is used on some pulleys (Figure 17-16). The tensioner pulley or an idler pulley is positioned so that it will increase the amount of wrap around certain pulleys. The amount of wrap and its width allow the belt to handle the horsepower requirement. Proper belt tension is usually maintained by a spring-loaded tensioner pulley (Figure 17-17). Some tensioners include

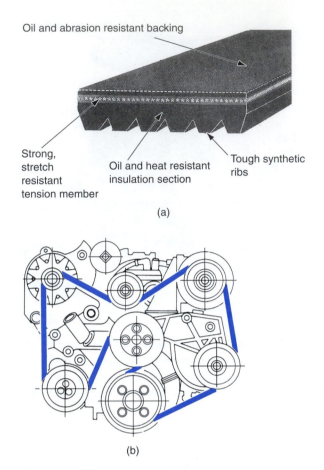

FIGURE 17-16 A cutaway view of a V-ribbed belt showing its internal construction *(a)*. *(b)* shows a typical belt routing and demonstrates why this belt is called a serpentine belt. Note that the water pump rotates in an opposite direction because it is driven by the back of the belt. *(Courtesy of Goodyear Tire & Rubber Company)*

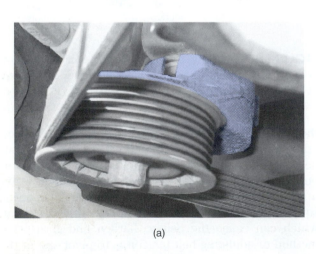

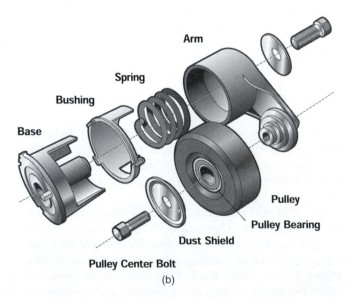

FIGURE 17-17 This idler pulley includes an automatic tensioner *(a)*. An exploded view is shown in *b*. *(b Courtesy of Gates Corporation)*

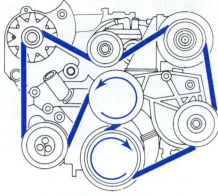

Serpentine belt:
fan and water pump
rotate counterclockwise

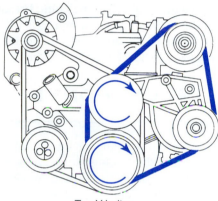

Two V-belts:
All pulleys rotate
clockwise

FIGURE 17-18 When a V belt is used, all the driven components rotate in a clockwise direction. With a serpentine belt, those components driven by the back of the belt rotate counterclockwise.

markings to show that a belt has stretched too far and should be replaced. It should be noted that the pulleys driven by the back of this belt, usually the water pump and fan, rotate in the opposite or counterclockwise direction; these parts are redesigned to operate properly in this direction (Figure 17-18). Some engines use two V-ribbed belts or a V-ribbed belt and a V belt.

17.5   RADIATOR

The radiator is a heat exchanger that gets rid of excess engine heat. Most radiators are of **fin-and-tube design.** Coolant flows through tubes from the inlet tank to the outlet tank. The fins are attached to the tubes to provide the air contact area. The fin-and-tube area is commonly called the **core** (Figure 17-19).

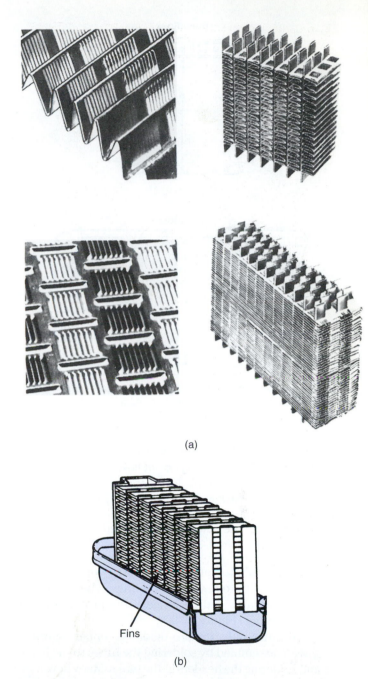

(a)

Fins

(b)

FIGURE 17-19 A radiator core is made up of tubes and fins (a) that join to a header and tank (b). (Courtesy of Modine Manufacturing)

Many older vehicles use **downflow** radiators: The flow direction is from top to bottom. Most newer vehicles use **crossflow** designs in which the flow is from one side to the other. A downflow radiator uses the natural flow direction (cooled water drops while heated water rises). A few engines use this principle in **thermosyphon** cooling systems, which have no water pump.

Downflow

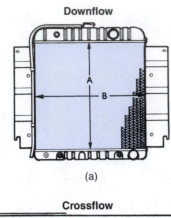

(a)

Crossflow

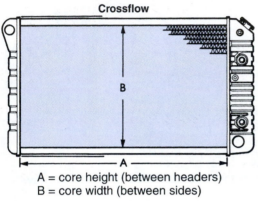

A = core height (between headers)
B = core width (between sides)

(b)

FIGURE 17-20   Most older vehicles use a downflow radiator design *(a)* in which the coolant flows downward. Most newer vehicles use a crossflow design *(b)* in which the coolant flows across the radiator. *(Courtesy of Modine Manufacturing)*

A crossflow radiator produces better cooling in modern vehicles with low, wide hood lines. The tubes in a crossflow radiator can be longer; this provides more time for cooling (Figure 17-20).

Most older radiators are made of copper or brass. They were assembled by soldering the tubes to the headers and soldering the headers to the tanks. Many newer radiators are made of aluminum. The core is vacuum brazed together, and on many, plastic tanks are held onto the core by crimped metal tabs. A specially shaped O-ring is used to seal the tanks to the core headers (Figure 17-21).

The radiator cap is usually mounted in the top tank of a downflow design and in the colder, lower-pressure outlet tank of a crossflow radiator. Some vehicles use a pressurized CRR with the pressure cap mounted on it; others have the pressure cap located in the upper radiator hose. On vehicles with an automatic transmission, a transmission oil cooler is mounted in the bottom or outlet tank. All newer vehicles use a **pressure cap** and a **coolant recovery reservoir (CRR).**

17.5.1   Pressure Cap

The pressure cap seals the cooling system so it will hold pressure. Pressure is used to raise the coolant boiling point so the engine can operate at a higher, more efficient temperature. A spring in the cap pushes the cap's gasket against a seat in the filler neck to form a seal. When coolant pressure gets high enough, it pushes the lower sealing gasket off the seat, and some coolant escapes to the CRR or out the overflow hose. Many modern vehicles use a 15-lb (103-kPa) rated cap (Figure 17-22).

Coolant pressure comes from the expansion of the coolant as it is heated by the engine. Coolant volume increases about 10% as it heats from 70 to 180°F (21 to 82°C).

As described in Section 4.5, raising the pressure of a liquid increases the liquid's boiling point. Pressure of 15 lb increases the boiling point of water to 250°F (121°C). With a coolant mix of 50% antifreeze, the boiling point at 15 psi is increased to 262°F (125°C) (Figure 17-23).

◀   CAUTION   ▶

Remember that many vehicles have coolant temperatures above the boiling point. Many sources recommend that the pressure cap never be removed from a hot engine. Releasing system pressure can cause immediate and violent boiling. Numerous injuries and at least one fatality have occurred from burns caused by boiling coolant (Figure 17-24).

As a cap is installed, the cam on the filler neck or the threads on some caps pull the cap downward to seat the cap's lower gasket against the seat in the filler neck. During a normal warm-up cycle, coolant expands to form pressure, and, as mentioned, a certain amount of coolant pushes past the gasket and leaves the radiator, either to the CRR or out the overflow tube.

During cooldown, the coolant contracts, and because of the pressure drop, the vacuum relief valve in the cap opens and allows coolant to return from the CRR (Figure 17-25). In older vehicles, air reenters through the overflow tube (Figure 17-26).

17.5.2   Coolant Recovery Reservoir

In older vehicles, a certain volume of air was kept in the radiator to allow for expansion. Air adds oxygen to the system; this leads to oxidation and corrosion. Air also

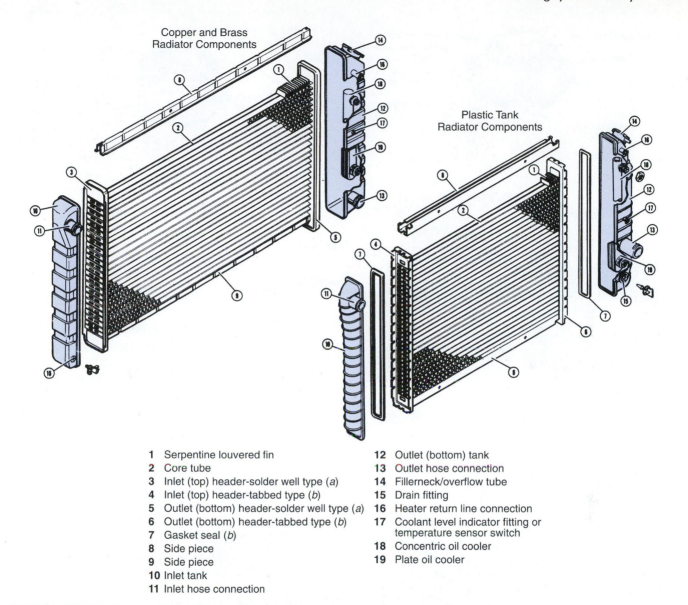

Copper and Brass Radiator Components

Plastic Tank Radiator Components

1 Serpentine louvered fin
2 Core tube
3 Inlet (top) header-solder well type (*a*)
4 Inlet (top) header-tabbed type (*b*)
5 Outlet (bottom) header-solder well type (*a*)
6 Outlet (bottom) header-tabbed type (*b*)
7 Gasket seal (*b*)
8 Side piece
9 Side piece
10 Inlet tank
11 Inlet hose connection

12 Outlet (bottom) tank
13 Outlet hose connection
14 Fillerneck/overflow tube
15 Drain fitting
16 Heater return line connection
17 Coolant level indicator fitting or temperature sensor switch
18 Concentric oil cooler
19 Plate oil cooler

FIGURE 17-21 Most older radiators used a brass or copper core with the tanks soldered in place (*a*). Many newer radiators use an aluminum or brass core with plastic tanks (*b*). (*Courtesy of Modine Manufacturing*)

mixes with coolant as it passes through the radiator, which reduces efficiency. An air or steam pocket in a water jacket can allow the temperature of some portions to reach critical points.

The CRR, also called an **expansion tank,** allows the cooling system to purge all air and be 100% full of coolant. In most vehicles, the CRR is simply a semi-transparent molded plastic container. Coolant level can be checked by looking at the coolant level; graduations indicate the correct level. The expansion hose from the radiator connects to the bottom of the CRR, and the CRR is vented to atmosphere. When the engine warms, expanding coolant flows into the CRR, and the level

rises. When the engine cools, coolant returns to the radiator and the level drops.

Most CRRs are nonpressurized, and they had a simple filler cap with a vent to atmosphere. Some modern vehicles use a CRR that is under cooling system pressure, and the pressure cap is mounted on the CRR.

17.5.3 Cooling Modules

Modern vehicles require more than one system to be air cooled; these systems can include the cooling system, A/C system, automatic transmission fluid, engine oil, power steering fluid, and incoming air charge from

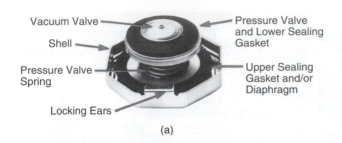

Vacuum Valve

Shell

Pressure Valve Spring

Locking Ears

Pressure Valve and Lower Sealing Gasket

Upper Sealing Gasket and/or Diaphragm

(a)

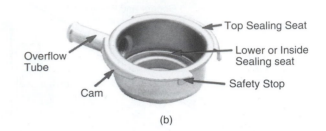

Overflow Tube

Cam

Top Sealing Seat

Lower or Inside Sealing seat

Safety Stop

(b)

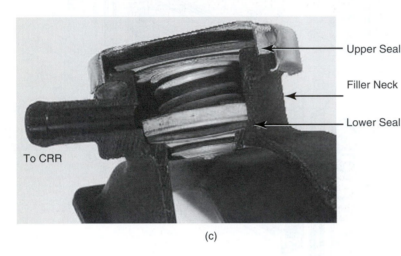

Upper Seal

Filler Neck

Lower Seal

To CRR

(c)

FIGURE 17-22 A pressure cap *(a)* and a radiator filler neck *(b)*. As the cap is installed, the cam portion pulls the cap downward to seat the lower sealing gasket firmly on the sealing seat *(c)*. *(a and b courtesy of Stant Manufacturing)*

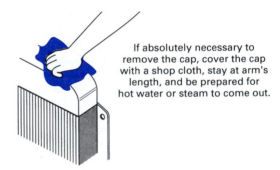

If absolutely necessary to remove the cap, cover the cap with a shop cloth, stay at arm's length, and be prepared for hot water or steam to come out.

FIGURE 17-24 Do not remove the cap from a hot system unless absolutely necessary. If you have to remove it, follow these precautions. Release of cooling system pressure can produce instant and severe boiling.

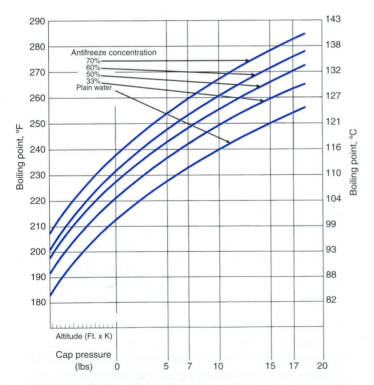

FIGURE 17-23 The boiling point of water increases with pressure and the addition of antifreeze.

a supercharger. If these units can be combined, the overall efficiency of these heat exchangers can be improved and assembly of the vehicle during manufacture is simplified and made easier. A cooling module combines some or all of these heat exchangers into a single unit that often includes the electric cooling fan assembly with shroud (Figure 17-27).

A cooling module also allows one component to give structural support to another, and this allows the overall weight and size to be reduced. Most modules are designed with connections of the quick-connect style.

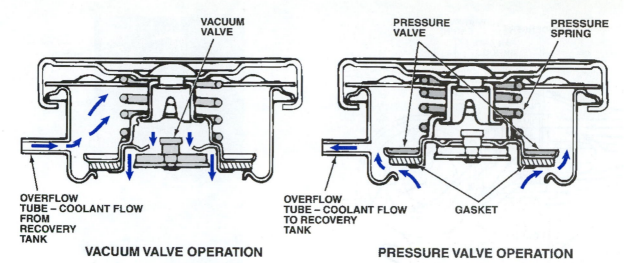

VACUUM VALVE OPERATION

PRESSURE VALVE OPERATION

FIGURE 17-25 The cap's pressure valve is opened when coolant pressure is greater than the pressure spring (*right*). This weighted vacuum valve opens from gravity when coolant pressure drops (*left*). Some caps use a small spring that holds the vacuum valve closed (not shown).

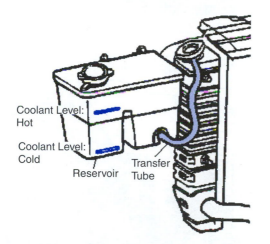

Coolant Level: Hot

Coolant Level: Cold

Reservoir

Transfer Tube

FIGURE 17-26 When the cap relieves pressure, coolant travels through the transfer tube to the reservoir. The coolant returns to the radiator during cooldown.

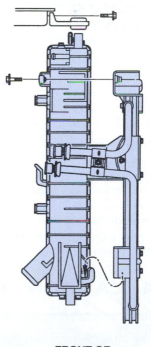

FRONT OF VEHICLE

FIGURE 17-27 This A/C condenser is attached to the radiator to form a cooling module. Some modules include an oil cooler for power steering or engine oil. (*Courtesy of Visteon*)

17.6 FAN

The fan ensures adequate airflow through the radiator while the vehicle is stopped or moving at low speeds. At cruising speeds, the fan is not needed because ram air through the grill supplies ample air. This airflow is improved by an air dam under the front bumper of some vehicles (Figure 17-28).

A fan requires power to drive it (about 2 to 6 hp). This power requirement varies with diameter, blade pitch, and number of blades. Larger diameter, higher blade pitch, or more blades move more air but also require more power and can be very noisy. Much design work has been done in shaping the blades to reduce both power draw and noise. Many fans have unequal blade spacing and blades

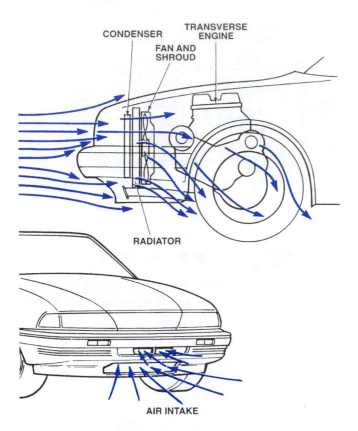

FIGURE 17-28 Air enters the radiator from the grill area above or below the front bumper. It exits through the engine compartment to the front wheel wells and below the vehicle. *(Reprinted with permission of General Motors Corporation)*

with curved tips to reduce noise. Most fans also operate in a **shroud** to improve airflow (Figure 17-29).

On most RWD cars, the fan is mounted on the water pump shaft and driven through a **fan clutch.** A few RWD vehicles use variable pitch fans with flexible blades. Most FWD cars use one or two electric fans.

◄ CAUTION ►

When working on a vehicle with the hood open, exercise caution around the fan. Fan blades can break and be thrown off with great force; at least one person has been killed when struck by a flying fan blade. Check a fan for cracks at the blades that might lead to breaking, and never stand in line with the fan of a running engine (Figure 17-30).

17.6.1 Fan Clutch

Most fan clutches are temperature-controlled fluid couplings and are called *thermal* or *thermostatic* fan

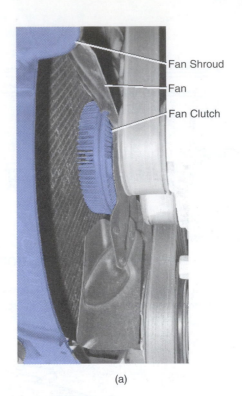

(a)

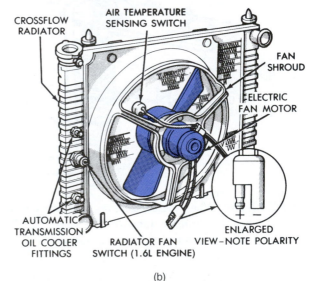

(b)

FIGURE 17-29 Most RWD vehicles drive the fan through a clutch that is mounted on the water pump shaft (a). Most FWD vehicles use an electric fan (b). *(b courtesy of DaimlerChrysler Corporation)*

clutches. They are designed to slip when cold and can only drive the fan to certain speeds when hot. There is also a nonthermal design that can only drive the fan up to a speed of about 1,200 to 2,200 rpm. A fan clutch improves fuel mileage because it reduces the fan's horsepower draw, and it also greatly reduces the noise level.

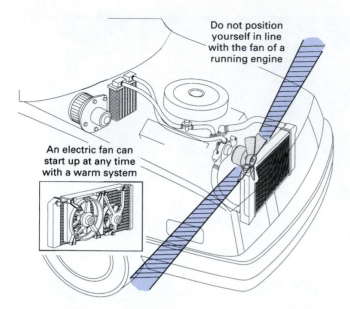

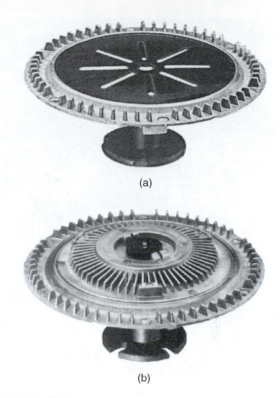

(a)

(b)

FIGURE 17-30 Use caution around a running engine. Things can get caught in the fan or belts, or a fan blade can break off and fly outward with great force. An electric fan can start up at any time on many vehicles. *(Courtesy of Everco Industries)*

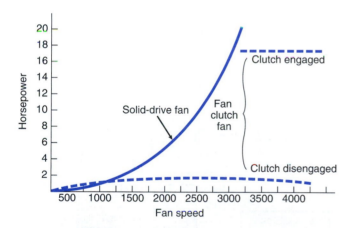

FIGURE 17-31 The horsepower draw of a solid-drive fan increases significantly as engine speed increases. With the clutch disengaged, draw is limited to about 2 horsepower (hp). With the clutch engaged, draw is limited to about 18 hp.

When a fan clutch is engaged, the increased airflow and noise level from cold to hot are quite noticeable (Figure 17-31).

The fan is bolted to the body of the fan clutch. The clutch plate inside the body is connected to the water pump shaft. A bearing on the shaft supports the body. The body also contains a reservoir in which silicone fluid can be stored. The fluid stays in the clutch cham-

FIGURE 17-32 A nonthermal fan *(a)* merely slips as speed increases; a thermal fan *(b)* disengages almost completely when it is cool. *(Courtesy of Stant Manufacturing)*

ber of a nonthermal or torque-limited fan clutch and can only transmit a small amount of torque, so it simply slips when the fan load reaches its torque rating.

When a thermal design unit is cold, a small portion of fluid is in the working chamber so that the clutch can only transfer a small amount of power. The fan can be driven to speeds of about 1,000 rpm. When the unit is hot, a thermostatic bimetal or coil spring moves to open a passage between the working chamber and reservoir, and silicone fluid fills the working chamber. This allows the clutch to transfer more power, and the fan speed increases to about 1,600 to 2,000 rpm (Figure 17-32).

17.6.2 Electric Fans

The fan blade is attached directly to the shaft of the electric motor; the motor mounting bracket often includes the shroud for the fan. Fan motors and fans of different sizes are used by vehicle manufacturers and are used as single units or in pairs. They can also be mounted as pusher fans in front of the radiator or puller fans behind it. Larger fans and fans with more blades can move more air, but they are noisier and require

FIGURE 17-33 This vehicle uses two electric fans (*arrows*) mounted in a fan shroud that helps improve the airflow.

larger motors, which in turn require more electrical current (Figure 17-33).

Fan motors are usually controlled by a **relay.** In some vehicles, the relay is controlled by the electronic control module, (ECM), body control module, (BCM), or powertrain control module, (PCM) and a temperature sensor or switch or body control module, (BCM). Some motor relays are controlled by a coolant temperature switch. These switches turn *on* when the coolant temperature goes above a certain point, say 200°F (93°C), and turn *off* when the coolant temperature drops a few degrees below the *on* point. Some dual fan units turn the second fan *on* if the coolant temperature continues to rise; the *on* setting is about 10 to 20°F above the first fan. Fan motors are also controlled by A/C operation. A fan can be turned on when the A/C is turned on or when the A/C high side pressure reaches a certain point. A dual fan unit can use both of these.

Another fan switch variation is that most systems use a simple high side pressure switch, and some units use a pressure transducer. The pressure transducer allows the control module to monitor high side pressure. When the pressure reaches a certain point relative to engine temperature and other factors, the control module turns a fan on or off (Figure 17-34).

Many fan relays are connected directly to B+ through a fuse link or circuit breaker; the circuit is not

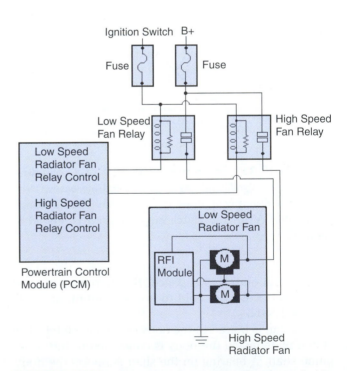

FIGURE 17-34 These two fan motors are controlled by two relays that are switched on and off by the PCM.

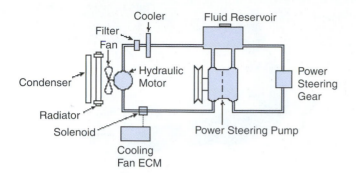

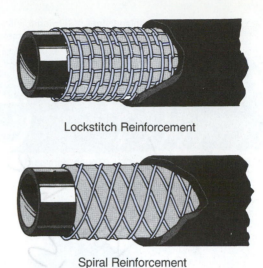

Lockstitch Reinforcement

Spiral Reinforcement

FIGURE 17-35 This cooling fan is driven by hydraulic pressure from the power steering pump. The hydraulic fluid flow is controlled by an electric solenoid that is controlled by an electronic module.

FIGURE 17-37 A cutaway radiator hose showing internal reinforcement and a heater hose showing spiral reinforcement. *(Courtesy of The Gates Rubber Company)*

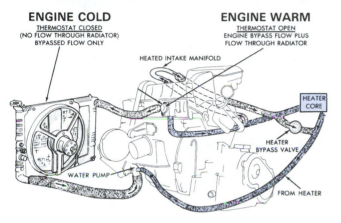

FIGURE 17-36 The upper and lower radiator hoses connect the radiator to the water pump and thermostat housing. Hoses also route coolant to the heater and intake manifold. *(Courtesy of DaimlerChrysler Corporation)*

controlled by the ignition switch. These fan motors can turn on anytime the conditions are right; do not put yourself in a position where you can be injured by the unexpected start-up of a fan.

17.6.3 Hydraulic Cooling Fan

Some modern vehicles use a cooling fan that is driven by hydraulic pressure from the power steering system (Figure 17-35). An electric solenoid valve controls the hydraulic flow to the hydraulic fan motor, and the solenoid valve is controlled by an electronic control module (ECM). This allows control of fan speed, as well as when it operates.

17.7 HOSES

Two large **hoses** connect the engine's water jackets to the radiator. The upper hose transfers hot coolant to the

radiator; the lower hose returns the coolant, which is now cooler, to the engine. These hoses must be flexible to allow the engine to move on the motor mounts. Hose flexibility also removes the need for close alignment of the connections between the radiator and engine. Hose flexibility also removes engine vibrations, which can shake a radiator apart (Figure 17-36).

Hoses are constructed around an inside tube of synthetic rubber. One or two layers (or plies) of woven textile are placed around this inner tube; then an outer layer of rubber is placed around the textile plies (Figure 17-37). To increase the life of the hose, better hoses use rubber materials that are resistant to oil, heat, and electrochemical degradation. Electrochemical degradation is caused by electrical current flow between the radiator and engine that causes small cracks in the inner hose liner; chemical action in these cracks breaks down the hose materials. Oil tends to swell and soften rubber, and heat tends to make it hard and brittle. Silicone rubber materials are used for severe-duty, high-heat conditions. Lower radiator hoses should always contain a springlike coil of wire or reinforcement to prevent them from collapsing from water pump suction. If the lower hose collapses, it can shut off the flow of coolant into the engine.

Some hoses are molded to a particular shape for a particular installation. Some hoses even have alignment marks to ensure they are installed so they will not be deformed. Hoses are also available in a straight form and in a flexible, corrugated form (Figure 17-38). One or more of the hoses used in modern vehicles can be

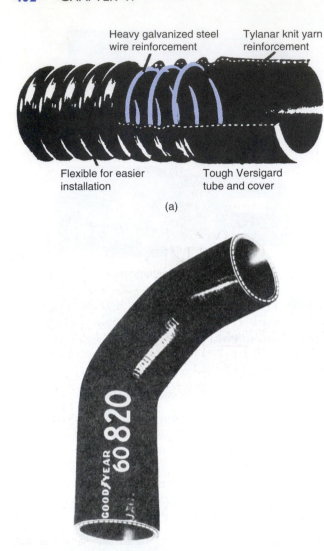

Heavy galvanized steel
wire reinforcement

Tylanar knit yarn
reinforcement

Flexible for easier
installation

Tough Versigard
tube and cover

(a)

(b)

FIGURE 17-38 Besides the straight form, radiator hoses are available in flexible forms (*a*) and molded shapes (*b* and *c*). *(Courtesy of Goodyear Tire & Rubber Company)*

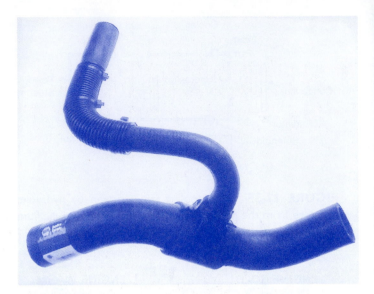

FIGURE 17-39 This branched lower radiator hose connects to the radiator outlet connection, the water pump inlet, and the coolant recovery reservoir.

17.8 GAUGES

The gauge indicates the engine's coolant temperature. Remember that the normal cooling system operating range is about 180 to 245°F (84 to 120°C). The lower end is the thermostat opening temperature, and the upper end is just below the coolant boiling point with the specified pressure cap and antifreeze mixture (Figure 17-41).

Most older vehicles used mechanical gauges that use a sending unit connected to the gauge by a thin capillary tube. The sending unit contains a gas that expands as it is heated. This gas pressure acts on a Bourdon tube to give a gauge reading (Figure 17-42).

Most vehicles today use an electric gauge that is essentially an ammeter. This gauge is connected to the sending unit in the engine by an electric wire (Figure 17-43). The sending unit changes resistance value as the engine warms up. This causes the gauge to respond to the increased current flow that results. Electric gauges require a voltage source that is more constant than that produced by an alternator; a constant voltage regulator or instrument voltage regulator is used in many gauge circuits.

Many modern vehicles use electronic displays to show instrument panel functions. These panels consist of electronic modules with an information sensor for each function.

Some older vehicles use one or two coolant temperature lights. A few vehicles have a green light that

branched or T-shaped; for example, the lower radiator hose of one passenger car has a branch that connects to the CRR (Figure 17-39).

Several types of clamps are available to make leak-proof connections. The better clamps can exert a high amount of clamping pressure evenly around the hose in a manner that does not cut the hose (Figure 17-40). One type of clamp uses a thermal plastic ring that is placed over the hose end and heated using a heat gun to shrink it and tighten it in place. This band has the ability to compensate for diameter changes as the hose and connector heat and cool. It is cut off to remove it. A spring-style clamp also allows for thermal expansion and contraction.

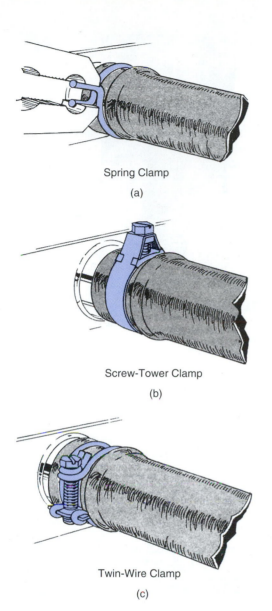

Spring Clamp
(a)

Screw-Tower Clamp
(b)

Twin-Wire Clamp
(c)

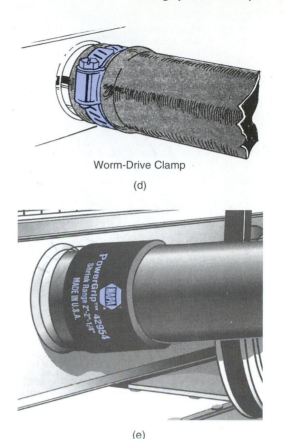

Worm-Drive Clamp
(d)

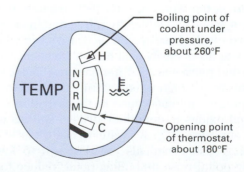

(e)

FIGURE 17-40 Common hose clamp types. Spring clamps *(a)* are common on OE installations; screw-tower clamps *(b)* and twin-wire clamps *(c)* were popular in the past; and worm-drive clamps *(d)* are popular replacements. PowerGrip clamps *(e)* are heat-sensitive material shrunk to fit using a heat gun. *(Courtesy of The Gates Rubber Company)*

comes on when the engine is at operating temperature, and many vehicles have a red light that comes on when the temperature is close to the boiling point. These lights use a simple circuit that goes from the light to the sending unit in the engine's water jackets. The sending unit is a temperature switch that closes at temperatures above a certain value.

Some vehicles use a *low coolant warning light* to warn the driver of a low coolant level. This light uses a switch mounted in one of the radiator tanks. When the coolant level drops below the switch, its contacts close, and this turns the light on. The three styles of temperature indicators require coolant to bring the temperature to the sending unit. If there is a sudden loss of coolant, the gauge will probably not respond, and the engine can overheat while showing a normal gauge reading.

Boiling point of coolant under pressure, about 260°F

Opening point of thermostat, about 180°F

TEMP

FIGURE 17-41 Most temperature gauges do not show the actual temperature; "normal" is 150 to 240°F.

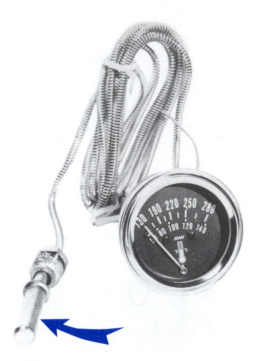

FIGURE 17-42 A mechanical temperature gauge uses a temperature bulb (*arrow*) installed into the water jackets.

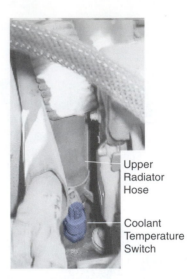

FIGURE 17-43 This coolant temperature switch (CTS) is mounted close to the thermostat and the outlet to the upper radiator hose.

◀ **CAUTION** ▶

Coolants, especially ethylene glycol but also propylene glycol, are toxic and also have a sweet taste so they are attractive to children and pets. In one year, 1990, 585 people ingested antifreeze; 26 of these victims went to intensive care, and 4 of them died. In Europe, several manufacturers add a bittering agent to antifreeze to make it less desirable.

FIGURE 17-44 This section of an antifreeze container gives important information about the capabilities of the product.

17.9   COOLANT

Coolant is the working fluid that transfers heat in a cooling system, much like the refrigerant in an A/C system. Water is the base coolant because it is plentiful, inexpensive, flows easily, and has an excellent ability to absorb and release heat. Water has drawbacks, though: It freezes at too high a temperature, boils at too low a temperature, and can cause metal corrosion (rust on steel and oxide on aluminum). The chemicals in high-quality antifreeze improve water to make it an excellent coolant. These chemicals are designed to lower its freezing point, raise its boiling point, reduce foaming, reduce cavitation, and prevent rust and corrosion. Some of the major chemicals used are the following:

- *Corrosion inhibitors*: Silicates, phosphates, and borates to help protect aluminum from corrosion, but silicates are abrasive to water-pump seals, leading to early failure. Extended-life coolants use carboxylate technology (a mixture of organic acids) for corrosion protection.
- *pH buffers*: To maintain proper acid–alkaline balance and prevent electrolytic corrosion.
- **Ethylene glycol (EG)** or **propylene glycol (PG)**: To reduce freezing point and increase boiling point.
- *Dye*: To provide color (Figure 17-44).

EG is the base for most domestic antifreeze brands. PG is the base for some domestic and European antifreezes;

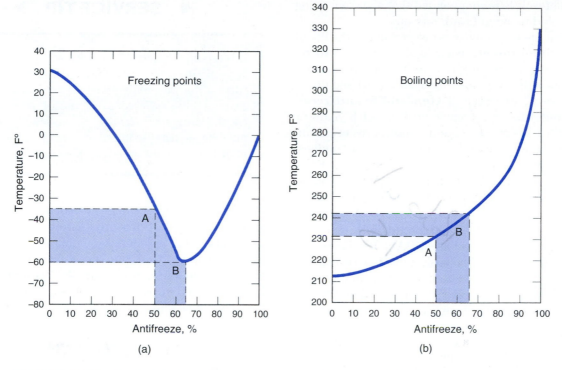

FIGURE 17-45 Coolant boiling point increases as antifreeze is added. The coolant freezing point drops as antifreeze is added until it reaches about two-thirds antifreeze. Recommended concentration is between 50% *(a)* and 66% *(b)*.

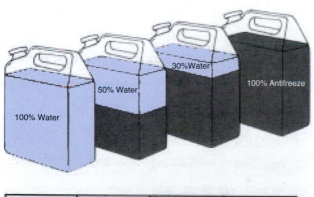

FIGURE 17-46 A 50% antifreeze mix provides a good range between freezing and boiling points; a 70% mix provides a broader range. Neither pure water nor pure antifreeze should be used. *(Courtesy of Gates Corporation)*

it is advertised as the safe antifreeze. Most manufacturers recommend a 50% coolant mixture of antifreeze and water (half and half) to get adequate corrosion protection. In very cold areas, the mixture can be more concentrated, but the limit is 67% (two-thirds antifreeze and one-third water). Higher antifreeze concentrations have a higher freezing point along with poor heat transfer (Figure 17-45). Antifreeze has a higher viscosity than water, so it does not flow as well; it also does not pick up and release heat as well as water (Figure 17-46).

EG and PG come from the base chemical ethylene oxide (EO), and both have the problem that if they are exposed to higher than normal temperatures, they become blackened, corrosive, and foul smelling in a relatively short period of time. Future emission requirements, especially with diesel engines, will probably increase coolant temperatures. Another coolant, Propanediol (PDO), is currently being developed and tested for high-temperature use. PDO is also derived from EO, and will probably be supplied with extended-life chemistries.

Both EG and PG are good antifreeze base chemicals. The biggest fault is toxicity, and PG is less toxic and does not have the sweet taste that EG has. These two antifreeze types should not be mixed. They have different specific gravities; the specific gravity of EG is higher. The antifreeze concentration of a mixture cannot be accurately tested with either a hydrometer or refractometer. It is recommended that a system using PG be labeled to avoid future mix-ups.

Coolant life in an engine is determined by the life of the **corrosion-protection** package. If allowed to remain in an engine too long, rust, corrosion, and erosion begin. Most antifreeze (usually dyed green) should be changed every 1 or 2 years. **Extended-life antifreeze** (dyed orange) has a recommended life of 5 years or 150,000 miles. These conventional antifreezes use an inorganic additive technology (IAT) consisting of amines, borates, nitrates, phosphates, or silicates. Early extended-life antifreeze uses an additive package based on **organic acids (OA)**. Zerex has recently developed an extended-life antifreeze, G-05, used in both domestic and import vehicles, OEM and aftermarket, that uses hybrid organic acid technology (HOAT). It is becoming very important to follow the vehicle manufacturer's recommendations concerning antifreeze type and change intervals. Extended-life and conventional antifreeze should not be mixed because it can reduce the service life to that of conventional antifreeze.

Coolant starts out as clear as water. Its familiar colors come from dye that is added. The dye is added to allow a quick check to see if the proper chemical is being used, to be able to quickly see the fluid level in the CRC, and to help get the proper fluid in the correct under-hood component. At this time, many vehicle manufacturers use a different coolant color. Zerex G-05 for Daimler-Chrysler is orange while the same product supplied to Ford Motor Company is yellow. Color is not a reliable indicator of the type of coolant being used in a vehicle.

◀ **SERVICE TIP** ▶

Most domestic original equipment (OE) and aftermarket antifreeze use the following color coding: Light green indicates a material using silicone–silicate inhibitors; orange indicates organic acid, extended-life inhibitors. Antifreeze can be either EG or PG based. There is no universal color coding, so foreign OE antifreeze can use red, blue, green, or orange dyes for any of the antifreeze types.

Aluminum radiator and heater cores are subject to erosion; the coolant flow wears into the metal until it becomes too thin to contain the internal pressure. The erosion rate increases as the amount of dirt, rust, hard water deposits, and abrasive material dropping out of antifreeze increases. Silicates with other antifreeze chemicals can form abrasives, which in turn wear anything they pass by, including soft aluminum and water-pump seals.

◀ **SERVICE TIP** ▶

It is recommended to replace coolant using a mixture of the same type and concentration of antifreeze as originally used. If replaced with an extended-life antifreeze, the duration is the same as the original coolant. Extended-life coolant must be used in the initial or first fill of the vehicle in order to obtain extended-life performance.

The old antifreeze that is drained out must be recycled or disposed of properly. Although most of the ingredients will biodegrade, coolant absorbs heavy metals—copper, lead, and zinc—from the engine and radiator, and these are toxic. As mentioned earlier, coolant should not be allowed to stand in an open container because children or animals may drink it.

17.10 ENGINE BLOCK HEATER

Engine block heaters are small, electrical-resistance heater units that can be mounted in the cylinder block. These heaters are plugged into ordinary 110-volt AC house current and are used in very cold areas to warm an engine while it is shut off. Block heaters provide easier engine starting and faster warm-up (Figure 17-47).

◀ **PROBLEM SOLVING 17-3** ▶

A friend asks you why his pickup may be overheating. The radiator core, hoses, and fan appear normal. When you look at the coolant in the radiator, you find it has a brown color, and there is a brown, slimy film on the valve of the radiator cap. What might be wrong with this system? What recommendations should you make to your friend?

Another friend has a similar complaint of an overheating car; it boils out coolant under a moderate load. When you look at the coolant level, you find that it is low and the coolant has a slightly brownish color. You fill the radiator, but you can find no sign of leaks with the engine either off or running. There are some streaks around the CRR that look like they might have come from hot coolant. What could be wrong with this system? What should you recommend your friend do?

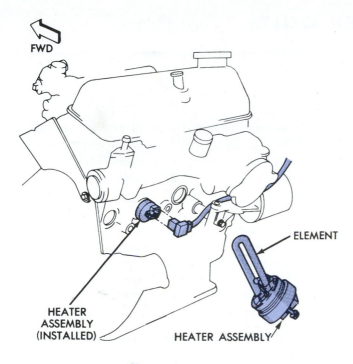

FWD

ELEMENT

HEATER
ASSEMBLY
(INSTALLED)

HEATER ASSEMBLY

FIGURE 17-47   A heater assembly can be installed in place of a core plug. The cord for this heater is plugged into common house current to warm the coolant and prevent freeze-up. *(Courtesy of DaimlerChrysler Corporation)*

REVIEW QUESTIONS

The following questions are provided to help you study as you read the chapter.

1. The vehicle's cooling system is designed to keep the engine at the _correct_ _op Temp_.

2. The plugs used to seal the large holes in the sides of the engine block are properly called _core_ _hole plugs_.

3. The _therm_ opens at a temperature of about 200°F to allow coolant to circulate between the engine and _Rad._.

4. While the thermostat is closed, _coolant_ will circulate between the engine and the _water pump_.

5. Many thermostats use a(n) _wax_ _motor_ to open the valve at the correct _Temp_.

6. The coolant flow is from the _Rad_ to the lower hose, and then it is _pump_ through the water jackets.

7. The coolant flow through most radiators is from the _inlet_ to the _outlet_ or from one _tank_ to the other.

8. Most modern vehicles use a(n) _V_ – _Rubber_ drive belt that is also called a(n) _serp_ belt from the way that it is routed around the pulleys.

9. Cooling systems use a pressure cap in order to raise the _boil point_ of the _coolant_

10. As an engine warms up to operating temperature, coolant will flow past the pressure cap to the _cool ree res_.

11. Do not remove the pressure cap of a hot system because the coolant will probably _boil violently_

12. A fan clutch helps reduce fan _Horse Pow Draw_ and _noise_ when a high airflow is not needed.

13. An electric fan can be mounted in front of the radiator and _push_ the air through it or behind the radiator and _pull_ the air through.

14. The ideal coolant mix for most vehicles is _50_ antifreeze and _50_ water.

15. Dirty coolant is a sign that the _coolant_ should be _flushed_

CHAPTER QUIZ

The following questions will help you check the facts you have learned. Select the answer that completes each statement correctly.

1. Modern cooling systems are designed to maintain an engine temperature of _____.
   - **a.** 150 to 270°F
   - **c.** 180 to 230°F
   - **b.** 100 to 160°F
   - **d.** 170 to 300°F

2. Two technicians are discussing thermostats and coolant circulation. Technician A says that the coolant does not circulate while the thermostat is closed. Technician B says that the heater doesn't blow warm air while the engine is cold because of this. Who is correct?
   - **a.** A only
   - **c.** Both A and B
   - **b.** B only
   - **d.** Neither A nor B

3. While discussing cooling system operation, Technician A says that the engine will overheat if the thermostat sticks in the open position. Technician B says that heater operation will be affected if the thermostat sticks open. Who is correct?
   - **a.** A only
   - **c.** Both A and B
   - **b.** B only
   - **d.** Neither A nor B

4. On most engine blocks, the coolant flow is into the _____.
   - **a.** top and out the bottom
   - **b.** top and out the top
   - **c.** bottom and out the top
   - **d.** bottom and out the bottom

5. Two technicians are discussing coolant circulation. Technician A says that coolant flows from the bottom to the top in older radiator designs. Technician B says that the coolant flows from one side of the radiator to the other in a crossflow design. Who is correct?
   - **a.** A only
   - **c.** Both A and B
   - **b.** B only
   - **d.** Neither A nor B

6. The boiling point of water with a 15-psi pressure cap is about _____.
   - **a.** 212°F
   - **c.** 250°F
   - **b.** 290°F
   - **d.** 300°F

7. The amount of power required to drive a fan is affected by the _____.
   - **a.** diameter
   - **c.** number of blades
   - **b.** blade pitch
   - **d.** All of these

8. Two technicians are discussing fan clutches. Technician A says that some fan clutches have a thermostatic valve that allows the clutch to drive the fan when it gets hot. Technician B says that a fan clutch allows a large fan to be used with a lower noise level and power loss. Who is correct?
   - **a.** A only
   - **c.** Both A and B
   - **b.** B only
   - **d.** Neither A nor B

9. An electric cooling system fan is controlled by _____.

   A. cooling system temperature

   B. A/C system operation

   Which is correct?
   - **a.** A only
   - **c.** Both A and B
   - **b.** B only
   - **d.** Neither A nor B

10. The best amount of ethylene glycol to mix into the coolant is _____.
    - **a.** 25%
    - **c.** 75%
    - **b.** 50%
    - **d.** 100%

◀ Chapter 18 ▶

COOLING SYSTEM INSPECTION, TROUBLE DIAGNOSIS, AND SERVICE

LEARNING OBJECTIVES

After completing this chapter, you should:

1. Be familiar with the preventive maintenance operations and adjustments necessary to keep a cooling system operating properly.
2. Be able to inspect a cooling system to determine whether it is operating correctly.
3. Be able to perform the standard cooling system tests to locate the cause of a problem.
4. Be able to R&R a faulty cooling system component.
5. Be able to complete the engine cooling system diagnosis and repair operations in the ASE Task List, Section C (Appendix A).

TERMS TO LEARN

angular misalignment	mechanical reverse flush
backflush	parallel misalignment
chemical flush	pH balance
coolant voltage	pressure test
finger check	refractometer
flush	reserve alkalinity (RA)
hydrometer	test strip

18.1 INTRODUCTION

Engine cooling systems require periodic maintenance to keep them operating properly. These checks range from checking coolant level and condition, inspecting belts and hoses, and replacing coolant. Properly maintained cooling systems normally give lifetime trouble-free operation. Coolant should be replaced before the inhibitor package breaks down so problems caused by corrosion, electrolysis, and erosion can be prevented.

◀ SERVICE TIP ▶

Electrolysis can cause pinholes in the radiator or heater core. An aluminum component will be discolored, black, and pitted; copper and brass components will probably develop blue-green corrosion. The pinholes tend to occur in the center of the heater core and an inch or so away from the radiator tanks or in the vicinity of the cooling-fan mounts.

Cooling system problems do occur, and these problems usually show up as leaks, overcooling, or overheating. Overcooling is first noticed by most drivers as poor heater operation in the winter; overcooling also causes poor engine performance, reduced fuel mileage, and excess engine wear. Overheating is usually more serious. More than one engine has been ruined by the effects of overheating, which include

409

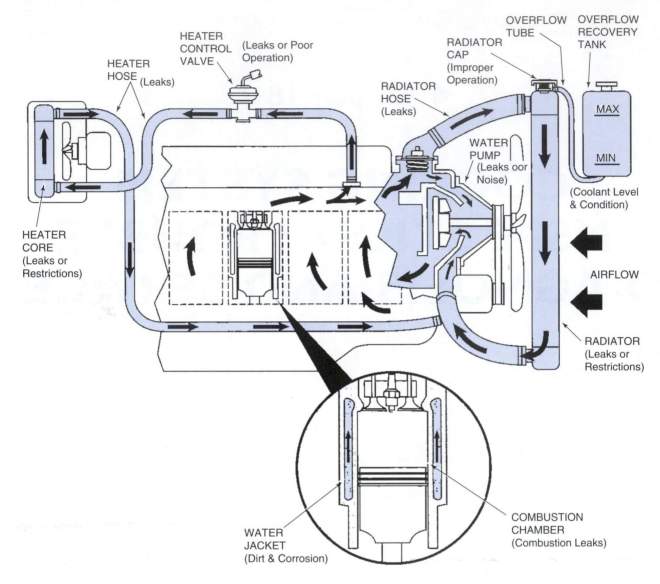

OVERFLOW TUBE

OVERFLOW RECOVERY TANK

HEATER CONTROL VALVE (Leaks or Poor Operation)

RADIATOR CAP (Improper Operation)

HEATER HOSE (Leaks)

RADIATOR HOSE (Leaks)

MAX

MIN

WATER PUMP (Leaks oor Noise)

HEATER CORE (Leaks or Restrictions)

(Coolant Level & Condition)

AIRFLOW

RADIATOR (Leaks or Restrictions)

COMBUSTION CHAMBER (Combustion Leaks)

WATER JACKET (Dirt & Corrosion)

FIGURE 18-1 Common cooling system problems; most of these can be located with a visual check.

warped and cracked cylinder heads and burned and badly scored pistons, cylinders, and valves. Several tests are used to locate cooling system problems, including visual and hand-feel checks, temperature tests, and pressure tests (Figure 18-1).

Cooling system service includes radiator and engine water jacket cleaning and flushing and the repair and replacement of faulty components.

◄ **SERVICE TIP** ►

Erosion is wear from dirty, abrasive coolant. Erosion normally occurs at the radiator or heater core inlet and tube ends.

18.2 PREVENTIVE MAINTENANCE OPERATIONS

Preventive maintenance operations are usually listed in the vehicle owner's manual and in the maintenance and lubrication section of the service manual (along with the maintenance schedule). These schedules usually call for regular inspection of the coolant level (some recommend this at each gasoline refill), annual inspection of the belts and hoses, and a change of the coolant at the recommended intervals.

18.2.1 Coolant Level

In a modern semiclosed system with a pressure radiator cap and coolant recovery reservoir (CRR), coolant level

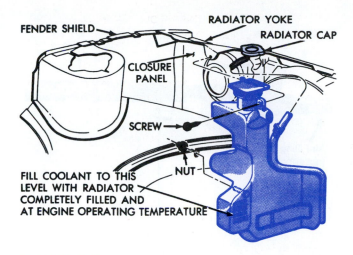

FIGURE 18-2 Coolant level in a modern system, using a coolant recovery reservoir, is checked at the reservoir. *(Courtesy of DaimlerChrysler Corporation)*

is checked by looking at the level in the semitransparent CRR. The cap does not need to be removed except to check coolant condition and cap performance (Figure 18-2).

◄ **CAUTION** ►

Extreme care should be exercised when removing the pressure cap from a system that is at operating temperature or above. Remember that coolant temperature can be above 212°F (100°C) and boil immediately if the pressure is removed.

◄ **SERVICE TIP** ►

Some technicians squeeze the upper hose. If it is hard from internal pressure, **do not remove the cap.**

◄ **SERVICE TIP** ►

When removing the pressure cap from a warm system, carefully follow these steps:

- Place a shop rag over the cap.
- Stay at arm's length from the cap.

- Carefully rotate the cap to its safety stop (Figure 18-3).
- Wiggle the cap as you check for system pressure.
- If there is escaping pressure, either step away until the pressure is released or cool the system down until the pressure release stops.
- If there is no escaping pressure, finish removing the cap.

The radiator of a CRR system should be full to the level of the sealing surface at the filler neck. A lower coolant level indicates a system leak, faulty cap, or leak in the CRR hose. The coolant level in a non-CRR system should be about 2 inches below the filler neck on a cold system and almost to the filler neck seat on a warm system. This lower level allows for coolant expansion as the system warms up (Figure 18-4).

18.2.2 Coolant Mixtures

As mentioned earlier, coolant is normally a mixture of antifreeze and water. In some areas, there is a legal definition for four types of coolant:

- *Engine coolant concentrate:* Essentially pure antifreeze
- *Prediluted engine coolant:* A 50–50 mixture of antifreeze and water
- *Recycled engine coolant concentrate:* Recycled EG that meets new coolant specifications
- *Recycled coolant:* A 50–50 mixture of recycled antifreeze and water

Antifreeze is commonly available as pure 100% antifreeze or in a 50% mixture as a new or recycled product.

Water can absorb more heat than antifreeze, but it freezes at 32°F (0°C), boils at 212°F (100°C), and allows corrosion and other contamination to occur. Antifreeze lowers the freezing point, raises the boiling point, and contains corrosion inhibitors, but it cannot transfer as much heat as water. The lowest freezing point occurs in a mixture of one-third water and two-thirds (66.6%) antifreeze. Also, corrosion inhibitors do not dissolve properly without water. With 100% antifreeze, the inhibitors can form deposits in the system and become insulation, raising the temperature inside the system.

Most sources recommend a 50% mixture, one-half water and one-half antifreeze; this ratio provides a

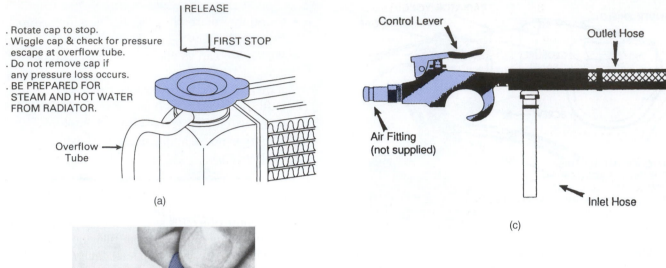

. Rotate cap to stop.
. Wiggle cap & check for pressure escape at overflow tube.
. Do not remove cap if any pressure loss occurs.
. BE PREPARED FOR STEAM AND HOT WATER FROM RADIATOR.

RELEASE

FIRST STOP

Overflow Tube

(a)

Control Lever

Outlet Hose

Air Fitting (not supplied)

Inlet Hose

(c)

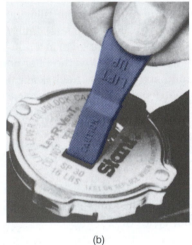

(b)

FIGURE 18-3 If necessary, follow these methods of removing the cap from a hot system (a). A safety cap has a lever that is raised to release any pressure from the system (b). The inlet hose of this coolant pressure reliever is connected to the radiator overflow hose, and the control lever is operated to safely remove any pressure from a system (c). (b courtesy of Stant Manufacturing; c courtesy of Wynn Oil Company)

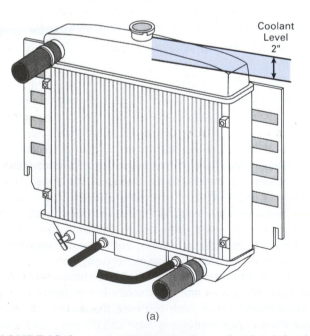

Coolant Level 2"

(a)

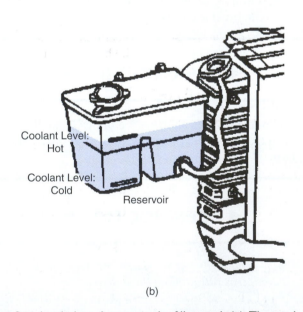

Coolant Level: Hot

Coolant Level: Cold

Reservoir

(b)

FIGURE 18-4 In an older system, the coolant level should be about 2 inches below the seat in the filler neck (a). The coolant level in a coolant recovery system is indicated on the recovery reservoir (b), and the radiator should be filled completely. (a courtesy of Everco Industries)

freeze protection to −35°F (−37°C). In very cold areas, the antifreeze portion can be increased to 67%; this mixture prevents freezing down to about −61°F (−52°C). The antifreeze concentration should be at least 40% but never greater than 67%.

◄ SERVICE TIP ►

EG can burn, and a mist of pressurized EG coolant can produce an explosion if it contacts an open flame.

◄ SERVICE TIP ►

A cooling system is more sensitive than a human to water quality. Poor quality water can cause serious damage in a cooling system. Many sources recommend using distilled water for the coolant mix.

18.2.3 Coolant Condition

Good coolant should have a bright yellow-green or orange color and a very slight slippery feel. Coolant normally deteriorates to a brownish, rusty color. As it loses its corrosion- and rust-protection abilities, rust forms on the iron parts and corrosion forms on the aluminum portions of the water jackets. Dirt and rust are also deposited on the horizontal surfaces and at the bottom of the water jackets. These are indications that the coolant has gone past the point where it should be changed.

◄ SERVICE TIP ►

A simple **finger check** (rubbing a finger around the inside of the filler neck) provides the technician with a quick way to check for faulty coolant and a dirty system (Figure 18-5).

◄ SERVICE TIP ►

Many technicians will lower the coolant level to expose some of the radiator tubes. This allows a limited visual inspection of the radiator tubes.

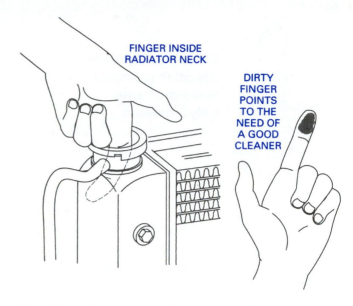

FIGURE 18-5 A simple check for cleanliness is to rub a finger around the inside of the filler neck. Any dirt on your finger indicates a dirty system that should be cleaned.

◄ SERVICE TIP ►

A brown, muddy sludge has been found in systems using Dexcool, an extended-life antifreeze developed by Havoline. The cause of this sludge has been attributed to incomplete bleeding that left air in the system.

A slightly dirty system should be **flushed** with plain water as the coolant is changed. A dirty or rusty system can usually be cleaned using a **mechanical reverse flush** or a **chemical flush;** these procedures are described in Section 18.4.1.

Another coolant check is for the antifreeze concentration to determine the freeze point. The freeze point can be measured using a hydrometer, refractometer, or test strips (Figure 18-6). A hydrometer measures the specific gravity of the coolant, and a refractometer measures its light-refracting qualities. The **hydrometer** is the least accurate, especially if propylene glycol or a mixture of EG and PG is used. Most hydrometers sold in the United States are calibrated for EG. Some **refractometers** are calibrated for both EG and PG. A refractometer is more accurate than a hydrometer, but it is also much more expensive. A **test strip** is dipped into the coolant, and this produces a color change. Comparing the color with a chart determines the freeze point.

Testing of Ethylene Glycol is normally performed with a Hydrometer.

Testing of Propylene Glycol is performed with a test paper. The color of the sample is then compared to a chart to establish the degree of protection.

FIGURE 18-6 Ethylene glycol–based coolant mixtures are commonly tested using a hydrometer or refractometer; test strips are used for propylene glycol mixtures. *(Courtesy of Four Seasons)*

(a)

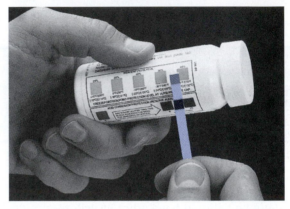

(b)

FIGURE 18-7 A test strip is dipped into the coolant *(a)* and the color change is compared with a chart *(b)* to determine freeze point, boil point, and acid corrosion protection. *(Courtesy of Environmental Test Systems, Inc., Elkhart, IN)*

Test strips are relatively inexpensive and are relatively accurate with EG, PG, and mixtures of the two. They also offer an advantage in that test strips check reserve alkalinity at the same time. Test strips can be saved or attached to the inspection sheet or work order to provide a record. Normally a 50–50 coolant mix with a freezing point of −34°F (−37°C) is recommended.

Reserve alkalinity (RA) is a check of the coolant **pH balance.** A coolant can become acidic and produce severe corrosion and electrolysis when the buffers for reserve alkalinity are used up. Some shops use a pH meter to check the level. Fresh EG coolant mixes should measure between pH 9 and 11; fresh OA antifreeze mixtures should be pH 8.3. As a general rule, pH should be between 7.5 and 10. A lower level indicates that the coolant is becoming acidic and corrosive. If the pH is above 11, buildup will occur.

Another check is for coolant electrolysis, also called **coolant voltage.** This quick and simple check measures the voltage in the coolant; less than 0.3 V is acceptable. Some sources recommend 0.1 V or less. A higher voltage reading indicates acidic coolant or the possibility of stray current passing through the coolant, possibly from an improperly grounded cooling fan mo-

tor. This problem has increased with radiators that have plastic tanks because they do not provide a good electrical ground path.

To measure coolant concentration and condition using test strips, you should:

1. Run the engine to mix the coolant thoroughly and to bring it to room temperature.
2. Dip the strip into the coolant, remove it immediately, and shake off the excess coolant.
3. Determine the freezing and boiling points by immediately comparing the color of the end pad with the color chart (Figure 18-7).
4. After 15 seconds, compare the second pad with the color chart to determine acid corrosion protection.

FIGURE 18-8 The plastic pump is used to draw a few drops of coolant and transfer it onto the measuring window. The window is then closed. *(Courtesy of Wynn Oil Company)*

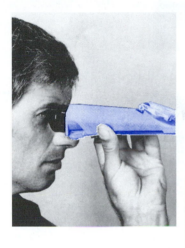

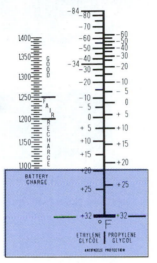

FIGURE 18-10 A hydrometer is read by drawing enough coolant into the unit to lift the float and noting the graduation at the liquid level.

FIGURE 18-9 Point the refractometer toward a light source and look through the eyepiece. The freeze point is indicated at the dividing line between dark and light (the edge of the shadow). *(Courtesy of Wynn Oil Company)*

3. Check the thermometer; adjust the temperature-calibrating sleeve if so equipped.
4. Read the scale at the level of the coolant on the float. On some units, a chart is used to read the freezing-point temperature by the letter indicated on the float (Figure 18-11).

To measure coolant concentration using a refractometer, you should:

1. Run the engine to mix the coolant thoroughly.
2. Clean the window and the plastic cover so they are clean and dry. Close the cover.
3. Transfer a few drops of coolant so the drops will run between the window and the cover (Figure 18-8).
4. Point the unit toward light and look into the eyepiece. The coolant protection is at the point between the light and dark portions of the scale (Figure 18-9).

To measure coolant concentration using a hydrometer, you should:

1. Run the engine to mix the coolant thoroughly.
2. Draw a sample of coolant into the hydrometer so the float is floating. Tap the hydrometer to ensure that the float is not stuck (Figure 18-10).

To measure cooling system voltage, you should:

1. Run the engine to mix the coolant thoroughly.
2. Shut off the engine, and connect the negative (−) lead of a digital voltmeter to the metal radiator filler neck, metal part close to the filler neck, battery ground, or engine ground.
3. Insert the positive (+) lead into the coolant, making sure it does not touch the filler neck or core, and read the meter (Figure 18-12). A reading of more than 0.1 V indicates a potential problem. *If electrolysis is suspected,* watch the meter while turning on or off the electrical devices that might be causing the problem; a change in the meter reading indicates a problem.
4. Start the engine as you watch the voltmeter reading. A higher reading during this dynamic check indicates an electrolysis caused by an engine electrical component.

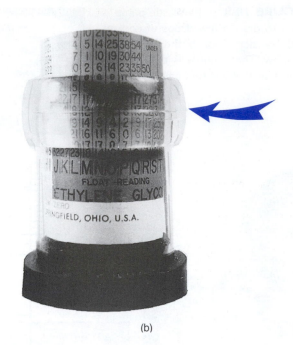

(a)   (b)

FIGURE 18-11   Many antifreeze hydrometers include a thermometer and slide. Set the slide to the thermometer reading *(a)* and read the freezepoint on the proper scale *(b)*.

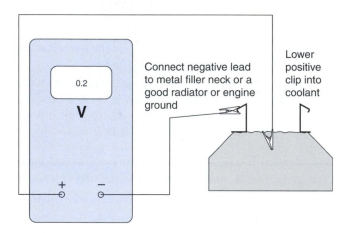

Connect negative lead to metal filler neck or a good radiator or engine ground

Lower positive clip into coolant

0.2

V

+   −

FIGURE 18-12   Radiator voltage is measured by clipping one voltmeter lead to a good ground or the filler neck of all-metal radiators. Dip the clip on the other lead into the coolant; a reading of 0.3 V or greater indicates a problem.

◀ **SERVICE TIP** ▶

To find the cause of a dynamic electrolysis problem, watch the voltmeter as a helper switches the vehicle's electrical devices off. A drop in cooling system voltage indicates the problem source.

◀ **SERVICE TIP** ▶

Many electrolysis problems are often caused by faulty or missing engine or transmission ground straps.

◀ **SERVICE TIP** ▶

Excess cooling system voltage can be caused by acidic coolant that should be changed. The dissimilar metals in a cooling system along with acidic coolant will create a battery.

REAL WORLD FIX: The 1993 Jeep had a severe leak at the lower radiator hose connection. Inspection showed that the lower radiator was severely eaten away, leaving a lot of blue-white corrosion deposits. Talking with the customer revealed that this radiator was only 6 weeks old.

FIX

Checking with an ohmmeter showed a lot of resistance between the radiator and the vehicle's frame. Inspection of the radiator and A/C condenser showed that one of the ground straps was missing and the other one was installed by a very loose bolt. Proper replacement of the missing ground strap and tightening of the other bolts along with repair of the radiator fixed this problem.

◀ SERVICE TIP ▶

A way to check for a faulty ground while measuring voltage drops is to have a helper connect a jumper to provide a ground as the component operates. One end of this jumper should be connected to the battery ground.

18.2.4 Changing Coolant

Dirty coolant should be changed and either recycled or properly disposed of. Many sources recommend changing coolant every 2 years.

To change coolant, you should:

1. Run the engine to bring the coolant to operating temperature and shut the engine off.
2. Position a container to catch the draining coolant and open the radiator drain (Figure 18-13).
3. Remove the radiator cap after the CRR has emptied.
4. Remove the cylinder block drain plug (V engines have two) and drain the coolant into a container (Figure 18-14).
5. Drain the CRR if it did not empty.

6. If the system is slightly dirty, close and replace the drain plugs, fill the system with clean water, and repeat steps 1–5. If the system is very dirty, back-flush the system as described in Section 18.4.1.
7. Replace the drain plug(s) and close the radiator drain.
8. Refill the system with a coolant mixture of 50% new or recycled antifreeze and 50% water. The water jacket portion of most engines refills quite slowly because the air has to bleed out through the small hole in the thermostat. Some systems have an air bleed valve that should be opened to allow the air to leave the water jackets (Figure 18-15).
9. Replace the radiator cap. Run the engine until the thermostat opens and the upper radiator hose becomes hot. On some vehicles, you should

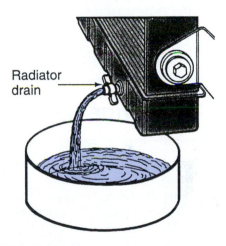

Radiator drain

FIGURE 18-13 Most radiators include a plug or petcock to allow draining the coolant. Be sure to catch the coolant for proper disposal. *(Courtesy of DaimlerChrysler Corporation)*

FIGURE 18-14 An in-line engine usually has one drain plug *(left)*; a V-type engine usually has a drain plug in each cylinder bank. *(Courtesy of Daimler-Chrysler Corporation)*

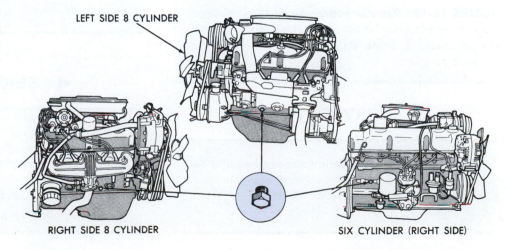

LEFT SIDE 8 CYLINDER

RIGHT SIDE 8 CYLINDER

SIX CYLINDER (RIGHT SIDE)

turn the heater on to open the valve and allow coolant to flow through the heater core.

10. Stop the engine. Fill the radiator to the filler neck seat and the CRR to the proper level.

11. Replace the radiator cap.

◄ SERVICE TIP ►

Leave the radiator cap in place as you begin draining the system; the coolant will be pulled out of the CRR. When the CRR is empty, remove the radiator cap to speed up draining.

◄ SERVICE TIP ►

If using pure antifreeze and water, locate the cooling-system capacity specification and pour one-half this amount of new or recycled antifreeze into the system. Fill the radiator with water.

◄ SERVICE TIP ►

If the cooling system is dirty, most sources recommend filling the system with clean water, running the engine until the thermostat opens, and then draining the water out. This should be repeated until clean water drains out.

◄ SERVICE TIP ►

If using extended-life antifreeze, distilled water is recommended. Chlorine from tap water can react with this antifreeze to reduce corrosion protection qualities.

◄ SERVICE TIP ►

Used antifreeze should be properly handled for several reasons. It is poisonous, but animals such as dogs and cats will drink it because it has a sweet taste.

FIGURE 18-15 Some cooling systems include a bleed valve to allow easy removal of air as the water jackets are filled.

◄ SERVICE TIP ►

Many areas consider antifreeze to be hazardous waste, and shops and individuals who pour antifreeze into the ground or down the drain may be subject to severe fines.

◄ SERVICE TIP ►

Some technicians have experienced breakage problems with plastic drain valves. They feel that disconnecting the lower radiator hose from the radiator hose is almost as fast as opening a drain valve and saves the problem of trying to find a replacement valve (Figure 18-16).

◄ SERVICE TIP ►

If a plastic drain valve that is threaded into a radiator tank breaks off, it can be removed using an old file. Heat the tang of the file, and push it into the center of the broken plastic. It should melt its way into the plastic. Let it cool for a few minutes, and then unscrew the broken part.

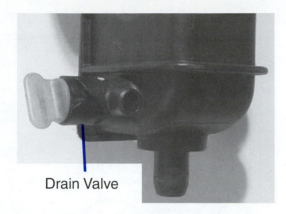

Drain Valve

FIGURE 18-16 This plastic drain valve is formed as part of the radiator tank. If the valve should break, the tank or radiator must be replaced.

Antifreeze-recycling machines allow shops to reclaim antifreeze for reuse. These machines use several different processes to filter out impurities; chemicals are added to restore the additives. Most recycling units start with dirty, used coolant and end up with a clean 50–50-mix coolant ready for reuse. Companies in many metropolitan areas provide recovery and reclaiming services (Figure 18-17).

At this time, many shops use an exchange unit to allow them to replace the coolant easier and faster as well as doing a better job by reducing the chance of air bubbles trapped in the system (Figure 18-18). These machines pump fresh coolant into the system as the old coolant is removed and stored in the machine. Some units include a vacuum fill procedure to remove any air pockets in the cooling system. Some coolant exchange units also are designed to recycle the coolant removed from the vehicle.

To change coolant using a coolant exchange unit:

1. Connect the machine to the vehicle. This is normally done by removing the upper radiator hose and installing a pair of adapters.
2. Follow the machine's operating procedure to complete the coolant exchange.

18.2.4.1 Air Locks Air locked in the water jackets, heater core, or hoses will prevent complete filling of the cooling system. The air is trapped by the closed thermostat or by a system design that has portions of the system above the filler cap. Systems with air bleeds reduce this problem by making it easier to remove the air at the air bleeds, but air bleeds are not used in all systems, and they can be difficult to locate when they are used.

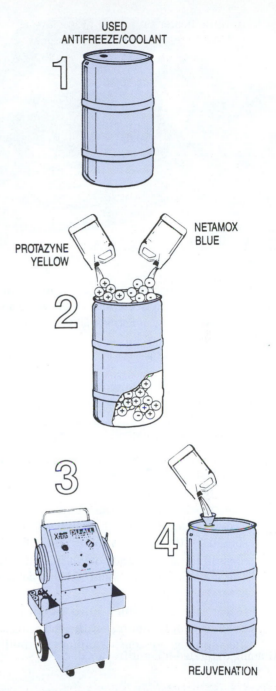

FIGURE 18-17 This antifreeze-recycling process adds two chemicals to the used coolant before it is run through the recycling unit. After reclaiming, new antifreeze is added to adjust the coolant concentration. *(Courtesy of Wynn Oil Company)*

A recent innovation is a tool that evacuates the cooling system through the cooling system filler opening (Figure 18-19). After pulling the system into a vacuum, a shut-off valve is closed to trap the vacuum. The coolant will be pulled into the system by

FIGURE 18-18 A coolant exchange unit is used to pull out the old coolant and replace it with a fresh water and antifreeze mixture. *(Courtesy of Robinair, SPX Corporation)*

the vacuum, completely filling the system in a short period of time.

To fill a cooling system using an airlift you should:

1. Insert the airlift unit into the radiator filler neck using the proper rubber cone to get a good fit.
2. Connect shop air to the airlift unit, and operate to develop a vacuum in the cooling system. You should see the upper radiator hose collapse.
3. Shut off the airflow, and note the vacuum gauge. The cooling system should hold a vacuum for several minutes.
4. Insert the airlift filler hose into the fresh coolant supply, and open the valve to allow the cooling system vacuum to pull the coolant in.

◄ **SERVICE TIP** ►

Air lock problems can be reduced by partially filling some of the components with coolant as they are replaced or blocking the thermostat open as described in Section 18.4.2.4.

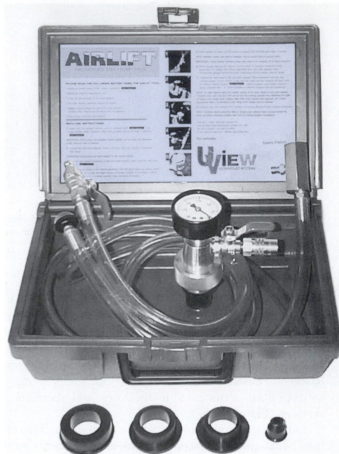

FIGURE 18-19 An airlift unit is designed to evacuate the cooling system of all air, check for vacuum leaks, and quickly refill the system completely with new coolant. It attaches to the radiator filler neck with another connection to a shop air hose and then to the coolant container. *(Courtesy of UView UltravioletSystems)*

◄ **SERVICE TIP** ►

An air lock can also be removed by connecting a hand vacuum pump to the CRR connection at the radiator filler neck. Operating the vacuum pump to reduce cooling system pressure will often pull pockets of air from the system.

REAL WORLD FIX: The 1996 Chevrolet Blazer (33,000 miles) has a noise problem; it sounds like water is sloshing around under the glovebox. The technician suspects that the evaporator drain is plugged. The drain was located and checked and found to be okay.

FIX

Following advice, the technician checked for a heater core air lock. A sludgy buildup was found at the heater core connections, so the system was flushed and the coolant was replaced. Making sure that all of the air was bled out of the heater core fixed this noise problem.

18.2.5   Drive Belt Inspection and Replacement

Engine drive belts should be checked periodically for damage and proper tension. If a belt shows excessive wear, severe glazing, rubber breakdown, or frayed cords, it should be replaced. Small cracks on the ribs of a V-ribbed belt are acceptable, but if chunks of ribs are missing, the belt should be replaced. As mentioned earlier, the failure of many belts cannot always be foreseen, so, to be on the safe side, many sources recommend belt replacement at 4- or 5-year intervals (Figure 18-20). The automatic tensioner on some vehicles includes a belt stretch indicator; if belt stretch of more than 1% is indicated, the belt should be replaced.

A belt that is too loose will slip. Slippage causes an annoying, screeching noise as the engine accelerates. It also causes glazing of the belt, which can cause more slipping. A belt that is too tight causes an excessively high load on the bearings of the components driven by the belt. Traditionally, belt tension is checked by pushing the center of the belt inward and then pulling it out-

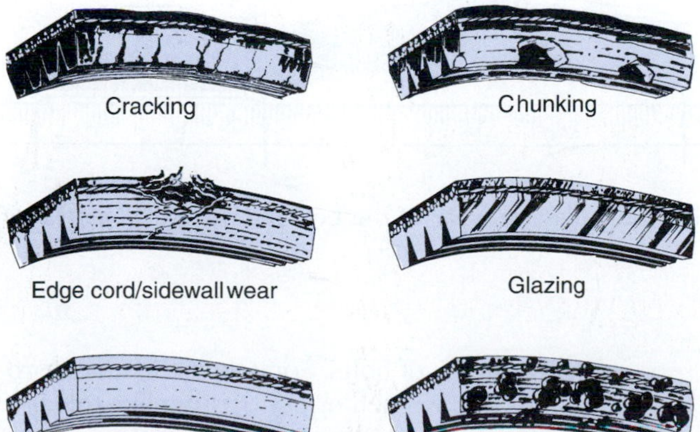

FIGURE 18-20 A drive belt should be replaced if it shows any of these faults. *(Courtesy of Gates Corporation)*

ward. The belt should deflect about 1/8 to 1/4 inch under a pressure of around 5 lb; this amount varies according to the length of the belt span. This is not a very accurate method of checking tension: Most manufacturers recommend using a belt tension gauge that is hooked onto the belt and uses a scale to show tension. This gauge is most accurate (Figure 18-21).

◄ SERVICE TIP ►

If the belt shows signs of failing early, check for **parallel** or **angular misalignment** (Figure 18-22). Either of these conditions can cause excessive belt temperature and shortened life (Figure 18-23). Pulley and sheave alignment is checked by sighting along the pulleys or placing a straightedge or round bar along the pulleys.

To quick-check for the cause of drive belt noise, you should:

1. With the engine running at idle speed, pour a small amount of clean water on the belt and listen for a noise change.

   If the noise increases, there is a belt tension problem.

   If the noise decreases, there is a belt alignment problem.

◄ SERVICE TIP ►

A V-ribbed belt will tolerate up to 1° of misalignment. A special checking tool using laser light has been developed.

To remove and replace a drive belt that uses a set tensioner, you should:

1. Locate the device that is used to adjust belt tension and loosen both the adjuster bolt and the pivot bolt (Figure 18-24).
2. Grip the belt at the center of a convenient span and pull outward quickly and firmly. This should completely loosen the belt tension, making installation easy.

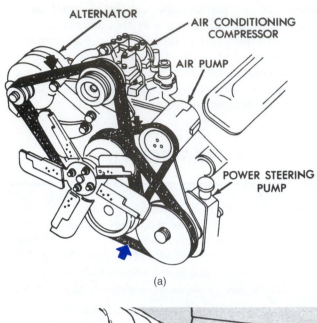

ALTERNATOR

AIR CONDITIONING COMPRESSOR

AIR PUMP

POWER STEERING PUMP

(a)

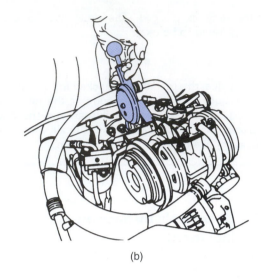

(b)

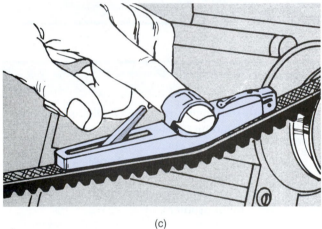

(c)

FIGURE 18-21 Drive belt tension can be checked by measuring how far the belt deflects under a light pressure *(a)* or by using a tension gauge, which is more accurate *(b and c)*. *(a and* b *courtesy of DaimlerChrysler Corporation;* c *courtesy of Gates Corporation)*

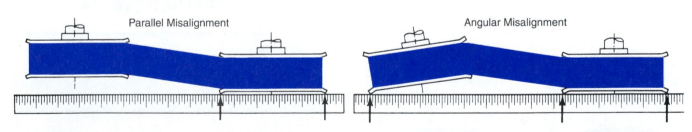

Parallel Misalignment   Angular Misalignment

FIGURE 18-22   Misalignment of the pulleys can cause belt noise and excessive wear of the belt and pulleys. *(Courtesy of Gates Corporation)*

3. Remove the belt.

4. Compare the old and new belts to ensure you have the correct replacement.

5. Place the new belt in position, making sure that it is seated in each pulley groove.

6. Swing the belt adjuster outward, tightening the belt to the correct tension, and tighten the ad-

juster and pivot bolts. Some units include a provision for a wrench or pry bar to make this procedure easier. A belt pulley jack can also be used. Do not use excessive prying force on fragile components (Figure 18-25).

7. Connect a tension gauge and check for correct tension. Readjust the belt if necessary (Figure 18-26).

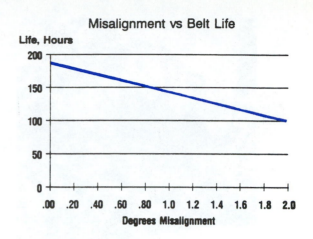

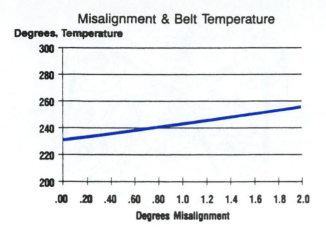

FIGURE 18-23   As shown here, a small amount of misalignment can increase drive belt temperature and wear. *(Courtesy of Gates Corporation)*

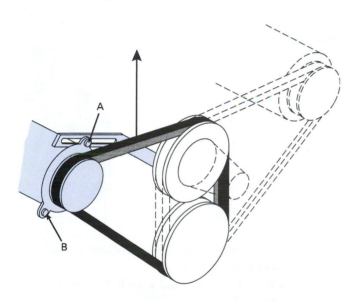

BELT REMOVAL
1. Loosen bolt A and pivot bolt B.
2. Pull outward at center of belt
   with a quick jerk.

FIGURE 18-24   To remove a drive belt, loosen the adjuster and pivot bolts and pull sharply at the center of the belt. This loosens the adjustment, making installation of the new belt easier.

8. Start the engine and check for proper belt operation. Excessive belt slap indicates a need for readjustment.

◄   **SERVICE TIP**   ►

It is recommended to recheck belt tension after 5 minutes of operation.

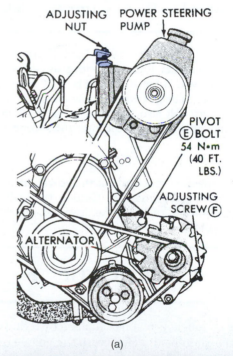

(a)

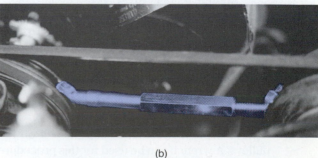

(b)

FIGURE 18-25   Depending on the installation, you can pry on the adjustable component using a screwdriver or bar, swing it using a wrench, move it using a threaded adjuster *(a)*, or use a pulley jack *(b)*. *(a courtesy of DaimlerChrysler Corporation)*

FIGURE 18-26   This type of belt tension gauge is hooked onto the belt and quickly released to measure belt tension.

REAL WORLD FIX: The 1990 Ford Explorer (165,000 miles) eats drive belts. It came in with a shredded drive belt, and a new belt was installed. It came back 30 miles later with another shredded belt. A new belt was installed. The second belt and a third belt also shredded in about 35 miles. The compressor clutch was replaced after the second belt failed.

FIX

A closed inspection revealed that the power steering pulley was not completely installed. Getting this pulley to its proper position and replacing the drive belt one more time fixed this problem.

◀   SERVICE TIP   ▶

Some technicians test belt tension by trying to rotate the alternator pulley (with the engine off) by pushing or pulling on a fan blade. If the pulley can be rotated, the belt is too loose.

To remove and replace a drive belt using an automatic tensioner, you should:

1. Note the routing of the belt.
2. Relieve the belt tension and slip the belt off the pulleys. A wrench can be used for this procedure on some tensioners; others provide for a pry bar (Figure 18-27).
3. Install the belt on some pulleys, rotate the tensioner, slide the belt into the proper position, and release the tensioner.

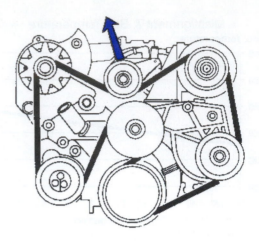

FIGURE 18-27   Moving the automatic tensioner outward allows the serpentine belt to be removed from the pulleys.

FIGURE 18-28   When a V-ribbed belt is installed, make sure the belt is positioned correctly in the pulley grooves.

4. Check to ensure proper belt placement on each pulley (Figure 18-28).
5. Start the engine and check for proper belt operation.

Automatic tensioners can also fail. At least one source recommends replacing the tensioner when the belt is replaced. A tensioner can be checked using the following procedure.

To check belt tensioner operation, you should:

1. With the engine running at idle speed, observe any tensioner movement. If it appears to bounce back and forth a large amount, the dampener portion is probably worn out.
2. Stop the engine. Using the proper tool, swing the tensioner through its travel. It should move smoothly against the spring pressure with no catches or free portions.
3. With the pulley unloaded, check for free play or rough bearing operation. Next, spin the bear-

ing; it should rotate smoothly for two or three revolutions.

18.2.6   Hose Inspection and Replacement

Radiator and heater hoses should be checked periodically. As with drive belts, potential problems can be difficult to see. Signs of failure include cracks, cuts, swelling, and hardening of the hose material. Some hoses become hard, stiff, and brittle, and others become soft and swollen. A hose can appear to be good on the outside, but the inner layer can collapse and partially block coolant flow. Squeeze and bend the hose as you check it for signs of these problems. As with a belt, some sources recommend replacing the hoses at 4- or 5-year intervals to prevent failure (Figure 18-29).

◀ SERVICE TIP ▶

Squeeze the hose near the connectors and compare the feel with the center. Electrochemical degradation usually occurs within 2 inches of the ends of a hose, and soft spots, gaps, or channels indicate a weak hose.

Oil damaged hose   Abrasion damaged hose

(a)

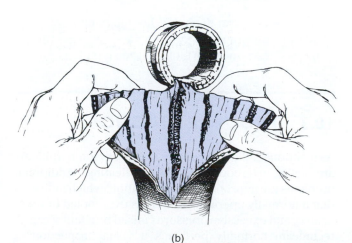

(b)

◀ SERVICE TIP ▶

The hose is usually stuck in place; to prevent damage to the connector, many technicians slice the end of the hose with a sharp knife. Then the hose end can be peeled loose (Figure 18-30).

To remove and replace a hose, you should:

1. Partially drain the coolant so the level is below the hose connections.
2. Loosen the clamp at each end of the hose.
3. Slide the hose off the connection.
4. Clean any rust or corrosion from the connection.
5. Slide the new hose with clamps (loose) over the connectors, engine end first, and rotate the hose on the connections until it is properly positioned and free of kinks. Some manufacturers recommend the use of a water-resistant sealant at these connections.
6. Position the clamps so they are right next to the bead on the connector and tighten them (Figure 18-31).

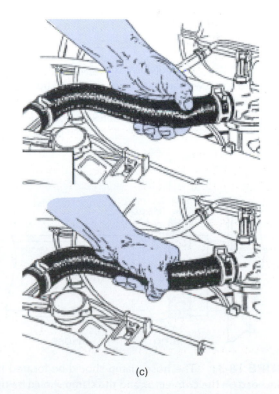

(c)

FIGURE 18-29   Oil and abrasion damage are seen during a visual inspection *(a)*. Electrochemical degradation, ECD *(b)*, can be detected by squeezing the hose. ECD is indicated if the hose feels softer at the ends *(c)*. *(Courtesy of Gates Corporation)*

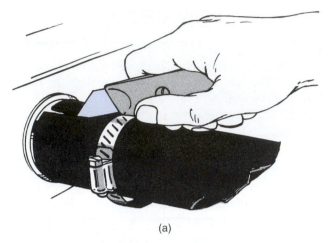

(a)

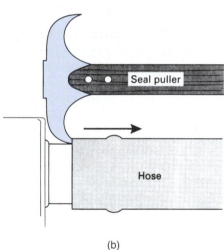

(b)

FIGURE 18-30 The quickest and easiest way to remove a hose is to slit it with a sharp knife *(a)*. If the hose is to be reused, a cotter pin puller or seal remover can be used to aid in removal *(b)*. *(a courtesy of Gates Corporation)*

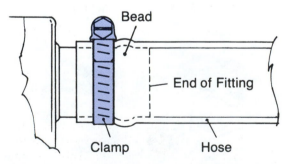

FIGURE 18-31 The hose clamp should be located next to the bead on the connector, and the clamp should be tightened to the correct torque.

FIGURE 18-32 Rubber will be squeezed up into the slots when a screw clamp is properly tightened.

7. Fill the cooling system, run the engine until it reaches operating temperature, and check for leaks as you retighten the clamps.

◄ SERVICE TIP ►

When replacing a radiator hose, you will often find a bunch of crud or corrosion on the outlet neck. This can be quickly cleaned using a piece of steel cable; rub the cable over the filler neck using a "shoe shine" motion.

◄ SERVICE TIP ►

A screw-type clamp should be tightened to 30 to 40 in.-lb of torque (the point where the hose rubber squeezes into the slots of the clamp) (Figure 18-32).

18.3 TROUBLE DIAGNOSIS

As mentioned, the three major cooling system problems are leaks, overcooling, and overheating. Additional problems are improper gauge operation, which indicates that a normally operating system is overcooled or overheated, and excessive pressure caused by a faulty cap. A technician normally performs a visual inspection; a check of the coolant antifreeze concentration, condition, and level; a **pressure test** on the cap and system

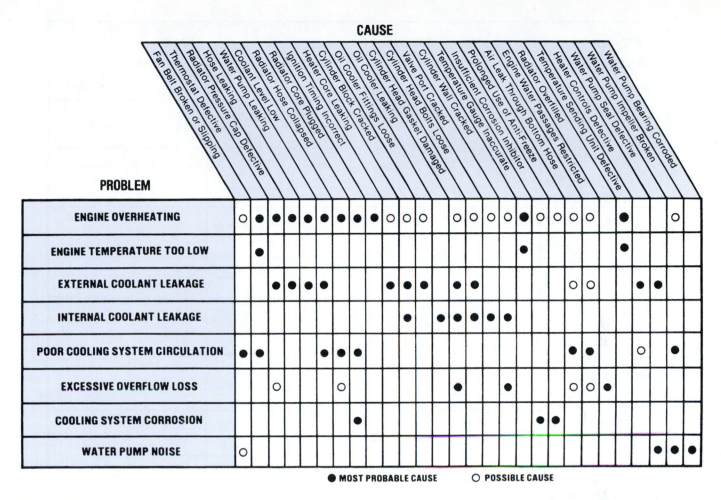

FIGURE 18-33 A problem-solving guide can be used to help locate the probable (●) or possible (○) cause of a cooling system problem. *(Courtesy of Wynn Oil Company)*

for leaks; a test for combustion leakage; a test of thermostat operation (if warranted by the inspection); and a check of the actual system temperature. The tests do not have to be performed in this order: The order depends on the equipment available, the nature of the problem, and the experience of the technician. A troubleshooting chart such as the one shown in Figure 18-33 is often followed to ensure that important items are not skipped.

18.3.1 Cooling System Inspection

Like system inspection for A/C diagnosis, cooling system inspection is used to locate any obvious problems that need correction. It is also a test that can involve all of your senses. Besides a visual inspection, you feel for bearing looseness, hard or soft hoses, temperatures of various items, and flow or pressure of coolant in a hose; you listen for malfunctioning water-pump bearings and gurgles or thumps inside the radiator and water jackets;

and you notice the smell of hot antifreeze leaking out of a system. Many shops use an inspection checklist to provide inspection information for the customer (Figure 18-34). The cooling system inspection consists of a number of steps.

To check a cooling system, you should

With the system cold and the engine off, the checks are as follows:

1. Remove the radiator cap and check the level, condition, and antifreeze concentration of the coolant.

2. Using a light, look for corrosion, dirt, and rust inside the radiator (Figure 18-35). Insert a finger into the filler neck and rub it around the surrounding area. Visible dirt or rust in the radiator or on your finger indicates a need for flushing.

| CUSTOMER _____ PHONE _____ DATE _____ |
| VEHICLE/MAKE _____ YEAR _____ LICENSE _____ MILEAGE _____ |

INSPECTION AREA	INSPECTION RESULTS					RECOMMENDATION
HOSES:	OK	HARD/ BRITTLE	SPLIT/ CRACKED	SOFT/ SPONGY	OIL SOAKED	REPLACE
UPPER RADIATOR						
LOWER RADIATOR						
BY PASS						
HEATER						
FANBELTS:	OK	FRAYED	SPLIT/ CRACKED	GLAZED	LOOSE	REPLACE
ALT./GEN.						
POWER STEERING						
A-C COMPRESSOR						
WATER PUMP:	OK	LOOSE SHAFT BEARING	BLEED HOLE LEAKS	GASKET LEAKS	FAN CLUTCH LOOSE	REPLACE/ POWER FLUSH
COOLANT RECOVERY TANK:	OK	DIRTY	EMPTY	REFILL	MISSING	INSTALL
RADIATOR CAP PRESSURE CHECK:	OK	SWOLLEN GASKET	BROKEN GASKET	CORRODED CAP	WEAK CAP	REPLACE
RADIATOR PRESSURE CHECK:	OK	FINS PLUGGED	RUSTY/ OILY	LEAKS	BLOCKED CORES	ROD OUT/ POWER-FLUSH
COOLANT:	OK	DIRTY	RUSTY	OILY	FOAMY	REPLACE/ POWER-FLUSH
THERMOSTAT:	OK	REPLACE/ OPEN-MISSING	STUCK/ CLOSED	FLUSH TEST	GASKET LEAKS	REPLACE

FIGURE 18-34 Many technicians use a checklist during cooling system inspection. The checklist provides a professional display of any problems for the customer and helps ensure that important checks are not skipped. *(Courtesy of Wynn Oil Company)*

3. Check the exterior of the radiator for stains, which might indicate a leak, and debris on the front or bent fins, which can interfere with airflow.

4. Check the drive belt(s) for possible damage and proper tension.

5. Check the hoses for visible damage and signs of leaking; bend and squeeze the hoses as you check them.

6. Check the water pump for signs of leakage. Try moving the pump shaft from side to side; there should be no perceptible movement.

7. *On RWD cars,* check the fan, fan clutch, and fan shroud. Fan blades should be secure and straight. The fan should rotate at the clutch, but there should be definite resistance. There should be no oil leaks from the fan clutch body.

Solder Bloom–Solder corrosion caused by poorly inhibited antifreeze. Tube-to-header joints are weakened, and corrosion can restrict coolant flow.

Internal Deposits–Rust and leak inhibitors can form solids that collect in the cooling system and restrict flow.

Fin Deterioration–A chemical deterioration of the fins most often caused by road salt or sea water.

Fin Bond Failure–A loss of solder bond between fins and tubes. Fins are loose in core. This causes loss of heat transfer and reduces the strength of the radiator.

Tube-to-Header Leaks–Failure of the solder joint results in coolant loss.

Leaking Tank-to-Header Seam–Failure of the solder joint or cracked headers is generally the result of pressure.

Blown Tank-to-Header Seam–Usually an indication that the radiator has seen extreme pressures.

Loose Side Piece–Can lead to flexing of the core and radiator tube failure.

FIGURE 18-35 The most commonly encountered radiator faults. Most of these problems require replacement of the radiator or tanks. *(Courtesy of Modine Manufacturing)*

Leaky Oil Cooler Fitting–Caused by failure of the solder joint between the radiator tank and oil cooler.

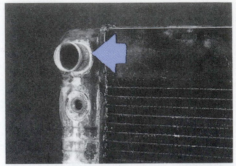

Leaky Inlet-Outlet Fitting–Leaks in this area of the radiator can be caused by fatigue or by corrosion of the solder joint.

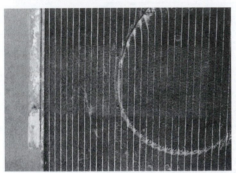

Fan Damage–Minor collisions of failed water pump can result in damage to the radiator.

Over Pressurization–Excessive pressure in the radiator by a defective pressure cap or engine exhaust gas leak can destroy the radiator.

Electrolysis–Stray electric current can cause excessive corrosion of metal components.

Electrolysis–Stray electric current can cause an electrochemical reaction that will produce voids in tubes.

Cracked Plastic Tanks–High stress in radiator can cause premature failure of the plastic tanks.

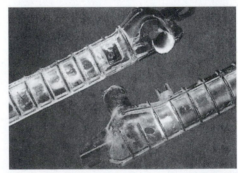

Steam Erosion–Steam can break down the plastic tank which will produce thinning and ultimately holes in the plastic tank. Frequently, white deposits are also found.

FIGURE 18-35 Continued.

FIGURE 18-36 If the fan is rotated, you should notice a definite drag of the fan clutch. Also check for excessive play in either a front-to-back or sideways direction (*arrows*).

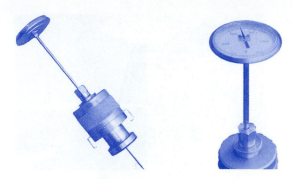

FIGURE 18-37 A thermometer installed in the radiator filler neck can be used to check the temperature of the coolant. The adapter is also used for pressure checks. (*Courtesy of Waekon Industries*)

Grip the tips of two opposite blades, and try to move the fan from side to side and from front to back. More than 1/8 inch of movement indicates a faulty fan clutch (Figure 18-36). *On FWD cars*, check the fan, motor, and shroud-mounting bracket for damage, proper mounting, and free rotation of the fan.

◀ **SERVICE TIP** ▶

If you suspect a leak, shine an ultraviolet, black light over the engine soft plugs, hoses, and other possible leak locations. Some antifreeze solutions glow and will reveal the leak. A fluorescent dye can be added to the coolant to make it glow under the black light. Pressurizing the cooling system will also make leaks show up.

With the engine running, the checks are as follows:

1. Place a thermometer into the radiator filler neck and start the engine.
   OR: check the upper radiator hose temperature using an infrared thermometer.
2. Squeeze the upper radiator hose. With the engine cold, the thermostat should be closed and there should be little or no flow through the hose.

3. Check the drive belts. They should be running true, with a small amount of whipping at the longest span or the last span before the crankshaft pulley. All pulleys and shafts should be running smoothly, with very little or no runout.
4. After 5 to 10 minutes, the engine should reach operating temperature, and the thermostat should open. At this time, coolant flow can be felt in the upper hose, and the hose temperature increases. The thermometer indicates the coolant temperature and the opening point of the thermostat (Figure 18-37).
5. Increase the engine speed as you squeeze the upper radiator hose. The flow inside the hose should increase as the water pump speeds up.
6. The electric cooling fan of a FWD car should start operation when the engine warms up, about 20 to 40°F above the thermostat opening point.

◀ **SERVICE TIP** ▶

On vehicles with two-speed electric fans, try to produce high-speed fan operation to ensure that it will work properly when it becomes needed.

◀ **SERVICE TIP** ▶

Infrared thermometers make temperature checks much easier; merely point the unit at the heat source to be checked. The temperature is then read on the unit's display (Figure 18-38).

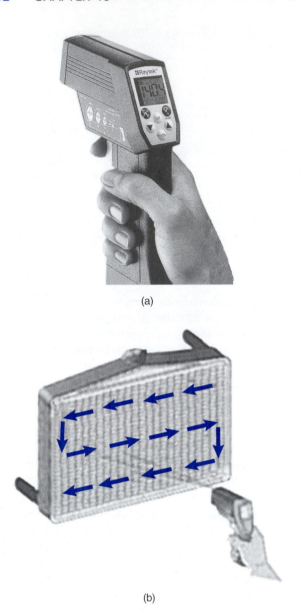

(a)

(b)

FIGURE 18-38 An infrared thermometer allows fast temperature checks. Merely point the unit at the spot to be checked, pull the trigger, and read the temperature. *(Courtesy of Raytek Corporation)*

With the system warm to hot and the engine off, the checks are as follows:

1. Compare the temperatures indicated on the thermometer and on the vehicle temperature gauge; they should be equal.
2. Listen to the cooling system. Light snapping, popping noises are normal heat expansion and contraction noises. A slight pressure release at the radiator cap (when in place) is also normal. Heavy thumping sounds from inside the engine indicate

overheating in localized areas; the noise is probably caused by an internal restriction.

3. On RWD cars, spin the fan. With the engine warm, a faulty fan clutch is indicated if the fan spins more than one revolution.

18.3.2   Pressure Tests

Pressure tests are used to check for leaks and proper operation of a pressure cap. A pressure test can also be used to check for an internal combustion leak.

There are several styles of pressure testers. The most common is a hand pressure pump with adapters that connect to the pressure cap and radiator filler neck. An adapter that connects into the system through the temperature sending unit port is also available for some hand pumps. Another style of pressure tester connects to the system through the coolant overflow hose. This unit is essentially a pressure regulator connected to shop air. A third style of tester replaces the radiator cap with an adapter that allows a pressure or temperature probe to be inserted. This unit can use a pressure regulator and shop air as a pressure source or measure the pressure generated by the system (Figure 18-39).

To test a cap using a hand pump tester, you should:

1. Remove the cap from the system and clean the cap gasket with water.
2. Select the proper adapter for the cap, immerse the cap in water to wet the gasket, and install the cap on the adapter and the adapter on the tester (Figure 18-40).
3. Slowly operate the tester pump as you watch the gauge pressure. The pressure should increase to a point and then stop increasing as the cap releases pressure; this point should be the pressure value of the cap. The cap should hold this pressure for 1 minute.
4. Release the pressure and repeat step 3 to make sure the test is accurate. If the cap releases pressure early or late or will not hold pressure, it should be replaced.

To pressure test a system using a hand pump tester, you should:

1. Fill the radiator.
2. Connect the pressure tester to the radiator filler neck (Figure 18-41). Adapters are required to connect the tester to some radiators.

(a)

(b)

FIGURE 18-39 Cooling system pressure testers include a style using a hand pump *(a)* and ones that use shop air pressure or cooling system pressure *(b)*. *(a courtesy of Stant Manufacturing;* b *courtesy of Waekon Industries)*

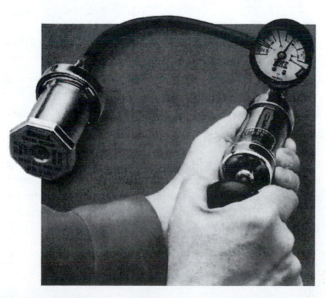

FIGURE 18-40 After wetting the cap gasket with coolant or water, it is placed on the adapter. Then the tester is pumped to the point where pressure is released. (This pressure should match the cap's rating.) *(Courtesy of Stant Manufacturing)*

Or remove the temperature sending unit, install the adapter into this opening, and connect the pressure tester to this adapter. Note that with this connection you are testing the cap also.

3. Slowly pump the tester to the pressure rating of the system or the pressure range indicated on the cap. If using the adapter so that the radiator cap is in place and the cap releases early, replace the cap.

4. Observe the pressure gauge: It should hold steady for at least 2 minutes. If the pressure drops, coolant is probably leaking out; check for leaks in the system.

5. If using the adapter so that the radiator cap is in place, increase the pressure using the pump and observe the coolant overflow hose. The cap should release pressure and cause flow through the hose at its rated pressure.

To pressure test a system using a pressure regulator and shop air pressure, you should:

1. With the system cool, remove the radiator cap, install the adapter, and install the pressure probe into the adapter.

Or remove the overflow hose from the filler neck and connect the pressure regulator unit to the filler neck connection (Figure 18-42).

(a)

(b)

FIGURE 18-41 A system's pressure is checked by connecting the tester to the radiator and bringing it up to the proper pressure (a). Adapters are available to fit the various filler neck styles (b). *(Courtesy of Stant Manufacturing)*

(a)

(b)

FIGURE 18-42 A pressure probe with regulator has been installed in the radiator neck using the same adapter shown in Figure 16-32b (a). Shop air can be put into the system using the fitting (*arrow*). A similar style of tester is shown in b. (a *courtesy of Waekon Industries*)

2. Connect a shop air hose to the test unit and increase the pressure regulator setting to the rated pressure of the system.

3. After the system pressure is reached, shut off the air supply and watch the pressure gauge. The system should hold pressure for 2 minutes. A leak is indicated if the pressure drops.

◀ **CAUTION** ▶

Be careful while using either type of pressure tester to check for combustion leaks. With the tester replacing the cap, there is a closed system with nothing to release excess pressure. You must be ready to relieve excess pressure in a harmless manner. Never permit the pressure in the system to exceed 20 psi. In a normal system, the pressure gradually increases as the coolant warms and expands. In a system with a combustion leak, the pressure can increase very rapidly.

To test for a combustion leak, you should:

1. Connect either the hand pump unit or the pressure regulator unit to the radiator filler neck.
2. Start the engine and observe the pressure gauge. A rapid pressure increase indicates a leak from the combustion chamber to the water jacket. Pulsations of the gauge needle also indicate combustion gases being forced into the water jacket. If this happens, you can short out the spark plugs until the pulsations stop to find the bad cylinder. Be ready to release excess pressure (Figure 18-43).

◄ SERVICE TIP ►

Some technicians completely fill the radiator and crank over the engine using the starter. A combustion leak is indicated by pressure pulses on the gauge.

18.3.3 Combustion Leak Checks

A combustion leak can be caused by a blown head gasket, warped head or cylinder block, or cracked head or

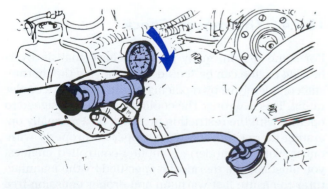

FIGURE 18-43 A combustion leak will cause a rise in system pressure if the engine is started. Be ready to relieve any excess pressure.

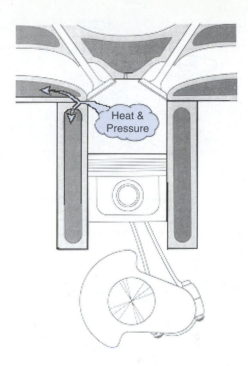

FIGURE 18-44 A combustion leak is caused by a crack or a faulty head gasket, which allows combustion pressure to enter the water jackets.

block. This type of leak allows hot, high-pressure gases to pass from the combustion chamber to the water jacket. The result is usually rapid overheating and deterioration of the coolant. Sometimes the leak allows coolant to flow into the combustion chamber; this can cause excess steaming from the exhaust or a hydrostatic lock in a cylinder during cranking (Figure 18-44).

Occasionally, an internal leak allows coolant to enter the oil. Minor leaks cause excess water droplets in the oil; major leaks can cause gray, repulsive-looking oil.

◄ SERVICE TIP ►

A simple test to determine whether there is water in the oil is to transfer a few drops of oil from the dipstick to a hot exhaust manifold. Plain oil will spread out and burn off as light-colored smoke. Any water in the oil will sizzle and spatter.

Checks for combustion leaks look for gas bubbles in the coolant or the presence of carbon dioxide (CO_2). CO_2 is indicated by a color change in the test fluid. Exhaust gas analyzers can also be used to test for CO or CO_2 in coolant, but great care should be exercised to prevent coolant from being drawn into the tester.

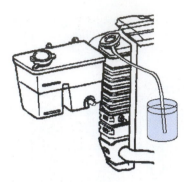

FIGURE 18-45 A simple check for a combustion leak is to immerse the overflow/transfer tube into a container of water and run the engine. Bubbles from the hose indicate a combustion leak.

◀ **SERVICE TIP** ▶

When using an exhaust gas analyzer, some technicians place a close fitting tube, about 6″ long, into the filler neck. This is used to direct any escaping gases to the tester probe. Many technicians insert the analyzer probe into the CRR because there is usually ample room above the coolant, and the CRR tends to trap any gases escaping from the cooling systems.

◀ **SERVICE TIP** ▶

Some technicians check for HC in the cooling system as an indication of a combustion leak, but this can be misleading because many chemicals can cause false HC readings. It is recommended, if using a modern combustion analyzer, to check for carbon monoxide (CO); a CO reading of greater than 0.02 parts per million (ppm) indicates there is a probable combustion leak into the cooling system.

To check for gas bubbles, you should:

1. Disconnect the overflow hose from the CRR and place it in a container of water (Figure 18-45).
2. Loosen the radiator cap so it will release pressure.

3. Start the engine and watch the end of the overflow hose. A stream of bubbles indicates a combustion leak or a suction leak at the water pump or lower radiator hose. The combustion leak rate increases if the load on the engine is increased.

To check for CO_2 in the coolant, you should:

1. Remove the radiator cap and partially drain the coolant so the level is 2 or 3 inches below the filler neck.
2. Start the engine and let it idle.
3. Partially fill the test unit to the correct level with the test fluid (Figure 18-46).
4. Place the test unit into the filler neck and draw air from the radiator through the test fluid using the aspirator bulb. Continue this step for up to 2 minutes.
5. Observe the test fluid. If it stays blue, there is no combustion leak. If the color changes from blue to yellow, there is a combustion leak.

◀ **SERVICE TIP** ▶

The exact cylinder that is leaking can usually be determined through a compression test. Another method is to leave the system connected to the regulated pressure tester for a period of time with the engine shut off. Pressure from the tester can force coolant to fill the faulty cylinder. If the spark plugs are removed and the engine cranked, coolant will be pumped out of the bad cylinder.

18.3.4 Thermostat Check

For some reason, many people believe that an overheating engine can be "cured" by removing the thermostat completely or by replacing it with one with a cooler rating. This is wrong. The cooling system is designed to operate with the restriction provided by a normally operating thermostat and cannot operate properly without it. With all modern, computer-controlled engines, you must use the thermostat specified by the manufacturer to ensure fast warm-up and proper emission-free engine operation. A faulty cooling system overheats and boils the coolant; all a thermostat does in a faulty system is reduce the time to boil.

(a)

(b)

FIGURE 18-46 A combustion leak tester is partially filled with test fluid (*a*). Working the test bulb draws gases from the system through the fluid (*b*). There is a combustion leak if the fluid changes color.

A thermostat that is stuck closed causes the engine to overheat; one that is stuck open causes overcooling, with slow, prolonged warm-up. Either of these conditions should show up during a visual inspection. The test described here is used to either confirm a suspicion or evaluate an unknown thermostat.

To test a thermostat, you should:

1. Force the valve of the thermostat partially open, slide a thin feeler gauge through the opening, and allow the thermostat to close and catch the feeler gauge.
2. Place a container of water on a stove or hot plate.
3. Tie a string to the feeler gauge and suspend the thermostat in the water so it does not touch the sides or bottom of the container (Figure 18-47).
4. Suspend a thermometer in the water near the thermostat.

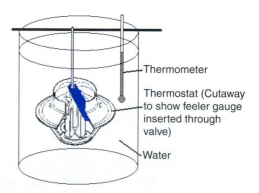

FIGURE 18-47 Place a thin feeler gauge into the valve portion of a thermostat and suspend it by a string in a container of water. Heat the water; the valve should open to let the thermostat drop. This should occur at the thermostat's rated temperature.

5. Begin heating the water and observe the thermostat. It should open and fall off the feeler gauge when it reaches operating temperature.

6. When the thermostat opens, note the water temperature.
   a. If the thermostat opens at a temperature within 10°F (18°C) of the rating stamped on it and opens completely, it is functioning properly and can be reused.
   b. If the thermostat opens too early (cooler) or does not close completely, it should be replaced.
   c. If the thermostat opens too late or does not open, it should be replaced.

Always replace a faulty thermostat with the one specified by the vehicle manufacturer. If the engine has a properly functioning thermostat and still overheats, something else is wrong.

REAL WORLD FIX: The 1996 Mazda MPV van (65,000 miles) overheats after a 10- to 20-minute drive. The thermostat has been replaced twice and the radiator once, but this did not help.

FIX

The technician removed the heater hoses to check the coolant flow and discovered that there was no flow. Checking further, it was found that the plastic water-pump impeller had cracked so that when it got hot, it would slip on the shaft.

AUTHOR'S NOTE

Feeling for coolant flow by squeezing the upper hose could have indicated this problem.

18.3.5   Fan Clutch Test

Some technicians have found that faulty fan clutches are a major cause of high A/C high side pressure and compressor clutch failure. In addition to the checks made during the inspection, the operation of a fan clutch can be tested using a fan clutch tester, strobe light tachometer, or timing light. When cold, the fan speed should be limited; when warmed up, the fan speed should be at or not above a specified rpm. The flashes of the strobe light make the fan and fan clutch appear to stand still when the flashes occur at the same frequency as the fan speed.

◄   SERVICE TIP   ►

A quick check is to observe the fan as you shut off a "hot" engine; with a good fan clutch, the fan will stop rotating almost as fast as the drive belt. If the fan continues to spin for a few revolutions, the fan clutch is probably worn out. Another check is made with the engine off: Spin the fan by hand; if the fan clutch is good, the fan will stop almost immediately.

To quick-check a fan clutch, you should:

1. Start the engine, and turn on the A/C to add heat to the radiator; place cardboard or shop cloths in front of the radiator to block the airflow.
2. A roaring, rumbling noise with an increase of airflow indicates that the fan clutch has engaged.

◄   SERVICE TIP   ►

A fan clutch should lockup at about 170°F (77°C) and release at about 150°F (66°C).

◄   SERVICE TIP   ►

With the fan clutch engaged, the airflow through the radiator should easily hold a piece of paper (some technicians use a dollar bill) against the radiator.

To test a fan clutch, you should:

1. Using a suitable marker, mark one of the fan blades and the water pump pulley; some technicians put a different number on each of the blades.
2. Start the engine and direct the strobe light toward the fan and pulley. Adjust the engine speed to 1,000 rpm and the strobe light speed so the fan and pulley appear to stand still. The fan and pulley should be close to the same speed.
3. Increase the engine to 1,500 rpm. If cold, the clutch should be slipping, and there should be a speed difference between the fan and pulley.
4. Block off the front of the radiator to increase the temperature so the fan clutch engages, increase the engine speed to 2,000 rpm, and recheck the fan speed. The fan speed should be limited to about 1,500 to 2,000 rpm.

18.3.6 Electric Fan Tests

Electric fans are powered through a relay and one or more switches or the ECM as described in Chapter 14. A faulty fan motor is removed and replaced. Other problems such as vibration or poor airflow can be caused by damaged or broken fan blades or a damaged shroud/housing. Reversed airflow can be caused by reversed connections at the fan motor.

◀ **SERVICE TIP** ▶

With the fan(s) running, carefully hold one end of a strip of paper near to the front or back of the fan; the paper should be blown toward the rear of the vehicle.

Cavitation is a disruption of the airflow that also causes poor airflow. You can test for cavitation by measuring the fan motor current draw.

To test for cavitation, you should:

1. Remove the fan so it can operate in the open with free airflow in and out. Be careful so neither you nor your clothing get's caught by the blades.
2. Connect the fan motor to a battery using the proper polarity and with an ammeter in series with one of the leads. While the motor is running, the amount of current draw should be indicated on the ammeter.
3. You can determine the effect of cavitation by laying the fan motor so the inlet side is flat on a bench top or floor and repeating step 2. You should be able to hear the motor run at a higher speed with a lower current draw; this tells you that the fan is moving less air.
4. Replace the fan, and remeasure the current draw. If the amount is less than what was measured in step 2, the fan is cavitating because of an airflow problem.

18.3.7 Water Pump Test

Water pump impeller erosion or corrosion can be caused by poor coolant service or use of the wrong coolant, and the result will be poor or no coolant circulation. Access to the water pump is fairly easy on many RWD vehicles, but water pump removal on many FWD

vehicles can be difficult. During this test, the water pump in a cold engine should be able to create pressure of about 10 to 15 psi (69 to 108 kPa); if it cannot create pressure, it is bad.

To test a water pump, you should:

1. Disconnect the supply heater hose from the heater, and plug the heater core pipe.
2. Connect a pressure gauge to the heater hose.
3. Start the engine and increase the engine rpm to about 2,500 rpm.
4. Note the pressure on the gauge. A pressure reading above 10 psi indicates a good pump; less than 10 psi indicates a probable failure.

18.4 COOLING SYSTEM SERVICE AND REPAIR

The major cooling system service and repair operations are flushing to clean out a dirty system and replacement of faulty components. Overheating can be caused by defective engine parts (e.g., a blown head gasket or warped head), but this text does not cover engine teardown. Many good information sources describe engine disassembly, inspection, and repair.

Radiator repair is a specialized skill that is normally performed by specialty shops. Many modern radiators use an aluminum core with tanks that are secured by bent or crimped connections. The tanks can be removed and replaced to allow replacement of faulty items in many vehicle dealerships; they normally have the tools and information required for these operations (Figure 18-48).

18.4.1 Flushing a System

A dirty, rusty cooling system can often be cleaned using a chemical cleaning agent and a pressure **backflush.** Heavy rust or scale buildup in the water jackets probably requires engine teardown and a thorough boil-out or bake-oven cleaning. Rust and dirt are insulators that slow heat flow to the coolant in the water jackets and from the coolant to the radiator. A 1/16-inch layer of rust slows heat flow as much as a 1/4-inch layer of iron.

Chemical flushing uses strong chemicals designed to loosen or dissolve oil film, rust, scale, and other debris in the water jacket or radiator. These chemicals are either poured into the cooling system and circulated by the water pump or pumped through the system by a flushing unit. If using either of these, be sure to follow the directions on the container or the flushing unit.

Pressure flushing is often called backflushing because flow is the reverse of the normal direction.

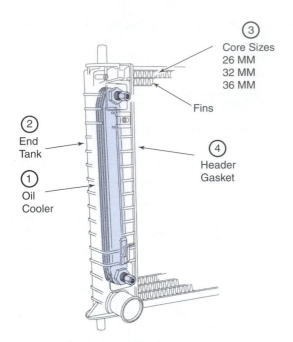

FIGURE 18-48 The end tank on some radiators can be removed to replace the tank, sealing gasket, or internal cooler. *(Courtesy of Visteon)*

Reverse flow helps loosen debris. This flow is often pulsed, using air pressure to break more material loose (Figure 18-49). The handheld backflush gun is an effective flushing tool but is becoming less popular because of the amount of operator time it requires. Machine flushing units can be attached quickly to a system; after the flushing operation begins, the operator can leave and perform other tasks.

> *To flush a system using a handheld flushing gun, you should:*

1. Add a flushing chemical to the radiator if the system is dirty enough to warrant it. Follow the directions on the container, which usually involve running the engine a prescribed length of time after it has warmed up. Drain the system and dispose of the spent cleaning solution in the proper manner.
2. Disconnect the upper radiator hose at the radiator and the lower hose at the engine.
3. Attach the flushing gun to the lower radiator hose; connect a hose to the upper radiator connector to direct water away from the engine (Figure 18-50).
4. Connect the flushing gun to a water hose and an air hose to a regulated air supply. Adjust the air pressure regulator to 20 psi.
5. Turn on the water and allow it to fill the radiator.

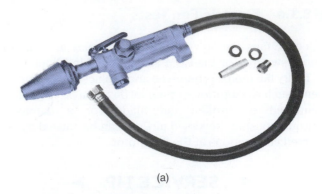

(a)

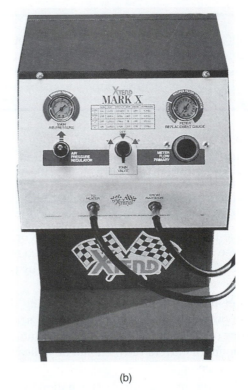

(b)

FIGURE 18-49 A flushing gun *(a)* and a flushing machine *(b)* can be used to flush a cooling system. This particular flushing machine will also recycle coolant. (a *courtesy of DaimlerChrysler Corporation;* b *courtesy of Wynn Oil Company)*

6. Operate the air valve in short bursts so the radiator stays full of water.
7. Watch the water flow from the radiator; repeat step 6 until the water runs clear.
8. Remove the thermostat from the engine and replace the thermostat cover.
9. Attach the flushing gun to the upper radiator hose (leading to the engine water jacket) and repeat steps 5 and 6 until the water running out of the engine is clear. When flushing the engine, the air pressure can be increased to 40 psi (Figure 18-51).

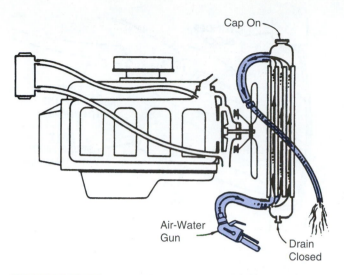

FIGURE 18-50 A radiator is backflushed by running water with added air bursts backward through the core.

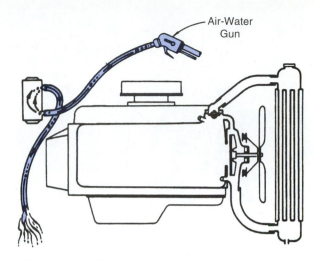

FIGURE 18-52 A heater core can also be backflushed, but be sure to keep the pressures low so as not to rupture the core.

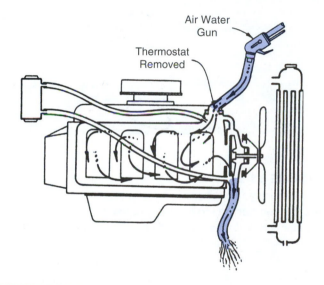

FIGURE 18-51 Water jackets are backflushed by running water with added air bursts backward through them. Be sure to remove the thermostat before backflushing.

10. The heater core can be flushed by connecting the flushing gun to the heater hoses and repeating steps 5, 6, and 7. Air pressure should be adjusted to 15 psi when flushing a heater core (Figure 18-52).

11. Replace the thermostat and radiator hoses, fill the system with a 50–50 mix of antifreeze and water, and check for leaks.

Most shops today use a flushing machine for coolant exchange. This machine is quickly attached to the vehi-

cle's cooling system at the upper radiator hose or one or both of the heater hoses. Then the machine is used to circulate a chemical cleaning agent through the cooling system until it is clean. Machine flushing uses a procedure that is similar to a coolant exchange (Section 18.2.4).

If the radiator still shows scale deposits, its flow can be tested to determine if it is restricted. A radiator shop usually has the equipment to boil out, rod, or replace the core in a very dirty radiator. The rodding operation involves removing the radiator tanks and running a metal rod through each of the tubes.

18.4.2 Component Replacement

Replacement of most cooling system components essentially follows a procedure of draining the coolant, removing the old part, installing the new part, replacing the coolant, and checking for leaks. The exact procedure to follow for each vehicle is described in the service information. Descriptions given here are to point out service operations performed by some technicians to ensure proper operation.

18.4.2.1 R&R Engine Core or Soft Plugs Core plugs are normally replaced when an engine is overhauled or when they begin leaking. The biggest problem typically encountered is getting access to the plug: It is often behind an exhaust pipe, motor mount, or starter. Normally the old plug is removed and a new one driven in place.

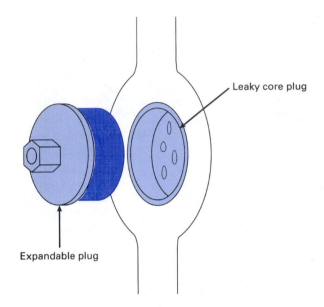

FIGURE 18-53 A leaky core plug can often be repaired by installing an expandable plug into the core plug.

◀ **SERVICE TIP** ▶

If a cup plug is in a hard-to-reach location, the old plug can be cleaned and left in place with an expandable rubber plug inserted into it (Figure 18-53).

◀ **SERVICE TIP** ▶

Many technicians coat the inner side of a metal plug with nonhardening gasket sealer or room temperature volcanizing (RTV) sealant to serve as a corrosion barrier and the side of the plug to serve as a sealant. Rubber expandable plugs should be installed dry.

To R&R a leaky core plug, you should:

1. Drain the coolant.
2. If practical, remove the old plug. This is normally done using a slide hammer or punch and pliers, as shown in Figure 18-54.
3. Clean any corrosion from the opening.
4. Coat the new plug with sealant and drive it into the opening. The driving tool should loosely fit

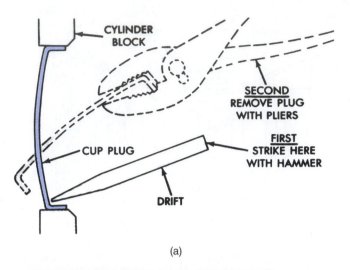

(a)

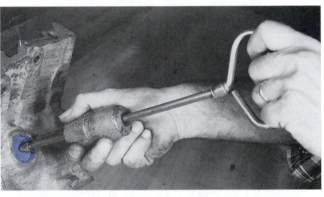

(b)

FIGURE 18-54 A cup plug can be removed by rotating the plug using a punch and hammer and pulling it out with pliers *(a)*. Another way to do this is to use a slide hammer with a puller screw *(b)*. *(a courtesy of DaimlerChrysler Corporation)*

the inner diameter of the plug. Try to position the plug so its inner edge is flush with the inside of the water jacket to eliminate a debris buildup pocket.

5. Refill the system with coolant and check for leaks.

18.4.2.2 R&R Fan and Fan Clutch Except for the tight fit between the radiator and some of the bolts, R&R of the fan and fan clutch is a fairly easy task. Be careful to tighten the mounting bolts onto the water pump shaft evenly so that a good, straight fit is accomplished. Improper mounting can make the fan and fan clutch run off center. This can cause vibration, which in turn can damage the water-pump bearings or shaft. If improper mounting is suspected, a fairly simple fan runout check can be made.

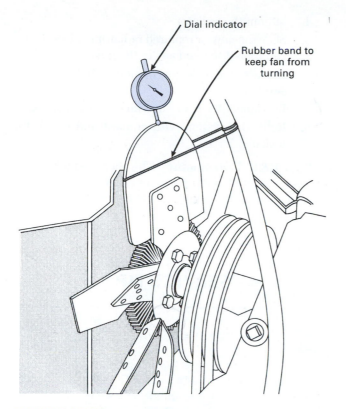

FIGURE 18-55 Fan runout is measured by holding the fan stationary using a rubber band, mounting a dial indicator at one of the blades, and cranking the engine. Excessive runout indicates faulty fan or fan clutch mounting.

To check fan runout, you should:

1. Disable the ignition system so the engine will not start.
2. Keep a fan blade from rotating by looping a strong rubber band over the blade and an engine part (Figure 18-55).
3. Crank the engine as you observe for side-to-side motion of the fan. It should stay still.

If the fan moves more than 0.010 inch, check the mounting to ensure that it is straight. If necessary, shim the mounting point to remove the runout. If the fan is damaged and requires replacement, be sure to replace it with a fan of the correct size and type.

◄ **SERVICE TIP** ►

If replacing a fan or fan clutch, pay attention to the direction of rotation. Most modern engines that use a serpentine, V-ribbed belt drive the water pump and fan off the flat, back side of the belt so it turns in a counterclockwise direction. Engines that use a plain V belt drive the fan and water pump from the inside of the belt, and the fan turns in a clockwise direction. Both the fan and fan clutch must match the direction of rotation (Figure 18-56).

FIGURE 18-56 If replacing a fan, make sure that the replacement is designed to rotate in the correct direction. *(Courtesy of Stant Manufacturing)*

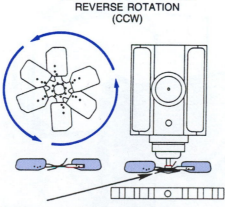

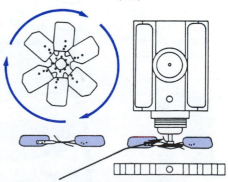

Some fan clutches thread onto the drive shaft from the water pump. They are removed by unscrewing them in a direction opposite to normal rotation. On some vehicles, a special wrench is required for this operation.

18.4.2.3 R&R Radiator

Probably the most difficult part of radiator removal is the disassembly of the oil cooler lines for automatic transmissions. On older vehicles, a flare fitting is used, and two wrenches are required for disconnection: one wrench to turn the fitting nut, and one to keep the fitting from turning. Some newer vehicles use a quick-connect coupling that requires a special tool.

To R&R a radiator, you should:

1. Drain the coolant.
2. Disconnect the upper and lower radiator hoses and the overflow hose from the radiator. On vehicles with automatic transmissions, disconnect the oil cooler lines.
3. Disconnect the shroud, if necessary, and remove the bolts that attach the radiator (Figure 18-57).

4. Lift out the radiator.
5. Slide the new or repaired radiator in place, being careful not to bend any of the fins.
6. Replace the radiator mounting bolts and the shroud.
7. Reconnect the hoses and lines to the radiator.
8. Refill the system with coolant and check for leaks.

18.4.2.4 R&R Thermostat

The thermostat in most vehicles is located under its cover at the upper outlet of the engine. In some vehicles, it is located at the lower coolant inlet.

◀ **SERVICE TIP** ▶

A thermostat must always be installed so that the heat motor or sensing portion is toward the hot water. A close inspection of their mountings shows that most thermostats fit into a recess (Figure 18-58). The gasket not only seals the cover but also prevents coolant flow past the thermostat. Some thermostats must be aligned as they are installed into their housing.

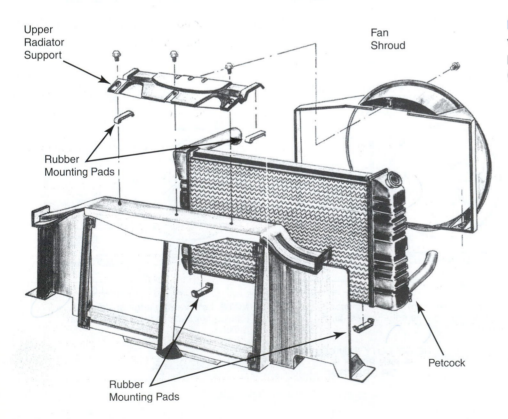

Upper Radiator Support

Rubber Mounting Pads

Fan Shroud

Rubber Mounting Pads

Petcock

FIGURE 18-57 An exploded view of radiator assembly showing parts removed during replacement. *(Courtesy of Everco Industries)*

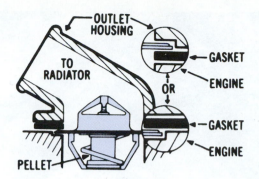

FIGURE 18-58 A thermostat is normally set in a recess in the engine or outlet housing; the gasket often prevents flow around the thermostat. *(Courtesy of Stant Manufacturing)*

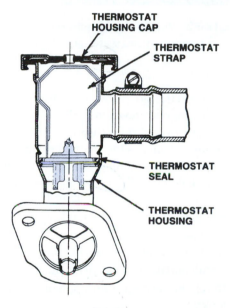

FIGURE 18-59 An exploded and cutaway view of a cap-mounted thermostat. *(Courtesy of Stant Manufacturing)*

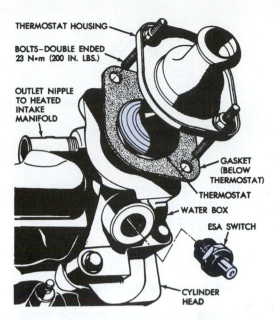

FIGURE 18-60 The thermostat is normally mounted near the heater hose outlet and temperature sensing (ESA) switch. *(Courtesy of DaimlerChrysler Corporation)*

◄ **SERVICE TIP** ►

Many thermostats have an air bleed hole or notch in them. On some, the bleed hole has a jiggle pin in it to keep it open. On vertically mounted thermostats, the air bleed should be positioned in the uppermost position to bleed as much air as possible.

To R&R a thermostat, you should:

1. Partially drain the coolant so the level is below the thermostat cover.

2. Disconnect the upper radiator hose at the thermostat cover and disconnect the bypass hose (if so equipped). On some vehicles, just remove the radiator cap–like thermostat cover (Figure 18-59).
3. Remove the thermostat housing bolts and the thermostat housing.
4. Remove the thermostat and gasket (Figure 18-60).
5. Clean the gasket surfaces and the thermostat recess.
6. Install the thermostat, new gasket, and cover. A sealant is usually recommended for the gasket.
7. Replace the bolts and tighten them to the correct torque.
8. Refill the system with coolant and check for leaks.

◄ **SERVICE TIP** ►

When replacing a thermostat, some technicians force the valve open and place an aspirin tablet in the valve to keep it from closing completely. The partially open valve allows the air from the water jackets to escape so the coolant can enter quickly. The tablet will dissolve shortly after the system is filled.

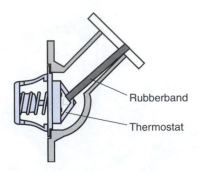

FIGURE 18-61   The rubber band is holding the thermostat in place in the housing. After the housing is fastened in place, the rubber band will be removed.

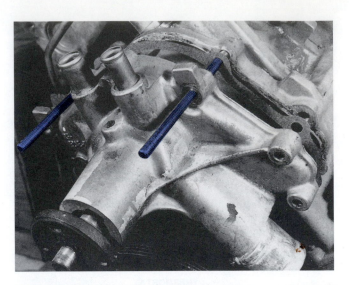

FIGURE 18-62   A pair of guide pins is being used to hold the gasket in position as this water pump is installed.

◀ **SERVICE TIP** ▶

Vertically mounted thermostats can be difficult to hold in position while the cover is replaced. A tip is to loop a rubber band through the thermostat and then slip it out after the cover is in place (Figure 18-61). Gaskets with an adhesive coating that will stick onto the housing can also be used to hold the thermostat in the correct position.

18.4.2.5 R&R Water Pump   As with core plugs, the biggest problem faced when replacing a water pump is often access to the bolts. On some engines, the water pump bolts also secure the timing chain cover, and replacement of the water pump can break the oil seal between this cover and the block. It is best to follow the manufacturer's replacement procedure.

To R&R a water pump, you should:

1. Drain the coolant and remove the drive belt. On RWD vehicles, remove the fan and fan clutch.
2. Remove the water pump mounting bolts and remove the pump. If necessary, use a hammer to tap the side of the pump to break the gasket loose.

3. Clean off the old gasket and sealant; clean out the pump impeller cavity in the block if it is exposed.
4. Install two guide pins (headless bolts) to hold the gasket in place, slide the gasket into place, and slide the water pump into place. A coating of gasket sealant or RTV sealant is often recommended for the gasket (Figure 18-62).
5. Install the bolts and tighten them to the correct torque.
6. Replace the fan and fan clutch.
7. Install and adjust the drive belt.
8. Refill the system with coolant and check for leaks.

◀ **SERVICE TIP** ▶

Some engines use a reverse rotation water pump that is driven by the back side of the drive belt (Figure 18-63). Standard and reverse rotation water pumps cannot be interchanged.

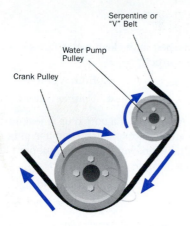

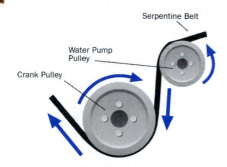

FIGURE 18-63 A belt-driven water pump can rotate either clockwise or counterclockwise depending on which side of the belt is used to drive it. *(Courtesy of Gates Corporation)*

REVIEW QUESTIONS

The following questions are provided to help you study as you read the chapter.

1. The coolant level in a modern vehicle should be at the *seal surface* on the CRR, and if the radiator cap is removed, it should be even with the sealing surface in the *filler neck* .

2. If removing the radiator cap from a hot cooling system, be very careful because the *coolant* might suddenly *boil* .

3. Dirty coolant indicates that the coolant should be *inspected* and probably that the cooling system should be *flushed*

4. Coolant freeze protection can be checked using a(n) *hydrom't* , *refract* , or *test strip* .

5. The most accurate checking method is the *refrac*

6. A reading of more than 0.3 V at the radiator filler neck indicates a potential problem of *acidity*

7. The normal coolant is *50* antifreeze and *50* water; in very cold climates, the percentage of antifreeze can be increased to *66* .

8. Used antifreeze should be *recycled* or disposed of in the *proper container* .

9. Early drive belt failure can be caused by *mis align* or improper *tension*

10. When a hose is replaced, the *clamp* should be positioned right next to the connector bead, and it is a good practice to recheck clamp *tension* after the engine has been warmed up and cooled down.

11. A radiator cap is tested using a(n) *press tester*

12. Bubbles coming up through the coolant in a radiator is a sign of a(n) *combustn leak* .

13. A faulty thermostat usually sticks *open* or *closed* , and it should be *replaced* with one that meets the manufacturer's specifications.

14. A dirty cooling system can be cleaned using a(n) *bade* flush, *chemic* flush, or *press* flush.

CHAPTER QUIZ

The following questions will help you check the facts you have learned. Select the answer that completes each statement correctly.

1. In a modern cooling system, the coolant level is checked at the
   a. radiator.
   b. thermostat cover.
   c. coolant recovery reservoir.
   d. None of these

2. While discussing coolant changes, Technician A says that the old coolant can simply be poured down the drain. Technician B says that used coolant must be recycled. Who is correct?
   a. A only
   b. B only
   c. Both A and B
   d. Neither A nor B

3. Two technicians are discussing coolant flow. Technician A says that you should not be able to feel a coolant flow through the upper radiator hose while the engine is cold. Technician B says that when the thermostat opens, the upper hose should start getting hot and you should feel a flow through it. Who is correct?
   a. A only
   b. B only
   c. Both A and B
   d. Neither A nor B

4. Technician A says that a cooling system should hold pressure for at least 2 minutes when its pressure is checked. Technician B says that the pressure tester can also be used to check for combustion leaks. Who is correct?
   a. A only
   b. B only
   c. Both A and B
   d. Neither A nor B

5. A thermostat that is stuck open causes the engine to overheat.
   a. True
   b. False

6. Technician A says that a leaky heater core may show up as a drip onto the carpet. Technician B says that you can test a heater core for leaks using a pressure tester. Who is correct?
   a. A only
   b. B only
   c. Both A and B
   d. Neither A nor B

7. Technician A says that fan clutch operation can be tested using a strobe light. Technician B says that the fan clutch should be locked up when the engine is cold. Who is correct?
   a. A only
   b. B only
   c. Both A and B
   d. Neither A nor B

8. Two technicians are discussing system flushing. Technician A says that you should flush a system in the direction of normal coolant flow. Technician B says that a system should be flushed until clean water flows out of the system. Who is correct?
   a. A only
   b. B only
   c. Both A and B
   d. Neither A nor B

9. Technician A says that if a core plug is leaking and is in a difficult location, an expandable rubber plug can be inserted into it. Technician B says that rubber plugs should always be installed dry. Who is correct?
   a. A only
   b. B only
   c. Both A and B
   d. Neither A nor B

10. Two technicians are discussing radiator removal. Technician A says that you should use two wrenches as you loosen the cooler lines to the automatic transmission. Technician B says that cooler line on modern vehicles might require special tools to disconnect the quick-connect–type coupler system. Who is correct?
    a. A only
    b. B only
    c. Both A and B
    d. Neither A nor B

11. Technician A says that the major cause of engine overheating is a faulty thermostat that opens at too high temperature. Technician B says that the bleed notch or jiggle pin should be at the top when installing vertically mounted thermostats. Who is correct?
    a. A only
    b. B only
    c. Both A and B
    d. Neither A nor B

12. Technician A says that after service, it is good practice to retighten hose clamps after the engine has been run and then cooled down. Technician B says that when coolant is replaced, the coolant level should be checked after the engine has been warmed up. Who is correct?
    a. A only
    b. B only
    c. Both A and B
    d. Neither A nor B

13. Two technicians are discussing antifreeze. Technician A says that green antifreeze should be changed every year or two to keep a cooling system clean. Technician B says that an overheating system can be kept from boiling by using straight antifreeze for a coolant. Who is correct?
    a. A only
    b. B only
    c. Both A and B
    d. Neither A nor B

14. Technician A says that the fan used with modern RWD vehicles always rotates in a clockwise direction, the same as the crankshaft. Technician B says that the fan clutch used on FWD vehicles can cause fan rotation in either direction. Who is correct?
    a. A only
    b. B only
    c. Both A and B
    d. Neither A nor B

◀ Appendix A ▶

ASE CERTIFICATION AND TASK LIST

Mechanics have the opportunity to voluntarily take ASE certification tests to become ASE-certified technicians. ASE is short for National Institute for Automotive Service Excellence. Certification helps technicians prove their abilities to themselves, their employers, and their customers, many of whom are suspicious of the automotive repair profession.

ASE certification requires that you pass one or more tests and have at least 2 years of automotive repair work experience. School training can be used to substitute for part of the work experience requirement, and you may take the test or tests before completing the work experience requirement. Initially you will receive the test score report; when the experience requirement is completed, you will receive certification.

There are eight automotive service tests, and one is A7, Heating and Air Conditioning. The A7 test has 50 questions that are taken from the following content areas:*

Content Area	Questions
A. A/C System Diagnosis and Repair	12
B. Refrigeration System Component Diagnosis and Repair	11
1. Compressor and Clutch	(5)
2. Evaporator, Receiver–Drier, Condenser, and Related Components	(6)
C. Heating and Engine Cooling Systems Diagnosis and Repair	6

*The content areas and task list are provided courtesy of the National Institute for Automotive Service Excellence.

D. Operating Systems and Related Controls Diagnosis and Repair	16
1. Electrical	(7)
2. Vacuum or Mechanical	(4)
3. Automatic and Semiautomatic Heating, Ventilating, and A/C Systems	(5)
E. Refrigerant Recovery, Recycling, and Handling	5

If you intend to take the A7 test and feel a need to study for it, all content areas are divided into groups of tasks. The tasks focus on the things that a heating and air conditioning technician should be able to do. For an up-to-date task list, call ASE at 703-713-3800 or go to www.asecert.org and request the Automobile Preparation Guide.

HEATING AND AIR CONDITIONING TEST TASK LIST

A. A/C System Diagnosis and Repair

1. Diagnose the cause of unusual operating noises of the A/C system; determine needed repairs.
2. Identify system type and conduct performance test on the A/C system; determine needed repairs.
3. Diagnose A/C system problems indicated by refrigerant flow past the sight glass (for systems using a sight glass); determine needed repairs.

4. Diagnose A/C system problems indicated by pressure gauge readings; determine needed repairs.
5. Diagnose A/C system problems indicated by sight, sound, smell, and touch procedures; determine needed repairs.
6. Leak test the A/C system for leaks; determine needed repairs.
7. Identify and recover A/C system refrigerant.
8. Evacuate A/C system.
9. Clean A/C system components and hoses.
10. Charge A/C system with refrigerant (liquid or vapor)
11. Identify lubricant type; inspect level in A/C system.

B. Refrigeration System Component Diagnosis and Repair

1. Compressor and Clutch

1. Diagnose A/C system problems that cause the protection devices (pressure, thermal, and control modules) to interrupt system operation; determine needed repairs.
2. Inspect, test, and replace A/C system pressure and thermal protection devices.
3. Inspect, adjust, and replace A/C compressor drive belts and pulleys.
4. Inspect, test, service, and replace A/C compressor clutch components or assembly.
5. Identify required lubricant type; inspect and correct level in A/C compressor.
6. Inspect, test, service, or replace A/C compressor.
7. Inspect, repair, and replace A/C compressor mountings.

2. Evaporator, Receiver-Drier, Condenser, and Related Components

1. Inspect, repair, or replace A/C system mufflers, hoses, lines, filters, fittings, and seals.
2. Inspect A/C condenser for airflow restrictions.
3. Inspect, test, and replace A/C system condenser and mountings.
4. Inspect and replace receiver–drier or accumulator–drier.
5. Inspect, test, and replace expansion valve.
6. Inspect and replace orifice tube.
7. Inspect, test, or replace evaporator.
8. Inspect, clean, and repair evaporator, housing, and water drain.
9. Inspect, test, and replace evaporator pressure—temperature control systems and devices.

10. Identify, inspect, and replace A/C system service valves (gauge connections).
11. Inspect and replace A/C system high-pressure relief device.

C. Heating and Engine Cooling Systems Diagnosis and Repair

1. Diagnose the cause of temperature control problems in the heater/ventilation system; determine needed repairs.
2. Diagnose window fogging problems; determine needed repairs.
3. Perform cooling system tests; determine needed repairs.
4. Inspect and replace engine cooling and heater system hoses.
5. Inspect, test, and replace radiator, pressure cap, coolant recovery system, and water pump.
6. Inspect, test, and replace thermostat, bypass, and housing.
7. Identify, inspect, and recover coolant; flush and refill system with proper coolant.
8. Inspect, test, and replace fan (both electrical and mechanical), fan clutch, fan belts, fan shroud, and air dams.
9. Inspect, test, and replace heater coolant control valve (manual, vacuum, and electrical types).
10. Inspect, flush, and replace heater core.

D. Operating Systems and Related Controls Diagnosis and Repair

1. Electrical

1. Diagnose the cause of failures in the electrical control system of heating, ventilating, and A/C systems; determine needed repairs.
2. Inspect, test, repair, and replace A/C-heater blower motors, resistors, switches, relay/modules, wiring, and protection devices.
3. Inspect, test, repair, and replace A/C compressor clutch, relays/modules, wiring, sensors, switches, diodes, and protection devices.
4. Inspect, test, repair, replace, and adjust A/C-related engine control systems.
5. Inspect, test, repair, replace, and adjust load-sensitive A/C compressor cutoff systems.
6. Inspect, test, repair, and replace engine cooling/condenser fan motors, relays/modules, switches, sensors, wiring, and protection devices.

7. Inspect, test, adjust, repair, and replace electric actuator motors, relays/modules, switches, sensors, wiring, and protection devices.

8. Inspect, test, service, or replace heating, ventilating, and A/C control-panel assemblies.

2. Vacuum/Mechanical

1. Diagnose the cause of failures in the vacuum and mechanical switches and controls of the heating, ventilating, and A/C systems; determine needed repairs.

2. Inspect, test, service, or replace heating, ventilating, and A/C control-panel assemblies.

3. Inspect, test, adjust, and replace heating, ventilating, and A/C control cables and linkages.

4. Inspect, test, and replace heating, ventilating, and A/C vacuum actuators (diaphragms/motors) and hoses.

5. Identify, inspect, test, and replace heating, ventilating, and A/C vacuum reservoir check valve, and restrictors.

6. Inspect, test, adjust, repair, or replace heating, ventilating, and A/C ducts, doors, and outlets.

3. Automatic and Semiautomatic Heating, Ventilating, and A/C Systems

1. Diagnose temperature control system problems; determine needed repairs.

2. Diagnose blower system problems; determine needed repairs.

3. Diagnose air distribution system problems; determine needed repairs.

4. Diagnose compressor clutch control system; determine needed repairs.

5. Inspect, test, adjust, or replace climate control temperature and sunload sensors.

6. Inspect, test, adjust, and replace temperature blend door actuator.

7. Inspect, test, and replace low engine coolant temperature blower control system.

8. Inspect, test, and replace heater water valve and controls.

9. Inspect, test, and replace electric and vacuum motors, solenoids, and switches.

10. Inspect, test, and replace ATC control panel.

11. Inspect, test, adjust, or replace ATC microprocessor (climate control computer/programmer).

12. Check and adjust calibration of ATC system.

E. Refrigerant Recovery, Recycling, and Handling

1. Maintain and verify correct operation of certified equipment.

2. Identify and recover A/C system refrigerant.

3. Recycle or properly dispose of refrigerant.

4. Label and store refrigerant.

5. Test recycled refrigerant for noncondensable gases.

Appendix B

TEMPERATURE–PRESSURE CHARTS

R-134a				R-12			
Temperature °C (°F)	Pressure kPa (psi)	Temperature °C (°F)	Pressure kPa (psi)	Temperature °C (°F)	Pressure kPa (psi)	Temperature °C (°F)	Pressure kPa (psi)
−9 (16)	106 (15)	38 (100)	857 (124)	−9 (16)	127 (18)	38 (100)	808 (117)
−8 (18)	115 (17)	39 (102)	887 (129)	−8 (18)	136 (20)	39 (102)	834 (121)
−7 (20)	124 (18)	40 (104)	917 (133)	−7 (20)	145 (21)	40 (104)	859 (125)
−6 (22)	134 (19)	41 (106)	948 (137)	−6 (22)	155 (22)	41 (106)	893 (129)
−4 (24)	144 (21)	42 (108)	980 (142)	−4 (24)	165 (24)	42 (108)	917 (133)
−3 (26)	155 (22)	43 (110)	1,012 (147)	−3 (26)	175 (25)	43 (110)	940 (136)
−2 (28)	166 (24)	44 (112)	1,045 (152)	−2 (28)	185 (27)	44 (112)	969 (140)
−1 (30)	177 (26)	46 (114)	1,079 (157)	−1 (30)	196 (28)	46 (114)	997 (145)
0 (32)	188 (27)	47 (116)	1,114 (162)	0 (32)	207 (30)	47 (116)	1,027 (149)
1 (34)	200 (29)	48 (118)	1,149 (167)	1 (34)	219 (32)	48 (118)	1,057 (153)
2 (36)	212 (31)	49 (120)	1,185 (172)	2 (36)	230 (33)	49 (120)	1,087 (158)
3 (38)	225 (33)	50 (122)	1,222 (177)	3 (38)	249 (36)	50 (122)	1,118 (162)
4 (40)	238 (35)	51 (124)	1,260 (183)	4 (40)	255 (37)	51 (124)	1,150 (167)
7 (45)	272 (40)	52 (126)	1,298 (188)	7 (45)	287 (42)	52 (126)	1,182 (171)
10 (50)	310 (45)	53 (128)	1,337 (194)	10 (50)	322 (47)	53 (128)	1,215 (176)
13 (55)	350 (51)	54 (130)	1,377 (200)	13 (55)	359 (52)	54 (130)	1,248 (181)
16 (60)	392 (57)	57 (135)	1,481 (215)	16 (60)	398 (58)	57 (135)	1,334 (194)
18 (65)	438 (64)	60 (140)	1,590 (231)	18 (65)	440 (64)	60 (140)	1,425 (207)
21 (70)	487 (71)	63 (145)	1,704 (247)	21 (70)	484 (70)	63 (145)	1,519 (220)
24 (75)	540 (78)	66 (150)	1,823 (264)	24 (75)	531 (77)	66 (150)	1,618 (235)
27 (80)	609 (88)	68 (155)	1,948 (283)	27 (80)	580 (84)	68 (155)	1,721 (250)
30 (85)	655 (95)	71 (160)	2,079 (301)	30 (85)	633 (92)	71 (160)	1,828 (265)
32 (90)	718 (104)	74 (165)	2,215 (321)	32 (90)	688 (100)	74 (165)	1,940 (281)
35 (95)	786 (114)	77 (170)	2,358 (342)	35 (95)	746 (108)	77 (170)	2,057 (298)

(Left groups labeled "Evaporator Range"; right groups labeled "Condenser Range.")

Note: Evaporator pressures represent gas temperatures inside the coil and not at the coil surfaces. Add to temperature for coil and air-off temperatures (4 to 6°C or 8 to 10°F). Condenser temperatures are not ambient temperatures. Add to ambient (19 to 22°C or 35 to 40°F) for proper heat transfer; then refer to chart.

Example: 32°C + 22°C = 54°C Condenser temperature = 1,377 kPa (R-134) or 1,248 kPa (R-12), based on 30-mph airflow.

Conditions vary for different system configurations. Refer to the manufacturer's specifications.

(Reprinted with permission of General Motors Corporation)

◀ Appendix C ▶

A/C SERVICE PROCEDURE DOCUMENTS

Proper A/C service procedures are described in documents developed by the federal government, the Society of Automotive Engineers (SAE), and the American Refrigeration Institute (ARI). Following is a listing of those that have a definite impact on modern A/C operations:

ARI 700–88 Purity Standard for Reclaimed R-12 Intended for Resale or Mobile Use.

SAE J51 Refrigerant 12 Automotive Air Conditioning Hose.

SAE J639 Safety and Containment of Refrigerant for Mechanical Vapor Compression Systems Used for Mobile Air Conditioning Systems.

SAE J658 Alternate Refrigerant Consistency Criteria for Use in Mobile Air Conditioning Systems.

SAE J659 Vehicle Testing Requirements for Replacement Refrigerants for CFC-12 (R-12) Mobile Air Conditioning Systems.

SAE J902 Passenger Car Windshield Defrosting Systems.

SAE J1627 Rating Criteria for Electronic Leak Detectors.

SAE J1628 Technician Procedure for Using Electronic Refrigerant Leak Detectors for Service of Mobile Air Conditioning Systems.

SAE 1629 Cautionary Statements for Handling HFC-134a During Mobile Air Conditioning Service.

SAE J1657 Selection Criteria for Retrofit Refrigerants to Replace CFC-12 (R-12) in Mobile Air Conditioning Systems.

SAE J1658 Alternate Refrigerant Consistency Criteria for Use in Mobile Air Conditioning Systems.

SAE J1660 Fittings and Labels for Retrofit of R-12 Mobile Air Conditioning Systems to R-134a.

SAE J1661 Procedure for Retrofitting R-12 Mobile Air Conditioning Systems to R-134a.

SAE J1662 Compatibility of Retrofit Refrigerants with Air Conditioning System Materials.

SAE J1732 HFC-134a (Refrigerant Recovery Equipment for Mobile Automotive Air Conditioning Systems).

SAE J1770 Automotive Refrigerant Recovery/Recycling Equipment Intended for Use with Both R-12 and R-134a.

SAE J1989 Recommended Procedure for the Containment of R-12.

SAE J1990 Extraction and Recycle Equipment for Mobile Automotive Air Conditioning Systems.

SAE J1991 Standard of Purity for Use in Mobile Air Conditioning Systems.

SAE J2064 R-134a Refrigerant Automotive Air Conditioning Hose.

SAE J2099 Standard of Purity for Recycled HFC-134a for Use in Mobile Air Conditioning Systems.

SAE J2196 Service Hose for Automotive Air Conditioning.

SAE J2197 HFC-134a Service Hose Fittings for Automotive Air Conditioning Service Equipment.

SAE J2209 CFC-12 Extraction Equipment for Mobile Automotive Air Conditioning Systems.

SAE J2210   HFC-134a Recycling Equipment for Mobile Air Conditioning Systems.

SAE J2211   Recommended Service Procedure for the Containment of HFC-134a.

SAE J2219   Mobile Air Conditioning Industry Criteria and Guidelines.

SAE J2297   Ultraviolet Leak Detection: Stability and Compatibility Criteria of Fluorescent Leak Detection Dyes for Mobile Air Conditioning Systems.

SAE J2298   Ultraviolet Leak Detection: Procedure for use of Refrigerant Leak Detection Dyes for Service of Mobile Air Conditioning Systems.

SAE J2299   Ultraviolet Leak Detection: Performance Requirements for Fluorescent Refrigerant Leak Detection Dye Injection Equipment for Aftermarket Service of Mobile Air Conditioning Systems.

SAE J2670   Stability and Compatibility Criteria for Additives and Flushing Materials Intended for Use in Vehicle Air-Conditioning Systems Using R-134a.

EPA SNAP-APPROVED REFRIGERANTS AS SUBSTITUTES FOR CFC-12

Refrigerant	Supplier	Chemical Composition	Lubricant Recommended	Desiccant Recommended	Label Color Background	Label Color Foreground
R-134a	many	100% HFC-134a	PAG POE	XH-7 or XH-9	Sky blue	Black
Freeze 12	Technical Chemical	80% HFC-134a 20% HCFC-142b	MO POE	XH-7 or XH-9	Yellow	Black
Free Zone RB-276	Refrigerant Gases	79% HFC-134a 19% HCFC-142b 2% lubricant	MO	XH-7 or XH-9	Light green	White
FRIGC FR-12	Intercool	59% HFC-134a 39% HCFC-124 2% R-600a	POE	XH-7 or XH-9	Gray	Black
FX-56, 409A*		60% HCFC-22 25% HCFC-124 15% HCFC-142b				
GHG 406A*	People's Welding	55% HCFC-22	MO	XH-9	Black	
McCool		41% HCFC-142b 4% R-600a	Alkylbenzene			
GHG-X4,	People's Welding	51% HCFC-22	MO	XH-9	Red	White
414A* Autofrost Chill-it		28.5% HCFC-124 16.5% HCFC-142b 4% R-600a	Alkylbenzene			
GHG-X5	People's Welding	41% HCFC-22 15% HCFC-142b 40% HFC-227ea 4% R-600a			Orange	
400						

Refrigerant	Supplier	Chemical Composition	Lubricant Recommended	Desiccant Recommended	Label Color Background	Label Color Foreground
GHG-HP	People's Welding	65% HCFC-22 31% HCFC-142b 4% R-600a	MO Alkylbenzene		Not yet developed	
Hot Shot, **414B**[*] **Kar Kool**	Icor	50% HCFC-22 39% HCFC-124 9.5% HCFC-142b 1.5% R-600a	MO	XH-9	Medium blue	Black
Ikon		25% HFC-152a 75% FIC-1311[**]	MO			
MP-39, 401A[*]		53% HCFC-22 34% HCFC-124 13% HFC-152a				
MP-66, 401B[*]		61% HCFC-22 28% HCFC-124 11% HFC-152a				
MP-52, 401C[*]		33% HCFC-22 52% HCFC-124 15% HFC-152a				
SP34E	Solpower	Composition claimed as confidential business information.				

[*]American Society of Heating, Refrigerating, and Air-Conditioning Engineers (ASHRAE) number.
[**]FIC, triodide fluorodocarbon.
Oils: MO=Mineral oil; PAG=Polyalkaline glycol; POE=polyolester.
All refrigerants subject to use conditions: Unique fittings and label required; barrier hoses required for refrigerants that contain HCFC-22.
Blank spaces indicate that information is not available.

UNACCEPTABLE REFRIGERANTS FOR AUTOMOTIVE USAGE

OZ-12/HC-12a, Duracool 12a, R-176 (Artic Chill), R-405A (G2015)

Service Fitting Sizes

	High-Side Service Port			Low-Side Service Port		
Refrigerant	Diameter	Threads per inch (TPI)	Direction	Diameter	Threads per inch (TPI)	Direction
R-12, before 1987	7/16 inch	20	Right	7/16 inch	20	Right
R-12, after 1987	6/16 inch (3/8 inch)	24	Right	7/16 inch	20	Right
R-134a	16 mm	Quick connect		13 mm	Quick connect	
Freeze 12	7/16 inch	14	Left	8/16 inch (1/2 inch)	18	Right
Free Zone	8/16 inch (1/2 inch)	13	Right	9/16 inch	18	Right
FRIGC	17 mm	Quick connect		15 mm	Quick connect	
GHG 406A GHG X-4,[*]	0.305 inch	32	Left	0.368 inch	26	Left
Autofrost	0.305 inch	32	Right	0.368 inch	26	Right
Chill-it	6/16 inch (3/8 inch)	24	Left	7/16 inch	20	Left
GHG X-5	8/16 inch (1/2 inch)	20	Left	9/16 inch	18	Left
GHG HP	NYT			NYT		
Hot Shot	10/16 inch (5/8 inch)	18	Left	10/16 inch (5/8 inch)	18	Right

[*]GHG X-4 is sold by two different suppliers, and there is a unique fitting for each.
NYT, not yet developed.

◀ Appendix E ▶

POTENTIAL COMPRESSOR PROBLEMS WITH R-134A

Some compressors have problems and experience failure in systems retrofitted with R-134a; others might experience problems that usually result from the retrofit. They are listed by the vehicle they were installed on and by the manufacturer or remanufacturer.

Audi Nippondenso units after date codes 1605 and up, 2893 and up, 3901 and up are okay; earlier ones should have the seal replaced.

Chrysler Dayton A590/C171 might not handle the pressure. A Sanden clone with casting numbers 709CA or 709 CC is okay. Remanufactured A590/C171 are probably okay. Mitsubishi scroll compressor (some models between 1988 and 1993) require control valve change.

Ford Tecumseh HR-980 and Panasonic/Matsushita (on Probes) use viton seals; not okay. FX15 might not handle the pressure; check the orifice tube for metal debris.

GM The following compressors will not work: V5 with blue labels and date codes from 1/88 to 8/89, R4 compressors with date codes from 1/1/90 to 6/18/93, all DA-6 (if the date code is after 1988, it is an HR6 and is okay), Nippondenso 10PA20 used on Corvette from 1988 to 1993, and Sanden 7-cylinder used on medium-duty trucks from 1990 to 1993.

Honda Keihin compressor will probably not handle the pressure. Conversion kits for a different compressor are available.

Moog Automotive, Temperature Control Division Rebuilts Remanufactured compressors since 1993 are compatible with both R-12 and R-134a. However, they do not recommend that an R-12 system using a DA-6 or FX15 compressor be converted. Replace the DA-6 with an HR6 or HD6 and replace the FX15 with an FS10.

Nissan V5 compressor used on Q45 requires replacement with new V6.

Saab Some Sanden 5-cylinder compressors use viton seals; not okay.

Toyota Units without the ink label *RBR* (rubber both refrigerants) require O-ring change at compressor block fitting.

458

◄ Appendix F ►

ENGLISH–METRIC CONVERSION TABLE

Multiply	By	To Get/Multiply	By	To Get
Length				
inch (″)	25.4	millimeter (mm)	0.3939	inch
mile	1.609	kilometer	0.621	
Area				
$inch^2$	645.2	$millimeter^2$	0.0015	psi
Pressure				
psi	6.895	kilopascals (kPa)	0.145	$inch^2$
psi	0.0703	kilogram/centimeter (obsolete system)	14.22	psi
psi	0.0689	bar	14.5	psi
psi	0.006895	megapascal (mPa)	145	psi
Volume				
$inch^3$	16,387	$millimeter^3$	0.00006	$inch^3$
$inch^3$	6.45	$centimeter^3$	0.061	$inch^3$
$inch^3$	0.016	liter	61.024	$inch^3$
quart	0.946	liter	1.057	quart
gallon	3.785	liter	0.264	gallon
Weight				
ounce	28.35	gram (g)	0.035	ounce
pound	0.453	kilogram (kg)	2.205	pound
Torque				
inch-pound	0.113	Newton-meter (N-m)	8.851	inch-pound
foot-pound	1.356	Newton-meter	0.738	foot-pound
Velocity				
miles/hour	1.609	kilometer/hour	0.6214	miles/hour
Temperature				

(degrees Fahrenheit − 32) × 0.556 = degrees Celsius

(degrees Celsius × 1.8) + 32 = degrees Fahrenheit

◀ Appendix G ▶

BOLT TORQUE TIGHTENING CHART

The tightening value for a particular nut or bolt is normally determined by the diameter and grade of the bolt, the material into which the bolt is being threaded, and whether the threads are lubricated. Torque value specifications are normally printed in the service manuals, but if none are available, the following chart can be used as a guide.

The following values are given in foot-pounds. They can be converted to inch-pounds by multiplying them by 12 or to Newton-meters by multiplying them by 1.356. These values are given for clean, lubricated bolts.

Sae Standard

Grade Size	1 and 2	5	8	Wrench Size Bolt	Wrench Size Nut
1/4	5	7	10	3/8	7/16
5/16	9	14	22	1/2	9/16
3/8	15	25	37	9/16	5/8
7/16	24	40	60	5/8	3/4
1/2	37	60	92	3/4	13/16

Metric Standard

Grade Size	5	8	10	12	Wrench Size Bolt
6 mm	5	9	11	12	10 mm
8 mm	12	21	26	32	14 mm
10 mm	23	40	50	60	17 mm
12 mm	40	70	87	105	19 mm
14 mm	65	110	135	160	22 mm

◄ Appendix H ►

REFRIGERANT NUMBERING SYSTEM

The procedure for determining the refrigerant number is rather tedious and is of no value to the refrigerant technician. It is included in this text to reduce some misconceptions and wild stories that have passed through the industry.

The system is based on the number of carbon, hydrogen, and fluorine atoms in the refrigerant molecule. It is a three-digit system with the letter "a" added to indicate a nonsymmetrical or asymmetrical molecule. Two methods can be used to detemine the number:

- C (minus 1), H (plus 1), and F. R-12 has 1 C (1−1=0); O H (0+1=1); and 2 F (2), to get 012, or 12.
- Add 90 to the number; the sequence is carbon, hydrogen, and fluorine. With R-12, 12+90=102, so this tells us there is 1 C, 0 H, and 2 F.

Look at the R-12 and R-134a molecules in Figure 2–9. You will see that the R-12 molecule is symmetrical; both sides are the same. The R-134a molecule is asymmetrical; the left and right sides are different so an *a* is added to it. There is an HFC-134 molecule that is symmetrical, but it is not used in automotive refrigerant systems.

Technically, we should use the name CFC-12, HFC-134a, or HCFC-22 to indicate that the refrigerant is a chlorofluorocarbon, hydrofluorocarbon, or hydrochlorofluorocarbon, but with an industry in which many people like to call everything "freon," using "R" for refrigerant is a good start. Those of you with better habits than this author can use the proper prefix.

The chemical name for CFC-12, dichlorodifluoromethane, tells us that the molecule has two (di) chlorine atoms and two fluorine atoms, and the suffix methane tells us there is one carbon atom. The prefix, di = 2, tri = 3, tetra = 4, penta = 5, and so on tells us the number of atoms. With carbon-based molecules, single C molecules are methanes, double C molecules are ethanes, three C molecules are propanes, and so on. HFC-134a, tetrafluoroethane, has four (tetra) F atoms, two H (not mentioned in the name), and the suffix ethane, telling us there are two carbon atoms.

This explanation is not complete; chemists use other designations to show bonds within the molecule and different number combinations for blend refrigerants. This numbering system is based on the carbon chain that the molecule is built around. In this system, HFC-134a is 1, 1, 1, 2 tetrafluoroethane.

◀ Appendix I ▶

NATEF TASKS: AREA VII, HEATING AND AIR CONDITIONING

These tasks have a priority: 90% of Priority 1 (P-1) tasks must be completed, 80% of P-2, and 50% of P-3 tasks must be completed. Additional information concerning NATEF certification can be obtained by calling the National Automotive Technicians Education Foundation, Herndon, VA, (703) 713–0100.

A/C System Diagnosis and Repair

Task & Priority	Textbook Section	Worktext
1. P-1	9.1 to 9.4.2	E 4, 5, 11, & 20
2. P-1		E 3
3. P-1		E 3
4. P-1	10.3 to 10.3.7	E 4, 5, 11, & 20
5. P-2	9.4.2	E 7
6. P-1	10.2, 10.3, & 13.3.2	E 8 & 9
7. P-1	14.2	E 18 & 19
8. P-2	14.2	E 44
9. P-1	13.3.7, 14.2.6, & 14.4	E 3

REFRIGERATION COMPONENT DIAGNOSIS AND REPAIR

Compressor and Clutch

Task & Priority	Textbook Section	Worktext
1. P-2	10.3.4	E 27
2. P-2	9.2.1 & 16.2.5	E 4, 5, & 63
3. P-2	9.2.1 & 14.2.2	E 28 & 45
4. P-1	9.2.1 & 14.2.1	E 44

Evaporator, Condenser, and Related Components

Task & Priority	Textbook Section	Worktext
1. P-3	10.3.4, 13.3.6, 14.2.1	E 39, 40, & 44
2. P-2	14.3 & 14.4	E 49, 50, & 51
3. P-1	9.2.1 & 10.3.4	E 12 & 53
4. P-1	14.4	E 52
5. P-2	14.4	E 14 & 53
6. P-3	9.2.1	E 13
7. P-3	14.4	E 13 & 53
8. P-3	14.4	E 12 & 53

Heating, Ventilation, and Engine Cooling Systems Diagnosis and Repair

Test & Priority	Textbook Section	Worktext
1. P-2	9.2	E 4 & 21
2. P-1	16.3.2 & 16.3.3	E 60 & 62
3. P-1	16.3	E 54 & 64
4. P-1	16.3.4	E 61
5. P-1	16.2.3 & 16.2.4	E 55, 56, & 57
6. P-1	16.2.4 & 16.4.1	E 56, 57, & 58
7. P-1	9.2	E 59
8. P-1	12.8	E 30
9. P-2	9.2 & 11.2.1	E 21 & 22
10. P-3	11.2.3 (TBD)	E 23

Operating Systems and Related Controls Diagnosis and Repair

Task & Priority	Textbook Section	Worktext
1. P-2	12.8 & 12.9.2	E 4 & 26
2. P-1	12.8 & 12.9	E 29
3. P-1	12.4	E 27 & 28
4. P-2	11.4.3	E 4 & 24
5. P-3	9.2	E 4, 24 & 31
6. P-3	11.3.2	E 24
7. P-3	9.2	E 4 & 25
8. P-3	9.2	E 31 & 32

Refrigerant Recovery, Recycling, and Handling

Tesk & Priority	Textbook Section	Worktext
1. P-1		E 34 & 35
2. P-1	13.3.2	E 8, 9, & 34
3. P-1	13.3.4	E 35
4. P-1	3.3	E 35
5. P-1	13.3.4.1	E 35
6. P-1	13.3.7 & 13.3.8	E 36, 37, & 38

Task List Priority Item Totals: 25 P-1, 11 P-2, and 9 P-3 *25 P-1 Tasks, 11 P-2 Tasks, 9 P-3 Tasks: 100% Covered*

◀ Appendix J ▶

KEY TO PROBLEM SOLVING

CHAPTER 7

Problem Solving 7-1:

You should expect a hot discharge hose, condenser, and receiver-drier. A problem is indicated if it is hotter than normal. Possible causes are overcharge, restricted condenser, missing condenser seals, and contaminated refrigerant; further tests are needed.

Problem Solving 7-2:

You should check the A/C fuse and if it's good, the clutch connection to see if it is getting power. These checks are described in Chapter 14.

Problem Solving 7-3:

Depending on ambient temperature, these conditions can be normal. You need more information, and this is provided in Chapter 12.

CHAPTER 8

Problem Solving 8-1:

The oily dirt indicates a probable refrigerant leak which is a bad sign.

Problem Solving 8-2:

The hissing sound is refrigerant passing through the orifice tube as the high and low pressures equalize. It is normal, and there is no problem.

Problem Solving 8-3:

The short cycles along with a non-working A/C system indicate a very low refrigerant charge. Checking refrigerant pressures and the system temperatures should confirm this problem.

Problem Solving 8-4:

The frost on the suction line is caused by the POA valve closing to prevent icing of the evaporator. This is a good sign that the A/C system is working properly.

CHAPTER 9

Problem Solving 9-1:

Poor heater output is often caused by non-hot engine coolant or poor flow through the heater core. To confirm these possibilities, check the coolant temperature to make sure it is hot, and check the temperature of the heater hoses. Both hoses should be hot, with the return hose a little cooler.

CHAPTER 10

Problem Solving 10-1:

Case 1: If the A/C air discharge is from the defroster ducts, there is a mode door failure, and it is defaulting to defrost. If this is a vacuum-operated system, there is probably a vacuum loss or severe vacuum leak. Check the vacuum supply to the control head. If the blower has no High Speed, the high blower relay has failed. Check the relay for proper voltage at the different terminals.

   Case 2: This system is defaulting to defrost. It has a problem in the vacuum supply circuit. Inspect the vacuum check valve and reservoir.

Problem Solving 10-2:

If the air discharge is not cold, either the control head temperature setting is set too high or the A/C is not working. The temperature setting can be read on the control head. You can confirm A/C operation by looking for compressor operation and feeling the suction line; it should be cold.

CHAPTER 12

Problem Solving 12-1:

Refrigerant pressure of 10 psi relates to a temperature of about 6°F (–19°C). Normal pressure for a system that is not running should be in the 60–80 psi range. This system probably has a low refrigerant charge.

Problem Solving 12-2:

If the TXV does not respond to thermal bulb temperature changes, it is bad. High low-side pressure can be caused by a TXV that is stuck open. High low-side pressure can also be caused by a restricted suction line or a faulty compressor.

CHAPTER 15

Problem Solving 15-1:

The high pressures and noisy compressor operation are being caused by the contaminated refrigerant. You should recover the refrigerant and send it off for recycling or disposal. After evacuating the system and charging it with the proper amount of clean refrigerant, it should work properly.

CHAPTER 17

Problem Solving 17-1:

The burned valves and warped head were caused by overheating. As the engine is being repaired, all possible causes for overheating should be checked and repaired.

Problem Solving 17-2:

Removing the thermostat is never a wise move. All possible causes for overheating should be checked.

Problem Solving 17-3:

Case 1: The coolant is old with worn out inhibitors and the cooling system is dirty. The rust and residue are probably reducing heat transfer. The cooling systems needs to be cleaned, flushed, and then filled with new coolant.

   Case 2: This is similar to Case 1 but more severe. There is a possibility of a combustion leak into the cooling system under heavy load. The recommendation would be the same as Case 1 with the addition of a check for combustion leaks.

ENGLISH-LANGUAGE GLOSSARY

Absolute pressure: Pressure measured above absolute zero pressure.

Absolute zero: The total absence of pressure or temperature.

A/C: Air conditioning; a device that controls the temperature and humidity of the air inside a vehicle.

Accumulator: The component in some A/C systems that contains the desiccant and provides a place to store reserve refrigerant. It is found in the low side.

Actuator: A device that moves another item, such as an air control door.

Aftermarket: An item or part installed after the vehicle was made; not made by the vehicle manufacturer.

Air conditioning: Control of cleanliness, humidity, movement, and temperature of air.

Air inlet door: The door that controls the source of air entering the A/C and heating unit.

Air lock: An incomplete filling problem encountered when filling a cooling system if the air inside the system cannot escape as the coolant is added.

Alternate refrigerant: An approved refrigerant type used to retrofit an R-12 system.

Ambient temperature: The temperature of air surrounding an object; the temperature of air outside a vehicle.

Ambient temperature sensor: A sensor that measures the temperature of outside air entering the vehicle.

Antifreeze: A substance mixed with water to lower the freezing point of the coolant.

Aspirator: A component that pulls air past the in-vehicle temperature sensor; it uses a Venturi principle.

Atmospheric pressure: The pressure of air around us; 14.7 psi at sea level.

Atom: The smallest particle of matter.

Automatic temperature control (ATC): A system that automatically adjusts the output of the heat and A/C system to provide the desired in-vehicle temperature.

Auxiliary gauge: The third gauge used to measure pressure on the outlet side of an EPR valve or STV.

Axial compressor: A compressor with pistons arranged around the center shaft.

Backflush: An operation that forces a liquid through a system in the reverse direction to clean the system.

Back seat: Turning a service valve all the way outward to allow flow from the compressor to the suction or discharge line.

Barrier hose: A hose with a nonpermeable inner liner.

Belt lock system: A strategy that will shut off the A/C compressor if it is operating slower that it should be to prevent a seized compressor from destroying the accessory drive belt.

Black death: A term referring to the black, gooey mess resulting from a catastrophic compressor failure.

Bleed: To loosen or open a fitting or hose to allow air to escape from a cooling system or heater.

Blend: A mixture of refrigerants to form a non-CFC refrigerant usable in an R-12 system.

Blend air: A system that mixes cold and warm air to get the desired temperature.

Blower fan: The fan that forces air through the evaporator and heater core and into the passenger compartment.

Blower speed controller: A solid-state control unit that regulates the blower speed from signals from the control module.

Boiling: Conversion of a liquid to a vapor that is accompanied by bubbles as vapor rises through the liquid.

Boiling point: The temperature at which a liquid boils.

Bowden cable: A cable or wire inside a housing used to control the position of a remote door, valve, or other device.

British thermal unit (Btu): A measurement of heat quantity; the amount of heat needed to increase the temperature of 1 lb of water 1°F.

Cabin filter: A filter in the HVAC system to remove small particles, like dust and pollen, and odors from the air.

Calorie: A measurement of heat quantity; the amount of heat required to increase the temperature of 1 g of water 1°C.

Capillary tube: A very thin, gas-filled tube used to sense temperature.

Celsius: Temperature scale based on 0° as the freezing point of water and 100° as the boiling point.

Centigrade: Same as Celsius.

Charge: The specific amount of refrigerant needed to properly fill a system; the act of putting the correct amount of refrigerant into a system.

Charging station: A piece of equipment that includes the things needed for normal A/C system service: gauges, hoses, valves, a vacuum pump, a means of measuring refrigerant, and a storage container for refrigerant.

Chlorofluorocarbon (CFC): A human-made compound that contains chlorine, fluorine, and carbon; R-12.

Climate control: The act of controlling the temperature, humidity, and purity of air.

Clutch: The device used to connect and disconnect the compressor pulley with the compressor shaft.

Clutch cycling switch: The temperature or pressure switch that turns the compressor off and on to prevent the evaporator from freezing.

Cold: The absence of heat.

Cold engine lockout: A device to prevent blower motor operation while the engine coolant is cold.

Compound gauge: A gauge that measures both a pressure and a vacuum; the low side manifold gauge.

Compressor: The component in an A/C system that compresses refrigerant vapor and causes that vapor to move through the system.

Condensation: Conversion of a vapor into a liquid.

Condenser: The component in an A/C system in which heat is removed and vapor is changed to liquid.

Conduction: Heat transfer directly through a material.

Contamination: R-12 or R-134a that contains 3% or more of noncondensable gas or a foreign refrigerant.

Control head: The panel where the controls for A/C and heat are located.

Convection: Heat transfer by circulation of a liquid or vapor.

Conversion fitting: A fitting installed over an R-12 service fitting to allow use of an alternate refrigerant.

Cool: The act of removing heat.

Coolant: A mixture of antifreeze and water used in the cooling system.

Corrosion: Chemical action that eats away a metal substance.

Cycling: A repeated off–on operation at regular intervals.

Cycling clutch: A method of controlling A/C temperature by cycling the compressor off and on.

Cycling clutch orifice tube (CCOT): A system that uses a fixed orifice tube and that cycles the clutch to prevent icing of the evaporator.

Dehumidify: Remove water vapor from air.

Delta T: An engineering term that refers to the difference in temperature between two points.

Desiccant: A drying agent found in the receiver–drier or accumulator that removes moisture.

Diagnostic trouble code (DTC): Numeric code used to indicate the nature of trouble or problems.

Dichlorodifluoromethane: Cl_2Fl_2C, CFC-12, R-12.

Difluoroethane: HFC-152a, R-152a.

Discharge: The act of removing refrigerant from a system (*see* Venting); the outlet side of the compressor.

Discharge line: The line that connects the compressor discharge port to the condenser.

Discharge pressure: High side pressure.

Drier: *See* Receiver–drier.

Drive belt: A belt driven by the crankshaft that drives the A/C compressor, water pump, and other engine accessories.

Dryer: *See* Receiver–drier.

Dynamic pressure: High and low side pressures in an operating system.

Engine coolant temperature (ECT) sensor: A device to monitor engine coolant temperature and convert it into an electrical signal.

Environmentally friendly: Procedures and products designed to prevent harm to Earth or its atmosphere; also called environmentally aware, environmentally conscious, environmentally safe.

Evacuate: To pump a vacuum into an A/C system to remove contaminated refrigerant and water.

Evaporation: The change of state from a liquid to a vapor.

Evaporator: The component in an A/C system in which heat is absorbed and liquid is changed to a vapor.

Evaporator pressure regulator (EPR) valve: A valve used to maintain evaporator pressure to prevent icing.

Expansion tube: *See* Orifice tube (OT).

Expansion valve: *See* Thermal expansion valve (TXV).

Fahrenheit: Temperature scale based on 32° as the freezing point of water and 212° as the boiling point.

Fan clutch: A device used to control the speed of the radiator cooling fan.

Filter: A device used to remove solid foreign particles from the refrigerant or coolant.

Fixed orifice tube: *See* Orifice tube (OT).

Flooding: A term that refers to overcharging a system so that liquid refrigerant fills an area.

Fluorocarbon: A compound that contains fluorine and carbon.

Flush: To clean a system by pumping a liquid through it.

Freezing point: The temperature at which a liquid freezes.

Freon: Brand name for some of the refrigerants developed and sold by Du Pont.

Fresh air: Air that enters the A/C and heat system from the outside.

Fresh air filter: A filter that removes dust and pollen from fresh air.

Front seat: Turning a service valve all the way inward to shut off the flow from the compressor to the suction or discharge line.

Fuse: An electrical device designed to open a circuit if there is excess current flow.

Gas: A vapor without any droplets of liquid.

Gauge pressure: Referring to a pressure scale in which 0 is equal to atmospheric pressure.

Gauge set: *See* Manifold gauge set.

Head pressure: The same as high side pressure.

Heat: A form of energy that raises temperature.

Heat exchanger: A device used to move heat from one item to another; a vehicle's condenser, evaporator, and radiator are heat exchangers.

Heat pump: A combination A/C and heater system in which the line connections at the compressor can be reversed to provide both A/C and heat.

Heater core: The component in a heater system that transfers heat from the coolant to the air.

Hg: The chemical symbol for mercury; vacuum is measured in inches of mercury ("Hg).

High-pressure cut off (HPCO) switch: A switch that stops compressor operation when high-side pressures get too high.

High-pressure relief valve: A valve in the high side of a system designed to open and release excessive pressure.

High side: Part of the A/C system that has high pressure and contains liquid refrigerant.

Humidity: Water vapor in the air.

HVAC: Heating, ventilation, and air conditioning.

HVAC air filter: A filter contained in the air distribution system that is designed to remove dust and pollen particles from the air stream.

Hydraulic fan: A fan-drive system that operates by hydraulic flow. It usually incorporates electronic controls.

Hydrochlorofluorocarbon (HCFC): A human-made compound that contains hydrogen, chlorine, fluorine, and carbon.

Hydrofluorocarbon (HFC): A human-made compound that contains hydrogen, fluorine, and carbon; R-134a.

Hygroscopic: The ability to readily take in and retain moisture.

Identifier: A piece of equipment used to determine the purity of a refrigerant.

In-car sensor: A temperature sensor that measures the temperature of the air inside the vehicle.

Insulate: Add a barrier to isolate or seal with a nonconductor.

Latent heat: Heat that causes a change in state without a change in temperature.

Leak detector: Equipment used to locate refrigerant leaks.

Liquid: A state of matter in which the atoms move freely but do not separate as in a vapor.

Liquid line: The line that connects the condenser outlet to the receiver–drier inlet or orifice tube and the receiver–drier outlet to the TXV.

Low side: Part of the A/C system that has low pressure and contains refrigerant vapor.

Magnetic clutch: *See* Clutch.

Malfunction indicator light (MIL): A light on the instrument panel to inform the driver that a malfunction or problem has occurred.

Manifold gauge set: Service equipment that consists of two pressure gauges, three or four service hoses, and two valves; used for pressure testing and servicing an A/C system.

Matter: The substance created when atoms join together.

Micron: A measurement for deep vacuum, 1,000 microns = mm, 25,400 microns = 1' Hg.

Mode door: A flap valve that moves to divert airflow to the floor, instrument panel, or windshield outlets.

Muffler: A device that quiets compressor pumping sounds.

Multiplexing: A system of sending two or more signals through a common circuit; microprocessors are required at each end of the circuit.

Noncondensable gases (NCG): Gases, such as air in an A/C system, that do not readily change to a liquid state as the refrigerant does.

OEM: Original equipment manufacturer.

Oil bleed hole: An orifice at the bottom of the accumulator that allows oil and some liquid refrigerant to flow to the compressor for lubrication.

Organic acid technology (OAT): The inhibitor package used with extended-life antifreeze.

Orifice tube (OT): The component in some A/C systems that provides a restriction to meter the refrigerant flow into the evaporator. It causes a pressure buildup in the high side and a pressure drop in the evaporator and low side.

Overcharge: Too much refrigerant in a system.

Ozone: A chemical link between three oxygen atoms (O_3).

Ozone layer: Layer that acts as a shield against ultraviolet radiation in the upper atmosphere.

Panel registers: Outlets in the instrument panel used to direct air into the passenger compartment.

Performance test: The standard diagnostic test of system pressures and temperatures to determine whether a system is operating properly.

Pilot-operated absolute (POA) valve: A valve used to maintain evaporator pressure to prevent icing.

Plenum: The chamber in the A/C and heat unit in which the cool and warm air are blended for the desired temperature.

Polyalkylene glycol (PAG): A synthetic lubricant used with R-134a refrigerant.

Polyolester (POE): A synthetic lubricant used with R-134a refrigerant.

Pressure: A force per unit of area. *See also* psi.

Programmer: An electronic device that controls ATC system operation.

psi: Pounds per square inch.

psig: *See* Gauge pressure.

Pulse width–modulated (PWM) blower speed: A method of controlling blower speed by changing the duty cycle.

Pump down: *See* Evacuate.

Purge: To flush a system with liquid refrigerant or dry nitrogen to remove all air or moisture; to thoroughly evacuate a system.

Radiation: Heat transfer from the sun's rays.

Radiator: The component in a cooling system that transfers heat from the coolant to air.

Ram air: Air forced through the condenser and radiator by the forward movement of the vehicle.

Receiver–drier: The component in some A/C systems that contains the desiccant and provides a place to store liquid refrigerant. It is found in the high side.

Recirculated air: Airflow into the A/C and heat system from the passenger compartment.

Reclaim: The act of removing all impurities from refrigerant so it is essentially identical to new, unused refrigerant. Reclamation is not performed in automotive service shops.

Recover: The act of removing refrigerant from a system so that it can be recycled for reuse.

Recycle: The act of using portable equipment to clean debris, oil, water, and noncondensable gases from refrigerant so it can be reused in a system.

Refrigerant: The agent in a liquid and vapor form in the A/C system used to absorb, transfer, and release heat.

Refrigeration: The use of mechanical means to remove heat.

Relative humidity: The amount of water vapor contained in air relative to the maximum amount it can contain at a given temperature.

Resistor: A device used in electrical circuits to reduce current flow or drop voltage.

Retrofit: The act of replacing the R-12 in a system with an EPA-approved refrigerant.

Saddle clamp: A fitting that is clamped onto a metal line to allow attachment of a service port.

Saturated vapor: A vapor that is in contact with its liquid in an enclosed space.

Schrader valve: A spring-closed valve used at A/C service ports.

Sealant: A one- or two-part chemical that is charged into an A/C or cooling system that is designed to seal small leaks.

Secondary loop system: An A/C system design that uses one cooling system contained completely under the hood and another loop to transfer heat from the passenger compartment to the primary cooling loop.

Semiautomatic temperature control (SATC):   A climate control system that can automatically maintain the air temperature and blower speed; the operator controls where the air is discharged.

Sensible heat: Heat that causes a temperature change without a change of state.

Service hoses: Hoses used to connect a manifold gauge set or charging station to a vehicle's A/C system.

Service ports: A fitting to which service hoses are attached.

Servomotor: A motor that is capable of positioning an air control door or other item to a particular position.

Short cycling: A condition in which the compressor cycles off and on too frequently.

Sight glass: A window in the liquid line or receiver–drier that allows observation of refrigerant flow.

Solid: A state of matter that has a fixed shape in which the atoms have restricted movement.

Static pressure: Pressure in a system that is not operating.

Stop leak: *See* Sealant.

Sub-cooling: Liquid that is cooled below the point of condensation; the decrease in temperature of the liquid leaving the condenser.

Suction line: The line that connects the evaporator outlet to the compressor suction port.

Suction pressure: Same as low-side pressure.

Suction side: *See* Low side.

Suction throttling valve (STV):   A valve used to maintain evaporator pressure to prevent icing.

Sunload sensor: A sensor that detects the amount of sunlight and radiant heat entering the vehicle.

Superheat: Vapor that is heated above the boiling point; the increase in temperature of the evaporator outlet above the inlet.

Temperature: Heat intensity measured in degrees.

Temperature-blend door: A door in the A/C and heat system that mixes cold and hot air to get the desired temperature.

Temperature sensor: A device used to determine a temperature and convert it into an electrical signal.

Tetrafluoroethane: HFC-134a, R-134a.

Thermal: Refers to heat.

Thermal expansion valve (TXV):   The component in some A/C systems that meters the refrigerant flow into the evaporator. It causes a pressure buildup in the high side and a pressure drop in the evaporator and low side.

Thermal limiter: A device that opens a circuit when the temperature gets too high.

Thermistor: A device used in electrical circuits that changes resistance relative to temperature.

Thermostat: An automatic device for regulating temperatures; used in a cooling system to control the circulation between the engine water jackets and the radiator.

Thermostatic switch: A control switch used in some A/C systems that monitors evaporator air temperature and opens the compressor clutch circuit to prevent icing.

Topping off: The act of adding refrigerant to a system without making any repairs.

Transducer: A device used to change an incoming signal of one type to an outgoing signal of another type.

Undercharge: A system that is low on refrigerant.

Under-dash unit: An industry name that refers to hang-on A/C systems; aftermarket systems.

Vacuum: A pressure below atmospheric; usually read in inches of mercury or microns.

Vacuum actuator: A device used to move air control doors.

Vacuum motor: *See* Vacuum actuator.

Vacuum pump: A device used to evacuate a refrigeration system.

Vapor: A gas; the gaseous state of a refrigerant or water.

Variable orifice valve (VOV):   An orifice tube with a valve that changes orifice size in response to refrigerant flow and pressure.

Venting: The act of releasing refrigerant or a gas into the atmosphere. Venting a refrigerant is illegal.

Viscosity: The relative thickness of a liquid.

Water valve: A device for controlling the flow through a heater core.

SPANISH-LANGUAGE GLOSSARY

A/C, air conditioning: Véase Air-conditioning (A/C).

Absolute pressure: Presión absoluta. Medida sobre Absolute Zero o sobre ausencia de presión y temperatura.

Absolute zero: Ausencia absoluta de presión o temperatura.

Accumulator: Acumulador. Un componente que está situado entre el compresor y el evaporador en el lado inferior del sistema. Este componente almacena el exceso de vapor refrigerante en un sistema de aire acondicionado que usa un tubo de orificio.

Actuator: Activador. Componente mecánico. Usado para controlar una o más piezas en el sistema de aire acondicionado como las puertas de control de entrada de aire.

Aftermarket: Mercado secundario. Mercado de piezas de repuesto fabricadas o reconstruidas por una segunda parte y no por el fabricante del vehículo.

Air inlet door: Puerta/aleta de entrada de aire. Componente del sistema de ventilación. Usada para controlar la cantidad de aire que entra al vehículo. Sea para el sistema de aire acondicionado o para el sistema de calefacción.

Air-conditioning (A/C): Sistema de aire acondicionado. Utilizado para controlar la temperatura y humedad del aire en el interior de un vehículo.

Align: Alinear. Ponerse al lado. Poner partes de la unidad en la posición correcta.

Alloy: Aleación. Metal que consta de un elemento o más que normalmente se añaden para aumentar la resistencia del metal base o darle propiedades importantes.

Alternate refrigerant: Refrigerante alterno. Gas refrigerante aprobado como buen substituto de gas R-12.

Alternator: Alternador. Generador de corriente eléctrica que produce corriente alterna pero que se rectifica a la corriente directa por medio de diodos. También se llama *AC generator (generador de corriente alterna)*.

Altitude: Altitud. Distancia medida hasta la tierra al nivel del mar.

Ambient air temperature: Temperatura ambiente. Temperatura del aire que rodea un objeto.

Ammeter: Amperímetro/amperómetro/ametro. Instrumento eléctrico que sirve para medir amperios (unidad de la intensidad de corriente eléctrica).

Ampere: Amperio. Unidad que mide la intensidad de corriente eléctrica. Llamada en honor de Andre Ampere (1775–1836).

Amplitude: Amplitud. Diferencia entre la cresta y el valle de una onda.

Analog: Análogo. Clase de instrumento del tablero de dirección/salpicadero que indica valores por medio del movimiento de un aguja o aparato parecido. Una señal análoga es continua y variable.

Anode: Ánodo. Electrodo positivo hacia el cual fluyen los electrones.

ANSI (American National Standards Institute): Instituto Nacional Americano de Estandares.

Antifreeze: Anticongelante. Evita el congelamiento del agua, al ser los dos mezclados, en el sistema de enfriamiento del motor.

API (American Petroleum Institute): Instituto Americano de Petróleo.

APRA (Automotive Parts Rebuilders Association): Asociación de Reconstructores de Piezas Automotrices.

ASE (National Institute for Automotive Service Excellence): Instituto Nacional de Excellencia de Servico Automotriz.

ASTM (American Society for Testing Materials): Sociedad Americana para Materiales de Prueba.

Atmospheric pressure: Presión atmosférica. La presión del aire a nuestro alrededor. Equivalente a 14.7 PSI a nivel del mar.

Atom: Átomo. La unidad más pequeña de materia que tiene características propias.

Atomize: Atomizar. Reducir a o separar en partículas diminutas.

Automatic temperature control (ATC): Control de temperatura automático. Sistema que controla la temperatura del interior del vehículo automáticamente.

AWG (American wire gauge system): Sistema americano de calibrador de alambre.

Axial compressor: Compresor axial. Compresor de gas refrigerante del sistema de aire acondicionado con pistones alrededor del eje central.

Backflush: Sondeo invertido. El forzar un líquido limpiador en sentido opuesto al cual circula el gas refrigerante.

Baffle: Plato deflector. Plato o blindaje que se utiliza para desviar el flujo de o un líquido o un gas.

Barometric pressure: Presión barométrica. Medida de presión atmosférica, en pulgadas de mercurio (Hg), que refleja la altitud y condiciones del tiempo.

Barrier hose: Manguera o conducto de conexión estanca(o). Clase de manguera para un sistema de aire acondicionado que incluye una cubierta por dentro para prevenir la fuga de refrigerante por las paredes de la manguera. Normalmente se requiere el uso de mangueras barreras con refrigerante HFC-134a.

Base: Base. Parte de un transistor que controla el flujo de corriente a través del transistor.

Battery: Batería. Aparato químico que produce voltaje por medio de dos metales distintos sumergidos en un electrolito.

Belt lock system: Sistema anti-amarre de la banda. Evita que un compresor de gas refrigerante arruine la banda en caso de mal funcionamiento.

Bidirectional communication: Comunicación bi direccional. Comunicación por computadora que utiliza los datos en serie como ambas entrada y salida de datos.

Black death: Término usado para describir un compresor de gas refrigerante con grandes fallas mecánicas internas. Estas fallas causan que el compresor despida unas pequeñas partículas de metal y también una sustancia un tanto viscosa y pegajosa.

Bleed: Purgar el aire. Sacar el aire de un sistema de enfriamiento del motor al abrir un grifo o al desconectar una manguera.

Blend: Mezcla. Mezcla de gases refrigerantes sin CFC que substituye al gas refrigerante R-12.

Blend air: Mezcla de aire. Mezcla de aire frío y de aire caliente para obtener una temperatura deseada.

Blower-motor: Motor del ventilador. Motor eléctrico con un abanico que circula el aire dentro del automóvil para calentarlo, enfriarlo y descongelarlo.

BNC connector: Conector BNC. Conector coaxial que normalmente se usa en los osciloscopios. Llamado en honor de su inventor, Baby Neil Councilman.

Boiling: Hervir. La conversión de un líquido a gas o vapor. Acompañado de burbujas en la superficie del líquido.

Boiling point: Punto de ebullición. La temperatura a la cual un líquido alcanza a hervir.

Bowden cable: Cable-en-guía. Componente usado para transferir una fuerza mecánica. Usado para controlar o cambiar la posición de un componente remoto.

Brinelling: Brinelling. Falla mecánica que describe una abolladura en metal, por ejemplo, la que ocurre cuando se aplica una carga a choque a un balero/cojinete. Llamado en honor de Johann A. Brinell, ingeniero sueco.

British thermal unit (BTU): Unidad térmica británica. Calor necesario para elevar la temperatura de una libra de agua un grado Fahrenheit (°F) al nivel del mar.

Brushes: Brochas/escobillas. Conductor de cobre o carbono que se utiliza para trasladar corriente eléctrica a o de una parte eléctrica que gira, como la que se encuentra en un motor o generador eléctrico.

Calorie: Caloría. Medida de cantidad de calor. La cantidad de calor requerida para calentar 1 gramo de agua a 1° centígrado.

Capacitance: Capacidad. Mide la carga que puede almacenar un capacitor/condensador dado la diferencia de potencial de voltaje. Se mide en faradios o en incrementos más pequeños, como microfaradios.

Capacitor: Capacitor. También se llama *condensor (condensador)*. Unidad eléctrica que puede trasladar corriente alterna pero que a la vez bloquear corriente directa; se usa en circuitos eléctricos para controlar las fluctuaciones de voltaje.

Capillary tube: Tubo capilar/capilario. Tubo Delgado lleno de gas. Usado para detectar/medir temperatura.

CCOT (cycling clutch orifice tube): Abreviatura que se usa para identificar un sistema de aire acondicionado que emplea un tubo con orificio para ciclar el embrague.

Celsius: Celsio. Escala de medida de temperatura basada en 0° como punto de congelamiento del agua, y 100° como su punto de ebullición.

Centigrade: Centígrado. Vea Celsius.

Centi-Stoke: (cSt); centímetro por gramo por segundo; unidad de medición de la viscosidad de un fluído.

CFC-12:   Refrigerante del aire acondicionado; también se llama *R-12*, cuyo nombre químico es diclorodifluorometano.

Charge: Carga. Cantidad específica de gas refrigerante a usarse para llenar un sistema de aire acondicionado. El acto de cargar un sistema de aire acondicionado con la cantidad de gas refrigerante correcta.

Charging station: Estación/máquina de carga de gas refrigerante. Contiene medidores, mangueras de servicio, válvulas, bomba de vacío/succión y un tanque de almacenamiento para gas refrigerante.

Chassis: Chasis. El bastidor, la suspensión, la dirección y la maquinaria de un automóvil.

Chassis ground: Tierra de chasis. En términos eléctricos, una tierra es el camino deseable para el circuito de retorno.

Check engine light: Luz de aviso del tablero controlada por la computadora del vehículo; también se llama *malfunction indicator light (MIL) la luz indicadora de mal funcionmiento.*

Circuit: Circuito. Un circuito es el camino de los electrones: fluyen de un fuente de poder, a través de una resistencia y vuelven a la fuente de poder.

Circuit breaker: Fusible interruptor de circuito. Unidad mecánica que abre un circuito eléctrico a caso de flujo de corriente en exceso.

Clamp: Abrazadera. Cincho ajustable usado para mantener la conexión de dos piezas diferentes.

Climate control: Control de clima/temperatura. Usado para controlar la temperatura, la humedad y la pureza del aire en el interior del vehículo.

Clutch: Embrague. Usado para conectar la polea y el eje central de un compresor de gas refrigerante.

Cold: Frío. La ausencia de calor.

Component: Componente. Una de varias piezas en un sistema.

Compound gauge: Manómetro/medidor compuesto. Usado para medir presión y vacío. Como el medidor de presión del lado bajo de un sistema de aire acondicionado.

Compressor: Compresor. Mecanismo que se emplea en sistemas de aire acondicionado para aumentar la presión y la temperatura del refrigerante.

Computer: Computadora. Mecanismo que puede realizar calculaciones matemáticas o lógicas de alta velocidad.

Condensation: Condensación. La conversión de un vapor al estado líquido.

Condenser: Condensador. Mecanismo como un radiador que se utiliza para condensar el refrigerante de un sistema de aire acondicionado.

Conduction: Conducción. Como la del calor a través de un metal u otro objeto.

Conductor: Conductor. Material que conduce electricidad y calor. Un metal que tiene menos que cuatro electrones en el nivel más alejado del núcleo.

Cone: Cono. El anillo de rodamiento interior de un cojinete.

Contamination: Contaminación. La contaminación de un sistema de aire acondicionado para gas R-12 o R-134-a. Aquella que contiene 3% de un gas no-condensable o de un gas refrigerante diferente o más.

Continuity: Continuidad. Grupo de instrumentos que se usa para revisar alambrado, circuitos, conectores o interruptores para rupturas (circuito abierto) o corto circuito (circuito cerrado).

Control head: Control principal. Contiene los controles para el sistema de aire acondicionado y para el sistema de calefacción.

Controller: Controlador. Nombre que se usa para describir una computadora o un módulo de control electrónico.

Convection: Convección. El acto de transferir calor por medio de la circulación de un líquido o vapor.

Conversion fitting: Adaptador/grifo de conversión. Instalados en sistemas donde el gas refrigerante R-12 será substituido con otro diferente.

Cool/to cool: Enfriar. El acto de remover calor.

Coolant: Agua de refrigeración/refrigerante. Mezcla líquida de anticongelante y agua en el sistema de enfriamiento del motor.

Corrosion: Corrosion. Desgaste químico o por reacción electroquímica.

Cup: Copa. El anillo exterior de un balero.

Current: Corriente. Flujo de electrones por un circuito eléctrico; se mide en amperios.

Cycling: Ciclo. El encender e interrumpir la operación del compresor de gas refrigerante en intervalos regulares.

Cycling clutch: Embrague de ciclos. Forma de control de temperatura al embragar y desembragar el eje del compresor de gas refrigerante en intervalos regulares.

Cycling clutch orifice tube (CCOT):   Tubo de orificio restrictor/medidor. Usado para evitar el congelamiento del evaporador. Ayuda a embragar y desembragar el eje del compresor de gas.

Data: Datos. Información que se usa como base para computaciones mecánicas o eléctricas.

DC (direct current) coupling: Acoplador de corriente directa. Una transmisión de señal que pasa ambas las señales de AC y DC al instrumento de medida.

Dehumidify: Deshumedecer. Remover humedad/vapor del aire.

Density: Densidad. Masa por unidad de volumen; peso específico.

Desiccant: Secador. Material secador que se usa en sistemas de aire acondicionado, como aluminio silicio o gel silica.

Diagnostic trouble code (DTC): Código de falla. Sequencia alfanumérica o numérica que indica una falla en el sistema de funcionamiento de un vehículo.

Dichlorodifluoromethane (CFC R-12): Nombre químico del gas refrigerante R-12. Contiene Cloro, Fluor y Carbón.

Dielectric strength: Resistencia diélectrica/potencial dieléctrico. Resistencia a la penetración eléctrica.

Digital: Digital. Método de despliegue que utilza números en vez de una aguja o aparto parecido.

Digital signal: Señal digital. Señal eléctrica que está o prendida o apagada sin otra opción.

Diode: Diodo. Aparato eléctrico que permite que la corriente fluya en una sola dirección.

Direct current (DC): Corriente directa. Flujo constante de corriente eléctrica que fluye en una sola dirección.

Discharge: Descargar/descarga. El remover gas refrigerante de un sistema de aire acondicionado. El lado de salida o de descarga del compresor de gas refrigerante.

Discharge line: Línea de descarga. El tubo, o manguera, que conecta el compresor de gas refrigerante y el condensador.

Discharge pressure: Presión de descarga. El lado conteniendo alta presión de gas refrigerante en un sistema de aire acondicionado.

Division: División. Segmento particular de una onda definido por la cuadrícula del despliegue.

DOT (Department of Transportation): Abreviatura para el Departamento de Transportación.

DPDT (double-pole, double-throw) switch: Conmutador bipolar de dos posiciones. Dos circuitos, dos posiciones.

Drive belt: Banda. Componente que conecta a la polea principal con varias otras poleas para así darles vuelta. Poleas como la del compresor de gas refrigerante, la bomba de agua, así como otros accesorios.

Duty cycle: Ciclo de duración. Porcentaje del período de un motor que el motor trabaja o reposa.

Dynamic pressure: Presión dinámica. La presión en un sistema de aire acondicionado en operación.

Eccentric: Excéntrico. Relación de dos componentes redondos que tienen centros distintos; componente que tiene dos superficies redondos, que no se ubican en el mismo centro.

EEPROM (electronically erasable programmable read-only memory): Memoria de acceso aleatorio programable y borrable electrónicamente.

Elastomer: Cuacho/goma.

Electricity: Electricidad. Movimiento de electrones libres de un átomo a otro.

Electrolyte: electrolito. Sustancia que, en solución, se separa en iones y se hace capaz de conducir una co rriente eléctrica; la solución ácida de una batería de ácido-plomo.

Electromagnetic induction: Inducción electromagnética. Generación de corriente en un conductor que pasa por un campo magnético. En 1831 Michael Faraday descubrió la inducción electromagnético.

Electromagnetic interference (EMI): Interferencia electromagnética. Señal electrónica indeseable.

Electromagnetism: Electromagnetismo. Campo magnético creado por flujo de corriente por un conductor.

Electromotive force (EMF): Fuerza electromotriz. Fuerza (presión) que puede mover electrones por un conductor.

Electron: Electrón. Partícula que lleva carga negativa y que tiene 1/1.800 la masa de un protón.

Electron theory: Teoría de electrones. Teoría que dice que electricidad fluye desde negativo ($-$) a positivo ($+$).

Electronic circuit breaker: Véase Positive temperature coefficient (PTC).

Element: Elemento. Sustancia que no se puede separar en otras sustancias distintas.

Emulsion: Emulsion. Dispersión de glóbulos de un líquido en otro.

Energy: Energía. Capacidad para llevar al cabo trabajo.

Engine control module (ECM): Módulo de control del motor. Unidad de mando que controla el combustible y las emisiones, tal como diagnósticos.

Engine coolant temperature (ECT):   Temperatura del anticongelante del motor.

Environmental Protection Agency (EPA): Agencia de Protección del Medioambiente. Agencia del gobierno federal que impone las leyes que tienen que ver con el medio ambiente. Estas leyes incluyen las que reglamentan la cantidad y contenido de las emisiones automoviles.

Environmentally friendly: De sentido ecológico. Procedimiento o producto diseñado ecológicamente para no dañar la tierra o su medio ambiente.

EPR (ethylene propylene rubber): Caucho de etileno-propileno. También una abreviatura para la válvula del aire acondicionado que se llama *evaporator pressure regulator (válvula reguladora de la presión del evaporador)*.

Ester oil: Aceite ester. Clase de aceite refrigerante.

Evacuate/to evacuate: Evacuar. El uso de una bomba de vacío para remover humedad/agua de un sistema de aire acondicionado.

Evaporation: Evaporación. El cambio de estado de un líquido a vapor.

Evaporator: Evaporador. Mecanísmo parecido a un radiador que se usa para absorber calor y para hacer que el refrigerante cambie de líquido a gas.

Evaporator pressure regulator: Regulador de presión del evaporador. Usado para prevenir el congelamiento del evaporador.

Expansion tube: *Véase* Orifice tube.

Expansion valve: Válvula de expansión: Usada para medir el flujo de refrigerante al evaporador. Ayuda a mantener presiones de gas altas y bajas en sus respectivos lados del sistema.

Fahrenheit: Escala de medida de temperatura basada en 32° como punto de congelamiento del agua, y 212° como su punto de ebullición.

Fan clutch: Embrague del abanico. Usado para controlar la velocidad del abanico para el enfriamiento del radiador.

Filter: Filtro. Usado para remover partículas extrañas o ajenas del gas refrigerante o del anticongelante.

Filter dryer: Filtro secador. Usado para remover humedad del gas refrigerante.

Fitting: Acoples, grifos. Usados para conectar dos piezas.

Fixed orifice tube: Tubo de orificio. Usado para medir el flujo de gas refrigerante al evaporador. Ayuda a mantener las presiones altas y bajas en sus respectivos lados en el sistema de aire acondicionado.

Flare/to flare: Acampanar. El aumentar el diámetro de la punta de un tubo para usarlo con otro conector de plomería.

Flooding: Inundar. El sobrecargar un sistema de aire acondicionado a grado que llena un área de gas refrigerante en forma de líquido.

Fluorocarbon: Flurocarbono. Composición de elementos químicos. Contiene Fluor y Carbón. Usados en algunos lubricantes, gases refrigerantes y en algunos repelentes.

Flush: Sondeo. Procedimiento para limpiar un sistema de aire acondicionado.

Foot-pound: Libras pies/pie-libra. Medida del esfuerzo de rotación. Una fuerza de una libra aplicada sobre un objeto a una distancia de un pie desde el centro de dicho objeto.

Freezing point: Punto de congelamiento. Temperatura a la cual un líquido se congela.

Freon: Freon. Marca de Dupont para refrigerante CFC-12.

Frequency: Frequencia. Número de veces una onda se repite en un segundo, que se mide en Hertz (Hz), en una banda.

Fresh air: Aire fresco. Aire que entra del exterior del vehículo a través de los conductos de aire del sistema de ventilación.

Fresh air filter: Filtro de aire fresco. Usado para remover polvo, polen y otras impurezas del aire fresco.

Friction: Fricción. Resistencia al deslizamiento entre dos objetos en contacto.

Fuse: Fusible. Componente eléctrico. Usado para interrumpir/abrir un circuito eléctrico en caso de alto flujo de amperes.

Garter spring: Muelle/bobina toroidal. Resorte usado en un cierre para ayudar mantener el labio del sello en el contacto con la parte móvil.

Gas: Gas. Un vapor sin ninguna parte en estado líquido.

Gauge: Calibrador. Calibres de alambre asignados por el sistema americano del calibrador de alambre; lo más pequeño el número del calibrador, lo más grande el alambre.

Gauge pressure: Presión medida. Escala en la cual 0 equivale a la presión atmosférica.

Gram: Gramo. Unidad métrica de la medida del peso igual a un 1/1000 de un kilogramo (28 gramos = 1 onza). Un dólar americano o un clip pesa alrededor de 1 gramo.

Grommet: Arandela. Un ojete generalmente hecho de caucho que se usa para proteger, reforzar o aislar alrededor de un hoyo o pasaje.

Ground: Tierra. Potencial posible más bajo del voltaje en un circuito. En términos eléctricos, tierra es el sendero deseable de circuito de regreso. Tierra puede ser también indeseable y puede proporcionar un sendero del atajo para un circuito eléctrico defectuoso.

Halogenated compounds: Compuestos halogenados. Sustancias químicas que contienen cloro, flúor, bromo o yodo. Estas sustancias químicas generalmente se consideran peligrosas y cualquier producto que las contiene debe ser deshecho según procedimientos aprobados.

Head pressure: Presión principal. *Véase* High side.

Heat: Calor. Una forma de energía. Causa aumento de temperatura.

Heat exchanger: Unidad de intercambio de calor. Usada para disipar o transferir calor. El panal/base de calefacción, el evaporador y el radiador de un vehículo son unos ejemplos.

Heat pump: Bomba de calor. Combina el sistema de aire acondicionado y el de calefacción. Las líneas de plomería del compresor son invertidas para obtener ambos aire acondicionado y calefacción.

Heat sink: Absorbente de calor. Generalmente, una unidad de metal con planos de derive que se usa para mantener frescos los componentes electrónicos.

Heater: Calentador. Componente que emite calor.

Heater core: Panal/base de calefacción. Parte del sistema de enfriamiento del motor. Componente que transfiere el calor del anticongelante al aire que entra al interior del vehículo.

Hertz: Hertz. Unidad de la medida de la frecuencia, abreviada Hz. Un Hertz es un ciclo por segundo. Llamado en honor de Heinrich R. Hertz, físico alemán del siglo diecinueve.

HFC-134a: Refrigerante automotriz del aire acondicionado, que también se llama R-134a, cuyo nombre químico es tetrafluoroétano.

Hg: Símbolo químico del Mercurio. Vacío se mide en pulgadas de Mercurio.

High pressure cut off (HPCO) switch: Interruptor de alta presión. Usado para desembragar la polea del eje del compressor en caso que la presión del lado alto exceda ciertos limites.

High pressure relief valve: Válvula de escape de alta presión. Usada para prevenir presiones en exceso en el lado de presión alta del sistema de aire acondicionado.

High pressure switch: Interruptor alta presión. Interruptor que se usa en un sistema de aire acondicionado para parar la operación del compresor cuando la presión alcance un nivel peligroso.

High side: Lado de presión alta. Parte del sistema de aire acondicionado con alta presión de gas refrigerante en estado líquido.

Horsepower: Caballo de fuerza. Unidad de fuerza equivalente a 33,000 librapies por minuto. Un caballo de fuerza iguala 746 W.

Hose: Manguera. Usada como parte de la plomería del sistema de aire acondicionado y del sistema de calefacción.

Humidity: Humedad. Vapor de agua en el aire.

HVAC: Se refiere a Calefacción, Ventilación y Aire Acondicionado.

Hydraulic fan: Abanico hidráulico. Modo de mover un abanico usando flujo hidráulico. Usualmente controlado electrónicamente.

Hydrochlorofluorocarbon (HCFC): Nombre químico.Contiene Hidrógeno, Cloro, Fluor y Carbón.

Hydrofluorocarbon (HFC): Nombre químico. Contiene Hidrógeno, Fluor y Carbón.

Hygroscopic: Higroscópico/hidroscópico. Término que se usa para describir la absorción de agua especialmente de humedad en el aire. La habilidad de absorber y retener humedad.

Identifier: *Véase* Refrigerant identifier.

Idler pulley: Polea de asistencia. Usada como una guía o para el ajuste de tensión de una banda.

In-car sensor: Sensor de temperatura interior. Detecta la temperatura del interior del vehículo.

Insulate/to insulate: Insular. Proteger una pieza con material no-conductivo.

Intermittent: Intermitente. Irregular; una condición que acontece sin una pauta fija, aparente o previsible.

ISO (Internationl Standards Organization): Organización Internacional de Estándares.

Kevlar: Kevlar. Marca de Dupont de fibras aramida.

Kilo: Kilo. 1.000; se abrevia «k»«K».

Latent heat: Calor latente. Calor que afecta un estado material sin afectar temperatura.

LCD (liquid crystal display): VCL. Visualizador de cristal líquido.

Leak detector: Detector de fugas. Usado para encontrar fugas de gas refrigerante.

Liquid: Líquido. Estado físico de un elemento en el cual sus átomos se mueven libremente pero sin separarse como lo hacen en un vapor.

Liquid crystal display (LCD): Visualizador de cristal líquido (VCL). Visualizador que usa cristales líquidos para desplagar ondas y texto en la pantalla.

Liquid line: Línea de líquido. Tubo de salida que conecta al condensador con la entrada del recipiente desecante o con el tubo de orificio restrictor/medidor y la salida del recipiente desecante a la válvula térmica de expansión.

Lock nut: Tuerca de seguridad.

Low pressure switch: Interruptor de baja presión. Se usa en un sistema de aire acondicionado para prevenir la operación del compresor cuando la presión en el sistema es demasiado baja para la operación segura.

Low side: Lado de presión baja. Parte del sistema de aire acondicionado con baja presión de gas refrigerante en estado de vapor.

Lubricant: Lubricante. Cualquier sustancia que se coloca entre dos superficies con el objetivo de reducir la fricción entre ambas.

Magnetic clutch: Embrague activado por medio de magnetismo. *Véase* Cycling clutch.

Male: Macho. Tipo de conector a unirse con un conector hembra.

Malfunction indicator lamp (MIL): Luz/lámpara de indicación de problemas/fallas. Esta luz ámbar de advertir que se ubica en el tablero/salpicadero puede llevar el nombre *check engine* o *service engine soon*.

Manifold gauge set: Manómetro o juego de medidores de presión. Compuesto de dos medidores. Usado para leer presiones de gas refrigerante en un sistema de aire acondicionado.

Micron: Micra. Unidad de medida que equivale a una millonésima de un metro (o milésima de un milímetro).

MIL: *Véase* Malfunction indicator lamp.

Millisecond: Milisegundo. Un milésimo de un segundo (1/1000).

Mineral oil: Aceite mineral. Un hidrocarbono refinado sin aditivos animales o vegetales.

Miscible: Miscible. Término que significa «capaz de ser mezclado».

Mode door: Puerta de aleta. Usada para redirigir el flujo de aire hacia el piso, al panel de instrumentos o al parabrisas.

Muffler: Silenciador. Usado para callar el bombeo del compressor de gas refrigerante.

Multiplexing: Multiplexación/multicomunicacion. Un sistema usado para poder enviar dos o más señales a través de un circuito común. Requiere un microprocesador para cada pieza en dicho circuito.

Non-condensable gases (NCG): Gases no-condensables. El aire en un sistema contaminado que no cambia al estado líquido como lo hace el gas refrigerante.

NTC (negative temperature coefficient): Coeficiente de temperatura negativo. Generalmente que se usa en referencia a un sensor de la temperatura (líquido refrigerante o temperatura aérea). Mientras que la temperatura se aumenta, la resistencia del sensor se disminuye.

Ohm: Ohmio. Unidad de la resistencia eléctrica; llamada en honor de Georg Simon Ohm (1787–1854).

Ohmmeter: Ohmiómetro. Instrumento de prueba eléctrico que se usa para medir los ohmios (unidad de la resistencia eléctrica).

Ohm's Law: La ley de Ohm. Ley eléctrica que dice que se necesita 1 voltio para mover 1 amperio por 1 ohmio de resistencia.

Oil bleed hole: Drenaje de aceite. Ubicado en el fondo del acumulador. Permite el drenaje y flujo de aceite y refrigerante en estado líquido para lubricar el compresor de gas.

Omega (Ω): Omega. La última letra del alfabeto griego; símbolo para el ohmio Ω, la unidad de resistencia eléctrica.

Open circuit: Circuito abierto. Circuito que no es completo y por lo cual no corriente fluye.

Organic acid technology (OAT): Nombre del paquete de inhibidores para uso con anticongelante de larga vida/duración.

Orifice tube (OT): Tubo restrictor/medidor. Usados en algunos sistemas de aire acondicionado. Mide el flujo de gas refrigerante al evaporador. Ayuda a mantener las presiones de gas refrigerante altas y bajas en sus respectivos lados del sistema.

O-ring: Sello de anillo. Usados para sellar conexiones de plomería del sistema de aire acondicionado.

Oscilloscope: Osciloscopio. Despliegue visual de ondas eléctricas en una pantalla fluorescente o en un tubo de rayos catódicos.

OSHA (Occupational Safety and Health Administration): Instituto de Seguridad e Higiene en el Trabajo.

Overcharge: Sobrecargar. Poner una excesiva cantidad de gas refrigerante en un sistema.

Ozone: Ozono. La combinación química de tres átomos de Oxígeno.

Ozone layer: Capa de Ozono. Capa de protección contra los rayos ultravioletas.

PAG (polyalkilene glycol): Abreviatura para *glicoles polialquilenos*.

Performance test: Prueba de funcionamiento. El acto de medir presiones y temperaturas de un sistema de aire acondicionado. Usada para diagnosticar y verificar la operación apropiada de dicho sistema.

Plenum: Pleno. Cámara en la cual se mezclan el aire frío con el caliente. Usado para adquirir una temperatura deseada.

POA (pilot-operated absolute): Abreviatura para una válvula de aire acondicionado que se llama válvula piloto de regulación de presión absoluta.

Polarity: Polaridad. Condición de ser positivo o negativo con relación a un polo magnético.

Polyolester (POE): Lubricante sintético usado en sistemas de aire acondicionado con gas refrigerante R-134a.

Positive temperature coefficient (PTC): Coeficiente de temperatura positivo. Generalmente se usa en referencia a un conductor o fusible interruptor de circuito electrónico. Mientras la temperatura aumenta, la resistencia eléctrica también se aumenta.

Potentiometer: Potenciómetro. Resistor variable de tres terminales que varía la caída del voltaje en un circuito.

Power: Poder. En términos eléctricos, voltios por amperios (poder = I × E) que se expresa en vatios.

Power train control module (PCM): Módulo de control del tren de fuerza. Computador en el vehículo que controla ambas la regulación del motor y las funciones de la transmisión.

PPM (parts per million): Partes por millón.

Pressure: Presión. Cantidad de fuerza usada por cada unidad de área. *Véase también* PSI.

Programmer: Programador. Usado para controlar temperaturas automáticamente.

PSI (pounds per square inch): Libras de presión por cada pulgada cúbica. Unidades de medida de presión.

PTC: *Véase* Positive temperature coefficient.

Pulse: Pulso. Señal de voltaje que aumenta o disminuye desde un valor constante y después vuelve al valor original.

Pulse width-modulated (PWM) blower speed: Velocidad de abanico controlada electrónicamente. Un procesador emite frecuencias moduladas al motor eléctrico del abanico. El procesador enciende y apaga este motor eléctrico intermitentemente. Así en turno cambia la velocidad del abanico.

Purge: Purgar. Usar el flujo de gas refrigerante en estado líquido o nitrógeno seco para remover toda humedad y aire fuera de un sistema. El acto de evacuar un sistema completamente.

R-12: Refrigerante del aire acondicionando que se llama también CFC-12; el nombre químico es diclorodifluorométano.

R-134a: Refrigerante del aire acondicionando automotriz que se llama también HFC-134a; el nombre químico es tetrafluoroletileno.

Race: Pista de rodamiento. Superficie interior y exterior fresada de un cojinete de bolas o de rodillas.

Radiation: Radiación. Calor transferido de los rayos del sol.

Radiator: Radiador. Componente del sistema de enfriamiento del motor. Usado para transferir el calor del anticongelante al aire que pasa a través de él.

Ram air: Aire forzado. Aire forzado a través del condensador y del radiador cuando el vehículo va en movimiento.

Receiver-drier: Receptor secador. Artefacto que se usa como un depósito y contenedor para el secador en unos sistemas de aire acondicionado automotrices.

Recirculated air: Aire en recirculación. Aire que pasa a través del evaporador y del panal/base de calefacción que viene del interior del vehículo.

Reclaim: Reclamación (de propiedades o estados originales). El acto de remover toda impureza de un gas refrigerante con fin de hacerlo como nuevo. Talleres de servicio no hacen reclamaciones.

Recover: Recuperar. Extraer el gas refrigerante de un sistema de aire acondicionado para reciclarlo y poderlo usar nuevamente.

Recycle: Reciclar. El reciclar gas refrigerante usando una máquina. Dicha máquina separa objetos extraños, lubricantes, agua y gases no condensables del gas refrigerante para poder usarlo nuevamente.

Reference voltage: Voltaje de referencia. Voltaje que se aplica a un circuito.

Refrigerant: Refrigerante. Un agente en estado líquido o de vapor. Usado en el sistema de aire acondicionado para absorber, transferir y disipar calor.

Refrigerant identifier: Identificador de gas refrigerante. Aparato usado para medir y determinar la pureza de un gas refrigerante.

Refrigeration: Refrigeración. El remover o disipar calor por medios mecánicos.

Relative humidity: Humedad relativa. Porcentaje de vapor de agua que podría estar en el aire comparado con la cantidad verdadera en el aire.

Relay: Relevador. Interruptor electromagnético que usa un brazo movible.

Remanufactured: Reconstruido. Término que se usa para describir un componente que se desmonta, se limpia, se inspecciona y se vuelve a montar utilizando repuestos nuevos o rehabilitados. Según la Automotive Parts Rebuilders Association (APRA), este componente mismo también se llama *rebuilt.*

Renewal: Recambio o pieza de recambio. UNA parte construida para ser usado como un repuesto para la parte del equipo original (OE).

Resistance: Resistencia. Oposición al flujo de corriente que se mide en ohmios.

Resistor: Resistor. Componente eléctrico. Usado para reducir amperaje o voltaje en un circuito eléctrico.

Retrofit: Modificación con fin de actualización. El sustituir gas R-12 en un sistema con otro gas previamente aprobado por la EPA (Agencia de Protección del Medio Ambiente).

Revolutions per minute (RPM): Revoluciones por minuto. Medida de cuán rapidamente un objeto gira sobre un eje.

Saddle clamp fitting: Abrazadera receptora. Permite la instalación de un conector de servicio un tubo del sistema.

SAE (Society of Automotive Engineers): Sociedad de Ingenieros Automotrices.

Saturated vapor: Vapor saturado. Gas refrigerante en estado de vapor en contacto con gas en estado líquido.

Schrader valve: Válvula-Schrader. Válvula cargada de resorte que se usa en los puertos de servicio del riel del combustible y el sistema de aire acondicionado. Inventado en 1844 por August Schrader.

Sealant: Sellador. Compuesto químico de una o dos partes. Usado para sellar pequeñas fugas en un sistema de aire acondicionado. Otros se usan en sistemas de enfriamiento del motor.

Secondary loop system: Sistema de vuelta secundaria. Usa un sistema de enfriamiento contenido dentro del compartimiento del motor (sistema primario) y otro en el interior del vehículo (sistema secundario). Circulación del sistema secundario al primario ayuda a transferir y a disipar el calor.

Semi-automatic temperature control (SATC): Control de temperatura semiautomático. Sistema que mantiene la temperatura del interior del vehículo y la velocidad del abanico automáticamente. El operador controla las salidas del aire.

Semiconductor: Semiconductor. Materia que es ni conductor ni aislador y que tiene exactamente cuatro electrones en el nivel exterior de átomo.

Sensible heat: Calor sensible. Calor que afecta la temperatura sin afectar el estado material.

Sensor: Sensor. Componente que reacciona con estímulo físico, como calor, luz, ruido, presión, magnetismo o movimiento que lo hacen transmitir señales eléctricas.

Service hoses: Mangueras de servicio. Conectan los medidores de presión de gas refrigerante a un sistema de aire acondicionado.

Service ports: Conectores de servicio. Permiten conectar las mangueras de servicio al sistema.

Servomotor: Servomotor. Servo motorizado. Mecanismo capaz de cambiar de posición. Usado para mover una o más piezas en un vehículo como lo son las puertas de salida del aire del sistema de ventilación.

Shelf life: Tiempo de durabilidad antes de la venta. Plazo de tiempo que algo puede permanecer en un estante de almacenamiento sin que el nivel de desempeño se reduzca del desempeño de un producto que se acaba de fabricar.

Shim: Lámina de ajuste. Espaciador de metal delgado.

Short circuit: Circuito corto. Circuito en que la corriente fluye pero evita un poco de o toda la resistencia en el circuito; una conexión que tiene como resultado una conexión «cobre a cobre».

Short cycling: Ciclo corto. Cuando el compressor de gas refrigerante embraga y desembraga con mucha frecuencia.

Short to ground: Corto a tierra. Circuito corto por lo cual la corriente fluye pero evita algo de o toda la resistencia en el circuito y fluye a tierra. Porque el suelo es generalmente acero en la electricidad automotriz, un corto a tierra (puesto a tierra) es una conexión «cobre a acero».

Sight glass: Ventana. Localizada en el tubo de alta presión o en el recipiente desecante. Usada para ver el flujo del gas refrigerante.

Solenoid: Solenoide. Interruptor electromagnético que usa un núcleo movible.

Solid: Sólido. Estado físico de una materia en el cual sus átomos no son libres de separarse.

Static pressure: Presión estática. Presión en el sistema de aire acondicionado cuando está apagado.

Subcooling: Congelar. Enfriar un líquido fuera de su punto de condensación. Como en el caso del refrigerante que sale del condensador.

Suction line: Línea de succión. El tubo que conecta el evaporador a la entrada del compressor de gas refrigerante.

Suction pressure: Presión del lado de succión. *Véase* Low side.

Sunload sensor: Sensor de intensidad solar. Usado para detectar la cantidad de luz solar y la cantidad de calor radiante en el interior del vehículo.

Superheat: Sobrecalentar. Calentar un vapor fuera de su punto de ebullición. El aumento de temperatura del lado de salida del evaporador comparado a la temperatura del lado de entrada.

Switch: Interruptor. Componente eléctrico. Usado para completar, interrumpir o cambiar una conexión en un circuito eléctrico.

Tell-tale light: Lámpara de aviso. Lámpara de advertir del tablero (a veces se llama *idiot light* (*luz de idiota*)).

Temperature: Temperatura. La intensidad de calor o frío medida en grados de una escala definida.

Temperature blend door: Puerta de mezcla de temperatura. Usada para mezclar aire caliente y frío que entran al interior del vehículo para así obtener una temperatura deseada.

Temperature sensor: Sensor de temperatura. De tecta diferentes niveles de temperatura y emite una señal eléctrica.

Tetrafluoroethane (R-134a): Nombre químico del gas refrigerante R-134a. (CF_3 - CH_2F). Contiene Hidrógeno, Fluor y Carbón.

Thermal: Termal. Palabra usada con referencia a calor.

Thermal expansion valve (TXV): Válvula termal de expansión. Usada en algunos sistemas de aire acondicionado. Mide el flujo de gas refrigerante que llega al evaporador. Ayuda a mantener presiones de gas altas y bajas en sus respectivos lados del sistema.

Thermistor: Termistor. Componente eléctrico. Varía la resistencia al flujo de amperes en un circuito eléctrico de acuerdo a su temperatura.

Thermistor: Termistor. Resistor que varía su resistencia según la temperatura. Un termistor de coeficiente positivo aumenta la resistencia cuando se aumenta la temperatura. Un termistor de coeficiente negativo aumenta la resistencia con una disminución de temperatura.

Thermoelectric principle: Principio termoeléctrico. Producción del flujo de corriente creado calentando la conexión de dos metales distintos.

Thermostat: Termostato. Artefacto que controla el flujo en un sistema basado en la temperatura tal como el sistema de refrigeración de motor.

Thermostatic switch: Interruptor termostático. Usado en algunos sistemas de aire acondicionado. Apaga

el compresor de gas de acuerdo a la temperatura del aire que pasa por el evaporador. Esto así previene que el evaporador se congele.

Throttle position (TP) sensor: Sensor del ángulo de apertura del acelerador. Sensor que indica la posición del acelerador a la computadora.

Topping off: Llenar hasta el tope. El adherir gas refrigerante a un sistema hasta llenarlo sin necesidad de hacerle reparaciones.

Torque: Torque/torsión. Fuerza que tuerce que se mide en libras pies (lb-ft) o Newton–metros (N–m), que pueda resultar en movimiento.

Torque wrench: Llave de tensión. Llave inglesa que registra la cantidad de torsión que se aplica.

Transducer: Transductor. Unidad de control eléctrica y mecánica que presiente la velocidad que se usa en sistemas de control de crucero.

Transistor: Transistor. Artefacto semiconductor que puede operar como amplificador o interruptor eléctrico.

TXV (thermostatic expansion valve): Abreviatura para un sistema de aire acondicionando que usa una válvula de expansión termostática.

Undercharge: Bajocargar. Poner una insuficiente cantidad de gas refrigerante en un sistema.

Under-dash unit: Unidad bajo el tablero. Componente de un sistema ubicado debajo del tablero en el interior del vehículo.

Vacuum: Vacío. Presión negativa (menos que la presión atmosférica); se mide en pulgadas o centímetros de mercurio (Hg).

Vacuum actuator: Activador operado por medio de vacío. Usado para controlar una o más piezas en el sistema de aire acondicionado como lo son las puertas de control de entrada de aire.

Vacuum motor: *Véase* Vacuum actuator.

Vacuum pump: Bomba de vacío o Bomba de succión. Utilizada para el proceso de evacuación de gas refrigerante de un sistema.

Vapor: Vapor. El estado físico de un gas refrigerante. El estado físico del agua.

Variable orifice valve (VOV): Tubo restrictor/medidor variable. Contiene un orificio que cambia en diámetro de acuerdo al flujo y la presión del gas que circula por el mismo.

Vehicle identification number (VIN): Número de identificación de vehículo. Número alfanumérico que identifica el tipo del vehículo, la planta de ensamblaje, el tren de potencia etc.

Venting: Ventilar. Dejar escapar gas refrigerante a la atmósfera. Considerado un acto ilegal.

VIR: Una abreviación de un antiguo tipo de sistema de aire acondicionado en una unidad, llamado *valves in receiver (válvulas en el receptor)*.

Viscosity: Viscosidad. La resistencia al flujo. El grosor relativo de un líquido o semilíquido. Una medida de que tal facilmente puede fluir un liquido.

Volatility: Volatilidad. Medida de la tendencia de un líquido para cambiar al vapor.

Volt: Voltio. Unidad para la cantidad de presión eléctrica; llamado en honor de Alessandro Volta (1745–1827).

Voltage drop: Caída de tensión. Pérdida de voltaje a través de un alambre, conector o cualquier otro conductor. La caída de tensión es la resistencia en ohmios por la corriente en amperios (la ley del Ohmio).

Voltmeter: Voltímetro. Instrumento eléctrico de la prueba que se usa para medir los voltios (la unidad de la presión eléctrica). El voltímetro se conecta en paralelo con la unidad o el circuito que se está probando.

Water valve: Válvula de paso de agua. Usada para controlar la cantidad de agua que pasa por el sistema de calefacción.

Watt: Vatio. Unidad eléctrica de poder; un vatio (1/746 hp) iguala el voltaje por la corriente (amperios). Llamado en honor de James Watt, inventor escocés.

Zener diode: Diodo-Zener. Diode especialmente construido (muy dopado) diseñado para operar con una corriente de corriente de retorno después de que se alcance un cierto voltaje. Llamado en honor de Clarence Melvin Zener.

INDEX

A

Above ground storage tank (AGST), 31
Accumulator
    low side operation, 88, 89–90, 91
    normal reading, 223
    refrigerant leak detection, 241
    system components, 132, 133, 134
Acids, RCRA control, 28
Actuators
    ATC, 269, 273–274
    ATC systems, 170, 172, 176, 177
    calibration, 298
    SATC, 170
Adsorption filters, 161
After blow module, 194–195
Aftermarket A/C units, 144–146
Aftermarket heating systems, 154–155
Aftermarket service manuals, 3
Air, contamination checks, 316–318
Air bags, 35–36, 284
Air bleeds, 258, 259
Air condition check list and performance report, 214–216
Air condition service training
    ASE task list, 499–451
    ASE task priorities, 462–463
    Clean Air requirements, 200
Air conditioner (ac) system
    abnormal conditions, 224–230
    basic description, 83–85
    charge level, 328–335
    clutch/clutch coil r&r, 350–357
    common repairs, 345–346
    component leak tests, 245
    component R&R guidelines, 381–382
    component replacement, 380–382
    compressor repairs, 346–350
    diagnostic test procedure, 191–193
    electronic diagnostic tool, 233–234
    evacuating, 327
    flushing, 318–322
    hoses/fittings R&R, 368–380
    in-car inspection steps, 184–185
    mode/function doors, 162
    performance test, 214
    performance test guidelines, 217, 218
    problem diagnosis, 188, 189–191, 198–201
    recharging, 306
    retrofitting, 335–341
    service check list 183
    servicing tips, 303–304
    shaft seal R&R, 357–363
    stress test, 224
    system noise, 195–196
    system odors, 194–195
    under hood inspection (engine off), 181, 183, 184, 185
    under hood inspection (engine on), 187, 188
Air distribution
    duct system section, 160
    HVAC division, 39
    system components, 157
Air doors
    air management problems, 255
    component, 157, 158
    duct system, 160–161
Air filtration, 161
Air flow,
    checks, 188
    control of, 159–160
    horizontal split, 163, 164
Air gap, 355, 357
Air inlet, 160–161
Air locks, 419–420
Air management, 39
Air management system
    common problems, 255–256
    components, 157, 158
    duct sections, 160–163
Air mix door, 162
Air quality sensors, 174
Airlift unit, 419–420

Alternating current (AC), 265
Ambient sensor, 173
American Refrigeration Institute (ARI), service
    procedure documents, 453–454
Ammeter, 289
Amperage, 289–292
Ampere-turns, 267–268
Amperes (amp), 264
Analog meter, 282, 283
Angular misalignment, 421, 422
Antifreeze
    coolant, 411–412
    coolant replacement, 418, 419
    RCRA control, 28
    waste disposal, 33–34
Armature, 117, 119, 120, 121
Asbestos, 29–30
Asbestosis, 29
ASE. *See* National Institute for Automotive Service
    Excellence
Asian red coolant, 34
Aspirator, 173
Atmospheric pressure, 54–55
Audi pink coolant, 34
Automatic temperature control (ATC),
    diagnostic flow chart, 192
    system components, 269
    systems, 158, 170, 171–172
Automatic tensioners, 424–425
Automotive waste
    chemical poisoning, 31–32
    RCRA control, 28
Awl, 10
Axial position, 95
Azeotrope, 68

B

Back seat, 209
Backflush, 439
Bar, 55
Barb, 136
Barb fittings
    attachment guidelines, 378
    hose repair, 374, 375
Barrel, 13–14
Barrier hose, 102, 103, 138, 139
Batteries
    disposal, 34
    RCRA control, 28
    storage, 35
Battery acid, 28
Battery Council International (BCI), 34
Beadlock, 136

Beadlock fitting
    attachment guidelines, 379
    hose repair, 373–374, 375
Belt drive inspection, 421
Belt lock, 173–174
Belt lock strategy, 269
Belt protection system, 173–174
Belts
    inspection, 421
    noise check, 421
    maintenance, 409
    preventative maintenance, 304, 410
Black death, 318
Bleed valve, 417, 418
Bleeds, 166
Blend air doors, 177
Blend door
    duct system, 162
    system checks, 256, 257
Blends, refrigerants, 59–60, 65
Blink code, 293, 296
Blood-born pathogens, 36
Blower motors
    air distribution system, 158, 167, 168–169
    air management problems, 255, 256
    ATC systems, 177, 178
    output devices, 267, 277–278, 292
Body control module (BCM), 263, 274–275
Boiling point
    conversion, 43
    coolant, 405
    coolant system, 385, 394, 396
    and pressure, 52–53
    R-12, 56–57, 59
    R-134a, 58, 59
    R-22, 57, 59
Bolts
    basic equipment, 5, 6, 7
    service tip, 13
    tightening torque chart, 368, 460
Bowden cable, 154
Brake dust, 30
Brake fluid, 30
Brake shoes, 30
Break cleaners, 29
British thermal unit (Btu), 42, 44
Bubble point, refrigerants, 68
Bubble-style crimp, 374, 379
Bubbles, leak detection, 234, 235, 237, 242
Bump cap, 15, 16
"Burp," 310, 318
Bus information system, 274
Bypass door, duct system, 162
Bypass valve, heating system, 151

C

Cabin air filter
  and air cleanliness, 45
  duct system, 161, 162
  replacements, 186
Cable adjustment, 257
Calibration adjustment, 204
Calibration codes, 2
Calorie, 42
Cap screw, 5, 7
Capillary tube, 129
Captive ferrule, 138, 139
Captured O-ring, 137
Carbon dioxide (CO_2)
  fire extinguishers, 20
  test steps, 436
Casting numbers, 3
Cellular construction, 152
Celsius, 42, 43
Center punches, 11
Center register discharge temperature, 223
CFC-12, refrigerant, 56–57, 58, 59
Charge level, 224–227
Charging cylinder, 330
Charging stations, 201, 203
Charging steps, 332–333
Chemical flush, 413
Chemical poisoning, 31–32
Chisel, 11
Chlorofluorocarbon (CFC), 56, 57
Circuit breaker, 266, 267
Circuit tester, 11
Clamping systems
 screw-types, 380
  spring locks, 370, 372
Clamps
  coolant system, 402, 403
  cooling hose replacements, 426
Clean Air Act
  ac service certification, 200
  and air conditioning, 28
  recovery container certification, 66
  Section 609, 64
  Section 612, 68
  venting ban, 305
Climate control, 39
Clutch assembly
  removal guidelines, 352–353
  repairs, 350–352
  replacement guidelines, 354–356
  system components, 117, 119–121
Clutch circuits, 274, 276
Clutch coil
  R&R, 350–356

testing, 289, 292
Clutches
  ASE task list, 450
  ASE task priorities, 462
  manufacturers, 351
  output devices, 267, 274, 276
  service tips, 354, 355, 357
Coaxial arrangement, 112
Coaxial swash-plate compressors, 112
Coaxial wobble-plate compressors, 115
Coil, 119
Cold engine lockout, 173
Combination wrench, 10
Combustion leak, 435–436
Comebacks, 180
Comfort zone, 42, 44
Complete circuit, 264, 265
Compound gauge, 201, 204, 206
Compression heating, 79–80
Compression ratio, 107, 110
Compressor bench checks, 364, 365
Compressor/clutch diagnostic chart, 192
Compressor inlet gauge, 208, 209
Compressor oil checks, 365–366
Compressors
  abnormal conditions, 229
  ac problems, 199
  ASE task list, 450
  ASE task priorities, 462
  causes of failure, 346, 348
  electric, 99–100
  installation guidelines, 348–349
  internal repairs, 363
  leak check guidelines, 365
  low side operation, 91, 93–94
  lubrication, 123–126
  model identification, 108, 117, 118
  oil checks guidelines, 366–367
  problems with R-134a, 458
  refrigerant leak detection, 241
  removal guidelines, 349, 350
  repair service tips, 347–349, 350
  replacement guidelines, 349
  rotation checking guidelines, 364, 365
  system components, 106–107
  types of, 95–100
  typical configuration, 109
Condensers
  ASE task list, 450
  ASE task priorities, 462
  blockage, 228, 229
  high side operation, 95, 99–101
  low side operation, 91
  refrigerant leak detection, 241

Condensers, *cont.*
    seals, 128
    system components, 127–128
Conduction, 48
Conductors, 264
Connecting wires, 266, 267, 268
Control devices
    ASE task list, 450–451
    ASE task priorities, 463
    ATC, 170, 171, 174–178
    electrical system component, 266, 267
    SATC, 170
Control head, 158, 165–169
Control modules, 263, 270, 271–273
Control panel and module, 269
Control valves, 149, 150, 151, 153–154
Convection, 48–49
Conversion fitting, 339, 340
Coolant condition
    maintenance, 409
    preventative maintenance, 413–417
Coolant exchange unit, replacement steps, 419, 420
Coolant level
    cooling system maintenance, 409
    preventative maintenance, 410–411, 412, 413
Coolant pump, coolant system, 390
Coolant recovery reservoir (CRR), 394–395, 397
Coolant system
    components of, 386
    function of, 385–386
    pressure tests, 432–435
Coolant voltage
    coolant condition, 414
    measurement steps, 415, 416
Coolants
    coolant system, 390–391, 404–406
    component, 386
    four types of, 411
    RCRA control, 28
    replacement , 409
    replacement steps, 417–418
    waste disposal, 33–34
Cooling fan circuits, 278–280
Cooling load, 77–78
Cooling modules, 395–396, 397, 398
Cooling systems
    ASE task list, 450
    component inspection/replacement, 409, 413–426
    component replacement services, 410
    diagnosing problems, 409, 426–439
    inspection checklist, 428
    inspection steps, 427–428, 431
    maintenance, 409
    maintenance tests, 410, 413–414

    problem-solving guide, 427
    service/repair, 410, 439–447
    types of, 78–81
Core, 393, 395, 441
Core hole, 387
Core hole plug,
    coolant system, 387
    replacement, 441, 442
    replacement steps, 442
Corrosion
    causes of, 248–249
    types of, 404
Corrosion-protection, 406
Corrosive materials, 27
Crankshaft, 107
Critical pressure, 53
Critical temperature, 53
Crossflow system, 393, 394
Cubic feet per minute (cfm), 324
Cut-in pressure, 93
Cutout pressure, 92–93
Cycling, heating system leaks, 248
Cycling clutch orifice tube (CCOT) system, 83
Cycling clutch system
    icing control, 92
    normal readings, 223
    testing, 218, 219
Cycling diagnostic trouble code (DTC), 249

D

Damper drives, 121–122
Debris, 304
Defrost, doors, 162
Defrost switch, 92
Delta T
    measurement guidelines, 231, 232
    refrigerant charge verification, 230
Denso compressor, 114
Department of Transportation (DOT)
    hazardous wastes, 33
    recovery container certification, 66, 312
Deposits, radiators, 429
Desiccant, 89
Dew point, 68
Dexcool, service tip, 413
Diagnostic identifier, 307, 308
Diagnostic link connector (DLC), 294
Diagnostic trouble code (DTC)
    coolant system, 385
    electronics, 293–296
    HVAC system, 263
    test procedures, 193
Dial indicator, 15

Diodes, 268, 269
   service tip, 284, 292
Direct current (DC), 265
Disc, 117, 119
Discharge line
   high side operation, 103
   low side operation, 91
Discharge pressure, 222
Discharge stroke, 107
Displacement, 107, 109
Disposal
   air-conditioner oil, 36
   antifreeze waste, 33–34
   brake fluid, 30
   contaminants, 65
   EPA rules, 30–31
   refrigerant oil, 36
   shop cloths, 17, 18
   solvents, 31–32, 33
   tires, 36
Diverter door, 162
Downflow system, 393, 394
Drive belts
   ac problems, 199
   automatic tensioners, 424
   coolant system, 390, 391–393
   replacement instructions, 184
   replacement steps, 421–424
Drive plate, 117
Drop in, 68
Dry chemicals, 20
Dual condenser, 101
Dual heating systems, 154
Dual-zone, 163, 164
Ducts
   air management components, 157
   three major sections, 160–163
Dyes, 404, 405, 406
Dynamic installations, 368–369

E

E-Z Clip system, hoses, 374, 375
Ear protection, 15
Economy retrofit (Type II) procedure, 337, 338
Electric compressor, 99–100
Electric control circuits, 168–169
Electric fans
   cavitation test steps, 439
   coolant system, 399–400
Electric pump, 151
Electric vehicles 151
Electrical circuits, 280–282
Electrical cords, 20

Electrical switches, 138–139, 140
Electrical symbols, wiring diagrams, 265
Electrical systems
   ASE task list, 450–451
   basic components, 266–268
   repairs, 298–300
Electricity, concepts, 264–266
Electrolysis
   cooling systems, 409
   corrosion, 248–249
   radiators faults, 430
   voltage problems, 416
Electromagnetic induction (EMI), 281–282
Electromechanical controls, 165, 166
Electronic control assembly, ATC, 170
Electronic control module (ECM)
   ATC, 170, 174–175
   HVAC system, 263, 270–274
Electronic diagnostic tools, 233–234
Electronic evaporator dryer module, 194–195
Electronic gauge sets, 208, 210
Electronic leak detectors
   detection method, 234, 235–236
   use guidelines, 241–242
Electronic scales, 330, 331
Electronic self-diagnosis, DTC, 293
Electronic service information, 3–4
Electronics, basic concepts, 268–274
Electrostatic discharge (ESD), 269, 282, 284
Engine
   ASE task list, 450
   energy conversion, 40–41
Engine block heater, 406–407
Engine coolant concentrate, 411
Environmental Protection Agency (EPA)
   asbestos exposure, 29
   hazardous materials list, 27
   oil disposal, 30–31
   oil filters disposal, 31
   Section 609 enforcement, 64
   SNAP-approved refrigerants, 455–456
Equipment, ac service, 200–201
Erosion
   cause of, 249
   definition, 410
   heating failure, 248
   radiators faults, 430
Esters, lubricants, 59
Ethylene glycol (EG)
   coolants, 413
   corrosion inhibitor, 404, 405–406
   disposal of, 33–34
European blue coolant, 34
Evacuate, ac system, 327

Evaporative cooling, 78, 79
Evaporator(s)
    air management system, 158
    ASE task list, 450
    ASE task priorities, 462
    and expansion drives, 85–87, 88–89
    icing control, 91–94
    leak inspection, 244
    low side operation, 88–89
    pressure controls, 93
    refrigerant leak detection, 241
    system components, 132, 133
Evaporator cores, plugged, 186
Evaporator outlet, normal reading, 223
Evaporator pressure regulators (EPRs), 93
Exhaust hose, 17
Expansion cooling, 80–81
Expansion devices, components, 128–132
Expansion drives, low side operation, 85–88
Expansion tank, coolants, 395
Expansion value, low side operation, 91
Extended life antifreeze, 406
Extruded tubes, 127

F

Fahrenheit, 42, 43
Fan belt, coolants, 390
Fan clutch
    coolant system, 398–399, 400
    R&R, 442, 443, 444
    test steps, 438
Fan runout, 442, 443
Fans
    coolant system, 386, 397–401
    radiators faults, 429
    R&R, 442, 443
Federal Motor Vehicles Safety Standard (FMVSS), 149
Feeler gauge set, 11
Female flare, 136
Female O-Ring, 136, 138
Ferrule, 373
Filter wrench, 11
Filters, 135–136
Fin and tube
    condensers, 100
    coolant system, 393
Finger check, 413
Finger-style crimp, 374, 378
Fingerprint, identifier, 309
Fins
    preventative maintenance, 304
    radiators faults, 429
Fire extinguishers, 20

Fittings
    ac hoses, 206
    O-ring styles, 376
    O-ring types, 368–369
    and radiators faults, 430
    and refrigerant lines, 104
    and refrigerants, 457
    spring lock connectors, 370–372
    threaded connectors, 369–371
Fixed orifice tube (FOT), 83, 130
Flame-leak detectors, 237, 238
Flap doors, 157, 159
Flare-nut wrench, 10
Flattened tube, 100
Flex Temp, probe, 219
Flooded, low side operation, 85
Floor-defrost doors, 162
Fluorescent dyes, leak detection, 234, 235, 237
Fluorescent tracers, use guidelines, 242–243
Flushing
    coolant condition, 413
    cooling system services, 410, 439–441
    maintenance, 306, 318–322
Flushing gun, guidelines, 440–441
Flux pole, 121
Fossil fuels, 76
Fractionizing, 68
Freeze plug, 387
Freezing point, conversion, 43
Freon, 55
Fresh air, 160–161
Front seat, 211
Function doors, 162
Functional test, HVAC system, 181
Fuse, 266
Fusible link, 266

G

Gage, 14
Gas, heat transfer, 50, 51
Gas bubbles, test steps, 436
Gasket scraper, 11
Gasoline handling, 35
Gauge
    coolant system, 402–404
    definition, 14
Gauge pressure
    pressure measurement, 55
    at sea level, 304
    troubleshooting chart, 202
Gauge rod, 14
Gauge system
    connection guidelines, 213, 214

disconnection guidelines, 214
normal reading, 225
Glide, refrigerants, 68
Global warming, 63
Gloves
automotive waste, 32
safety tips, 15
Go-no-go identifier, 307
Goo, debris, 318
Grade, bolts, 6, 7
Greenhouse effect, 63
Ground, electricity, 264–265
Ground circuit, 267
Grounded circuits, problems, 281
Groundout, 195
Gut pack, 363

H

Halide torch, 237
Hammers
service tip, 13
tool chest, 10, 11
Hand pump test, cooling system, 432, 433
Hand tools
basic equipment, 8–13
borrowing, 12
brand names, 12
safe use, 13
Hand valves, 201, 205, 207
Hang-on units, 145
Hard code, DTC, 293
Hazard Communication Standard, OSHA, 28
Hazardous waste materials
definition of, 27
Hazard Communication Standard, 28
RCRA control, 28
and shop personnel, 26
HCFC-22, refrigerant, 56, 59, 64
Head pressure, 222
Heat
as energy, 40–42
flow of, 47–48
intensity, 42–43
measurement of, 42–43
mode/function doors, 162
quantity, 42, 44–45
transfer rules, 76
Heat exchanger, 48, 76
Heater core
a/c door component, 158
coolant circulation check guidelines, 251
description of, 152
heating load, 76, 77

heating system component, 149, 150
hybrid vehicles, 151
leak check, 252, 253
R&R, 252, 253
Heater system
ambient temperature, 249, 250
components, 149, 150
infrared thermometer checks, 250
Heating, HVAC division, 39
Heating load, 76, 77
Heating systems
ASE task list, 450
ASE task priorities, 462
common problems, 248, 249
Heating, ventilation, and air conditioning (HVAC) system
air filter, 161
air filter replacement, 254, 255
ASE task list, 451
ASE task priorities, 462
diagnostic test procedure, 191–193
divisions of, 39
electric servomotors, 167
inspection procedures, 181
no/insufficient cooling, 181–182, 191, 193
purpose of, 39–40
system noise, 195–196
system odors, 194–195, 255
HFC134a, refrigerant, 56, 57–59, 65
High performance retrofit (Type I) procedure, 337, 338
High pressure cutoff (HPCO) switch,
high side operation, 102
retrofitting, 336
High side
air conditioner operations, 94–102
air conditioning systems, 83
normal pressure reading, 223
High-efficiency particulate air (HEPA), asbestos, 29
High-resistance circuit, 280
Highly saturated nitrile (HSN), 369
Hoisting
safety requirements, 18–19
sequence, 21–23
Hood, 17
Hoses
ac pressure checks, 201, 203, 204, 205–208, 209, 214, 242
air condition systems, 102, 103, 104
coolant system, 388, 401–402, 403
coolant system component, 386
cooling system inspection, 425
cooling system maintenance, 409
cooling system replacement, 425–426
heating system component, 149, 152–153
heating system repair, 250–251

Hoses, *cont.*
  inspection of, 185
  leak repairs, 369, 373
  preventative maintenance, 410, 412
  refrigerant leak detection, 241
  replacement guidelines, 373
  system components, 135–139
Hot gas bypass valve, 93, 95
Humidity, 44
Hybrid organic acid technology (HOAT), 34
Hybrid vehicles, heating system, 151
Hydraulic cooling fan, 401
Hydrocarbons, 307
Hydrochlorofluorocarbon (HCFC), 56, 57
Hydrofluorocarbon (HFC), 56, 57
Hydrogenated nitrile butadiene rubber (HNBR), 368, 369
Hydrometer, 413–416
Hygroscopic lubricants, 124

I

Icing switch, 92
Identification systems, 1–3
Identifiers, 305–309
Ignitable material, 27
Infrared thermometer
  system inspection, 431–432
  use, 187, 200, 217, 219, 250
Inlet hose, 149
In-line filters, 135–136
  installing steps, 322, 348
  maintenance, 306, 326
In-line piston compressor, 110–111
Insulators, 48
Interior ventilation, 161
International Automotive Technicians' Network (IATAN), 4
International Mobile Air Conditioning Association Foundation (IMACA)
  ac service training, 200
  check list & performance report, 214
  retrofitting refrigerants, 336, 337, 338

J

Jewelry, safety tips, 15, 16, 32
Jiggle pin, 389
Jumper wires, 282

K

Kilopascal (kPa), 55
Korean blue coolant, 34
Kyoto Protocol, 64–65

L

Latency period, 29
Latent heat, 51
  of condensation, 51–52
  of evaporation, 51–52
  of fusion, 52
Lead-acid batteries, 34
Leaks
  ac problems, 199, 200, 201
  cooling system, 409, 426
  in radiators, 429, 430
  tests for, 431, 436
Length, metric conversion table, 459
Line restriction, 227–228
Lines
  air condition systems, 102–103
  system components, 136
Lip seal
  removal steps, 358, 360
  replacement guidelines, 358
  shaft seal R&R, 358, 359
  system components, 123
Liquid, heat transfer, 50–51
Liquid line
  high side operation, 103
  low side operation, 91
Live flushing, 322
Load, output devices, 267
Lock washer, 8
Loctite, nut sealant, 8
Lokring fitting, 376–377
Low side
  air conditioner operations, 83–94
  air conditioning systems, 83–84
  normal pressure reading, 223, 224
Lubrication, 123–126
Lung cancer, 29

M

Magnet, 11
Male flare, 136
Male Insert O-Ring, 136
Male O-Ring, 136, 138
Malfunction indicator lamp (MIL)
  coolant system, 385
  ECM, 271, 273
  OBD, 249
Manifold gauge set
  ac pressure checks, 204, 205–208, 209
  evacuating steps, 327, 328
Manual system, temperature control, 158

Material Safety Data Sheets (MSDS), hazardous materials, 28
Matter, forms of, 50
Measurement, service procedure, 13
Measuring tools, types of, 13–15
Mechanical refrigeration, 78–79, 80
Mechanical reverse flush, 413
Mechanical systems, ASE task list, 451
Mercedes yellow coolant, 34
Mesothelioma, 29
Metal lines
   lokrings, 377
   repair of, 378
   replacement guidelines, 373
Meter, 286
Metric bolts
   sizes, 6, 7
   torque tightening chart, 460
Metric conversion table, 459
Micrometer, 13–14
Micron, 324, 325, 327
Micron filter, 161
Mid seat, service values, 211
Mill file, 10
Mineral oil
   lubricants, 123–124, 125
   seal removal, 358, 360
Misalignment, belts, 421–423
Mobile Air Conditioning Society (MACS)
   ac service training, 200
   component repair frequency, 345–346
   retrofitting refrigerant, 336
Mobile vehicle air circulation (MVAC), Section 609, 64
Mode doors
   ATC systems, 177
   duct system, 162–163
Molecular sieve, 89
Montreal Protocol, 64
Muffler, 136
Multi-V belt, 391
Multimeters, 282, 283, 288, 290
Multiplex, EMC, 274, 275
Multiposition switch, 168

N

National Institute for Automotive Service Excellence (ASE)
   certification program, 449
   Clean Air Act training, 200
   heating/ac test task list, 449–450
   heating/ac task priorities, 462
   heating/engine cooling systems diagnosis/repair, 450
   operating systems/related controls diagnosis, repairs, 450–451
   refrigerant recovery, recycling/handling, 451
   refrigeration system component diagnosis/repair, 450
National Institute for Occupational Safety and Health (NIOSH), 29
Nitrile butadiene rubber (NBR), 368
Noncondensable gasses (NCG), 306
Normally closed (NC) relays, 267
Normally open (NO) relays, 267
Nuts, 6, 7, 8

O

O-rings
   ac fittings, 136, 137–138
   coolant system, 394, 395
   compressors,122
   separating, 368
   variety of, 368–369
Occupational Safety and Health Act (OSHA)
   asbestos exposure, 29
   definition of, 26–27
   Hazard Communication Standard, 28
   health rights, 27
   inhalant regulations, 32
Ohm's law, modern version, 284
Ohmmeter, 287–288, 289
Ohms (Ω), electricity, 264
Oil
   and component replacement, 381
   compressor repairs, 347
   level check guidelines, 367
   levels checking/correcting, 322–323
   RCRA control, 28
   as refrigerant, 60
   storage of used, 31
   waste disposal, 30–31, 36
Oil charge, 323
Oil filters
   RCRA control, 28
   waste disposal, 31
On-board diagnostics (OBD), 249
One-piece beadlock, 374
Open circuits, 280
Orbiting piston compressor, 98, 99
Organic acid (OA), 406
Organic acid technology (OAT), 34
Orifice tube (OT) system
   abnormal conditions, 230
   air conditioning, 83–85
   high side operation, 94–102
   low side operation, 87–88, 94

Orifice tubes
  low side operation, 87–88, 91
  remover/installer kit, 382
  system components, 130–132
Original equipment manufacturer (OEM)
  fitting repairs, 377, 378
  hose repairs, 379
  service manuals, 3
Out-gasses, 310
Outgassing, 124
Outlet hose, 149
Output devices, 266, 267–268
Outside air door, 160–161
Overcharge
  abnormal conditions, 228
  low side operation, 90–91
Overcooling, 409, 426
Overheating, 409–410, 426
Ozone layer, 62, 63

P

Paint, RCRA control, 28
Panel-defrost doors, 162
Parallel circuit, 265
Parallel flow, 100, 101
Parallel misalignment, 421, 422
Partial charge, 328, 329
Particle filters, 161
Particulate filter, 161
PASS, fire extinguishers, 20
Peltier effect, 77
Performance test
  ac system, 214, 217
  interpreting readings, 221–224
"Perk" waste disposal, 31
Personal safety equipment
  described, 15, 16
  hazardous materials, 27
pH balance, coolants, 414
Phillips screwdriver set, 10
Pilot operated absolutes (POAs), 93
Pin punches, 11
Pinch bar, 11
Piston compressors
  high side operation, 95, 96, 97
  system components, 106–107
Pitch, 5, 6
Plastic drain valve, 418, 419
Plenum
  air management system component, 157
  duct system section, 160, 162
  fabrication of, 160

Pliers, 10
Pollen filter, 161
Poly-V belt, 391
Polyalkaline glycol (PAG)
  ester, 59
  lubricants, 123–124, 125
Polyolester (POE)
  ester, 59
  lubricants, 123–124, 125
Positive temperature coefficient (PTC)
  heating load, 76–77, 78
  protection devices, 266–267
Potentiometer, 165, 167
Pounds per square inch absolute (psia), 55
Pounds per square inch gauge (psig), 55
Power source, 266
Prediluted engine coolant, 411
Pressure
  air conditioning systems, 84, 85
  boiling points, 52–53
  definition of, 54
  measuring, 55
  measuring systems, 57
  metric conversion table, 459
  performance categories, 222
  radiators faults, 430
  refrigerant boiling points, 59
  at sea level, 316
Pressure caps
  coolant system, 394, 396, 397
  inspection tests guidelines, 432
  removal guidelines, 411, 412
Pressure checks, 198, 201–208
Pressure regulator, 433–434
Pressure relief valve, 126–127
Pressure sensor, icing control, 93
Pressure switch
  icing control, 92–93
  low side operation, 91
Pressure test, coolants, 426–427
Pressure transducer, ATC systems, 174
Pressure-temperature (P-T) relationship
  air contamination checks, 316–318
  refrigerants, 71
  water, 56
Pressure-temperature (P-T) relationship chart, 54, 452
Prevailing torque nuts, 8
Preventive maintenance, purpose of, 304
Propylene glycol (PG)
  corrosion inhibitor, 404–406
  disposal of, 34
Protection device, 266
Pulley, clutch assembly, 117, 119, 120, 121

Pulse width modulation (PWM)
    blower motor circuits, 277–278
    control heads, 165, 167
Punches
    service tip, 13
    tool chest, 11

Q

Quick Detect, sealant contamination, 309
Quick-connect coupling
    heating system, 153
    heater system problems, 250, 251

R

R-12
    compressor configuration, 109
    container, 69, 70
    container pressure, 317
    fitting sizes, 457
    hose connections, 204, 208, 212
    and ozone layer, 62–63
    phase out, 64
    purity standard, 307
    refrigerant, 56–57, 58, 59
    refrigerant identification, 305–306
    retrofitting procedure, 338–340
    SNAP-approved substitutes, 455–456
    system temperature/pressure, 201, 203, 204
    temperature-pressure chart, 452
R-22, refrigerants, 56, 57, 59
R-134a
    compressor configuration, 109
    compressor problems, 458
    container, 69
    container pressure, 317
    hose connections, 205, 208, 213
    refrigerant, 56, 57–59, 59, 65, 69, 70, 72
    retrofitting, 335–340
    service couplers, 210, 211
    service ports, 208
    system temperature/pressure, 201, 203, 204
    temperature-pressure chart, 452
R-152a, 72
Radial compressor, 111
Radial pistons, 95
Radiant heat, 49, 50
Radiators
    coolant system, 393–394
    coolant system component, 386
    cooling system services, 410
    common faults, 429–430

hoses, 386
R&R steps, 444
specialized repairs, 439
Radio frequency interference (RFI), 281
Radioactive material, 27
Ram air pressure, 157–158
Reactive material, 27
Real world fix
    Acura (1991), 271
    Acura (1993), 227
    BMW (1993), 255
    BMW 535i (1985), 252
    Buick (1988), 186, 255
    Buick (1992), 297
    Buick (1999), 298
    Cadillac (1990), 279
    Cadillac (1994), 296
    Cadillac (1995), 282
    Cadillac DeVille (1996), 383
    Cadillac De Ville (2000), 225
    Camry (1988), 291
    Camry (1991), 273
    Chevrolet Blazer (1996), 420–421
    Chevrolet Lumina (1995), 193
    Chevrolet Malibu (2001), 277
    Chevrolet Monte Carlo (1996), 297
    Chevrolet motorhome (1984), 307
    Corvette (1988), 276
    Dodge Caravan (1988), 188
    Dodge Caravan (1989), 254
    Dodge Caravan (1992), 184
    Dodge Caravan (1993), 26, 329
    Dodge Caravan (1996), 285, 297–298
    Dodge Colt (1993), 244
    Dodge Intrepid, 280
    Doge RAM van (1998), 290
    Ford Explorer (1990), 424
    Ford Explorer (1991), 350
    Ford Explorer (1995), 271
    Ford Explorer (1996), 186, 256, 330
    Ford LTD (1987), 259
    Ford Taurus (1997), 228, 278
    Ford van (1996), 226
    Ford Windstar (1995), 291
    GMC pickup (1992), 296–297
    GMC Yukon (1999), 193
    Honda (1989), 271, 336
    Honda Civic (1992), 229
    Honda Prelude (1993), 300
    Infiniti (1990), 321
    Jaguar (1993), 321
    Jeep (1993), 416–417
    Jeep Cherokee (1993), 296

Real world fix, *cont.*
  Jeep Cherokee (1998), 280
  Jeep Grand Cherokee (1994), 383
  Lexus (1990), 229
  Lincoln (1991), 354
  Lincoln Town Car (1995), 294
  Mazda (1996), 228–229
  Mazda MPV (1996), 438
  Mercedes (1986), 357
  Mercedes-Benz (1984)
  Mercedes-Benz (1992), 271
  Mercedes-Benz (1999), 278
  Mercury Grand Marquis (1994)
  Mercury Mountaineer SUV (1997), 230
  Mitsubishi (1991), 276
  Nissan Maxima (1990), 297
  Nissan Pathfinder (1992), 350
  Oldsmobile 98 (1995), 295
  Plymouth Horizon (1988), 230
  Plymouth Voyager (1990), 338
  Pontiac Bonneville (1992), 259
  Pontiac Bonneville (1993), 186
  Pontiac Bonneville (1994), 249
  Pontiac Grand Am (1995), 252
  Pontiac Grand Am (1997), 226–227
  Saab (1986), 186
  Saab (1993), 293
  Saturn (1992), 229
  Subaru Legacy (1997), 280
  Suzuki Sidekick, 293
  Taurus (1990), 347
  Toyota 4Runner (1995), 226
  Toyota Supra, 290
  Volkswagen Jetta (1994), 277
  Volvo (1997), 342
Rear air distribution systems, 169–170
Rear window defroster, ATC systems, 178
Receiver-drier(s)
  accumulator, 89
  ASE task list, 450
  high side operation, 101–102
  low side operation, 91
  system components, 132–133, 134–135
Recharging, 306, 328–335
Reciprocating piston, 106
Reciprocating piston compressors, 95
Recirc, 160
Recirculation air door, 160
Recirculation, duct system, 160
Recover, definition, 65
Recovery
  contaminated refrigerant, 314–315
  preventative maintenance, 305–306
  refrigeration, 309–316

Recovery container certification, 66
Recovery/recycling/recharging units, 201
Recycle
  definition, 65
  refrigerants, 305, 306, 312, 315–316
Recycle engine coolant concentrate, 411
Recycle Guard, 309, 310, 311
Recycled coolant, 411
Reed valves
  piston compressor, 107
  removal guidelines, 363, 364
  replacement guidelines, 363, 364
Refractometers, 413, 414, 415
Refrigerant (s)
  abnormal conditions, 228
  ac pressure checks, 213
  ac problems, 199, 200
  ac process, 50, 55–60
  ASE task list, 451
  ASE task priorities, 463
  charge level, 90–91
  charge level verification, 230
  and Clean Air Act, 28
  common types, 56–60
  containers, 68–70, 74
  contamination of, 305, 306–307
  disposal of contaminated, 65
  hose repair, 377, 378, 379–380
  HVAC divisions, 39
  identification steps, 305, 307–308
  identifier, 307–308, 309
  illegal, 72
  leak detection methods, 234–244
  low side operation, 89–91
  new research, 63–64
  numbering system, 461
  physical properties, 67
  RCRA control, 28
  recovery of, 305, 309–313
  recovery of contaminated, 315
  recovery/recycling, 65
  recovery steps, 313–314
  recycling steps, 316
  repair/recovery, 180
  retrofitting choices, 335
  safety precautions, 72–73
  SNAP-approved substitutes, 455–456
  verification guidelines, 231
Refrigerant containment switch, 336
Refrigerant handling systems, 201
Refrigerant leak
  detection guidelines, 238, 239
  electronic detector guidelines, 241–242
  service tips, 239–240, 241–242

Refrigerant management center, 201
Refrigerant oil, 36, 60
Relative humidity (RH)
    definition, 44
    evaporative cooling, 78
    measuring, 220
Relays
    control devices, 267
    fan motors, 400
    system components, 140–142
Relief valves, compressor, 126–127
Removing and replacing (R&R), 298
Reserve alkalinity (RA), 414
Resistance, 287–289
Resistors, 168
Resource Conservation and Recovery Act (RCRA), 27–28
Restrictors
    heating system, 153
    heating system problems, 250
    vacuum circuits, 166
Retrofitting
    maintenance, 329, 335–341
    procedural steps, 340–341
    refrigerants, 58
Reverse coolant flow, 390
Right-to-know laws, 28
Rockwell hardness test, steel, 5
Roof pack, 145–146
Rotary compressor, 95–97, 107
Rotary door, 159–160
Rotating field, 117
Rotor, 117, 120, 121
Rotor pulley, 354–355
Rovac system, 81
Rub-through, 242

S

Safety
    coolant system, 398, 399
    pressure caps, 411
Safety equipment, 304
Safety glasses, 11, 15, 16
Safety tips
    hand tools, 13
    for technicians, 15–17
Saturated vapor, 53, 54
Scan tools, DTC, 293, 295, 296
Schematics, electricity, 265
Schrader valve
    removal of, 239
    service ports/valves, 210, 212
Scotch yoke, 107, 108, 112
Scotch yoke compressor, 95–96

Screw driver set, 10, 11
Screw-tower clamp, 403
Scroll compressor
    high side operations, 95–100
    system components, 107
Seal cartridge, 122
Seal protector, 358, 361
Seal seat, 122
Sealants
    identification steps, 309, 310
    maintenance, 341–342
    refrigerant contamination, 307
Seals, 304, 335
Seams, 429
Secondary condenser, 101
Self-locking nuts, 6, 7, 8
Semiautomatic temperature control (SATC)
        systems, 158, 170
Sensible heat, 51
Sensing bulb, 129
Sensors
    ATC, 269–271, 272
    ATC systems, 170, 171, 172, 173–176
    SATC, 170
Series circuit, 265
Serpentine flow, 100, 101
Serpentine V-ribbed belt, 391, 392
Service
    information sources of, 3–4
    manuals, 3
    procedure documents, 453–454
Service hose
    ac system checks, 201, 205, 206, 208, 209, 210
    service unit, 211–213
Service ports
    ac system checks, 208, 209, 210, 211
    refrigerant leak detection, 241
    service units, 212
Service unit, 211–214
Service valves, 211
Shaft seals
    R&R, 357–363
    system components, 122
Shock control, 18
Shoes, safety tips, 15, 16
Short cycle, 142
Shorted circuits, 281
Shrink tube, 300
Shroud, 398, 399
Shutoff valve, 206, 207, 211
Sight, ac systems, 84
Sight glass
    low side operation, 91
    normal reading, 223

Sight glass, *cont.*
  receiver-drier, 135
  refrigerants, 219, 220
Significant New Alternatives Policy (SNAP)
  approved refrigerants, 455–456
  section 68, 72, 612
  t-p ressure relationships, 71
Sliding mode door, 159
Slugging
  compressor damage, 332
  low side operation, 88–89
Small cans
  charging steps, 334
  refrigerants, 68, 69
Smart control heads, ECM, 271
Smart motors, ECM, 271
Society of Automotive Engineers (SAE)
  bolt torque tightening chart, 460
  contaminant standard, 306
  hoisting/lifting standards, 18–19
  leak detection standard, 236
  recovery/recycling standards, 65, 66
  service procedure documents, 453–454
  steel classification, 4
Socket set, 8–9
Soft code, DTC, 293
Soft plugs
  coolant system, 387
  replacement, 441, 442
  replacement steps, 442
Solar sensor, ATC systems, 175
Solder bloom, radiators, 429
Solid matter, heat transfer, 50
Solid state electronics, 268–269
Solvents
  chemical poisoning, 31–32
  hazardous waste, 33
  RCRA control, 28
  waste disposal, 31–32, 33
Special tools
  compressor repairs, 346, 348
  lokrings, 377–378
  O-rings, 368
Spindle, 14
Spontaneous combustion, 17
Spring clamp, 402, 403
Spring lock coupling
  fitting repairs, 370–372
  O-rings, 368–369
Starved, low side operation, 85
Static installations, 368
Stationary field, 117
Steel classification, 4–5
Stop leaks, 341

Stratosphere, 62, 63
Strength ratings, steel, 5
Stress test, guidelines, 224
Stud, 5
Sub-cooling
  condenser, 99, 100
  measurement guidelines, 231, 232
Subcondenser, 101
Subcool, 53
Suction filter screen, 350, 351
Suction line
  high side operation, 103
  low side operation, 92
Suction pressure, 221
Suction stroke, 107
Suction throttling valve (STV)
  evaporators, 132, 133, 138
  model names, 144
  pressure regulation, 93, 94
  system components, 142–143
Suction value, 91
Sulfuric acids, 35
Summer thermostat, 389
Superheat, 53, 128
Swash plate
  compressor, 95, 96
  system components, 107, 108, 109, 112, 113
Switch
  control devices, 267
  compressor, 126–127
  system components, 140–142

T

Tank certification, 312, 313
Tanks, radiators faults, 429, 430
Technical service bulletins (TSBs)
  diagnostic test procedures, 191
  heater core repair, 249
  OEM information, 4
Technicians, safety tips, 15–19
Tecumseh compressor, 108, 109, 111
Telescopic gauge, 14
Temperature
  ac system, 84
  conversion equations, 459
  coolant system, 385, 387
  performance categories, 222
Temperature check
  ac problems, 198, 200
  infrared thermometer, 187, 200, 217, 219, 250
Temperature door, 162
Temperature sensing thermistor, 92
Temperature-blend door, 161

Temperature-controlled switch, 92
Temperature-pressure charts, 54, 452
Terminal, removing, 298
Terminal repair set, 297, 298
Test light, 282, 283
Test strips
    coolant condition, 413–414
    measurement steps, 414
Themoelectric device, 77
Thermal cycling, 153
Thermal energy, 40
Thermal expansion valve (TXV) systems
    abnormal conditions, 230
    air conditioning, 83–85
    expansion devices, 128–130
    high side operation, 94–102
    low side operation, 85–87, 94
    rear units, 144
    replacing/installing, 382–383
    testing guidelines, 232–233
    on vehicle checks, 232, 233
Thermal fuse, 121
Thermal switch, 227
Thermistors
    ATC systems, 173
    sensors, 270
    solid-state sensor, 142
Thermostats
    coolant system, 387–390
    coolant system component, 386
    checks, 436–437
    inspection steps, 437–438
    repair/replacement, 444–446
    repair/replacement steps, 445
Thermosyphon system, radiators, 393
Thimble, 13–14
Threaded fasteners, 5–8
Three-way design thermostat, 149
"Thunks," 185, 256, 257
Tires, waste disposal, 36
Tools. *See* Hand tools, Measuring tools, Special tools
Topping off, 65, 328, 329
Torque
    metric conversion table, 459
    tightening specification chart, 368, 460
Total Environmental Warming Impact (TEWI)
        index, 64–65, 72
Toxic material, 27
Transducers
    electricity, 270
    solid-state sensor, 142
Trouble tree, diagnostic chart, 188–191
Tubing size, 84
Twin-wire clamp, 403

Two-cylinder V compressor, 111
Two-part seal
    removal guidelines, 359, 361, 362
    replacement guidelines, 362–363
    shaft seal R&R, 357–358, 359
Type I, retrofitting procedures, 337, 338
Type II, retrofitting procedures, 337, 338

U

Ultrasonic leak detector, 236, 261
Ultraviolet radiation, 62
Undercharge, 90
Underground storage tank (UST), 31
Unified National Coarse (UNC), fasteners, 5
Unified National Fine (UNF), fasteners, 5
Utility knife, 11

V

V belts
    coolant system, 391–393
    misalignment tolerance, 421
Vacuum
    definition, 55
    leak checks, 259
Vacuum actuators, 165, 166, 168
Vacuum check, leak detection, 234, 235
Vacuum control circuit, 165–166, 167
Vacuum control system
    air management system checks, 258–259
    ASE task list, 451
    troubleshooting guidelines, 260–261
Vacuum diaphragm, 153–154
Vacuum motor, heating system, 153–154
Vacuum pumps
    ac pressure checks, 201, 203
    evacuating steps, 327, 328
    leak tests, 245–246
    oil levels, 325–326
    rating systems, 324
    service tips, 326
Value grinding compound, 12
Valve core depressor, 206, 210
Valve core tool, 11
Valve cores, 208, 209
Valve in receiver (VIR)
    expansion devices, 129, 130
    serviceable unit, 135
Valve plate, 364
Valves, 157
Vane compressor
    high side operations, 95–98
    repairs, 347
    system components, 107, 108

Variable displacement compressor
   high side operation, 98
   low side operation, 93–94
Variable displacement wobble-plate
      compressors, 115–117
Variable orifice valve (VOV)
   description, 131–132
   low side operation, 87
Vehicle emissions control information (VECI), 2
Vehicle identification number (VIN), 1–2
Vehicles, lifting, 18–19, 21–23
Velocity, metric conversion table, 459
Vent, 65
Vented, refrigerants, 305
Vernier caliper washer, 14–15
Visual inspection, 181, 182
Voltage, measuring, 285–287
Volts (V),electricity, 264
Volume, metric conversion table, 459
VW/Audi pink coolant, 34

W-Y

Washers, 8
Waste disposal. *See also* Disposal
   contaminated blends, 65
   regulation of, 30–36
   shop cloths, 17, 18
Water
   coolant mix, 411–412
   fire extinguishers, 20
Water jackets
   coolant system, 387
   coolant system component, 386
   cooling system services, 410

Water pumps
   coolant system, 390–391
   coolant system component, 386
   repair/replacement, 446–447
   repair/replacement steps, 446
   test steps, 439
Water quality, coolants, 413
Watts, 43, 264
Weight, metric conversion table, 459
Winter thermostat, 388–389
Wintergreen oil, service tip, 6
Wires
   corrosion, 284
   electrical system, 266, 267, 268
   splicing, 299–300
Wiring diagram
   electricity, 265
   reading tips, 292
Wobble plate
   compressor, 95, 96
   system components, 107, 108
Workplace hazardous materials information systems
      (WHIMS), 28
Worm-drive clamp, 403
Wrench(es)
   adjustable, 12
   bolt gauge, 8
   thread size, 7
Wrench set, 9, 10, 11
York compressor, 108, 109, 111

Z

Zeotrope, 68, 70
Zexel compressor, 108, 115